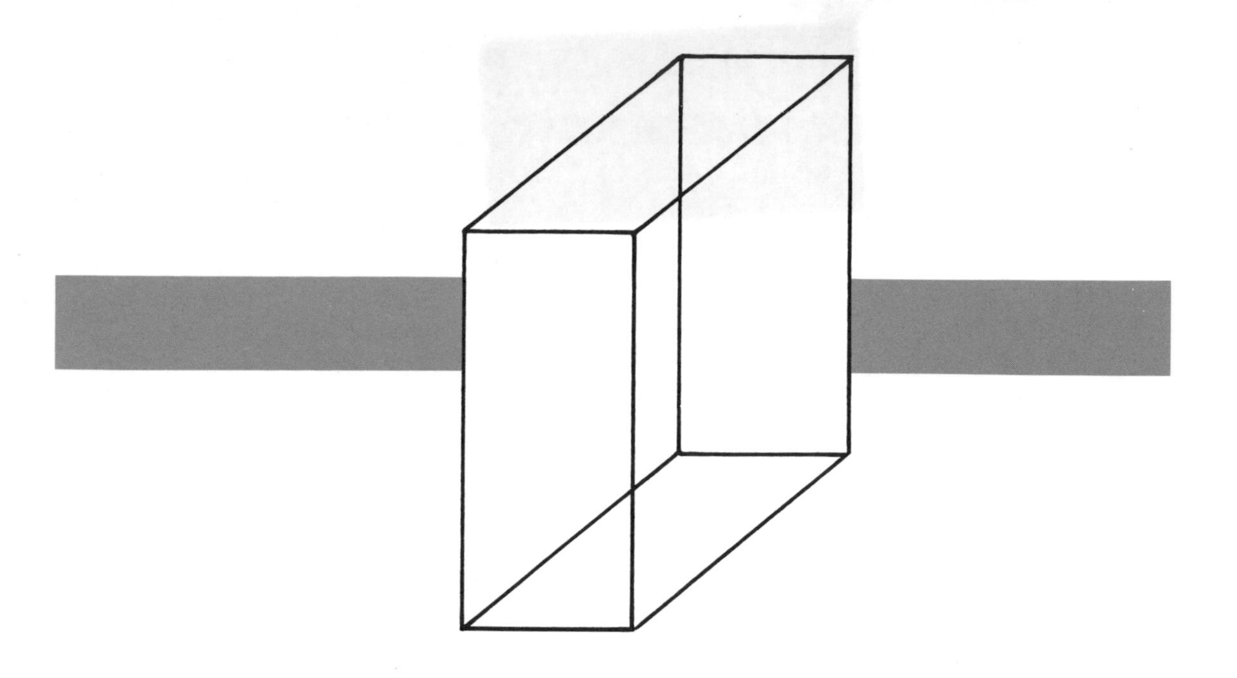

CAD/CAM HANDBOOK

Eric Teicholz

Editor-in-Chief

Graphic Systems, Inc.

Cambridge, Massachusetts

McGraw-Hill Book Company

New York St. Louis San Francisco Auckland Bogotá
Hamburg Johannesburg London Madrid Mexico Montreal
New Delhi Panama Paris São Paulo Singapore
Sydney Tokyo Toronto

THE McGRAW-HILL DESIGNING WITH SYSTEMS SERIES

ERIC TEICHOLZ
CONSULTING EDITOR

Stitt *Systems Drafting: Creative Reprographics for Architects and Engineers* (1980)

Daryanani *Building Systems Design with Programmable Calculators* (1980)

Stitt *Systems Graphics: Breakthroughs in Drawing Production and Project Management for Architects, Designers, and Engineers* (1984)

Teicholz *CAD/CAM Handbook* (1985)

Stitt *Designing Buildings That Work: The Architect's Problem Prevention Sourcebook* (1985)

Orr *The Architect's CADD Primer* (1985)

Gerlach *Converting to Designing with A/E Systems* (1986)

Library of Congress Cataloging in Publication Data

Main entry under title:

CAD/CAM handbook.

(The McGraw-Hill designing with systems series)
1.CAD/CAM systems—Handbooks, manuals, etc.
I.Teicholz, Eric. II.Title: C.A.D./C.A.M. handbook.
III.Series.
TS155.6.C36 1985 620'.00425'02854 84-4365
ISBN 0-07-063403-3

3 4 5 6 7 8 9 0 HAL/HAL 8 9 8 7 6 5

ISBN 0-07-063403-3

The editors for this book were Joan Zseleczky and Susan B. West, the designer was Mark E. Safran, and the production supervisor was Sally Fliess. It was set in ITC Zapf Book Light Roman by Byrd Data Imaging Group.

Printed and bound by Halliday Lithograph.

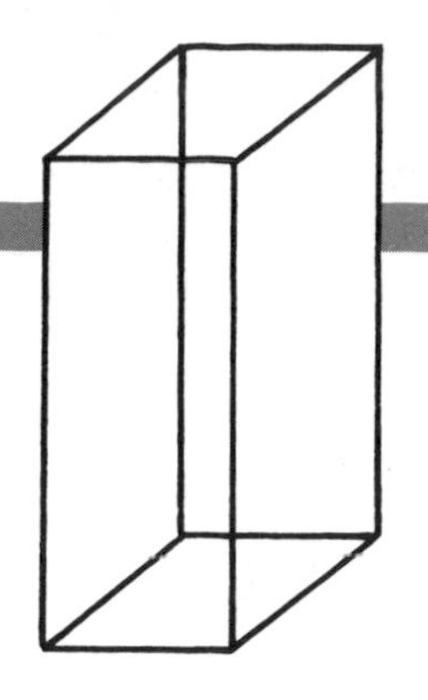

Contents

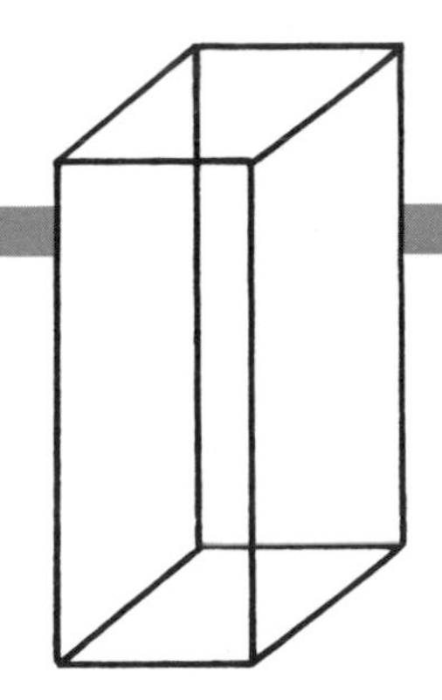

Contributors

Tom Bakey, President, Tom Bakey Associates, Sunnyvale, California (Chapter 12: Piping and Instrumentation Diagrams)

Jerry Borrell, Editor-in-Chief, *Digital Design*, Boston, Massachusetts (Chapter 13: Solid Modeling)

Aaron Cohen, Principal, Aaron Cohen Associates, Croton-on-Hudson, New York (coauthor Chapter 5: Ergonomics)

Elaine Cohen, Principal, Aaron Cohen Associates, Croton-on-Hudson, New York (coauthor Chapter 5: Ergonomics)

Charles Evans, Evans Engineering Co., Greendale, Wisconsin (Chapter 10: Electrical Applications)

Anthony W. Horn, President, Horn Center of Drafting, Houston, Texas (Chapter 9: Mechanical Drafting)

Alex Houtzeel, President, Organization for Industrial Research, Inc., Waltham, Massachusetts (Chapter 17: Process Planning and Group Technology)

William L. Howard, Corporate Director, Fairchild Industries, Germantown, Maryland (Appendix C: Large Systems)

Peggy Kilburn, President, Program Advisory Board, *S. Klein Newsletter*, Sudbury, Massachusetts (coauthor Chapter 4: Market Projections)

Stanley Klein, Editor-in-Chief, *S. Klein Newsletter*, Sudbury, Massachusetts (coauthor Chapter 4: Market Projections)

Carl Machover, President, Machover Associates, White Plains, New York (Chapter 2: CAD/CAM: Where It Was, Where It Is, and Where It Is Going)

Megatek Computer Graphics, San Diego, California (Chapter 18: Glossary of Computer Graphics Terms)

Robert D. Miller, Senior Staff Engineer, Operations Support System, FMC Corp., Chicago, Illinois (Chapter 7: Understanding and Measuring Productivity)

William J. Mitchell, Graduate School of Architecture and Urban Planning, UCLA, Los Angeles, California, and Principal, The Computer Aided Design Group, Santa Monica, California (Chapter 11: Architecture, Engineering, and Construction)

Joel Orr, President, Orr Associates, Danbury, Connecticut (Chapter 3: Tools: Hardware and Software; Appendix B: Minicomputer Systems)

Roger S. Pressman, President, R. S. Pressman and Associates, Inc., Orange, Connecticut (Chapter 16: Numerical Control)

Ronald C. Reeve, Jr., Chief Executive Officer, Reeve Consultants Inc., Columbus, Ohio (Chapter 15: Robotics)

Allan H. Schmidt, President, Allan H. Schmidt Associates, Concord, Massachusetts (Chapter 14: Cartography)

Eric Teicholz, President, Graphic Systems, Inc., Cambridge, Massachusetts (Chapter 1: Introduction to the Handbook; Chapter 6: System Selection and Acquisition; Appendix A: Microcomputer Systems)

Gary W. Zera, President, Zericon, Racine, Wisconsin (Chapter 8: Managing Systems Effectively)

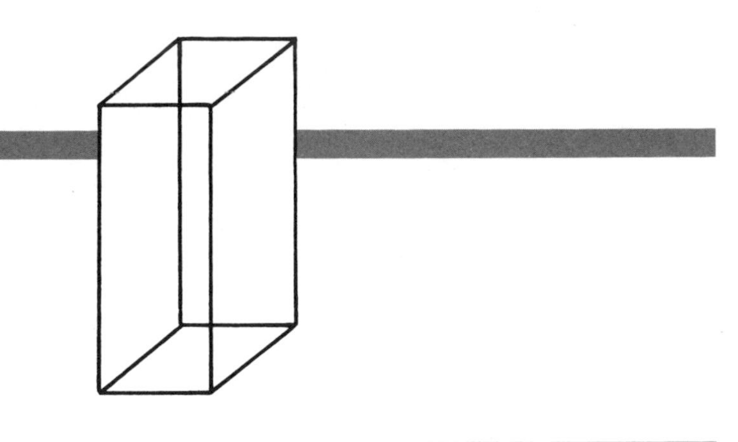

Preface

The *CAD/CAM Handbook* attempts to assess the current status of computer-aided design/computer-aided manufacturing (CAD/CAM) technology: how to effectively acquire and use this technology, how CAD/CAM technology is currently used by various segments of industry, and how it is evolving.

CAD/CAM technology is 15 years old. The capabilities of CAD/CAM systems have evolved from simple two-dimensional drafting systems to sophisticated integrated three-dimensional design, drafting, and engineering systems.

Another important development is the integration of CAD/CAM with computer-integrated manufacturing (CIM). Examples of the integration of these two technologies include such processes as material requirements planning, robotics, group technology, and process planning, The productivity and economic benefits that can be gained from the use of current CAD/CAM technology are well documented throughout this handbook. As CAD becomes integrated increasingly with CAM, these benefits will increase correspondingly—particularly manufacturing productivity.

I would like to acknowledge and thank the 19 individuals that contributed to the production of this book. I would also like to thank Martha Osler and Judy Teicholz for all of the proofreading and administrative support provided. It is to all these people that I would like to dedicate this book.

Eric Teicholz

ABOUT THE EDITOR

Eric Teicholz is president of Graphic Systems, Inc., a Cambridge-based CAD/CAM consulting firm. The company has done extensive consulting and publishing in the area of system evaluation, procurement, and management. Mr. Teicholz has been involved in CAD/CAM since 1968—both as an academic at Harvard University and, more recently, through his consulting company. He has published numerous professional and technical papers and is the author of *McGraw-Hill A/E Computer Systems Update* and coeditor of *Computer Graphics and Environmental Planning* and the *CIM Handbook* (forthcoming).

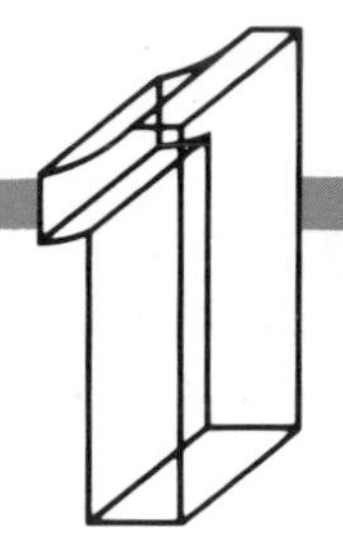

Introduction to the Handbook

by

Eric Teicholz

1.1 PURPOSE

This book is written for those students, professionals, and organizations who are either using or considering the use of computer-aided design and computer-aided manufacturing (CAD/CAM) systems. The book is comprehensive and covers all aspects of basic CAD/CAM technology including hardware and software tools; current and projected market segmentation; the acquisition, evaluation, and management of systems; and applications and capabilities of current small, medium, and large systems.

✓ 1.2 INTRODUCTION

Until the last few years, CAD/CAM systems have been used almost exclusively by large aerospace and automotive companies. With the advent of less expensive hardware (particularly microprocessors) and more extensive and powerful applications software, the purchase of cost-effective CAD/CAM systems for design, drafting, and analysis is possible for almost any drafting, engineering, or manufacturing firm. This recent acceptance of CAD/CAM technology by end users has dramatically affected the way in which products are designed and manufactured.

✓ The productivity and economic benefits of CAD/CAM, although difficult to measure objectively (see Chaps. 5 and 6), are well documented and include the following:

1. ***Improved Drawing Quality, Management, and Maintenance.*** CAD/CAM systems operate most efficiently when standard drawing details and operating procedures are present. CAD/CAM software necessitates precise input, edit, output, and management procedures—thereby forcing users to be explicit about drafting and data management procedures.
2. ***Early Discovery and Reduction of Errors.*** CAD/CAM results in greater drawing accuracy than with manual drafting methods. For example, numerous drawing overlays or layers (the ability to store data in different computer memory locations) are available with most systems. Layers can be used to store different aspects of a drawing, such as multiple building stories, heating, ventilation, and air conditioning (HVAC) layouts, reflected ceiling plans, and electrical or structural information.

   Both time savings and error reductions can be derived from storing and subsequently selectively retrieving and combining (overlaying) these data, using the layers provided with most systems—especially if a firm has experience using pin-bar drafting methods. An overlaid (combined) display visually depicts interferences and inconsistencies in the data. Additional errors are reduced, since most CAD/CAM systems have "semiautomatic" dimensioning capabilities which automatically determine line and arc lengths.
3. ***Integrated Design.*** A single, central database that is used for both design and analysis results in a cohesive (integrated) rather than a fragmented (discontinuous) design process. This, in turn, has the additional advantage of encouraging the use of cost-saving repetitive details. Both intradisciplinary and interdisciplinary functions benefit from a cohesive database.
4. ***Simulation.*** Several systems currently available have three-dimensional data representation capabilities, thereby allowing for isometric or perspective visualization of a design without resorting to physical models.
5. ***Time Reduction.*** Productivity (efficiency) gains for automated, rather than manual, drafting range from 2:1 to 8:1 for most applications. Time savings are also realized by using standard libraries and details which result in shorter project span times and in faster detection of problems before they become critical. All these factors allow users to accept tightly scheduled projects that could not normally be accommodated.
6. ***Training.*** CAD/CAM operator instruction provides for more direct training procedures, since the training involves an explicit preestablished set of methods related to system use.

7. ***Management Enhancements.*** CAD/CAM results in a controlled information flow that produces better monitoring of cost expenditures and better control, security, and maintenance of data.

✓ In general, CAD/CAM systems both improve the quality of a design and result in shorter product cycles because of increased lead time from a project's conception through the production of working drawings. The development of a single database for a project results in error reduction, better management control, and more feedback for the client. All these benefits result in more efficient drafting and design which, in turn, result in cost savings for the company.

At present, the full potential has not yet been realized for even greater responsiveness, accuracy, and productivity in product design by further integration of CAD and CAM processes. The existence of a single, accurate, and commonly accessible database that is widely used is not yet a reality but will become commonplace for successful and productive manufacturers in the near future.

1.3 HANDBOOK ORGANIZATION

The handbook is organized in four major sections: the first being an overview of CAD/CAM; the second dealing with aspects of the acquisition, evaluation, and management of systems; the third with specific CAD/CAM application areas; and the fourth with current overviews of microcomputer, minicomputer, and large systems.

In Part 1, the overview section, there are four chapters:

1. Carl Machover describes the past, present, and future of CAD/CAM and presents numerous case studies of current users from a variety of disciplines.
2. Joel Orr writes about the hardware and software tools that comprise CAD/CAM systems.
3. Stan Klein and Peggy Kilburn look at market projections for hardware, software, and systems related to CAD/CAM.
4. Elaine and Aaron Cohen discuss various issues related to the ergonomics of systems.

Part 2 on process-related issues contains three chapters:

1. Eric Teicholz describes the process of selection, evaluation, and acquisition of CAD/CAM systems.
2. Robert Miller writes on understanding, measuring, modeling, and calculating CAD/CAM productivity factors.
3. Gary Zera discusses CAD/CAM management by dealing with issues such as personnel, database procedures and structure, and types of CAD and CAM interfaces.

Part 3 relates to major application segments of CAD/CAM systems and contains ten chapters.

1. Anthony Horn describes the benefits and components of CAD/CAM mechanical drafting software, including procedures for the development of mechanical databases.
2. Charles Evans discusses advantages and aspects of using CAD/CAM systems for electrical design and drafting applications, including electrical schematics and printed- and integrated-circuit-board design and drafting.
3. William Mitchell writes on the current and potential use of CAD/CAM technology for architectural, engineering, and construction applications.
4. Tom Bakey describes how a process and instrumentation (P & ID) drawing is created and edited on a typical CAD/CAM system.

5. Jerry Borrell discusses the state of the art and potential of using CAD/CAM systems for solid and geometric modeling.
6. Allan Schmidt writes about current applications and trends of using CAD/CAM software for producing and analyzing topographic and thematic maps.
7. Ronald Reeve describes various aspects of industrial robots, including their role in manufacturing, CAD/CAM interfaces for robots, and the role of artificial intelligence in robotics.
8. Roger Pressman discusses numerical control systems and programming and their current and future application in the automated factory.
9. Alex Houtzeel describes group technology and computer-assisted process planning—two exciting new technologies related to using CAD/CAM systems for manufacturing processes.
10. A glossary of computer graphics terms, originally published by Megatek Computer Graphics, is included at the end of Part 3.

The final section of the book, Part 4, describes capabilities of existing small, medium, and large CAD/CAM systems. Part 4 contains three appendixes:

1. Eric Teicholz provides an overview of microcomputer systems and includes several case studies.
2. Joel Orr describes both the current status of minicomputer CAD/CAM systems and an overview of issues that are relevant to all systems.
3. William Howard describes vendors and capabilities of large multiterminal systems.

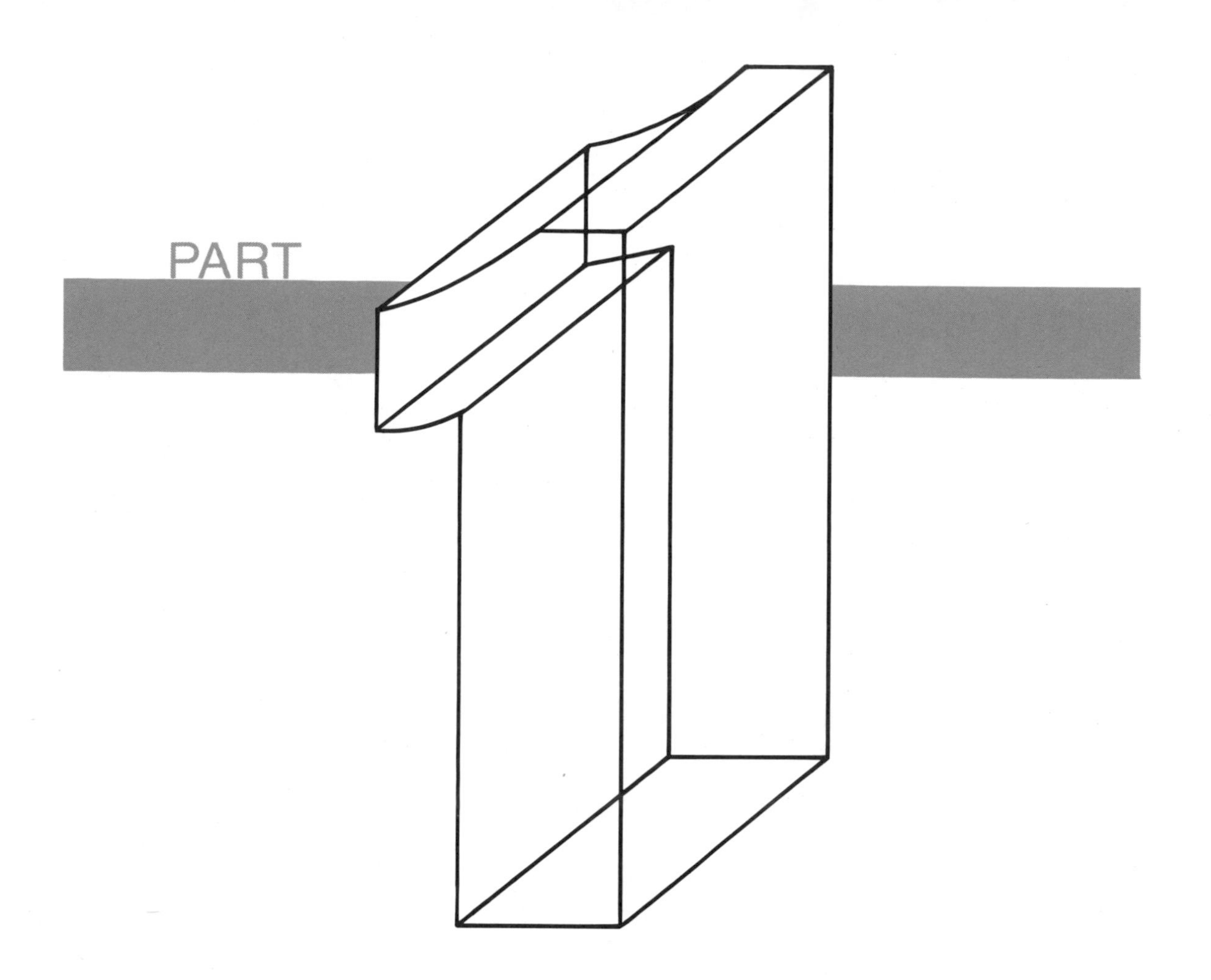

PART 1 OVERVIEW

CAD/CAM: Where It Was, Where It Is, and Where It Is Going

by
Carl Machover

2.1 INTRODUCTION

In 1983, computer-aided design and computer-aided manufacturing (CAD/CAM) was expected to be a $1.5 billion industry—part of a $3.5 billion computer graphics industry. By the end of 1983, more than 44,000 CAD/CAM workstations were expected to be in place, servicing the needs of an estimated 70,000 drafters and engineers. At least five companies [Computervision, Intergraph, Calma, Applicon, and International Business Machines (IBM)] were expected to deliver $150 million worth or more in CAD/CAM systems in 1983, and the growth is expected to continue at about 30 percent per year. At least five more companies (Control Data Corp., Hewlett Packard, Prime, Sanders, and Tektronix) were expected to deliver more than $100 million in goods and services in 1983 to CAD/CAM users and system suppliers.

Not bad for an industry that almost did not exist 15 years ago! In fact, Computervision, Intergraph, Prime, and Applicon were not in business 15 years ago. Calma had just been founded. While the other companies were in business, their CAD/CAM involvement was minor or nonexistent.

In this chapter we will cover some of the origins of CAD/CAM, describe some current applications, and discuss some future trends.

2.2 WHERE IT WAS

This is not a formal history of CAD/CAM—such a history should be researched, footnoted, complete, and accurate. This is more in the nature of a brief, personal history of a field in which I have been involved for 25 years. Most of the material in this section was adapted from an article, "A Brief Personal History of Computer Graphics," written by me and published in *Computer Magazine*, November 1978.

2.2.1 In the Beginning

It can be persuasively argued that the first computer graphics systems appeared with the first digital computers. Massachusettes Institute of Technology's (MIT) Whirlwind computer had cathode-ray tube (CRT) graphic displays in the control room (Fig. 2.1). Another early use of computer graphics as a human-machine interface was the SAGE (semiautomatic ground environment) air-defense command and control system of the middle 1950s. SAGE converted radar information into computer-generated pictures. SAGE also introduced the light pen, which allowed the operator to select information by simply pointing at the appropriate target displayed in the CRT (Fig. 2.2).

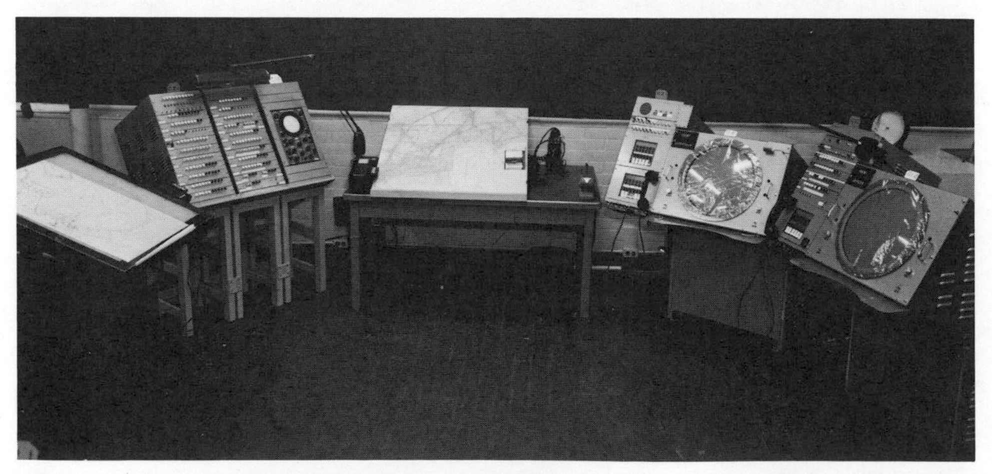

Figure 2.1 Portion of Whirlwind computer control room. (*Courtesy of Mitre Corp.*)

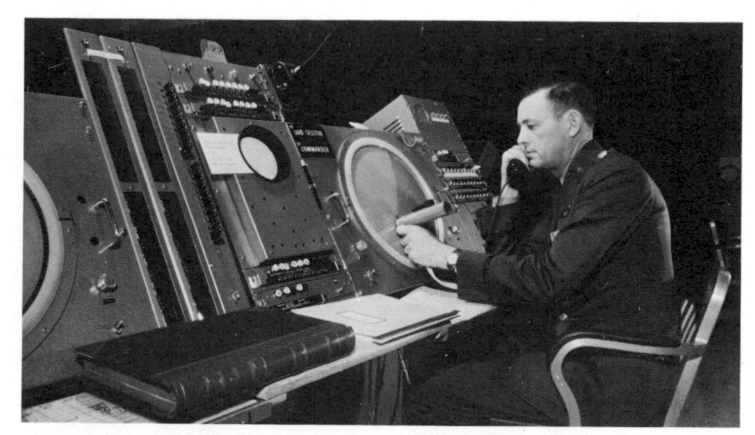

Figure 2.2 Experimental SAGE operator consoles. (*Courtesy of Mitre Corp.*)

In a nonmilitary environment during the 1950s and early 1960s, the TX1 computer at MIT featured a similar type of interactive graphics console. One of the early Digital Equipment Corporation (DEC) interactive computer graphics displays, the Type 30, was modeled after the MIT TX1 system (Fig. 2.3). Another early DEC development evolved from the Type 30 experience—the DEC338, introduced in 1968, was probably the first intelligent graphics terminal commercially available.

Figure 2.3 Digital Equipment Corporation Type 30 display. (*Courtesy of Digital Equipment Corp.*)

2.2.2 The Middle 1960s

A milestone in the development of computer graphics was the pioneering work of Dr. Ivan Sutherland, whose 1963 MIT doctoral thesis describing Sketchpad contained some of the seminal data-structure work laying the theoretical basis for computer graphics software.[1]

Also around 1963, MIT's Steve Coons (now deceased) began developing surface-patch techniques, ideally suited for CAD. Another historically significant graphics program began independently at General Motors (GM). DAC/1 (design augmented by computer) evolved into a major CAD effort and has become a key element in the design of GM cars and trucks (Fig. 2.4). (Ed Jacks and Don Hart had key roles in the GM effort.) The DAC/1's IBM Alpine display evolved into the IBM 2250 graphics console, which was introduced with the IBM System/360 computer series in 1964.

At about the same time, S. H. Chasen put together a team at Lockheed-Georgia to

Figure 2.4 General Motors DAC/1 (design augmented by computer) installation. *(Courtesy of General Motors Research Laboratories, Warren, Mich.)*

investigate the use of computer graphics for numerical control (NC) part programming, Lockheed's first effort in computer graphics and CAD/CAM.

Itek's Digigraphic program was also proceeding at the same time as Sketchpad and DAC/1. Under the influence of Thurber Moffett and Norm Taylor, the Digigraphic product became the basis for Control Data Corp.'s interactive computer graphics line, which subsequently evolved into a variety of systems.

The early to middle 1960s was a fertile period for computer graphics and CAD. By October 1966, even the *Wall Street Journal* recognized the activity and wrote about computer graphics and CAD. Major U.S. aerospace corporations like Lockheed, McDonnell Douglas, and Boeing began to explore the use of computer graphics for aircraft and missile design. IBM organized a program called Project Demand, and worked with Lockheed, McDonnell Douglas, North American Rockwell, Rolls Royce, and TRW in an effort to evolve CAD and, ultimately, CAM techniques. Project Demand may have influenced the design of McDonnell's CADD and Lockheed's CADAM (computer-aided design and manufacturing) programs.

Figure 2.5 shows David Prince's perception of the technological milestones that led to the development of computer graphics during this period.[2]

In the middle 1960s, manufacturers of commercial CRT graphics terminals, who offered CAD/CAM systems and components, included:

Control Data Corporation (CDC)

Digital Equipment Corporation (DEC)

Ferranti

Information Displays, Inc. (IDI)

International Business Machines (IBM)

Sanders

Systems Engineering Laboratory (SEL, now part of Gould)

Univac

In the early 1960s, "computer graphics" was by no means the universal term for the technology. Devices were called electronic displays, computer-controlled displays, information displays, and evaluated data displays. The British called their displays VUBU (visual unit backup), and CAD was often called automatic drafting.

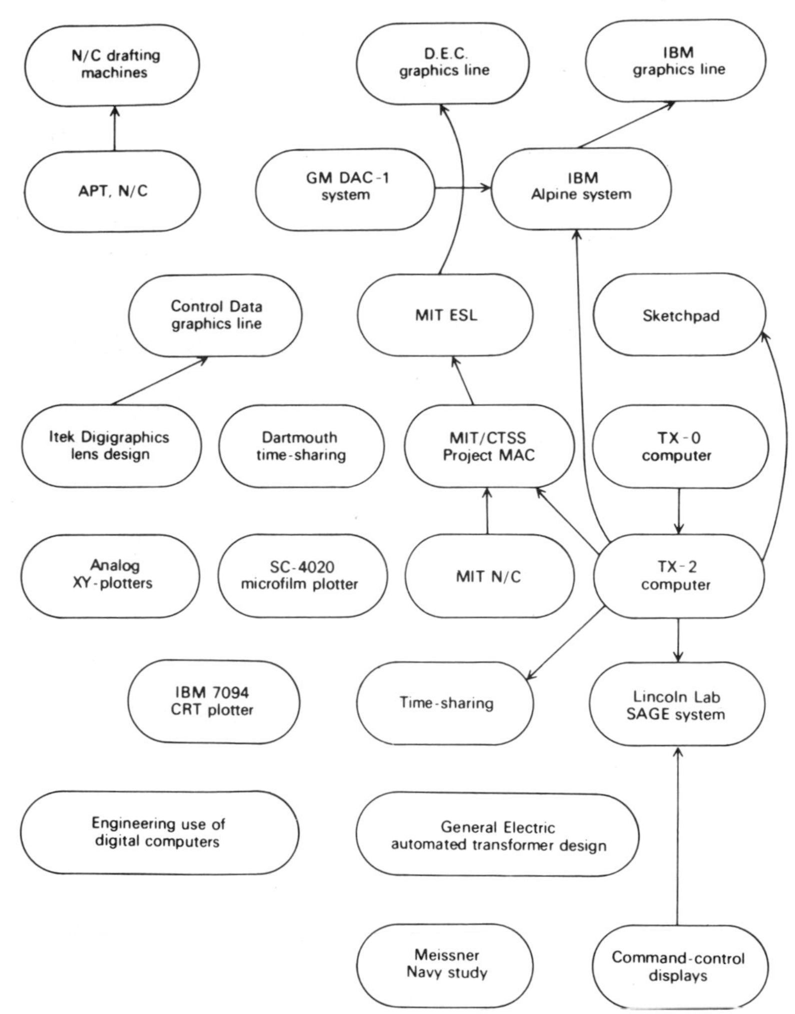

Figure 2.5 Technological milestones leading to computer graphics. (*Courtesy of Addison-Wesley Publishing Co.*)

2.2.3 Storage-Tube Displays

Although Tektronix is now synonymous with storage tube display terminals, it is worth remembering that "way back" in 1965, Bolt Beranek and Newman (BBN) offered the Teleputer terminal using an early 5-inch Tektronix storage tube (Fig. 2.6). This product was used as a mid-1960s computer-aided engineering (CAE) timesharing system. Further, Tektronix was not the first company in the marketplace with the larger storage-tube terminal. That honor is shared by Computer Displays with their ARDS terminal (Fig. 2.7) and Computek with their 400 series terminal (Fig. 2.8). These first systems, which came out in about 1968, used the Tektronix 611 6 × 8 inch storage tube and offered terminals in the $12,000 to $15,000 range. Tektronix then entered the marketplace with the T4002A at about $9000, followed shortly by the 4010 at about $4000 (Fig. 2.9). With the introduction of the 4010, Tektronix was able to dominate the storage-tube display market and, to a large extent, the computer graphics market.

As an indication of technological progress, in the spring of 1983, Tektronix introduced a new line of color raster graphic terminals, including the 4105, a 60 frame per second noninterlaced terminal with a large screen and about the same addressability as a relatively static, monochromatic 4010, at about the same price.

The storage-tube products succeeded in opening up computer graphics to literally tens of thousands of new users. Prior to the introduction of the storage-tube terminal, users were faced with initial investments of $50,000 to $250,000 for hardware alone; the

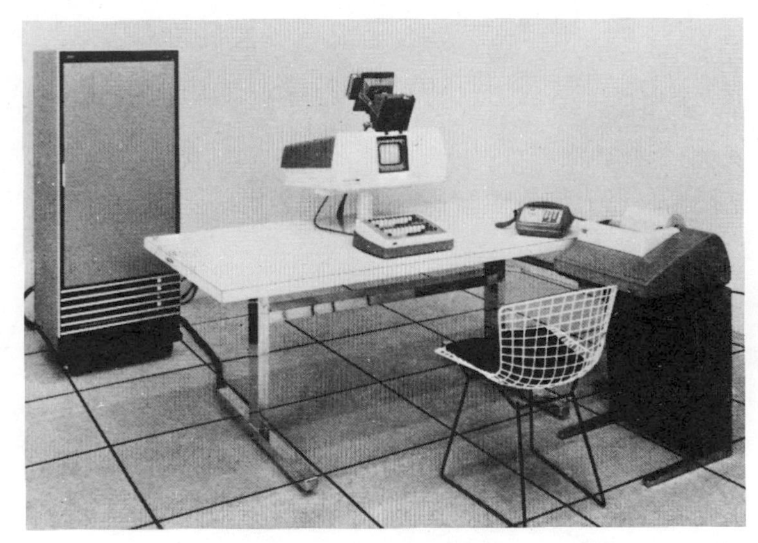

Figure 2.6 BBN Teleputer, an early system using a 5-inch storage tube. (*Courtesy of Bolt Beranek and Newman Inc.*)

cost of software was extra (and usually indeterminate!). These early systems had cost per console-hour figures in the range of $50 to $250. The storage-tube systems had much lower initial costs and could be configured into systems that were costing in the range of $20 to $40 per console-hour. Responding to this low-cost marketplace, manufacturers using other technologies (such as stroke-writing refresh tubes, scan converters, plasma displays, and raster displays) began to offer terminals in the same low-price range.

2.2.4 Hard-Copy Devices

Hard-copy devices are an important element of computer graphics and CAD systems. An early workhorse was the California Computer Corp.'s (CalComp) 565 drum plotter (Fig. 2.10), introduced in 1958. The Tektronix dry silver copier, Model 4610, offering a fast, dry hard-copy capability for under $5000, was introduced about 1970, and it was a major

Figure 2.7 ARDS terminal manufactured by Computer Displays, Inc. (*Courtesy of Adage Inc.*)

Figure 2.8 Computek, Inc., Model 400 storage-tube terminal. (*Courtesy of Computek.*)

contribution to the growth of computer graphics. Now, electromechanical plotters and electrostatic plotters are available in the same price range.

2.2.5 User Input Devices

In the early systems, the users were limited primarily to keyboards, light pens, joysticks, and trackballs. The graphic tablet (as opposed to the electromechanical digitizer) appeared in the late 1960s and the early 1970s.

Figure 2.9 Early Tektronix computer graphics products. (*Courtesy of Tektronix.*)

Figure 2.10 CalComp 565, an early digital incremental drum plotter. (*Courtesy of CalComp, photographed by Bill Butterfield Commercial Photography.*)

2.2.6 Software

The growth we see now has been made possible by a rapid expansion of a wide variety of software packages. It was characteristic of early systems that once the user received the hardware, the burden of making the hardware work with a computer was pretty much the user's problem. That situation has gradually changed over the last two decades, so that a wide variety of proprietary packages are now available that simplify the generation of images, plots, and other graphics. Since the early 1970s, complete turnkey systems have become available that almost entirely isolate the user from software issues. The system is delivered to the user as a problem-solving device, capable of immediate application at the user's facility. Typical of these early systems were products supplied by Computervision (Fig. 2.11) and Information Displays. Although these were primarily drafting systems (CAD),

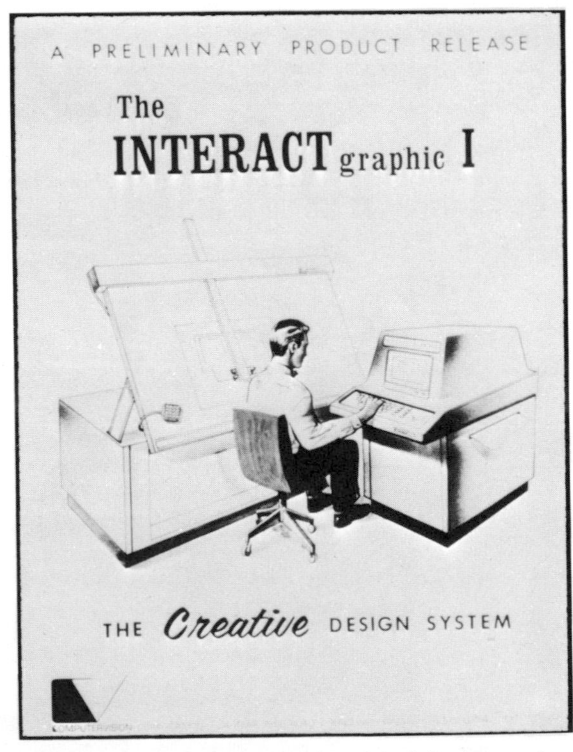

Figure 2.11 Computervision's original business plan cover.

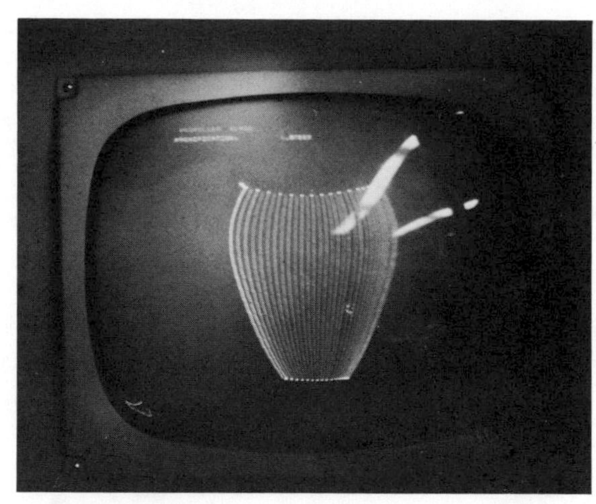

Figure 2.12 National Engineering Laboratories numerical control display.

some, like the Univac-driven IDI unit used by the National Engineering Laboratories in East Kilbride, Scotland, were involved in the development of tool paths for NC machining of turbine blades (Fig. 2.12).

2.2.7 Growing Pains

In the late 1960s and early 1970s, a number of new computer graphics companies were organized. Listed below are just a few of these companies which now offer CAD/CAM products or components and the dates on which they were founded or on which they became active in computer graphics.

Adage (1965)
Applicon (1969) (now part of Schlumberger)
Calma (1968) (now part of GE)
Computervision (1969)
Evans & Sutherland (1968)
Houston Instrument (1968) (now part of Bausch & Lomb)
Imlac (1968)
Lundy (1970)
Megatek (1972) (now part of United Telecommunications)
Ramtek (1971)
Talos Systems (1974) (now part of Sanders)
Summagraphics (1972)
Vector General (1969)
Zeta Research (1969) (now part of Nicolet-Zeta)

Through the 1960s and early 1970s, computer graphics and CAD were considered by many to be expensive toys that could be justified only by government agencies, *Fortune* 500 companies, and university research environments. Computer graphics was effectively known as a "solution for no known disease," and seminars proliferated that asked the question, "Why is computer graphics always a year away?"[3,4]

In 1969, the author estimated that there were probably no more than 100 graphics terminals installed in 1964. That number grew to about 50,000 by 1977 and will probably be in excess of 8.8 million by 1985 (including personal computers with graphic capability).

The applications that could be described in the 1960s included CAD in the aircraft and textile industries, management information systems, simulation, process control, computer-aided education, pattern recognition, graphic arts, and computer-generated movies. Graphics are certainly still being used in these areas, and market penetrations are considerably higher now than they were in the middle 1960s.

CAD now dominates the integrated-circuit (IC) field. A 1978 market study reported that almost 75 percent of all IC design activities were carried on with computer graphics systems.[5]

Another fine view of the CAD/CAM past is given in "Historical Highlights of Interactive Computer Graphics" by S. H. Chasen, published in *Mechanical Engineering*, November 1981. For a good flavor of the 1960s, there are several bibliographies that are of interest, particularly the bibliography "Computer Graphics for Architecture and Design."[6]

2.3 WHERE IT IS: CAD/CAM CASE STUDIES

Today, CAD/CAM can mean

- Computer-aided drafting
- Computer-aided design
- Computer-aided manufacturing

The range of functions normally described in CAD/CAM is illustrated by Fig. 2.13 (adapted from Control Data Corp. data). For a variety of reasons, including available software and the need for a "hard-dollar" basis for justification, most CAD systems are still used for drafting. True design software is not readily available, and true design systems may be too expensive to justify by a first-time user. The dominant CAM application is in the NC environment. Undoubtedly, the concentration on drafting and NC will change in the future (see Sec. 2.4), but drafting and NC clearly dominate CAD/CAM applications today.

CAD/CAM is used in mechanical; electrical and electronic; architect, engineering, and

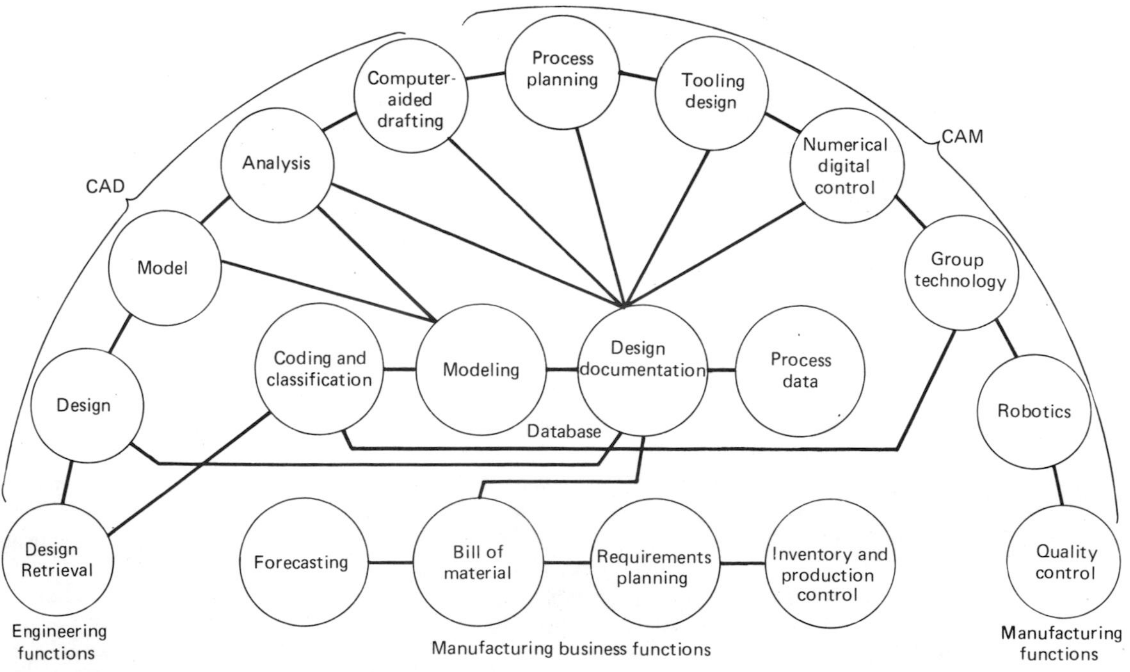

Figure 2.13 Integrated engineering manufacturing system. (*Adapted from Control Data Corp. data.*)

Table 2.1 CAD/CAM Systems Forecasted Growth, 1980–1989

Year ending	Est. system growth, %	Systems installed during year	Workstations installed during year	Total (cumulative) installed systems	Total (cumulative) workstations
1979	—	—	—	3200	12,000
1980	40	1200	4500	4400	16,500
1981	40	1600	6300	6000	22,800
1982	40	2200	8800	8200	31,600
1983	40	3000	12,300	11,200	43,900
1984	40	4200	17,200	15,400	61,100
1985	35	5600	19,600	21,000	80,700
1986	30	7500	26,200	28,500	106,900
1987	30	10,000	35,000	38,500	141,900
1988	30	13,000	42,200	51,500	184,100
1989	30	16,900	54,900	68,400	239,000

NOTE: MAC estimates that there are the following:
About 1,000,000 engineers and about 300,000 drafters in the United States
About 260 U.S. manufacturing companies larger than $1 billion per year
750 U.S. manufacturing companies between $100 million and $1 billion per year
30,000 U.S. manufacturing companies between $5 million and $100 million per year

Source: Prepared by Machover Associates Corporation.

construction (AEC); mapping; and other applications. Table 2.1 shows the estimated and forecasted cumulative installations in these areas from 1979 to 1989, while Table 2.2, adapted from "CAD/CAM Review and Outlook" by Thomas P. Kurlak, Merrill Lynch, Pierce, Fenner and Smith, Inc., September 14, 1982, shows the market size, share of market, and growth. Mechanical applications represented the largest CAD/CAM market from 1979 to 1983, making up 38 percent of all CAD/CAM systems sold in that period. The sales volume grew 13.3 times from 1979 through 1983. Mapping, although a relatively low share of the market (12 percent) between 1979 and 1983, showed the highest growth—increasing almost 17:1 between 1979 and 1983. The growth in mapping has slowed down, however, in the last 2 years (1982 to 1983), while growth in the AEC areas has been highest in that period.

Representative CAD/CAM application case studies follow. Because of space limitation, only a few of the thousands of installations and organizations can be discussed in this section. Selection was based on publicly available information.

2.3.1 Aerospace Industry

Most major aerospace companies worldwide have incorporated CAD/CAM in their engineering and manufacturing disciplines. Their initial efforts date back to the early 1960s. Several, such as Daussault (CATIA), Lockheed (CADAM), McDonnell Douglas (CADD),

Table 2.2 Estimated Worldwide CAD/CAM Market by Application ($ Millions)

	1979	% growth	1980	% growth	1981	% growth	1982	% growth	1983	% growth	Cumulative 1979–1938 Total	Cumulative 1979–1938 % market
Mechanical	128	+85	225	+75	360	+60	443	+23	545	+23	1700	38
Electronic	98	+84	167	+66	233	+40	300	+29	410	+37	1210	27
AEC	58	+100	87	+50	138	+59	200	+46	302	+50	785	18
Mapping	32	+100	73	+128	111	+52	144	+30	180	+25	540	12
Other	18	+82	20	+11	30	+50	63	+110	83	+32	215	5
Total	334	+87	572	+71	872	+52	1150	+30	1520	+32	4450	

and Northrup (NCAD), actively market their programs developed in-house to companies in competitive or related industries. Many aerospace companies have systems supplied by outside vendors as well as systems developed in-house.

BOEING COMMERCIAL AIRPLANE COMPANY

A typical aerospace industry application at Boeing Commercial Airplane Company is described in the following section adapted from "Boeing Unveils New 757: On Time/On Schedule with CAD/CAM" by K. C. Chartrand, which appeared in *Computer Graphics News*, January/February 1982.

On January 13th [1982], the Boeing Commercial Airplane Company's first 757 was rolled out for its public debut at the Renton, Wash. facility. . . . With its sister craft, the wide-body 767, the 757 represents a new generation of commercial airliners that incorporate the latest commercial aviation technology. Remarkably, both planes were produced on schedule and slightly under budget. This feat is credited largely to the unprecedented application of computer-aided design and manufacturing (CAD/CAM) techniques to production of both the 767 and the 757. In fact, the 757 production effort marks the greatest use of CAD/CAM to date by the commercial aircraft industry. . . .

The design of this new jet benefited from a battery of technological improvements and innovations. Foremost among these are improved aerodynamics, a better power plant, reduced overall weight, and a new flight deck. . . . None of them could have been implemented without the direct and intensive application of CAD/CAM. . . .

Boeing encouraged its subcontractors, who were responsible for 45 percent of the work on the 757, to join it in implementing high productivity CAD/CAM technology. The company has used computers to control manufacturing operations since 1958, but the 757/767 programs are the first in which it has made extensive use of both CAD and CAM. The chief virtue of these technologies in the aircraft industry is that they permit the correction of costly design errors and inconsistencies before tooling—or fabricating—is begun, offering substantial savings of both time and money. The CAD program at Boeing currently includes the application of three basic computerized elements:

- *Lofting programs use preliminary baseline designs* (which specify range, number of passengers, wing area, and so on) to mathematically define the surface of the craft with extreme precision. These contours are ultimately transformed into detailed technical drawings and data sets for release to manufacturing units.
- *Automated program tool (APT) software language programs are used to drive electronic plotters* that produce mechanical drawings. Boeing's engineers use APT for much of their early design work, finding it especially effective in defining families of similar, contour-related parts such as fuselage frames.
- *Interactive computer graphics are used to complete drawings begun on the APT system* and to create new finished drawings independently. The data representing an engineer's drawing are stored in the computer's memory; they can then be fed into automatic plotting machines that produce drawings, or transferred directly to manufacturing use.

All of these techniques were used by Boeing's 757 design team to produce drawings and data sets from which the aircraft was built. The 757 program has incorporated CAM to an unprecedented degree; however, the penetration of computer techniques in manufacturing remains far less extensive than in engineering—about 7 percent in tool design, for example.

For at least one of Boeing's major subcontractors, Avco Corporation's Aerostructures Division in Nashville, Tenn., the 757 program was the first broad-based use of CAM technology. Avco's engineers . . . reviewed Boeing's data for ambiguities or discrepancies that would cause problems in manufacturing. When such problems were discovered, Avco's engineers devised a possible solution and submitted it to Boeing. Boeing's designers then either approved the proposal or drew up one of their own. This close working relationship resulted in a remarkable degree of CAD/CAM integration. . . .

One of the best applications of a true CAD/CAM link at Boeing is the manufacture of sheet metal components—the myriad brackets, gussets, hangers, etc., that go into an airframe. Before CAD/CAM, these parts were laboriously guided on manually operated routers, using individual templates as masters, and the average manufacturing cycle was two to three weeks. Now, with Boeing's CAD and CAM departments accessing the same data base through the same terminals, the manufacturing engineer simply adds changes and supplementary information directly to the designer's specifications. The system automatically generates control data for two numerically controlled routers. The current CAM flow time in this integrated system is one hour.

CAD played a dual role in the 757's aerodynamic design; it replaced the traditional draftsman's table in original design work, and it was used to support a graphic, dynamic analysis of the design. . . .

In terms of fuel efficiency, the engines are naturally the most important part of the airplane. The Boeing 757 is offered with two types of engines: the Rolls-Royce RB 211-535C and the Pratt & Whitney PW2037. Both engine-makers used CAD/CAM extensively in their development. . . .

CAD/CAM's contribution to weight reduction took two basic forms: added precision in design and manufacture, and the ability to employ new, lightweight, composite building materials. . . .

CAD/CAM was not only used in the development of the 757 cockpit, it is an integral part of the instrumentation. The cockpit was designed entirely on Boeing's CAD system and manufactured from the same data base. . . .

As demonstrated by the 757, the overall benefits of CAD/CAM implementation in the aircraft industry are many, and they are gaining recognition within the industry. Analysts are cheered by increased productivity, better management control, greater design freedom, shorter lead times, greater operating flexibility, improved reliability, reduced maintenance, reduced scrap and rework, and so forth. Virtually everyone agrees, however, that the greatest benefit of CAD/CAM is that it makes it possible to build better airplanes—like the Boeing 757.

2.3.2 Automotive Industry

The three major American automobile manufacturers—Chrysler, Ford, and General Motors—are heavily involved in CAD/CAM. Each uses a combination of in-house-developed software and turnkey systems in a variety of applications. Each has several hundred CAD workstations installed and each has described plans for increasing integration of CAD with CAM. Extensive use of CAD/CAM is also seen in European and Japanese automobile manufacturers, including Peugeot, Renault, Mercedes, Volkswagen, Leyland, Fiat, Toyota, Nissan, and Mazda. At least one company, Ford of Europe, began to market its in-house-developed program through Prime to Ford subcontractors and other potential users.

FORD MOTOR COMPANY

A representative automotive application at Ford Motor Company is described in the following section adapted from "Graphics at Ford Motor Co. Chassis Engineering" by J. W. Adler and R. J. Ortland, which appeared in the Ford Motor Company newsletter, *Computer Graphics Viewpoint*, April 1983.

In November of 1981, a group of carpenters and millwrights descended on a large traditional drafting room and, using circular saws and impact wrenches, dismantled and disposed of some 50 eight-foot drafting boards, clearing a 4,500 square foot area. Thus began the implementation of Ford Chassis Engineering's 1981–1983, $7 million computer graphics expansion project, which would more than double the 1981 graphics design capacity at Chassis, introduce the Prime network and a centralized computer facility, and further enhance capabilities in the area of structural analysis. . . .

Chassis Engineering was introduced to computer graphics over ten years ago, initially using the Computer CV-1 system, and later the Ford SURFX system. However, the first major effort to implement computer aided design at Chassis was in 1977, with the acquisition of Gerber design stations, linked to an online digitizer and plotter, for which unique software was developed. Today, eight Gerber stations are used primarily for tolerance stacking and certain special purpose, stand-alone programs, such as centerline detailing, tire profiles, spring-deflection geometry analysis, and rack and pinion gear studies.

As development of the Ford graphics system progressed, it was found to be well suited for automotive chassis design and finite element analysis applications. A rapid rate of growth was maintained from 1978 to the present with the Ford system being emphasized in three successive expansion projects.

Facilities provided for in the recently completed expansion project feature through-the-wall installations of the Lundy UltraGrafs, with glare resistant screens. This provides the users with an office environment—normal temperature, sound and lighting levels—while the equipment is housed in isolated service corridors. . . .

A full range of computer graphics applications are currently found at Chassis encompassing Computer Aided Design (CAD), Computer Aided Analysis (CAA), and Computer Aided Manufacturing (CAM).

Chassis CAD applications cover a wide variety of components: wheels, brakes, fuel systems, suspensions, exhaust systems, engine mounts, frame crossmembers, steering gears, steering columns, and controls. Approximately seventy percent of Chassis computer graphics drafting applications involve design and packaging work, essentially all of which is three-dimensional. Tolerance stacks account for an additional 20 percent and detailing represents 10 percent.

Computer graphics, for example, was used to develop converters and associated air systems to accommodate several carline packages for both function and fit, achieving optimum clearances and maximum commonization of parts. The dynamic rotation and surfacing capabilities offered by the Ford system were particularly useful for complex routings and clearance checks.

Computer Aided Analysis, especially Finite Element Analysis (FEA), is used at Chassis to reduce the number of design iterations and subsequent prototype build and testing costs. Over three million dollars annual savings were associated with the 1981–83 graphics expansion. FEA methods provide analysts with: location and magnitude of high stresses, estimates of fatigue life, prediction of deflection of parts where stiffness affects function, and vibration analysis, such as determining natural frequencies and mode shapes of components and systems. Interpretation of FEA results has been aided significantly by the introduction of color graphics to display stress distributions, and by using the Lundy dynamic capabilities for modal analysis.

In addition to finite element work, Chassis Engineering also uses the mechanism program ADAMS on the CYBER 176 and Prime computers to analyze forces and kinematics for generalized linkage designs. . . .

Computer Aided Manufacturing is a logical extension of the three-dimensional design/analysis process. This was demonstrated by Steering Engineering's total CAD/CAM approach to the design of the 1984 Mark VII steering column shroud. . . .

It is planned that within four years 90 to 100 percent of all drafting work in Chassis Engineering will be done using computer graphics.

2.3.3 Electrical and Electronic Applications

Perhaps the earliest application of CAD was for schematic and wiring diagram production. Applications have expanded to include printed-circuit (PC) board layout (with automatic wire routing and automatic component placement), and IC, large-scale integration (LSI), and very large-scale integration (VLSI) design (including schematic entry, logic and circuit simulation, mask layout, gate array layover, and fault simulation).

INTERNATIONAL BUSINESS MACHINES (IBM)

The following section is adapted from "The Interactive Wiring System" by F. D. Skinner, which appeared in *IEEE Computer Graphics & Applications,* April 1981. It describes a system developed and used by IBM.

The Interactive Wiring System [IWS] is a highly interactive graphic application originally developed for the embedding of overflow wires on cards, boards, and other high-level (nonchip) packages. IWS has since been expanded to support component placement, I/O assignment, and service (voltage or test point) net manipulation. This application, part of IBM's EDS—Engineering Design System, operates on a System/370 based graphics configuration, . . . which consists of an IBM S/370 host processor linked to one or more graphic subsystems through a 5098/N5 sensor-based control unit. This link operates at 277K bytes per second and allows each graphic subsystem to be placed up to one mile from the host processor. A graphic subsystem contains a standard IBM 1131/3D 32K-word (64K-byte) central processor, a GCU—graphic control unit, and up to three GDUs—graphic display units (which are IBM 2250/4 CRTs with extended order sets). . . .

IWS/370 represents the first attempt to use interactive graphics to support the large variety of card, board, planar, and module packages used throughout IBM and to provide interfaces from and to the Physical Design (PD) subsystem. . . . The PD subsystem and IWS/370 complement each other, the former being used for functions such as logic entry, global automatic wiring, global checking and release to manufacturing, the latter being used for dynamic incremental changes in component placement, I/O assignment, service point assignment, and wire embedding, and for access to limited autoroute and checking functions. . . .

IWS/370 was first released to the IBM design community in mid-1977 and has been continuously enhanced since then. Many functions have been (and are being) added as the result of user feedback to the IWS/370 development group. . . .

A variety of design criteria underlie the IWS/370 data base structure and the display techniques used to permit interaction with the model represented by the data base. Performance is paramount. IWS/370 has been designed to permit responses to trivial actions (80 percent of a user's activity) within one second, with some responses quicker than 0.15 second. Such response rates are considerably faster than those suggested by reports of other interactive physical design systems. However, a system response time of 1.5 seconds has been found to degrade performance by about 50 percent when compared with response times of less than 0.75 second. Experienced users are expected to cause attentions at an average rate of one action every two seconds. While such performance has not been possible at all user locations, it has been achieved at some locations and remains the design target.

The second most important criterion is prevention of design errors ahead of time rather than notification after the fact. It is the author's [F. D. Skinner's] belief that these two criteria—performance and error prevention (and other less important criteria)—can be best achieved by using a directed beam refresh CRT display, with a light pen as the principal interactive tool, and some very specific logic functions available within the display order list. . . .

The organization of IWS/370 is based on the firm conviction that the user is in charge and should be able to explicitly perform any individual function. Only after the user has been given such capability is consideration given to providing recursive or automatic functions. Automatic functions are limited to those which can be accomplished within a reasonable response time (one to ten seconds) and which leave the user with as much control as possible.

Before [using the] IWS/370, a designer must employ the logic entry capabilities of the PD subsystem to specify the package (card, board, etc.), components, and net structure to be realized; the package and all components must be available to the system in a library. . . .

[Available functions include:]

Component Placement. Selecting the component option on the main menu provides access to various functions for controlling component position and orientation. . . .

I/O Editing. Selecting the I/O option on the main menu provides access to a variety of functions for the review and reassignment of package I/O's. . . .

Service Net Editing. The service net menu provides functions for the review and editing of voltage and test-point nets. . . .

Wire Editing. Selection of wiring data for editing is initiated through one of four main menu options: all nets, user group, check group, or overflows. The subset of nets comprising the user group is determined solely by the user and can be changed at any time. . . .

Utilities. An extensive set of utilities allows the user to change control options, perform limited checking, generate output, and apply some of the automatic functions to a wider set of nets. . . .

IWS has been well received by the IBM design community, with a consistent growth in its usage since its release in 1977. Data obtained from the many users who designed cards and boards during the 1977–1979 period show

- Improvement in turnaround time of 30 to 50 percent,
- Reduction of computer center and director labor costs of up to 70 percent, and
- Reduction of total cost of up to 50 percent, even though both computer center and labor costs have increased substantially since 1977.

Experience at one IBM site indicates that an individual with physical design experience can become productive with IWS in about two weeks, as opposed to a period of six to eight weeks with the batch physical design subsystem.

Incorporation into the system of ideas from IWS users has been one of the major factors in user acceptance of IWS/370. Many functions—especially some of the checking utilities—have been added as a direct result of user feedback. . . .

VIA SYSTEMS

Graphic systems for VLSI design are becoming common. One such system developed by VIA Systems (formerly DMT Corporation) is described in the following section adapted from "A Lower Cost Graphics System for VLSI Design, Design Rule Checking and Pattern Generation" by R. M. Jennings and T. H. Edmondson, *Computer Aided Design*, July 1982.

Just as there is no one "best" circuit technology, there is no best design methodology or CAD toolset for LSI and VLSI design.

Designers quickly learn that there are four basic design methodologies of current interest. Listed in increasing order of layout complexity, they are: gate arrays (uncommitted logic arrays), standard cells, symbolic layout, and hand crafted. . . .

However, all of these design technologies can, and should, be treated as variations on a basic hierarchical (structured) design methodology. . . . [This system is] a combination of 16-bit and 32-bit processors. In such a configuration, massive computational problems, such as logic simulation, placement, and routing, are resident on a 32-bit machine, such as the VAX11/780. Graphics creation and editing functions are performed on a 16-bit machine and networked to the 32-bit machine as appropriate. . . .

The system accepts inputs from commercial graphics system, such as Applicon 870 and 860 and Calma GDSI and GDSII; also, IC layouts can be directly generated using traditional mask images and symbolic layout. The system outputs in Applicon and Calma formats, as well as pattern generation formats. In addition to graphics file inputs, the system accepts pattern generation data in MANN, Electromask, and MEBES formats. This data is reconstructed as a graphics file for manipulation and editing.

Since a major function of the system is to process "foreign" files and to efficiently generate pattern generation output, several additional functions are supported. As examples:

- All touching and overlapping figures (90 degrees, 45 degrees) on specified source layers can be merged into single polygons, subject to input validity rules. This provides substantial reductions in pattern complexity and number of exposures.
- Entire layers can be oversized or undersized. To maintain connectivity, an automatic compensation algorithm ensures that adjacent figures continue to touch after shrinking; also, oversizing does not create new overlaps.

For original layout creation, online design rule checking (DRC) is supported; in this function, illegal figures are flagged by the system as the user attempts to create them. Tests include minimum interior spacing, polygon orthogonality, open polygons, repeated points, and illegal angles.

In batch mode, for files created on the system or for "foreign" files, all figures on a specified layer are checked on the same basis as in the online mode.

Single layer external checks find pairs of figures within a single layer closer than a given distance and copy them into an output file. Test conditions include line-to-line, line-to-corner, corner-to-corner, and "doughnut" violations.

Multilayer external checks find figures on one layer that are closer than a given distance to figures on a second layer. Other tests check enclosures between two layers. Pairs of figures on specified layers, one of which overlaps the other, are examined.

The distance between parallel sides of the inner and outer figures is compared to a test distance, and those pairs with too narrow a border are written into an output file as possible violations. . . .

Both online and batch DRC checks were enumerated earlier. However, it should be noted that the major thrust in the development of this system was the need to reduce the time required to perform design rule checks. Without a hierarchical structure in both design and DRC, it would be impossible to process VLSI circuits on a small machine.

Symbols (cells) are checked at the time they are created and can then be treated as black boxes during higher level DRC.

Since the data structure is organized for mask design, and mask design only, significant efficiencies are obtained both on the graphics system during mask design output and on the pattern generation machine itself.

Software fractures figures, expands cells and arrays, eliminates gaps and overlaps, minimizes the number of exposures, and sorts the data for the chosen output machine. Scaling and imperial/metric conversion are also supported.

2.3.4 Architecture, Engineering, and Construction (AEC)

Between 1979 and 1983, it is estimated that about 18 percent of the value of CAD systems sold were sold to the AEC segment. By 1983, the AEC market was the fastest growing segment of CAD/CAM.

EVERETT I. BROWN COMPANY

The activity of one company, Everett I. Brown Company, Indianapolis, Indiana, is described in the following section adapted from "Graphics for Architecture" by Patrick K. Brown, which appeared in *Computer Graphics World*, March 1982.

> Foreseeing total computerization of building design in the next five to ten years, the Everett I. Brown Company has developed one of the first computer graphic networks for computer aided building design (CABD). This system speeds the execution of all architectural and engineering drawings, resulting in reduced construction and life-cycle costs, eliminating redundant drawings, simplifying and expediting design and drafting work, and giving facilities managers the data and drawings they need.
>
> Departments and professionals within the Everett I. Brown Company are diverse, and include architects, engineers (civil, structural, mechanical, electrical and process), attorneys, CPA's, artists and interior designers, construction managers and superintendents, as well as a rapidly growing number of experts in computer graphics. . . .
>
> In 1978, we purchased a system from M&S Computing, now called Intergraph Corporation. We started in graphics with a DEC PDP 11/34, an 80 megabyte hard disk, three workstations and a Calcomp 960 plotter. Through our first project, this was enough. For the second project, however, we replaced the 80 megabyte disk with a 300 megabyte disk. Presently we have more than 2.65 billion bytes of memory on line.
>
> Early in 1979 we added a fourth workstation and a second 300 megabyte disk. In early 1980 we upgraded the PDP 11/34 to an 11/70, added four additional second generation workstations, another 300 megabyte disk, a 2780 emulator to allow us to communicate with the IBM world, and several pieces of peripheral equipment.
>
> In November 1980, we added our first remote workstation cluster and since then have had as many as three separate remote operations at any one time. Just last July we added a second PDP 11/70, two 675 megabyte Winchester disks (dual porting them to allow access off either system), two third generation raster workstations, a second Calcomp 960 plotter and an electrostatic plotter. . . .
>
> Very recently we installed a PDP 11/23 based system in our McLean, Virginia office. It includes two additional workstations (one with a color raster)—allowing us to operate remote workstations off an 11/70 in Indianapolis, locally off the 11/23 in McLean, or allows the 11/23 to talk with the 11/70 or with any of our remote terminals in client's offices.
>
> In later 1981, we acquired half interest in Mid-States Engineering Co., Inc., an Indianapolis-based photogrammatic and engineering service firm. Mid-States had the first U.S. commercial installation of the Wild Heerbrugg/Synercom Wildmap system, enabling direct digital conversions to a data base from photogrammetric stereo models. They combine aerial mapping with a fully-integrated computer graphics system for site design and engineering, land use planning, and computerized mapping and land data systems.
>
> The integration of ours and Mid-States' computer systems has resulted in what we believe to be the most comprehensive computer graphics engineering and design capability available anywhere. Putting them together means that site survey, planning, new construction, remodeling, and facilities management drawings can all be done on the same computer system using the same data base. . . .
>
> Most architects don't know about such things as computers, production, and investment decisions. Many architecture firms, despite their size, are not prepared to use the technology implicit in computer graphics. . . .
>
> With just three years of computer graphics experience, Everett I. Brown Company had four generations of workstations. The typical architecture and engineering company has some almost insurmountable problems. Not only is there a profound lack of architectural and engineering software, but lack of adequately trained people as well. Along with rapidly changing hardware, comes a bewildering variety of hard-to-evaluate options. Three-dimensional designing is easier and faster, but extremely expensive. In many cases it is unproven, and only the largest firms can afford it. . . .

We always looked at the next largest thing. From basic drafting—using the computer as a substitute for pencil and T-square—we went to cells. These tiny clusters of lines and symbols are the next biggest scale. Here we are using the computer as a substitute for a drafting template. Then we built the next largest scale: "macros", small programs that are clusters of cells or pre-drafted elements, written and drawn. Finally, we are increasingly moving towards still larger scales, calling up whole data bases of complex information. Once we mastered producing drawings, we sought new worlds to conquer.

From production we looked to the next largest context: the overall project. As soon as we could, our computer aided ability was expanded to include all the other data and activities surrounding a project (i.e. programming, estimating, environmental and energy analyses, operating and maintenance costs, plus all of the in-house functions that administer a project). Once the physical design of a project was completed, establishing a data base for the entire project was the next step.

Now having started small, we have looked at the next largest thing: the control of a client's projects over time. Under the title "facilities management", we can build a data base that relates the history and performance of old facilities to ongoing construction. . . .

There is little doubt that within five to ten years computer graphics will be the accepted way to do nearly all architectural and engineering designs and drafting. Companies that start using this technology now will have a big jump on their competition. Implementing graphics takes time. The hardware will cost less next year, but the software may not. But this is not very important when you consider the cost of "people-ware". Labor costs keep climbing. . . .

Make no mistake about it. Computer graphics are here to stay. The opportunities for new and more comprehensive applications by architects and engineers are almost endless.

2.3.5 Other Manufacturing Industries

COMPO INDUSTRIES

In 1983, about 5% of the CAD/CAM sales went into miscellaneous manufacturing industries. Typical of these applications is that of Compo Industries, which is described in the *Computervision Corporation 1982 Annual Report.*

Compo Industries designs and fabricates injection molds for shoe manufacturers. Its customers provide specific shoe designs from which Compo creates sets of shoe molds in every size.

"Making molds requires considerable skill," explains Mark Dane, vice president of Engineering, "and few young people are getting into it. Five years down the road, we could face a severe problem because a lot of senior machinists will be retiring, and their skills will just disappear. Consequently, the decision to purchase CAD/CAM went very, very fast."

Compo uses a Computervision Designer V CAD/CAM system—CAD to design shoe molds, and CAM to machine the finished mold designs.[*]

Joseph Lewis, Compo's director of CAD/CAM Applications, feels that it is impossible to separate CAD from CAM in his operation. "If we just developed the CAD portion, we couldn't machine the parts we had designed. The Computervision system is one package. We chose it because CAD and CAM are integrated beautifully."

According to Scott Somerville, CAD/CAM manager, "customized software lets a designer spend one hour on a mold and save 20 hours of machining."

The system does many tedious, repetitive tasks, freeing designers to use their creative skills on the actual design on the shoe. "Really what we're doing," says Lewis, "is allowing our designers to spend a lot more time working where there's the highest return on investment."

2.3.6 Mapping

SOUTHERN BELL TELEPHONE

About 12 percent of the value of CAD/CAM systems installed between 1979 and 1983 are used in mapping applications. A number of telephone companies, for example, have installed CAD systems to provide up-to-date map and detailed plant information. A

[*]Computervision and Designer are registered trademarks of Computervision Corporation.

representative system, installed at Southern Bell Telephone, Atlanta, Georgia, is described in the following section. This section is from an article which appeared in *Telephone Engineer and Management Directory,* July 1981, vol. 46, and was reprinted in *Mapping and Earth Sciences, Production Application Profiles,* publication number DGC007AO, published by Intergraph Corporation in 1982.

In August 1981, Southern Bell Telephone, headquartered in Atlanta, Georgia, took the first step in an extensive overhaul of its outside plant record keeping system. At Ft. Lauderdale, Florida, one of its six operating areas, the company installed an Intergraph interactive computer graphics system designed to fully automate the outside plant record keeping process and generate information to meet the requirements of engineering, operating and accounting personnel. . . .

This fully-operational system provides immediate access to up-to-date map and detailed plant (equipment) descriptive information in formats tailored to each type of user. For the local environment, the system offers interactive graphics, and full analysis and reporting capabilities for record maintenance and volume job processing. For the remote environment, the system generates microfilmed maps to be used in conjunction with interactive alphanumeric terminals for daily inquiry, analysis and reporting. And, for the mobile environment, the system provides microfilmed maps for field location of equipment and for the identification of field configurations. . . .

Until recently, manual map and record keeping has been sufficient, but the sheer size of Southern Bell's network—13 million telephones, connected by 93 million miles of cable running underground and suspended from 1.5 million poles—made an automated facilities information management system a necessity. . . .

Hardware for the Ft. Lauderdale system includes an Intergraph 780 Central Processor with magnetic tape and disk drives, eight interactive graphics workstations for digitizing and maintaining plats, two electrostatic plotters to generate quick copies of information displayed on the workstation screens, seven alphanumeric terminals for record input and maintenance, and a large format electrostatic plotter. . . .

On a daily basis, Southern Bell must initiate hundreds of field installation projects in order to maintain and extend service to its growing customer base. When Network Services issues a work request, Bell personnel must respond with a so-called "work print" prescribing what to install and where to install it. These individuals work from plats, also known as "outside plant records," each one detailing the equipment in a small section of the operating area. Besides consulting plats and record ledgers, outstanding work orders must be referenced so that the instructions issued do not conflict with work already in progress. Previously, each of these steps was performed by hand—all maps were hand drafted, and ledgers were updated by hand. Each needed to be kept meticulously up-to-date to avoid discrepancies that could cost thousands of dollars. In all, the all-manual process was tedious and offered the everpresent potential for posting backlogs and errors.

The Intergraph FIDS system replaces this manual system with a central digital database designed to store all plats and associated descriptive records for the entire area. The FIDS Work Authorization Processing/Tracking Subsystem enables Bell to rapidly access plats from the database for display on the workstations' high resolution 11" screens. Accompanying records for a displayed plat are accessed interactively by entering a "fence" command into the display. When a certain type of record is specified by the operator, the system automatically searches the database and displays the desired equipment record on the workstation screen. Once a work print is drafted, changes to the plat are rapidly posted back to the central database using the workstation cursor and specialized commands from the system's Telephone Applications Menu. . . .

Outside plant records (plats) often contain drawings of planned construction in addition to drawings of facilities as they are presently configured. The proliferation of projects in various stages of completion, oftentimes overlapping on the same part of the network, has greatly complicated the plat and record update process. For example, with the traditional manual system, more than one individual can be working with the same plat which creates the potential for conflicting changes to be scheduled.

The FIDS system eliminated the potential for these conflicts by virtue of its central database and its resident security features. . . .

Telephone mapping and records keeping practices have been well defined for years, but they have always been vulnerable to individual interpretation. Without realistic means to fully enforce standards under the manual system, map symbology and annotation varies, leading to confusion and errors by users.

To resolve the standardization problem, the Southern Bell System is equipped with data entry and automatic editing routines which fully enforce Southern Bell standards. Any data entered which violates code is not accepted and is annotated as an error requiring correction.

Other features in the system include

- Cable size pair number validation
- Cable throws-automatic ripple processing
- Automated loop makeup reporting
- Accounting applications

2.3.7 Utilities

SOUTHERN COMPANY SERVICES, INC.

Utilities were one of the early adapters of CAD—utilizing the technology in a variety of applications. One typical application at Southern Company Services, Inc., is described in the following section adapted from an Applicon case study published in 1979, "Automated Drafting System Levels Manpower Loading and Improves Drawing Quality at Southern Company Services," publication number M4108.

Southern Company Services, Inc.—a subsidiary of the Southern Company—provides technical and other specialized services to the Southern Company and its four electric utilities in the Southwest: Alabama Power, Georgia Power, Gulf Power, and Mississippi Power. Based in Birmingham, Alabama, with offices in Atlanta and New York, SCS provides a complete range of engineering and technical services necessary for the planning and design of all the electric-generating facilities in the Southern electric system. About 1200 people are employed in the engineering area, with approximately 800 directly involved in power plant design. Plans for an average of 8 to 10 plants are usually in process at SCS at any given time.

As power generation technology advanced, plant designs have become more and more complicated. Additionally, increased government intervention in the design process, especially in the area of pollution control regulation, required many thousands of extra engineering hours.

This expansion in the number and scope of projects has demanded that close attention be given to ways in which resources can be used more effectively and increasing costs can be held to a minimum. Southern Company Services decided to evaluate automated drafting as one method of increasing drafting efficiency. . . .

After extensive evaluation of the technology and methods of automated drafting, Southern Company Services installed, in January of 1976, a computer graphics system to be used primarily for the production of diagrammatical drawings. The interactive system, designed and manufactured by Applicon Incorporated of Burlington, Massachusetts, consists of a Digital Equipment Corporation minicomputer, three drafting workstations, a high-speed flatbed plotter, and associated computer peripheral hardware. It allows operators, some of whom have no drafting training, to create drawings, based on engineering-supplied sketches, in a more timely, cost effective, and efficient method than manual drafting techniques had previously allowed.

During the process of system implementation planning, Southern Company Services management decided that the best method of operation would be to centralize the automated drafting functions in one group. As Martin L. Brannon, SCS's Supervisor of Methods Studies and Applications, explains, "This method of centralization allows for a concentration of manpower. When we implemented our first automated drafting system for diagrammatic work, we believed that by keeping all of that particular type of work in one area, we could maintain one level of drafting manpower and minimize the 'float' we were experiencing in those design groups whose major output was diagrammatical drawings."

Drawings created in automated drafting are more visually pleasing, and the symbology is more standardized for clarity. Most revisions can be accomplished both more quickly and more easily than with manual methods, and each revision appears as clear and uncluttered as a new drawing. Uniformity of the appearance of drawings makes them more easily verifiable, as well as simpler to read to the field construction people working from them. Drawing production times have decreased significantly. . . .

Willard C. Payne, Supervisor of Automated Drafting at SCS, explains the procedure in his department as follows: "When an engineer from one of our mechanical or electrical design groups needs a piping and instrumentation diagram, elementary diagram, wiring diagram, function control diagram, or simple dimensional drawing such as a control panel layout, he no longer has to sit down and discuss his requirements with a drafter. Instead he merely free-hand sketches what he wants and sends it to our group. Our operators work from this rough sketch to produce a new drawing on the system. Creating a new drawing may take eight hours or less, depending on the size and complexity of the drawing.

A ballpoint pen on bond paper check plot is produced on the system plotter in about ten minutes and, after an initial verification by the Automated Drafting personnel, it is sent back to the engineer for verification. The engineer indicates any necessary revisions or updates on the drawing and returns it to Automated Drafting. There, an operator redisplays the drawing (which has previously been stored on magnetic tape) and performs the necessary revisions.

According to Mr. Payne, "Most revisions can be accomplished in about 30 minutes. The quality of the revisions produced on the Automated Drafting System is an improvement over those done manually, since new additions do not have to be squeezed in as they were manually. Instead, whole sections of the drawing can be moved about and spread to make room. In the same way, if whole sections are deleted, the drawing can be condensed. Text and symbols appear uniformly spaced throughout the drawing, making it easier to read.". . .

Since the installation of the first system in 1976, Southern Company Services has expanded its Automated Drafting Group to include another three-terminal system. The Group now operates three 8-hour shifts per day, five days a week, with a total of 18 operators actively producing drawings. Approximately 30 newly created or revised E-size (34 × 44") drawings are plotted each day, about 6,000 each year. These drawings, stored both on magnetic tape and on microfilm, are carefully catalogued for easy retrieval. . . .

2.3.8 CAD/CAM for the Smaller Company

Historically, CAD/CAM systems were the tool of large companies. To make the initial investment of about $500,000, a company needed to have about 20,000 hours of manual drafting and design time per year—which meant that the company's annual volume was about $50,000,000 per year or more. And, in fact, even into the early 1980s, it was estimated that over 80 percent of CAD/CAM systems were installed in organizations of that size or greater. There were exceptions, of course. Either smaller companies "bit the bullet" on the major expenditure because they anticipated appropriate returns, or they began to acquire low-cost CAD systems (under $100,000) which began to appear on the markets around 1980. Two small-company applications are described in the following section adapted from "You and Your Computer, Designed for Productivity" by Tom Wolpert, which appeared in *Venture*, January 1982.*

H. THOMAS KELLER, INC.

Thomas Keller, president of H. Thomas Keller, Inc., a Highpoint, N.C., furniture design company, foresaw the possibilities for CAD in his organization when he saw the graphics package on a home computer in a retail shop. Keller, who had no prior experience with industrial computers before he purchased his system, uses it for his own $1 million (sales) company, and he set up another division, called Meta Vision, a computer service bureau, to rent out time on the CAD system to help justify the initial expense. He charges users $50 an hour, or $65 an hour if Meta Vision does the work.

Keller purchased his CAD system for $300,000 from Information Displays, Inc. (IDI) of [Armonk,] N.Y. While IDI provided the basics, Keller developed his own listing of symbols used to execute complex graphics commands tailored to furniture design. "There are literally thousands of components to furniture design," says Keller. "And we're developing a symbol for each. It's a huge task." The IDI CAD System, which Keller chose because its

*Reprinted from the January 1982 issue of *Venture*, The Magazine for Entrepreneurs, by special permission. 1982, Venture Magazine, Inc., New York, N.Y.

software was best suited to the ornate curved lines necessary in furniture design, employs a light-pen used directly on the monitor screen. And, training has not been difficult for the 10 employee company. Says Pat Leonard, systems manager of Meta Vision: "We've been able to train people to work at their manual speed in two or three days. In another week, they're able to significantly increase their output. We've been extremely pleased with the results so far."

RAM AERIAL MAPPING

It is not only architects and other sorts of designers who have put CAD systems to work in their offices. Ram Aerial Mapping, a Newton, N.J.–based company which provides topographical maps to utilities, construction companies, and municipalities, purchased a system in 1980. Edward Drelich, president of Ram Aerial, chose a configuration sold by Datatech of Boston, and spent $100,000, including software, to obtain the capabilities he needed. . . . Drelich was familiar with the turf, having worked in electronics and with computers for close to 20 years; however, even allowing for that experience, the easy integration of the system into his company has been remarkable. "They came and unloaded it one afternoon, and it has worked since then with no hitches," he says.

Drelich's system differs somewhat from other CAD applications. The machine is not used strictly for design, although it is composed of the basics found in a CAD system . . . . But, it has a special device called a stereo plotter which enables Ram to produce maps representing three dimensional landscape features from aerial photographs. In addition, Drelich plans to eventually use the system to handle normal data processing tasks, such as payroll and accounts receivable. . . .

The availability of low-cost CAD systems has been of special interest to the small (less than 10-person) architecture office. One such user is described in the following section adapted from "Cold Climate Cultivates Creative CADD," which appeared in *Design Graphics World,* May 1983.

WILLIAM BERGENTHAL

Not long ago, Alaskan architect William Bergenthal was faced with a problem. His increased workload (usually a situation an architect looks forward to) meant he would have to either turn down business (not desirable) or hire more people. Fortunately for Bergenthal, he discovered an alternative solution, computer aided design and drafting (CADD).

William founded A2D2, his one-man architectural firm, in 1977. His projects include both commercial and residential developments which he handles from his Anchorage home.

During a period with an extremely heavy workload, Bergenthal looked into the possibility of a CADD system in order to help handle the tasks. "Work here is seasonal," he explained, "and I didn't want to hire more people for the short-term."

The CADD system Bergenthal decided on was TOUCH 'N DRAW from Arrigoni Computer Graphics, Inc. The complete system is made up of a desktop computer, a file manager, a digitizing tablet, a plotter, and software. . . .

Bergenthal cited several reasons for purchasing a CADD system. "I thought it would do everything I wanted, and I was very impressed with the software," he stated. "And the equipment didn't require a special computer room, making it possible for me to work from my home."

Installed in May 1982 [the CADD system], Bergenthal began training on it immediately. "I was given four eight-hour days of training," said Bergenthal. "I was also given a toll-free number to call if I had any questions."

Initially, Bergenthal plans to use the CADD system on a project for the largest lumber company in Alaska. As part of a major expansion, the company plans to add several facilities. He'll use the computer to design the first facility. As an ongoing project he can then modify those plans for facilities to be added later.

According to Bergenthal, the main benefit of using CADD has been the speed with which he can produce drawings. "I'm able to work faster," he stated, "and my drawings are extremely accurate." . . .

Not only is the CADD system a help in the creative process, but it's also an effective marketing tool. "More clients come my way because of the CADD system," Bergenthal said. "Everyone is interested in computers these days, and if you offer something different, you have edge."

Also, by 1980, traditional turnkey companies began to offer "starter kits" to provide entry-level systems for small companies. A mold design application is described in the following paragraph adapted from the *Computervision Corporation 1980 Annual Report*.

INDIANA DIE CAST TOOL, INC.

Indiana Die Cast Tool, Inc. [Franklin, Indiana], designs and machines plastic molds for customers in the television, appliance and computer industries.

A Computervision CAD/CAM system has reduced by one third the time to prepare designs and drawings for molds and has greatly improved the efficiency of shop-floor operations. The results are reduced costs and shortened development cycles.

Indiana Die Cast Tool, Inc. is a family owned business with 50 employees and annual sales of less than $3 million. The company serves customers having diverse requirements for complex plastic molds where speed of delivery is crucial.

When the company management decided in 1977 to install a CAD/CAM system to integrate design and manufacturing, it was initiating an important new competitive strategy for a firm of limited size.

Not only did the Computervision Designer system streamline and shorten design turnaround times, but it also optimized the transfer of information between design and manufacturing groups to bring a better product to market faster.[*]

At Indiana Die Cast Tool today, a designer builds a model of a mold with the assistance of a Computervision [the CAD/CAM] system, revising, modifying and varying elements ten times faster than could be accomplished manually. Herbert English, company president, reports, "We can completely design and prepare drawings in one-fourth to one-third the time previously required." . . .

2.4 WHERE IT IS GOING

Over the next few years, we can expect both technology and application enhancements and expansion in CAD/CAM.

2.4.1 Technology

From a technology standpoint, there will continue to be the conflicting pressures of higher performance and lower cost. This will result in:

- Higher-resolution color displays probably moving to 2000 lines by the mid-1980s (60 frames per second noninterlaced) to create more realistic images.
- Continuing pressure for improved ergonomics since the user community and some of the federal and state organizations are beginning to consider legislation regarding the use of visual display terminals.
- A large number of simultaneous colors, as display images move from line or schematic drawings to full shaded pictures, will become more common. Typical CAD displays will probably push toward 500 to 1000 colors simultaneous.
- Real-time manipulation of shaded images—initially manipulation of previously generated images—then reduced time to generate new images.
- Growing use of voice, sight, and gesturing devices for operator interface. By mid-1980s, for example, continuous speed voice input will probably be a common feature in CAD/CAM systems.
- Much more functionality (both picture manipulation *and* applications) built into systems as hardware or firmware.
- Increasing use of microcomputers (especially as they move to 16-bit and 32-bit CPUs over the next few years) as lower cost, somewhat lower functionality stand-alone

[*]Computervision and Designer are registered trademarks of Computervision Corporation.

systems, and as part of a local-area or wide-area network, or as highly intelligent workstation front ends for large mainframe-based programs, particularly computer-aided engineering (CAE).

- Continuing demands for quick-look and final-output quality color hard copy. In the next few years, we should see improved techniques (that is low cost per copy) for producing engineering-sized multiple-color hard copies at costs similar to black-and-white (or blue-line) copies used today.
- Growing use of "soft-copy" terminals on the shop floor so that the latest versions of a drawing can be distributed without concern that the hard copy on hand has not been appropriately modified and therefore does not represent the latest version.
- Automatic and semiautomatic engineering drawing digitizers will become more common. By applying EXPERT programs, increasingly sophisticated pattern recognition will be incorporated into the systems.

2.4.2 Applications

From an applications standpoint, pressures will continue to integrate manufacturing and drafting and design, create systems for users not presently taking advantage of CAD/CAM, and refine present techniques for true design (goal seeking), group technology, process planning, quality control, and robotics. Expected developments in the next few years include:

- Growing skill in computer-integrated manufacture (CIM). CAD systems will be increasingly able to account for special manufacturing requirements in the design phase. Systems will begin to tie into present materials requirement planning (MRP) systems. It will probably be well into the 1980s and early 1990s before CIM for mechanical applications becomes as common (and as sophisticated) as the level of CIM achieved in today's PC, IC, and VLSI worlds.
- Specialized users who have developed unique programs for their applications or industry can be expected increasingly to bring these programs to market, either as third-party software or as turnkey systems.
- Decreasing costs for systems (some adequate CAD systems in the $5000 to $10,000 range) will open the use of CAD to an ever-increasing number of small companies. *As appropriate software becomes available,* we will probably see the use of CAD growing in the small architecture office, machine shop, tool and die shop, technical writing and documentation shops, and small civil engineering offices. As data interchange standards [such as the Initial Graphic Exchange Specification (IGES)] become refined, we will see increasing pressure by contractors to force subcontractors to accept CAD and CAM databased material rather than conventional drawings.
- As we learn more about the "goal-seeking" aspects of the design process, we will see increasing availability of EXPERT programs that are essentially software mimics of the way an expert analyzes a problem and reaches a decision. Closely associated with artificial intelligence, these more "bounded" programs will probably begin to be quite common in CAD/CAM systems by the end of the 1980s.
- EXPERT programs will also be a prime element in computerized process planning, which should become common by the late 1980s.
- Increasing use of group technology can be expected over the next decade. In a sense, CAD makes it too easy to create a new design (not necessarily in itself costlier, but costly because of manufacturing implications). Group technology can provide a mechanism for desirable standardization.
- As the use of flexible manufacturing systems (FMS) and manufacturing cells becomes more common, CAD/CAM systems can be expected to provide more quality control and robotics features.

2.5 SUMMARY

Perhaps, in a larger sense, the principal impact of the growing use of CAD/CAM will be in the way in which we organize to do business. Walls between engineering and manufacturing will crumble, some traditional specialties (like manufacturing engineering or process planning) may disappear, absorbed into other disciplines (like design), and relationships between contractors and subcontractors will change. In any case, these changes represent exciting problems and opportunities for us all.

REFERENCES

1. Sutherland, I. E.: "Sketchpad: A Man-Machine Graphic Communication System," TR-296, MIT Lincoln Laboratory, Lexington, Mass., January 1963.
2. Prince, M. David: *Interactive Graphics for Computer-Aided Design*, Addison-Wesley Publishing Co., Reading, Mass., 1971.
3. "Interactive Graphics: Where is the Market," Symposium sponsored by Keydata Corporation in Boston, Mass., May 13, 1969.
4. "Why is Computer Graphics Always a Year Away?" Symposium sponsored by Battelle Seattle Research Center in Seattle, Wash., July 31 to August 1, 1973. Proceedings published as "Computer Graphics," *ACM SIGGRAPH Newsletter*, vol. 8, no.1, Spring 1974.
5. "Computer Graphics Equipment, Software and Services in the Manufacturing Industries," no. 490, Frost & Sullivan, New York, N.Y., April 1978.
6. Milne, Murray (ed.): *Computer Graphics in Architecture and Design*, Yale School of Art and Architecture, Yale Corporation, New Haven, Conn., 1969.

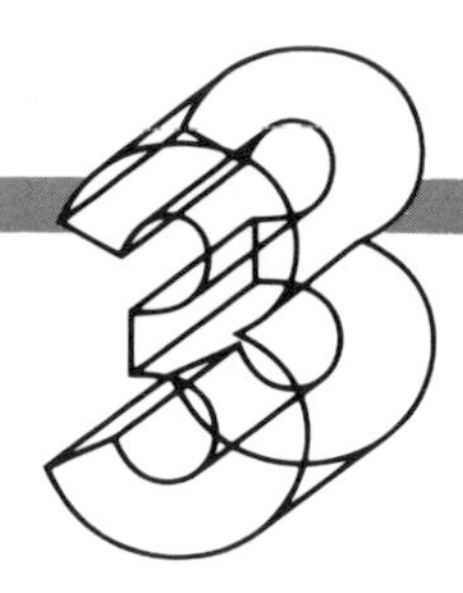

Tools: Hardware and Software

by
Joel Orr

3.1 GENERAL

It is no longer possible to understand the functioning of a machine by simple visual examination. Since the invention of the computer, the intelligence that operates within the heart of the machine is invisible. That intelligence, of course, is computer software, which is discussed later in this chapter. Hardware is what you see when you look at a computer-aided design and computer-aided manufacturing (CAD/CAM) system.

Only a small portion of CAD/CAM system hardware is unique to CAD/CAM systems. The computation devices are common to all computer systems, as are the communication devices. Graphical displays and input and output devices are shared with business graphics, mapping, animation, simulation, and other graphics systems. The only uniquely CAD/CAM devices are special interfaces to numerical control units and robots.

The components of a CAD/CAM system are input devices, displays, output devices, computation devices, and communication devices. Each of these is discussed in its own subsection. The first three fall into two broad categories that correspond to the two basic systems for encoding pictorial information for computer manipulation. These two systems are called *vector* and *raster* and are described in the next section.

3.1.1 Vector Graphics

With vector encoding, an image is represented in terms of the lines it comprises. Each line is defined by the coordinates of its endpoints; curves are described by using very short straight-line segments or can be represented by polynomial approximations.

A vector input device typically looks like a large drafting table, with a movable part called a *cursor*. The cursor is placed over the point whose coordinates the operator wishes to determine; the operator then presses a button, causing the coordinates of the location indicated by the cursor to be stored. This process is called *digitizing*. The operator moves the cursor to another position and digitizes that point, indicating (by means of a button) whether or not it is connected to the previous point.

Most vector graphics displays are cathode-ray tubes (CRTs). The displays are similar to plotters, except that an electron beam is the writing device (tracing the outline of the drawing) and the phosphor-coated front of the CRT is the drawing medium.

A typical vector output device is a pen plotter, in which a pen is moved under computer control from point to point on a piece of drafting medium. The plotter moves the pen just as a person would draw lines on paper, with the pen in contact with the drafting medium as it moves to draw the line. The pen lifts and moves to a new point (without touching the medium) to start a new line.

3.1.2 Raster Graphics

In the raster method, the entire picture area is divided into small homogeneous cells as if by a grid. Each such cell is colored in some way, like a tile in a mosaic, with all tiles having the same size and shape. In the simplest form, each cell contains either a color or the absence of color. In more complex systems, each cell contains one of a range of colors and shades. These cells are called picture elements or *pixels*.

The quality of a raster picture depends on two parameters: the number of pixels per unit of area (resolution) and the range of colors and shades permitted each pixel. Of course, the smaller the pixel and the greater the variety of available colors and shades, the better the picture will look.

Raster input devices do not distinguish individual lines but take in the entire image, pixel by pixel. Typical devices are TV cameras (with digitized output) and digital facsimile machines.

In raster CRT displays, the electron beam always traverses the same path. The only thing that changes from one pass (or frame) to the next is the beam intensity, which changes on a pixel-by-pixel basis. An image is thus created by light and dark dots, evenly sized and spaced.

Raster output devices generate images one line of pixels at a time (as do electrostatic plotters) or a single pixel at a time (as do digital facsimile receivers). It is, of course, possible to use a vector input device, such as a digitizing tablet, with a raster display or hard-copy output unit. Off-the-shelf hardware and software can take care of the conversion from one format to the other, albeit at some cost.

Figure 3.1 Intelligent vector and raster refresh displays. (*Courtesy of Megatek.*)

3.2 INPUT DEVICES

3.2.1 Functions

Three major functions are served by graphic input devices. First, they are used to get pictures into the computer, such as maps, seismograms, and engineering drawings, as well as continuous-tone imagery, such as remotely sensed data and advertising art. Second, the devices are used in conjunction with interactive graphics displays to control a cursor that moves on the face of the display. The area of a small digitizing tablet is "mapped" to the face of the display in such a way that the motion of a stylus or other type of cursor on the tablet controls the corresponding motion of a cross or other marker on the graphics display.

A third use of graphic input devices is function selection; this happens in three ways. The first way is with menus, which are specially designated areas of digitizer boards that are laid out similarly to keyboards. They have function names and symbols placed inside of grid cells. The computer system associated with the digitizer "knows" that when a point is digitized within that area, it is to activate the selected function rather than simply enter the *XY* coordinates of the point into the database. The second way is with a screen menu, where by using the graphic input device as a cursor control unit, instructions are selected on a graphic display. The third way is by using the stylus of the digitizing tablet to draw simple characters or symbols which are recognized by the associated computing system as cues, invoking certain commands.

3.2.2 Features

The main operational features of input devices are listed below.

- ***Size of Input Document Allowed.*** Where applicable, this varies widely; digitizers as small as 8 inches square and as large as 4 × 5 feet are available.
- ***Resolution, Accuracy, and Repeatability.*** Resolution usually means, "How close together can two points be and still be recognized as two separate points?" Accuracy in the plane is difficult to define, but basically it refers to the correlation between measurements determined by the graphic input device and real-world measurements. That is, if a line is known to be a foot long and the digitizer says it is 1.001 feet long, then that is a measure of the accuracy of the digitizer. Repeatability means that if a point is digitized and redigitized many times, how small will the range of values be? These terms are frequently used very loosely and should be carefully defined within the context of each individual piece of equipment under consideration before making a decision based on them.
- ***Device Intelligence.*** Many input devices contain powerful microcomputer systems. A user must determine how much intelligence is required for tasks such as rotation, translation, and other forms of encoding in relation to the system into which the input device is to be integrated.
- ***Raster or Vector Format.*** If the data are ultimately going to appear in vector format, it is likely that a vector input device is needed. If the data are to be manipulated in raster format, a raster input device is required. It is possible to gather data in raster format and to convert it to vector format; however, this requires highly specialized and expensive software. Similarly, vector data can be converted within a computer into raster format slightly more easily than the conversion in the other direction. However, these considerations must be carefully examined, as conversions typically make extensive use of processor resources.
- ***Color Discrimination.*** Some input devices, in particular raster scanners, are capable of discriminating among different colors in the source materials.
- ***Operational Environment.*** It is important to specify the conditions under which the device is expected to operate—temperature, humidity, dirt, and so on.
- ***Computational Environment and Interfaces.*** Will the device have to operate with existing systems or software? It is important to specify precisely what systems and software the device will have to support.

3.2.3 Types

DIGITIZER BOARDS

Description. Digitizer boards are electromechanical vector graphic input devices that typically resemble a drafting board with a movable stylus or reticule called a *cursor*. They are used to enter drawings into computer graphics systems by taping the drawing to the surface of the digitizing board and placing the cursor over points whose coordinates are to be entered. Often called simply *digitizers*, the major subgroups are

- ***Free-Cursor Digitizers.*** The cursor is a low-mass device at the end of a flexible piece of wire.

- ***Constrained-Cursor Digitizers.*** The cursor slides along a gantry that traverses the entire digitizing board area.
- ***Motorized-Cursor Digitizers.*** The actual cursor motion is effected by motors, driven by an operator-controlled joystick.

Salient Features. Free-cursor digitizers allow greater ease of use with menus where the cursor must be moved about quickly from one location to another, while constrained-cursor digitizers provide the capability to work in an upright mode and for the operator to release the cursor without having it fall to the ground. Motorized digitizers combine the best features of both free-cursor and constrained-cursor units but usually add some expense. Available resolution is to 0.001 inch. Available accuracy is to 0.003 inch. Digitizer boards are available on an off-the-shelf basis in sizes from simple 11 × 11 inch tablets to 48 × 60 inch backlit translucent boards. Other sizes can be produced on special order.

Price Range. Small, low-resolution units are available for as little as $600. Large, motorized, backlit, high-accuracy units cost $20,000 and more.

JOYSTICK, TRACKBALL, MOUSE

Description. All three of these devices contain potentiometers (variable resistors), the settings of which can be used to control various graphical functions, such as the location of a cursor upon a display screen. The joystick consists of a spring-loaded stick that can be tilted in any direction. The direction of the tilt is usually used to indicate the desired direction of motion for the cursor, while the angle of inclination determines the speed of cursor motion.

The trackball resembles a billiard ball. It is partially ensconced in a pocket, inside which are potentiometers that are normally used to control cursor position. The ball is rolled with the palm of the hand; the cursor is usually made to move in the direction of the roll at a rate corresponding to the rotational speed of the ball.

Mouse is the name given to a graphic input device that functions, in essence, like an upside-down trackball. The mouse is rolled about on any flat surface; the cursor is caused to move in a direction corresponding to the direction of motion of the mouse wheels, or ball, and at a corresponding rate.

Salient Features. These devices are generally used for cursor positioning. While users often indicate distinct preferences for one or another, studies indicate that there is no inherent superiority to any of them; all are approximately equal in terms of ease of use.

Price Range. These devices cost between $100 and $750.

LIGHT PEN

Description. The light pen is a stylus-shaped pointing device that senses light emanating from a display screen. Through timing measurements, the system is able to determine the point on the display at which light is being detected. Light pens sometimes contain light-sensing electronics in the stylus; in other configurations, optical fibers are used to route the screen light to the light-detection circuit.

Salient Features. Proponents of the light pen claim that its similarity to the traditional tool of the drawing maker is a great advantage, as in the directness of the pointing action. Detractors cite low resolution and the need to hold the pen up to the screen (supposedly excessively fatiguing) as reasons not to use this device.

Price Range. Light pens cost from $150 to $400.

POTENTIOMETERS

Description. Potentiometers are variable resistors, like volume controls on radios. Banks of potentiometers are used on some systems for controlling a variety of graphic input functions, such as entering rotation angles. In Tektronix direct view storage tube (DVST) displays, potentiometers (sometimes called *thumbwheels* in this context) are used to position the cursor on the display.

Salient Features. Potentiometers are convenient devices for entering relative magnitudes.

Price Range. Potentiometers cost from $100 to $800.

GAZE-DIRECTED INPUT UNIT

Description. Gaze-directed units bounce a low-power laser beam off the eyeball of the user to determine the direction of gaze. This information can then be used like any other positional information.

Salient Features. This unit is an experimental device, developed to enable pilots of high-speed military aircraft to manipulate controls when other resources fail. It has been used experimentally at MIT Architecture Machine Group in conjunction with a spatial data management system to enable an operator to select objects by looking at them.

Price Range. Prices for gaze-directed input units are in the low thousands.

THREE-DIMENSIONAL DIGITIZERS

Description. There are a variety of apparatuses on the market that enable the user to position a probe or cursor in space and obtain cartesian, spherical, or cylindrical coordinates. These are useful for digitizing three-dimensional objects, such as engineering models.

Salient Features. Resolution, accuracy, and digitizing space dimensions vary from ¼ inch to micrometers. Cost increases exponentially with accuracy.

Price Range. Three-dimensional digitizers cost from $600 to $300,000.

STEREO COMPILERS

Description. Stereo compilers have been used to collect data from stereo pairs of aerial photographs for a number of years. Many of these units have now been computerized by the addition of digital shaft encoders. Though expensive, stereo compilers are typically extremely stable and highly accurate from a mechanical point of view. However, they are slow and not convenient for low-resolution digitizing.

Salient Features. Stereo compilers have resolution and accuracy down to several microns. They are designed for use with 9-inch photographic plates and are not easily modified for other formats.

Price Range. Stereo compilers cost from $65,000 to $500,000.

"WHOLE-EARTH" DIGITIZERS

Description. Whole-earth digitizers are inertial navigation devices converted for surveying use. They contain a gyroscopically stabilized platform which is calibrated at a position of known coordinates and elevation, then transmits in digital form coordinates of the new location to which it is moved. They are now being used in conjunction with satellite navigation systems.

Salient Features. Still in the experimental stage, whole-earth digitizers are expected to revolutionize large surveying projects.

Price Range. Whole-earth digitizers cost $150,000 and up.

LINE FOLLOWERS

Description. Line followers are a type of equipment that electromechanically identifies lines and follows along, transmitting the coordinates of points at which the line changes in direction, thus providing pure vectorized output. They are semiautomatic in operation and require a full-time operator.

Salient Features. Line followers are highly accurate, operate at moderately high speed, and are extremely expensive. They are useful primarily for highly convoluted linear imagery, such as topographic maps with little or no text, since they do not handle text easily.

Price Range. Line followers cost $50,000 and up.

TOUCH DIGITIZERS

Description. Touch digitizers act as overlays for CRT displays. They sense the location of physical contact. They are used primarily for menu selection and secondarily for cursor control. Several types are on the market and employ different technologies.

Salient Features. Touch digitizers resolve down to 0.01 inch.

Price Range. The cost of touch digitizers can run from $800 to $3000.

RASTER SCANNERS

Description. Raster scanners are drum or flatbed devices containing a strong light source and a precision diode array or other light-sensing device. The head traverses the image area in a raster pattern and transmits on a pixel-by-pixel basis information to the controlling computer.

Raster scanners are relatively fast input devices but provide no intelligence along with the data. That is, there is no way of telling from the input of a raster device that two pixels are associated with a particular line. Currently, no text recognition is available either. However, raster scanners are the leading candidate for the input end of the fully automatic digitizing devices, which are probably no more than 3 years away.

Salient Features. Raster scanners resolve up to 1200 lines per inch and have an accuracy similar to their resolution. They have a speed up to 30 minutes for a 40×60 inch area, depending on resolution.

Price Range. Prices for raster scanners are $40,000 and up.

TV CAMERAS

Description. Regular video TV cameras can be used as raster input devices. The analog output of the TV camera is simply converted into digital format by standard electronic means. The resolution of the TV camera depends on the optics placed in front of a Vidicon tube or charge-coupled device array.

Salient Features. TV cameras are relatively low-cost raster input devices.

Price Range. TV cameras cost $3000 and up.

3.3 DISPLAY DEVICES

3.3.1 Functions

Graphics displays provide the CAD/CAM system user with a window into the mind of the system. Models that exist only in mathematical form can be viewed on the graphics display. If the display is large enough—as in the case of projection displays—it can be used for sharing the model with other users, as in meetings.

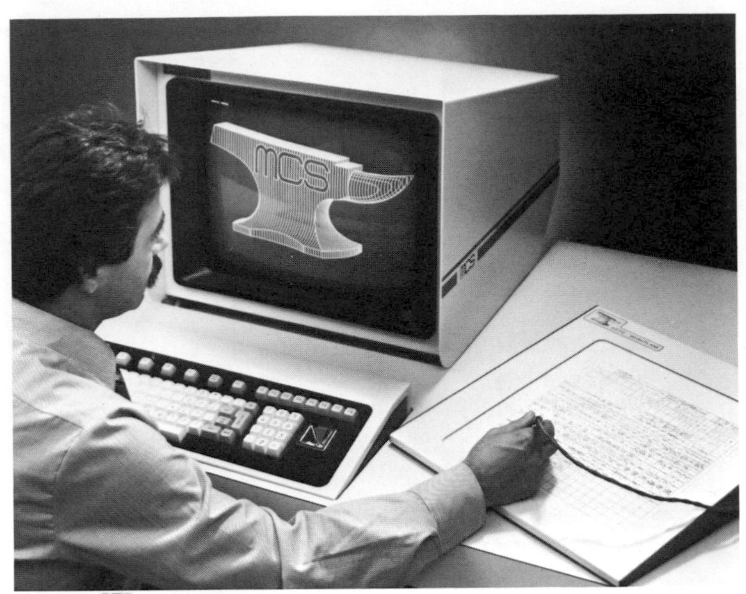

Figure 3.2 A workstation, consisting of an intelligent raster refresh display, a digitizing tablet, and a keyboard. (*Courtesy of MCS.*)

3.3.2 Features

Graphics displays are characterized by the following features:

- ***Resolution.*** As in input devices, resolution refers to how close two points can be together and still be separable. The range of resolutions for commonly used graphics displays is from 200 × 300 points or pixels to 4000 × 4000 points or pixels.
- ***Display Size.*** This may vary from about 2 inches diagonal up to 24 feet diagonal for projection displays.
- ***Speed.*** The ability of the display to show dynamic images depends on the speed at which it can redraw the image on the display. This is usually measured in microseconds or nanoseconds per pixel.
- ***Number of Vectors.*** This applies primarily to vector refresh displays in which the number of vectors—expressed sometimes in vector per inch—is limited.
- ***Color.*** The number of colors that can be simultaneously shown varies generally with the price of the unit. There are displays with as few as two colors up to as many as millions of possible colors.
- ***Physical Operating Environment.*** Some displays are more sensitive to temperature, humidity, and vibration than others. In some situations the display may itself affect the environment, as in the case of high-security installations, which require displays that are shielded so that they do not radiate information into the environment.
- ***Interfaces.*** Displays vary widely by available interface. Standards—RS232C, GPIB, etc.—are usually supported; specialized parallel and serial interfaces can often be ordered.
- ***Software Support.*** There are some de facto standards in graphics display command sets, such as those of the Tektronix 4010, Tektronix 4027, and DEC VT 100. A display manufacturer will often say a display is "Tektronix compatible."
- ***Light Output.*** This varies from dim, requiring a partially darkened room, to very bright. While specification sheets will sometimes express this factor in footcandles or lumens, it is generally more useful for the user to judge by demonstration.

- ***Hardware Function Generation.*** Some displays have local graphic "intelligence" and are able to generate various geometric shapes, such as circles, ellipses, curves, and rectangles, based on simple commands. Another common feature is "polygon fill," in which an enclosed area can be filled or flooded with a specified color. The speed of the fill function varies considerably from one unit to another. Local text and line font generation are also sometimes available. Other functions include alternative displays, meaning that there is sufficient memory for the terminal to store locally more than one screenful. Panning, zooming, and dragging are other functions that are sometimes implemented locally.
- ***Programmability and Local Memory.*** Many displays are actually complete graphics computers and can store data and be programmed.
- ***Hard-Copy Interface.*** Many graphics displays offer simple interfaces to common hard-copy output units, such as the Tektronix 4631 or the Versatec V-80.
- ***Input and Interaction Devices.*** Graphics displays generally come with some form of graphic input device. On Tektronix displays, this is usually thumbwheel cursor controls or a joystick. Other displays might include a tablet or a mouse. Not all displays offer all types of input devices.

Figure 3.3 A dual-screen workstation. (*Courtesy of Intergraph.*)

3.3.3 Types

There are several different types of graphics displays; cathode ray tubes are, by far, the most common.

CATHODE RAY TUBE (CRT)

Description. The common television picture tube is an example of a CRT. It is an evacuated glass bottle, the inside front of which is coated with a material called a *phosphor,* which has the property of emitting visible light when struck with a stream of electrons.

In *refresh* CRTs, the picture is redrawn at least 30 times per second—usually from local memory—so that the viewer has an impression of a constant image being displayed. There are vector refresh CRTs—also called directed beam or calligraphic—

in which the electron beam draws the lines of the image being displayed. These are characterized by high resolution (4000 × 4000), high dynamics, and high cost.

In a raster refresh CRT, the beam traverses the same path over and over, creating an image by becoming stronger and weaker and thus illuminating or not illuminating the phosphor dots over which it passes. Color is available on both vector and raster refresh CRTs; however, it is much less expensive on raster CRTs.

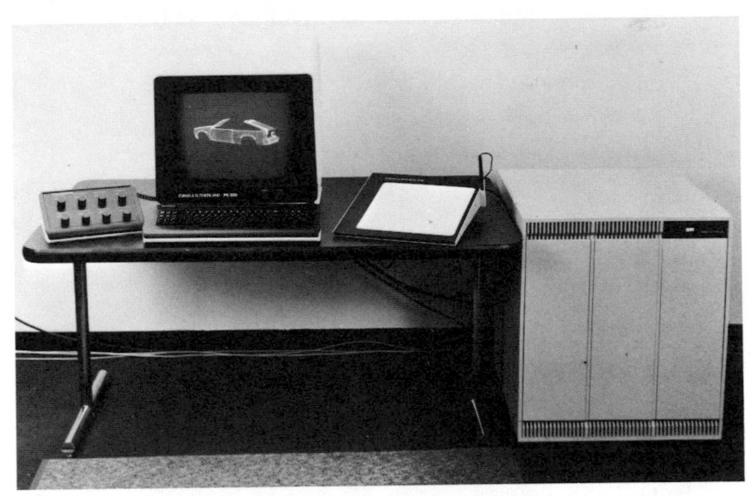

Figure 3.4 A vector refresh display. (*Courtesy of Evans and Sutherland.*)

In *storage* CRTs, the image is actually stored on the face of the display. Thus, the main electron writing beam need draw the picture only once. The electronics of the CRT retain the image on the display with no need for refresh memory. Storage tubes (also called DVSTs—direct view storage tubes) are characterized by extremely stable high-resolution images. Lines, however, cannot be individually erased; the entire image must be erased and redrawn without the undesired line. Another disadvantage is that light output is relatively low.

Combination storage and refresh displays are available in which part of the image can be stored and part displayed in vector-refresh mode. Storage displays are manufactured only by Tektronix.

Salient Features. CRTs are by far the most common type of graphics display. They consume relatively large amounts of power and require high voltages for image generation. There is also a potential radiation hazard with every CRT. Because of mass production of television sets, these are by far the least expensive type of graphics displays.

Price Range. CRT prices start at $50.

PLASMA DISPLAY

Description. In a plasma display a thin (1-inch) glass envelope is filled with an inert gas, such as neon. There are usually two sets of electrodes at right angles to each other that do not touch at the point where they appear to cross, being separated by a critical distance. A voltage applied across one electrode from each of these pairs causes the gas at their juncture to ionize. The gas then enters the plasma state of matter—an intermediate state between liquid and gas having characteristics of both; in this state it emits visible light. Very little current is required to keep the gas ionized and it can be switched on and off very quickly—in a matter of nanoseconds.

Salient Features. Plasma displays are flat, can be transparent, possess high light output and low power, and are relatively expensive. Color is still experimental.

Price Range. The prices of plasma displays start at $3000.

LIGHT-EMITTING DIODE (LED) DISPLAY

Description. In LED displays, the LEDs are bunched together, each one constituting a pixel in a raster display. Both monochromatic and color displays of this type have been assembled. Uses for LED displays are primarily military.

Salient Features. LED displays possess extremely high light output and medium power consumption and they are very expensive.

Price Range. LED displays start at $25,000 for a complete intelligent terminal.

LIQUID CRYSTAL DISPLAY (LCD)

Description. LCDs have become common and popular in watches and toys. The liquid crystal material is amorphous until submitted to an electric field, at which point it behaves like a crystal, reflecting light in one direction, depending on polarization. The LCD is a passive display, requiring an external light source. It is not commonly used for major commercial applications but has the potential for being so used.

Salient Features. LCDs have extremely low power consumption, are very flat, and are inexpensive to manufacture in quantity.

Price Range. No practical models are available for true graphics use at this time.

ELECTROLUMINESCENT PANEL

Description. As in the LCD, an electric field is used to create an image pattern. The electroluminescent panel, however, contains a chemical compound, such as zinc sulfide, which emits visible light when exposed to an electric field.

Salient Features. Electroluminescent panels have extremely low power consumption and can be made not only on glass but on flexible materials too. They have high light output and are relatively inexpensive to manufacture.

Price Range. Small quantities of displays are currently available for $500 and up.

PROJECTION SYSTEMS

Description. Various means are used to project an image onto a screen. Available projection systems include CRT projectors, diffraction light values, liquid crystal projectors, and a laser scan unit. The most common is the CRT projector, in which a CRT (or three of them for color) is mounted in such a way that its light output is passed through a special lens system and directed onto a screen. These are relatively inexpensive and have relatively low light output, sufficing for images that can easily be viewed in partially lit rooms.

Diffraction light valves use a complex mechanism that consists of an oil film and diffraction plates to enable a very bright light to be modulated by a color video signal. These are much more expensive than CRT projection units and have much higher light output and resolution. Images up to movie theater size can be viewed in relatively high ambient lighting.

There are not many liquid crystal projection units on the market. They are between the CRT and the diffraction light valve in cost. These are monochromatic and can display extremely bright images by using a liquid crystal to modulate a bright light beam.

Only one type of laser-photochromic film exists; it is called the Laserscan and is manufactured in England.

In it, a laser is directed in much the same way as the beam of a vector refresh CRT; the laser, however, "writes" on photochromic film—film that is temporarily clarified by exposure to light. A bright light is then projected through the film to produce a large image on a frosted glass screen. The film can be moved forward like a scroll, and within 20 minutes will "forget" the lines that were written on it. This unit produces very large, very sharp displays.

Price Range. Costs are $2000 and up for CRT projection systems, $20,000 and up for diffraction light valves, $15,000 and up for liquid crystal, and $300,000 for the laser scan unit.

3.4 OUTPUT DEVICES

3.4.1 Functions

Hard-copy output is the interface between the computer-aided design and drafting (CADD) system and the non-automated world. Output devices are primarily used to generate images on human-readable media. The output can be used in the same way as manually created drawings, thereby minimizing the trauma of automation for the user organization—at least temporarily.

3.4.2 Features

Output devices have the following features.

- ***Media.*** Standard output media include paper, Mylar, kronar, linen, vellum, and photosensitive film. Some types of output devices—e.g., pen plotters—can handle a wider range of media than others—e.g., electrostatic devices. Devices also vary widely as to the dimensions of the output they provide.
- ***Speed and Throughput.*** Do not confuse these two parameters. The time required to draw a particular type of line may be irrelevant to start-to-finish time in your application. *Both* parameters must be considered in the context of what you will be doing with the hard-copy device. For example, a flatbed pen plotter may have a pen motion speed far in excess of that of a given drum plotter; however, in an application requiring 25 plots at a time, the drum plotter could show greater throughput. Requirements should be defined in terms of plots per day rather than inches per second. In a related vein, pen plotter speed figures can be deceiving in another way, unless the devices' acceleration rates are known. For example, a 40 inch per second pen plotter that needs to accelerate in a straight line for 35 inches to attain that speed is going to be spending most of its time plotting at considerably lower speeds. Pen plotter accelerations currently range from under 0.5 to 6g. Pen plotter speeds range from about 3 inches per second to over 40 inches per second. With regard to electrostatic and other raster plotters, while output rate is usually constant, the computer time required to rasterize a vector plot is not! This parameter should be checked carefully.
- ***Resolution, Accuracy, and Repeatability.*** These terms are similar to those used for input devices. *Resolution* usually means, "How close together can two points be plotted and still be two separate points?" Resolution may also determine how smoothly curves are plotted.

  Accuracy could mean different things to different people. Users should define it for their own use, then let the suppliers know their definition. One definition is "How different from 1 inch is a plotted 1-inch line?"

  Repeatability means, "If four points are plotted in the corners of a plotting area, then plotted again, how close will the second set of points be to the first?" Remember that in the case of graphic computer output microfilm (COM), it may be necessary to consider the parameters of the "blowback" unit (the apparatus used to enlarge the COM output in normal office use) as well as those of the COM unit.
- ***Character, Curve, and Pattern Generation.*** Many graphic hard-copy devices today contain hardware character, curve (usually conic sections), and pattern generators. These features can greatly increase productivity—*if* the application is capable of taking advantage of them. They do in hardware tasks that were

heretofore accomplished in software—namely, the drawing of lines that make up the characters, curves, and patterns of the output. The controlling device has only to issue an appropriate code for, say, the letter "A"; the character generator produces the lines that make up the letter. Similarly, the hard-copy device generates patterns or curves based on succinct control codes from the controlling device, rather than having to receive commands defining all the points in a pattern or curve. Before deciding to require any of these features, make sure they will be useful in the intended application(s).

- ***Raster or Vector Format.*** Raster devices "paint" pictures by letting the point of image creation cover the area of the drawing in a line-by-line area-filling pattern, much like a commercial television set. Vector devices paint from point to point, with the point of image creation traversing the component lines of the drawing. Electrostatic plotters are examples of raster devices, while pen plotters are vector devices.

  Although there are other considerations, the format in which data are to be used should have some effect on the selection of a raster or vector hard-copy device. Vector devices need data in vector format, while raster devices are happiest with data in raster format. It is certainly possible to convert from one format to the other; however, such a conversion is typically a computer-consuming task. Since most graphic data at this time are stored in vector format, raster device vendors offer rasterizing processors as options with their gear. Vector devices, until recently, had a clear advantage in resolution over raster devices; raster technology has now almost caught up. However, vector devices still have a clear lead in resolution per dollar.
- ***Color.*** Color is fun, but expensive. If just colored lines are needed with only small areas in color, pen plotters will do. If you need color-filled areas in quantity, you can select from electrostatic color plotters, color ink-jet plotters, the various color matrix (impact) printers, color thermal printers, or color computer output film (COF) units. Remember that, for small quantities, the cost of color copies is almost negligible; it is well worth your while to use color if you can.
- ***Operating Conditions.*** What type of environment will the machine work in? Not all hard-copy output devices can survive dirty environments or extremes of temperature, humidity, or line current fluctuations. Who will run it? Will it have a dedicated operator, or will the night security guard be instructed to push the red button when the paper box is empty? These considerations should be expressed in the statement of requirements.
- ***Software.*** Some device suppliers provide certain programs free with the device and charge for others.

3.4.3 Types

PEN PLOTTERS

Description. Pen plotters are electromechanical devices that move a marking or scribing device and a piece of marking or scribing medium in relation to each other. Major subgroups are the following:

- Stationary-medium plotters, such as flatbeds, in which the drawing medium does not move (but the writing device does)
- Moving-medium plotters, in which the drawing medium is moved along at least one axis

Salient Features. Some moving-medium devices, such as drum plotters, can produce many plots in sequence, while stationary-medium units usually have a more limited working area. Available resolution is to 0.0005 inch, and available speeds are 3 to 40 inches per second. Pen plotters require point-to-point (vector) data. A plotter can usually hold two or more different pens—different colors, line widths, etc.

Figure 3.5 A D-size pen plotter. (*Courtesy of Bruning.*)

Price Range. Desktop units cost between $600 and $10,000. Large high-precision, high-speed devices go to $125,000. A continuum of prices and features is available.

ELECTROSTATIC PLOTTER

Description. A row of nibs (typically 100 to 200 per inch) is used to place point charges on a band of special paper stepping past it, usually at a constant rate of about 1 inch per second. The paper then moves through a toner bath; toner adheres to the charged spots and is baked on at a subsequent step in the process. Electrostatic plotters are available in widths of up to 72 inches. This "television" drawing pattern is called a raster. Separate rasterizing controllers are available as options from some firms, reducing the computation burden on the host computer.

Salient Features. Electrostatic plotters require raster data. They are typically more expensive than pen plotters and can be used as line printers. They operate silently with a constant drawing rate, usually about 1 inch per second, independent of drawing width or complexity. Maximum resolution is 300 points per inch. Electrostatic plotters can plot on dimensionally stable media, whether clear, opaque, or translucent. Color is available.

Price Range. Depending on width, nib density, and color, costs are from $4000 to $102,000.

GRAPHIC COMPUTER OUTPUT FILM (COF)

Description. Graphic COF units contain a high-precision CRT on which images are drawn. An internal camera—usually shutterless—is pointed at the CRT. The COF controller controls the drawing of images and the motion of the film. Exposed COF film is then developed in the usual photographic way. Some COF units allow the use of instant Polaroid film.

COF units come in two distinct categories: small COF units and computer output microfilm (COM) units. The small units that are now available are designed to offer a low-cost solution to the problem of color hard copy. These contain relatively inexpensive cameras and produce output on 8 × 10 inch, 4 × 5 inch, or 35-millimeter film. Their resolution is low to medium-high horizontal lines over the image area.

By contrast, COM units are far more expensive, have far greater resolution, and contain picture- and character-generation electronics. Blowback units are available that can accurately enlarge a 35-millimeter graphic image to engineering C or D size.

Most COF devices, including COM, have an optional apparatus that interposes color filters between the CRT and the camera, making color output possible. Some COM units can "draw" in either raster or vector mode; others can mix modes. Instead of a CRT, some units use a laser or electron beam to write directly on film in a lensless camera system.

Salient Features. Film sizes for COM are 35, 16, and 105 millimeter fiche, 105 millimeter full frame. Other COF film sizes are 8 × 10 inch for single image and multiimage and 4 × 5 inch.

Resolution. For COM points, resolutions are 512 × 512 to 16,384 × 16,384 (useful resolution depends on spot size). Few drawings take more than 12 seconds to draw. Other COF units have resolutions of 500 to 2000 horizontal lines. Output resolution depends on the resolution of the display.

Price Range. Costs are $3500 to $30,000 for the small COF units; others range from $120,000 to $450,000.

IMPACT PRINTER-PLOTTERS

Description. A wide range of devices produce images on paper by impact through an ink-bearing ribbon. Included in this group are daisy-wheel and thimble printers; matrix, belt, chain, and drum printers; Selectric printers; and others. These units produce graphic images in a dot-by-dot fashion or by using different characters in a raster pattern. Virtually all such units are primarily printers, secondarily plotters. Most have bidirectional paper feed. A number of impact matrix printers use multicolor ribbons to produce color dot plots.

Salient Features. Resolution is generally limited to 100 points per inch. Most units are not designed to plot quickly.

Price Range. Input printer-plotters cost from $1,000 to $25,000.

THERMAL AND ELECTROPHOTOGRAPHIC PRINTER-PLOTTERS

Description. These plotters are similar to impact printer-plotters except in the method of producing an image. Thermal devices use a heat process to bring out images on special paper; electrophotographic devices employ a dry silver-coated photosensitive paper that is developed by a heat process. Gray-scale reproduction is available on some models; color is also available.

Salient Features. See "Impact Printer-Plotters."

Price Range. Costs range from $1,000 to $7,000 and $12,000 for color.

LIGHT OR LASER RASTER PLOTTER

Description. A light or laser beam is used to write in a raster pattern on film with great precision.

Salient Features. These plotters resolve up to 1000 lines per inch.

Price Range. Costs are $50,000 to $250,000.

COLOR INK-JET PLOTTER

Description. The image is generated by three or four ink-jet sprays, each channeling a different primary color (or black) to paper. In higher-priced models, the paper is attached to a spinning drum. The ink jets traverse the spinning drum longitudinally, forming a raster image on the paper. In lower-priced units, a similar arrangement obtains, except that the paper is advanced as in a standard line printer. Color plots with up to 15,625 different shades can be produced.

Salient Features. The drawing size is to 22 × 34 inches with a point size to 0.008 inch. Resolution is to 150 points per inch. Expensive units produce plots with excellent color characteristics; others are limited by the quality of their inks. Minimum plot time is 1 minute. Cost of materials is $0.10 to $3 to $4 per plot.

Price Range. Ink-jet plotters cost as little as $700 and as much as $70,000.

COLOR COPIER

Description. In color copiers, a laser is used to transform computer-generated color separations into electrostatic images on the copier's selenium-coated drum. The drum then attracts colored toners, which are applied and baked onto paper (or clear plastic, for transparencies). Interfaces exist for most color terminals.

Salient Features. Drawing size is to 8½ × 11 inches and resolution is to 100 points per inch. Color copiers produce relatively low-cost, high-quality color hard copy and can also be used as regular color copiers.

Price Range. These units cost from $30,000 to $50,000.

CRT FLATBED PLOTTERS

Description. A CRT head is mounted on a flatbed plotter and is used to expose large sheets of film in a dark environment.

Salient Features. This is an experimental model.

Price Range. A CRT flatbed plotter will cost around $350,000.

PHOTOPLOTTERS

Description. A photoplotter is similar to a pen plotter except that a light beam is used to write on film in a dark room.

Salient Features. Photoplotters are highly precise and are used for printed-circuit (PC) board and large-scale integrated circuit (LSI) masks.

Price Range. Photoplotters cost from $20,000 to $250,000.

THREE-DIMENSIONAL DISPLAYS

Description. There are currently two demonstrable three-dimensional displays on the market, one commercially available, the other not yet funded for marketing.

The commercially available system is called SPACEGRAPH and comes from Genisco Computers Corporation. It employs a vibrating vinyl mirror that is synchronized with images appearing on a CRT to present a virtual three-dimensional image to the viewer, who sees the reflection of the CRT in the mirror.

The other unit has no name as yet. It is available for viewing at the MIT Innovation Center. The display consists of a board of LEDs mounted on edge on a turntable. As the turntable rotates, the LEDs corresponding to the instantaneous intersections of the plane of the display and the three-dimensional model are turned on, then off; this occurs at approximately 2° intervals. Since the board spins at a high rate, the net effect is of a three-dimensional image floating in space.

Salient Features. The MIT unit is more of a true three-dimensional display, in that it can be viewed in normal room lighting from virtually any angle. The Genisco unit, however, is commercially available. Applications include subsurface mapping, medical imaging, mechanical design, etc.

Price Range. SPACEGRAPH costs $59,000. No price is available yet on the MIT unit.

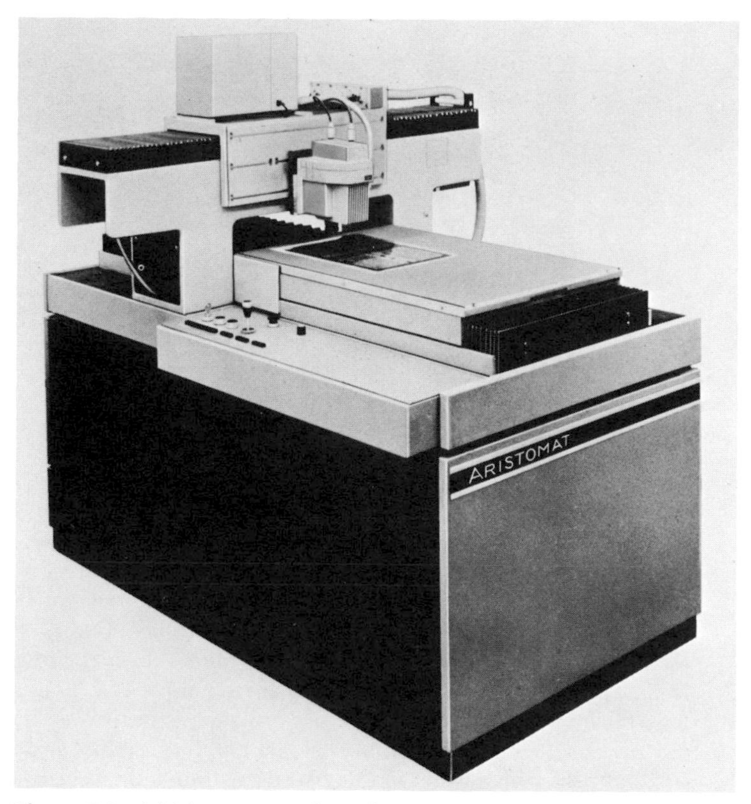

Figure 3.6 A high-accuracy photoplotter. (*Courtesy of Aristomat.*)

3.5 COMPUTATION DEVICES

The programmable computing part of a CAD/CAM system is not as simply categorized as the graphics peripherals. Boundaries between previously well-defined groups have become quite fuzzy. In general, there are three sizes of computation devices: large, medium-size, and small.

Large computation devices would be (erroneously) called "mainframes" by most people. This category embraces computers such as the IBM 370 and 30XX Series, the CDC Cyber Series, and the Univac 1100 Series. Some would put the DEC VAX 11/780, the DG MV8000, and the Prime 750 in this category; others would place the IBM 4331 in the medium category.

Medium-size systems use computers such as the PDP-11 Series by DEC, the Data General Eclipse and Nova units, or the Hewlett-Packard 1000 machines. These used to be clearly characterized by having a 16-bit word length (a computer's word length is the size of its basic unit of data). However, there are a number of 32-bit word length minicomputers today, such as the Data General MV4000, and the DEC VAX 11/750.

The small computation devices are usually based on microcomputer chips (*chip* means integrated circuit). These include the 8-bit ZILOG Z80, INTEL 8080, INTEL 8085; the 16-bit INTEL 8086 and 8088 and the ZILOG Z8000; and the 16/32-bit Motorola M68000 and INTEL 4/32. One of the problems in categorizing these devices is that the memory-addressing capabilities and computing power of the M68000 microprocessor are in some ways equivalent to those of machines hitherto denoted as mainframes.

Table 3.1 shows the main computation devices in use today and the systems in which they are used. The list is divided roughly by the number of workstations that can be supported by the device and also by the type of work that the device can do.

There has long raged a battle over whether 32-bit computation devices are essential for CAD/CAM or are merely optional. As might be expected, this is not an easy issue for the user to resolve. Intuitively, one would expect 32-bit computers to be more powerful than

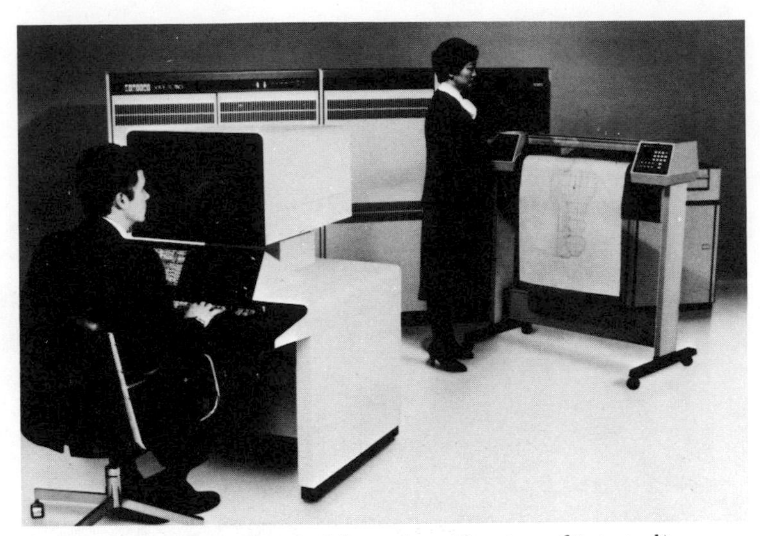

Figure 3.7 An interactive graphics system. (*Courtesy of Auto-trol.*)

16-bit computers, in that they handle a larger number of bits at one time. However, because of the sophistication of modern electronic circuitry, there is little in the way of two-dimensional graphics that 32-bit computers do that cannot be done almost equally well by 16-bit machines. In fact, there are a number of CAD systems on the market based on 8-bit microcomputers, whose performance is not worse than the worst of the 16-bit machines. Of course, three-dimensional graphics, solids, and analytical tasks do benefit substantially from a wider word. Two-dimensional drafting, however, can be done almost equally well on smaller computers.

Table 3.1

Computation device	Systems
Z80 8-bit microprocessor	Sigma Design, ERD, Arrigoni
6502 8-bit microprocessor	Cascade, T&W
8086 16-bit microprocessor	Tektronix 2D Drafting System, AVERA, Aydin, T&W
H-P 16-bit microprocessor	Bruning
DEC PDP-11 16-bit computer	Bausch & Lomb, Applicon, Intergraph, Synercom, Palette, ICS, McAuto UNIGRAPHICS, Telesis, Computool, Redac
DG Nova 16-bit computer	Summagraphics
DG ECLIPSE 16-bit computer	McAuto UNIGRAPHICS, Calma, CDC
Proprietary 16-bit microprocessors	Computervision, Vector, Automation
HP-1000 16-bit computer	Holguin, Gerber, Scitex
IBM Series/1 16-bit computer	IBM FASTDRAFT
M68000 16/32-bit microprocessor	Auto-trol, MENTOR, Cascade, Calma
DEC VAX 32-bit computer	Intergraph, Applicon, McAuto UNIGRAPHICS, Euclid, Auto-trol, Calma, TRICAD, MDSI, SCI-CARDS
Prime 32-bit computer	Medusa
SEL 32-bit computer	GRAFTEK
Perkin-Elmer 32-bit computer	CADAM
IBM 32-bit computer	CADAM, CATIA
Sperry Univac 36-bit computer	UNIS*CAD
Harris 48-bit computer	MCS-ANVIL
CDC 60-bit computer	CDC-ICEM (CD-2000, CDC-Synthavision, EDL)

From the point of view of programming, the user of the system is seldom involved with the actual computer to an extent that the word length would make a difference. User programming languages free the high-level user from concern with low-level issues such as word length.

Figure 3.8 A desktop CADD system. (*Courtesy of Bruning.*)

3.6 COMMUNICATION DEVICES

Nothing is unique about the communication devices required for CAD/CAM systems; they are the same ones used to communicate among computers in general. Networks of various types are becoming more popular among CAD/CAM system users as the need for local graphics power and central files becomes more evident.

3.7 SOFTWARE

Software is the "intelligence" within the "mind" of the computer. The term is used to refer to both programs and data. *Programs* are sets of instructions to the computer, indicating to it a series of actions to take; *data* is the term used for the information on which these actions are performed in response to the instructions of the program.

Programs can be batch or interactive. In working with a batch program, the user enters data but does not interact with the computer during the processing of the data. An example of a batch process is the entering of a list of coordinates describing a three-dimensional model for submission to a structural analysis program. Only the output of the analytical program gives the user feedback—the user cannot tell if things went wrong during data entry or processing until the entire analysis is complete. Typically, users of a batch program will submit a job and then turn their attention elsewhere rather than await the results; in some environments, the results may not arrive until a day or two later.

Interactive programs, on the other hand, provide a variety of immediate responses to the user. The user, in turn, can respond by modifying earlier actions or performing additional ones. For instance, the user of an interactive program may enter a point on a digitizing tablet; the system responds by flashing the point on a display. The user can then enter another point and request that a line be drawn between the points; the system responds by displaying the results.

Most CADD systems are interactive; however, it is appropriate in some instances to consider batch programs. A good example is the DS-1 schematic digitizing program from Design Aids, Inc. It accepts input from digitizers in batch mode and produces plots as output. Rough schematics are entered; neat drawings are plotted out.

Just as there are vector and raster hardware devices, there are also vector and raster data formats. In the vector format, the coordinates of the endpoints of lines are stored to describe a picture; in the raster format, codes describing the contents of the picture elements, or pixels, are stored in sequence.

Almost all CADD systems store data in vector format only. This format is more compact than raster format for most current CADD applications; that is, it requires less computer storage. Some recent technical publication systems store both raster and vector data; the raster data enable them to assimilate, edit, and reproduce continuous-tone imagery (in screened form).

CADD software includes the following categories: .

- Graphics
- Analysis
- Data Management
- Other

These are described in Secs. 3.8 through 3.11.

3.8 GRAPHICS

Graphics CADD programs fall into four categories:

- Plotting routines
- General-purpose libraries
- General-purpose end-user packages
- Special-purpose end-user packages

Routines are program segments that can be used by programmers to create programs but are usually incomplete from the end user's viewpoint; *libraries* are collections of routines. In our usage, *end-user packages* are complete programs in the sense that they can be used by nonprogrammers.

Each type of graphics software is described in the following sections.

3.8.1 Plotting Routines

Most pen and electrostatic plotter manufacturers provide plotting routines with their equipment. These are program segments—usually in Fortran, because of its popularity as a scientific computing language—that free the programmer from having to address the plotting device at a low level of command. For example, a common plotting routine is LINE; arguments passed to LINE are usually coordinates of endpoints, in some convenient units, such as inches. Were it not for routines like LINE, programmers would have to understand and program for the basic mechanical characteristics of the plotter—number of steps per inch, pen settling time, etc.

These routines usually comprise segments such as CIRCLE, TEXT, CONIC, and other basic pictorial elements; they are often provided gratis by vendors to purchasers of their plotting devices. (Many new plotting devices actually incorporate these routines into their firmware, or permanent internal software.)

3.8.2 General-Purpose Libraries

Some software firms market sets of routines that encompass many more functions than those in plotting routines and that will work with a variety of graphics devices. Such routines include digitizing functions, symbol creation and management, display manipulation (pan, zoom, etc.), and others—anything a programmer might want to do with a graphics input or output device. Unlike plotting routines, these libraries are not generally given away; they are sold and supported as independent software products. Examples are DI-3000 from Precision Visuals, Boulder, Colorado; DISSPLA from ISSCO, San Diego, California; GDDM from IBM, White Plains, New York.

3.8.3 General-Purpose End-User Packages

As we noted above, an end-user package is designed for use by nonprogrammers. General-purpose graphics program packages of this type enable the user to create, edit, manage, and produce graphics output from a computing system.

An example of this type of software is the two-dimensional drafting program, DRAGON, from Compeda Limited (now a division of Prime Computer Company). DRAGON runs on a number of different computers and supports a range of displays and input and output devices. It provides the user with a full range of basic drafting commands for drafting in almost any engineering discipline—mechanical, electronic, architecture, civil, etc. Some of these packages have sophisticated three-dimensional capabilities, such as Euclid from Matra Datavision, Massachusetts; others are more limited.

The principal difference between turnkey CADD systems and this type of software is that some sacrifices of efficiency and responsiveness must be made by vendors of these packages in order to maintain compatibility with a wide variety of computers and devices; turnkey system vendors can afford to fine tune their systems for such characteristics.

3.8.4 Special-Purpose End-User Packages

Some graphics programs are designed to perform a narrow range of functions, such as metal-building component drafting or waveform and timing diagram plotting; these are examples of special-purpose end-user graphics packages. Their primary function is graphical, although they are not designed to be used in the creation of a wide variety of functions, and they can be used by nonprogrammers.

3.9 ANALYSIS

Analysis programs come under the heading of design software. Models created on a CADD system can be passed to analysis programs. Often, the results of the analyses can also be viewed in graphical form. For example, a three-dimensional model of a bracket can be created on a CADD system, then used to create a mesh for finite-element analysis. After analysis, the deflected mesh can be visually superimposed on the original to enable the user to fully appreciate the analysis results. In electrical design, a schematic can be entered, then submitted to a circuit analysis program; outputs from electrical analysis programs are usually in alphanumeric form.

Analysis software is frequently of the batch variety. Many popular analysis programs require substantial computing power. CADD system computers are usually too small for extensive analysis software to be run along with the interactive graphics programs; arrangements are therefore common in which models are transmitted to larger computing systems by means of telecommunications.

Some forms of analysis are part of interactive graphics systems. Linear, area, and volume measurement, as well as determination of mass properties of closed bodies, are capabilities common to several of the leading CADD systems. In electronics applications, certain types of design rule checks can also be performed on the interactive systems without exacting undue penalties in terms of system responsiveness.

Structural, thermal, hydraulic, aerodynamic, and other forms of engineering analysis programs can derive their input from CADD systems. Creation of the model on the CADD system is usually much more efficient than any other form of data entry to the analysis programs.

3.10 DATA MANAGEMENT

Managing design and drafting data is more complex than managing purely textual information because of the data's pictorial nature. Pictures occupy relatively large amounts of computer memory; they often contain a wealth of diverse components whose classification is difficult and they must frequently be accessed by several members of a project team simultaneously. This set of requirements makes it inconvenient to use the standard filing schemes that are indigenous to the operating systems of most computer systems.

Most vendors of CADD systems have not given sufficient thought to the data management issue. Techniques that work well in a single-system environment may be wholly unsuited to an installation with 10 CADD systems. It is far too easy to create duplicate names and lose track of drawings for this issue to be treated lightly.

It seems that most CADD vendors have not appreciated the fact that the CADD database totally supplants the function of the print room—at least for those drawings that are in the automated system. This function is a complex one and is further complicated by the existence of long-standing and time-honored traditions with regard to drawing numbering and duplication; some of these traditions are functional, while others are not. Furthermore, it may be desirable to share data among a variety of systems made by different vendors; existing CADD data management schemes do not allow for such a possibility.

3.11 OTHER

Other types of software are sold in conjunction with CADD. These include code for computer-aided process planning, robot programming, PC board routing and placement, group technology (classification and coding), and various other software products that are not CADD but interface nicely to CADD.

3.12 SUMMARY

Hardware, as we said at the beginning of this chapter, is the *visible* part of CAD/CAM system; it is the portion of the system that contacts the world. However, the finest hardware, neatly assembled, well-interfaced, accurate, stable, and reliable, is absolutely useless without appropriate software. The bottom line is that when selecting a CAD/CAM system, most users should focus on overall performance rather than on technical issues like word length.

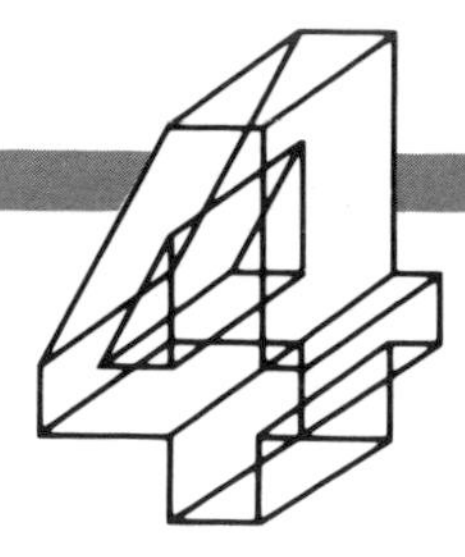

Market Projections

by
Stanley Klein
Peggy Kilburn

4.1 OVERVIEW

4.1.1 Scope and Objectives

In its brief history, the computer-aided design and computer-aided manufacturing (CAD/CAM) market has been like shifting sands. First, it was the turnkey systems approach—a total solution provided by a single vendor—that swept over the CAD/CAM user community. Then, in a do-it-yourself movement, the use of a host computer coupled with third-party software began to attract user favor in a big way. And now, at the time of this writing, it is the so-called engineering workstation, either stand-alone or networked, that has caught the user community's fancy.*

It is to help prospective and current CAD/CAM users cope with such transient technology phenomena that prompts this chapter. It is intended to provide an economic frame of reference, with insights into CAD/CAM's financial implications. The goal is to help the reader to understand where the CAD/CAM market came from and where it is headed, in order to help him or her plan accordingly.

Specifically, this chapter addresses such questions and issues as:

- What is the scope of the CAD/CAM market, and how did it grow to its current size?
- What is the relationship of CAD/CAM to computer graphics, and who are the leading companies?
- What has been the role of venture capital in the field? The role of entrepreneurship?
- What are the high-growth application areas in CAD/CAM? What forces are giving rise to this growth? What growth rates are anticipated for the different market segments?
- Also, how has the CAD/CAM market changed over time, and how will it continue to change? What are the new developments likely to reshape the market?
- Where can I go for more information on the subject?

With a knowledge of the above, one can gain a perspective on how to capitalize on the burgeoning opportunities in the CAD/CAM and computer graphics field. This may be either as a vendor seeking to enter CAD/CAM markets as a supplier or as a user enjoying CAD/CAM's benefits—and its challenges.

4.1.2 Relationship of CAD/CAM to the Computer Graphics Market

Simply stated, computer graphics refers to the use of the computer and related technologies to create and manipulate pictorial information in digital format. The specialized industry contains more than 500 hard-core vendors who manufacture computer graphics hardware, software, systems, and services (timesharing, job shop, etc.).

CAD/CAM is but an application area of computer graphics. It comprises some 75 percent of the computer graphics marketplace and, as a result, is the "tail that wags the dog." The starting point in all of CAD/CAM and its semantic derivatives, computer-aided engineering, computer-integrated manufacturing, etc., is simply the engineering drawing stored in digital format. It is this picture database that leads to virtually all the benefits that a user can derive from CAD/CAM technology, including such seemingly remote uses as job estimating, inventory control, and financial analysis.

PUTTING COMPUTER GRAPHICS IN PERSPECTIVE

Since its earliest beginnings, the computer graphics field, once virtually synonymous with CAD/CAM in a practical sense, has been characterized by robust growth and a strong

*As this book goes to press, it is the personal computer applied to CAD (DC-CAD) that promises to open up CAD technology to the largest user base ever.

element of entrepreneurship. In 1981 the computer graphics industry approached $2.5 billion in size and was increasing at a 50 percent annual rate. Such growth is understandable, since of all revenues generated by the computer industry, computer graphics accounts for less than a 5 percent market share. Hence, opportunity for growth obviously abounds.

Just as stunning are the comparative CAD/CAM figures. Its penetration into the engineering marketplace is less than 10 percent (and even this is a generous estimate), again signifying the availability of opportunities to users and vendor alike, albeit a plethora of new companies keeps popping up to seize these opportunities virtually as quickly as they arise.

This is not to say that the computer graphics industry is a pip-squeak. By no means! According to a detailed demographic analysis published in the 1984–1985 *S. Klein Directory of Computer Graphics Suppliers*, some 69,000 people were employed in some 500 computer graphics companies in 1983 to 1984. Moreover, vendor activity tends to be concentrated in four regions of the United States: Boston, San Francisco, Los Angeles, and metropolitan New York, in that order.

What this means is that one-third of the computer graphics industry is less than 5 years old! With 40 companies, at least, having entered the computer graphics field in 1982 for the first time, the industry has become even more youthful. The recent steep recession took a toll as well, it should be noted, knocking out Abt Computer Graphics, a business graphics company, and Nicolet CAD, a computer-aided drafting concern.

Interestingly, computer graphics has had two false starts prior to its current growth surge. This time the market surge is certain to be lasting because the same technological forces affecting all of the computer field—namely, ever greater memory densities on semiconductor chips, ever more powerful microprocessors, and the cumulative buildup in software—affects the memory-intensive, computational-heavy, and software-rich computer graphics CAD/CAM field even more so. Not only are CAD/CAM costs plummeting as a result, but the technology is a recognized productivity tool as well—and a very cost-effective one at that. Indeed, the economic breakthrough that opened up the computer graphics field can be traced to a single event in 1978. That is when IBM cut memory prices by a drastic 40 percent. From that point on, the field has mushroomed, as prices continue to decline in virtually all hardware categories.

PUTTING CAD/CAM IN PERSPECTIVE

Throughout computer graphics' volatile history, it is CAD/CAM that has been the pacesetting application—the most dynamic market for pictorial information systems. And this will continue to be so over the next 5 years at least. CAD/CAM benefits are now well documented and have been well publicized—virtually in every country around the globe.

Noted computer graphics consultant Carl Machover forecast that the total CAD/CAM market in 1982 would approximate $1 billion and then increase to as much as $4 billion by 1986, a growth rate of some 40 percent annually.

Continuing his analysis, Machover estimated that 80 percent of all CAD/CAM users had to be companies sufficiently large in size to generate at least $50 million in revenues annually. Such volume was a prerequisite to be able to cost-justify an investment in CAD/CAM that could easily total $0.5 million for hardware alone. The net result: only about 2000 companies in all the United States could afford to "go" CAD/CAM.

That state of affairs is now changing, as the result of the introduction in recent years of low-cost turnkey systems (see Table 4.1) that are priced at less than $100,000. CAD/CAM is now a viable proposition for companies having sales as little as $5 million a year, which encompasses some 30,000 companies in the United States. And the price of some computer-aided drawing systems based on Apple, IBM, and other personal computers has even moved down into the $25,000 range and less.

Machover left no doubt about the future trend to lower-cost technology. Out of the approximately $800 million market for CAD/CAM systems in 1981, low-cost turnkey systems accounted for less than 4 percent, or $30 million total. That proportion is expected to climb to 15 percent by 1986, or $700 million. By that time, the overall market itself will have soared to $4 billion, suggesting that the low-cost segment of CAD/CAM will grow twice as fast as the overall market. (Table 4.1 presents a rundown on low-cost turnkey CAD system vendors, their application specialties, and addresses.)

4.2 CAD/CAM MARKET HIERARCHY: COMPANY SALES AND MARKET SHARE

Low-cost systems, however, are no panacea. Although they can be ideal in executing dedicated drafting or design jobs, many of the low-cost machines lack the attributes offered by high-end systems, especially the power to do engineering analysis, to manipulate large databases, and to handle big number-crunching tasks as required in solids modeling, for example. That is why the suppliers of high-end turnkey systems who offer these capabilities will dominate in the marketplace. Such vendors supply all the necessary hardware (terminals, printers/plotters, digitizers, film recorders, and the like) and software (operating systems and industry-specific applications packages). They supply these in a complete ready-to-use package along with documentation, installation, and user training, with maintenance available on a contract basis. More and more, too, such system vendors are offering data communication and networking capabilities as well as database management tools. As users become more sophisticated CAD/CAM implementers, such adjunct capabilities become essential. (Figure 4.1 depicts the market shares of the major turnkey vendors.)

The zigzagging of the CAD/CAM market has also prompted the turnkey vendors to sail off on a new tack. At one time, these vendors attempted to be vertically integrated, providing their own proprietary application software to run on their own proprietary hardware. The dominant supplier, Computervision Corp., has gone so far as to create its own central processor, a unique approach among the vendors who typically rely on computers supplied by Digital Equipment Corp. and, at the low end, on microprocessors from Motorola. But now, all systems vendors—including Computervision—are encouraging the use of third-party software acquired from nonrelated parties to run on their own systems. It is increasingly clear that no one vendor can supply all the software necessary to meet all user needs, especially at CAD/CAM's high end. Examples of such software suppliers include CADAM, McNeal-Schwendler, Manufacturing & Consulting Services, and Structural Dynamics Research Corp.

This third-party software strategy really got started in earnest about 2 years ago when IBM, Prime Computer, Digital Equipment, and other computer manufacturers began vigorous campaigns to market their computers into CAD/CAM applications. Thus, they provided users with an alternative to a turnkey systems solution—more of a do-it-yourself arrangement. Users could now turn to their own general-purpose host computers, integrate graphics peripherals and other hardware, and employ third-party CAD/CAM software packages.

Turnkey vendors have thus begun to do the same. And as yet another competitive response to such direct use of host computers by CAD/CAM implementers, these turnkey vendors have also made a transition from 16-bit word length computers to more powerful 32-bit computers that can implement many more CAD/CAM functions, such as engineering analysis, database management, and solids modeling. Most successful in making the transition was Intergraph Corp., whose skyrocketing sales in 1982 took away the limelight from Computervision.

In CAD/CAM, however, change is the only constant, and at the time of this writing, yet another market trend is emerging, a turn to engineering graphics workstations, essentially self-contained stand-alone systems, frequently desktop-size machines, that can be networked to each other and/or to a central computer and database, if desired. The philosophy behind this development is one engineer, one computer! Such workstations incorporate state-of-the-art microprocessors, in particular, the Motorola 68000. Archetype of the class is Hewlett-Packard's model 9000 series, which is built not around a 16-bit microprocessor, but rather around a true 32-bit microprocessor—a first in the field. (Figure 4.2 depicts the projected shift in CAD/CAM computer configurations.)

So far our discussion has referred to CAD/CAM in a generic sense. But actually, the

Table 4.1 Low-Cost CAD/CAM Suppliers

ARCHITECTURAL

ARRIGONI COMPUTER GRAPHICS CO.
231 O'Connor Drive
San Jose, CA 95128
(408)286-2350

AUTO-TROL TECHNOLOGY CORP.
12500 North Washington Street
Denver, CO 80233
(303)452-4919
Also 3-D mechanical

AYDIN COMPUTER SYSTEMS
401 Commerce Drive
Fort Washington, PA 19034
(215)643-0600

CALCOMP (California Computer Products)
2411 W. La Palma Avenue
Anaheim, CA 92801
(714)821-2541

GRAFCON CORP.
5510 South Memorial
Tulsa, OK 74145
(918)663-5291

GRAPHIC CONSTRUCTIONS, INC.
320 S. Boston Avenue
Tulsa, OK 74101
(918)582-7446

INTERGRAPH CORP.
One Madison Industrial Park
Huntsville, AL 35807
(205)772-2180

ELECTRONICS

IC and VLSI Design

APPLICON, INC.
32 Second Ave.
Burlington, MA 01803
(617)272-7070
Also mechanical

AVERA CORP.
200 Technology Circle
Scotts Valley, CA 95066
(418)438-1401

DAISY SYSTEMS CORP.
2118 Walsh Ave.
Santa Clara, CA 95051
(408)727-5100

MENTOR GRAPHICS CORP.
10200 S.W. Nimbus Avenue, G-7
Portland, OR 97223
(503)620-9817

THREE RIVERS COMPUTER CORP.
720 Gross St.
Pittsburgh, PA 15224
(412)621-6250

VIA SYSTEMS, INC.
11 Concord Street
Nashua, NH 03060
(603)889-4197

VALID LOGIC SYSTEMS INC.
650 N. Mary Ave.
Sunnyvale, CA 94086
(408)773-1300

Printed-Circuit Boards

DESIGN AIDS, INC.
27822 El Lazo Blvd.
Laguna Niguel, CA 92677
(714)831-5611

GERBER SCIENTIFIC INSTRUMENT
83 Gerber Road West
South Windsor, CT 06074
(203)644-1551

RACAL-REDAC, INC.
One Redac Way
Littleton, MA 01460
(617)486-9231

SUMMIT CAD CORP.
5222 FM 1960 W. 102
Houston, TX 77069
(713)440-1468

TELESIS CORP.
21 Alpha Road
Chelmsford, MA 01824
(617)256-2300

MECHANICAL

AM BRUNING
1800 Bruning Drive West
Itasca, IL 60143
(312)351-2900

APPLICON, INC.
32 Second Avenue
Burlington, MA 01803
(617)272-7070
Also IC design

CAM-APT, INC.
166 Railroad Hill St.
Waterbury, CT 06722
(203)575-9300

CASCADE GRAPHICS DEVELOPMENT
1000 S. Grand
Santa Ana, CA 92705
(714)558-3316
Software, "Apple"-based

COM-CODE CORP.
1977 Chevrolet Street
Ypsilanti, Michigan 48197
(313)483-0295
Software only

DATA TECHNOLOGY, INC.
4 Gill Street
Woburn, MA 01801
(617)935-8820

DRAFTING DYNAMICS, INC.
4615 Industrial Avenue
Suite H
Simi Valley, CA 93063
(805)522-5471

ENGINEERING SYSTEMS CONSULTANTS, INC.
1801 Staring Lane
Suite 103
Baton Rouge, LA 70808
(504)769-2226

HEWLETT-PACKARD
Desktop Computer Division
3404 E. Harmony Road
Ft. Collins, CO 80525
(303)226-3800
Software

HOLGUIN ASSOCIATES
5822 Cromo Drive
El Paso, TX 79912
(915)581-1171

INTERACTIVE COMPUTER GRAPHICS, INC.
13541 Tiger Bend Road
Baton Rouge, LA 70816
(504)292-7570

INTERNATIONAL BUSINESS MACHINES CORP.
1133 Westchester Avenue
White Plains, NY 10604
(914)696-1255

K & E COMPANY
20 Whippany Road
Morristown, NJ 07960
(201)285-5169

PHOENIX AUTOMATION, INC.
100 Argyle Avenue
Ottawa, Ontario K2P 1B6
Canada
(613)235-7744

STRUCTURAL PROGRAMMING, INC.
83 Boston Post Road
Sudbury, MA 01776
(617)443-5366

SUMMAGRAPHICS CORP.
35 Brentwood Avenue
Fairfield, CT 06497
(203)384-1344
Also mapping

T & W SYSTEMS, INC.
18437 Mt. Langley
Suite B
Fountain Valley, CA 92708
(714)963-3913

TERAK CORP.
14151 N. 76th St.
Scottsdale, AZ 85260
(602)998-4800

TEKTRONIX, INC.
P.O. Box 500
Beaverton, OR 97077
(503)682-3411

Table 4.1 Low-Cost CAD/CAM Suppliers (*Continued*)

MECHANICAL (CONTINUED)

TRISKELION INTERNATIONAL CORP.
Courtyard
112 Merton Street
Toronto, Ontario, Canada M4S 2Z8
(416)482-7008

VECTOR AUTOMATION, INC.
Village of Cross Keys
Baltimore, MD 21210
(301)433-4202

Three-Dimensional

AUTO-TROL TECHNOLOGY CORP.
12500 North Washington Street
Denver, CO 80233
(303)452-4919
Also AEC

BAUSCH & LOMB
1300 East Anderson Lane
Austin, TX 78752
(512)837-2959

CADLINC INC.
1872 Brummel Ave.
Elk Grove, IL 60007
(312)228-7300

GERBER SYSTEMS TECHNOLOGY, INC.
40 Gerber Road East
South Windsor, CT 06074
(203)644-2581

MANUFACTURING AND CONSULTING SERVICES, INC.
17942 Cowan Avenue
Irvine, CA 92714
(714)540-3921

McDONNELL DOUGLAS AUTOMATION
Box 516
St. Louis, MO 63166
(314)232-6546

SIGMA DESIGN, INC.
7306 S. Alton Way
Englewood, CO 80112
(800)525-7050

MAPPING

GEOBASED SYSTEMS
725 W. Morgan Street
Raleigh, NC 27603
(919)834-9313

JAMES W. SEWALL CO.
147 Center Street
Old Town, Maine 04468
(207)827-4456

SUMMAGRAPHICS CORP.
35 Brentwood Avenue
Fairfield, CT 06497
(203)384-1344
Also mechanical

SYSTEMHOUSE, LTD.
99 Bank Street
Ottawa, Ontario K1P 6B9
Canada
(613)263-9734

MISCELLANEOUS

INFORMATION DISPLAYS, INC.
28 Kaysal Court
Armonk, NY 10504
(914)273-5755
Technical documentation

MICROTEX
80 Towbridge Street
Cambridge, MA 02138
(617)491-2874
Mold design

RESOURCE DYNAMICS INC.
655 Madison Avenue
New York, NY 10021
(212)486-9150

Source: "CAD/CAM Backgrounder: Issues & Insights," *The S. Klein Newsletter on Computer Graphics,* Sudbury, Mass., 1982.

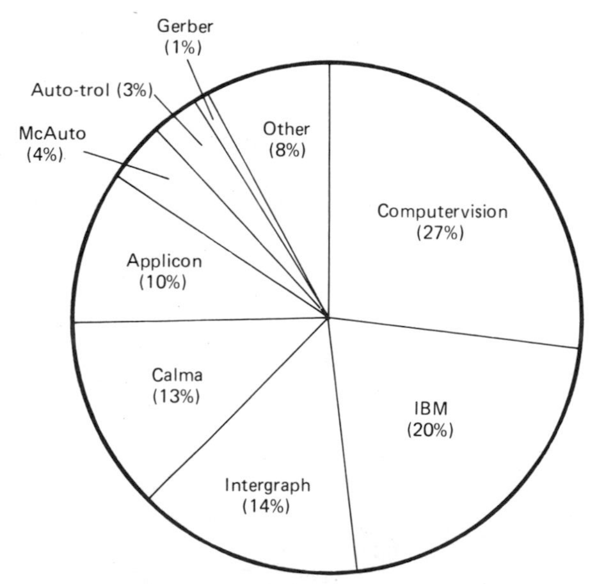

Figure 4.1 Estimated 1983 turnkey vendor market share (percent of total revenues by company). (*From Thomas Kurlak, "CAD/CAM Review & Outlook,"* The S. Klein Newsletter on Computer Graphics, *Sudbury, Mass.*)

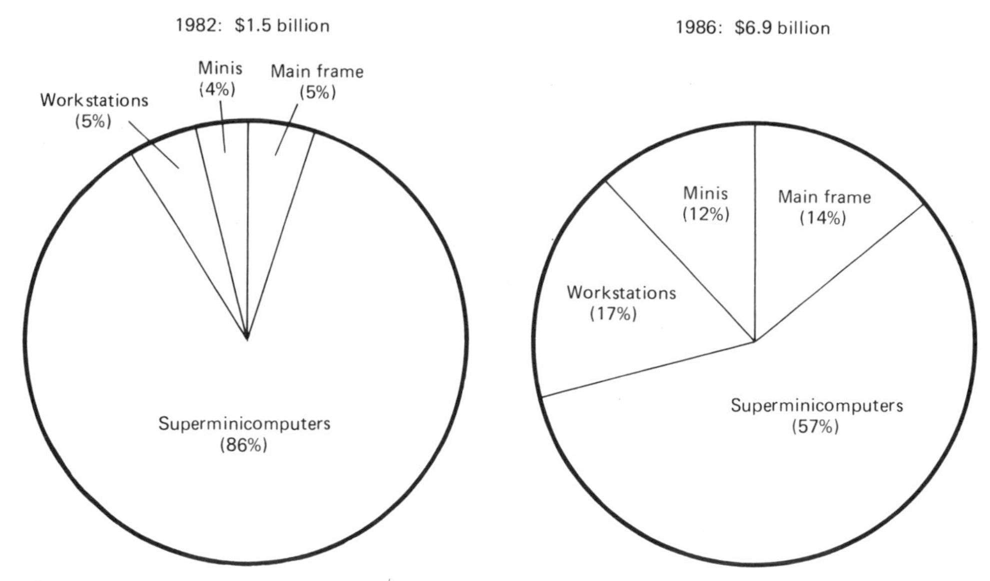

Figure 4.2 The CAD/CAM market by computer configuration (as a percent of total industry revenues), 1982 vs. 1986. (*From Jay W. Cooper, "CAD/CAM Review,"* The S. Klein Newsletter on Computer Graphics, *Sudbury, Mass.*)

technology can be further refined to refer to the specific engineering disciplines and, for that matter, to activities outside of engineering per se, such as architecture, interior design, facilities management, and publications systems. But of all the specialties, it is mechanical CAD/CAM that has traditionally been the largest and most rapidly increasing application area, resulting from its value to the automotive and aerospace industries in particular.

CAD/CAM analyst Tom Kurlak at Merrill Lynch forecasts that mechanical CAD/CAM will dominate the marketplace by 1991, representing 60 percent of the total CAD/CAM market, or $13 billion in absolute numbers. This forecast holds even though mechanical CAD/CAM's growth rate recently slowed in response to the economy's downturn, especially for the automotive and aircraft industries.

As concerns the electronics CAD/CAM market, Merrill Lynch sees this segment as having a greater immediate growth rate than mechanical: 29 percent in 1982, 37 percent in 1983, owing to CAD/CAM's expanded use in integrated-circuit (IC) design and the trend toward custom circuits designed by users rather than by semiconductor houses.

The architecture, engineering, and construction (AEC) market, however, is to show the lustiest growth. Kurlak forecasts a 50 percent growth rate in 1982 and 1983. Mapping CAD/CAM, according to him, will also show greater short-term growth than mechanical CAD/CAM despite the fact that mapping's growth rate in 1983 (25 percent) is forecast at half of what it was in 1981 (52 percent). (Figure 4.3 depicts the market outlook by application categories.)

4.3 HOW THE CAD/CAM MARKET HAS DEVELOPED

4.3.1 User Perceptions And Its History of Growth

The technical ability of the computer to economically store and display data graphically has grown at an extraordinary rate from a novelty concept in the early 1960s to a multibillion dollar industry in the early 1980s. Indeed, computer graphics is an extremely powerful human-machine interface—it is a person's ability to communicate with the computer through pictures, an effective device as old as caves. And computer graphics' prized application—CAD/CAM—has been hailed as the key to productivity improvement in industry, business, commerce, and education.

The growth of CAD/CAM was stimulated by four major catalysts: the military; the aerospace, automotive, and electronics industries; universities; and venture capital. In the earliest stages of development, the military was the only sector with sufficient resources to cost-justify CAD/CAM usage. The military-aerospace sector fostered the development of early technological breakthroughs in CAD/CAM in the 1950s and is credited with popularizing its concept in the late 1960s. Similarly, the nonmilitary aerospace, automotive, and electronics industries were quick to recognize the value of CAD/CAM in their operations, beginning in 1959. In addition to spawning the technology, both these sectors were developing the trained workforce that would form the basis of the CAD/CAM industry as it now exists. As well, the development of software technology in universities led to the establishment of software firms by their alumni. Finally, the role of venture capital became increasingly significant as the industry's growth became so explosive that entrepreneurs could no longer provide sufficient capital on their own to establish new firms.

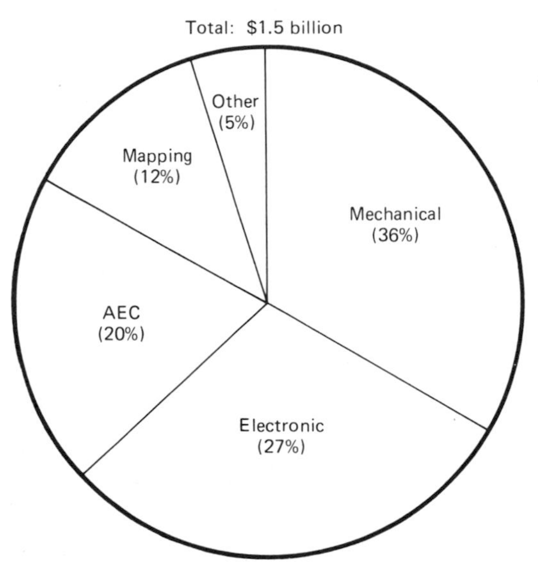

Figure 4.3 The CAD/CAM market by application (as a percent of total industry revenues), estimated for 1983. (*From Thomas Kurlak, "CAD/CAM Review & Outlook,"* The S. Klein Newsletter on Computer Graphics, *Sudbury, Mass.*)

The sharpest fluctuation in growth in the computer graphics market occurred in 1969 when the number of new company formations almost doubled. This event coincided with a strong stock market and an abundance of venture capital and signaled the beginning of a keen interest on the part of industry in computer graphics tools and techniques.

Nevertheless, the industry was still puny back then. Indeed, prior to 1976, it could be said that virtually no CAD/CAM market existed. At that time, the total computer graphics market for all applications was a mere $200 million, and CAD/CAM accounted for nearly half of that total, which of course did not make for a giant industry either. Characteristic of its meteoric growth, however, between 1976 and 1980, the CAD/CAM industry grew at a 60 percent annual rate.

The year 1978 represents a particularly important turning point. That is the year when a major decline occurred in computer memory prices, which was led by a 40 percent one-shot reduction by IBM. It was this trigger mechanism that, virtually overnight, rendered computer graphics cost-effective.

4.3.2 Vendor Evolution: An Entrepreneurial Paradise

The burgeoning CAD/CAM marketplace that has ensued from the developments just discussed turns out to have created an ideal environment for entrepreneurs to move into unfilled niches, starting new companies to fill industrial needs. So great is the proliferation that on average, a new company emerges every 2 weeks. Examples abound.

- Start-up company ANA Tech Corp., for example, in Littleton, Colorado, has devised a data capture system that "efficiently converts paper drawings to a computer-usable format," according to president David R. Grover, who also reports that his company is on the verge of completing a second round, $2.5 million venture financing to underwrite production.
- After quitting a marketing vice president position at Lexidata Corp., Martin Duhms founded New Media Graphics Corp. and using financing from nonestablished venture capital sources, has created a display generator that overlays computer graphics onto television images.
- Within a 2-week period, three companies—Qubix, Impres, and XYVision—all announced turnkey systems aiming to bring the full firepower of computer graphics onto the labor-intensive technical publishing field. Here, stand-alone workstations are used to integrate text, line art, and halftones into fully composed and paginated documents. With such systems, both drawings and text may be edited, formatted, stored, displayed, and reproduced automatically—all interactively. These three companies raised more than $5 million from the venture capital community *just to do initial development work*.
- Catronix Corp. is another start-up company founded under the sponsorship of the State of Georgia and located at the Georgia Institute of Technology. This company's contribution is CAD software that employs "a new algorithm" for executing three-dimensional modeling. What constitutes the breakthrough is that the program resides not on a mainframe but on a minicomputer and costs only $50,000.

Stories are legion of CAD/CAM professionals who left good jobs at established vendors to launch out on their own. In April 1979, MIT computer science graduate and 7-year Applicon veteran Michael Dickens, along with two Intel alumni, Mark Flomenhoft and James Taggert, put up $150,000 of their own money to found Avera Corp. Its first product: A desktop interactive computer graphics system targeted at IC design and schematic entry. One year later, Avera raised more than $1 million from two venture capital groups. The technology is changing so fast that Avera's pioneering products have become relatively obsolete. Unable to manage its growth and such rapid change, the company is now seeking a buyer.

Software development chief Thomas Bruggere resigned from Tektronix in 1980 to start up Mentor Graphics Corp. Its first product is a CAD/CAM system positioned in the marketplace as having the capability to do engineering analysis in electronic circuit design. Joe Sliwkowski has the distinction of having been employee number 9 at Computervision. With this background, he became the technical brainstorm behind Telesis Corp., founded in 1980 with a uniquely designed stand-alone, electronics turnkey system positioned to attract first-time CAD/CAM users.

Similar anecdotes also abound in computer graphics applications sectors outside of CAD/CAM as well. Randy Wise relinquished a lucrative career in the oil and energy field to start up Graphic Communications, Inc. Its specialty: Business graphics turnkey systems, at first, and more recently, business graphics software that runs on the IBM Personal Computer.

An especially interesting pioneer is Irwin Jarett, a certified public accountant and computer graphics guru combined, who has single-handedly taken on the accounting and financial community. His goal is to educate financial professionals on the use of computer graphics, especially as a way to present and interpret balance sheet and income statement data. He calls his company Fingraph, a contraction for financial graphics.

And in yet another field, facilities management, the renowned furniture manufacturer Herman Miller Inc. has become a fledgling supplier. It now offers to the general market its interior design software, originally developed in-house to meet its own needs. This is typical of how a hard-core user of computer graphics technology becomes a hard-core vendor.

4.3.3 The Role of Venture Capital

Whatever hurdles face the CAD/CAM entrepreneur, having access to funds is not among them. Venture capitalists view the emerging computer graphics field—and most especially CAD/CAM—as having extraordinary potential and seek to uncover viable business plans, originated by either ongoing firms needing expansion capital or visionary, competent entrepreneurs searching for start-up funding. Venture capitalists typically aim to grow a company to between $20 to 50 million in 5 to 7 years, ultimately to have the company go public, with net proceeds going toward repaying short-term loans, expanding production facilities, purchasing capital equipment, and increasing working capital.

In recent years, security values on publicly owned computer graphics companies have doubled, quadrupled, and even climbed tenfold after going public. Early computer graphics investors have amassed substantial equity gains in Computervision, Intergraph, ISSCO, Apollo, Adage, Evans & Sutherland, and Applicon (now merged into Schlumberger Ltd.). Recently (June 1984), much of those gains have been given back as the stock market slumped. Nevertheless, the venture capitalists managed to make large gains in the boom cycle. They await the next upturn with great anticipation.

Traditionally, the interest of venture capitalists has been highest in manufactured products and sophisticated turnkey systems, with software and service-based ventures seeming less attractive. But even that fixation is changing. During the summer of 1982, energy services supplier Impell Corp. paid $5 million to obtain a 25 percent equity interest in CAD/CAM software supplier Manufacturing and Consulting Services, Inc. And coincidentally, two software companies, Precision Visuals and Fingraph, each independently raised outside venture capital virtually within the same week in March 1983. Hardware and turnkey systems are still favorites among venture capitalists, but software definitely is no longer an outcast.

Some traditional sources of venture capital for CAD/CAM include the American Research and Development Corporation, Boston; The Palmer Organization, Boston; Frederick Adler, Esq., New York City; J. H. Whitney & Co., New York City; and Sutter Hill Ventures, Palo Alto.

4.3.4 Competitive Forces Compelling Growth in the CAD/CAM Market

Compared to CAD/CAM's virtually phenomenal potential, its current usage could well be described as antediluvian. In U.S. manufacturing, penetration is variously estimated at between 5 and 10 percent of potential users, with penetration in other sectors even lower; in Europe the extent of penetration is lower still. Most CAD/CAM systems today are used to handle very rudimentary design and analyses; those used in architectural and mechanical applications serve as little more than automated drafting tools.

The principal reason for CAD/CAM's relatively slow acceptance can be attributed to a general resistance to change, and more especially a latent fear of automation. There is no doubt that acquiring a CAD/CAM system is a giant step for any company, particularly smaller, unautomated firms. Automation in general and CAD/CAM in particular changes the entire complexion of a company. Personnel changes are required; either existing staff will need to be trained on the systems, thus requiring arrangements and adjustments to be made for their regular responsibilities during training, or new staff will have to be hired to operate the system.

The economics of the company will change once the system is operative; more work can be handled in less time, and staff will be freed for more creative endeavors. Does the company have more and creative work to occupy its staff? Even speech patterns will change as staff acquaint themselves with and become proficient in CAD/CAM jargon. Each person involved—from manager to operator—will need to adjust his or her way of thinking and planning to some degree. And all people involved will—or should—find the time to keep up with the latest technological advances, constantly monitoring for new developments to ensure that their CAD/CAM system keeps pace with needs. With all the adjustments necessary, even where there is full appreciation of CAD/CAM's many benefits, it can be almost frightening for the new user.

Nonetheless, the growth rate of the CAD/CAM market has been spectacular even during recessionary periods, though absolute growth does slow down during protracted slumps. This otherwise relentless growth occurs because CAD/CAM has, like a self-fulfilling prophecy, created a market for itself. Public knowledge of its benefits has augmented its desirability to an extent that CAD/CAM is becoming an economic necessity. Management is becoming increasingly aware of CAD/CAM's benefits, including increased productivity, improved product quality, ability to respond more quickly to market demand, and freeing staff from tedious, repetitive, time-consuming tasks for more creative efforts. Companies which have adopted CAD/CAM hold a strong competitive edge against their nonautomated counterparts. Moreover, managers are being pressured by their own staffs to provide the latest in modern technology.

There are, in essence, two driving forces in the CAD/CAM market: users and technological development. It is difficult to pinpoint which of the two are compelling a greater amount of growth in the market. Most certainly, to maintain their market share, each vendor will need to become more sensitive to the concerns and demands of its users. For example, a common complaint became evident in a survey of CAD/CAM users by the market and research planning firm, INPUT: a serious lack of understanding on the vendor's part vis-à-vis particular applications. Users reported an unsatisfactory amount of adjustment necessary to optimize their systems' effectiveness.

Thus, it can be observed that what drives the CAD/CAM market is *both* the new technological developments and the users themselves. The most successful CAD/CAM companies of tomorrow, the ones with the deepest market penetration and the ability to hold their positions, will be the ones which are simultaneously user-*anticipatory*, even more than user-responsive, are at the forefront of technological developments, and are directed by management that can handle explosive growth.

4.4 OUTLOOK: HOW AND WHY THE MARKET IS CHANGING

It is no exaggeration to say that the CAD/CAM market is undergoing dramatic changes. Indeed, changes occur virtually every day—in terms of vendors entering and leaving the market, technological breakthroughs, company successes, and user sophistication. The majority of changes, however, seem to be user-dependent; as user CAD/CAM sophistication grows, the demands on vendors increase. Elements that were once thought luxuries, or even frivolities, are now capturing user attention and demand. Effective development of such capabilities could well reshape the current market structure. For instance,

Color. Originally thought of as an expensive toy, color in CAD/CAM is a capability for which users seem willing to pay a premium. The development of cost-effective color hard copy is the next necessary step, and it will be available soon with the advent of new thermal transfer and ink-jet technologies now coming on the scene.

Solids Modeling. This capability enables assemblies, surfaces, and intersections to be clearly delineated via the automatic generation of isometric and exploded views and detailed dimensioned and assembly drawings. Solids modeling can automatically determine a part's surface area, volume, weight, moment of inertia, center of gravity, and other such properties.

Making such capabilities available to users (in fact, *determining* what users will need) is, and will continue to be, tantamount to any CAD/CAM company's success. There is a great deal of work to be done in this area. Users surveyed by market researchers Frost & Sullivan were critical of turnkey vendors for "being too hardware oriented, [attempting to] mold users to their systems, offering software of lower quality than their hardware, and not being supportive." The same survey determined that independent software dealers were considered to be more responsive, to provide better support, and to have lower-cost software that is both machine- and device-independent.

Further, there is a growing concern among users regarding exchange of data between different systems, particularly for turnkey systems, which eventually are likely to be interfaced to an organization's other computer systems. This concern has led to widespread support of the Initial Graphic Exchange Specification (IGES), a CAD/CAM standard that enables graphics databases prepared on one vendor's CAD/CAM system to be used on other vendors' equipment as well. At least 35 companies have committed themselves to support IGES.

The market research and planning firm INPUT conducted on-site interviews with 250 end users and vendors and found that "system integration directed at achieving optimal utilization of a CAD/CAM system is of keenest interest to users." Such integration is largely an internal management problem that users must grapple with within their own organizations. However, vendors must lay the groundwork for automated design and drafting to directly tie into engineering analysis and database management, including creation of the links to the manufacturing process. Whoever does the best job of advancing such integrated technology will win over vast markets!

4.5 FINAL REFLECTIONS

The field of CAD/CAM seems much like a Disney world; capabilities that were unheard of, for the most part even unimagined, 10 and 20 years ago are today's common practices—on their way to becoming outmoded. And like many of today's CAD/CAM entrepreneurs, Walt Disney was a visionary, so anxious to proceed with his innovative, creative ideas that several times he was just a breath away from financial disaster, having committed then-gargantuan sums of money to develop concepts that were considered outlandish and speculative.

But Disney was careful to match creative and technological genius with equal genius in business strategy and management. Without such a balance, any rapidly growing organization or industry may find itself well on the way to an unrecoverable collapse. It cannot be emphasized too strongly that the technical genius in CAD/CAM must be buttressed by competent management equipped to handle explosive growth.

Ergonomics

by
Elaine Cohen
Aaron Cohen

The most recent estimates indicate that substantially more than 7 million workers use video display terminals (VDTs) on the job each day. And the number continues to rise. One out of every five architects will have a computer-aided design (CAD) workstation by 1990, for example.

The expansion of VDT technology is not without difficulties, however. Complaints are surfacing. A surprising number of computer-aided design and computer-aided manufacturing (CAD/CAM) users report they have experienced pain or stiffness in the neck and shoulders while working at the machines. Indeed, 90 percent of all VDT operators make the same complaint, 89 percent complain of headaches, 88 percent of back pain, and 83 percent of periods of severe fatigue or exhaustion. Users have eye problems, including eyestrain (93 percent), tearing or itching (79 percent), burning (77 percent), and blurring (78 percent). Furthermore, speculation continues that the radiation emanating from all electronic equipment—and video display units in particular—contributes to cataracts and birth defects. This speculation has not quieted, even in the wake of the publication of the results of a major scientific study in which researchers failed to confirm any relationship between VDT radiation levels and human disease.

Speculation also exists that CAD/CAM operators work under conditions that are psychologically and mentally stressful. CAD/CAM equipment tends to be complicated. Some units contain dual screens, a keyboard and keypad, light pen, digitizer, plotter, printer, and the central processing unit (CPU). Complicated equipment causes blood pressure to rise as attempts are made to make the unfamiliar function. New CAD/CAM users are often in a constant state of worry. They fear they may do something wrong and cause the system to "crash." Thus the potential exists for major state and federal legislation, particularly for assembly line workers. The legislation will have little impact upon those who perform the more creative tasks. This latter group becomes too absorbed in the work to be performed and tends to ignore health rules.

5.1 A NOTE ABOUT RADIATION AND THE CRT

All electronic equipment emits low-level radiation. When electrons, for example, jump from higher atomic orbits to lower ones, light is given off. This is the ultimate source of light—and light is one form of radiation. It is part of the electromagnetic spectrum. The process works in reverse also. Light or other forms of radiation strike electrons and cause them to jump from lower orbits to higher ones. The phenomenon is called *excitation*. If the radiation has enough energy, it can make the electron jump completely out of the atom and cause the atom to become ionized. Such radiation is called *ionizing radiation*. When an atom is excited, its chemical bonding properties change. It may become detached from a molecule, changing the molecule's chemistry.

Radiation, then, can cause chemical reaction. If radiation has enough energy, it can even change the structure of the nucleus and turn atoms into different elements. Where living tissue becomes involved, any change in the atoms that make up the DNA (the blueprint for life) can cause cancer or, at the least, prevent the DNA from replicating properly.

Table 5-1 illustrates the electromagnetic spectrum, ranking the waves in order of increasing frequency. The only difference between light, radio waves, and x-rays is the wavelengths and average energy in electron volts. As the frequencies increase, the effects on matter become more pronounced.

Ionizing radiation comes in two forms, electromagnetic waves and charged particles. An electromagnetic field is produced by charged particles, which also affect electrons. The faster the particles, the more electrons they can affect. VDTs are sources of fast charged particles. Electrons strike the phosphor coating on the screen and give off light. The pattern is repeated at least 30 times a second, tracing whole figures so that viewers will see stable pictures.

At the far end of a cathode-ray tube (CRT) (Fig. 5.1) is a source of electrons which accelerates electrons from a hot wire through a typical potential of 10,000 volts. The electrons are deflected by a strong potential in an oscilloscope, or by a magnetic field in a television tube, to the screen of the CRT. If this energy were converted into a single x-ray, it

Table 5.1 Radiation and the CRT

Wave type	Wavelength	Average energy, electron volts	Effects on matter
Radio	1000 m to 10 cm	0.0001	None at atomic level
Microwave	10 cm to 1 mm	0.01	Fine, small molecular effects
Infrared	1 mm to 0.001 mm	0.1	Excites molecular structure
Visible light	7×10^{-4} mm to 3×10^{-4} mm	1.00	Excites electrons
Ultraviolet	10^{-4} mm to 10^{-7} mm	10.0	Ionizes outer electrons
X-rays	10^{-7} mm to 10^{-11} mm	1000.0	Ionizes inner electrons
Gamma rays	10^{-12} mm to 10^{-15} mm	10^6	Excites nucleus

Source: Eric Maloney, "Visual Display Terminals, Are They Hazardous to Your Health?" *Microcomputing,* July 1981, pp. 43–58.

would be very dangerous. Happily, the probability is small. Besides, if an x-ray were produced, it would have to travel through the phosphor, the glass walls of the tube, and about 2 feet of air to reach the operator. Since x-rays ionize every atom with which they come in contact, losing some energy to each, a single x-ray reaching the operator could be compared to driving a car through a stadium filled with basketballs—or around New Mexico with only 2 gallons of gas.

Although the immediate effects of small doses of ionizing radiation appear minimal, scientists are worried about the long-term, cumulative effects. The average person receives about 200 millirems per year from sunlight and normal surroundings. It is a well-known fact that sunlight causes skin cancer. There are even fears that artificial lighting does the same. Many people complain they experience headaches, dizziness, and nausea from fluorescent lighting. If this is the case, what about problems stemming from the use of CRTs?

As mentioned, claims that radiation emanating from common office equipment may be biologically harmful tend to be discounted, as the adverse effects have not been verified. But, then, using CRTs for many hours each day is a recent phenomenon. It may take years before difficulties become apparent, and by that time CRTs may no longer be used. The fact is that ophthalmologists are treating more young people with cataracts than ever before. There is a nagging fear that a definite link between cataract formation and CRT use exists.

Such physical and psychological problems should not come as a surprise, especially to those familiar with the history of industrial development. Just as mechanical devices

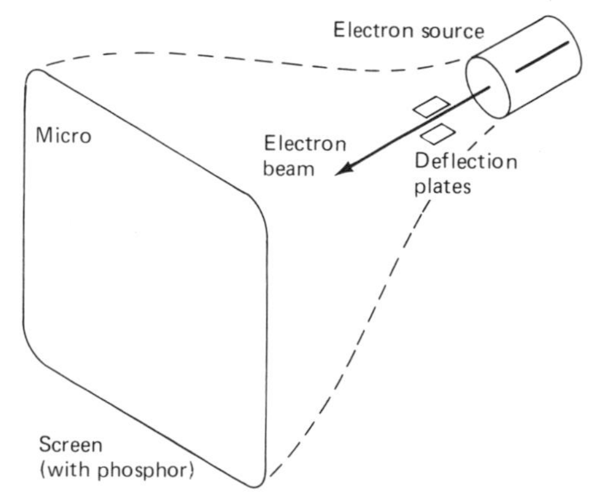

Figure 5.1 A diagram of a cathode ray tube (CRT). The CRT can be used as a CRT display, a television picture tube, or an oscilloscope.

created factory environments that were at first modified, and later dominated, by machines, the same circumstances are bound to occur in the office vis-à-vis electronic equipment. When mechanization first began in the industrial sector, little recognition was taken of the plight of the laborers. Their needs and desires were discounted. They were considered human machines. The situation was depicted in the literature and art of the nineteenth century. Eventually new and better working environments were created. Laws were even changed to protect those on assembly lines.

Today it is widely recognized that people are not very good machines (Fig. 5.2). They perform badly where tasks are repetitive. The whole thrust of the electronic revolution is to employ people at what they do best: the associative, creative, and cognitive. But until that can be fully instituted, electronic equipment actually makes some jobs worse, not better. Factory machine processes, for example, take place in a certain order. Such rigidity has been translated into the office. People must accommodate to electronic equipment rather than vice versa. They have to learn entirely new methods of function. Secretaries who once had many tasks to perform are now mere machine operators, required to sit in front of word processors at least 6 hours per day, eyes glued to the screen, ears plugged by the dictation-device earphones, fingers on the keys, and feet resting on the dictation-device foot pedal. Musculoskeletal stress is one result. Boredom is another. To make matters

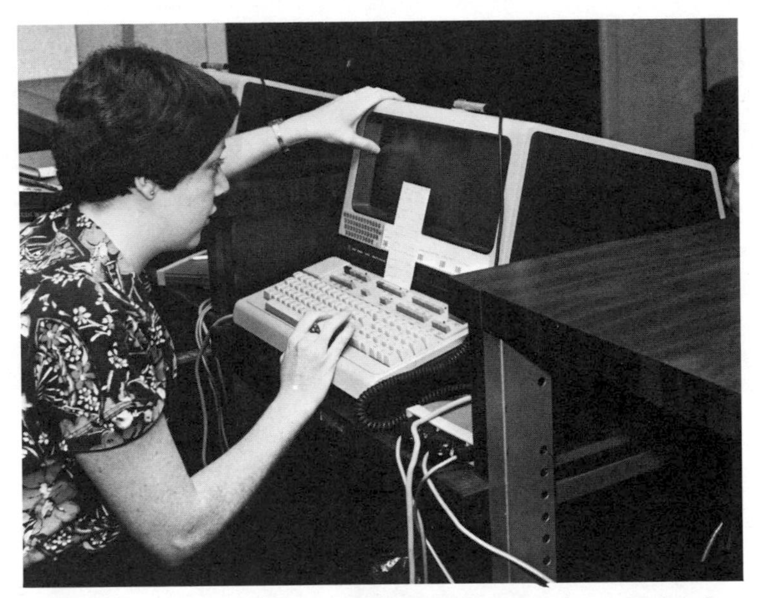

Figure 5.2 People are not very good machines. They perform badly where tasks are repetitive. The whole thrust of automation is to employ people at what they do best—the associative, creative, and cognitive. (*Courtesy of U.S. Army Library, Pentagon.*)

worse, in the name of productivity, electronic gadgets can count the number of transactions the word processing operators perform each day.

Because of the difficulties this new environment presents, the study of operator-machine interface is of major interest. The management of these studies often falls into the purview of the designer. That is because the installation of automated equipment involves space planning, renovation, and refurbishing. Therefore, picking the most comfortable hardware (as opposed to software), installing it properly, and keeping it fine-tuned should be coordinated by the same central authority that manages the general environment.

5.2 ERGONOMICS

For the designer, current operator-machine research can be broken into two major disciplines which interrelate: equipment design and workplace design. Together they are known as human factors engineering or ergonomics. Ergonomics has been defined as the technology of work design. The focus of ergonomics is upon the tasks that humans perform and how the workplace and the equipment help or impede those tasks. It encompasses:

1. The tasks and their management [e.g., definition, input-output requirements (Fig. 5.3), basic skills (training), and needs of and interactions with other workers and other departments]
2. The architectural location of the task [e.g., location within the building envelope in relation to fixed elements such as stairwells, elevators, windows, heating, ventilators, and air conditioning (HVAC), and electric and telecommunication power]
3. The workstation design (e.g., the general microenvironment including task and storage requirements, visual and acoustical needs, and special equipment)

The functions of the tasks and their management are usually the responsibilities of the client departments. Managers within the departments use various techniques to create, rearrange, or discard tasks. A favored method is to chart task flow. A popular flowchart is that originally developed by systems analysts to analyze the logic of computer programs (Fig. 5.4). Today, it is often used to determine the logic of a task and its individual steps. Most flowcharts use standard symbols for easy visualization: rectangles signify processing steps; diamonds, decision points; circles, connectors; and so on.

5.3 THE MACRO-, MIDI-, AND MICROENVIRONMENTS

It is the designer's job to facilitate task management for client departments by enhancing the architectural and interior design. This is done by attempting to integrate the macro-, midi-, and microenvironments into one coherent whole (Fig. 5.5).

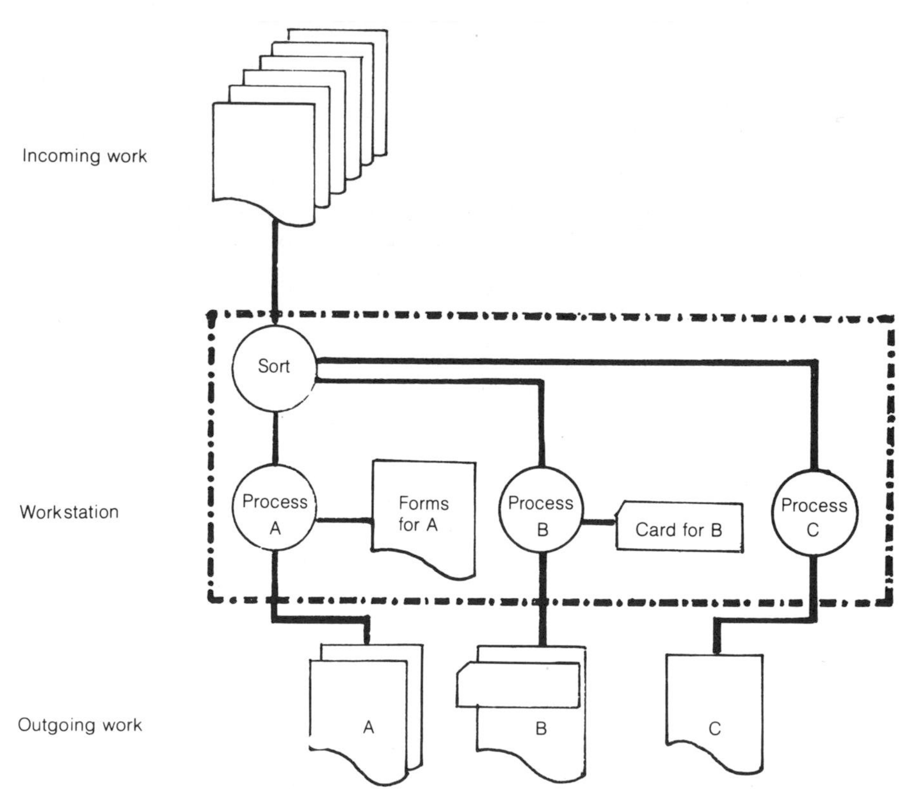

Figure 5.3 Input-output requirements.

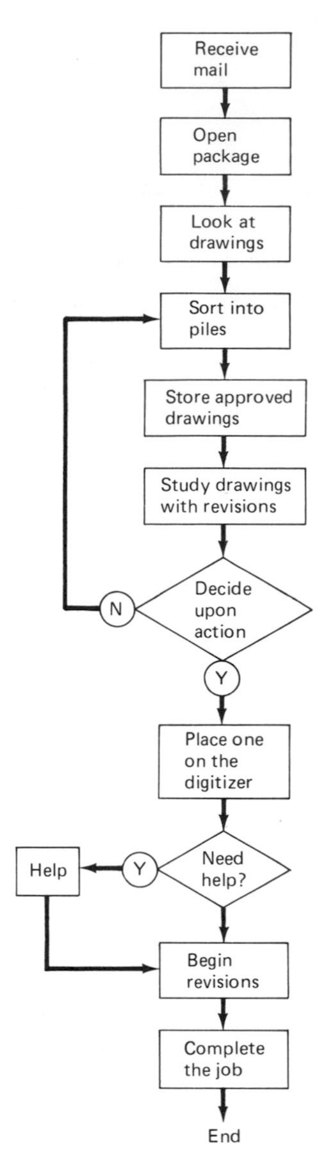

Figure 5.4 A flowchart.

Typically, macroenvironments are designed by architects and engineers who tend to be most interested in the large interior and exterior building elements (Fig. 5.6). As major design determinants, these elements modify layout flexibility. For example, for an office building to have as many rental units as possible, generally its core should be in the center to allow interior spaces to be subdivided with ease vis-à-vis traffic flow. An office building created for only one tenant has the cores on the ends, allowing maximum floor space for the layouts. In another example, a floor area with a constriction in the middle—placed there, perhaps, for aesthetic relief—prevents logical expansion from one space to another. Ceilings that are too low prevent spaces from being used for specific purposes. Poor electric and telecommunication power distribution in the first instance require extensive retrofitting to accommodate developments in automation.

On the other end of the scale are the microenvironments (Fig. 5.7). Individual CAD/CAM workstations may be designed by interior designers, space planners, vendors, or end users. Often there is little or no communication between the building and workstation designers. This is understandable when integrated CAD/CAM workstations are purchased directly from original equipment manufacturer (OEM) catalogs. In situations in which the building has been in existence for many years, it is also understandable. Unhappily, the same phenomenon occurs even when equipment and workstations are separately purchased and are then installed into brand new buildings. Illogical situations occur. CAD/CAM facilities are erected without proper ventilation or not enough space. Workflow patterns are not translated into reasonable layouts. It is essential, therefore, to set up lines of communication to integrate equipment and work flow criteria into a coherent design.

The lack of integration nearly always affects the midienvironments. The midienvironments are designed as overlapping responsibilities of the building architects or engineers, on one hand, and the interior designers, space planners, or end users on the other. Typically, midienvironments are areas shared by many people (Fig. 5.8). A major midienvironment may be the file room vault which contains, among other things, older out-of-date hard-copy drawings sometimes required by the CAD/CAM group. The location of the file room vault is the responsibility of the architect or engineers, but the layout is that of the interior designers, space planners, or end users. In the most dysfunctional arrangement, the file room vault is far away from the CAD/CAM group and can only be reached by passing through several other departments, riding the elevator, or walking a long distance. The situation may be caused by macroenvironmental features of the building, perhaps the location of the core. Security may be another reason. Or the vault may be located next to a large group of very active users. Since the CAD/CAM group is rather small, location next to the vault is considered relatively unimportant.

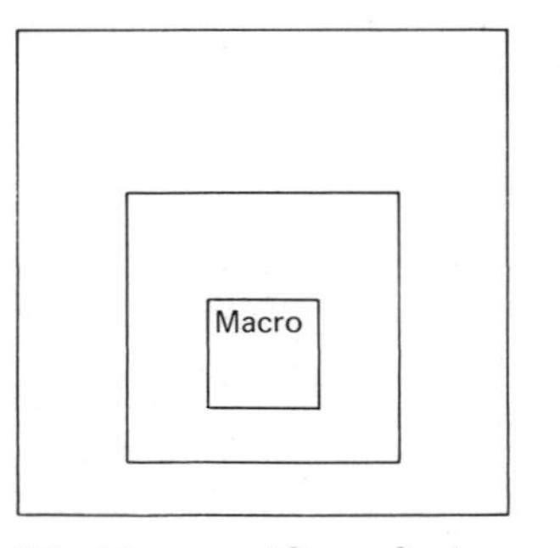

Figure 5.5 Macro-, midi-, and microenvironments.

As indicated, the ergonomics of the mac-

Figure 5.6 Macroenvironments are designed by architects and engineers who tend to be most interested in the large interior and exterior elements. (*Courtesy of Murphy/Jahn Architects, photographed by James R. Steinkamp.*)

ro-, midi-, and microenvironments encompass the psychological as well as the physical. For example, people walking into a CAD/CAM facility expect to see a receptionist. If one is nonexistent, the first person they see becomes, in effect, the receptionist. This is a problem which causes hardship for those seated near the entranceway. They are constantly interrupted by visitors seeking answers to directional questions.

Figure 5.7 Microenvironments include individual workstations and are typically designed by interior designers or space planners. (Courtesy of Steelcase.)

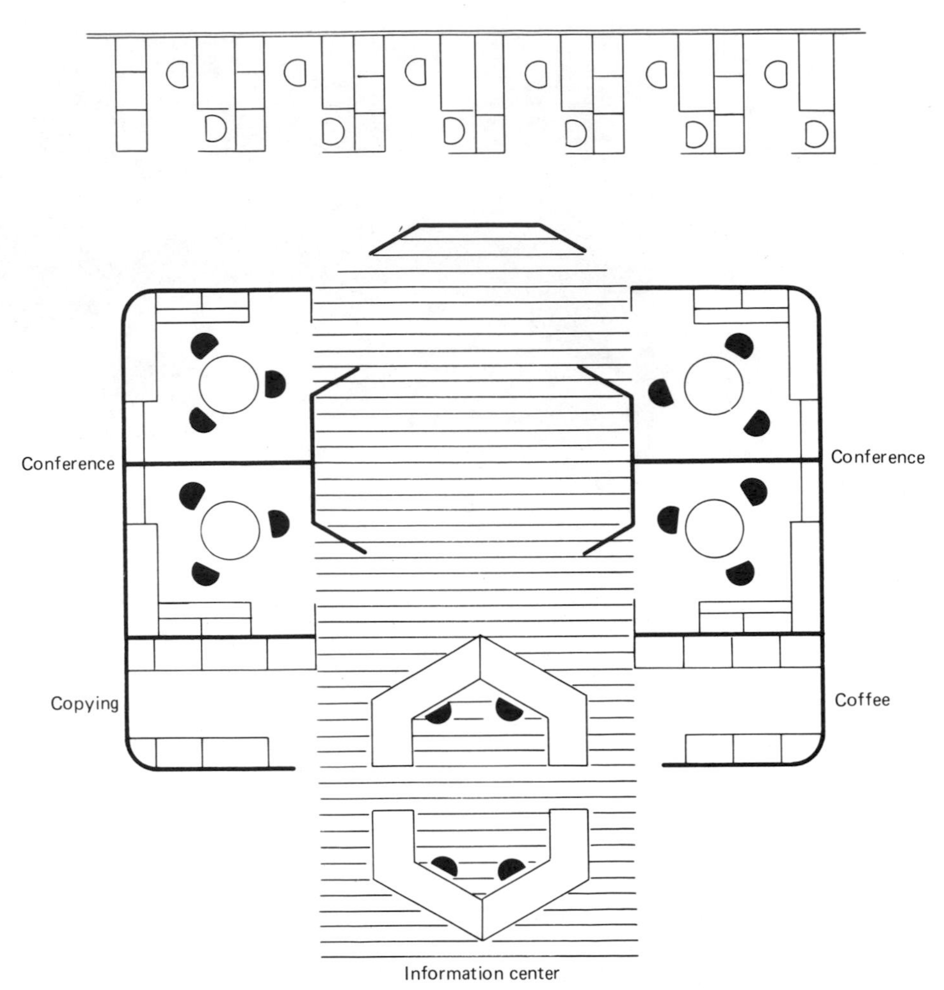

Figure 5.8 The shared spaces are the midienvironments and are the overlapping responsibilities of architects or engineers and interior designers or space planners.

First impressions are extremely important. Merchandisers are aware that initial impressions of retail establishments must impart important information to the potential buyer if the store is to be successful. The same is true about a CAD/CAM facility. The aesthetics and ambience must relate that it is creative and functional at the same time.

Psychological aspects are dependent upon social training. Several years ago, it was fashionable to locate electric switches approximately 3 feet from the floor. The thinking was that the hand naturally hangs close to that position. The problem was, however, that most people were used to electric switches which are located higher on the wall. When the lights were out, they groped about, unable to find the too-low switches. People had trouble finding them even when the lights were on. The practice disappeared.

Most people tend to think of ergonomics in terms of physical design, however, rather than psychological effect. The handicapped, for example, have been vociferous in their opposition to ordinary revolving doors. Where these doors are the only entrance, access for the handicapped is impossible. For the handicapped, barrier-free design is ergonomic design (Fig. 5.9).

5.4 THE ELDERLY OFFICE WORKER

The CAD/CAM planner must take into consideration that the population is aging (Fig. 5.10). Many companies have a mandatory retirement age, but senior citizen groups are vigorously lobbying to make such rules illegal. If this occurs, a whole series of problems in

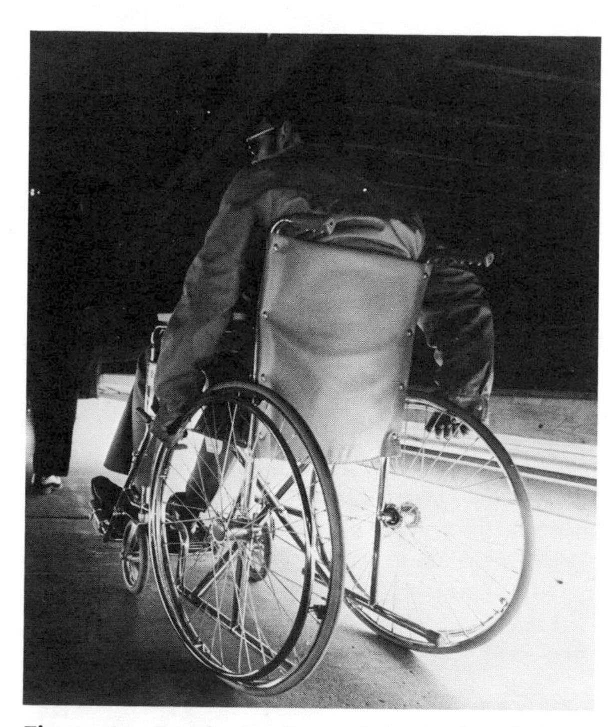

Figure 5.9 For the handicapped, barrier-free design *is* ergonomic design.

the work environment will begin to result, related to the physical well-being of the elderly. Muscular strength, for example, falls off with age. At the age of 60 a person has about 60 percent of the strength he or she had at age 30. Lifting heavy objects becomes difficult. Bending over and picking up cartons of printout paper can cause severe back strain. Compounding the problem are the dizziness and imbalance that result from reaching too low or too high. Then, too, the elderly have an increased fear of falling. Tripping hazards must be minimized. Floors must be level and carpets without minor tears. Stairwells should have sturdy banisters, and bathrooms should have grab bars.

Vision and hearing also degenerate with age. The eyes have difficulty accommodating to variations in lighting levels. Task-ambient lighting, so popular these days because it saves energy, may have to be used more judiciously. In many instances, there is too much variation in the level of light, temporarily blinding those with poor eyesight as they walk from one place to another. Older people also have reduced ability to see in areas of low-level illumination. Accidents may be waiting to happen.

Figure 5.10 The population is aging. Accommodating the elderly worker has begun to modify facility design.

Hearing loss is another problem. A child can hear a sound frequency of 20,000 hertz. By the age of 30, most people can hear only up to 15,000 hertz. By age 50, the limit is 13,000. Although hearing aids are widely available, they are not always satisfactory. Phone companies provide many of their hard-of-hearing customers with amplifiers, loudspeakers, and loud ringers. (Of course, the inability to hear as well as one used to may be a benefit. Noise in the office may not have to be reduced.)

The elderly also suffer when temperature variations are extreme. Today many companies attempt to follow guidelines for winter and summer thermostat settings. The lower winter temperatures, in particular, may adversely affect older people and make them unproductive. Chairs are another area of concern. Older people have difficulty getting out of chairs that are too soft or too low. Seats must not be lower than an individual's compressed seat height. Armrests which are the same length of the seat help the older worker to rise out of the chair. Backrests must offer firm support. Many older people like hardback chairs. These sturdy chairs give them a sense of security.

5.5 THE ELECTRONIC OFFICE

It matters very much, then, whether a specific CAD/CAM task is to be performed by a man or a woman, or a younger or an older person (Fig. 5.11). For that reason, adjustable furnishings are suggested. Until recently, for example, few men were typists. Typing was considered "woman's work." Typing runoffs and machine tables were designed with women in mind. They tend to be too low for men. Their clearances are not sufficient.

Figure 5.11 It matters very much whether a physical task is to be performed by a man or a woman, a younger or an older person.

Today, typing on CAD/CAM equipment is an androgynous task. Both men and women use the keyboards and keypads. Furthermore, sexual stereotyping is beginning to disappear. There are more male secretaries now than there were several years ago. Male word processing operators are common. For these men, equipment that is too low causes backache. Insufficient room under typing runoffs cramps the legs and causes pain.

To accommodate the average male, the average runoff should be 25 inches from the floor, rather than the 24 inches suggested for women. The runoff should adjust between 22.8 and 26.8 inches from the floor to accommodate 95 percent of the American adult population. Here, it should be noted that the U.S. military recommendations for the height of the home row keys of computer keyboards used by some planners are too high for women. This standard is 24¼ to 31 inches from the floor. At those heights the keyboard is above elbow height for the smaller adult female.

If typing runoffs were designed for women, the desks and drafting tables were designed with men in mind. Many women find that desks and table tops are too high. To accommodate 95 percent of the American adult population, desktops, for example, should be adjustable between 25 and 30 inches from the floor.

Most of the better furniture companies attempt to accommodate people in the 5th to 95th percentile in weight and height, or 90 percent rather than 95 percent of the adult population. They find it is too costly to produce furniture for the additional 5 percent. Other fine furniture companies use the concept of the average person and limit their lines altogether. That explains why chairs, desks, and tables from one manufacturer are comfortable for one group, while another group prefers some other company's product line.

Unfortunately, there is no average person. Heights, weights, body types, joints, and every other physical attribute vary from person to person. Those who are average in two dimensions make up only 7 percent of the population; those in three, about 3 percent; and those in four, less than 2 percent. Where furniture is expected to be used by many different people and is not flexible, a variety of seating and desk types is suggested.

Architectural clearances, including safety regulations, on the other hand, try to accommodate 99 percent of the people. The logic is clear: If there is sufficient room for nearly all of the tall people to pass, then everyone else will be able to pass as well. Ninety-nine percent of the citizens of this country are less than 6 feet 8 inches tall. It is not a coincidence that systems furniture manufacturers feature doors on partitions that are 6 feet 8 inches or higher (barroom-style doors excepted).

Systems furniture companies make flexible products in an attempt to use only one line to accommodate as many different people and jobs as possible (Fig. 5.12). Computer furniture companies attempt to design flexible furnishings to accommodate many different people but which are specific for certain job types and equipment (Fig. 5.13). It is not uncommon to find CAD/CAM furniture that features handles and levers which adjust the desks and tables in a variety of ways. While some planners believe that some furniture lines are flexible, durable, and attractive products exactly right for the job, others feel that ordinary drafting furniture can play the same role. Of course, it matters exactly what that role is. If a CAD/CAM station is expected to accommodate three different shifts per day, it may be important to have furniture that can adjust at a touch of a lever, especially if one operator is very tall and another is extremely short. On the other hand, if there is only one shift and one operator, such flexibility is a cost that can be saved. Furthermore, it matters whether the operator is expected to sit in one basic position for the length of the shift or

Figure 5.12 Systems furniture and panel systems in particular are designed to accommodate a variety of tasks. (*Courtesy of Herman Miller.*)

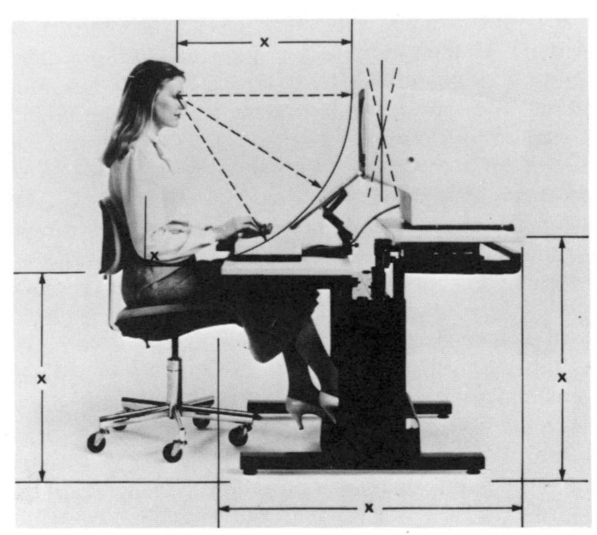

Figure 5.13 Computer furniture companies attempt to design flexible furnishings that are specific for certain job types and equipment. (*Courtesy of Wright Line, Inc.*)

move around and do several different tasks. Where the operator can move around, a good adjustable chair may be all that is required.

The correct relationship between chair, table, and equipment height affects comfort and productivity. Figure 5.14 shows some typical dimensions. Keyboards, for example, situated so that the elbow is raised more than 3 inches cause neck, shoulder, and upper back muscles to ache. The same is true of paper-and-pencil tasks. To keyboard, the angle of the wrist should not be greater than 10°, and the angle between the upper and lower arms should not be more than 80 to 120°.

Several CAD/CAM machines use keyboards that are not attached to the video display

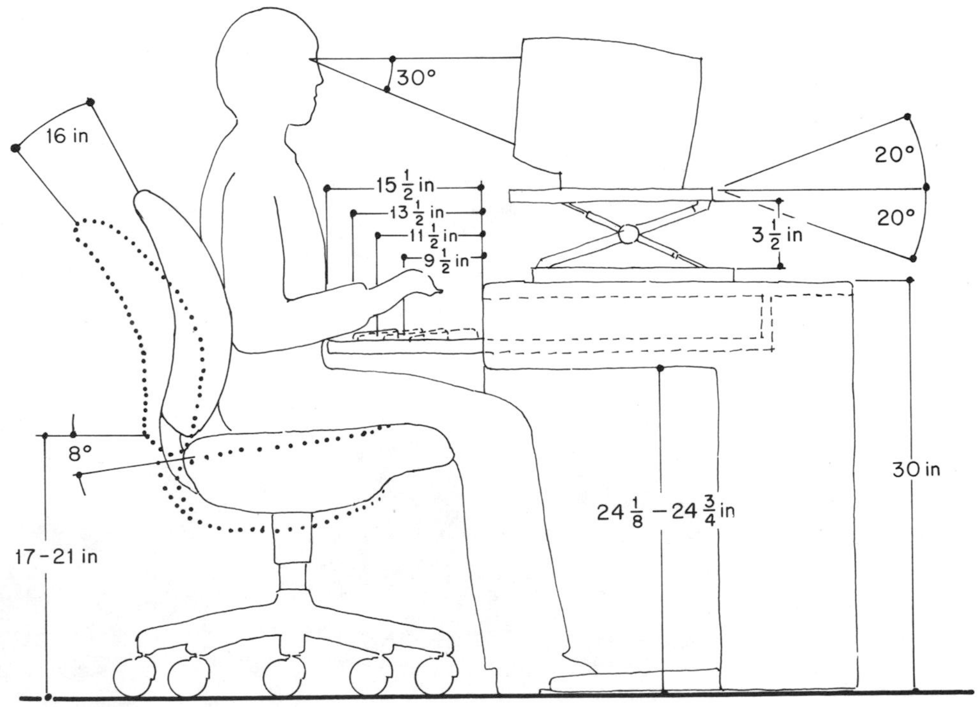

Figure 5.14 Typical dimensions.

screen but rather link to it by means of infrared rays. Others use extralong electric tethers. These tethers are up to 5 feet long. Although the tethers tend to be unsightly, they are extremely popular with programmers and analysts. The people can sit in a variety of comfortable positions. Some keyboard in their laps. In several cases, people keyboard on the floor, with their papers spread about their workstations in neat piles. (This, of course, is impossible to accomplish if one must use a keypad with one hand and draw with a light pen on a VDT with the other.)

The ability to change position is essential. It is difficult for anyone to sit still for any length of time. While sitting quietly, men move approximately 50 times an hour, while women move 40 times.

The distance of the hands from the body to the center of the keyboard is not as critical if one can move around. The common castered swivel office chair allows this movement—provided that the arms approach the keyboard comfortably. The recommended distance from the center of the torso to the center of the keyboard is no more than 11 inches. For very tall people, or those with extremely long arms, the preferred distance may be greater.

Eye-screen distances, on the other hand, are more critical for many people. Figure 5.15 shows the visual field. Some people have to sit closer than others in order to see. Bifocal users have particular problems. The lower lens is used for viewing close objects, while the upper lens is for distance. If the video display screen is at an inappropriate angle, the person wearing bifocals has to crane the neck and tilt the head upward, while looking down. The position is extremely uncomfortable. For those who do not use bifocals, the center of the screen should be between 10 and 20° below the horizontal plane of the eye height. That is because the head slumps as one reads. Some researchers recommend that the top of the screen also be below eye height, while others are just as vociferous that the top line of the display be 10 to 15° below the horizontal plane, with no portion at an angle greater than 40° below the horizontal. The variety of suggestions implies a screen that can

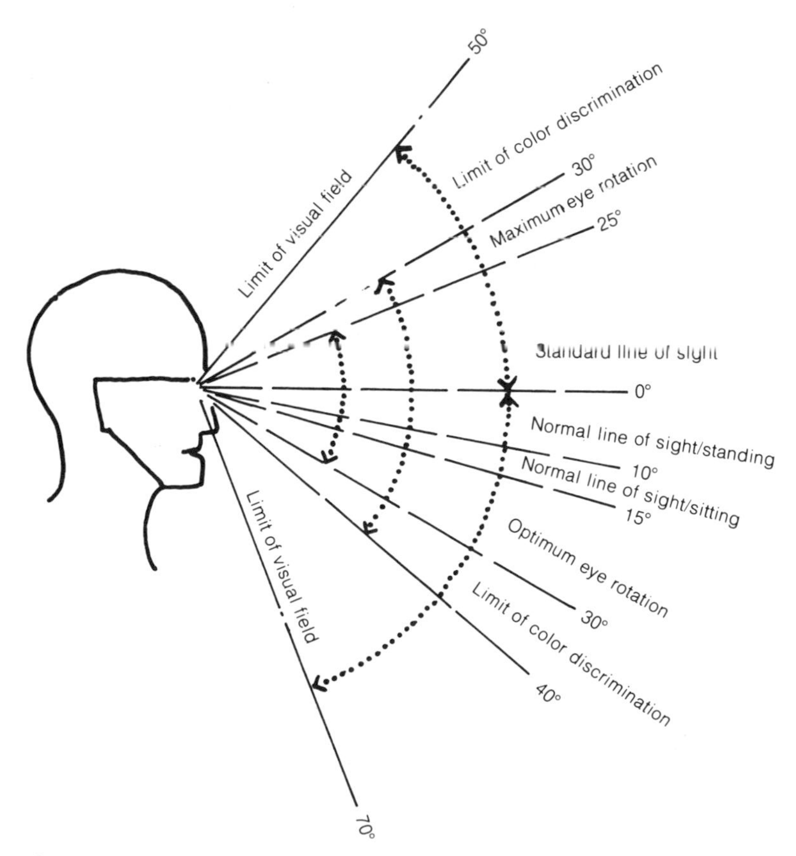

Figure 5.15 The visual field.

be tilted at will. Screens that tilt are recommended, especially where several different people are expected to use them for extended periods of time. Furthermore, many people like to be able to turn the screens from side to side, to angle them toward or away from themselves. The ability to do so enables one to change body positions. Lazy Susans are one desktop aid, although a console that is light enough to rearrange is a less costly suggestion.

Glare is an extremely difficult problem for many video display users. Operators should be able to adjust screen brightness and contrast. Lighting levels should be between 500 and 700 lux, depending on visual demands of other tasks performed in the work area. Drapes, shades, and blinds are recommended for windows that are in close proximity, and the terminals should be adjustable with respect to the windows and overhead lighting. Screen hoods are sometimes used, although antiglare filters have become more popular. Recessed, covered, or baffled direct lighting or indirect lighting fixtures are suggested.

Eyestrain may be caused by staring at the flashing cursor on a CAD/CAM VDT. It may also be caused by the glare on the display screen from light reflected from windows, shiny work surfaces, keyboards, too-bright lighting, or lighting incorrectly positioned in relation to the screen. It is also a function of the contrast between the bright lettering on the display and the dark lettering on printed matter. One's eyes must accommodate constantly. To combat these problems, CAD/CAM manufacturers equip their high-resolution screens with nonreflective glass. For screens that do not contain nonreflective glass, a nonreflective filter can be purchased. Many screens also tilt and swivel, which allows operators to find more comfortable body positions and, at the same time, reflects glare away from the user. Task lights that tilt and swivel are also recommended. Some screens feature brightness contrast and the ability to change lettering size or the color of the phosphors. Green lettering is favored by some people, while orange lettering is favored by others. Both groups claim these colors are easier to view for long periods than black or white. Digital flat screens—which produce less heat and provide flicker- and distortion-free displays—will probably become industry standards in a few years.

Ergonomics also involves the structure and makeup of the keyboard and keypad (Fig. 5.16). The original typewriter keyboard was created to keep the most active keys away from one another, so that they would not jam. The resulting design is known as the "qwerty," for the first six alphabet characters on the second row (the first row contains numeric characters). In an electronic age, the qwerty is unnecessary. Several companies have attempted the manufacture and distribution of new keyboards. To date, the new keyboards have not sparked wide interest. Their use would require massive operator

Figure 5.16 Ergonomics also involves the structure and makeup of the video display terminal and keyboard. (*Courtesy of Wright Line, Inc.*)

retraining. As it is, operators complain about minor variations in keyboard style from one manufacturer to another.

Keyboard designers have found that dished keys are necessary for extensive typing; otherwise, fingers literally slide around the keys. Since computers are electronic, the click must be built in; the operation is naturally silent. Most people need the click to "know" when keys are struck. For some operators, function keys are confusing. Great strides have been made to simplify keyboard style and link it with friendlier software. Separate number pads are often added to facilitate mathematical calculations, for example.

To alleviate tension, a 15-minute coffee break after 2 hours of continuous work at a keyboard under moderate workload is suggested. In fact, this is suggested for concentrated work on any CAD/CAM machine. Where there are problems viewing the screen, a 15-minute break is recommended after an hour. The same is true of extremely repetitive tasks under a very high workload. Postal workers labor in teams and change tasks at given intervals throughout the day.

Printers are another area of ergonomic research. Unfortunately, impact printers produce noise that adds stress to the environment, especially where CAD/CAM facilities are already overcrowded. Plotters and jet spray and thermal and laser printers make considerably less noise. Boxes which dampen the noise are widely available. They typically contain high-absorption, peak-and-valley acoustical foam, cooling fans, and clear plastic covers.

European workers are demanding that dot matrix printers have a noise level below 55 to 60 decibels, significantly lower than the 71 decibels produced by most printers manufactured in the United States. To comply, several U.S. manufacturers now offer sound dampening for the printers: clear plastic covers over the page exit and polyurethane foam in special spots in the machines.

Printers cause other problems. High-speed printers give off noxious fumes. Many printers are difficult to feed. Their paper can be heavy. Location may be circumscribed by

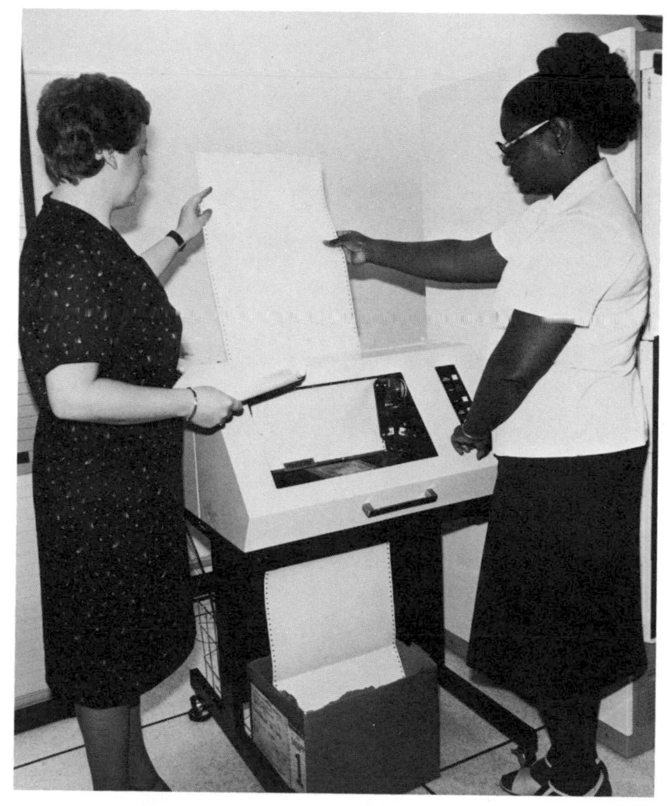

Figure 5.17 Printers are noisy. Many are difficult to feed. Location may be circumscribed by feed requirements and paper size. (*Courtesy of U.S. Army Library, Pentagon.*)

feed requirements and paper size (Fig. 5.17). If the printer is expected to work continuously, paper storage should be in close proximity and the logistics worked out. Otherwise back strain and frustration will result. Back strain may also result from picking up heavy disk packs or computer boxes. Disk packs may weigh more than 20 pounds. Computer equipment is typically packed in cumbersome boxes.

Computer rooms are notorious for their noises and their temperatures (Fig. 5.18). The noises come from the various mechanical operations such as disk and tape drives. Air conditioners are also noisy and, to make matters worse, often throw out too much cold air for comfort. Computer rooms may also contain radiation hazards. Even bigger hazardous potentials relate to electric shock. Malfunctioning equipment or dangling wires are always a danger. Cleaning fluids present other problems. Solvents used for maintenance give off toxic fumes, especially dangerous for those allergic to them.

Heat buildup is not a problem of the computer rooms alone. A rough rule of thumb is that each VDT and printer produces the same heat as a human being. Thus, if an area contains 50 employees and 50 machines, the HVAC system should be designed for 100 people. Obviously, printers and other machinery that work continuously produce more heat. They require special ventilation.

In addition to the ergonomic design of the computer rooms, VDTs, printers, and plotters are requirements for the chair. Manufacturers have concentrated their efforts on office chairs and drafting stools these last few years, for they appear to be key to operator comfort. Today's swivel, castered chairs and stools are different from their forerunners (Fig. 5.19). Some feature synchronized articulation. The seat and back construction moves as the body moves. Most chairs allow back-attitude control which locks the chair into several different positions, from relaxed to totally upright. Almost all feature height control; the seats can be raised or lowered from the average 16 to 17 inches above the floor. Many adjust from 13.6 to 20.6 inches to accommodate the majority of the adult population. Certain chairs are so adjustable that they move up and down hydraulically, with very little effort at all. Chairs come with seat-attitude control also. Here, the seat front lowers from the standard 6° pitch to 5° in order to accommodate shorter people, or raises to 8° to suit the tallest. Tension adjustment of the seat and back to suit individual weight and body heights is another feature.

Properly contoured back support of the lumbar curve is the critical task of the office chair (Fig. 5.20). The recommended angle is between 95 to 105°. The angle combines with

Figure 5.18 Computer rooms are notorious for their noises and temperatures. The noises are by-products of the mechanical operations of certain equipment. Air conditioners may keep the electronic equipment functioning but chill human operators. (*Courtesy of Dynatech Data Systems.*)

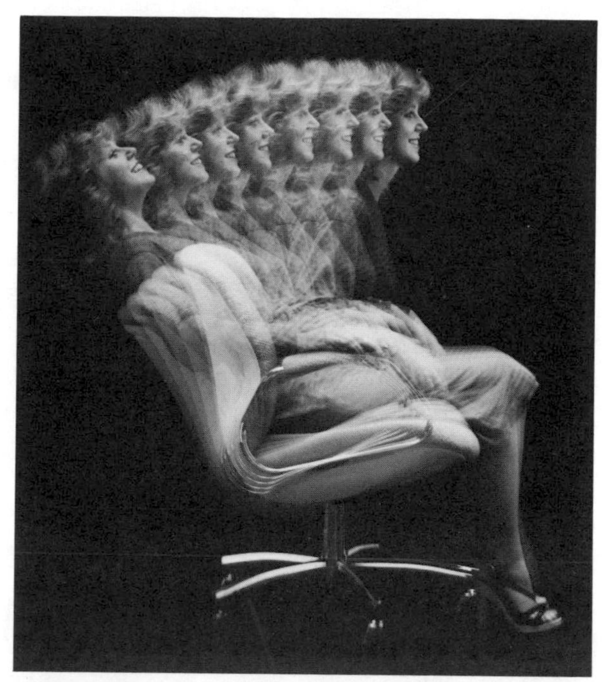

Figure 5.19 Today's swivel castered chairs are different from their forerunners. Many contain back and seat constructions which move as the body moves. (*Courtesy of Steelcase.*)

the lumbar curve to reduce pressure on the buttocks, as the buttocks should support slightly more than half of the total body weight. The balance of the weight should be divided between the upper torso, supported by the chair back, and the feet. It is essential that the feet rest on the floor. Short people find that their inability to touch the floor with their feet results in muscle strain and a cutoff of circulation to the legs. A seat and back pocket "nests" the body, aligning thighs, buttocks, and upper torso. The pocket must not be confining. Rather, the user must be able to move around freely as positions are changed. Side-to-side contour is also important. If a chair is contoured too high, it will cause pressure on sensitive projections of the thigh bones. Some contour, however, is necessary to cushion the base of the pelvis.

Another ingredient in picking the correct chair is the depth. Seat depths of less than 13 inches do not allow adequate support under thighs, while those greater than 16 inches will not accommodate small women. The front edge of the seat comes in contact with the back of the leg of a small woman, forcing her to sit toward the front or to slide away from backrest support. The result is poor posture. On the other end of the scale, seat lengths of 18 inches are required for fuller thigh support for very tall people. It affords them greater comfort.

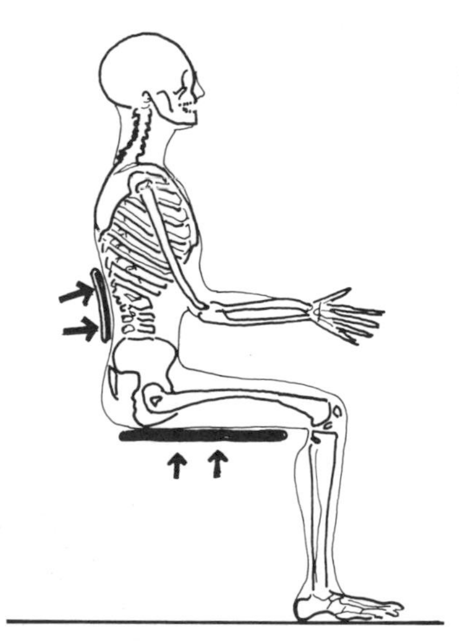

Figure 5.20 Properly contoured back support of the lumbar curve is one critical task of the office chair. Another is to provide firm support for the lower buttocks and the upper thighs.

Beyond seating requirements are the primary, secondary, and tertiary task requirements of the microenvironment. A common complaint is that there is little desktop room to take notes. Electronic equipment

Figure 5.21 Electronic equipment does not do away with pencil-and-paper tasks. A common complaint is that designers give little consideration to the primary, secondary, and tertiary task requirements of the microenvironment. (*Courtesy of U.S. Army Library, Pentagon.*)

does not do away with pencil-and-paper tasks (Fig. 5.21). Many people have *more* paper with which to contend. A common printout paper size is 14¾ inches by 11 inches. Since printouts are produced by continuous feed, the lengths of many documents are multiples of 11 inches. When data must be checked, the reader may want to scan several multiples at once. Then, too, printouts are often bound in book form. An open book is 24 inches deep, including the binder. At the very least, the desktop must be 24 inches deep to handle an open printout book and 36 inches deep to hold three lengths of printout paper. For a graphics terminal, the desk may be 5 feet deep to hold blueprints and such.

The desktop must be large enough to hold the electronic equipment. Some terminals are very bulky. Several intelligent terminals with built-in telecommunications devices and the ability to send and receive at 1200 baud are nearly 3 feet square. Other terminals are less bulky but are an amalgam of separate devices for which space must be found: a video display unit, keyboard, controller, disk drive, disk storage, and modem. Furthermore, many electronic devices can be upgraded. Space must be made for the peripheral devices which allow this upgrading to occur. Of course, many systems allow peripherals to be stacked one on top of the other, and thus minimize space. On occasion, a specially fabricated shelf is required to separate the pieces so that their normal vibration or heat does not interfere with each other's operation.

Some manufacturers supply workstations for their equipment. It is not uncommon, for example, for word processing systems to come built into their own desks. This is certainly true of many CAD/CAM systems.

The favored workstation design for many electronic tasks is L- or U-shaped. In an L-shaped design, it matters whether the worker is right- or left-handed. If the person is right-handed, the terminal should be to the right of the desk. When the person is working with paper and pencil at the desk, all major tasks are located to the right. The opposite is suggested for the left-handed person. The idea is to increase handling speed.

Where handling speed is important, good ergonomic design is essential. A major mailroom furniture and equipment supplier suggests that mailroom processing commence to the left of the doorway. Although the overwhelming majority of Americans are right-handed and instinctively turn to the right (left-handers turn to the left), once mail is delivered, every other process is on the right.

Of course, humans are adaptable. Unless the desks are extremely dysfunctional, the wrong-handed desk will cause only minor annoyance for most people. Many contend with telephones installed on the wrong side and do not even know it. Few notice that if they pick up the phone in their right hand, they must change hands to take notes. For right-handed people, the phone should be to the left, and for left-handed people to the right. Many designers split the difference and center the phone. Also of concern is the height of workstation partitions for visual and acoustical privacy. A 48-inch-high panel, while sufficient to block the horizontal line of sight for the overwhelming majority of women, will not do so for the taller men. Ninety percent of American women have a horizontal line of sight that varies between 45 and 48½ inches. The line of sight for the male population varies between 47 and 50¾ inches (Fig. 5.22). Indeed, there seems to be a notable lack of data used by many professionals in the furniture and building industries. Too much of what is designed is based on ideas that are outdated or are for different population groups. Many Americans are stouter today than their counterparts in the 1950s. By 1976, for example, the 5th, 50th, and 95th percentiles for body breadth grew to 18.8, 20.9, and 22.8 inches. With a 3-inch allowance for winter clothing, the figures can be rounded off to 22, 24, and 26 inches. Figure 5.23 shows typical standing and reaching dimensions. Figure 5.24 shows typical seated dimensions. Many local, state, and national codes use a 22-inch incremental factor for corridors. A corridor which is only 44 inches wide is not sufficient to let most people pass.

Ethnicity is also a significant factor in body size. The Hispanic population in Miami tends to be smaller than the more Nordic population of Minneapolis. Socioeconomic factors also affect body dimensions. The nutrition available to those with higher incomes creates freedom from disease and contributes to body growth. Socioeconomic status often determines the amount of education available. College graduates tend to be taller than their high school graduate counterparts. Does this mean that people in the executive suite are taller than those working on the loading dock? Or in the clerical areas? The answer is a resounding yes. In several major corporations the chairman, president, and top executives are well over 6 feet. Americans unconsciously give taller people greater authority. This may explain why the furniture in the executive suite tends to be much larger than elsewhere in the office.

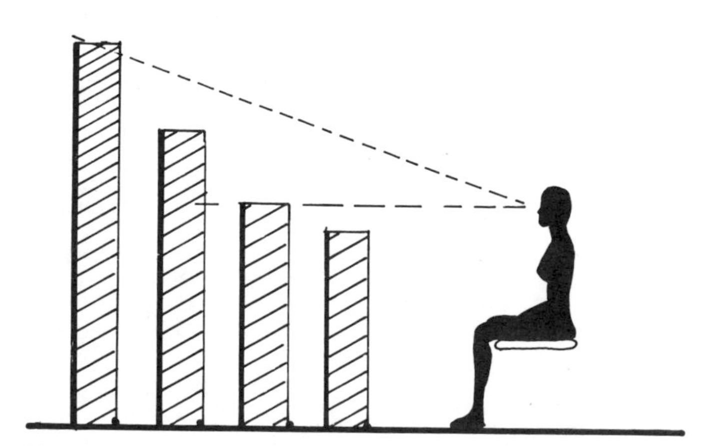

Figure 5.22 The horizontal line of sight for the seated U.S. male population varies between 47 and 50¾ inches while that of the female varies between 45 and 48½ inches.

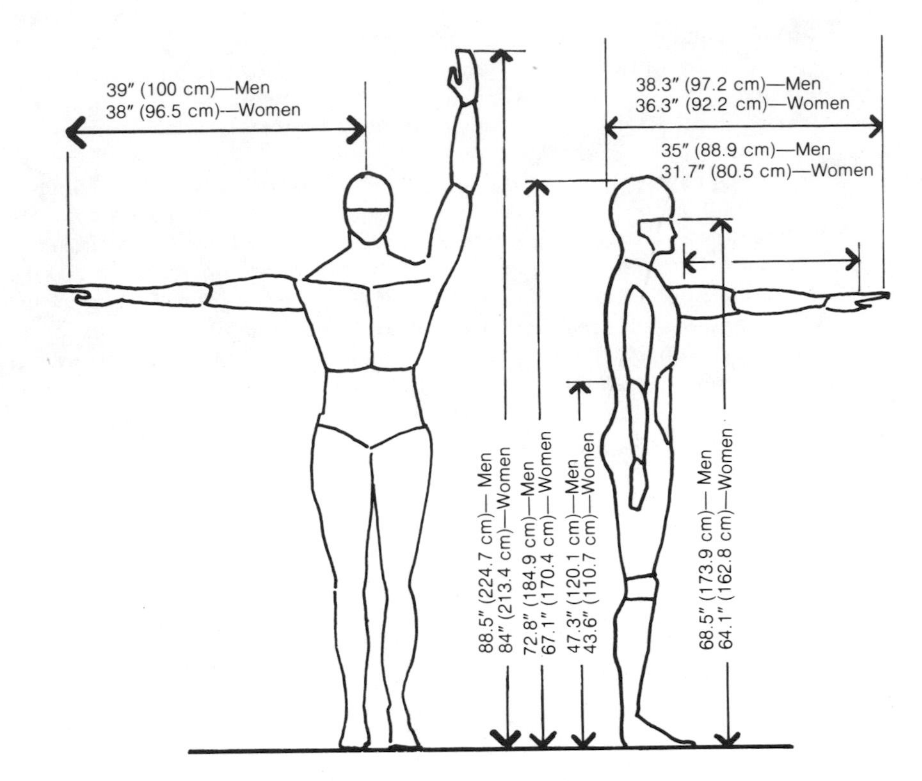

Figure 5.23 Typical standing and reaching dimensions.

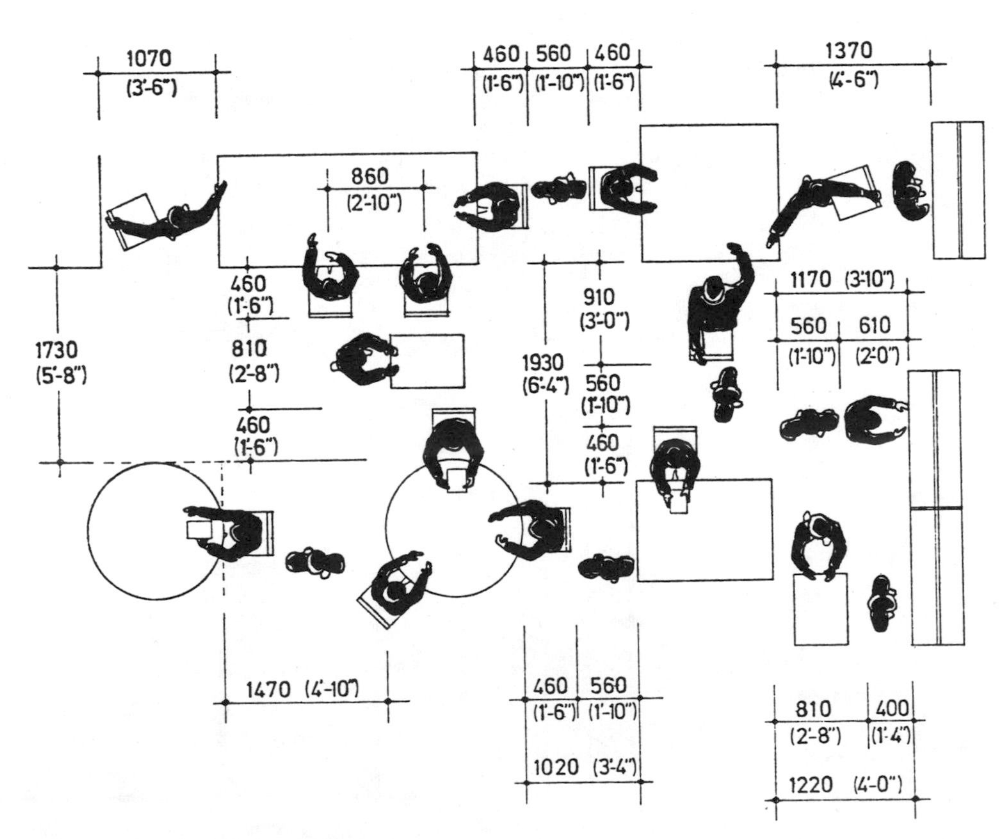

Figure 5.24 Typical seated dimensions.

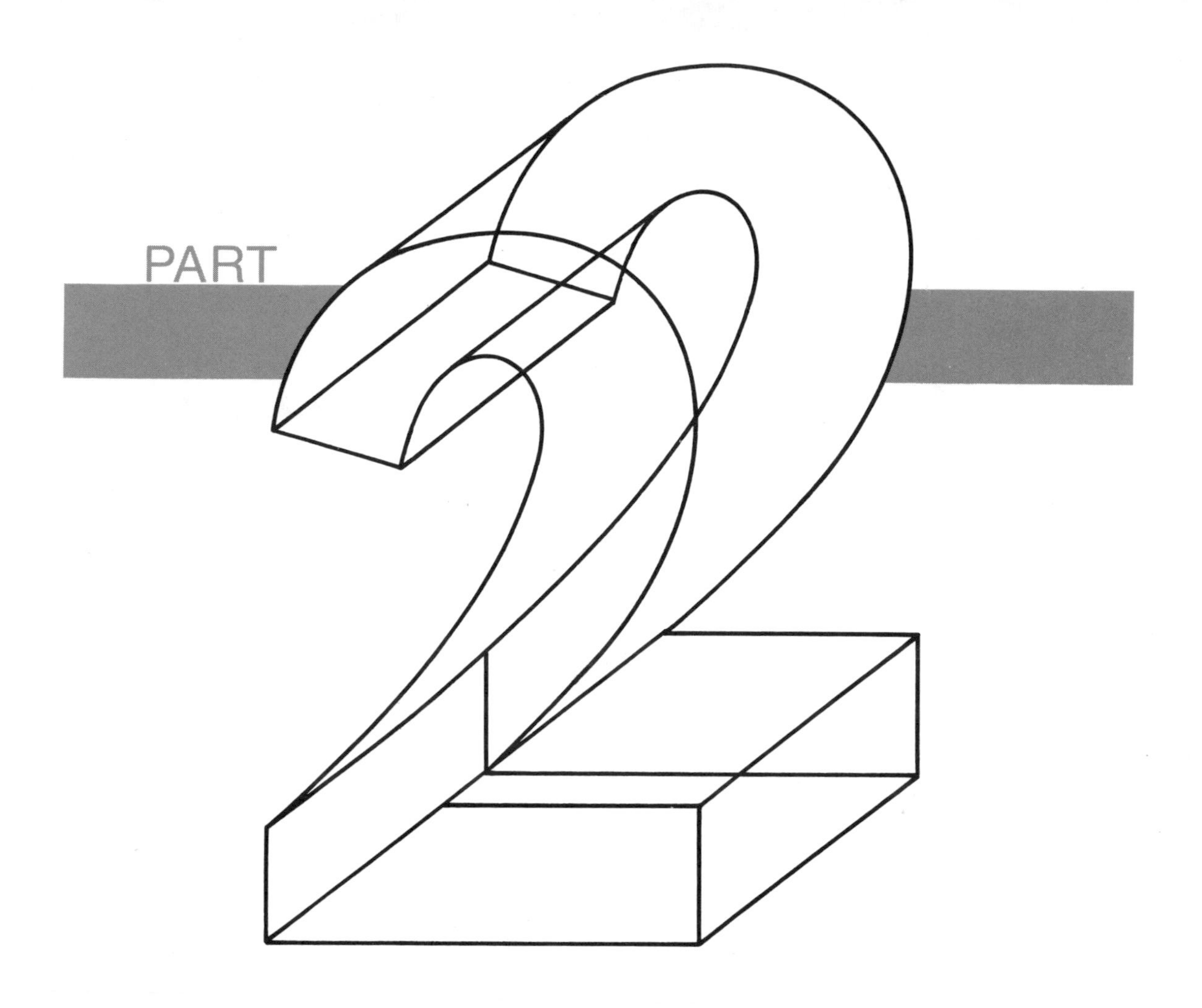

CAD/CAM PROCESS

System Selection and Acquisition

by

Eric Teicholz

6.1 INTRODUCTION

This chapter is written to provide a procedural framework for those interested in procuring a computer-aided design and computer-aided manufacturing (CAD/CAM) system. Its objectives are twofold. The first is to provide a guide for performing a general systems analysis to determine if CAD/CAM is relevant to the operations of a company, and the second is to describe how to select an appropriate system. The procedure presented has been used by a wide spectrum of design, drafting, and manufacturing companies.

6.1.1 Process Overview

The selection and acquisition process consists of two primary tasks—the first being a preliminary CAD/CAM feasibility study and the second a detailed systems analysis and system evaluation. The preliminary analysis is conducted in a relatively short time span and answers the question as to whether design and drafting automation is, or might be, appropriate to an organization. The second phase, an extension and refinement of the first, is more comprehensive and detailed in scope and is designed both to produce a set of specifications, which is contained in a request for proposal (RFP), for purchasing a CAD/CAM system and to provide criteria for evaluating different systems and vendors.

Specifically, the analysis and selection process is made up of the following tasks:

- Preliminary study
- Information and organization analysis
- Manual costs definition
- System requirements definition
- Writing the RFP
- Vendor evaluation and selection

6.1.2 Options for Implementation

The means by which automated techniques are implemented in a design, drafting, or manufacturing firm is an important consideration. The use of a dedicated in-house computer, for example, represents just one option. Others include the use of timesharing companies and/or service bureaus. No matter what option a firm selects, it is important to understand the important policy and organizational, as well as initial and recurring, implications of CAD/CAM. Each alternative should be considered at a conceptual level before one is selected for additional analysis.

In timesharing, a firm normally rents a terminal, such as a CRT terminal, for in-house use. The firm pays a monthly fee to the timesharing vendor for data storage and program access and uses application-specific programs on an as needed basis by communicating between the vendor's computer and the user's terminal—normally over voice-grade telephone lines, but sometimes over faster and costlier dedicated telephone lines.

Principal advantages of timesharing are twofold: a company need not make large capital expenditures for computer hardware or worry about technical obsolescence, and the firm can use software from a variety of sources, offered by one or more timesharing companies, while simply paying for the time used. Disadvantages of timesharing include the normally slow speeds (sometimes taking up to 1 hour) of sending large graphic data files across voice-grade telephone lines, the usually high costs associated with data storage and program access, and the lack of control over hardware, databases, and software.

With service bureaus, a user firm delivers input data to the bureau's computer and the bureau performs the processing, and then delivers the finished product. Turnaround time can take from 1 day to several weeks depending on the size of the job, how busy the bureau is, and whether additional data analysis is performed.

Service bureaus are usually expensive, slow, and can possibly have design security problems, but, like timesharing, they also have several advantages. First, they provide access to skilled personnel already acquainted with a particular hardware system. This is important because it can take over 6 months to become proficient on a sophisticated CAD/CAM system. Second, service bureaus often have specialized input and output equipment that a user might not be able to justify as an in-house investment. Third, service bureaus might provide backup drafting services during peak periods for firms. Service bureaus share with timesharing companies the advantage of performing an educational function by helping a company learn about CAD/CAM and its effect on an office. Finally, service bureaus specializing in particular applications such as architecture or electronics often have prestored libraries of standard drafting symbols that are of potential use to a company employed in a similar application.

6.2 PRELIMINARY STUDY

The preliminary or feasibility study analysis is initiated in order to review and document the current operational procedures of a firm and to select which areas are most amenable to automation. The effectiveness of current methods of operation must be objectively documented and evaluated before the potential of automation can be determined.

6.2.1 Task Objectives

As the practices of engineering, design, and manufacturing become increasingly complex, innovative new tools are needed to support day-to-day operations. Management is increasingly turning to computers, and to computer graphics in particular, for engineering design and drafting support. The primary objective of the preliminary study is to demonstrate to management the potential risks and benefits of automation.

At the end of this analysis, management should have enough information either to terminate the study or to continue with a more detailed and labor-intensive comprehensive analysis. Management should furthermore be aware of the functional feasibility and of the approximate cost savings of using CAD/CAM rather than manual methods. This "go" or "no-go" decision on the part of management relies heavily on relevant experience, coming either from in-house staff or from an experienced consultant.

The use of an outside consultant can offer many advantages in performing this task. Although consultants will not reveal details of other clients' applications, they can cite many examples of the conditions under which CAD/CAM will and will not work. A consultant can provide a level of experience and a degree of objectivity which are not always available with in-house staff. When a consultant is used, it is important to get regular progress reports so that both the client and consultant can determine if they are on the right track.

6.2.2 The Role of the Evaluation Team

The in-house evaluation team has overall responsibility for CAD/CAM selection, acquisition, and installation. The team should not be so large as to restrict decision making, and both management and technical staff should be represented. Specific responsibilities of the team include the development of time and dollar budgets for members, the determination of major milestones, and regular and frequent management reporting. The head of the team should be responsive to the goals or concerns of the company, have good communications skills, and be thoroughly familiar with all aspects of a firm's operation and long-range management objectives. This individual should be the only company source of contact for vendors.

Besides undertaking the preliminary feasibility analysis, to be described below, the team members should educate themselves to the greatest extent possible as to the current status and capabilities of existing CAD/CAM systems. This can be accomplished by attending trade shows, conferences, and seminars; visiting similar CAD/CAM installations; talking to vendors; and conducting a literature review.

6.2.3 Preliminary Analysis: Micro and Macro Issues

The preliminary study phase is meant to allow for the consideration of as many feasible automation alternatives as possible before the detailed analysis takes place. Functional appropriateness and economic risk and reward analyses are the task objectives. For the sake of expediency, simplifications and assumptions should be made, provided they are clearly articulated. Data acquired during this task is refined during the detailed systems analysis.

A number of micro (small-scale) and macro (large-scale) issues must be addressed by the evaluation team. Examples of macro issues might include

- Total scope of the processes being investigated
- Functional areas of company
- Organization of company
- Growth objectives
- In-house technical expertise (skill groups)
- Current decision-making procedures regarding technology
- Expectations regarding automation
- Goals and objectives regarding CAD/CAM
- Desired payback for CAD/CAM
- Potential technical interfaces for varied levels of automation
- Potential service of decentralized offices

Micro issues might include

- Differentiation of drafting and other skill-group tasks
- Coordination of work tasks
- Output formats
- Development of graphic standards (if nonexistent)
- Dispensation and protection of the database
- Frequency, types, and priorities of work tasks
- Potential automation interface areas
- Potential adaptation of existing computer facilities (if present)
- Magnitude and quality of existing process and task documentation—both clerical and technical.

To determine what design, drafting, or manufacturing operations might be appropriate for automation, one must determine the information flow of these procedures.

6.2.4 Candidate Tasks for Automation

In order to identify those tasks that are most amenable to automation, a company should look at its entire design, drafting, and manufacturing processes. The study should not be restricted to any particular department, since an integrated CAD/CAM facility yields the greatest time and cost dividends. One should also consider long-range planning goals to speculate how a company might evolve in the future.

Computers should be implemented for well-defined tasks where the speed and accuracy of machines yields high dividends. Candidate tasks for automation should incorporate one or more of the following characteristics: be labor-intensive, be critical in nature, be easily understood and definable in terms of input and output procedures, and be highly repetitive. Candidate functions containing these characteristics include:

- Word processing
- Accounting functions, including project control
- Work involving material takeoff from bill-of-material extraction software
- Design and drafting that results in automated preparation of engineering design and production drawings

The most likely drafting tasks for automation are those that are repetitive in nature—either at a micro (a drawing detail) or a macro (an entire process) level. For example, micro repetition might be present for a component manufacturer that designs products that are both variations of a common design and that use standard elements or symbols arranged in a variety of ways and minimally edited. A macro repetitive process might involve the repetitive design and analysis of various types of electrical circuits or turbines. A third type of repetitive process involves taking into account the number of revision cycles of a drawing. For example, the design of a nuclear power plant might involve a unique design but contain numerous revision cycles.

Another task that is a likely subject for automation is one that is prone to manual errors that would not be present with most CAD/CAM systems. Use of features such as automatic or semiautomatic dimensioning, drawing overlays, and integrated comprehensive databases all reduce certain types of design and drawing errors. In industries where this is critical (e.g., aerospace, automotive, manufacturing), error reduction is an important factor in considering and justifying the use of CAD/CAM.

6.2.5 Task Results and Preliminary Cost-Benefits Analysis

Recommendations should be made to management regarding the functional feasibility of automating specific design or drafting tasks. A preliminary cost-benefits analysis can be made to provide information on risks and approximate cost savings that can be realized.

This cost analysis is accomplished by taking preliminary process descriptions or diagrams (see Sec. 6.3.1), assigning average time estimates to the tasks, and using productivity gains (see Sec. 6.4.1) to determine potential time and cost savings accomplished with automation.

For example, a typical design and drafting sequence in an architectural office might consist of the sequence of operations shown in Fig. 6.1.

The evaluation team conducting the cost analysis then assigns estimated manual hours to each of the above tasks, which are then totaled. The team or a consultant then makes an estimate as to the productivity gain that will be realized by using an "average" CAD/CAM system. Finally, these productivity gains are translated into dollar and time savings—taking hardware and software purchase and operating expenses into account.

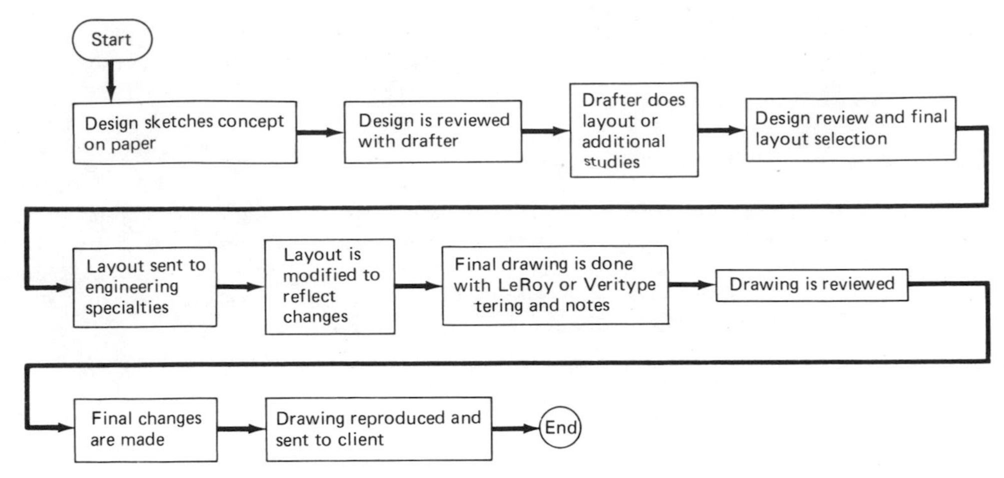

Figure 6.1 Typical design and drafting sequence of operations in an architectural office.

Many assumptions must be made in conducting this preliminary cost-benefits analysis and results must be evaluated in this context.

6.3 DETAILED TASK ANALYSIS

The purpose of an in-depth systems analysis is to gather information to decide which functions of a CAD/CAM system will be most beneficial for a company. Tasks that are labor and cost intensive might not be necessarily amenable to automation. Alternatively, tasks that realize the greatest productivity gains with automation might only constitute a small percentage of a company's work load.

At this point in the acquisition and selection process, the investigating firm is considering CAD/CAM as a real option. Assumptions made during the feasibility analysis stage must be reexamined. The purpose of this analysis is to develop a detailed set of technical specifications that can provide data for CAD/CAM cost-justification models and be incorporated into the RFP.

6.3.1 Work Process Diagrams

One way to represent a company's information flow is with diagrammatic flowcharts. Flowcharts are graphic models that have been employed by computer programmers for over 25 years. Normally, rectangles are employed to represent tasks, diamonds for decision points, and arrows for information flow (see Fig. 6.2).

Process flowcharts are normally developed in a top-down or hierarchical manner. That is, the initial flowchart developed should contain data related to major design processes. Next, subprocesses should be diagrammed, and so forth—with each flowchart increasing in detail definition until individual tasks and resources are identified. A corresponding hierarchical coding scheme can be developed, similar to the Dewey decimal system for library books, whereby diagrams can be cross-referenced to each other. Design review, drawing revisions, and feedback loops should all be included in the process analysis.

Such a detailed analysis can require considerable effort in a large firm. A firm should therefore start where there will be the largest potential savings, since the CAD/CAM system might be justified by automating just a few design or drafting operations.

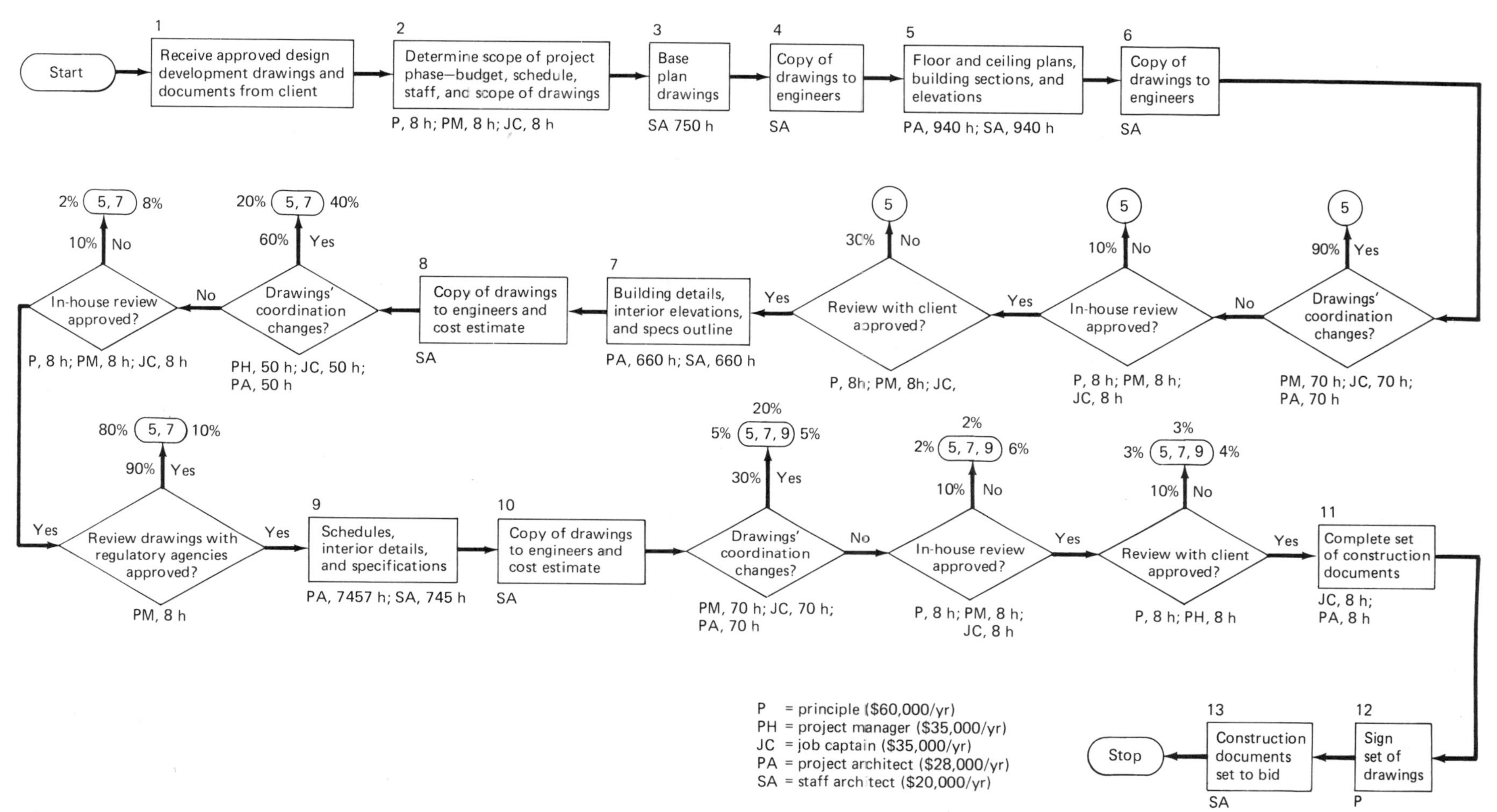

Figure 6.2 Construction documents phase of the architectural design process for $10 million office building, 133,000 square feet, $75 per square foot.

6.3.2 Management Analysis

An important objective of the systems analysis is to evaluate senior management objectives in terms of CAD. The focus of such a study is on corporate structure and the potential technical and managerial integration of CAD/CAM in the firm and, if relevant, its associated offices. Once again, the analysis should include a further refinement of management's attitudes, initially gathered during the feasibility analysis, regarding the following issues:

- Desired applications for automation
- Projected work flow
- Key financial issues
- Capital equipment planning
- Personnel selection and training
- Installation procedures
- Purchase or leasing equipment decisions
- Desired payback period
- Method of amortizing capital equipment

Some of this information can later be used for cost analyses for CAD/CAM justification.

6.3.3 Outcome of the Systems Analysis

At the end of the detailed systems analysis, the investigating firm should have a thorough understanding of the disciplines that have potential for automation, the percentage of the total work load (by discipline and drawing types) that will be affected by automation, the current and projected drawing loads (by application), and the stages where repetitive drafting takes place.

The outcome of such an analysis is, in part, the determination of a features list (list of functions) which is incorporated into the RFP. The systems analysis can take from 3 days to over 6 months based on the magnitude of the processes being investigated; the CAD/CAM sophistication of the user; the amount of organization, use of standard procedures, and repetitive details; and, finally, the size and organizational complexity of the firm itself.

All the findings should be documented in a summary report consisting of the results of the systems analysis. This report represents an initial benchmark whereby the in-house evaluation team specifies automation implications of management, technical objectives, and findings. The report provides a common basis for understanding of proposed functional capabilities of the CAD/CAM system.

6.4 MANUAL COSTS DEFINITION

Before the costing process takes place, one should review the drafting, design, and manufacturing work process diagrams to see what improvements can be made. One does not want to automate wasteful procedures. Almost all companies can find procedures for streamlining, eliminating, or generally expediting current manual design and drafting procedures.

The costing procedure is straightforward. A firm should take into account that work functions are only partially eliminated by automation and that a certain amount of human effort will always be required. One first determines average hourly rates for each of the skills used in the work process diagrams. These are entered on the diagrams themselves along with the estimated number of hours required to perform the delineated tasks. Taking repetitive iterations (feedback loops) of certain procedures into account, the total cost of that process is then tallied and multiplied by the number of times it is performed per month or per year. When all of the design, drafting, or manufacturing processes are summed in this manner, they should equal a firm's expenditures for these tasks (minus vacations, sick time, and other realistic time losses).

A variation of using a single average cost to perform a particular task is to use the maximum cost for the performance of a skill, a, the minimum cost for that same skill, b, and its average cost m, to calculate a mean expected cost for a task C, using Eq. (6.1).

$$C = \frac{a + 4m + b}{6} \tag{6.1}$$

One can also use Eq. (6.1) for time estimates by substituting maximum, minimum, and average task hours instead of rates to determine the most likely time needed to complete a particular task. People take varying amounts of time to perform the same task. The equation is meant to take uncertainty into account.

6.4.1 Estimating Cost Savings with Automation

There are a number of mathematical formulas that pertain to equipment payout period, productivity, turnaround time, error reduction, and other factors (see Chap. 8) that are used to estimate cost saving of using automated rather than manual procedures. Tom Bakey, president of Tom Bakey Associates in Sunnyvale, California, has identified six such methods that take design and drafting factors affected by CAD/CAM into account (see Figs. 6.3a to d).

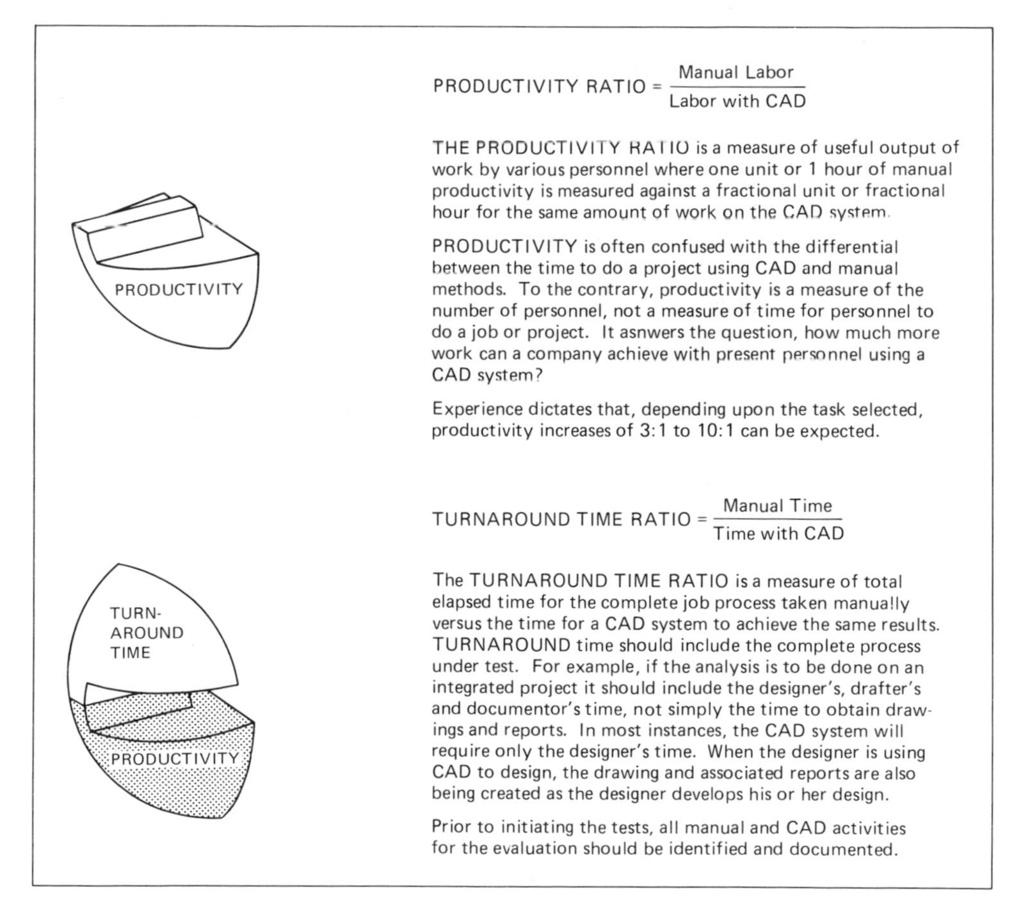

Figure 6.3a Productivity ratio, turnaround time ratio.

$$\text{ERROR REDUCTION RATIO} = \frac{\text{Manual Potential for Error}}{\text{Potential for Error with CAD}}$$

THE ERROR REDUCTION RATIO is a measure of the susceptibility for the chances for error while operating under the manual method versus the CAD system operation. It can also be considered as a method of analyzing the reduction in processing errors, i.e. copying transposition, translation, look up, and changes.

This factor, considered by many as subjective and elusive, can be isolated and, under proper management control, can become one of the most influential elements in the economic analysis. Personnel make mistakes and errors are present in every organization. Pinpointing those areas prone to error is essential for more efficient performance with or without CAD. Once isolated, they can be evaluated with respect to the differences between CAD usage and manual methods.

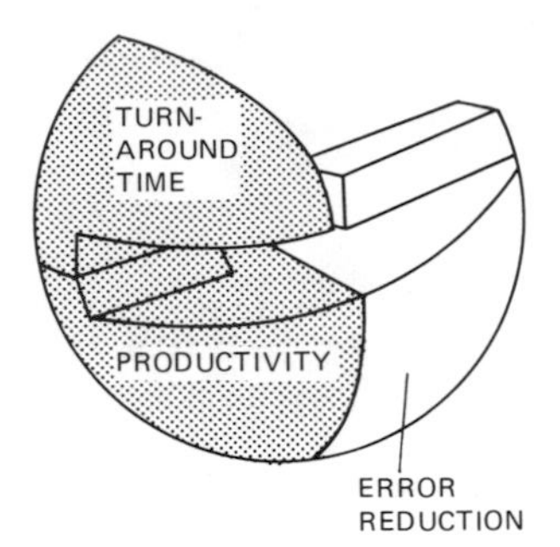

$$\text{OFFICE SPACE COST IMPACT} = \frac{\text{Annual Cost (CAD)}}{\text{Annual Cost (Manual)}}$$

OFFICE SPACE COST IMPACT is a measure of the impact of the CAD system on office space allocation. The impact is expressed as a ratio between present space cost allocations and the cost to operate CAD in a similar environment.

The impact takes into consideration three elements:

- The difference in the number of personnel between CAD when installed and present manual methods
- The amount of space required for each operation (CAD versus manual)
- The cost for the space allocated

Space requirements vary from company to company along with associated cost, but the office space cost impact ratio is an excellent relative measure and should reveal significant differences between CAD and manual space cost allocations.

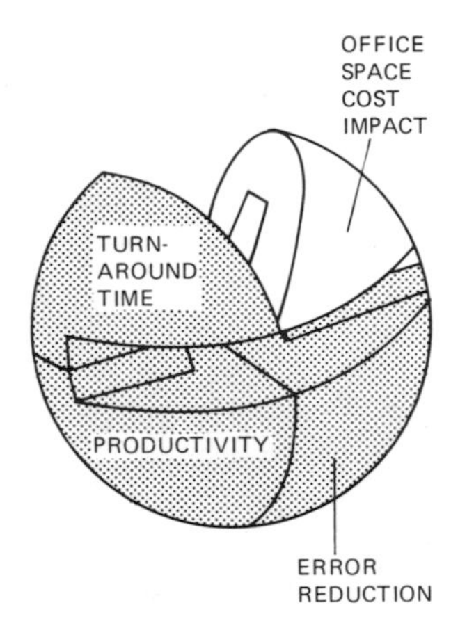

Figure 6.3b Error reduction ratio, office space cost impact.

Productivity gains, as just discussed, are the savings achieved by accomplishing a task with CAD/CAM rather than manual methods. For example, if it takes a fixed number of drafters 20 hours to produce a set of drawings manually and 10 hours to accomplish the same task with a CAD/CAM system, the productivity ratio gain is

$$\text{Productivity gain} = \frac{20}{10} = \frac{2}{1} = 2 \tag{6.2}$$

A company can therefore expect a 2:1 productivity increase for this task by using a CAD/CAM system. When systems are efficiently operating after an initial learning curve (from 3 to 9 months), management can expect the productivity (efficiency) gains shown in Table 6.1 over the same task performed manually (compiled from a survey conducted in 1981 by Daniel J. Borda of Arthur D. Little, Inc., Cambridge, Massachusetts).

Measuring productivity is not a precise science, and in the following quotation Daniel J. Borda explains how he derived the factors listed in Table 6.1.

> The tabulated Productivity Factors were compiled from a survey of 350 engineering and manufacturing organizations of which 95 organizations responded. These factors were compiled from the information received. We have to keep in mind that no standards exist as

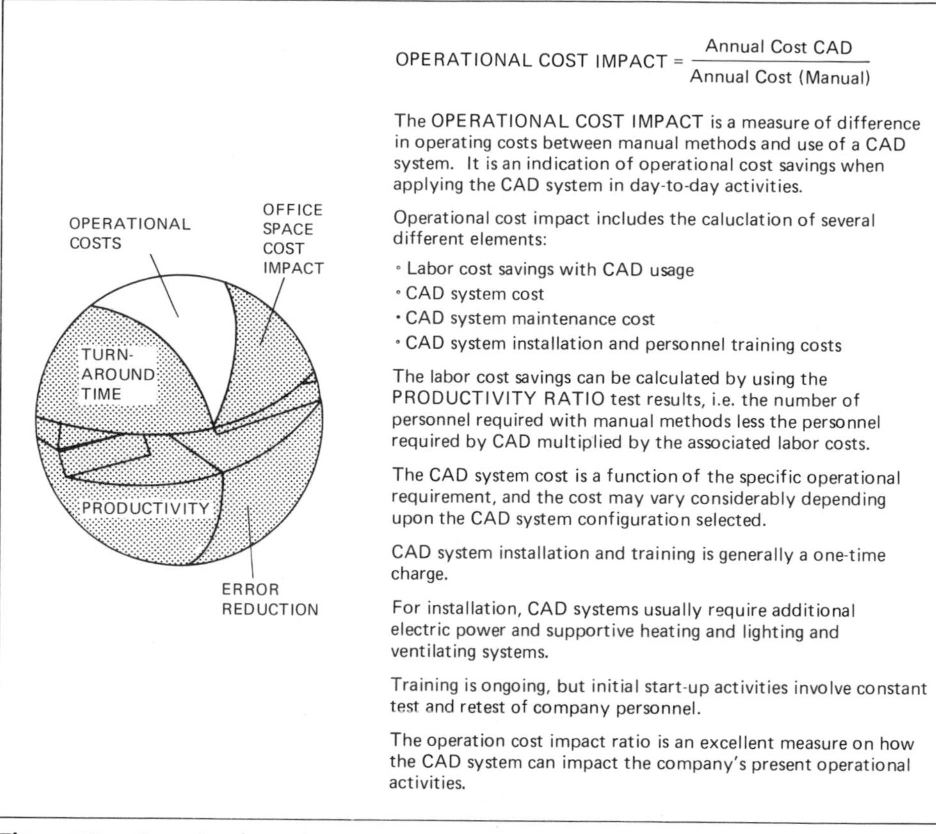

Figure 6.3c Operational cost impact.

to how productivity should be recorded. These 95 organizations used about a dozen different methods which cannot be mathematically added and averaged. However, we added and averaged these factors because they could then be used to identify an overall range that can be expected in industry. It is well to remember that increased productivity in industry does not simply mean more work done in fewer hours. The ultimate purpose of CAD/CAM is to produce a higher quality product (or to design a product that could not be practically designed manually) at a lower cost.

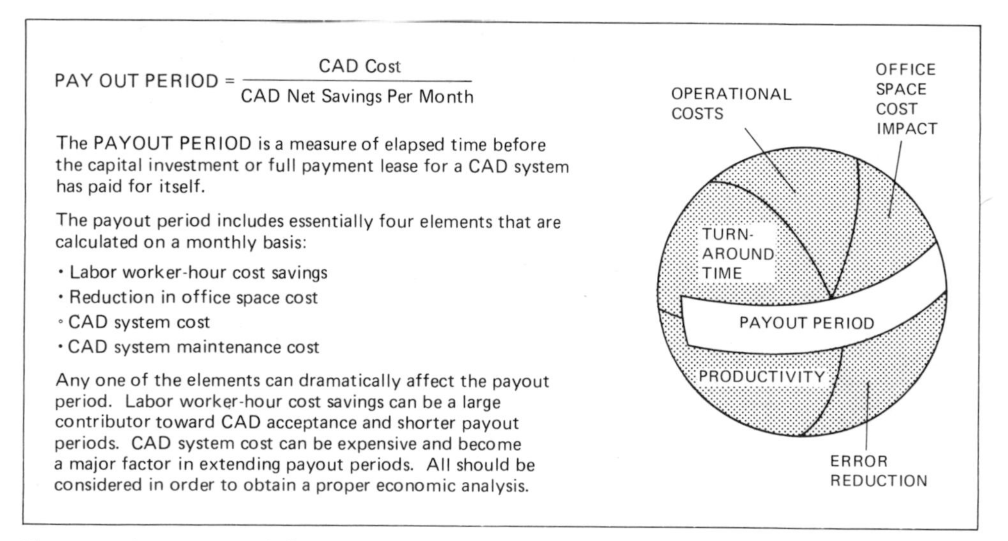

Figure 6.3d Payout period.

Table 6.1 Productivity Gains Using CAD/CAM

Application	Productivity Improvement Factor	
	Average	Range
Wiring	4.5:1	16–2
Publications	4.4:1	10–2
Design studies	4.3:1	20–2
Schematics	4.2:1	20–1.5
Sheet metal	3.8:1	20–1
Plant layout	3.4:1	10–1
Piping	3.2:1	10–1
Structural modeling	3.1:1	5–1
Civil engineering	3.0:1	20–1
Mechanical details	2.4:1	8–1
Integrated circuits	18.4:1	100–10
Engineering analysis	6.0:1	20–1.5
Template	5.8:1	6–3
Numerical control applications	5.6:1	10–1.5
Mapping	5.1:1	30–0.5
Charts	4.7:1	10–2
Structures detailing	4.7:1	25–1
Printed circuits	3.3:1	6–2

6.4.2 What to Automate First

CAD/CAM priorities are based on responses from senior management, from the heads of functional departments, and from the evaluation team. These priorities are based on cost-effective desired productivity increases for the various CAD/CAM application areas.

By this time, the evaluation team has prioritized the list of desired CAD/CAM functional tasks which are to be incorporated into the RFP. More important, the features list serves as criteria against which candidate systems can be tested, ranked, and compared—thus facilitating the determination of a "short list" or subset (see Sec. 6.7.1) of vendors. By prioritizing the required and desired system features, the user ensures that no critical functions are excluded from the system.

6.5 SYSTEM REQUIREMENTS DEFINITION

Once the cost justification analysis has been performed, a firm can decide which features of a CAD/CAM system are most important to a company. Although processes have been identified that are the most cost- or labor-intensive, available CAD/CAM systems might not be able to perform such tasks. One must therefore look at the highest-priority task for which existing CAD/CAM systems have demonstrated capabilities. One can ascertain near-future (3 years) CAD/CAM capabilities with a reasonable degree of assurance. One should not, however, cost-justify a system based on proposed or future system capabilities.

The objective of the system requirements task is to develop a short- and long-range plan for CAD/CAM implementation. These plans should be reviewed by management before incorporation into the RFP. The short-range plan should be in writing, should incorporate objectives for a 1- to 3-year time span, and should include the following information:

- Management priorities derived from Sec. 6.3.2
- An ordered list of tasks and processes that can be economically automated
- A description of tasks, departments, and people that will be affected by automation
- Estimated hardware, software, and operating costs for automation
- Estimated cost savings with automation

- Estimated effects of automation on company management and organization
- Implementation plan

The long-range plan should be an extension of the short-range plan but should include information on costs and personnel requirements for a 3- to 5-year time frame. Information on additional projected applications software development, estimated new hardware purchases, and potential new system's integration should all be included. Additional factors relating to the management of a CAD/CAM facility are found in Chapter 8.

There are a number of specific factors to consider in developing the short- and long-range plan. They are discussed in detail throughout this handbook. Included in this chapter is an abbreviated list of considerations for each of the major components of a CAD/CAM system.

6.5.1 Database

The primary database question is whether a two- or three-dimensional data representation is needed. Microcomputer systems are primarily two-dimensional in nature while most minicomputer-based systems offer both two- and three-dimensional capabilities. Systems offering both two and three dimensions are differentiated by how easy it is to alternate between two- and three-dimensional data representation. Electrical applications generally require only a two-dimensional database while manufacturing and architectural and engineering applications require three-dimensional data representation. It is estimated that over 75 percent of drafting is two-dimensional. A firm should make sure of their immediate and long-range data representation requirements. When in doubt, a firm should choose a three-dimensional system.

6.5.2 Mechanical Drafting

Drafting represents an application that is the common denominator of all CAD/CAM system. How easily drawings are created and modified is of critical importance in systems selection. Factors to consider include

- Availability, extensiveness, and ease of creation of application-specific component libraries
- Ease and types of edit capabilities
- Ability to perform group or associative functions
- Ability to merge text and graphics
- Availability and ease of use of a high-level graphics language
- Extent of available geometric primitives or building blocks (e.g., point, line, arc, curve, surface, solid generation, text, grid, shading capabilities)
- Extent of available graphic data transformational functions (e.g., create, modify, delete, copy, move, mirror, rotate, transform, insert, boolean operations)
- Extent of available viewing commands (e.g., pan, zoom, window, color, rotate, generate perspective)
- Extent of available analytic commands (e.g., locate, area, length, volume, angle, center of gravity, other mass property calculations)
- Extent and flexibility of bill-of-material extraction and report generation

6.5.3 Applications Software

Each application software package has its own specific set of performance specifications that should be considered. General considerations related to evaluating application-specific software include the following:

- Ease of input and output procedures
- Ability to perform the desired performance functions
- Ability to handle current and projected work loads
- Ease of use
- Support, documentation, frequency, and quality of updates
- External database interface support

6.5.4 Operating System

A computer's operating system controls both basic hardware functions and input and output procedures to peripheral equipment. Questions that are relevant to operating systems include the following:

- How easy is it to start up the system (called *bootstrapping*)?
- How easy is it to transmit data between peripherals?
- What is the number of terminals the system will support?
- How are system hardware and software priorities determined?
- How are errors handled?
- What types of audit trails are generated? (For example, does the system have the ability to automatically save drawing command sequences?)
- What types of system and job accounting can be performed?
- What are the file management capabilities?
- How much flexibility is there regarding high-level software development?

6.5.5 Communications

Data communication for CAD/CAM systems includes the ability to provide for graphic and textural communication between computers, from computer to remote terminals, and between computers and a remote host computer. This can be accomplished in a variety of ways, such as with voice-grade telephone lines using a modem or with higher-speed direct communication lines. Acoustical couplers required for voice-grade communication are slow (transmitting and receiving from 30 to 120 characters per second), while high-speed communication modems can transmit and receive from 120 to 960 characters per second. Large graphic file communication requires high-speed lines.

A second communication consideration relates to data communication and networking protocols that are supported by vendors. This is especially important if a CAD/CAM system manufactured by one vendor is required to communicate with databases generated from systems of other vendors. Data exchange standards, such as the Initial Graphic Exchange Specification (IGES) from the National Bureau of Standards, are beginning to emerge and to be supported by vendors.

6.5.6 Database Management

A database management system is a complex software package that allows for users to define, maintain, and protect files and to create reports. Points to consider include the following:

- Types of initialization, access, modification, and data security provided
- Ease of copying, deleting, initiating, merging, moving, and renaming drawing files
- Ease and flexibility of report generation capabilities
- Ease of cataloging parts and assemblies

6.5.7 Documentation, Training, and Support

Considerations of importance in this category include the following:

- Vendor response time for service calls
- Completeness and clarity, quality, updates, and types of documentation provided
- Availability and quality of online instruction aids
- Types, costs, and quality of hardware and software support
- Availability of local parts inventories
- Types and quality of both on-site and vendor-based training
- Availability of vendor-developed contract software
- Service experience with other similar firms

6.6 WRITING THE RFP

An RFP enables the firm to select from several systems the one that best meets its multifaceted needs and requirements. There are two basic approaches for the development of an RFP. The RFP can either detail the company's information needs and define precisely how desired functions are to be performed or, alternatively, require the vendor to define how a CAD/CAM system's features are performed—based on the company's desired functional requirements. The first approach requires a sophisticated evaluation team and a great deal of time (and expense) to generate an appropriate RFP. This approach also mandates the use of controlled or timed benchmarks (important basic drawings) to be used for system comparisons (see Sec. 6.7.2). The second approach enables an RFP to be written without detailed performance specifications by instead requiring vendors to state how desired features are accomplished within their system.

An RFP can be from 15 to over a 100 pages, depending upon the level at which information needs have been defined by the user firm. At the very least, however, enough data should be included in the RFP so that a vendor response can address the following issues:

- General systems capabilities and how and why they respond to the firm's needs
- Detailed hardware specifications (including memory needs and workstations)
- Application software and operating system recommendations and specifications
- Support and maintenance
- Education, training, and documentation recommendations
- Acceptance and inspection testing procedures
- Installation and environmental requirements
- Shipment and delivery schedules
- Warranty conditions
- Terms and conditions

In order to facilitate optimal and complete responses from the vendors, the RFP should be as clear, concise, and specific as possible. However, if detailed information needs are not specified within the RFP, a firm can select the second RFP development approach, which requires vendors to specify how certain functional capabilities are performed. For example, one can ask a vendor to describe how he or she provides the capability of defining the location of a coordinate point, or one can specify that a point must be defined by methods such as digitizing, explicit coordinates, end of an entity, origin of an entity, intersection of two entities, delta displacement, on a grid point, on a surface, projected along a vector and dropped onto a surface, normal to a surface, and so forth.

To summarize, an RFP can either contain explicit performance criteria for functional requirements or request a vendor to supply information on how desired functions are performed on the vendor's system. Finally, the RFP should contain examples of typical drawings that are illustrative of important drafting functions of the company.

Examples of major RFP sections of a typical CAD/CAM proposal would include the following:

1. ***Introduction and General Conditions.*** This section contains general background information, objectives of the CAD/CAM system, structure of the user organization, motivation for using CAD/CAM, projected growth of the system, user experience, selection procedures and criteria, minimum functional requirements, and projected work loads.
2. ***Company Description and User Groups.*** This section defines work tasks for departments that will initially be using the CAD/CAM system. Information on location (to determine workstation communication needs), departmental work loads, and organizational structure should be included.
3. ***Hardware and Operating System.*** This section covers performance specifications for the various hardware devices. Hardware to be specified includes the processor, disk and/or magnetic tape drives, graphic CRT workstations, alphanumeric displays, digitizers, hard-copy devices, line printers. Operating (computer) system software should also be specified in terms of desired system security, file management, text editors, and response times under various system loading conditions.
4. ***Drafting and Applications Software.*** This part contains specifications for application areas of interest. For example, specifications for the mechanical design and drafting package would contain data relevant to desired geometric graphic primitives (building blocks) for drawing creation, types of dimensioning (i.e., English or metric) desired, and analytic and drawing manipulation properties that are required.

   For generation of printed-circuit or electrical diagrams, the RFP might contain information on how the drawing should be organized and accessed (database representation), analytic features, and postprocessing capabilities. For wiring diagram applications, data should be specified for diagram creation and editing, parts libraries, diagram construction and editing, report generation, and verification.
5. ***Support.*** The support section of the RFP should contain requirements for documentation, training, and maintenance.

Finally, depending upon a company's size and sophistication, vendor-supplied services such as education, training, and documentation can become as important as selection of the physical hardware and software itself. Visits to relevant vendor sites and talks with other users are obviously critical as well. Examples of RFPs can often be obtained from the vendors themselves.

6.7 EVALUATION AND VENDOR SELECTION

A number of factors must be considered in the selection process that relate to software, hardware, and the vendors themselves. Communications, documentation, user feedback, and the system's future hardware and software growth potential (often called its *modularity* and *extensibility*) must all be measured in terms of utility and performance.

Capabilities to be considered in the evaluation and selection of a CAD/CAM system include the following:

1. ***Functional Capabilities.*** This relates to the system's ability to support the desired software functions (i.e., the features list). This is probably the most important system comparison criterion. A ranking can be obtained by evaluating each of the functions on the features list, listing an importance factor for each function, multiplying this by how well each vendor satisfies the criterion, and accumulating a total score for each vendor. It is important to take subjective human factor considerations into account.
2. ***Online Storage Capacity.*** Hardware can be ranked in terms of its primary and secondary storage capacity, taking the storage efficiency (data structures) of various systems into account.
3. ***Data Communications Capability.*** Communications, or computer networking, is the ability for computers to "talk" (by sending data and programs) to one another. It is used between systems or between a system and a central (or host) computer. If requirements call for such network links, the user should determine their throughput implications. That is, CAD/CAM drawing production should be measured with the communication links turned on and off during system evaluation.
4. ***Reliability and Maintenance.*** A system's reliability directly affects productivity. Repair time can be reduced by such factors as built-in diagnostics, flip-out equipment racks, forced-air cooling, and good diagnostic software. Microprocessor-based CAD/CAM systems do not require special cooling, mechanical, and power considerations, while minicomputer and mainframe systems do.
5. ***Potential Growth.*** A system's potential relates to its ability to accommodate growth in a number of areas: expansion in terms of application software, the ability of the system to be integrated with other systems, and the ability for a processor (by adding more memory) to support several edit workstations simultaneously.
6. ***Documentation and User Groups.*** Documentation relates to user, system, and programming manuals; videotapes; online tutorials; and other teaching aids. The system manuals should be complete and easy to use, with examples and sample work sessions. All other things being equal, vendors with active user groups (companies or individuals that meet and communicate with vendor representatives about system problems and application software development priorities) should be selected.
7. ***Vendor Competence.*** Questions related to evaluating the vendor, besides documentation and user groups, include the following:
   - ***a.*** What is the cost, quality, and availability of maintenance?
   - ***b.*** Does the vendor allow the company to acquire hardware directly from the manufacturer?
   - ***c.*** What are the magnitude, frequency, and quality of hardware and software updates?
   - ***d.*** What is the local hardware spare parts inventory?
   - ***e.*** What is the vendor background and interest in your company and application area?

6.7.1 Developing a Short List of Vendors

Vendors normally require at least a month to respond to RFPs. A firm should, however, immediately request a letter from the vendor stating if the vendor plans to respond to the RFP. Once vendor responses are received, they should be immediately checked for completeness and omissions. If the vendor has not included the requisite data, the vendor should be contacted and the omission corrected.

The buyer can now initiate the first vendor screening process to obtain a short list of vendors. This involves taking the prioritized list of desired features and noting all critical or "must" features for the proposed CAD/CAM system. This list of mandatory performance specifications can be easily summarized if the RFP contains a summary list of hardware and software performance specifications. The vendors that do not provide any mandatory requirements should be eliminated for consideration at this point.

An additional screening of vendor systems can be obtained if the vendors are ranked. This can be accomplished by listing how well each vendor satisfies the mandatory system performance specifications by using an arbitrary scale (e.g., where 1 = marginally satisfied, 2 = satisfactory, and 3 = exceptional). The potential CAD/CAM user firm then totals the scores related to how well each system satisfies the required functions and thereby derives a preliminary vendor ranking.

6.7.2 Benchmarking

Benchmarking is an evaluation procedure conducted to test important desired features of a vendor's CAD/CAM system. It provides a second screening mechanism before the final vendor determination. The process is valuable both for the vendors, in learning about and demonstrating required functional tasks, and for the buyer, in gathering data on a system's human factors (see Chap. 5).

Conducting controlled benchmarks for validating drawing productivity gains is almost impossible. It involves the timing of specific tasks on different systems. This is difficult because one cannot replicate such factors as operator skill, operating environment, and system loading conditions. Yet one can get a relative feel for how long various tasks require on various candidate systems. To obtain this relative sense of the time required for task performance, one should try to simulate the vendor's recommended proposed system as closely as possible.

Benchmarks consume from 1 to 2 days. The potential CAD/CAM buyer should therefore have eliminated all but three or four systems by this time. The benchmarking process is straightforward and consists of the following:

- Select subsets of typical drawings that illustrate as many of the "must" capabilities of the functional requirements as possible. About five or six benchmarks are usually enough to test a company's most important design or drafting criteria.
- Conduct the benchmarks on similarly sized systems approximating the eventual operating environment as much as possible. The vendor should be aware of your benchmark objectives and of what you are testing. A few surprises are permissible to test a system's flexibility, but even these should be planned to limit confusion. Benchmarks can also be used to test system features such as data transfer between components, accounting features, and database management capabilities.
- Evaluate and document results. Evaluation should be done at the vendor's site if possible to enable the vendor to answer any questions that might arise, and while impressions are still fresh.

Scores and vendor rankings can be obtained for each of the vendors by multiplying the system property being tested by a weighting factor that reflects the relative importance of that property. Subjective human factors considerations should also be reflected in your evaluation. Human factors consist of all or a subset of the following:

- Person-machine interfaces
- Workstation design and layout
- Ambient lighting conditions
- Command and parameter language capabilities
- Ease of menu creation and use
- Help files and online tutorials
- Ease of learning
- Other factors that affect the users' attitude toward the system

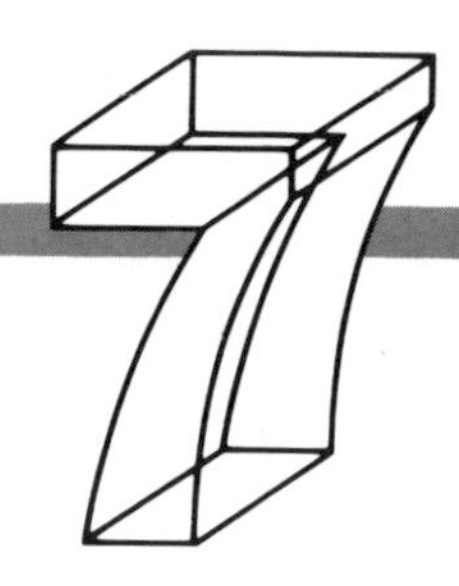

Understanding and Measuring Productivity

by
Robert D. Miller

7.1 PRODUCTIVITY: AN OVERVIEW

The topic of productivity, or perhaps better stated as lack of productivity, has become a common topic of discussion in American business and even to some degree in American homes. Americans are beginning to understand that our very standard of living, and certainly the standard of living our children will enjoy, is highly dependent on how productive each individual worker can become.

7.1.1 Productivity: Input and Output Relationships

Simply put, productivity is the relationship of total output to total input. Productivity can be expressed in many ways. It is the ratio of dollars generated from sales to the dollars required to produce a product and get it to the marketplace. It is the number of assemblies leaving a manufacturing department to the total resources consumed in creating them. It is the number of tool designs output to the number of designers required to make them.

Improved productivity is obtained by increasing the number of units output without a proportionate increase in input. Conversely, productivity gains can also be achieved by leaving output values at status quo and, through improved engineering, better production planning, newer machine tools, better management, etc., obtaining a reduction in the total amount of input resources required.

A decrease in productivity is likely to occur when the required input resources increase without a corresponding increase in units output. Inflation, worn-out machines, poor manufacturing methods, excess scrap, design without regard for manufacturing considerations, poor inventory management, and poor management strategy are a few of the reasons for a disproportionate growth in input costs. Decreasing output levels without equivalent decreases in input costs can also lead to reduced productivity. Management-labor problems, poorly maintained capital equipment, and softening markets with high fixed overheads are a few of the reasons this may happen.

7.1.2 Productivity: A Relative Measurement

Because productivity is relative, a company that was once very profitable may find that by doing nothing different at all, their competitive edge may be slowly diminished. This happens as competitors take greater steps to decrease their manufacturing costs per unit output. What may have once been an acceptable rate of productivity may no longer be adequate to stay competitive. Productivity becomes significant by making comparisons; that is, comparisons to how something used to be, the way it is now, or how much input a competitor may require to generate the same number of units output. The very nature of the free enterprise system leads to stiff competition which mandates every company be on a constant vigil to improve productivity.

7.1.3 Productivity and CAD/CAM Systems

Business elements such as government bureaucracy are generally productivity decreasers and are not easily changed, while other elements are more easily influenced by local management. One technique that managers of many companies have found to improve significantly the productivity of professional and technical staff is the use of computer-aided design (CAD) and computer-aided manufacturing (CAM) systems or CAD/CAM. Some of the benefits from using CAD/CAM which improve productivity are obvious and easily quantified, such as an increase in drawings output from a drafting department, while many other benefits, and possibly the most significant ones, are less tangible and very difficult to measure, such as the effects of better engineering. These long-term benefits may take as many as 5 to 10 years from implementation to be realized. In fact, managers of many companies currently using CAD/CAM systems are still unsure of how they will benefit most from the technology.

7.2 MEASURING CHANGE AND CALCULATING PRODUCTIVITY

This section deals with how to identify and measure the changes that occur when CAD/CAM systems are used and how to calculate an accurate productivity ratio. It is not the intent to state specifically all possible benefits from using CAD/CAM or to suggest the specific method to be used to quantify benefits. This section suggests possible ways to better understand and measure these changes and discusses how quantified change data may be used to evaluate productivity increases, or decreases. Every company is different, and the realization and quantification of actual benefits must be done on an individual basis.

Productivity calculations based on measured change should meet three basic criteria. First, they must reflect all possible benefits, including those that are difficult to measure. Second, they must be accurate in comparing baseline and measured input and output data. Third, they must be consistently applied and compared over time. If these criteria are carefully considered, a productivity calculation can be a very powerful managerial tool. A productivity measurement method which yields results that are incomplete, inaccurate, and inconsistent will do little to direct managers to problem areas and is likely to lead to incorrect decisions. Conversely, a well-defined, accurate, and consistently applied productivity measurement can lead to the following benefits:

1. Productive, realistic attitudes of managers and users
2. Good short- and long-term system growth decisions
3. Visibility of the most productive applications
4. Problem identification and resolution

These benefits provide ample motivation to recommend a good system for measuring and calculating productivity.

7.2.1 Measuring Change

One commonly used method of measuring change is to simply ask CAD/CAM system users for their opinions. Although far from empirical, this method is not without value. Many examples could be cited of CAD/CAM system users who sincerely believe they are many times more productive than they had been using manual techniques. Their skill, experience, and judgment are the basis for these opinions. With these CAD/CAM users, attitudes are usually positive and constant progress is typically made toward improved productivity.

When poorly designed quantitative measurement tools have been implemented in such organizations, the results are usually disastrous. Management attitudes become negative, shortsighted decisions are made, and users become frustrated and lose interest in earnestly striving to make the system work. Productivity falls off.

The major shortcoming of user opinion is that over time, system users tend to lose sight of what it actually took to complete a task without the CAD/CAM system. This can be overcome by having estimators who still do manual work predict what it would have taken to do a job manually. This method of measuring change still is quite subjective and can be improved by gathering real data from past experience.

A common malady from not having a well-applied system for measuring productivity change is the resulting disparity between users and managers. It is common to hear users say they are significantly more productive on the system than on the board and would quit before going back to old methods. In the same organization misinformed managers may be doubting the value of the system and seriously considering going back to manual methods.

Reporting productivity without a consistent method is much like reading the newspaper. The front page is filled with horror stories while the unsung heroes are hidden on the back page. A good scheme of measuring, recording, and publicizing both positive and negative results of a CAD/CAM system will bring the facts of what is really being accomplished to "the front page" for all levels of personnel to see rather than a sensational headline of perceived problems.

DEVELOPING A BASELINE

An accurate measurement of change is only possible if there is a well-documented baseline from which productivity improvement can be gauged. Many managers, whether using CAD/CAM or not, collect extensive data as a part of their existing control systems. These data could be used as a baseline for evaluating CAD/CAM productivity changes. If these data do not exist or are not adequately comprehensive, a system should be developed for gathering them. Great care should be taken to see that sufficient data items are monitored to allow measurement of the most important system objectives.

Measuring change can be done on any scale—from a corporate profit and loss level to discrete work elements of a drafting technician. The kind of baseline data collected should always reflect the intent of the measurement and the objectives of the system. A statement of total dollars saved since the CAD/CAM system was installed may be all the factory manager wants to know, while the engineering manager may need to know which applications are best suited for the system. The drafting supervisor may require a completely different level of detail, such as which operators produce best on the system. The knowledge of how a productivity ratio will be used is a prerequisite to knowing what baseline data to gather.

For example, suppose a CAD/CAM system were implemented in a company specializing in tool design. Possible baseline data could include the following:

1. Total number of tool designers
2. Current levels of output per designer measured by
   a. Drawing size
   b. Drawing complexity
   c. New and revised drawings
3. Overhead costs per designer
4. Average number of revisions per tool design
5. Average number of times designers must be consulted during tool build
6. Frequency of reworked tooling because of design errors
7. Amount of repeat business by customers
8. Length of time required to quote a job

These are only examples of possible baseline data and should not be considered as a complete list. Because many significant benefits from using CAD/CAM are often unexpected, every effort should be made to predict what activities will change and include them in the baseline data. Research into companies currently using a similar system for a similar application can provide insight into what baseline data should be tracked.

Like any data, great care must be taken in gathering and using baseline data. Methods used for gathering the baseline data should be reviewed and approved by all those whose data they are. This agreement proves invaluable when progress is reported later on. Functional managers should know that productivity data, both baseline and measured, belong to them and can be used effectively as a managerial tool.

Adequate documentation of methods used for collecting baseline data ensures consistent use and collection of the data. Baseline data should be collected over a long enough period of time to obtain a representative sampling. To account for changes in manual methods, baseline data may be taken from a rolling average. Adequate time periods and rolling averages tend to smooth out the effects of unusual situations and add credibility to the eventual usage of baseline data.

It may not always be appropriate to make new measurements of productivity with respect to the original base. From time to time the base may change. For example, if all drafting is done with T squares and triangles at the time a computer graphics system is initially purchased, the change in output would be calculated from that base. If, however, the manual methods were to change by the addition of manual drafting machines, it would no longer be valid to compare the added benefit of the computer graphics system to the T square and triangle base. Productivity ratios must compare new measured values to the currently implemented best alternative. Use of a rolling baseline also helps to account for the change in manual methods.

MEASURED DATA

Once a good baseline has been established from which comparisons can be made, a procedure can be established for measuring change obtained from the CAD/CAM system (measured data). The very same methods developed for measuring baseline data can be applied, and in fact should be applied, to measured data. The same list of objectives used to determine elements of baseline data lead to the collection of similar data at the new output and input levels. Efforts to measure change from using CAD/CAM can be done either at the macro level or by evaluating discrete activities. Usually, the managerial perspective is obtained from the sum of identified discrete elements.

Just like baseline data, measured data from using CAD/CAM are more accurate if measured over a substantial period of time. Measuring performance over time tends to smooth out unusual circumstances and provides a fairly representative view of the new data.

EXTERNAL CHANGE VARIABLES

To determine accurately what effect a CAD/CAM system really has on overall productivity, a manager must be aware of all other changes in the organization which may affect the performance of his or her employees. What may appear to be the results of CAD/CAM may actually be the exceptional performance of a new employee. A special retirement program causing the most-experienced engineers to leave the company may more than offset the improved productivity of the remaining less-experienced engineers. Fear of being laid off because of a slow economy may have motivated employees to work much harder than ever before, clouding the productivity issue. In some cases the "Hawthorne effect" may have affected performance. In other words, employees may improve their performance just because they know they are being watched and given special attention.

Management awareness of change variables external to the CAD/CAM system and their resultant effects on individual productivity is essential to good management, whether assessing the effects of CAD/CAM or not.

7.2.2 Calculating Productivity

Once accurate, reliable, and consistently applied data are available for the baseline and the measured period, several options are available for calculating productivity. Regardless of the method used, productivity calculations must reflect all of the measurable effects of the system for both input and output values. If possible, each of these items should be quantified and given a dollar value. On first glance many will say that most data items are intangible and cannot be expressed in terms of dollars. Rarely, however, does a problem occur in a business that does not cost money. For example, a fitup problem discovered during manufacturing that could have been resolved in the design phase can result in excessive tooling costs, poor assembly methods, and excessive manufacturing engineering overhead, all of which are tangible and measurable.

Every business is different, and this section cannot begin to suggest how to quantify every possible benefit from CAD/CAM for each business; the intent is simply to emphasize the value of doing it. If after all ideas have been exhausted, some items remain intangible, then attached to the productivity ratio should be a list of such items with examples of how each benefit manifests itself, e.g., improvement in morale of employees.

OUTPUT AND INPUT CHANGE RATIOS

The method for calculating productivity most frequently used is simply a measure of the output at some measured time, O_m, over the output at some baseline time, O_b. This rather simple technique is helpful and can be used effectively to measure the rate of change over time. It does not, however, take into consideration the significant increase in input costs required to create the resultant change in output. For example, after the purchase of a CAD/CAM system a manager may find that it now takes three times as much money to produce twice as many drawings.

Let us consider a different approach to productivity measurement, one proposed by the American Productivity Center. Think of change in output not as a productivity ratio but simply as an output change ratio. Real productivity P reflects all the input costs associated with obtaining some change. For the moment, let us calculate productivity as the ratio of output O to input I, which is sometimes thought of as an efficiency ratio.

$$P = \frac{O}{I} \tag{7.1}$$

According to John W. Kendrick in his book *Understanding Productivity*, significance in productivity is derived by making comparisons. A more meaningful productivity ratio could be calculated then by comparing the change in output ΔO over some period of time to the change in input ΔI over the same period of time.

$$P = \frac{\Delta O}{\Delta I} \tag{7.2}$$

The only mathematically valid way of making this comparison is to have the same units in both the numerator and denominator. If great care is taken early on, all calculable variables will be expressed in dollars. If this is not possible, ratios, which are without units, can be used in the equation.

THE PRODUCTIVITY RATIO

If output change is measured against many discrete performance objectives, output change ratios can be combined by using the average for all objectives, or they can be weighted to reflect the system's performance with respect to the company's prioritized objectives. Well-publicized, formally agreed-upon weighting factors should be assigned well in advance of the first formal evaluation. An output change ratio OR can be calculated from the following equation.

$$\mathrm{OR} = \frac{(O1_m/O1_b \times \mathrm{WT}) + (O2_m/O2_b \times \mathrm{WT}) + \cdots + (On_m/On_b \times \mathrm{WT})}{n} \tag{7.3}$$

Where O_m = measured period
O_b = baseline period
WT = weight
n = number of objectives evaluated

An input change ratio can be calculated by summing all input costs for both baseline and measured periods and calculating the ratio.

$$\mathrm{IR} = \frac{\Sigma I_m}{\Sigma I_b} \tag{7.4}$$

By comparing OR and IR, we begin to see whether our investment of resources in computer graphics has been productive. The American Productivity Center has termed

Table 7.1 Weighted System Objectives

Priority	Objective	Weight
1	Increase new business from faster quoting, more competitive design costs, and more accurate design	0.35
2	Decrease the number of tools requiring rework because of design errors	0.30
3	Reduce lead time for quoting	0.20
4	Increase the number of designs output per designer while keeping the number of designers constant	0.15

this a *productivity index*. However, because it is a ratio that reflects the real value of an investment, it can simply be called *productivity P*.

$$P = \frac{\text{OR}^*}{\text{IR}^\dagger} \tag{7.5}$$

A SAMPLE PRODUCTIVITY CALCULATION

An example of how this method can be applied may be helpful. Consider the same tool-design firm mentioned earlier under "Developing a Baseline." Company objectives which led to the initial procurement of the CAD/CAM system are prioritized and listed in Table 7.1. Baseline data gathered prior to system implementation should be used for making comparisons and must support each stated objective. Using the very same procedures as for baseline data, measured data (with the CAD/CAM system) should be gathered and carefully documented. If adequate control structures for recording input and output values have been effectively installed, measured data will be readily available. Using these data, the hypothetical calculations in Table 7.2 were made.

The dollars shown in Table 7.2 would likely be the summation of many more discrete items evaluated individually. For many in the organization, these discrete elements may be of greater benefit than the final calculation. For example, the CAD/CAM system manager may find that a particular new software feature allowing interference checking on the

* From Eq. (7.3).
† From Eq. (7.4).

Table 7.2 Weighted Output Data

Objective	Baseline, \$/month	Measured, \$/month	OR	Weight	Weighted OR
New business (attributed to CAD/CAM)	5000	15,000	3:1	0.35	1.05
Rework tools because of design error	6000	1500	4:1*	0.30	1.20
Quote lead time required	10,000	5000	2:1*	0.20	0.40
Design output	1000†	800†	2:1*	0.15	0.30
					2.95‡

*Output change ratio calculated as baseline period costs vs. measured period costs to reflect a decrease in costs from using CAD/CAM.
†Dollars per design.
‡Overall OR = Σ of weighted ORs = 2.95.

Table 7.3 Input Data in Dollars

	Labor, $I1$, \$/month	Overhead, $I2$, \$/month	Total, I, \$
I_m	12,000	6000*	18,000
I_b	10,000	1000	11,000

*Increased overhead for the measured period is attributed to the cost of the CAD/CAM system, and additional labor cost is for a system manager.

system significantly increases the visibility of potential problems. He or she may also find that in spite of all efforts to further reduce lead time for quoting, no significant change is evident. Reaching conclusions of this type is only possible if productivity data are gathered at a sufficiently detailed level.

Continuing the example, IR may be calculated by using Eq. (7.4). Table 7.3 illustrates this calculation.

$$\text{IR} = \frac{I_m}{I_b} = \frac{18{,}000}{11{,}000} = 1.64$$

Productivity may now be calculated as per Eq. (7.5).

$$P = \frac{\text{OR}}{\text{IR}} = \frac{2.95}{1.64} = 1.8$$

Analyzing the summation of all input and output change ratios provides a rational overall understanding of how well an investment in CAD/CAM may be paying off. Analysis of the discrete elements relating to each objective which contributes to productivity provides necessary information on what must be changed to improve productivity.

7.3 THE DYNAMIC NATURE OF PRODUCTIVITY

Understanding why productivity levels are what they are and how to change them requires experience, good judgment, and adequate data. Many factors influence productivity, and a good system manager must be able to evaluate which are affecting the system.

7.3.1 Training and Productivity

Adequate training has a critical influence on productivity. Insufficient training stretches out learning curves and leads to user frustration. Concentrated, well-focused training builds confidence in users and results in higher productivity levels and shorter learning curves.

Training and productivity are inseparable. Training must be an ongoing activity, beginning when the system is first introduced. Users should be encouraged to look constantly for new and better ways to do similar tasks. This formal perpetual training yields a long, positive-sloping learning curve and reduces the likelihood of premature plateaus. Figure 7.1 illustrates the effect of continued training on productivity.

7.3.2 Human Engineering and Productivity

The ease with which a CAD/CAM system allows the transfer of ideas into a well-organized computer database and eventually a finished product is called *human engineering*. Human engineering has a very significant impact on productivity and the slope of a learning curve. A well-engineered system has sufficient flexibility to allow for the individuality of engineers in problem solving. Ten people probably have ten different approaches to solving a problem; forcing them all to use a single method just because it is the only one available stifles creativity and yields a decrease in productivity.

7.3.3 Hardware and Productivity

Both hardware and software are critical to good productivity. Hardware must be reliable, easy to operate, and responsive enough to keep up with the thought processes of the user. Poor response time leads to lower productivity from less overall system throughput, poor concentration, and user frustration.

Response time should be considered as more than just the time required to execute a single command; command structures are different from system to system. Response time can also be considered on a larger scale, i.e., length of time required to complete some well-defined set of geometric construction activities. For example, one system may have excellent response time on individual commands but requires that each finite command be executed individually. Another system with only average response time may allow the combination of individual commands into macro-type statements, resulting in the same overall throughput. Even in these cases, however, user frustration from waiting for results from the combined commands may have a negative impact.

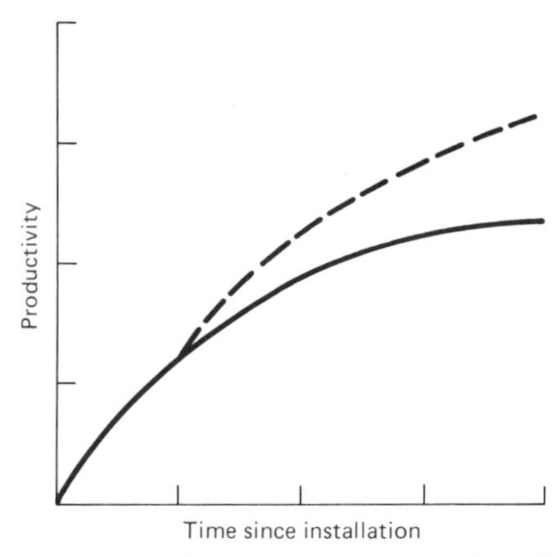

Figure 7.1 Productivity curve with (dashed line) and without (solid line) retraining of CAD/CAM users.

7.3.4 Software and Productivity

Adequate software is vital to achieving high productivity. Many software packages commercially available are very general-purpose in nature and can be used for many different applications; others are developed to fill a specific need. Although the general type of software is convenient and initially appealing, specific applications-oriented software for each individual application usually leads to higher productivity in the long run.

Numerical control (NC) software, for example, may be very generalized and allow the same general command structure for punch presses, lathes, mills, and drills. This is the fastest approach a vendor can take to reach as many customers as possible as quickly as possible. Over time, most vendors will eventually be pressured by market demand to provide specific software tailored to each NC application. Finely tuned, specific application-oriented software can automate a high percentage of work elements which are otherwise left to be done manually; the result is higher productivity.

7.4 SUMMARY

Armed with the understanding of how to measure change and calculate productivity, and knowing what factors influence productivity, a CAD/CAM system manager can more effectively manage the use of the system. As well-focused change strategies are implemented, it is possible to "take a snapshot" using meaningful productivity measurements, determine what effect the change strategy has had, and formulate new plans. If this is done over a long period of time, a productivity curve will continue on an upward slope, yielding much higher productivity in the long term. A productivity calculation should be thought of as a valuable tool for all levels of management and used constructively.

There is no simple turnkey method to measure change in output from the use of CAD/CAM. By following these basic guidelines and through careful thought and planning, the methods discussed in this section can be adapted to most situations.

The long-term effect of this approach to system evaluation and management will be a more finely tuned organization and a CAD/CAM system capable of delivering a higher return on your investment.

BIBLIOGRAPHY

American Productivity Center: *How to Measure Productivity at the Firm Level,* 1979.

A. T. Kearney, Inc.: "Where Improving Productivity Saves Big Money," *Business Week,* Nov. 20, 1978.

Kendrick, John W.: *Understanding Productivity: An Introduction to the Dynamics of Productivity Change,* The Johns Hopkins University Press, Baltimore, Md. 1978.

Miller, R. D.: *Understanding CAD-CAM Productivity,* National Computer Graphics Conference, 1981.

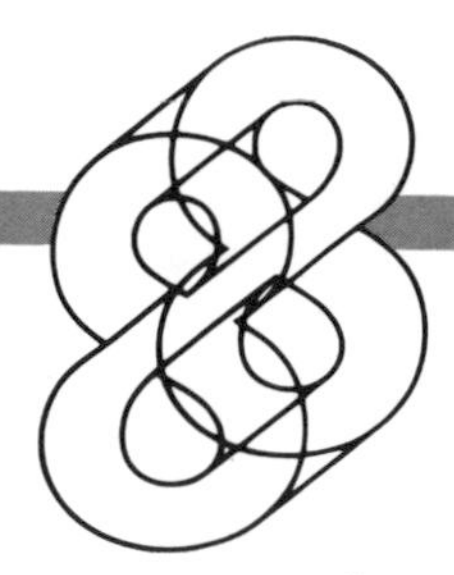

Managing Systems Effectively

by
Gary W. Zera

8.1 INTRODUCTION

Industrial organizations remain under constant pressure to increase productivity in order to maintain or gain a competitive advantage in their marketplace. Companies who are slow in reducing the cost of bringing their product to market will almost certainly have a difficult time maintaining a competitive position.

Efforts to increase productivity through optimization of existing systems have reached the point of diminishing returns. Companies are looking for more than the small incremental increases in efficiency that occur when traditional productivity systems are optimized. Implementation of an integrated computer-aided design and computer-aided manufacturing (CAD/CAM) strategy has, within the last few years, been adopted by industry in general as the most realistic and rewarding path to increased productivity.

The philosophy of how to make the transition from a manual or computer-assisted design and manufacturing system to an integrated CAD/CAM system is still evolutionary in nature and continues to change, with both dramatic successes and failures occurring.

During the introduction of computer graphics technology into an industrial environment, where productivity is the key issue, there is neither the time nor the desire to totally devise new concepts and methodologies throughout the implementation process. There currently exists sufficient documentation, accumulated by experts in the field, to allow proven techniques to be applied during start-ups of CAD facilities by first-time graphics users.

8.2 IMPLEMENTATION STRATEGY

The implementation of a CAD/CAM project is an exciting and unique opportunity to make a major contribution to an organization's productivity and future success. Excitement and enthusiasm should, however, be tempered with an awareness that—like many new technologies—the magical promise of increased productivity that computer graphics brings to industry has been somewhat oversimplified from an implementation point of view.

Proper implementation of a CAD system should take into account the long-term organizational needs early in the project's life cycle. This helps avoid unnecessary mistakes in structuring the initial database and makes the system manager's job easier by avoiding costly and time-consuming restructuring of an engineering database when integration with manufacturing becomes a reality. In most cases the CAM portion of the project is virtually nonexistent when the CAD system is being implemented. Every phase of the CAD strategy must be carefully planned. Direction by an individual accountable to both engineering and manufacturing is mandatory if implementation of a comprehensive plan is desired.

While managers generally recognize that great care must be taken during the initial definition phases of a CAD/CAM project, in many cases the greatest emphasis is placed upon vendor selection rather than upon analyzing and documenting the flow of work within the organization. While careful vendor analysis is important, the choice of one vendor over another will not usually make or break the project. Proper application of management resources will, however, make the difference between a dynamically productive environment and one that becomes static through lack of innovation and coordination. In addition to understaffing, management expectations, political environment, and a desire to please often lead to levels of frustration and stress that can adversely affect the project. The pressure to be productive at the facility level while dealing with computer hardware and software instability often does not leave the system manager with time to conceive and develop new plans and strategies properly.

During the project definition phase it is important that managers tightly define and document procedures to be followed during system implementation. As mentioned earlier, this is when the start-up starts, not after system installation. Adequate management resources must be committed to the project from the beginning, with the responsibility to follow through after the vendor selection process is completed.

8.3 MANAGEMENT RESOURCES

There are four management resource areas that should be addressed by companies contemplating a CAD/CAM project.

- Corporate CAD/CAM manager
- CAD/CAM steering committee
- CAD/CAM task force
- Graphics system managers

8.3.1 Corporate CAD/CAM Manager

Large multidivisional organizations require a person to devote full attention to the organization of a structured CAD/CAM environment. Smaller companies starting with a single system can initially give strategic responsibility to a strong system manager but should be prepared to give him or her additional personnel to help with the day-to-day activities of running the system. The CAD/CAM manager will be responsible for all CAD/CAM activity within the corporation.

The reporting hierarchy should be devised in such a way that this individual is in a bipartisan position, equally accountable to both manufacturing and engineering, with vested authority to arbitrate disputes and implement strategic plans pertaining to the integration of CAD and CAM. While it is important that this individual have a previous working knowledge of engineering and manufacturing applications, he or she should also have extensive graphics applications experience. In addition, the corporate CAD/CAM manager must possess organizational and planning skills essential to building viable groups and making effective decisions.

The most significant challenge for the CAD/CAM manager is to select and install a graphics system with minimal disruption to the existing environment while maximizing the overall impact on the organization from a productivity point of view. More than likely the system will be justified with a return on investment of less than 2 years. Because the project will be highly visible, rapid implementation is essential.

In light of this, a primary objective of the CAD/CAM manager should be to establish as many procedures and develop as many preinstallation databases as possible before the first graphics system arrives. A highly coordinated effort is required, demanding the resources of many managers and specialists with an intimate working knowledge of pertinent company processes.

8.3.2 CAD/CAM Steering Committee

A CAD/CAM steering committee is normally established to help select a vendor. This group should take on the additional responsibility of seeing that detailed flowcharts of those design and manufacturing processes of the organization that are likely to be impacted by CAD/CAM are prepared in advance. All interdivisional idiosyncrasies should be noted for possible conformance to convention or for waiver where a change would not be feasible. This is a major effort and should enlist the expertise of data processing systems experts.

The steering committee should establish a task force responsible for the ultimate definition of applications and procedures. In developing graphics strategies it is important that the participants view themselves as internal consultants while evaluating current procedures. Changes in procedures are often required to accommodate a new system. It is natural to cling to established practices, especially when the benefits are not readily apparent. Often during the implementation of a new technology, the early users incur a higher cost in order to build a database usable by the rest of the organization. While the long-term benefits can be impressive, this may not be consoling to those first involved in the plan unless some adjustments are made in departmental budgeting strategies. It is important that organizational groups even remotely impacted by CAD/CAM be represented at least initially.

Representatives from purchasing, legal departments, and accounting can pose many legitimate questions concerning warranty, maintenance, payback, etc. that can slow or even halt implementation at the last minute. If purchasing is surprised with a request to process a large order from a vendor it is not familiar with, delays to answer questions will take valuable time. The accounting group is more likely to accept assumed productivity ratios and intangible benefits if they have become somewhat familiar with computer graphics technology and concepts through involvement and vendor presentations.

8.3.3 CAD/CAM Task Force

While many time-consuming tasks are involved in the definition of a CAD/CAM database structure, managers with a good overview of general procedures (but who are no longer close to the day-to-day activities of their departments) are able to rely on subordinates (a CAD/CAM task force) with hands-on experience to outline company procedures in detail. This will establish the basic criteria for a graphics database structure.

If engineering is going to be the primary initial user of the system, some training considerations should be taken into account for manufacturing personnel. Bringing manufacturing into the loop early provides engineering with valuable information concerning manufacturing's database requirements. Advanced graphics training enables personnel whose responsibility it is to define database structures, to understand what they are expected to define. Often the steps involved in describing company procedures are intricate and detailed. It is beneficial to expose the individuals required to outline the organization's workflow to the principles of flowcharting for problem solving. An in-house course or seminar on the subject is one approach. A textbook or, at the very least, a formal set of guidelines should be distributed to task force members.

8.3.4 Graphic System Manager

If the position of corporate CAD/CAM manager has not been filled by the time a system manager is required, many database issues may not have been addressed and will be left up to the system manager to sort out. It may be difficult for a system manager without vested authority to enlist the cooperation of higher-level individuals while establishing basic procedures. A top-down philosophy supportive to the system manager should be adopted to assist in the attainment of corporate graphic goals.

The system manager needs to remain close to the day-to-day operation of the system. Initially, he or she will be too busy to deal effectively with long-term integration strategy. Precious time will be lost to the organization's need to implement a long-term CAD/CAM plan if upper management does not take on certain aspects of long-term planning. It is not unheard of for the system manager to spend a good percentage of the first year solving software problems.

If a corporate CAD/CAM manager takes on the responsibility of directing application definition and the vendor selection process, it may be wiser to wait until the vendor is identified before settling on a system manager. A paradox sometimes develops as to which comes first, the vendor or the manager. It may be true that an experienced graphics manager can manage any vendor's graphic system, as most systems are conceptually similar. A manager who has previous experience on a particular system is usually able to bring that system up to speed more quickly than a system he or she is not familiar with. This is particularly important when developing databases before installation, as the system manager may be involved in directing software development with graphics service bureaus having the same brand of graphics equipment as the organization intends to acquire.

As the number of feasible vendors approaches one or two, the search for a system manager can be more specific. It is ideal to hire a system manager about 6 months before the arrival of the hardware. There is usually adequate time to accomplish this, since organizational purchasing activities and vendor lead times usually average 6 months from the time the vendor is actually decided upon.

The system manager should have previous graphics experience but should not be expected to be the systems programmer, since the system manager will be busy handling the day-to-day definition of projects by application and work load. Initially the system manager should supervise construction of the computer graphics facility and development of software and geometric databases and write procedures not previously established through the efforts of a CAD/CAM task force.

8.4 SITE PREPARATION

Initial space planning and layouts can begin before the final vendor decision is made. The actual request for funds may have to be coordinated with approvals for the computer graphics hardware.

A timetable should be established based on the task with the longest lead time. Often this turns out to be the paperwork needed to initiate action within the organization. The following list is arranged with tasks ordered as they might occur.

1. Select site
2. Propose site layout
3. Determine environmental requirements
4. Determine power requirements
5. Define furniture and supply storage requirements
6. Prepare facilities drawings
7. Request quotations
8. Prepare request for expenditures
9. Start construction of facilities

As a general guide the reader should be aware of some of the following points:

1. The area chosen to house the central processing unit (CPU) and design area should be chosen with future expansion and accessibility by the user community in mind. Lead times for computer room expansion can be painfully long in some organizations. Proper planning will minimize growing pains when a second and third CPU are installed.
2. Pen plotters are noisy and distracting and should not be located too close to designers trying to concentrate.
3. Electrostatic plotters should not be in the CPU room because they can contaminate the air with paper dust or chemicals.
4. Modular walls are easier to rearrange and make designing a comfortable work area easier. They are also more expensive than permanent walls.
5. It should be kept in mind that new installations are often showcases and visitors will be common.
6. Graphics terminals give off heat, and adequate air circulation is important for user comfort and equipment reliability.
7. Glare from lighting can be eliminated by polarizers of mesh screen that fit over most cathode-ray tubes (CRTs).
8. Ambient light is becoming less of a problem because newer displays are brighter. Some can be used in normal office environments.
9. Computer room power should be checked by a solid-state voltage monitor before installation and for at least a week under operating conditions.
10. A larger air conditioner than needed should be installed. Air conditioner failures can cause computer circuits to be overstressed without actual failure. This can cause numerous intermittent problems.
11. The computer room should be designed so that traffic is minimized. Printers requiring frequent access should be located in the design area.
12. Additional power should be installed for future expansion of CPUs and disk drives to avoid delays when new equipment is installed.
13. Allowance should be made for extra telephones in the CPU room to handle modem communications and for a phone for service personnel.
14. Computer room construction should be carefully coordinated to coincide with delivery of hardware.

8.5 CENTRALIZED VS. DISTRIBUTED FACILITIES

Initially a centralized graphics facility where users can communicate with each other about system operation will provide a better environment for learning. If design groups and manufacturing personnel are spread out or located in different buildings, then a nucleus facility can be established and future expansion could include remote terminals.

If more than one system is being installed, then centralization of the CPUs with a nucleus design to remote areas can be considered right away. The advantages of a centralized facility are:

- Ease of maintenance
- Better control over scheduling
- Less duplication of effort by technical support personnel
- Lower installation costs
- Centralized structured training

The disadvantages of a centralized graphics facility usually become apparent when stations are required at distances greater than 2000 feet and require special telephone hookups or communications hardware. This brings into play a more complex set of issues dealing with capital, response time, and database management requirements usually associated with a complex data processing environment and is discussed under the topic of networking.

When a central computer is down for repairs or maintenance, all users are affected and are unable to work until the problem is corrected. Most mainframe vendors have very good uptime records; however, no computer operates indefinitely without some downtime. In the future stand-alone terminals with their own CPUs linked via inexpensive high-speed networks will allow engineers and drafters to utilize microprocessor-based personal computers with sophisticated graphics capabilities, eliminating many of the problems associated with expansion of existing facilities and centralized computing. The "terminal optimization technique" will prevail (the right computing tool for the right job), with very expensive and sophisticated computers capable of doing solids modeling and other high-level work located in a central facility. Sketching and two- and three-dimensional geometry creation can be done at the engineers' and drafters' workstation on inexpensive microprocessors capable of transferring their databases to the larger centralized graphics facility for extremely complex tasks.

Figure 8.1 is a typical floor plan of a centralized graphics area.

8.6 SYSTEM MANAGER AND THE DESIGN GROUP

The graphic system manager is required to interact with engineering managers and operating personnel concerning the day-to-day activities of the graphic system. The system manager may also be chartered to direct some or all the activities associated with graphics orientation within his or her operating group.

Initially the system manager will be required to assume both sales and public relations roles and should keep in mind at all times that he or she will have to live with the promises made concerning the benefits of computer graphics.

Comprehensive orientation provides managers with the tools to select graphics operating personnel effectively and make assessments as to which projects are suited to graphics.

The following issues should be addressed during the orientation program and before personnel selection commences.

- Presentations and equipment demonstrations
- Management training
- Productivity expectations
- Productivity vs. utilization
- Open vs. closed shop issues
- Project definition
- Database requirements
- Role of graphics service bureaus

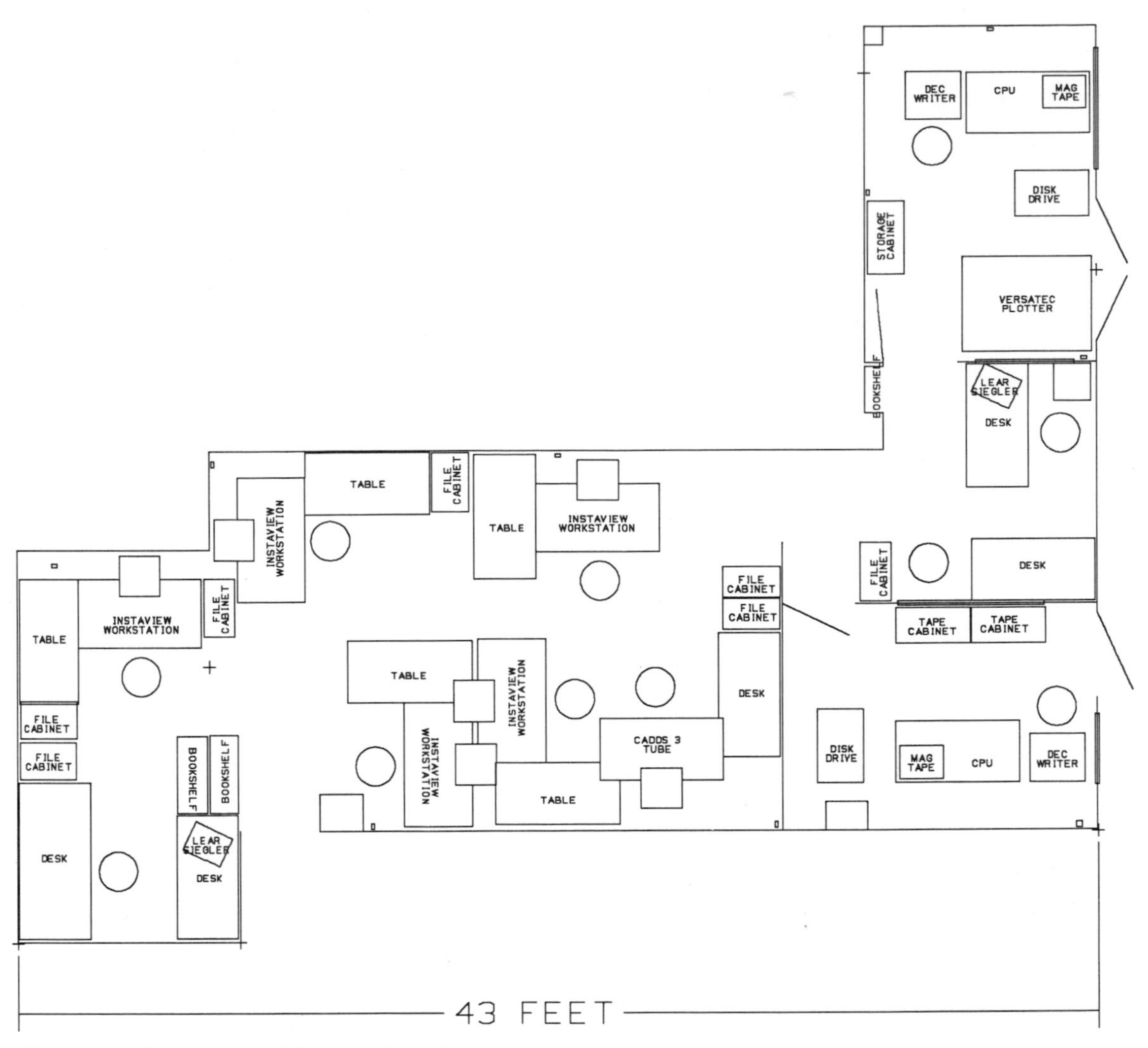

Figure 8.1 Computer graphics room layout.

- Shift considerations
- Personnel selection
- Learning curve

The objective of management orientation is to instill an awareness of the impact that computer graphics will have on the day-to-day activities of the engineering or manufacturing departments. It is important that supervisory personnel realize that changes in operating procedures are required to achieve long-term benefits in productivity. All personnel, whether they be potential system users or managers, should be exposed to some aspect of computer graphics.

8.7 PRESENTATIONS AND EQUIPMENT DEMONSTRATIONS

Initially a group presentation by the vendor should be made to key engineering and manufacturing managers and supervisory personnel. This initial presentation should include:

- An overview of CAD/CAM
- Description of hardware and functions

- Presentation of applications
- Future product offerings

The vendor should be requested to keep the presentation low-key from a sales point of view and make every effort to be instructional. Consultants can be very helpful in giving managers a realistic perspective of what to expect from CAD/CAM and should be considered for on-site lectures.

A follow-up demonstration of the vendor's capabilities should be scheduled at the vendor's regional office by technical support groups addressing various applications.

Little time should pass before the general work force is given an orientation, since there will undoubtedly be rumors and questions concerning the impact of computerization on the department. If possible, a departmental orientation schedule should be published to assure all personnel of some involvement in the orientation process. The orientation of key personnel before the general work force will give management time to anticipate many questions concerning shift work, job security, and the like.

8.8 SPECIALIZED MANAGEMENT TRAINING

Ideally every manager who will define projects to be executed on the graphics system should receive basic training. Training can usually be accomplished at the regional vendor's office. In addition, colleges that have installed graphics hardware offer a wide range of basic and applications courses, as do graphics service agencies. In some cases arrangements can be made to use the equipment of a neighboring company.

Although most managers are not required to operate the graphics system after it is installed, previous graphics training can prove invaluable during project definition. The main objective of this training is not necessarily to learn how to use the brand of equipment being acquired by the organization, but to teach basic graphics concepts common to all graphics systems, including:

Simple geometric construction
Mirroring
Translation
Stretching
Extraction of geometry from existing files
Merging of geometry into existing files
Dimensioning and text entry
Associativity of dimensions to geometry
Associativity of geometry to views
Layering concepts
Difference between two-dimensional and three-dimensional construction techniques

CAD/CAM will be a major factor in the organization's future success, and as graphics becomes a part of everyday activities, managers will be required to conceive of new ways to use graphics in engineering and manufacturing. Continuing education should be considered part of a professional engineer's job description. Participation in associations dealing with graphics issues and applications generates new ideas and aids in the development of professional relationships with other graphics users. The system manager should be active in professional associations and encourage other managers and engineers to participate.

8.9 PRODUCTIVITY EXPECTATIONS AND PROJECT DEFINITION

Before task definition is attempted, the facilities manager should convey to management some understanding of what a graphics system does best. It is important that management understand that some tasks are more productive than others and that the capabilities of the system should be kept in mind when evaluating the type of work to be done on the system.

Most graphics systems are justified on the basis of productivity estimates for conceptual design work, detail drawing, parametric generation of families of parts, and some manufacturing applications. It has been difficult to establish exact productivity ratios for different types of work on a graphics system because of the lack of data for graphics-generated drawings. Generally, experienced designers and drafters can estimate jobs from a manual point of view. This will allow the establishment of a baseline. Implementation of a graphics accounting system from the outset will enable productivity measurements to be made.

Most graphics systems have accounting logs which keep track of how long drafters or designers are using the system (see Fig. 8.2). Some systems are sophisticated enough to be used for extensive reporting of system usage. Others provide only basic information and require enhancement to be truly useful. In most cases additional programs are required to generate graphical output rather than simple alphanumeric reports.

8.10 CAD/CAM PAYBACK

CAD/CAM payback is postulated on the concept of reusing the drawing database for as many applications as possible, reducing or eliminating the need to recreate geometry for finite-element modeling, mass properties, and numerical control (NC) tool-path generation and tool fabrication. For many of these applications it is desirable to have a three-dimensional database. In applications such as sheet-metal fabrication where flat patterns are difficult to visualize and bend allowances are difficult to calculate, payback is difficult to estimate.

New concepts in budgeting strategies, taking into consideration value added in the creation of a graphics database, should be initiated at the corporate level. This encourages development of a graphics database that will benefit the entire organization. This situation is based on the database creator's effort to develop a database that is usable for other engineering or manufacturing applications. The database creator normally will be

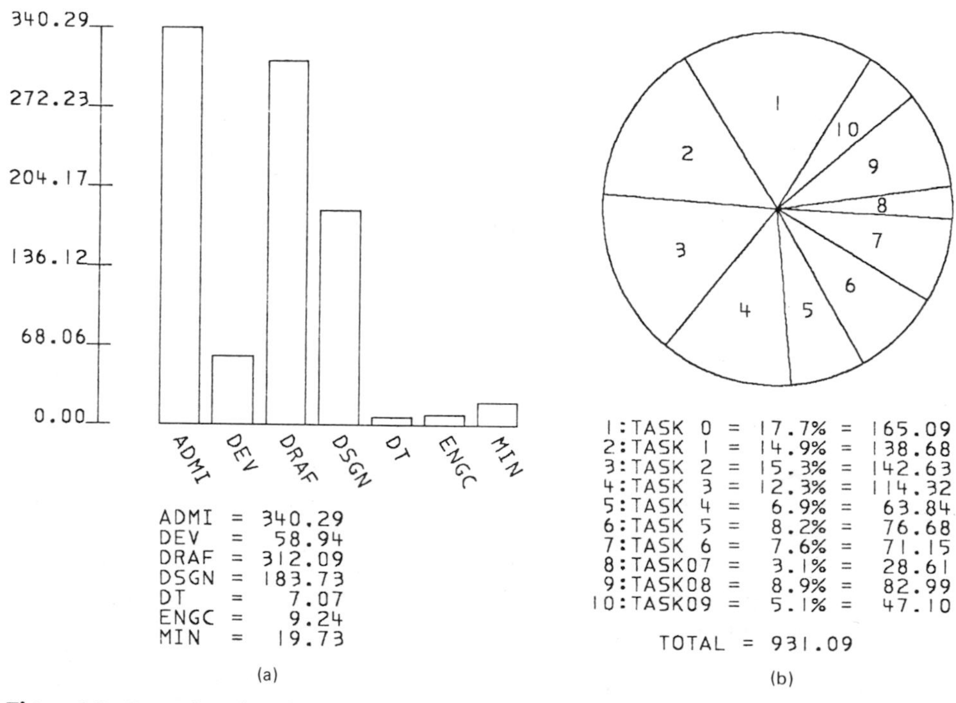

Figure 8.2 Examples of productivity reporting system. (*a*) Hours per department; (*b*) hours per task.

required to add more data, or organize the data in such a way that more time will be spent in the initial creation of the database than if reuse of the data were of no concern.

If some provision is not made for equitable project budgeting, the initial users of the system will incur penalties which can manifest themselves in the form of resistance to work in three dimensions. Some potential resistance may be overcome as design changes clearly become faster to make in three dimensions. Error detection because of interference and missing features in difficult-to-visualize areas may offer additional justification for three-dimensional databases.

Before development of a three-dimensional database, careful evaluation of the number of times the database will be used should be made to ascertain whether the investment is justified. An across-the-board decision to create all graphics in three dimensions may not be cost-effective. Not all manufacturing applications benefit from a three-dimensional model. NC tool-path generation of axial symmetrical components to be machined on a lathe requires only a two-dimensional profile. If a great deal of 4- and 5-axis machining requiring complex tool movements is done, the case for a three-dimensional database becomes stronger.

In addition, complex parts created in three dimensions enable tooling and fixture designers to create designs using the model geometry directly as a construction aid. In engineering groups, similar use of the model can be utilized to design test fixturing required in the prototype stages of a new project. Mold and pattern making is still very much an art form, and much work needs to be done in this area to understand how a three-dimensional database can be best used when making a one-of-a-kind pattern for casting applications.

The payback for detail drafting is not as high as for many design-oriented tasks. The payback on detail drafting is proportionate to the number and types of changes required on a design after it is considered ready to detail. If the design has been fairly well established and frozen in the layout stage, the payback may be less than obtained from conceptual design work. If the design is still unresolved and many geometric changes are required, then the graphics system will be beneficial. If the database is developed in three dimensions, a change to one view will often be all that is required if the database is view-associative. Changes made in one view will be reflected in all views of the drawing, eliminating the need to change geometry manually in each of several views. In addition, if the dimensioning software supplied by the vendor is also related to the geometry in the database, then dimensions will update automatically to correspond with changes in geometry.

In all views, associative features are extremely powerful and will increase throughput. The disadvantage of associativity in a database is its negative impact on response time as a result of additional overhead required by the computer to keep track of complex associative relationships.

The lack of associativity in some systems is claimed to be the main reason for high throughput when manipulating geometry and dimensions. In a nonassociative system the dimensions must be deleted and recreated by the user when geometry is changed. The key question concerning dimensioning associativity would be, "Do we change our drawing enough to justify the constant overhead of the associative feature?" The debate may become academic as new technology develops, bringing very inexpensive computers with the power of a mainframe within the reach of all users. These computers will ultimately handle most of the overhead encountered in associative systems and satisfy the most experienced users' requirements for speed and responsiveness.

8.11 DRAWING CHANGES AND PROJECT BUDGETS

While changes are normally faster using a graphics system, they can also cause a project to go over budget if engineers request more changes than they would otherwise make when manually working on the drawing board. This often occurs when designers recognize the ease of changing designs on a graphics system, and they are sometimes not as conscientious when communicating their original concepts to layout drafters.

When jobs are submitted to graphics, a work order should be included with an estimate of the computer hours required. A record of changes and revisions should be kept with cumulative hours recorded at each change as an aid in measuring productivity. Many times, in a well-intentioned effort to achieve perfection, a designer, nearing completion of a project under budget, will continue to make refinements and request changes that would be out of the question on the drawing board because of their extensive nature, perhaps even requiring an entire redraw on a clean sheet of paper.

Normally changes made on a graphics system are much faster than changes on a manual drawing, with the exception of minor alterations in text which require only a simple erasure that takes a few minutes on a manual drawing. Even the slightest change to a drawing on a graphics system requires a minimum setup time similar to any machine tool. The amount of time required to make minor changes will be dependent upon factors such as whether the drawing file is online or must be restored from tape.

Usually, active files are maintained online if possible, and this is not a factor. In addition, getting on a terminal and activating a drawing takes 5 minutes with 5 minutes to make the change and file the drawing and another 10 minutes to make a plot, adding up to a minimum of 20 to 30 minutes to make the most minor change to a drawing.

8.11.1 Manually Changing CAD Drawings

In some cases manual changes to a CAD drawing may be required. It is extremely dangerous to change a CAD drawing manually unless it can be ascertained that the database will be updated to correspond with the released version. One method of accomplishing a minor change is to change the part number. This has disadvantages in that it affects the paperwork load of the department and sometimes the entire organization.

An alternative method is to implement a CAD change request form, which allows a manual change to be made with the requirement that the database is updated within a minimum period of time. Obviously, this is risky if the follow-up system fails and the CAD database is not brought up to date. However, if a deadline needs to be met and a large volume of minor changes are delaying the release, a CAD change request form might prove to be a workable alternative.

8.12 PROJECT DEFINITION

The ideal situation is one in which decisions concerning project definition do not have to be made and all work can be accomplished on the graphics system. Because of the capital-intensive nature of CAD systems, a phased plan taking several years to implement is normal. Choosing the most productive work for the system is not always straightforward.

As the size of the design database increases on a graphics system, the need for additional terminals may increase more rapidly than a company can afford. This necessitates a careful analysis of which work should be directed to graphics first.

After evaluation of the type of work done within a particular group, there are three approaches that can be taken when defining projects to be accomplished on the system.

1. Major projects, such as an entire tractor composed of many different applications, offering a mix of both high- and low-payback work (some portions of the project may offer no short-term payback)
2. Specific portions of many projects offering the highest immediate payback, with no concern for long-term reuse of the database
3. Specific portions of many projects offering long-term payback through companywide reutilization of the database

The difficult decisions of project definition are minimized by newly developed systems having full two- and three-dimensional geometry capability and the ability to interface to existing turnkey systems with costs in the $15,000 range per design station. Companies who use optimization techniques to match the work to the computer should be able to implement a normal 5-year graphics plan within the scope of a 1- or 2-year capital plan.

8.13 PRODUCTIVITY VS. UTILIZATION

Initially, many company managers feel that the primary measure of a successful CAD project is the attainment of full-time system utilization in the shortest possible time. This can result in an intense effort to load the system with work, ignoring a preconceived strategy. Keeping the system busy may give the appearance of a productive environment, but it is unlikely that the system will be optimized through this approach. The number of hours the system is utilized does not necessarily equate with productivity.

It is important not to be as concerned with the volume of work initially as much as the quality of work. A longer learning curve is required for designers working in three dimensions than in two dimensions. Designers and mechanical drafters may require extensive training, depending on the complexity of the software. The larger and more diverse the trained staff becomes, the better the chances are that the system will be properly utilized.

Full utilization can be the measure of productivity where the system was purchased for one specific application such as detail drafting or facilities planning. However, even the simplest application requires an organized approach to library building and database structure. It is possible to consider these requirements in advance and be prepared to place trained operators on the system upon installation.

8.14 OPEN VS. CLOSED SHOP

The question of whether to implement a closed or open shop will be determined largely by the type of work done on the system. A closed shop is an internal service group composed of permanent graphics operators or designers. The closed shop sells the services provided by its graphics staff to various departments or divisions. The extent of available services such as design and drafting is limited only by the abilities of personnel employed by the graphics department.

Normally a closed shop is employed when a company decides to convert an existing manual database to graphics and the work requires little interaction with groups paying for its services. Digitizing existing layouts of integrated or printed circuits and map data are good applications requiring less experience. This offers an economical method of developing a graphics database. Occasionally a graphics system is justified for a specific application such as facilities planning, where a relatively small group of individuals will work on the system, or for detail drafting.

Because a closed shop is a specialized service, it is often the most economical way of accomplishing large volumes of repetitive work. Alternate shift operations may be easier to staff, since it is more realistic to hire and train new employees for positions requiring limited skills.

Generally, because of the narrow scope of work done in a closed-shop environment, more sophisticated design and drafting work benefits from an open-shop atmosphere. Start-ups may be slower in an open shop since a larger base of users is trained for longer periods of time. As higher-level users are trained, they will begin to recognize applications which are best suited to graphics. There will be more casual users on the system who will come and go with each new project. During the first year, usage may be sporadic while the user base is growing. Open time should be used for training and software development if there is some concern by upper management about system utilization.

8.15 PERSONNEL ORIENTATION

A general orientation of the work force should be scheduled before the CAD selection process begins. Periodic divisional or departmental staff meetings present an ideal opportunity to present the company's plan to implement graphics within the organization. A vendor presentation is appropriate at this time. Key management personnel should preface the presentation with a brief statement as to the organization's future plans and the benefits expected to be derived from graphics.

After the vendor presentation, management should be prepared to offer assurances that an opportunity exists or will eventually exist for all engineers and drafters to participate in the graphics plan. If this is not the case, a modified orientation strategy will be required. However, in most organizations it is recognized that eventually drawing boards will be obsolete.

Managers should expect questions concerning job security. Many employees will be concerned about being replaced by a computer. This is a carryover from the early days of data processing when many clerical tasks were automated. The same situation does not exist in engineering and manufacturing departments, where drafters and designers are highly skilled individuals. The graphics system should be viewed as a new type of drawing instrument that gives designers and drafters greater flexibility to do a job. They will be free to spend time solving engineering problems more creatively rather than struggling to lay down perfect letters.

Individual creativity will always be recognizable whether done on the drawing board or on a graphics system. The fact that designers can do their jobs faster will allow the luxury of exploring more options than they could in the past. This will create better designs, which will in turn increase the profits of the organization. The company will be free to use additional profits and time to expand its product line, thereby creating a more stable and secure environment for its employees.

Employees generally have little concept of how geometry is created on the graphics system and often feel that they will have to become programmers to operate the system. Senior employees may be especially fearful of becoming involved with the system if they are not reassured that age is not a factor. In fact, experience and exposure to the company's applications will more often give a senior employee an advantage over a younger, less-experienced person. This is especially true for detail drafting applications where knowledge of engineering standards plays an important role in a person's ability to turn out good drawings. Often an explanation of what "interactive" and "user friendly" mean will aid in helping nongraphics personnel understand how easy it is to learn to use a graphics system.

8.15.1 Personnel Selection

During the management orientation process, determinations should be made concerning the type of work to be done on the system. This information is useful in establishing the correct ratio of designers to detailers and other specialists to be trained on the system and helps avoid work-load and scheduling conflicts from developing.

A typical situation causing a system overload can occur when a new project is placed on the graphics system. Assume that six designers work full-time for several months on a six-station graphics system to bring conceptual design layouts to a point where detail drafting can start. The work they have created will keep 12 detailers busy for the same period. This work load will require a full first- and second-shift utilization of the system to accomplish the work within a given time frame. During this time the original designers will not be able to continue on to new design work on the graphics system until the detailing work is complete. If new product design priorities take precedence over detailing, then it is likely that some detailing of designs created on the graphics system will be offloaded to the drawing board for manual drafting, creating a mixed database of manual and CAD drawings. In addition, improper work-loading will sometimes create the erroneous assumption that the system is somehow the cause of a deadline problem and that work must be moved back to the drawing board to be completed on time.

Once initial project work loads can be established, personnel selection can take place. The very best people should be chosen for the first group to be trained. The return on investment from the first group is proportionate to the quality and skill level of those trained. The top performers in the group are usually the most difficult to give up for training. Commitment to graphics and some reshifting of work loads have to be made by managers and engineering supervisors. Any tendency to train individuals who can be spared from a project because they are not as heavily relied upon for their contribution should be avoided.

The initial core of graphics users will provide major support to subsequent groups as they are trained. The core group will set the example for the next group of trainees. They will be emulated by others, and if the initial users are the most innovative in their use of the graphics system, the path to increased productivity will be shortened.

Many techniques and procedures will be developed based upon recommendations of the first users of the system. Not making the proper commitment to training can result in a static graphics environment limited by the potential of the users. No system manager, regardless of skill, can make up for lack of user capability. Capability refers to the skills required to do high-quality design or drafting work in a manual environment.

It is more important that a person have good design or drafting skills rather than previous computer graphics experience. It is easier to teach an individual to use a computer graphics system than it is to teach mechanical design or drafting principles. Occasionally companies will hire experienced graphics operators without the same level of skills they would require of an individual applying for a position of the same responsibility in a nongraphics environment.

In most cases the criteria for selecting graphics personnel are no different than for any other type of hiring situation, and good personnel practices should be followed. The best workers on the drafting board will be the best on the graphics system. A positive attitude and curiosity are good attributes to have. An inquisitive nature is generally part of most engineers' makeup and is a valuable asset when exploring the capabilities of a graphics system. Aggressive individuals will not be intimidated by a computer.

The failure of a person to adapt to graphics can usually be traced to a previous attitude problem. Very few individuals fail because of an inability to comprehend the system command structure. In many cases preconceived ideas or fears can give the impression of a poor attitude and can be overcome with proper orientation.

8.15.2 Personnel Training: General

Actual training can be accomplished in several ways. A certain number of training "credits" normally are included with the purchase of a system. These credits can usually be applied at the vendor site or sometimes the vendor will make the services of an instructor available for on-site training after the system is installed. In addition, the vendor may offer basic and advanced training at district and regional offices throughout the country.

Training at the vendor's headquarters provides a formal and structured environment and also provides the opportunity to interact with other users of your vendor's equipment. Tours of the vendor's facility can also be informational for key supervisory people. Usually, it is a good idea to send several key managers and some of the initial core group to the vendor's site for training. Training at the vendor's site has the additional advantage of relieving the trainee from his or her everyday responsibilities and allowing full concentration on the subject.

If economics become a problem, regional offices offering training are sometimes located within daily driving distance. However, graphics vendors normally maintain their senior staff at headquarters, and the potential differences in instructor skill levels should be considered when choosing a training location.

In large organizations with several systems, in-house training programs are sometimes established. In many cases training of this type is advantageous because it can be better oriented to the company's particular procedural and applications needs. If the company has the luxury of maintaining a corporate training center, the advantage of removing the trainee from his or her working environment and reducing travel costs are combined.

In addition to formal classroom training, many vendors offer videocassette and audiocassette self-instructional courses that allow the user to train at the system without the presence of an instructor when open time exists. Normally courses of this type are intended for basic training and cover the major features of the system. This type of training will get a user started but should not be considered adequate for work requiring sophisticated use of the system. A designer doing two-dimensional layout work in mechanical design could probably do well with this type of training, but a person working in three-dimensional mechanical applications or complex integrated- or printed-circuit routing applications will require more advanced training.

8.15.3 Personnel Training: Applications

Applications training is also offered by most vendors in specific subject areas. Programmers, finite-element modelers, NC programmers, piping designers, and electrical designers require advanced courses usually not taken concurrently with basic training. A period of operational experience is usually required to understand the basic command structure of the system before taking advanced applications courses. The operating system course is usually taken by an individual responsible for file management and for backup of design data. Often this is the system manager and programmer. In addition a system operations specialist is normally required to handle day-to-day administrative activities such as:

- Daily and weekly tape backups
- Menu development
- Library development and organization
- Restoration and removal of parts from disk
- Maintenance of plotter supplies
- Execution and monitoring of batch jobs
- Administration of procedures
- Answering operator questions

The time required to get users up to speed will vary by application. A user doing repetitive digitizing can be productive within 2 weeks of training. Detail drafters may take 6 months. Engineers and designers working in three-dimensional design may take a full year to become expert users of the system. A rule-of-thumb formula indicates that a user will usually attain a productivity level equal to the drawing board within 3 months and will become fully productive on the system after 9 months to a year.

A certain number of users should be trained before the system arrives. However, if there is too great a time span between training and system arrival, much of what is learned will be forgotten. Vendor training just before or on-site after the system is installed is normal procedure. If a faster start-up is desired, alternative techniques can be employed. Users can be trained ahead of time at the vendor site, and computer time can be purchased at a service bureau many months before the system arrives.

A valid argument can be made for making use of a service bureau's graphics system in the case when a new project is contemplated and will have to be started on the drawing board due to the unavailability of a newly ordered system. Utilization of a service bureau can give a company a head start if proper cautions are exercised concerning database compatibility. Even databases created on a like system can be somewhat incompatible if created on a different software revision. Most vendors offer software converters for their own line of computer graphics equipment. However, there is always at least 20 minutes of conversion time required per drawing and sometimes several hours of rework in the converted-drawing database to realign views and relocate dimensions that may have gone astray during conversion. If this occurs, then other questions about the drawing integrity arise and the drawing will probably have to be checked again. All of this can amount to a heavy penalty for an early start-up.

This does not mean that use of another graphics system is not a good way to get started early. The safest way is to simply use equipment that will be identical in every way to the system that has been ordered. An experienced system manager will be able to ascertain that everything is in order.

8.16 MULTISHIFT OPERATIONS

Soon after start-up, system usage often increases to the point where a second system or a second shift is required to handle work loads. Because of the large capital investment required to acquire additional computer hardware, a second shift is usually implemented. The obvious advantage of operating a second shift is a conservation of capital resources. Turnaround time on designs is also shortened.

The advantage of maintaining a single shift is that communication problems do not develop when questions arise which may have to wait until the next day for resolution. It is also difficult to motivate technical people to work night shifts.

The easiest way to make better use of the system before starting a full second shift is to start working earlier in the day. A 6 A.M. to 6 P.M. shift, for example, increases system utilization by 50 percent and poses no great hardships on the department users.

It may make sense in some situations to limit the designers' time on the system to 4 hours per day, optionally giving the drafter 8 hours if necessary. A ratio of 2 design hours to 4 drafting hours is required in many types of engineering work. Proper scheduling helps avoid a situation where designers create more drafting work than can be completed on the system within a given time frame. If this occurs, some drafting may have to be completed on the drawing board to meet deadlines.

8.16.1. Flexible Hours

If a full second shift is ultimately needed, some overlap in working hours between designers and drafters is recommended. A 2 P.M. starting time for the second shift will normally provide enough overlap for communications between designers and drafters. Another alternative is to have designers start on the graphics system at 6 A.M. and work until noon, when a second shift would take over. This requires the second shift to work only until 8 P.M.

8.16.2 Running Batch Jobs at Night

Unfortunately, even the best choice of work may not offer enough return on investment to justify two-shift operation upon initial evaluation. However, three-shift operation of a CAD system offers no assurance that more work will be accomplished than in a two-shift operation. Proper organization of the work to be done during the first and second shifts may eliminate the need of a third shift and, in some companies, even reduce the need to operate a full second shift.

Computers are good at running large computational programs without human intervention, and this capability can be used in a graphics operation to reduce late-night human operation of the system.

Certain tasks such as plotting and routine database maintenance are time-consuming and require little or no user interaction and can therefore be done as "batch" jobs at night. In addition, plotting and database maintenance are CPU-intensive and negatively impact the responsiveness of the system from the user's point of view.

It is not uncommon for a graphics user to spend approximately 8 percent of his or her system time waiting for electrostatic plots to be completed. Normally the majority of checking plots are not required immediately and can be scheduled to be generated by the computer unattended, utilizing the batch-processing capability of the system. This allows the tasks to be executed automatically at a predetermined time each night. Any routine task taking more than 15 minutes and requiring no interaction from the user should be evaluated as a potential batch job for nights.

Other than plotting, there are routine database maintenance and diagnostic activities which may take another 30 minutes per user. Drawing database compression and checking are routine tasks usually executed by the operator as the number of geometric changes made in a drawing accumulate. As changes are made to a drawing, it may become more fragmented or scattered on the disk, increasing filing time and file activation. If these activities are scheduled during off hours, the designer or drafter will realize increased system efficiencies during prime time.

Proper management of system resources often requires additional systems personnel, since these activities take time to plan and organize. In most cases basic command files will need to be written to execute batch activities at night.

8.17 DATABASE AND PROCEDURES DEVELOPMENT

A substantial amount of preliminary database development is required before a system is usable for production work. The following list covers the most important areas:

- Company standard drawing formats and title blocks
- Commonly used drawing decals, charts, and symbols
- Daily, weekly, and monthly data backup procedures
- Standard file-naming conventions (companywide)
- Parts libraries
- Layering conventions
- Drawing release procedures and associated software
- Released drawing archiving procedures
- User authorization and protection scheme
- System utilization accounting programs
- Graphics departmental forms
- Operator procedures

The above items fall into three general categories:

1. Graphics files to be created for use on the graphics system
2. Written procedures to be followed by system users and support personnel
3. Software programs to be written for use on the system

8.17.1 Graphics Service Bureaus For Start-Up Assistance

Service bureaus can play a key role helping establish a new graphics facility for preinstallation database development. The system vendor should be able to assist in the location of graphics service bureaus using their equipment. Good service bureaus will have a competent staff of designers, detailers, and software personnel. Because graphics service bureaus are profit-motivated, they will have implemented many procedures to increase efficiency.

It is highly desirable to supervise the initial work of a graphics agency. Consider it worthwhile to have the system manager travel to the service bureau and work with them for the period of time necessary to define the work desired. In addition, the system manager can ascertain whether the bureau's staff can adequately perform the desired tasks.

The experience a graphics service bureau has gained in doing contract work for customer applications will prove invaluable and will suggest procedures and present opportunities not possible to obtain in any other way. In addition to assisting in a faster setup, the service bureau's experience will lower the probability of hastily conceived database structures requiring rework later.

8.17.2 Graphics Department Procedures Manual

An operator's procedures manual makes the job of orienting new users easier and saves the system manager time in answering questions. The operating manual also assists in the adherence to standard operating procedures.

Drawing construction technique should not be left totally up to the operator. Old drawing board habits, such as drawing roughly to scale, must be left behind. Drawing to the nominal and precisely to scale is an absolute requirement for most applications where the database is to be used for critical applications. There are exceptions by application, such as facilities planning, where digitized databases are acceptable and greater accuracy would only serve to increase database development time and cost.

The following is a table of contents for a typical graphic system departmental user's manual.

I. System start-up and shutdown
   - A. System power up and initial boot up of multiple systems
   - B. Regular log-in procedure
   - C. Crash recovery procedure
   - D. Nightly shutdown
   - E. Total shutdown of all systems
   - F. Emergency procedures
     1. Air conditioning failure
     2. Power outage
     3. Head crash
     4. Fire

II. Part naming convention
   - A. Copying and moving a part
   - B. Multiple-sheet drawings
   - C. Part construction phase
   - D. Checking phase
   - E. Revision phase
   - F. Release phase
   - G. Experimental phase
   - H. Production phase

III. Drawing conventions and techniques
   - A. Developing a construction strategy
     1. Identifying central geometric features
     2. Identifying symmetrical elements in the part
     3. The advantages of proper planning
   - B. Filing procedures
   - C. Units and scale
     1. Units
        - *a.* Database precision and round-off error in metric
        - *b.* Use of datums and subdatums
     2. Scale
   - D. Layering
     1. For internal engineering drawings
     2. For manufacturing drawings

E. Saving and restoring display images and layering combinations for quick recall
F. Formats
   1. Drawing setup
   2. Menu-driven programs for drawing setup
   3. Menu-driven programs for drawing parameter setup
   4. Temporary construction borders
   5. Final formats
   6. Title-block routines
   7. Change blocks
   8. Engineering parts list
G. Geometric construction
   1. Stages of the detailing procedure
   2. Geometry insertion
   3. In-stream commands for display manipulation
   4. Two-dimensional construction
   5. Three-dimensional construction
   6. Grouping and layering for machined surfaces
   7. Draft and surface generation for NC pattern making
   8. Removal of extraneous geometry from three-dimensional models
   9. Use of parametric programs for geometry construction
   10. Using the graphics system to classify part shape after geometry completion
H. Layout construction techniques
   1. From scratch
   2. From existing geometry
   3. Maintaining nodal associativity to retain currency of associated details
I. Detail construction techniques
   1. From scratch
   2. From a layout
   3. From a three-dimensional model
   4. Maintaining extended model associativity to retain currency with assembly layouts
J. Assembly-drawing techniques
   1. Use of programs for batch insertion of detail geometry for the automatic creation of assembly drawings
K. Sectioning
   1. The cut-plane method
   2. The cut-surface method
   3. The Z-clipping method
L. Dimensioning
   1. Parameters
   2. Insertion
   3. Repositioning
   4. Change
M. Decals, charts, notes, symbols, geometry
N. Plotting
   1. When and how to batch-plot checking drawing
   2. When and how to batch-plot released drawings

IV. Drawing route flowchart

V. Location of most current version of a part

A. Search over network architecture
B. Search of all system nodes
C. Search of archival files

VI. Engineering change procedure

VII. Operator responsibility

  A. Maintenance
  B. Meetings

VIII. Forms

  A. Bug sheet
  B. Layer log
  C. Release form
  D. Advance ECS number form
  E. Suggested improvement request form
  F. Plot request form
  G. Engineering drawing change notice

IX. Database maintenance

  A. Check database
  B. Pack database
  C. Sorting the database
  D. Regenerate graphics
  E. How to handle a problem part
    1. Dead entities
    2. Fatal errors
      a. When not to file over existing parts
      b. Use of alternative filing names for database protection
      c. When to attempt part recovery or go back to list filing
    3. Loss of graphics precision
    4. Response-related issues
    5. Database extents problems

8.17.3 File-Naming Conventions

Standard file-naming conventions should be established before any production work is done on the system. A good file-naming structure can:

1. Assist in locating files on the system
2. Enable the system manager to tell what phase of the design cycle drawing files are in
3. Monitor file activity
4. Aid in the removal of released drawings from the disk if required
5. Control revisions of released files
6. Monitor system utilization by project or part number

In general, a properly structured file-naming convention allows tracking of a part through initial creation, checking phases, experimental release, revisions, production release, and removal from the disk for archival storage.

8.17.4 Drawing Release Procedures

Drawing release procedures can be simplified through the use of manipulation of file names in conjunction with a drawing release form. Such a form can be attached to the CAD drawing as it progresses through the design process. A simple matrix with dates in and out for every iteration in the process will assist in maintaining a clean disk. Typically a form would have the following headings.

	Date	Date	Date	Date	Date	Date
CAD dept. in						
CAD dept. out						
Checking						
Project eng.						
Metallurgist						
Chief Eng.						
Coding						
Return form to graphics for removal from disk						

Unless the facility has unlimited disk capacity, the released parts will need to be taken offline to make room for other work in process. The previous procedure will signal the CAD department when a part is officially released, if the release is delayed or if it has become inactive for some reason. It is also desirable to know the part status since the part file may be competing for valuable disk space and should be temporarily removed from the disk. When it is needed, it can be restored from the monthly backup tapes.

8.18 MULTIDISK OPERATION

During the first 2 years of production, a facility might require 10 reels of tape for archival storage (1000 drawings). This amount of data would require two 300-megabyte disk packs at 50 megabytes per 2400 feet of tape recorded at 1600 bits per inch. A second disk drive would allow the use of disk packs for archival storage with additional tape backup for added protection. Multiple disk drives allow data to be removed and restored to the system more quickly. In addition, more data can be stored online at one time.

When drawing files are restored to the system, one of the disk drives can be shut down without stopping the computer or interfering with the user activity on the system. The files on the archival disk can be transferred to the working disk, at which time the archival disk can be removed and another archival disk can be installed to restore additional files if necessary.

Utilizing a disk pack for archival storage allows data previously stored on five tapes to be quickly and randomly accessed, whereas the data on magnetic tape can only be accessed serially. If the data sought are on the end of the tape, as long as 10 minutes could be required to locate the desired file. If numerous files are sought, it is very likely that all five reels of tape would have to be searched. The process could take longer than is desired for release and revision of drawings in a dynamic design environment. Up to four disk drives can be added to most minicomputer-based graphics systems and may be as important as adding more terminals when considering throughput.

Additional benefits in system performance and operations management are realized when a two or more disk drives are added to a graphics system.

1. The risk of the system being out of commission due to a disk malfunction is reduced, thereby avoiding lost production time.
2. Database portability and organization can be better maintained.
3. Users desiring special security conditions may remove packs if desired and store them however they wish.
4. Separate disk packs can be assigned to individual projects, as is common practice in large data processing environments.
5. User response is less impacted by the mechanical limitations of the disk, since twice as many read-write heads will be accessing data simultaneously.

6. Fragmented, noncontinuous files can be reduced by moving files with a disk-to-disk copy nightly or at lunchtime. A disk-to-disk copy takes approximately 15 minutes as opposed to several hours if a tape-to-disk transfer is required.
7. If periodic software reloading is required to reduce errors and maintain software stability, a master software pack can be installed in the system and duplicated whenever it is convenient. Again, the time required is only 15 minutes for the average 300-megabyte disk drive used on many turnkey graphic systems.

8.19 GRAPHICS DATABASE STRUCTURE

While defining database structures, a system manager should fully understand the associative aspects and attributive functions of the graphics database. Associativity will affect many future applications.

There are two types of graphics database structures.

1. ***Nodal.*** Graphics databases constructed in this manner maintain associative relationships with other graphics files on the graphics system.
2. ***Nonnodal.*** Graphics files created in this manner are unique to that drawing and carry no associativity.

8.19.1 Drawing Formats

The nodal concept is expanded upon in the following example of drawing format usage. Title-block formats are normally created as nodal databases. A nodal database is one that becomes a master reference when stored on the disk of a graphics system. When the nodal format is used in combination with a part file, a "one-way" associative relationship is created from the nodal file to the part drawing. The nodal format, as viewed in the part drawing file, is a reflection or copy of the master format and can be deleted from the part drawing but cannot be modified. Only a change in the master format will be reflected in the part drawing.

While the format is visible in every part it is associated with, when viewed on the display, it does not physically reside in the part database when it is filed. This results in a significant compression of data as compared to the same format created in a nonnodal form that requires the format to be duplicated physically in each drawing file. As the format represents from 10 to 75 percent of the space required for a drawing, the savings in disk storage can be dramatic.

In addition to data compression, another major advantage of utilizing nodal databases for standard geometry is associativity. If company drafting standards require a change in the appearance of a standard symbol, one change to the master nodal drawing file will be reflected in all drawings having an instance or "pointer" to that symbol.

8.19.2 Nodal Text Applications

Graphic text can also be nodal and offers additional opportunities to automate processes such as:

Title-block data entry
Data charts on drawings
Release of drawings
Revision text changes in drawings
Assembly drawing text
Bill-of-materials extraction
Computer-aided process planning

The use of nodal text and nongraphical attributes offers almost unlimited opportunities to automate routine processes. Drawing title blocks should contain text nodes for the entry of text in standard locations and heights. Text nodes are nongraphic instances in a drawing that can be assigned attributes, such as name, text height, and text justification. In addition, attributes can be assigned, such as color, part number, and, in some cases, function. Text nodes should be used in all areas of a drawing where there might be a future requirement to address or extract data from the drawing through a software program. The use of text nodes should be considered for use in all areas of the drawing which will be affected by drawing release procedures—such as part number changes, revisions, and bill-of-materials information.

Using the text node approach from the outset allows the user of the system to fill in title-block information by using a menu-driven, user-written program to "annotate" blank nodes. As the text height and font information will have been previously stored on the node, the operator need only respond to questions asked by the program concerning part number, material, drawing scale, etc. As the information is entered by the user, it is automatically located on the proper node and becomes part of an intelligent database which can be extracted or changed any time the particular node is addressed by another program.

This concept is one of major importance, and standard procedures should be established before any production work is done on the system. A mixture of drawings created in manual graphics mode will not be usable by programs designed for nodal title blocks and will require rework to bring them into specification. This does not imply that the actual drawing release software need be developed before work can begin. The blank node entries into the title block, however, provide the focus around which the programs will operate and can be created in the nodal drawing format before the actual software which addresses them is written.

All charts, drawing decals, and user-created symbols in a drawing can utilize nodal text and save a great deal of time in drawing construction. Often a clerical person can fill in data charts or assembly drawing part numbers.

8.20 RELOADING IMPORTANT DATA FILES

Database maintenance sometimes requires periodic removal of files from the disk. In a start-up situation, there will be only a few files to reload, and commonly a system manager can begin by keeping some of these on one or several tapes. As the graphics system grows, there will be more special files than can be kept track of, and it becomes more important that a master tape be kept current with the latest revision of these files. This can cause undue frustration trying to locate misplaced files quickly while users are waiting for the system to come back up. A separate tape should be maintained to keep nodal and other important files together. This will allow efficient reloading and prevent the possibility of files not being reloaded at all. Some of the files falling into this category are

Drawing formats
Title-block and drawing release programs
Special plotting-device files
Special line-font files
User-written programs
User-developed menu files
Menu graphics files
Daily, weekly, monthly backup files
Special symbol libraries
System configuration and device codes

8.21 DATABASE LIBRARY DEVELOPMENT

Development of standard libraries of commonly used components increases the productivity of a graphics system by allowing the user to take advantage of predefined geometry to build assemblies. In some cases a previously created part may be similar enough to a new design concept that minor modification of the old version will yield a new part in less time.

Components or common shapes within components which are used repetitively are the best candidates for a library database. Libraries may be nodal or nonnodal depending upon the particular application.

8.21.1 Parametric Component Libraries

Component libraries can be created in the following ways:

1. Created manually as required
2. Created automatically through parametric programs for commonly shaped parts

Manual creation is usually reserved for more complex components which may be required for reuse but do not lend themselves to creation through a program which could take advantage of common shapes.

Parametric creation of components is a technique which allows the entry of variables in a program to generate geometric shapes. Parametric programs take advantage of the mathematically predictable relationships that exist between common shapes found in components (such as nuts and bolts).

Variable input to a graphics system for parametric geometry creation can be accomplished in either of the two following ways.

1. The operator of the system can execute a program to create a component, such as a bracket with three bends. The program would prompt the user to enter the material thickness, angle of bends, radius of corners, overall length, etc. The program would then create the geometry.
2. A somewhat more sophisticated parametric technique can be used if an organization has installed a group technology program of computerized coding and classification of similarly shaped parts. Nongraphical alphanumeric data tables can be read into the graphic system from the group technology computer. The parametric program would then be written to read the variables directly from the computer file, requiring the operator to simply execute the program and enter the part number of the component he or she would like the program to create.

   This technique may make several hundreds of families of components available, totaling tens of thousands of parts. A unique program would be required for each family. After the components are created and used, it may not be desirable to maintain the entire component library on the system.

8.21.2 Data Compression

The use of parametric programs offers a significant opportunity to compress geometric data into nongeometric form through the use of alphanumeric data tables. Fully described geometry requires more disk space than its base description in alphanumeric listings of the parts' dimensions in a text file. The exact amount of increased space is a function of the particular graphics vendor's database structure. However, comparisons made on several graphics systems indicate that an alphanumeric text file describing 1600 components required 1 megabyte of disk space, while their geometric counterpart required 64 megabytes, giving a compression of 64:1. The implication is clear, and if the program used to create the geometry is fast enough to give the impression that the part actually resides on disk in its geometric form, large databases of standard components could be maintained online at all times.

8.22 COMMUNICATIONS AND NETWORKING

As an engineering database grows and additional graphics systems are installed in different geographic locations, the issue of how to make the database universally available becomes important. It is usually desirable to have as much of the database as possible online at all times. If this is not possible, then the most active portions of the database should be kept available to ease user access to drawing files.

There are three methods of maintaining an online database,

1. Addition of disk drives to existing graphics systems
2. Storage of data centrally on data processing or engineering computers
3. Use of distributed local area networks

Additional disks can be added to most minicomputer-based systems. Usually four drives are the maximum that can be installed on one system, although more may be added if the operating system will support several disk controllers. Eventually data that are not active may have to be removed when the maximum disk capacity of the system is reached. However, if additional CPUs are required to support more design terminals, then disk drives may also be added, allowing the database to be maintained online.

Cost of storage is another consideration. In the past, turnkey vendors have charged substantial premiums for peripheral equipment. This practice has been generally adopted to offset the cost of software development which is usually "bundled" into the price of a turnkey graphics system. A more recent trend has been toward "unbundling" and pricing software separately, bringing turnkey vendors' peripheral hardware prices into line with original-equipment manufacturers' pricing structures.

If separate graphics facilities exist and are more than several thousand feet apart, a method of transmitting files from one to another will be required. Normally phone line links are established with telephone modems on each computer. The advantage of this type of distributed arrangement is that the creating facility always has fast access to its own files. Other groups wishing to access files on a less frequent basis will not be greatly impacted by the additional time taken to transfer graphics files over the telephone. Typically, unless expensive dedicated phone lines are established, the rates of data transfer over the phone will be restricted to 4800 to 9600 bits of data per second.

8.22.1 Data Transfer Statistics

Graphics files are often large and take considerable time to transfer at the commonly used 4800 bit per second rate. Data transfer throughput will vary depending on the noise level of the phone line. Communications hardware and software are designed to make certain that digital data arrive at their destination looking the same as they did before transmission. Digital data must therefore be compared with data at the sending facility. If a match is not established, the data must be retransmitted. The effective throughput will be a function of the number of retries required to get a good data match on the receiving system.

TYPICAL DATA TRANSFER RATES

Table 8.1 represents the actual time required to transfer a 4.3- megabyte (34-megabit) file. The transmission consisted of 10,000 lines, points, and arcs. There was no annotation or dimensioning associativity in the database. Table 8.2 gives the actual time required to transfer an average graphics 0.5-megabyte (4-megabit) file.

Table 8.1

Rated transfer rate, kbits/s	Approximate throughput, kbits/s	Actual time, min
460.00	18.00% = 80	5.6
19.2	30.00% = 5.7	77.0
9.6	30.00% = 3.1	141.0
4.8	60.00% = 2.8	159.0

Table 8.2

Rated transfer rate, kbits/s	Approximate throughput, kbits/s	Actual time, min
460.00	18.00% = 80	0.6
19.2	20.00% = 5.7	9.0
9.6	30.00% = 3.1	16.3
4.8	60.00% = 2.8	18.4

If active work files are required on a daily basis, a tolerable time from the user viewpoint must be established to determine how graphics files are to be stored and transmitted over networks. In a distributed environment where a programmer can plan ahead, a 10- or 15-minute wait might be tolerable. In the case of a detail drafter accessing five or more drawings a day, the same 10-minute wait decreases throughput by 1 hour per day or 12 percent.

CENTRAL ONLINE STORAGE

Central storage offers advantages in control over the database and allows the database to be accessed from all authorized points in the organization. Central storage is sometimes considered more economical from a cost-per-byte perspective. Again, this depends upon the cost of adding incremental disks at the CAD facility vs. the central computing facility. The additional cost of communications hardware and software will affect the cost effectiveness of central or distributed storage. If 4800 bits per second data transfer rates are unacceptable from the user's standpoint, then more expensive communications links will be required. Communications links are technologically feasible in the 50-megabit range and, more commonly, 10 megabits per second over distances 5000 feet or less through local area networks.

8.22.2 Local Area Networks

Local area networks offer high-speed communications at a relatively low cost, usually around $1000 to $2000 per CPU or terminal on the network. The main problem encountered in the desire to use new technology in networking (such as Ethernet) is that it must be made compatible with the large installed base of existing graphics systems. Developers of low-cost workstations will ultimately make the connection to solve the proprietary interface problem created by the current generation of incompatible turnkey systems.

8.22.3 Long-Distance Networking

At distances greater than 5000 feet, public communication carriers offer services at various rates of speed. Table 8.3 gives relative communications costs.

The issue of communications is complicated by new developments in technology. In addition, there is a lack of standardization in the communications marketplace.

Table 8.3 Approximate Costs for Various Communications

Type	Speed	Line costs	Initial hardware and software costs
Phone	300–4800	Standard phone	Modem
Leased line	9600	$100–200 per month	Modem
	56 Kbits/s	$1500 per month plus	DMA
	1.5 Mbits/s	$1500 per month plus	$6000
Microwave	1.5 Mbits/s	$1500 per month or private	$12,000
Satellite	1.5 Mbits/s	$40,000 per month	$12,000

8.23 INTERFACE TO MANUFACTURING

Data movement and reuse of the graphics database offer perhaps the most significant opportunity to improve productivity in a CAD/CAM environment. The speed with which data are transmitted over a communications network may not be as important as *how* the data are organized.

There are four phases of establishing an intelligent communications network for the purpose of merging and extracting geometric and nongraphic data from both new and existing databases throughout an organization.

1. Development of an integration plan
2. Designing of integration architecture
3. Development of integration utilities
4. Development of network utilities

8.23.1 Integration Plan

The integration plan evolves from an analysis of long- and short-term needs. Objectives include

- Improvement of data quality
- Improvement of data availability
- Ease of data movement

8.23.2 Integration Architectures

"Who needs what data" will determine what the integration architectures look like. The exchange of specific data will be required by application programmers. NC programmers, for example, require only the geometry required to generate tool paths. Extraneous geometry may reduce the value of the database to the end user and will take longer to transmit over a network, thereby reducing throughput. In general, manufacturing needs will determine the drawing database layering conventions and the organization of nongraphic attributes of the CAD database.

8.23.3 Integration Utilities

In order to transmit a specific geometry to a particular application group, a set of formatting programs will be required to interrogate an engineering database and thereby extract only what is required by a specific application. A typical application subset will allow database utility programs to search directories for correct application drawings nested within a master part database. Only the necessary part parameters and application data are transmitted over the communications network.

The need for very high-speed communications networks can be reduced by avoiding the transmission of extraneous geometry and annotation over the network. The objectives of the integration utilities should be to:

1. Increase transparency to the end user, allowing the existing data to be used
2. Minimize risks associated with "overdistribution" of data

8.23.4 Network Utilities

Software protocols will be required to make communication links between various vendors of computers. Network utilities should conform to the International Standards Organization (ISO) open-systems architecture reference model for data communications. Application-level programs will be required to interface the system to the highest-level network software. In some cases, high-level software will not be available from vendors of communications hardware. In this situation, interfaces for some systems may have to be written in-house or contracted for from a software firm.

8.24 SUMMARY

The introduction of CAD technology into the engineering community is a relatively new phenomenon for many companies. Manual drafting techniques have not essentially changed for thousands of years. A new, more adaptive perspective of the engineering and manufacturing community will be required by workers as computers have an impact on their everyday activities. A major effort will be required by management to reorient and retrain the general work force if the increases in productivity offered by CAD/CAM technology are to be realized.

Management will be required to exercise greater planning skills when installing various modules of a CAD/CAM system. New systems will be expected to interact and integrate with existing engineering, manufacturing, and business systems. To implement an integrated CAD/CAM system successfully, a larger commitment to management resources will be required than is usually associated with the operation of a turnkey graphics system in an engineering environment.

The engineering and manufacturing community will undergo extensive change as CAD/CAM technology matures and becomes fully adopted by industry in general.

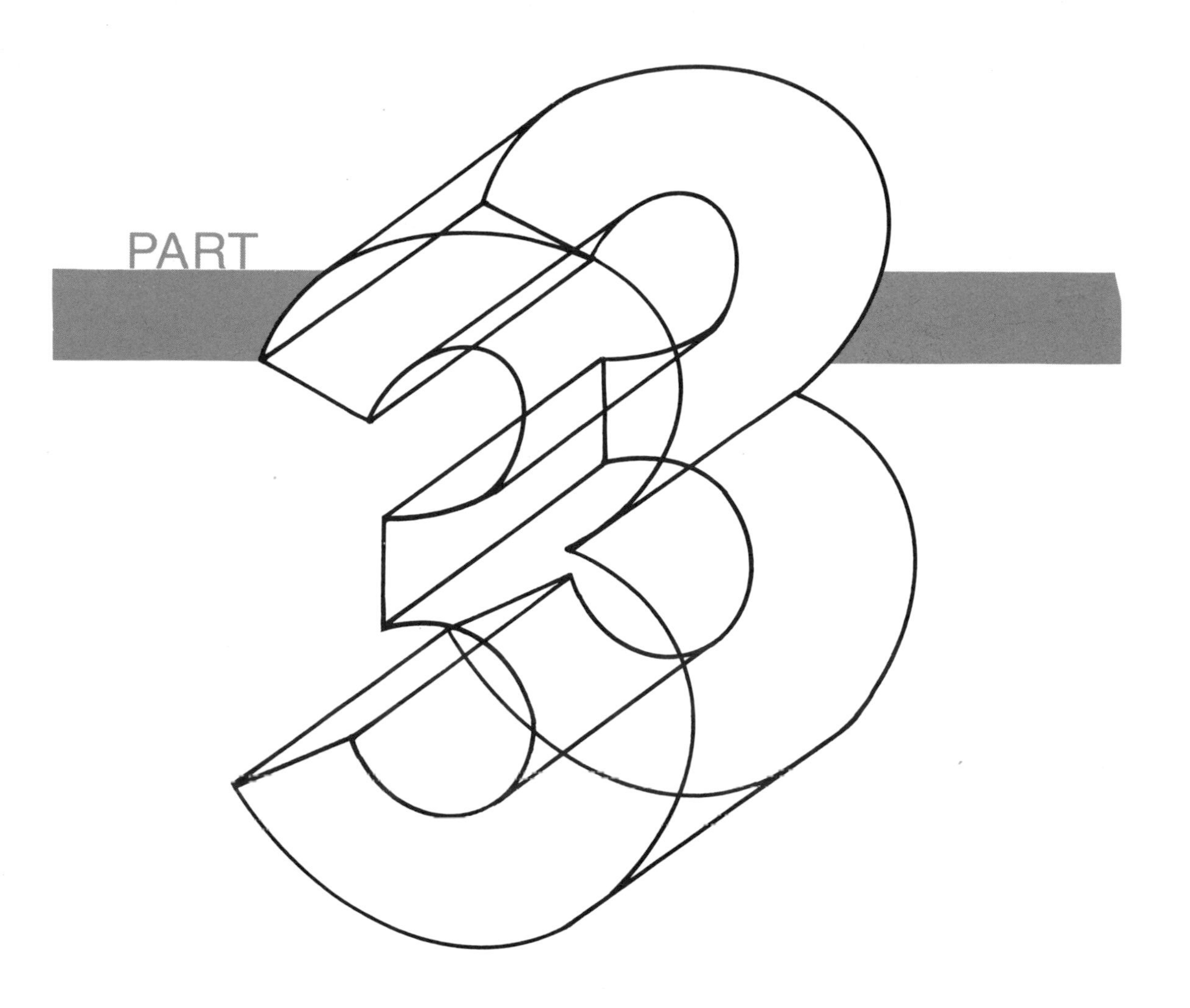

PART 3

APPLICATIONS

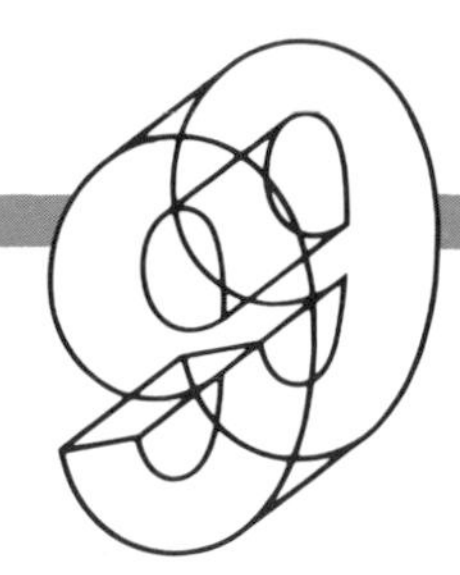

Mechanical Drafting

by
Anthony W. Horn

9.1 INTRODUCTION

9.1.1 Initial Questions

Would you like to be able to draw three times faster than you now draw by hand? How about eight times as fast? When you have been working all day on a complex machine assembly drawing and you suddenly realize that one of its critical dimensions is incorrect, would you like to be able to simply put the proper number onto the sheet and watch the drawing correct itself immediately and automatically? These are no longer incredible questions. Computer-aided design (CAD) systems are doing these things every day, as well as other things that are impossible with conventional drawing methods.

There are a number of very sound reasons for you to consider CAD as a viable mechanical drafting and design tool (see Table 9.1). When these reasons are considered, along with the facts that computer technology is continually improving and hardware and software costs keep decreasing, it is inevitable that within a few years CAD will be the standard drafting and design technique.

Table 9.1 Reasons Design and Manufacturing Firms are Shifting to CAD

Design	Manufacturing	Marketing
Increased productivity	Increased productivity	Excellent marketing tool
Lower drafting costs	Lower drafting costs	Faster project turnaround time
Faster project turnaround time	Lower NC programming and fixture design costs	Better interdepartment communications
Extended design time	Less waste and better verification before manufacturing	Company retention of competitive advantage
Improved quality and consistency	Improved interdepartment communications	Incentive for attracting high-quality personnel
Ability to retain competitive advantage	More accurate cost estimates	More accurate cost estimates
Incentive for attracting high-quality personnel	More efficient change orders	Improved quality and consistency
More efficient change orders		
Staff decentralization		
Improved interdepartment communications		
Improved design analysis		
Greater creative opportunities		
More accurate cost estimates		
Improved filing system		
Better project control		

9.1.2 Types of Mechanical Drawings and Information

Mechanical drafting and design involve a variety of different types of drawings: details, assemblies, sections, developed patterns, and illustrations. These drawings all show the geometric shape and size of a designed part or assembly. They also contain many other pieces of information: standard instructions to the machinist for making the part, material specifications, special procedures, catalogue order numbers, etc.

All these drawings contain two basic categories of data: coordinate-geometric data and descriptive data. The shapes on the drawing convey the first type of information, while the notations, dimensions, and symbols convey the other. CAD systems have all been designed to produce drawings in the same format. CAD systems are essentially data processing systems with easy-to-use, powerful, geometric display capabilities. The higher-performance systems are more versatile in their ability to link together graphic and nongraphic data and have more powerful drafting and modeling capabilities.

9.2 BASIC CAD TWO-DIMENSIONAL DRAFTING

9.2.1 Drawing a Line

One of the fundamental tasks a drafter repeatedly performs is the drawing of a straight, scaled line. Using CAD, drawing a line is begun by specifying its type (a wide variety of line types are available for selection) and its beginning point. To locate a starting point the operator either positions the cursor on the display screen or types in a starting point in x and y grid coordinates. Positioning the cursor on the screen is done by a variety of methods: using a joystick (see Fig. 9.1), thumbwheels, electronic stylus on a tracking data tablet, and the like (see Chap. 3). Once the starting point has been chosen, the operator signals the system by probing an electronic data tablet with a stylus (see Fig. 9.2), and a small square of light appears under the cursor, indicating a current point has been entered (see Fig. 9.3).

Next, the operator uses a "protractor" and "scale" (numeric keypad) area on the tablet to enter the direction and length of the line. Two quick probes with the stylus on the tablet

Figure 9.1 Moving the cursor on the display screen using a joystick.

Figure 9.2 Data tablet used for command input.

enter these commands, and the system promptly displays a scaled line on the screen (see Fig. 9.4). The number of actions required includes the locating of the cursor and several quick probes on the tablet. The normal time for such a basic set of tasks is approximately 5 to 10 seconds.

Compare the CAD method to the conventional method of drawing a line.

1. Select a starting point on the paper and align the straightedge.
2. Draw a light layout line.
3. Move the straightedge out of the way.
4. Pick up a scale and orient it correctly.
5. Accurately measure and mark the proper length.
6. Realign the straightedge.
7. Darken in the line.

The normal time to accomplish all this, for a good drafter, is approximately 30 to 45 seconds (depending on the difficulty in reading and marking the scale). Significant productivity gains start at this basic level.

9.2.2 Circles

Drawing circles and arcs on a CAD system is easy to do. To draw a circle, the operator locates the center with the cursor on the display and probes the tablet to enter this point (see Fig. 9.3). Then the CIRCLE command and the circle diameter are entered by probing the data tablet, and the system responds with the required circle (see Fig. 9.5*a* and *b*). Ellipses are done the same way. In the case of polygons, the center is located and the system asks the number of sides required. The operator enters the desired number, and the polygon is displayed. Polygons of any diameter and virtually any number of sides can be drawn.

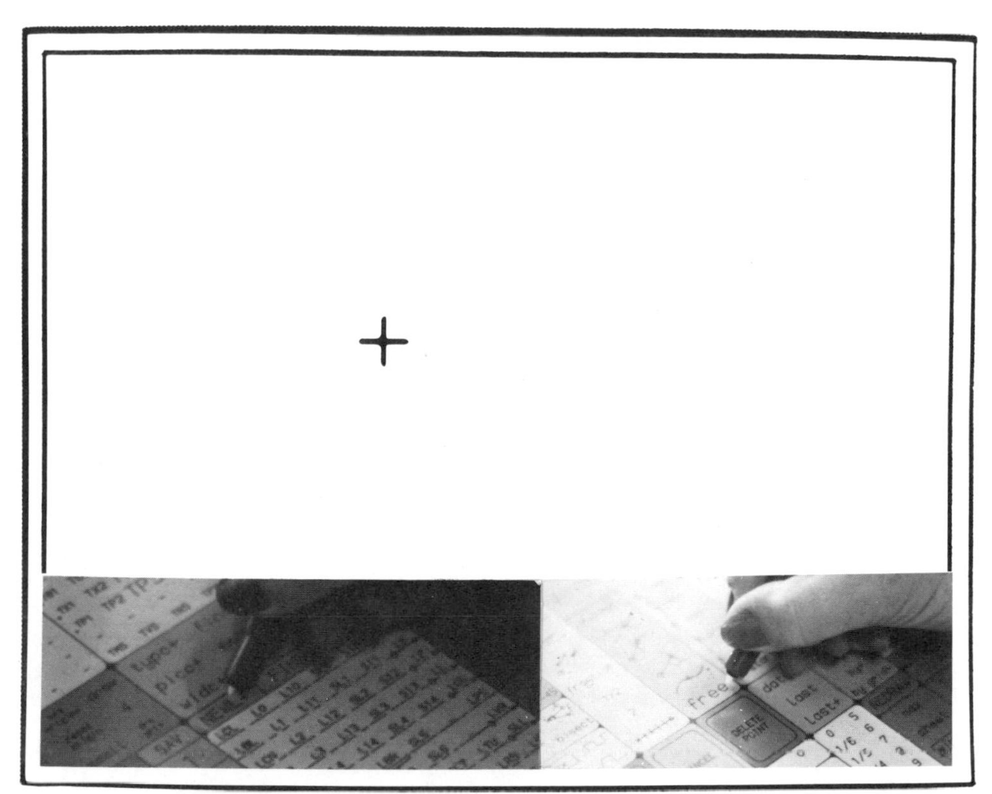

Figure 9.3 Beginning a line. Here the operator specifies a line type and its point of origin.

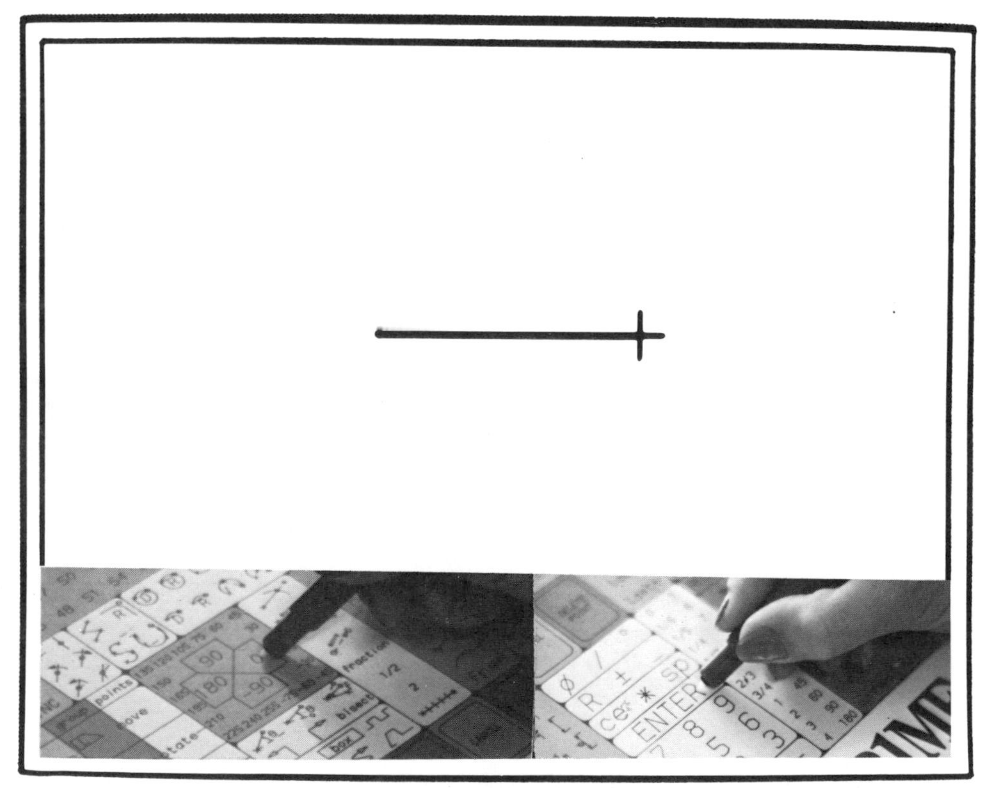

Figure 9.4 Drawing a line. Here the operator instructs the system to draw a line in "direction 0°, distance 4 inches."

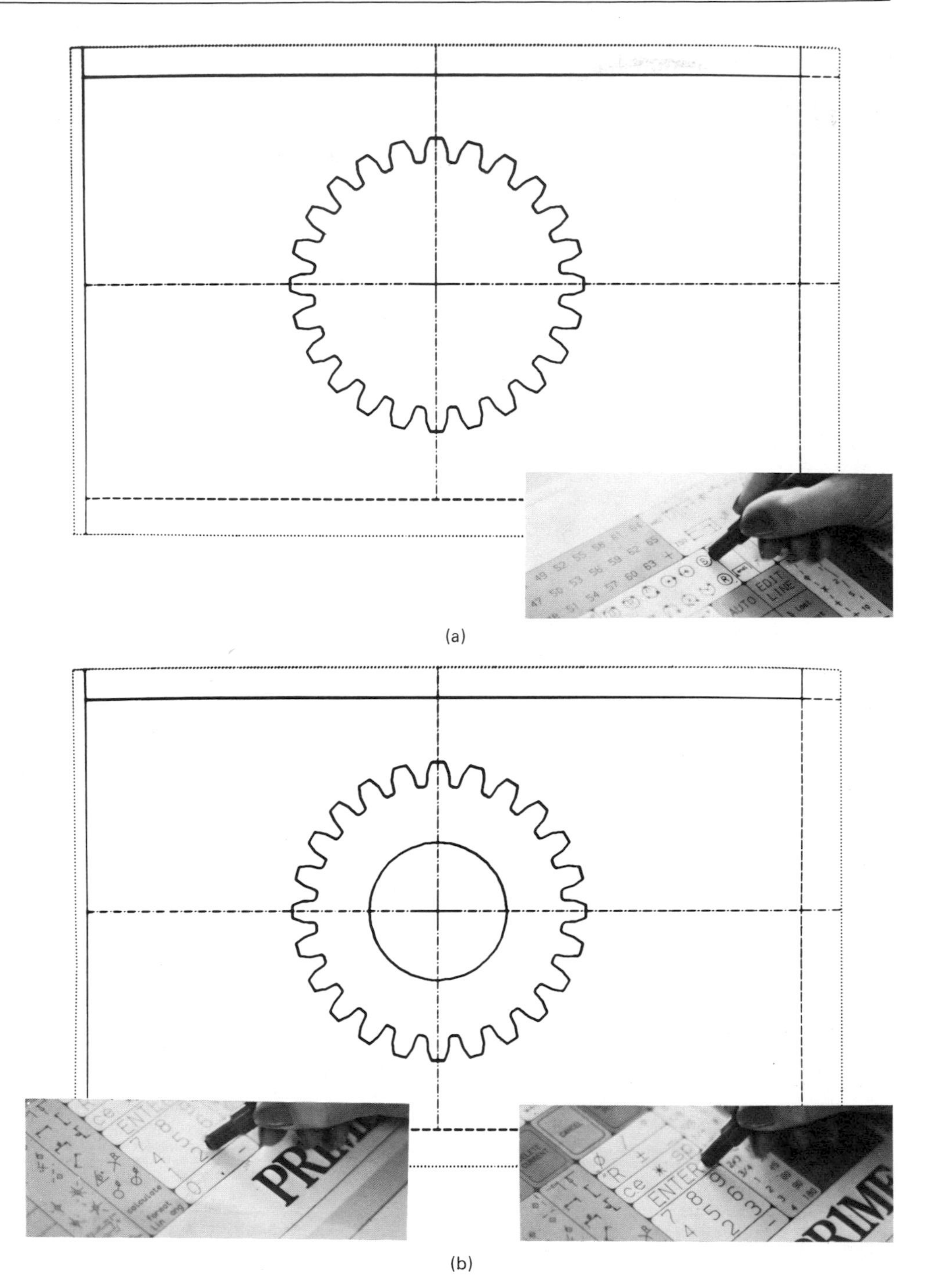

Figure 9.5 Drawing a circle.

9.2.3 Entering Notes and Text

To enter titles, labels, and notes on the drawing, the operator probes the tablet for a particular type of text font. The notation itself is entered through the typewriter keyboard, and after probing an ENTER command, the text appears centered on the cursor. If repositioning is needed, an adjustment grid on the tablet can be probed to reposition the text (see Fig. 9.6).

Many systems have a variety of text fonts available in the libraries. Typical choices

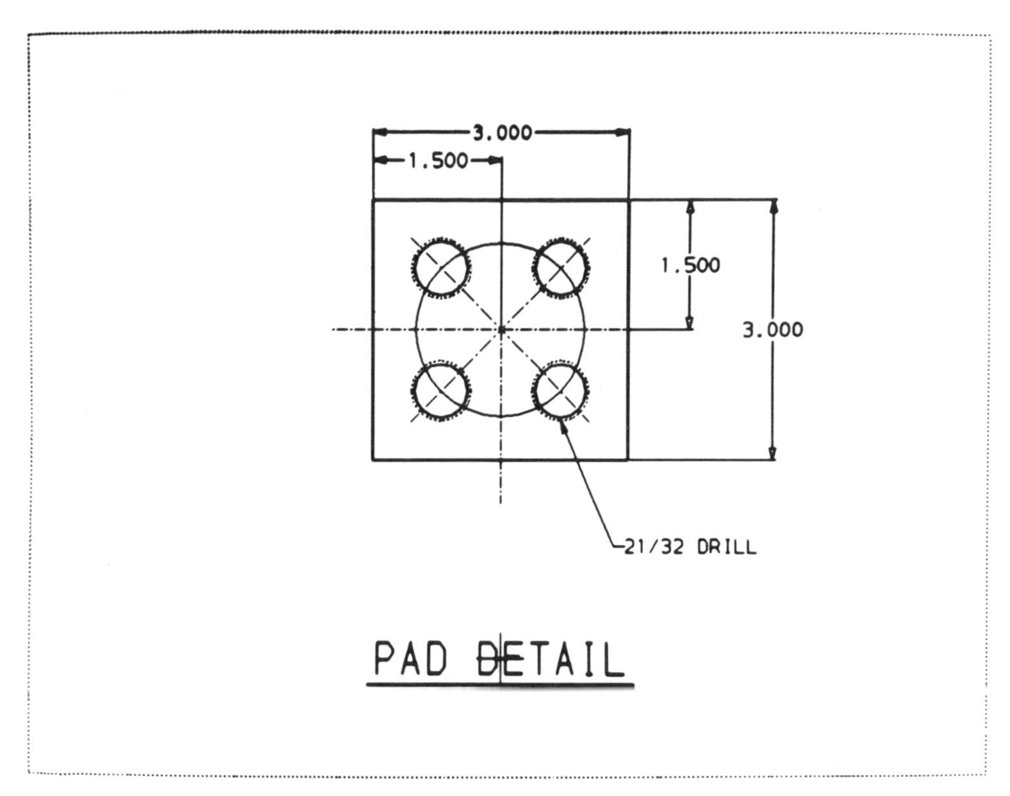

Figure 9.6 Entering notes and text on a CAD system.

include Leroy, English Times, Block, and Speed Font. Height, spacing, justification, and font type can be specified or interactively changed to any desired setting. An excellent feature is the ability to take complete paragraphs that are entered through the text editor and enter them as a whole on the sheet. This is called the TEXT MERGE command, and if the system does not have this feature, it may require a tedious line-by-line entry onto the sheet.

9.2.4 Special Characters

Some CAD systems provide all the special characters normally associated with engineering and mathematical calculations in addition to the alphanumeric characters normally associated with typewritten notes (see Fig. 9.7). These special characters are entered onto the sheet by typing in a code for each particular symbol.

@10	=	²
@11	=	³
@12	=	≠
@13	=	⩽
@14	=	⩾
@15	=	≃
@16	=	≈
@17	=	±
@18	=	√
@19	=	℄
@20	=	α
@21	=	π
@22	=	¢
@23	=	∅
@24	=	Ω
@25	-	~
@26	=	µ
@27	=	°
@28	=	θ
@29	=	Ä
@30	=	Å
@31	=	Ø
@32	=	Ö
@33	=	Ü
@34	=	ä
@35	=	å
@36	=	ø
@37	=	ö
@38	=	ü
@39	=	β

Figure 9.7 Special characters.

9.2.5 Dimensions

One of the biggest time-savers on a CAD system in two-dimensional drafting is the dimensioning capabilities. To dimension an outline, the operator typically must position the cursor over the desired text position on the screen and probe a location point. Then the operator must move the cursor in the vicinity of each point to be picked up in the dimension string and probe the tablet for each entry (see Fig. 9.8).

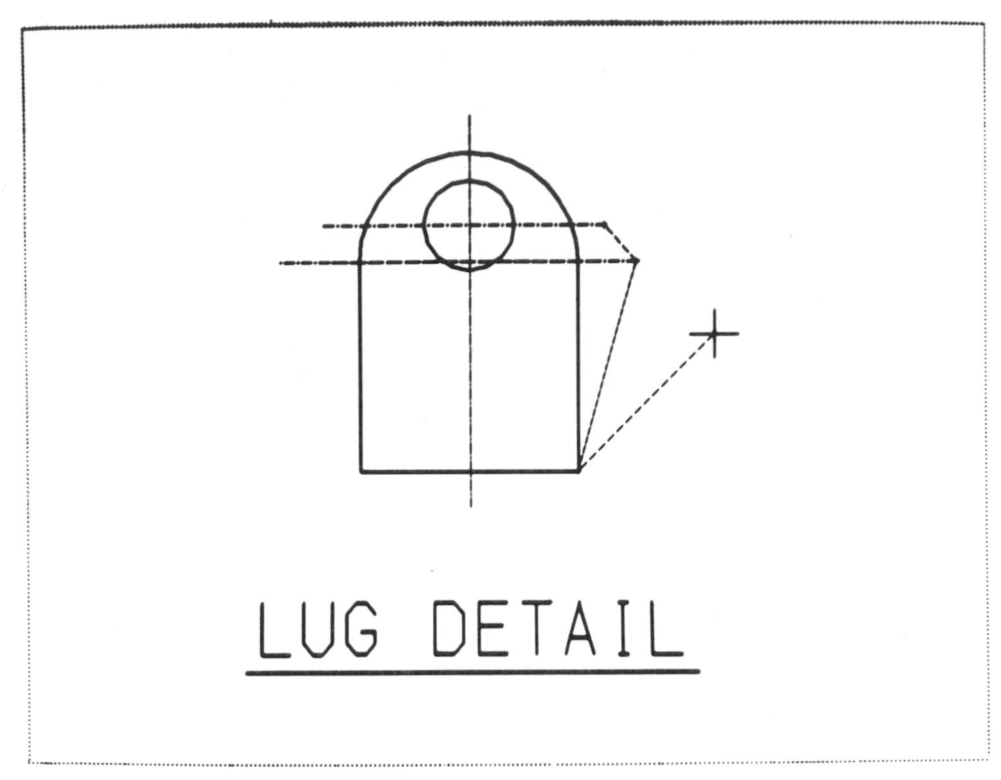

Figure 9.8 Dimensioning an outline.

Once the row of dimensions has been specified, a single probe on the tablet directs the system to calculate all distances and display the dimension string (see Fig. 9.9). Normally, displays appear printed out to three decimals. The operator has the choice of CHAIN, BASELINE, or DATUM dimensions. Tolerance ranges as well as American National Standards Institute (ANSI) or International Standards Organization (ISO) formats may be selected. Some systems work in either metric or English units. Another desirable feature is the ability to input and output dimensions in feet and inches as well as fractions. This feature is of high value, since it saves converting units and allows direct scaled input.

9.2.6 Layers

CAD systems structure a drawing into a series of layers, comparable to using a collection of transparent overlays when drawing with conventional techniques. The obvious difference is that on the CAD system, the layers are handled electronically rather than physically. Generally, outlines are placed on one layer, centerlines on another, dimensions on yet another, and so on (see Fig. 9.10). By using such layering assignments, the operator can produce drawings with selected information on them. For instance, a drawing plotted using layers number 1 and number 4 would show only outlines and dimensions, but not general notes (layer 6) or crosshatching (layer 5).

Layering allows flexibility in both the viewing and the plotting of a drawing. For instance, a drawing can be used for both sales and production through selective plotting of recorded data. On the sales drawing, the outlines could be shown by having layer number 1 turned on. Sales information could be entered onto the drawing placed on layer number 20. When using the drawing for a sales presentation, layers number 1 and 20 only could be plotted. To use the same drawing for production, the operator would turn off layer number 20 (containing sales information) and complete the drawing by adding dimensions, cross-hatching, general notes, etc.

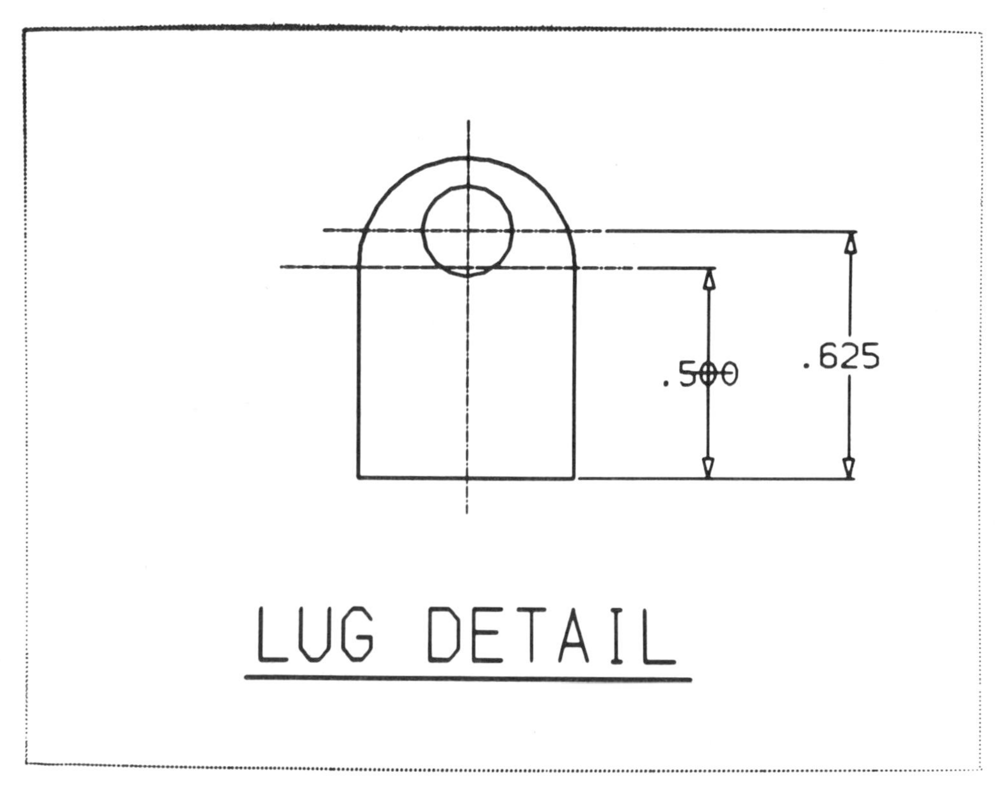

Figure 9.9 Once the row of dimensions has been specified, a single probe on the tablet directs the system to calculate all distances and display the dimension string.

9.2.7 Cross-hatching

Crosshatching capabilities (see Fig. 9.11), like many other features, vary widely. Some systems require the operator to trace the desired area to be crosshatched; other systems automatically crosshatch certain "active" lines. Some systems have numerous crosshatch patterns available in the libraries. This is a beneficial feature, but the importance of it depends on how easily the system allows the operator to create new patterns through repeated cross-hatchings with multiple line types. For instance, an aluminum pattern is composed of one set of solid lines at 45°, followed by another set of dashed lines superimposed at −45°. Such a pattern can be done very easily if it is stored in the pattern

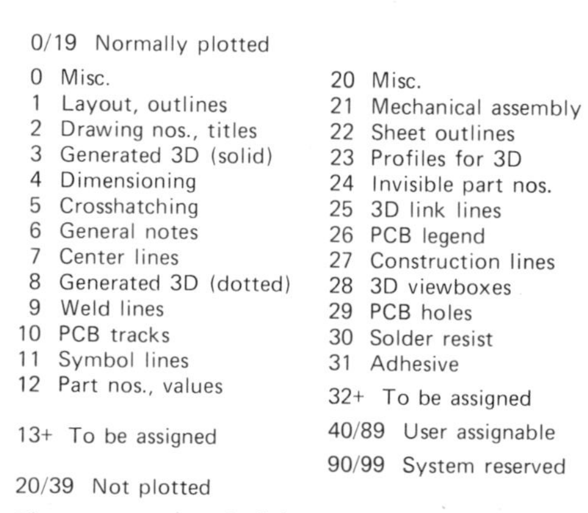
0/19 Normally plotted

0 Misc.
1 Layout, outlines
2 Drawing nos., titles
3 Generated 3D (solid)
4 Dimensioning
5 Crosshatching
6 General notes
7 Center lines
8 Generated 3D (dotted)
9 Weld lines
10 PCB tracks
11 Symbol lines
12 Part nos., values

13+ To be assigned

20/39 Not plotted

20 Misc.
21 Mechanical assembly
22 Sheet outlines
23 Profiles for 3D
24 Invisible part nos.
25 3D link lines
26 PCB legend
27 Construction lines
28 3D viewboxes
29 PCB holes
30 Solder resist
31 Adhesive

32+ To be assigned

40/89 User assignable

90/99 System reserved

Figure 9.10 Typical layering conventions for CAD systems.

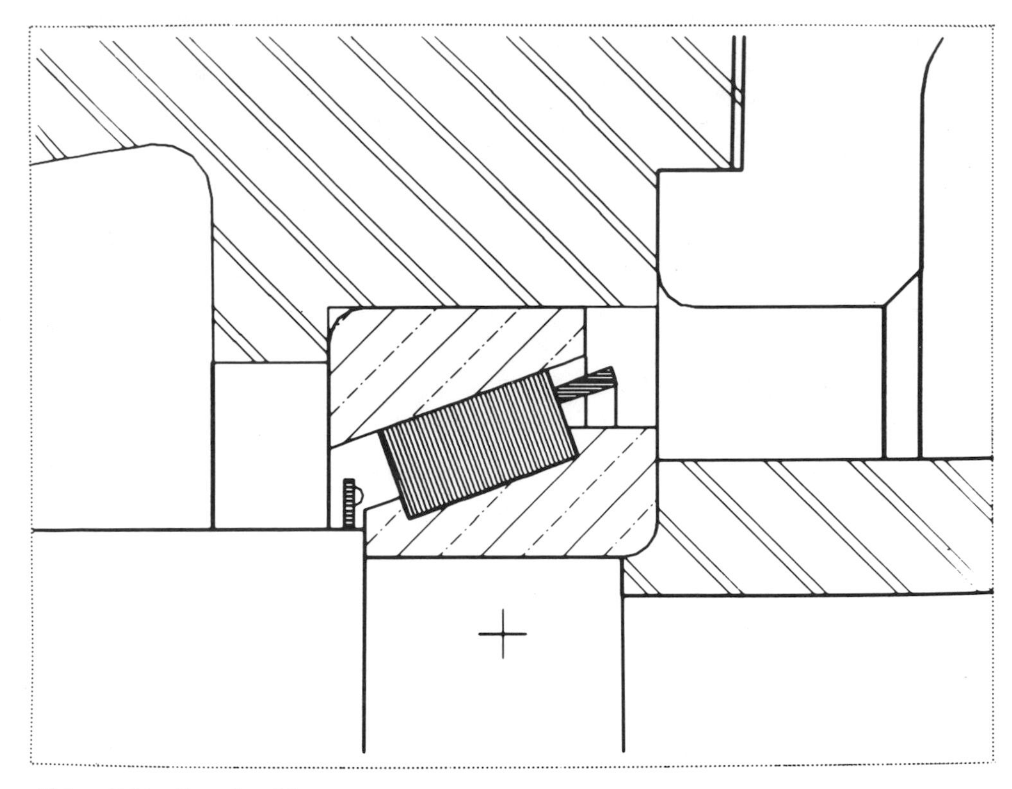

Figure 9.11 Cross-hatching.

library or if the system allows simple multiple passing. However, it can be a tedious assignment if the system requires tracing the figure outline before each pass.

9.2.8 Construction Lines

Advanced construction line capabilities can include constructing tangents to specified circles (see Fig. 9.12*a*) creating the outline of a tapered part (see Fig. 9.12*b*). Once the outline has been constructed, the part can be drawn in finished form by tracing over the construction lines with solid lines and removing them (Fig. 9.13).

9.2.9 Grids

CAD systems are based on a standard cartesian coordinate system, which locates points in terms of x, y, and z coordinates. Most systems allow interactive displaying and use of an xy grid to help in locating points on the drawing (Fig. 9.14). Usually this grid can be selectively viewed and switched from active to inactive status. When the grid is displaying in 1/4-inch increments and it is switched to the active mode, all points entered onto the sheet will snap to the nearest grid intersection. This creates, in effect, a drawing that is constructed to a 1/4-inch tolerance. If the operator needs a small grid displayed, the system can show a 10×10 grid around the last point constructed. Other grid commands might include reset origin, set grid size, or draw every nth grid line.

9.2.10 Grouping and Transformations

A timesaving feature found on most systems is the capability of grouping elements in a group line and manipulating them temporarily as a unit (Fig. 9.15). This enables the operator to transform (move, rotate, magnify, mirror) them or erase them all at once.

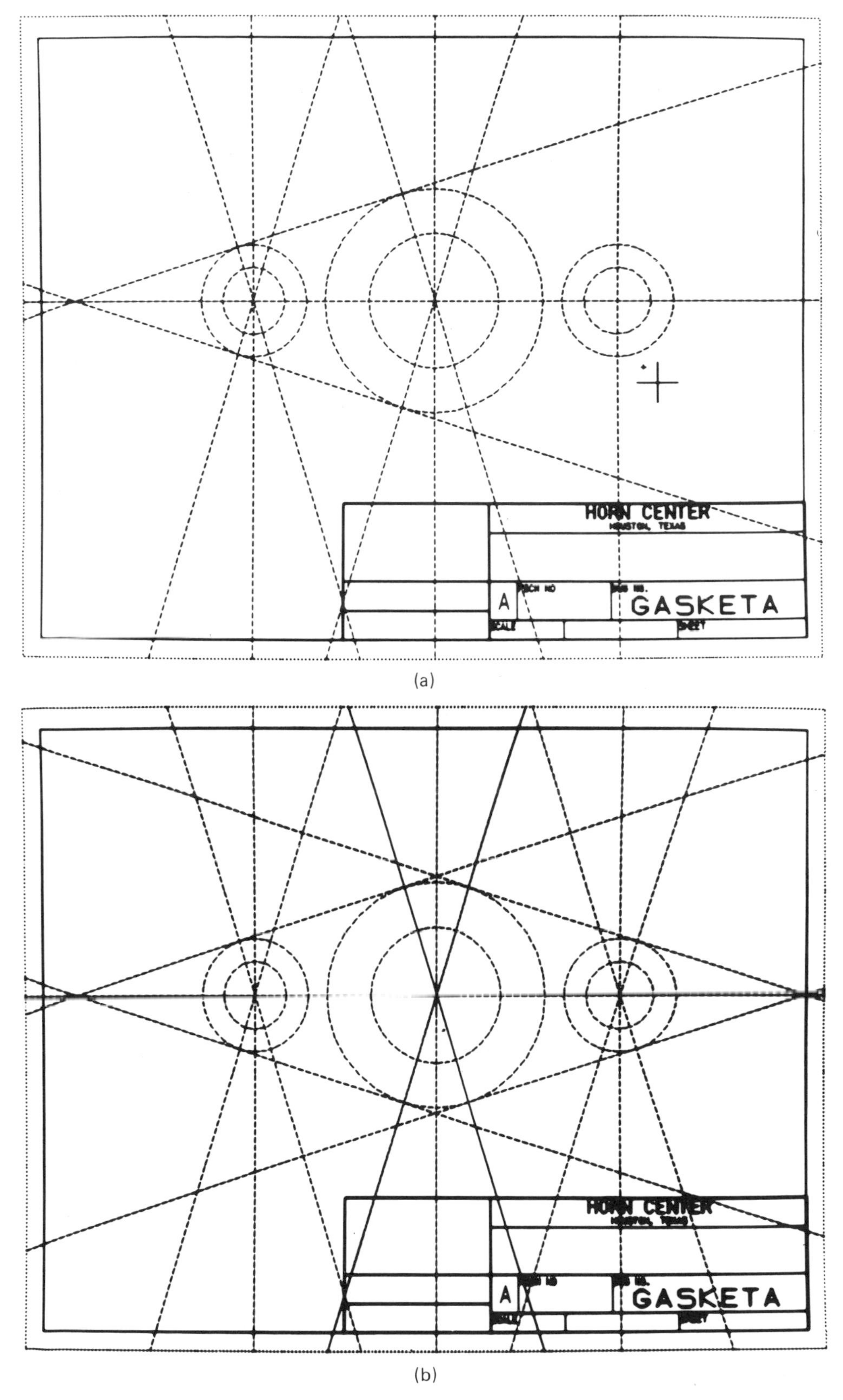

(a)

(b)

Figure 9.12 Constructing (*a*) tangents to specified circles, which (*b*) creates the outline of a tapered part.

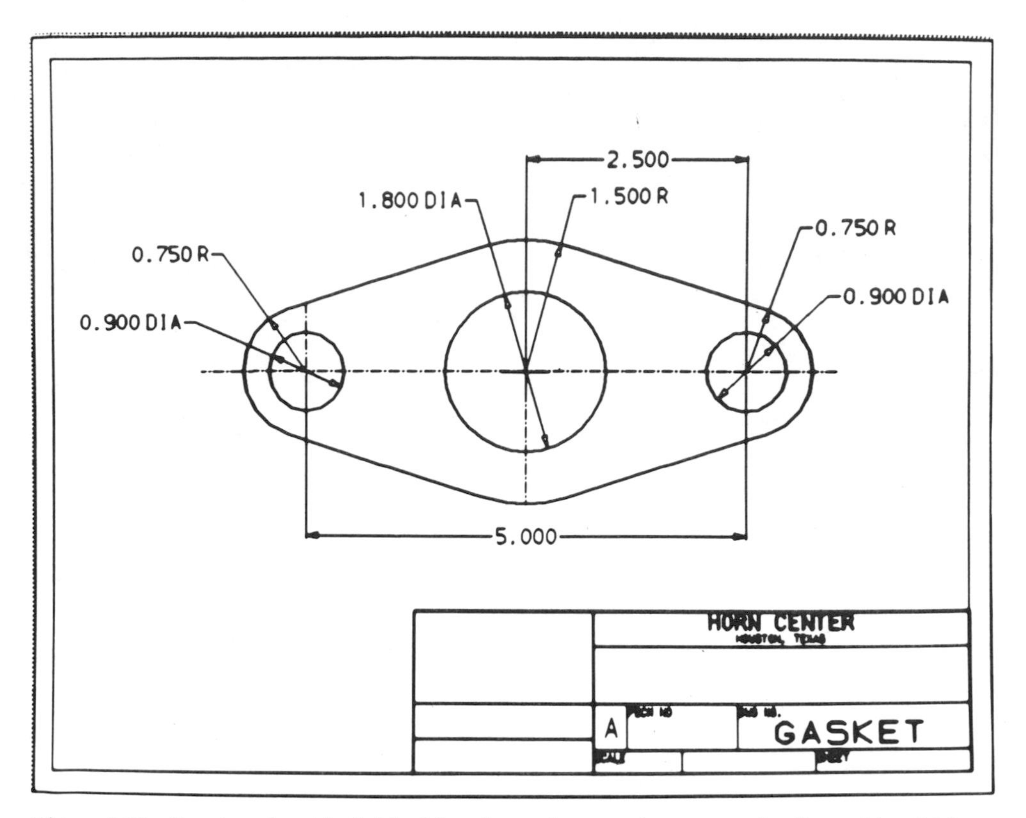

Figure 9.13 Drawing of part in finished form by tracing over the construction lines with solid lines and removing them.

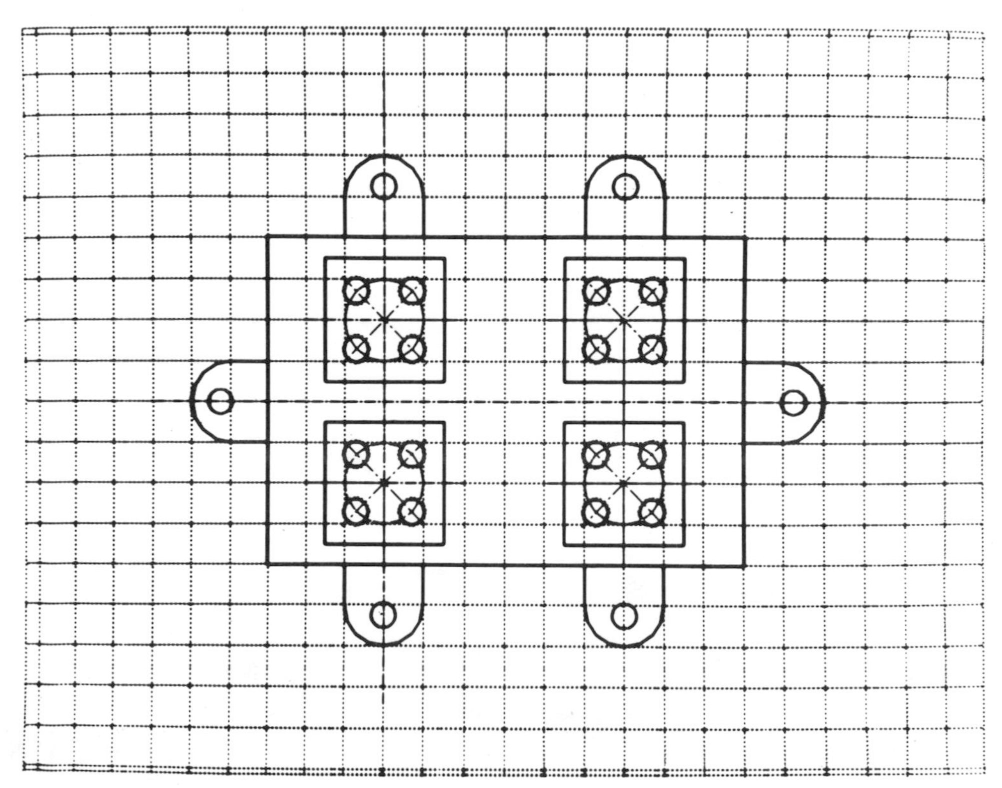

Figure 9.14 Use of an xy grid to help in locating points on a drawing.

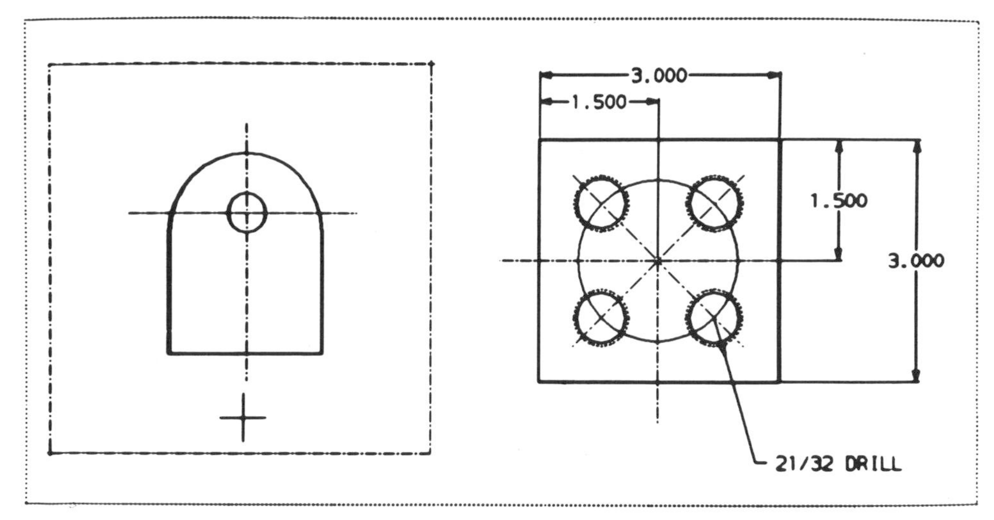

Figure 9.15 Grouping of elements in a group line and manipulating them temporarily as a unit.

Furthermore, the group may be sent to a temporary storage location in memory to be called back again several times during the course of a drawing as a repetitive detail. This frees the operator from having to draw something more than once. In Fig. 9.15, a part has been grouped and unloaded (sent to temporary storage).

After the various detail groups have been stored, they may be called back onto the sheet and rotated, magnified, mirrored (transformed) to construct an assembled view (Fig. 9.16).

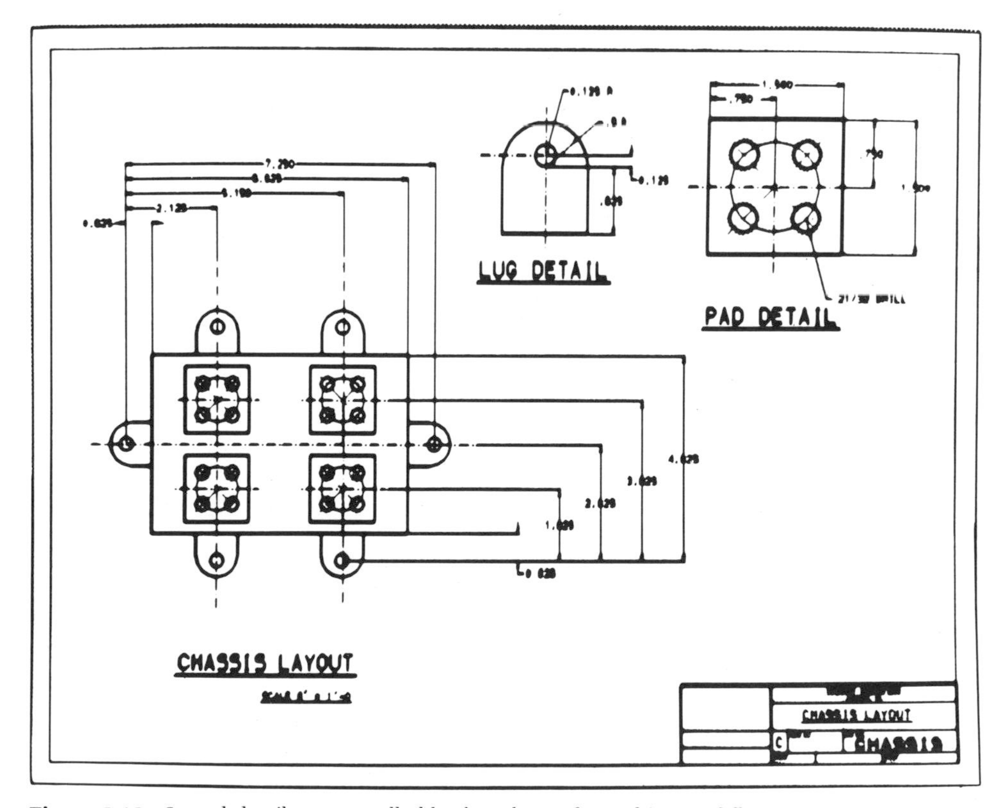

Figure 9.16 Stored detail groups called back and transformed into a different view.

9.3 MECHANICAL CAD SOFTWARE

9.3.1 Overview

Versatility and elegance in CAD comes from two sources: the hardware devices themselves (all have inherent limitations) and the software (programs) that operates on the hardware. Many available systems are sold as turnkey units, so evaluation of these must be done on the entire package.

Generally, the most striking differences among systems result from their variations in software capabilities. Two systems with comparable hardware can perform vastly different levels of tasks because of software differences. Hardware can be seen and compared, but software takes closer evaluation and understanding before one can be sure of what the system can actually do.

Mechanical CAD software consists of various combinations of programs and data files from the following categories:

1. Drawing administration
2. General drafting and geometrics
3. Bills of materials
4. Graphic data analysis
5. Solids modeling
6. Three-dimensional viewing
7. Model analysis
8. Application software
9. Interfaces to third-party software
10. Database management

Look at Fig. 9.17 for a block diagram of these program groups. Each of these software programs performs some specialized task required in a drafting-design environment. No system on the market today contains a full complement of working programs from every single group. Some design systems have been configured through extensive user input to perform almost all of these various functions, but commercially marketed systems do not.

9.3.2 Symbol Libraries

Some vendors offer a mechanical symbol library as part of their system. Generally these symbols consist of typical fasteners, washers, etc. It is also possible to include such things as typical patterns, as well as tolerance and finish marks (although these may be considered under another category).

A well-documented library can account for significant productivity gains because it relieves the operator from drawing a repetitive figure or detail more than once. Things to consider when reviewing offered libraries include the appropriateness to your particular needs and the ease with which the symbols can be retrieved and loaded onto a sheet. It is advantageous to have at least several hundred symbols available for immediate use. If there is a lot of searching and loading from storage media onto a current disk before use, there will be wasted time resulting in lower productivity.

It is worthwhile to request an actual demonstration of symbol creation and use when looking at any particular system before purchase. No matter how many symbols are provided with the system (if any), there is always a need to create special ones. The number of steps and the degree of difficulty in creating and storing symbols vary with each system, so this is a good point for comparison.

If library security and protection rights are important, these should be considered also. Some firms prefer to have a central control over all symbols, giving full access rights to use by all drafters and designers but not allowing them the right to overwrite or delete an

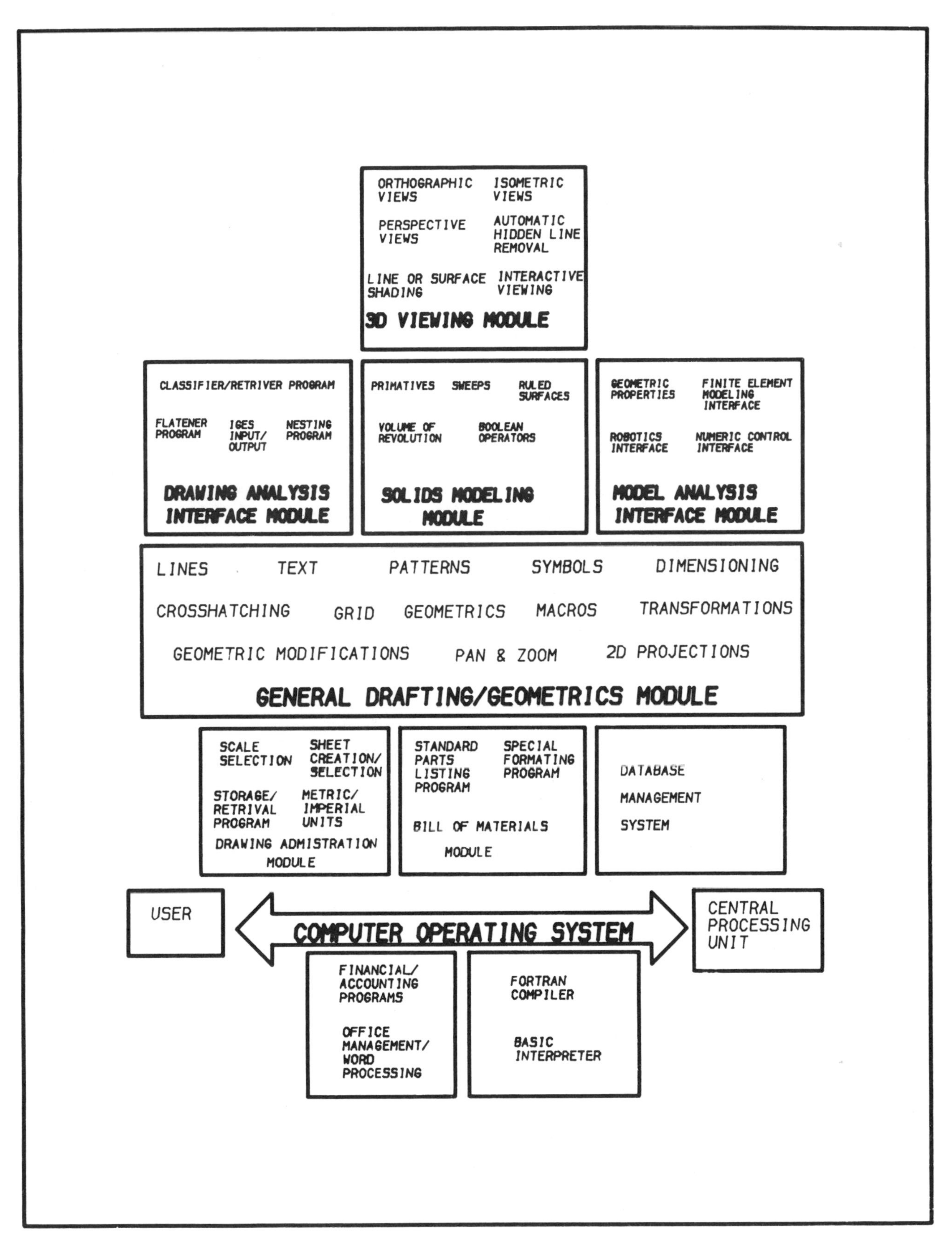

Figure 9.17 Block diagram of mechanical CAD software.

existing library symbol. This maintains uniformity on all documentation and also protects important details from inadvertent loss.

9.3.3 Flattening Programs

Flattening programs are available as purchased software on some commercial systems. These programs take a three-dimensional part and unfold it into a flat pattern layout. Conventionally, designers calculate bend allowances and angles using calculators or tables to arrive at the necessary setbacks and tangents. With multiple bends this gets increasingly difficult, so the automating of these tasks saves a lot of effort.

Once the developed patterns have been completed, they may be nested on some systems through a nesting and flame-cutting program. Generally these programs allow interactive orientation and placement of parts on the display while automatically maintaining a minimum clearance between parts. These packages also allow use of the leftover material from interior voids and will report on the number of pieces fitted onto the sheet as well as the percentage of plate utilized.

On some systems it is possible to create numerical control tapes by simulating the tool path on the displayed layout (see Chap. 16). The operator normally has to command the sequence of machining, the beginning and exit points of the cut, bridges between parts if necessary, and the required clearances for cutting or burning. Once tool paths have been generated, the system can output either a source program or a cutter location file, depending upon the particular software capabilities.

9.3.4 Bill of Material

Bill of material programs are available on some CAD systems. These programs vary widely in their ability to record and output specifications along with the graphics of the drawing. Usually these programs count piece-mark symbols on the sheet and format the data stored inside them. Inside each piece mark are several data entry locations (Fig. 9.18). Each of these entries has a different classification of text automatically assigned to it by the program, so that the system recognizes all entries of type A text to be item number, all entries in type B text to be name, etc. As the system scans the sheet, it formats the entries into columns and outputs a bill of material file (see Fig. 9.19).

Parts listing programs get more versatile when they allow the operator or system administrator to modify the format. This opens up the choices of available formats for each user to shape as needs dictate. Bill of material programs are an excellent example of CAD systems being extended beyond simple graphic tasks and taking on data processing tasks. When these programs are utilized thoughtfully and fully into the users' operations, they can provide accurate and extensive parts lists and material takeoffs automatically.

9.4 DEVELOPING A MECHANICAL DATABASE

9.4.1 Overview

Mechanical database is the name of the collection of elements and their attributes,* symbols, details, macros, and application programs in a CAD system. The schema of a database and its ability to associate various types of descriptive data with the graphic coordinate data are major determinants in the database's effectiveness in creating reports, bills of material, etc.

As the CAD system is used and the symbols, drawings, and documentation accumulate, the mechanical database becomes as valuable a resource to the company as the hardware itself. The need to organize, use, and protect these data effectively becomes one

*Attributes include such things as position, type, and erasability.

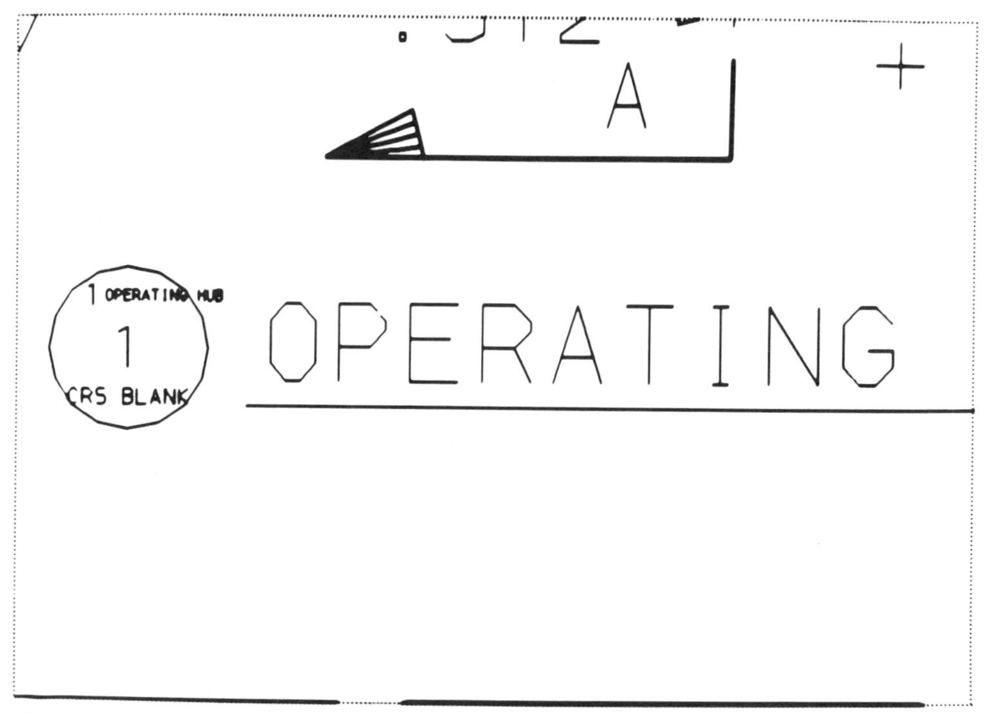

Figure 9.18 Detail of a piece-mark symbol showing locations for entry of text used to make a bill of material. These piece marks can be scanned by the system to output a bill of material for the sheet.

of the central issues in getting the most out of the system. Ideally, the symbols, standard details, macros, and user programs should be an independent collection of accessible data, available to all operators and programmers. This allows flexible and full use of the data, since they are not defined in a particular document or user directory only. A

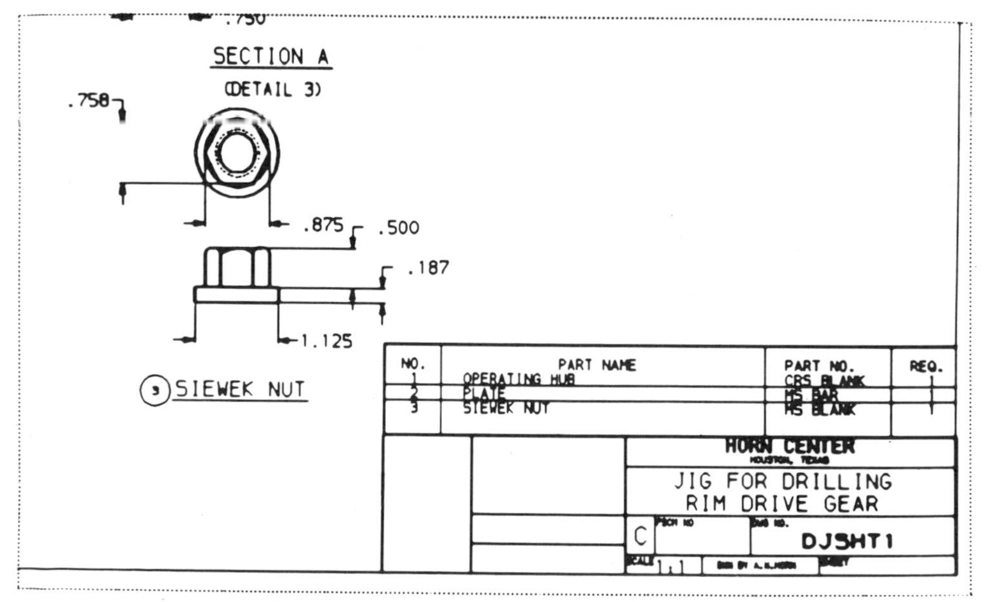

Figure 9.19 Finished bill of material. All the data listed were generated automatically by the system by reading and sorting the data contained in the piece marks.

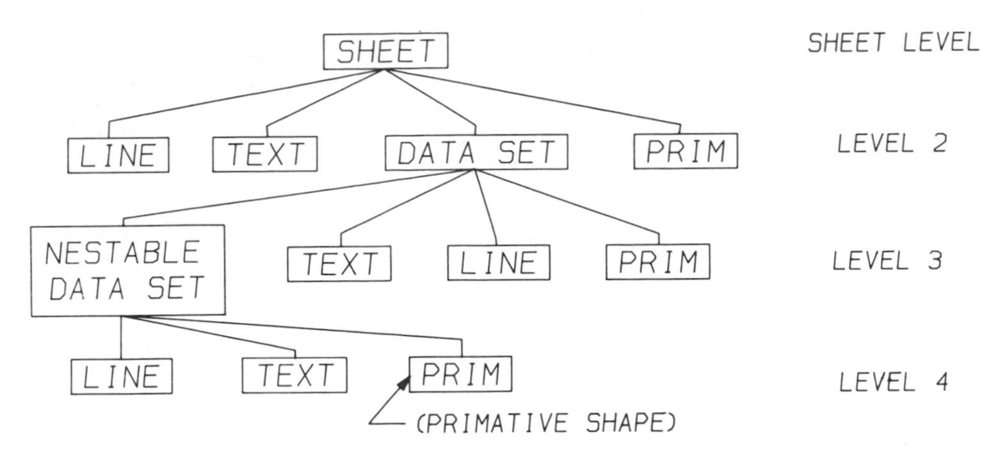

Figure 9.20 Typical mechanical database structure.

properly set-up organization makes the efficient managing of data much easier from the start.

Most mechanical CAD systems have hierarchical database structures* (see Fig. 9.20). This is effective and appropriate for mechanical design because machines are essentially hierarchical in character, i.e., assemblies, subassemblies, and elements.

Some of the more advanced systems offer a feature called *database management*. Database management systems (DBMS) allow and facilitate describing, modifying, manipulating, and maintaining data for multiple applications. Basically, DBMS works by using a single data occurrence in multiple structural relationships accessed by many different users. This reduces duplication and inconsistencies in different files. The DBMS program contains internal pointers separate from the data; these pointers facilitate searches and updates through multiple access methods (direct, keyed, or calculated). These programs include specific commands to maintain and manipulate the database as needed. For instance, once a project has been designed and documented, the system can be asked to provide a schedule of parts based on various parameters. The operator may need a list of components supplied by vendor A or the most expensive purchased items listed in descending order. For firms wanting extensive querying and reporting capabilities, using DBMS can be an invaluable tool in fully implementing and utilizing a CAD system.

9.4.2 User-Generated Symbols

One example of building up a database occurs in the creating of standard symbols. No matter what system is chosen, it is inevitable that the users will be generating their own unique additions to the symbol libraries. The easier this is to do and the more variety allowed and space available for these figures, the better.

User-generated symbols frequently consist of special fasteners or details which often occur in a particular specialty. Symbols are usually created as data cells, or sets. To create a symbol, the operator instructs the system to open up a new data set for input. The graphics of the symbol are then created using special set lines. Next, specifications are entered into the set using a special text.

On more advanced systems, each specification heading is entered using a different type of text, which allows the system to retrieve specific data as ordered. For instance, the operator can ask for a count of all items of a particular type, the total cost of a particular group, or the expected delivery time of a necessary component. Such a capability falls under the heading of database management and is commercially available on some systems (see Chap. 3). After completing the graphics and specifications, the data set is closed and the symbol is stored in the system library as a numbered file. Copies of it may

* Other types of database schemas include Network and Relational.

be called up for use repeatedly on future sheets, and its associated data can be retrieved as needed for parts lists, reports, etc.

Symbols and detail files can be tremendous time-savers because it means literally that the user only has to draw something one time. After that it will be stored somewhere, allowing the transfer of its relevant information to a new sheet, with modifications added as necessary to complete the task. This is one of the major sources of CAD productivity gains.

9.4.3 User-Generated Macros

Command files written in CAD command language are called *macros* or *quickactions*. These are user-generated programs that execute a particular group of drawings or administrative tasks. For example, a macro can be written which links the necessary sequence of commands to automatically set up a new drawing sheet in the proper scale, units, and sheet size then asks the operator to input a drawing title. Macros can also be something as versatile as a program that draws a particular shape to be manufactured by the user's company. The operator can run the program, and as it processes, it pauses and asks the operator to specify certain critical dimensions. Once the system receives the needed specifics, it goes ahead and accurately draws out the part, crosshatches it automatically, and dimensions it. If the user's company manufactures a family of products, such macros can greatly automate the drawing process.

Any repetitive operation is a potential candidate for becoming the subject of a macro. The key to writing these files easily lies in the versatility and fullness of the CAD command language and its syntax. The more flexible and varied the commands, the greater the productivity gains possible.

Before advanced macros can be written, the system must be capable of pausing in the midst of executing such a file and allowing operator input of a specific number before it continues to process the file. This capability is not available on some of the lower-cost automated drafting systems, but its inclusion adds a great deal to the number and types of macros which can be developed.

9.4.4 User-Generated Programs

As a CAD system gets more fully used, it can be customized to do specific tasks through user programming. This can involve taking generated graphic data and using certain critical dimensions as input into a computer analysis program. The CAD data are processed by the computer according to the program instructions to calculate useful properties or results, such as geometric analysis, or automatically sizing molds from drawn castings through the use of known shrinkage allowances. Purchased applications software is done the same way. This software involves general cases and frequently tackles problems too difficult for an average user to attempt.

User programming is an extremely inviting area to investigate because the payoffs are so rewarding in terms of the drafting and design hours saved through automating various tasks. These programs are written in BASIC or Fortran and may require the computer to perform numeric calculations or reformat certain groups of data. Once the program has finished its analysis, its results are produced in a usable form for the CAD system to comprehend as command input so that it may continue to draw a modified or new display as ordered by the program.

Programming skills can add a great deal to the usefulness of a CAD system because they let the users expand the system's capabilities to suit their own needs. If there is some particular problem or activity the system is not able to accomplish, a program can often be written to achieve that result. Needless to say, this can get very costly if too much programming effort is required. The ideal situation is to have a system with extensive capabilities built in and develop a limited number of specialized programs to integrate it as fully as possible into normal business operations.

9.5 SOLIDS MODELING

9.5.1 Introduction to Solids Modeling

Solids modeling (see also Chapter 13) is one of the major advances in CAD systems to become commercially available recently. The term *solids modeling* is used to describe a program that instructs the computer how to build an accurate mathematical model of a three-dimensional object (see Chap. 15). There are a couple of ways this can be done, but once the object has been mathematically described, the information can be used in many application programs. For instance, the system may be ordered to generate various orthographic and perspective views of the model automatically. Other applications might apply the output from the modeling program as input into an NC program, or it can be used to program intelligent robots, describing the three-dimensional shapes they manipulate. The mathematical model becomes the key to numerous downstream applications.

Even though they have been under development since the late 1960s, until 1982 only a few solids modeling systems were actually in existence. By the end of this decade, they are expected to be making widespread contributions into the way mechanical parts are being designed, documented, and manufactured.

There have been two main reasons for the rapid emergence of this technology. First has been the refinements in computers themselves, which allow smaller computers to handle the massive calculations required for solids modeling. Only recently the development of "super minis" has taken place; these super minicomputers have the power that previously only existed on huge mainframe computers. Second, there has been a need to enhance the productivity of CAD systems beyond the level of simple automated drafting packages.

The basic difference between a conventional CAD system and a system capable of solids modeling is that the computer is programmed to build a model of a solid object that recognizes the connections between edges and surfaces. Early attempts at three-dimensional representations used a wire-frame model to describe the object. This was ambiguous because the wire frame can represent either a solid or a void. The model is not clearly defined because it does not represent the relationship between the edges and the surfaces. The next step beyond a simple wire frame is to cover the wire frame with mathematically defined surfaces. This enables the computer to generate realistic views and to instruct milling machines how to mill the surface of the model, but it is still incomplete because it does not represent a solid mass. A cloaked surface can still enclose a solid or a void.

Important in evaluating solids modeling systems is the extent to which the vendor has been able to interface the results of the modeling calculations with application and analysis programs. For instance, if finite-element modeling is required, there should be easily implemented interfaces to the major industry programs such as ANSYS and NASTRAN. If NC is being implemented, there should be direct interfaces to APT and COMPACT II (postprocessors should also be available for a wide variety of machine tools).

The step up from wire-frame models to solids models represents a significant improvement in CAD technology. The difference between them is comparable to the difference in using a straightedge versus an automated drafting system because of the complexity involved in modeling the surface connectivity. However, the results possible from these systems are much more extensive than has been heretofore possible, and they represent the current state of maximum performance and technology.

9.5.2 Technical Illustrations

One of the most radical impacts made by CAD is occurring in the realm of technical illustration. CAD systems are demonstrating they can deliver large productivity gains over conventional techniques (the computer-animated films of today reveal the potential).

Once a mathematical model of the part has been built in the computer, various views can be rendered by the viewing programs. These vary in scope from limited viewing to full

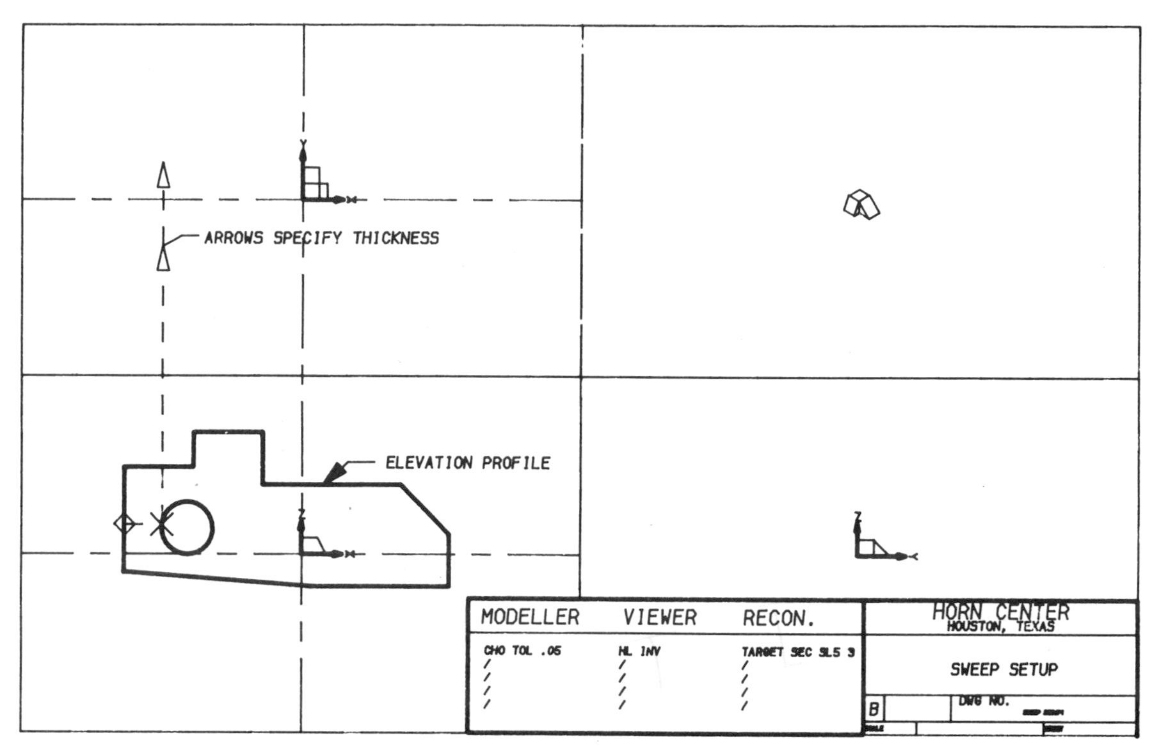

Figure 9.21 Elevation view of a plate, with the thickness specified by the "link" line arrowheads in the plan view. This is basically all the information needed by a solids modeling system to generate a model and specified views of the part.

interactive viewing capabilities. When these viewing programs let the operator specify the station point and viewing angles, they allow virtually any three-point perspective desired. When these are coupled with fully automatic hidden line removal capabilities, the time savings are enormous; drawings that used to take days now can be modeled in a matter of minutes.

Parts can be illustrated by constructing them in several different ways, depending on the system. Some large vendors still require the drawing to be generated as a wire frame first, then processed further into a solid; others have software that directly generates several types of solids. Once modeled, the view can be shaded in smooth tones.

Some powerful systems use standard drafting techniques to model a part. These are boundary file representation (B-rep) modeling systems [another type, constructive solid geometry (CSG) systems are also common]. In this approach, a particular view is drawn (elevation, plan, etc.), and the depth is specified in another view (see Figs. 9.21 through 9.24). The computer takes that information and uses it to model the part. These systems are sometimes configured to allow boolean operations (see Fig. 9.25), which give the added versatility necessary to model more complex sculptured shapes (see Chap. 13).

CAD makes it possible to set up an illustration and documentation department electronically; this involves coupling the CAD system to a text processing system, then merging these on a composition system. The output of the composition system can be processed in a typesetting system, producing a finished, printed, illustrated page.

9.6 CONCLUSIONS

9.6.1 General Considerations

Evaluating and choosing a mechanical CAD system can be a difficult task at best, and an impossible one without advanced preparation. Use the checklist at the end of this chapter

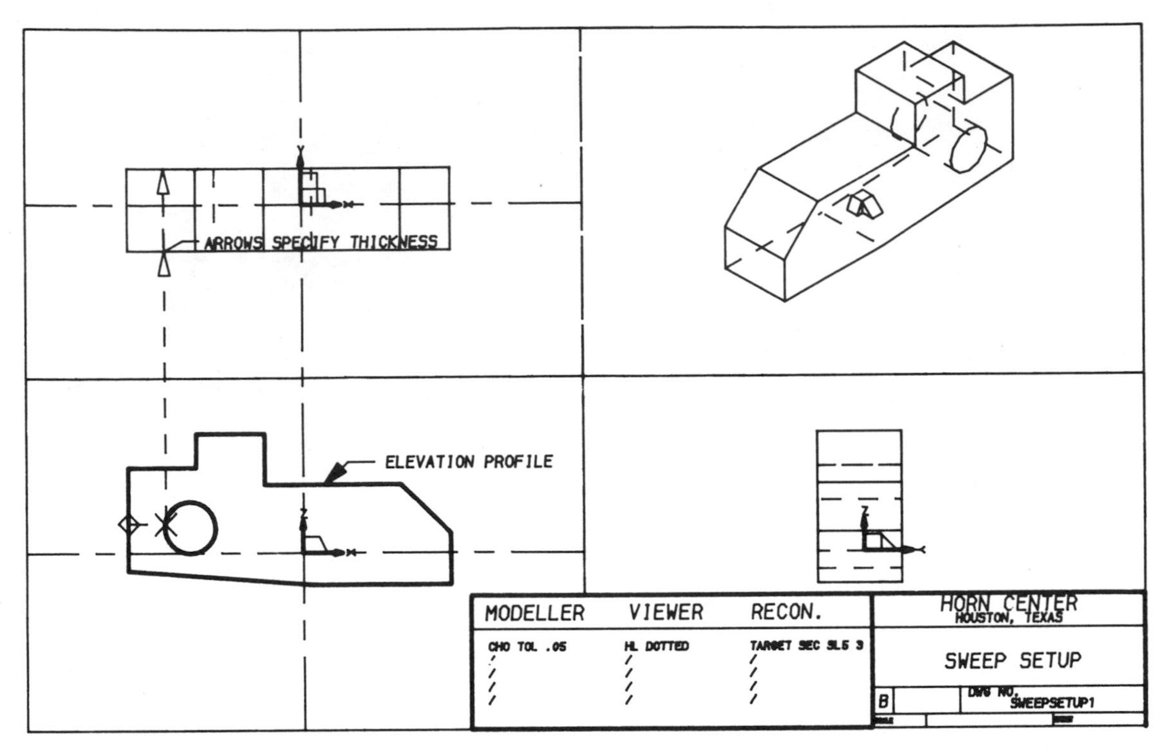

Figure 9.22 After having the shape and thickness given as shown in Fig. 9.21, the system automatically generates a finished set of views.

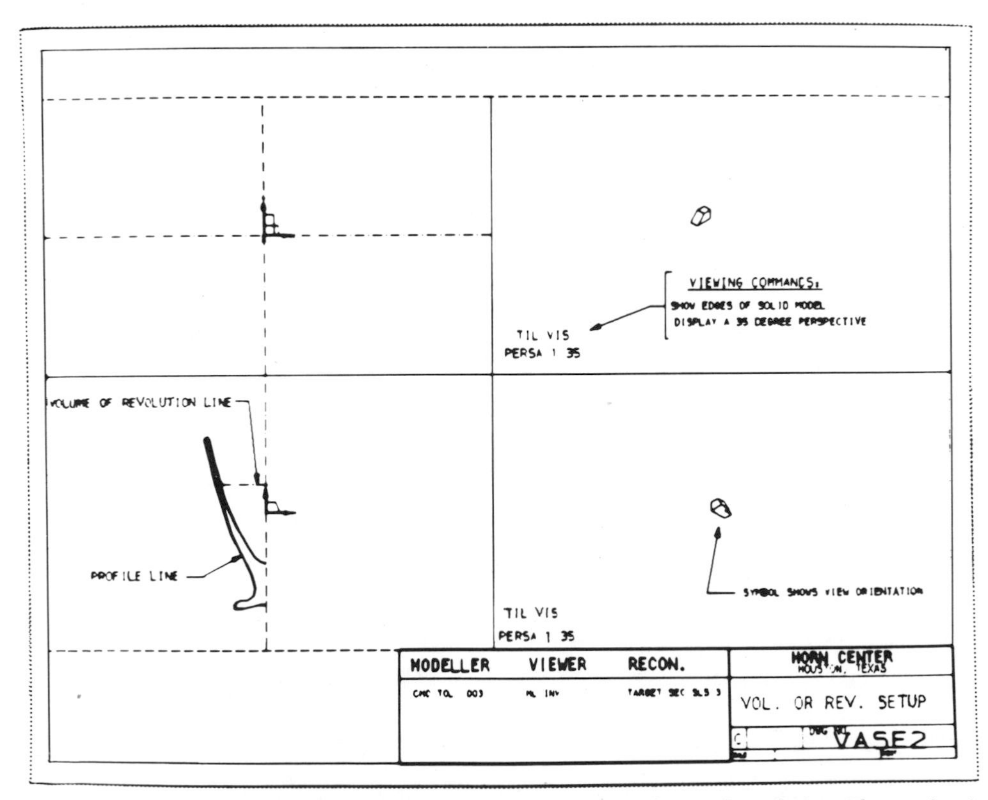

Figure 9.23 The required information needed to generate a volume of revolution. The section is shown in the elevation view and will be rotated around the vertical centerline.

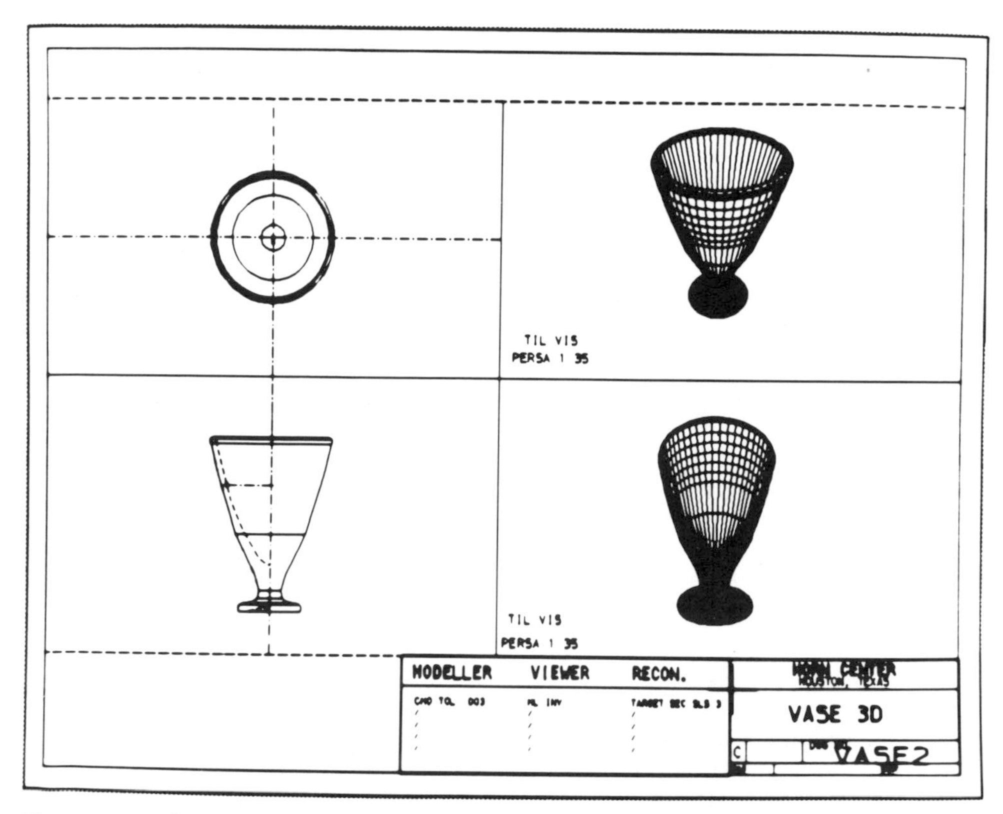

Figure 9.24 The completed volume of revolution as generated from the data input in Fig. 9.23.

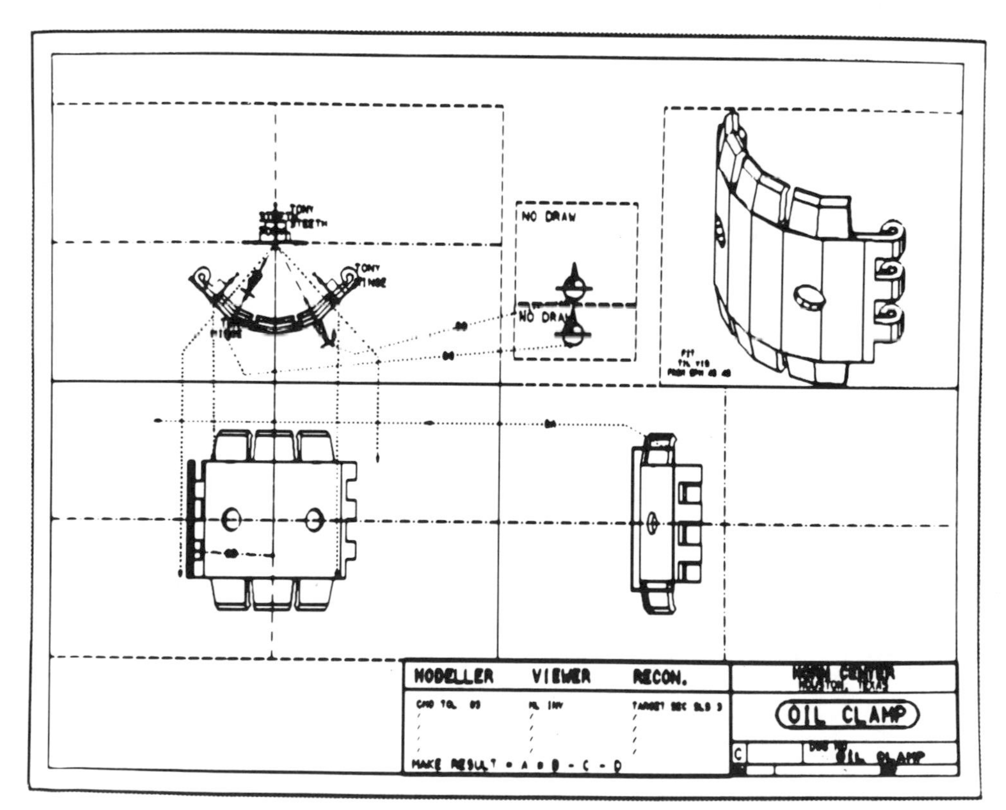

Figure 9.25 A generated sculptural shape composed by assembling several shapes through a boolean operation. This can be commanded through a one-line statement saying MAKE RESULT = A + B − C, where A, B, and C are components of the finished assembly.

as an overview of system capabilities, adding any features or capabilities you might need in particular. General considerations should also include:

A. Physical layout

1. Number and location of workstations
2. Environmental conditions
3. Amount of storage needed

B. Implementation

1. Productivity expectations
2. Interfacing to other systems and computers required
3. Report writing capabilities required
4. Job accounting required
5. Organization and personnel limitations

C. Vendor

1. Support record
2. Stability
3. Testimonials from other users

Probably the single biggest mistake made in the selection process is lack of study and planning. It is essential to allow enough time to become acquainted with basic CAD features and capabilities before narrowing the selection search to a few systems. In this regard CAD evaluation seminars or basic CAD operator courses are worthwhile because the amount of time and money invested to become trained in a thorough manner is small compared to the overall system costs.

Finally, it is well to recognize the dynamic aspect of the CAD industry. To enter into the full-time use of this equipment requires both a major expenditure and a commitment to constant development. Probably no other industry is changing as rapidly; it seems that every month some new development or capability is announced. This means that CAD is not something to learn and put into rigid use, but rather a dynamic educational process that is open to new applications and ideas. This constant newness is what makes CAD somewhat intimidating, but it also opens the way for large application rewards now and numerous creative possibilities in the near future.

9.6.2 Features Checklist

A. Drawing administration

1. Multiple scale selection
   a. Any sheet scale
   b. Any temporary scale
2. Metric or imperial units
3. Variety of drawing sheets
   a. Collection of library sheets
   b. Easily created new sheets
4. Friendly filing system
5. Security*
   a. Multilevel passwords
   b. Assignable protection rights
6. Database management*

* Indicates advanced system.

B. General drafting

1. Lines
   a. Multiple types
   b. Easily editable†
   c. Active lines* coupled segments
   d. Special lines*† double, weld, etc.
2. Curves
   a. Smooth function
   b. Ellipse
   c. Parabola
   d. Cubic
   e. Bezier*
3. Shapes
   a. Circles, arcs, ellipses
   b. Polygons
4. Construction lines*†
   a. Easy to use
   b. Numerous entry options
   c. Deletable with single command
   d. Geometric constructions
5. Dimensioning
   a. Manual (specified) dimensions
   b. Semiautomatic dimensioning†
   c. Automatic dimensioning*†
   d. Geometric modification through dimension changes*†
6. Layering
   a. Easy to turn layers on or off
   b. Automatic layering assignments of elements
7. Cross-hatching
   a. Numerous patterns available
   b. Easily defined crosshatch area†
   c. Easily constructed new patterns*†
8. Transformations†
   a. Includes MOVE, ROTATE, MAGNIFY, and MIRROR
   b. Operates on current and new elements, groups, and points
   c. Text maintained legible*
9. Grouping elements†
   a. Easy access to storage
   b. Simple loading and unloading
   c. Responds to transformations
   d. Multiple delete options on groups
   e. Type change of grouped elements*†
10. Symbols
    a. Easily constructed and stored
    b. Can include associated specifications*†
    c. Large storage capacity

C. Solids modeling*†

1. B-rep system
   a. Includes sweeps, volume of revolution, ruled surfaces
   b. Boolean operations
   c. Automatic hidden line removal

* Indicates advanced system.
† Indicates feature with major impact on productivity.

2. CSG system
   a. Wide variety of primitives
   b. Boolean operations
   c. Automatic hidden line removal
3. All systems (B-rep and CSG)
   a. Line shading
   b. Surface shading
   c. Viewing programs
      (1) Standard views (orthographic and isometric)
      (2) Interactive viewing
      (3) Dynamic rotation
      (4) Dynamic pan and zoom

D. NC programming*†

1. Tool-path verification
2. Interfaces to APT and Compact II
3. Three- to five-axis machining

E. Flattener and nesting programs*

1. Allows use of interior voids
2. Automatic clearance
3. Percentage of use readout

F. Other desirable features†

1. Help facility
2. User friendly
3. Color capability
4. Good workstation ergonomics
   a. Majority of data input through tablet or menu, not keyboard
   b. Fast response time
   c. Access to source code
   d. Hooks into database*
   e. Expandability

* Indicates advanced system.
† Indicates feature with major impact on productivity.

Electrical Applications

by
Charles Evans

10.1 INTRODUCTION

This chapter discusses electrical drafting and design principles as they apply to the use of computer graphics equipment in the production of manufacturing drawings and machine-compatible tapes for the computer-controlled assembly of electrical circuits. After a review of basic principles of electrical drafting and design, the section discusses the limitations of traditional practices and the reason for the use of computer graphics systems in doing work that was previously done by hand on a drafting board. The advantages of computer graphics systems are discussed for the design of schematics, printed-circuit boards, and integrated circuits. Next follows a general discussion on how a computer graphics system is used in electrical design and drafting work, and how the system aids the designer and drafter in checking the work. A specific computer graphics system is assumed to be available, and the reader is treated to a detailed discussion of the procedures and techniques used by the designer and drafter. Illustrations are included to show completed drawings that can be made from the database.

10.1.1 Electrical Drafting and Design Principles

During the conceptual design studies for a new electrical circuit, a map or diagram of the circuit must be made and studied. Even the simplest circuit cannot be adequately explained, analyzed, or constructed without the use of an appropriate diagram. The diagrams that are used for this purpose are called *block diagrams, logic diagrams, schematic diagrams,* or *wiring diagrams.* Each of these diagrams utilizes symbols that represent the components or packaged circuits that make up the overall circuit being designed. The symbols are then connected by straight horizontal and vertical lines in such a way as to describe the circuit.

Block diagrams do not completely describe an electrical circuit but do indicate the complexity of the circuit, what it is supposed to do, and what its main features are. The symbols used in block diagrams are almost entirely simple rectangles.

Logic diagrams are similar to block diagrams in that they describe the logical progression of electrical signals in a circuit as they go from one component or logic element to another. However, the symbols take forms that are unique to a particular function, and the diagrams are used only for digital control circuits.

Schematic diagrams describe the picture of an electrical circuit in further detail, supplying enough information for complete analysis of the circuit. Standard symbols are used and complete electrical connections are shown in such a way that the circuit can be most easily understood.

There are two types of schematic diagrams:

1. ***The Traditional Electronic Schematic.*** In this schematic, the source of signal or power is on the left side of the drawing, and the destination or use of the signal or

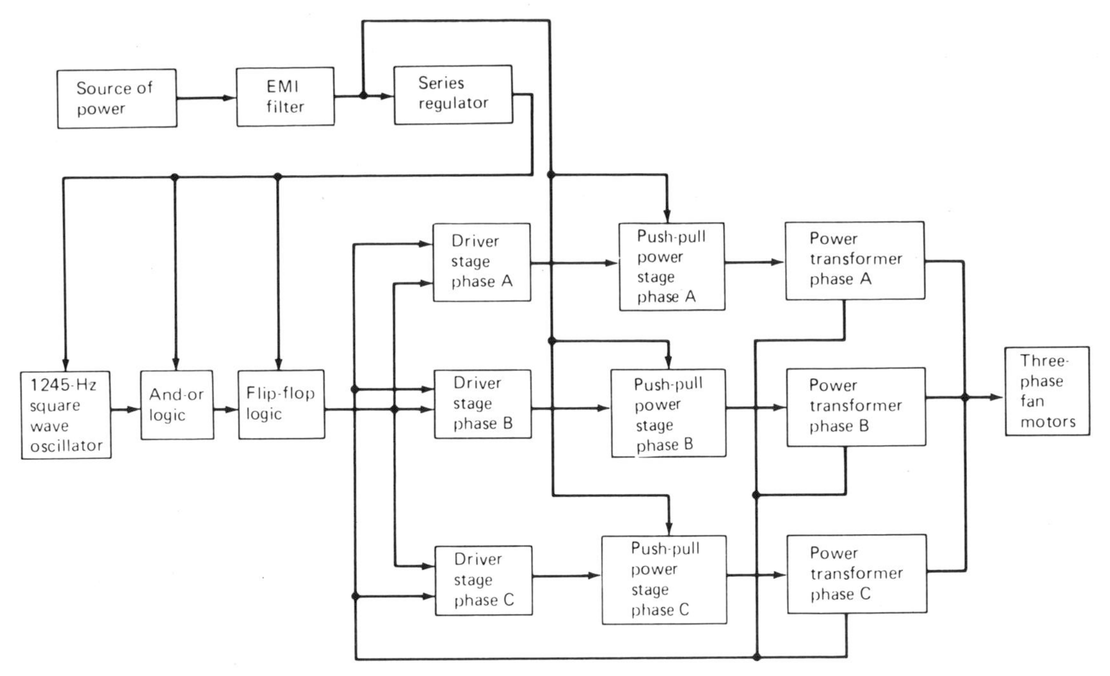

Figure 10.1 Block diagram.

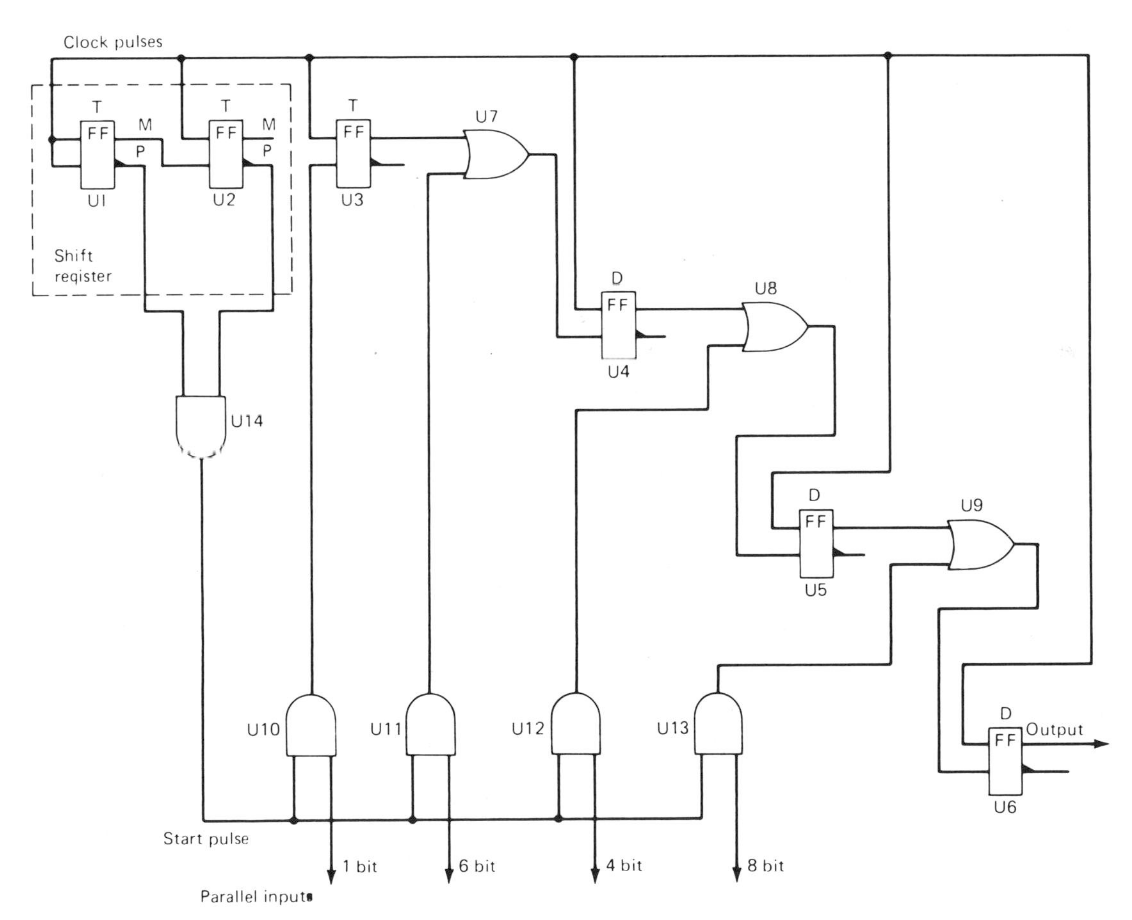

Figure 10.2 Logic diagram.

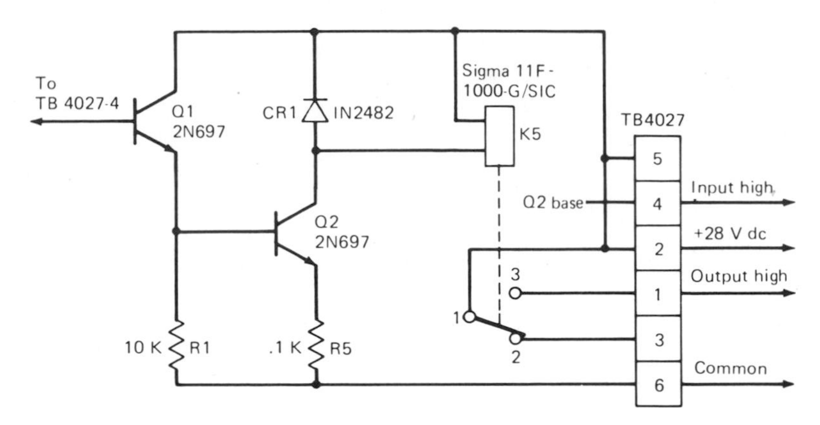

Figure 10.3 Schematic diagram.

power is on the right-hand side of the drawing. Signal flow is generally from left to right and from top to bottom of the drawing. The highest voltage level is at the top of the diagram, and the lowest voltage is at the bottom of the diagram.

2. ***The Elementary or Ladder Diagram.*** This diagram arranges the circuit so that the signals are like rungs on a ladder, strung between vertical lines that represent levels of voltage. The lowest voltage is the vertical line at the right and the highest voltage is the vertical line at the left. The rungs of the ladder are arranged so that the first signal to be activated in an operating sequence is at the top of the ladder.

The lines between the symbols on a schematic may or may not represent actual wires that are connected between components in an electrical assembly. On an actual assembly a wire may go to one part and a second wire may connect to the same terminal of that part, but it may not appear this way on the schematic. The schematic is not necessarily a visual representation of the way that the wires look on an actual assembly. It is drawn so that a circuit can be understood, not so that it can be constructed a certain way. For most complex electrical circuits, or circuits that utilize special construction techniques, a wiring diagram is also needed.

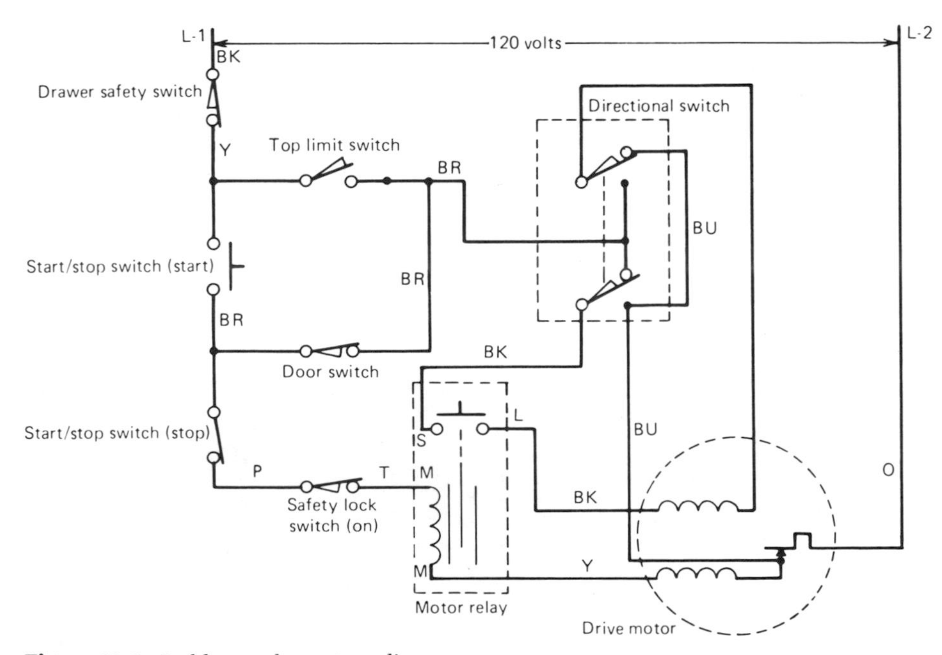

Figure 10.4 Ladder or elementary diagram.

A wiring diagram is an actual picture of the circuit as it appears on a completed assembly. It is used not for analysis or explanation of a circuit but as an assembly drawing in the shop. Enough details are shown on the wiring diagram so that the technician can identify where the wires are to go, to what terminals they are connected, and what kind of connection is made. Special forms of wiring diagrams are made where printed circuits or integrated circuits are used. For these advanced types of circuits, the wiring diagrams consist of a number of drawings and photographic films, some of which are used like templates in the manufacture of printed-circuit boards or integrated-circuit packages.

Printed-circuit boards consist of copper foil bonded to one or both sides of an insulating base material. On some complex circuits, a number of boards are sandwiched together to make a multilayer board so as to accommodate the additional electrical connections. In most manufacturing situations, the foil-covered board is first covered with a photosensitive material. A photographic film is made to the exact size of the board. This photographic film shows a pattern of the circuit on it. The pattern is made in such a way that, when the film is placed over the board, light can pass through it only in those areas that represent the conducting materials in the circuit. The light that passes through the film hardens the photosensitive material on the board in those areas. The board is then placed in an etching bath, which removes all copper except the areas where the photosensitive materials have been hardened. The etched board then represents a base to which electronic components can be assembled. The remaining copper left on the board supplies the connections between the components. The connections are usually soldered, using automated soldering techniques. Wherever there is a connection to be made, an area of copper is left on the board and a hole is drilled through the board at this location. This copper area is called a *pad.* Wherever a connection has to be made from one side of the board to the other, a pad is placed on both sides and a hole is drilled at this location. This type of connection is called a *via* or *feedthrough.*

A printed circuit is described by a number of different drawings for manufacture of

Figure 10.5 A printed circuit. (*Courtesy of Diana Mehail.*)

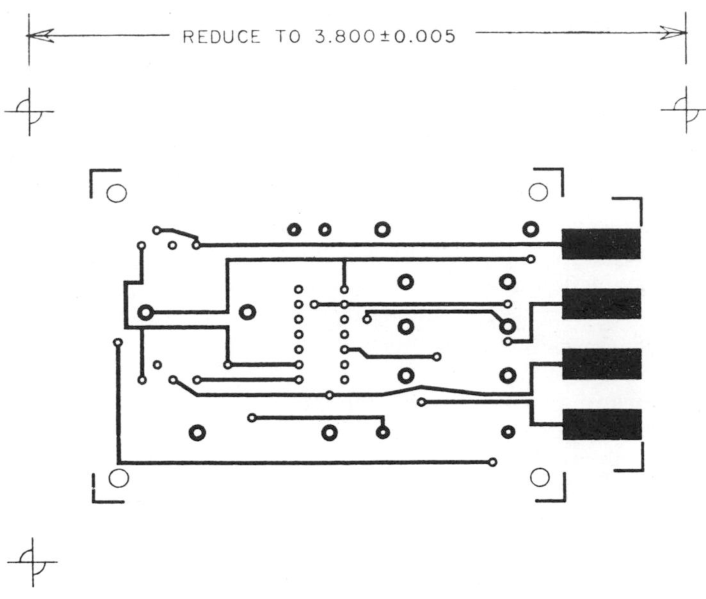

Figure 10.6 Layout pattern, printed-circuit board, connection side.

the board itself as well as assembly of components to it. These drawings will now be described.

1. ***Master Layout Drawing.*** A drawing must be made to describe the copper pattern on the board, for each side of the board, and for each layer of a multilayer board. An accurate photographic reduction of the drawing must be made, and it must consist of opaque and transparent areas, precisely located.
2. ***Silk Screen Drawing.*** A drawing must be made of the assembly markings to be made on the board, including outlines and orientations of the components that are to be

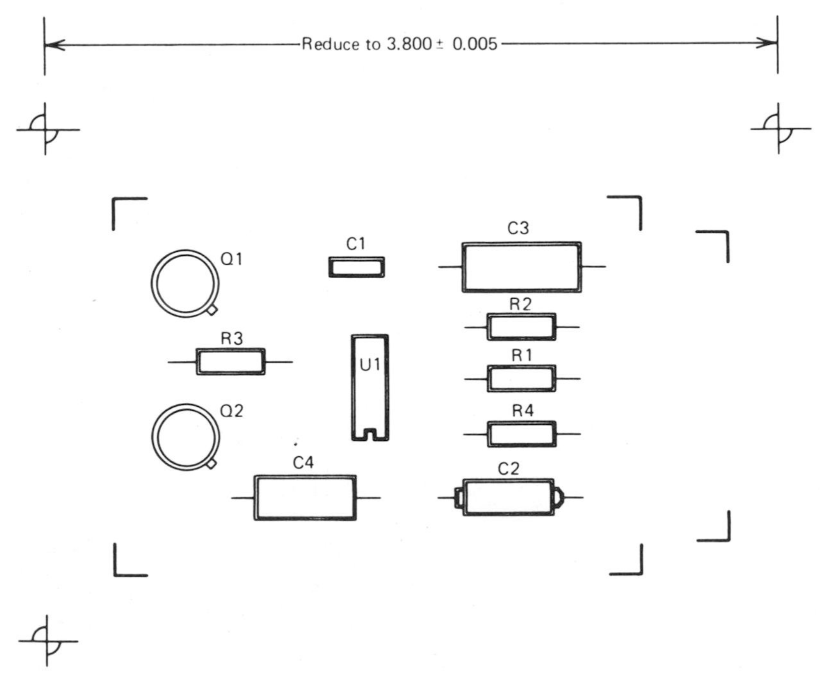

Figure 10.7 Silk screen drawing, printed-circuit board.

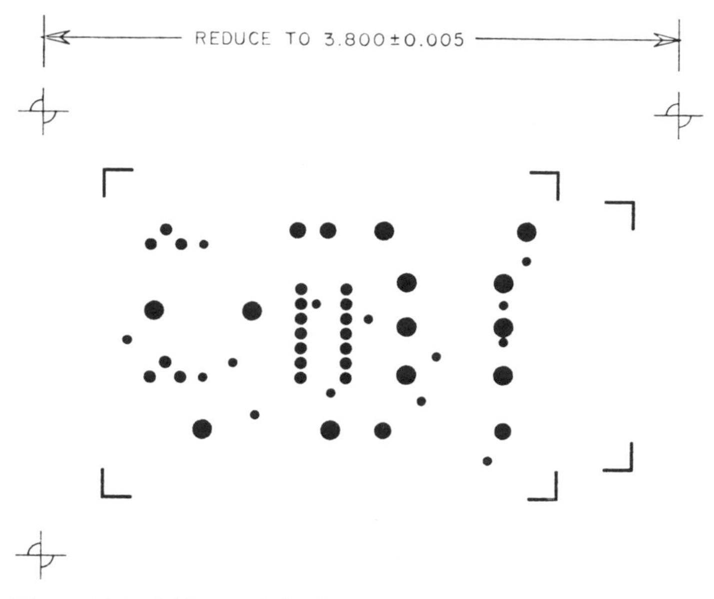

Figure 10.8 Solder-mask drawing, printed-circuit board.

assembled to it. This drawing is also photoreduced, and a stencil must be prepared from it to place the markings on the board, using a silk screen printing process.

3. ***Drilling and Machining Drawing.*** A drawing must be prepared of the holes and other machined cuts that must be made in the board.
4. ***Solder-Mask Drawing.*** If automated soldering techniques are used, a drawing must be made of the areas on the board to which solder must adhere, such as pads to which connections must be made. This drawing is also photoreduced and is used like a stencil to place solder-resistant material onto the board so that solder will not adhere in those areas.

Integrated circuits are built on semiconductor crystals. The oxidized surface of the crystal is painted with a photosensitive material. It is then covered with a mask that admits light in one area and blocks light in another area. The transparent portions of the mask admit light to the crystal, which hardens the photosensitive material which has been painted on it. The oxide surface of the crystal is then etched with a solution that does not affect the light-hardened area. Gaseous semiconductor impurities are then introduced into the areas that have been exposed by the etchant. These impurities diffuse into the crystal. The surface of the crystal is then oxidized again, and the photoetching process is

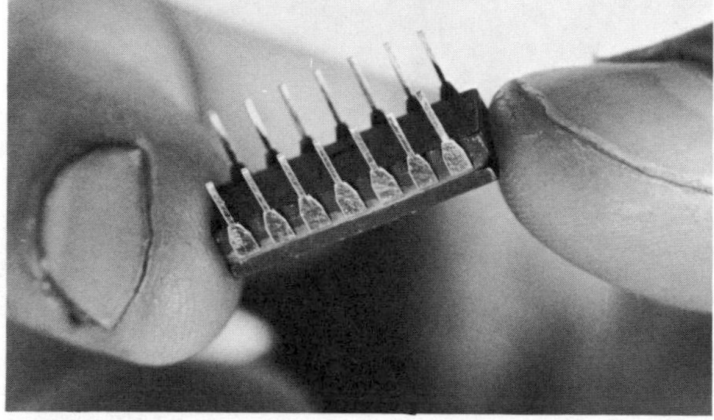

Figure 10.9 An integrated circuit. (*Courtesy of Diana Mehail.*)

repeated. A different type of gaseous impurity is then introduced into the exposed areas. Because of the differences in conductivity and other characteristics of the impure areas of the semiconductor crystal, an electronic circuit can be constructed. Each layer of oxidized material and impure areas constitutes a complex circuit layout. The resulting crystal is called a *chip*. Connections to the chip are then made at various points, and it is packaged in a plastic or metal case. The connections are brought out to terminals that protrude from the case.

In both the integrated-circuit layouts and the printed-circuit layouts, the mask that is transparent in some areas and opaque in others is constructed from a photographic film. The photographic film is a reduced copy of a layout that is made by the electrical designer, either by traditional drafting methods or by the use of a computer graphics system.

10.1.2 More Production Needed by Electrical Designers

The complexity of electrical circuits is increasing at a great rate. A generation or so ago, the engineer gave a rough schematic to a drafter, and the skills of the drafter were limited to just making the lines straight and the drawing easy to follow. The complexity of circuits has grown, and electronic technology has also grown by leaps and bounds. Electronic circuits have become groups of semiconductor crystals connected into complex control schemes (such as in computers or computer-controlled systems) and communication circuits (such as in radio and television equipment). The circuits are assembled to printed-wiring boards or printed-circuit boards, and the numbers of wires are reduced. However, now packaging design is more important—the drafter has to design the layout of the wiring boards and gain more specialized drafting skills. Some of the packaging involves laying out the circuits on a semiconductor crystal, producing a microminiature electronic package. In recent years, circuit complexity has increased to such a level that some printed-circuit boards are built in eight or more layers, sandwiched together, and have tiny components assembled to both sides. Integrated circuits are being built in such a way that one tiny electronic package houses a complete computer. Techniques have been developed for depositing complete electronic components as thick as 1 micrometer or less on an insulated base to produce complete microminiature circuits. This requires many tedious hours of drafting and design time. The circuit complexity is becoming so great that the electronic packages are impossible to design by traditional methods. Drafters and

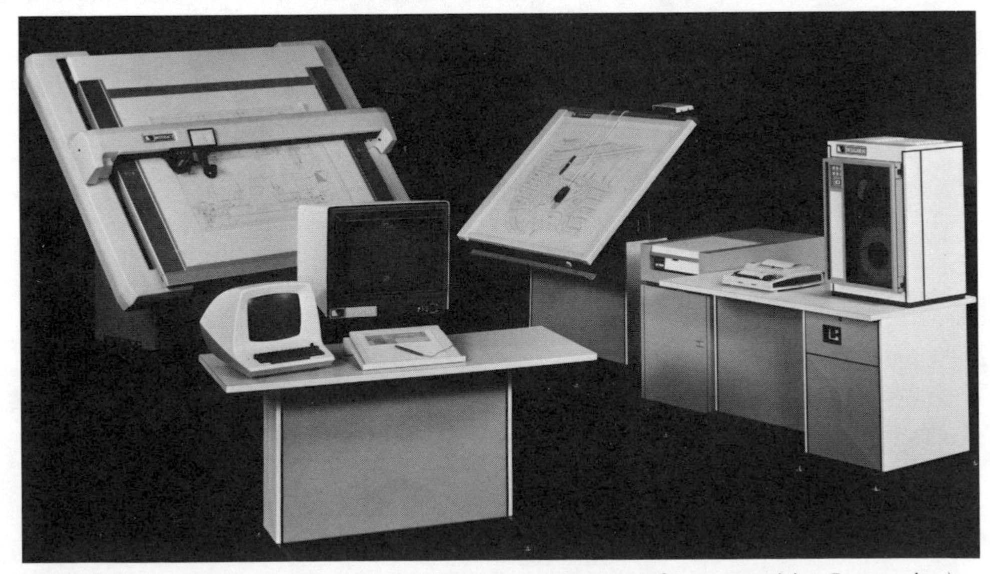

Figure 10.10 Interactive computer graphics system. (*Courtesy of Computervision Corporation.*)

designers are being forced to use interactive computer graphics equipment for this design work. The computer graphics systems are so sophisticated that they will, with little or no help from the designer, place components in logical positions, route the connections between them, check for errors between the schematic and the physical layout, check for errors in labeling as well as errors in logic or circuit connections, and produce parts lists and signal lists automatically for extremely complex circuits involving dozens and even hundreds of components, and involving thousands of connections.

10.1.3 Limitations of Standard Drafting Practices

For some complex circuits, the design cannot be completed by traditional methods. The traditional methods involve circuit patterns on large sheets of vellum. This is just too slow and tedious, leading to employee fatigue and errors. Printed-circuit patterns are frequently too dense and too precise for manual layout methods. To be off by a mil or two on multilayer circuit boards causes expensive circuit failures and difficult fabrication techniques. Even minor modifications to a circuit require many hours of drafting time and checking time. Computer graphics equipment can easily make small changes and then do the checking automatically.

Documentation for large-scale electronic circuits is more difficult, and yet more important. Bills of materials and other production data are more important now. Manual methods of documentation require many labor-hours for every newly designed piece of electronic equipment.

When drawing an electronic schematic or ladder diagram, an electrical drafter spends many hours endlessly copying and recopying standard symbols and circuit connections with pencil and paper. When a mistake is made or a change in design occurs, an area of a drawing must be erased completely and redrawn, requiring many tedious labor-hours.

10.2 ADVANTAGES OF COMPUTER GRAPHICS SYSTEMS FOR ELECTRICAL DESIGN AND DRAFTING

10.2.1 Schematics

For making schematics, a computer graphics system can have scores of standard symbols, drawing formats, and standard circuit configurations stored in its database, which can easily be called up and placed on a drawing with one stroke of an electronic digitizing tool. Large groups of symbols can have their sizes, orientations, and locations specified and changed before or after being put on the drawing by similar simple strokes of the electronic pen. Minor or major drawing changes can easily be made without working with large sheets of paper, electric erasers, or various kinds of manual drafting tools and materials.

If a system is properly set up and the operator properly trained, drawings can be made 5 to 10 times faster than with conventional manual drafting techniques, and with greater precision.

If a portion of a circuit must be moved on a drawing, a simple command entered on the graphics terminal will move that portion from one drawing position to another and erase the original markings from the drawing. If a repetitive circuit feature is encountered, the operator only needs to draw it once and, with a simple command, copy it automatically to other locations on the drawing.

The computer graphics system can be used to assist in checking an electrical drawing. Incorrectly labeled components and illogical connections are identified (such as two parallel signal paths between the same connecting points). Missing connections to electronic components are found. Errors between an engineer's schematic and the production wiring diagram can be identified and located automatically by the system.

10.2.2 Printed Wiring and Integrated Circuits

If the drawings are used for making printed circuits or integrated circuits, many additional errors can be identified and located by the system. The graphics system can compare a schematic with any of the printed-circuit board drawings and determine if there are errors between them. Electrically, the printed-circuit board must reflect the same connections as the schematic. If they do not match, the system will identify and locate them and show them to the operator by highlighting them in some way. The system will identify errors in labeling the silk screen drawing of the board. If these errors can be found and eliminated, a component will be prevented from being connected incorrectly, and the wrong component prevented from being assembled to the board. The system will identify situations where a run will cross another run inadvertently on the same side of the board. The system will identify and locate situations where inadequate clearance has been maintained between runs on a board or between pads.

A computer graphics system will speed up the design of a printed circuit by choosing the best location for a component based on its knowledge of the schematic and the connections that are to be made to the component. The system will choose where vias or feed-throughs are to be located, and will determine the paths that the runs take between components with a simple command on the terminal. The system can take these actions regardless of the number of layers a printed-circuit board has.

These capabilities are extremely advantageous for complex circuits requiring multilayer printed-circuit boards. The circuits can become so complex that a human being cannot, without help, do the design work. The number of decisions involved are beyond the capability of the designer to lay out with traditional taping methods.

The system features can extend to the total number of drawings required by the circuit board manufacturing process. Silk screen drawings, master layout drawings, drilling and machining drawings, and solder-mask drawings can all be made by the system without additional input by the operator or designer. Simultaneously with the automatic placement of components and automatic routing of their connections, the system can be easily programmed to make these other drawings.

The use of the computer graphics system to prepare an integrated-circuit layout from a logic diagram or schematic is similar to the method of preparing a printed-circuit layout from a schematic. Instead of the designer being concerned with the placement of components, routing, and fabrication of a printed-circuit board, he or she makes a system layout or floorplan layout, subsystem layout or macrocell layout, mask layout, mask fabrication, and then fabrication of the integrated circuit.

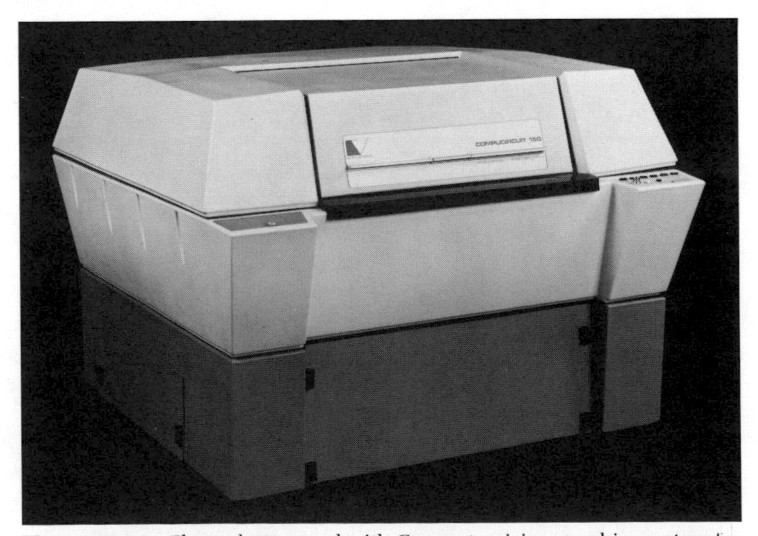

Figure 10.11 Photoplotter used with Computervision graphics system for electrical design work. (*Courtesy of Computervision Corporation.*)

10.2.3 Manufacturing Interface

Using a computer graphics system, a direct link can be made from the designer's desk to numerically controlled equipment that drills holes in the circuit boards, prints information onto them, inserts components into them, solders them all in the right places—all with a high level of quality. The system uses magnetic recording tape that can be used to program photoplotters and numerically controlled machining equipment. Photoplotters produce, directly from tape, negative photographic films that are used in photoetching and silk screening the required patterns on the circuit boards. Numerically controlled drill presses utilize the tapes produced by the system to drill the hundreds of small holes that are needed in the boards. Numerically controlled machines utilize tapes produced by the system to select and insert components automatically into the drilled circuit boards.

10.3 CAD AS AN AID TO ELECTRICAL DESIGNERS AND DRAFTERS

10.3.1 Graphics Database

In using a computer graphics system, the electrical designers and drafters make use of a large group of predrawn symbols that have been stored in the database. When the system is first installed, the operators must spend many hours drawing standard symbols that can be used later. Symbols for common electrical components such as capacitors, resistors, and diodes are made available to place onto the drawing with a single touch of a function key on the graphics terminal. A filing system is set up to manage the library of stored parts. The predrawn symbols provide uniform size, orientation, shape, and line thickness for the drawings. Complex symbols, such as those depicting integrated-circuit packages, plug-in circuit boards, or multipin connectors, can be inserted on a drawing with the single touch of a function key. These same symbols can be moved, removed, or modified easily by a simple touch of a function key.

10.3.2 Nongraphical Database

Filed with the predrawn symbols are nongraphical characteristics that have been assigned to the symbols during their construction on the terminal. Nongraphical characteristics are developed by

1. Using special forms of graphic entities that are available in the system software. These entities may include lines or text having special characteristics that are used solely for electrical drawings.
2. Assigning certain graphical entities to specific layers. The system software allows for overlays to be made for specified entities. These are often referred to as layers or levels. They can be thought of as transparencies, each transparency having markings that add more definition to the existing graphics. By assigning certain entities to given layers, the entities can have special significance on the drawing.
3. Assigning properties to a symbol or certain entities on a symbol. A predefined list of properties can be assigned by the operator. These properties do not appear as a part of the graphics but contain special characteristics that are recognizable by the system. These special characteristics can be assigned to a symbol, or an entity in a symbol, by assigning a given property to it.

When the graphical parts of a symbol are inserted into a drawing, the symbol insertion includes these nongraphical characteristics.

10.3.3 How These Features Help the Designer

Some advantages of inserting predrawn symbols onto a drawing have already been discussed. Additional advantages accrue from

1. The precision with which they can be inserted
2. The fact that text can be associated with the symbols and connecting lines
3. The nongraphical characteristics that are inserted with the symbols

These advantages assist the designer to draw neat, easily understood diagrams efficiently and quickly. In addition, the power of the computer helps the designer check the drawings for accuracy and completeness. By associating text with a symbol, the system can identify and list component identifications and signal identifications. By associating text with connecting lines, connecting lines can be associated with given symbols and be identified as well. The nongraphical characteristics that are a part of each symbol can be used to set up a self-checking routine, whereby the designer uses the system to prevent certain errors from creeping into the circuit diagram. For example, if a terminal on one of the symbols is not connected anywhere, the system will identify that as an error. Thus, the designer will be notified that an additional connection must be shown on the drawing.

The computer graphics system allows the designer to exercise more creativity and makes his or her job less tedious. This is especially true with the more complicated circuits involving large numbers of multiterminal components. It is very frustrating for a designer to spend days working on the layout for a printed-circuit board and then find another connection that has to be made "from here to there" because of either an error or an engineering change order. Invariably, the layout becomes less than ideal, and new errors are often introduced in the revised layout. Using the computer graphics system, software features allow much of the placement of components and layout of runs to be completed before the designer has spent much time on the circuit. The designer then merely edits the layout, providing for features that the system does not have the human judgment to provide.

10.4 PRODUCTION OF AN ELECTRICAL SCHEMATIC OR WIRING DIAGRAM

10.4.1 Description and Basic Use of a Typical System

There are many models of computer graphics systems available for electrical design work. The rest of the discussion on using these systems will be devoted to a particular system and software package with which the author is familiar so that typical operating techniques can be discussed in detail.

The system on which the discussion will be based is a Computervision CGP-100. It is based on a 16-bit minicomputer. The drawings are made by use of Computervision's CADDS 3 software. It has a teledisplay terminal with keyboard, a digitizing tablet to which a menu is mounted, a graphics display screen, and a digitizing pen, all mounted on a flat surface at standard table height.

The workstation is one of four that are connected directly to the main computer system in an adjoining room. It uses a 300-megabyte disk, driven by a disk drive mounted in the main housing. The system includes a nine-track high-speed tape drive and a telewriter terminal. The tape drive allows permanent storage and retrieval of graphics data and software programs. The telewriter terminal is operated like the teledisplay terminal at the workstation. However, the telewriter does not provide a display of any graphics data. Instead, it is used to generate text files, issue commands for recording and reading tape, plotting drawings, system programming, and system management. It does provide a paper-tape record of any alphanumeric information that is fed into or out of the system. A

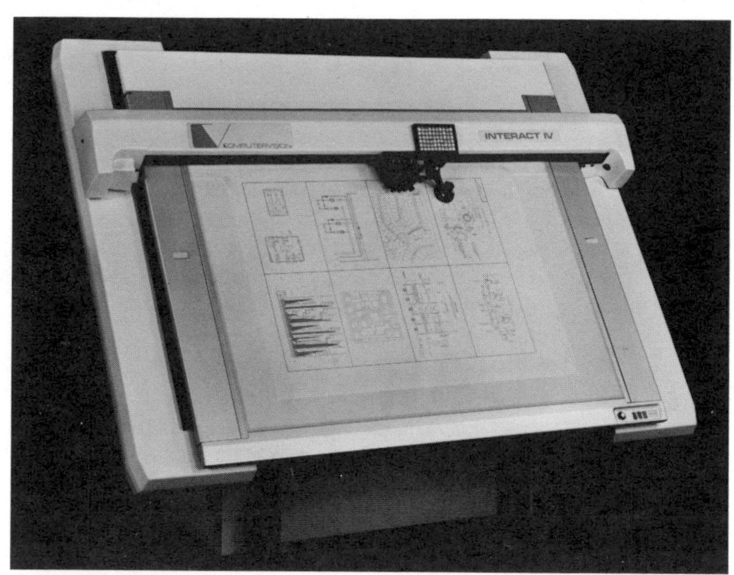

Figure 10.12 Computervision Interact IV plotter. (*Courtesy of Computervision Corporation.*)

Computervision Interact IV pen plotter is used to make hard copy of the drawing on vellum.

The computer graphics system is under the supervision of a system manager. The system manager starts the system, loads the appropriate software from the library of tapes, and clears the system for use by an operator at one of the workstations. There will be no discussion about the specific procedures that the system manager uses, since those functions are usually not the responsibility of the electrical designer. After the designer has been notified that the system is operative, he or she then logs in on the system and becomes an operator on the terminal. The logging-in procedure is specified by the system software as modified by the system manager and company policy.

The operator uses part names which are in accordance with standard procedures set up by the system manager and approved by the supervisor of the design department. The part name must be structured in such a way that the main catalogue of parts or equipment

```
◆◆TASK00 INITIATED◆◆

SYSNEWS.&BLD.LLLNEWS
 1-16-81 12:53:03


◆◆◆◆◆◆◆◆◆◆◆◆◆◆◆◆◆◆◆◆◆◆◆◆◆◆◆◆◆◆◆◆◆◆◆◆◆◆◆◆◆◆◆◆◆◆◆◆◆◆◆◆◆◆◆◆◆◆◆◆◆◆◆◆◆◆◆◆◆◆
◆◆◆◆◆                                                                ◆◆◆◆◆
◆◆◆◆◆                  COMPUTERVISION CORPORATION                    ◆◆◆◆◆
◆◆◆◆◆               SOFTWARE RELEASE REVISION 10-03-G                ◆◆◆◆◆
◆◆◆◆◆                                                                ◆◆◆◆◆
◆◆◆◆◆◆◆◆◆◆◆◆◆◆◆◆◆◆◆◆◆◆◆◆◆◆◆◆◆◆◆◆◆◆◆◆◆◆◆◆◆◆◆◆◆◆◆◆◆◆◆◆◆◆◆◆◆◆◆◆◆◆◆◆◆◆◆◆◆◆
0>CADDSCLR
 CADDS 3  REV 10-03-G  1-19-81 10:13:16
INITIALIZE CADDS PARAMETERS?
TYPE OK TO CONTINUE
OK
0A00 REGEN SECTORS AVAILABLE
TYPE OK TO REALLOCATE

    2560 (0A00) SECTORS ALLOCATED FOR REGENS

PART NAME:ET.S.3.1
 CREATING NEW PART
:
```

Figure 10.13 System is ready for operator to make a drawing.

is at the beginning and the specific part or circuit name or number is at the end, separated by periods. For example, suppose the part is the schematic for an electronic transducer. The part name could be

ET.S.3.1

where ET is the class of drawings that are used to describe the electronic transducer, S is the class of drawings used to describe an electrical schematic of the transducer, 3 is the number of the schematic to be drawn, and 1 is the revision of schematic number 3.

After the operator types the part name, the RETURN button is pushed and the system responds with a prompt symbol. Now the operator starts making the schematic on the terminal by entering commands on the keyboard.

The commands can be roughly separated into four parts:

1. Verb
2. Noun
3. Modifier
4. Data input

Parts of the command are expressed in terms of shortened forms of commonly used words. For example, the word *insert*, which is a verb, is shortened to INS. The verb is a word that is used to denote what action is to take place.

In some cases, the complete command is given by the verb. When the command is finished, the RETURN button is pushed. When a drawing is completed and is to be filed on the disk, the operator issues the command FILE and the system stores the drawing in its memory, after it is given an appropriate part name.

In most cases, the verb is followed by a noun. The noun indicates that an entity is to be inserted or changed in some way. An entity is any elementary graphic element such as a line, a circle, or a predrawn symbol.

In some cases, the complete command is expressed by a verb and a noun, followed by RETURN. For example, if everything on a drawing is to be erased, the command is ERS ALL, followed by RETURN.

In many cases, the verb and noun are followed by a modifier. The modifier defines information about the noun expression that is to be acted upon. The kind of modifier that is to be used is determined by the noun that precedes it. For example, the command INS

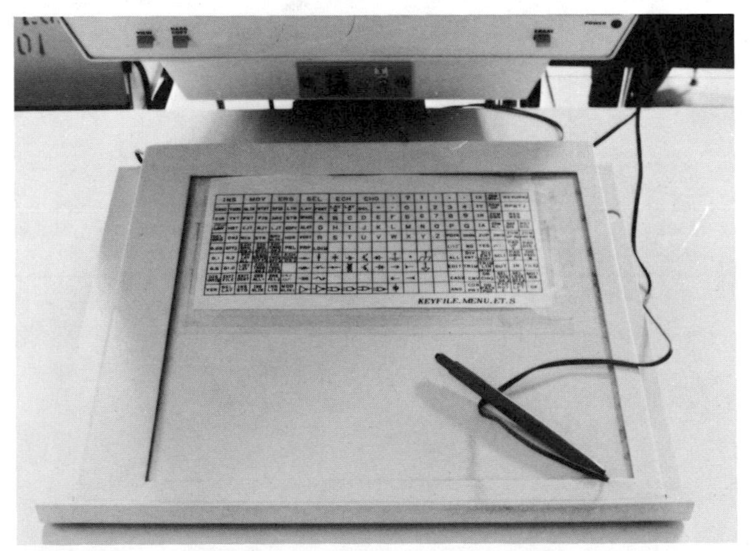

Figure 10.14 Electrical menu in place on graphics terminal tablet. (*Courtesy of Diana Mehail.*)

LIN is followed by VERT, indicating that a vertical line is to be made. INS is the verb, LIN is the noun, and VERT is the modifier. The noun LIN identifies an entity representing a line on the drawing.

After the verb-noun-modifier phrase has been entered, the operator enters the data input mode of the command, signified by the entry of a colon. Data in this mode are entered by using the keyboard or the electrical digitizing pen. When the pen is used, the act is referred to as *digitizing*.

For the system that is being discussed, use of the keyboard is minimized by the use of a menu. When using a menu, a section of the digitizing tablet is used for digitizing actual word phrases as parts of the command for inserting an entity. Because of the software capability of the system, it is possible to program the tablet so that it utilizes a keyfile stored in the system. To utilize this keyfile, the menu is taped to the upper half of the tablet. Then the command RST KEY is issued to the system using the keyboard. The system asks for the name of the keyfile to be restored, the operator types the name, and, after a few seconds, the system restores the keyfile in such a way that the tablet can be used to insert words, phrases, or an entire command with one stroke of the digitizing pen. By using the menu, complete commands are entered without even touching the keyboard. However, the teledisplay screen will show the same characters on it that were obtained using the keyboard, and the graphics display will also be the same as was obtained with the keyboard.

Complete assembly drawings and detail drawings can be made with the graphics system by inserting lines, circles, or predrawn symbols using the techniques just described.

10.4.2 Using the System for Electrical Applications

For electrical applications, four categories of the system capabilities are recognized.

1. Use of nodal entities
2. Parts insertion techniques
3. Layering
4. Nongraphical properties and files

Nodal entities differ from simple entities such as circles, arcs, and lines in that they have nongraphical features as well as special rules for insertion and use. The names of some common nodal entities and their shortened forms are listed as follows:

Nodal figure	NFIG
Connect node	CNOD
Text node	TNOD
Nodal lines	NLIN
Nodal text	NTXT

Nodal figures are parts that are stored in the system database and that have nodal entities inserted onto them. They have special names assigned to them and are constructed for the purpose of insertion into a larger, more complex drawing.

A connect node is a nodal entity that signifies the beginning or end position of an electric connection. It appears as a small diamond on the graphics screen.

A text node is a nodal entity that serves as a seat for text to be inserted into an electrical drawing. It is also used for setting the specifications of the text that will be eventually inserted onto an electrical drawing. The specifications may include the text height, font style, layer, association with a nodal entity, and a nongraphical property. The text node appears as a small isosceles triangle on the graphics screen.

Figure 10.15 Nodal line, with a connect node at either end.

A nodal line is the entity that produces an electric circuit on a drawing. A nodal line always begins and ends at a connect node, thereby forming an electric connection between two points.

Nodal text is textual information on an electrical drawing and is used to indicate terminal identifications, reference designations, part numbers, or circuit values, among other things. The text on an electrical drawing is inserted as a nodal entity because it is always associated with nodal entities and is only used on drawings that contain nodal entities. Nodal text is usually inserted at a text node, and the system recognizes it as being associated with the text node.

Most mechanical design drawings that are made on the graphics system do not utilize nodal entities. One may then wonder why electrical drawings require them. The answer is that nodal entities allow greater capabilities of the computer graphics system to be utilized. Nongraphical properties and other features of nodal entities are utilized for automatic checking of shorts and opens in circuit diagrams that are made on the system. Nodal entities allow generation of bills of materials, wire lists, and signal identification lists. They also simplify the design of printed circuits and integrated circuits, using the computer graphics system. For example, using nodal entities, software packages can be used that provide for automatic placement and insertion of components onto printed-circuit board outlines and automatic routing of conducting paths between preplaced components on the printed-circuit board. In short, nodal entities provide for rapid and precise, error-free design of schematics, wiring diagrams, printed-circuit boards, and integrated-circuit layouts.

10.4.3 Development of Symbols

To use a computer graphics system for electrical design applications, a parts library must be prepared that contains various symbols and component outlines. These parts must be drawn, using nodal entities, and filed in the library for later insertion into schematics and printed-circuit board designs. They are given part names and then inserted as nodal figures onto a circuit design drawing.

Figure 10.16 Schematic symbol, with text nodes and connect nodes.

To make a symbol, a grid is put on the screen and a feature in the system software causes all digitized entities to "snap" to the nearest grid point. This ensures that the symbol is precisely made and allows for easier use of the symbol when employing it on a schematic. In construction and use of the symbol, the termination points are located so that they fall on a standard grid pattern that is used in construction of the schematic drawings. When inserting the symbol onto the schematic, the location of the digitized entry is the X0Y0 position that existed on the screen when the symbol was made. This position is called the *subfigure origin* and is indicated by a + sign on the drawing. When making the symbol, the subfigure origin is located on the symbol graphics at a standard location for schematic construction. A standard location is used to assist the operator in using the symbol to make a schematic.

Elementary entities, such as lines and circles, are used for the graphics of each symbol. Connect nodes and text nodes are then added to the symbol. Connect nodes are put on the symbol in the exact locations to which connections are made when using the symbol on a schematic. They are put on a different layer than the graphics. The standard layer for this is layer 1. Text nodes are added to the symbol to represent locations and specifications for the text that is used to describe:

1. Terminal identifications
2. Reference designation
3. Part code value representing the exact component specification

If there are two terminals, two text nodes are added to the symbol for terminal identification using another layer, usually layer 2. The same number of text nodes are used for terminal identification as there are numbers of terminals on the symbol. Text nodes for reference designators and part code values are then added in such a location as will be acceptable for text location during schematic construction. These text nodes are put on different layers also, usually layers 3 and 4. In some cases, additional text nodes are added to the symbol on an unused layer for cross-referencing purposes.

All text nodes contain complete specifications on the text that will be placed on the schematic when the symbols are used. These specifications include text height, justification, font style, and the like.

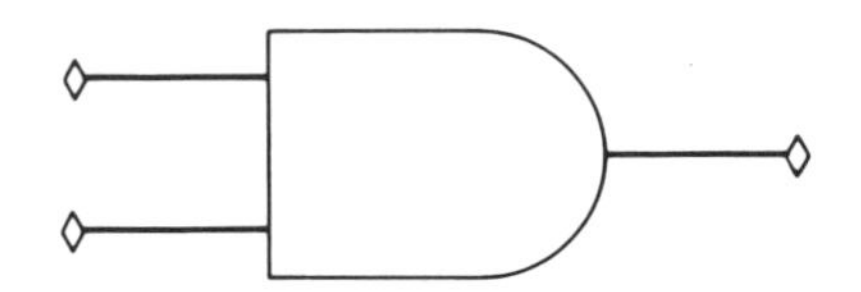

Figure 10.17 Logic symbol with connect nodes.

10.4.4 Diagram Construction

A standard grid size is chosen, and the system is programmed so that all digitized entries are forced to go to a grid intersection. Symbols are then inserted as nodal figures onto the drawing in the locations that will provide for the best schematic layout, using layer 0. They are inserted in much the same places that they would be located if they were placed manually. Even though layer 0 is used, the nodal figures that are inserted retain the original layering concept that was established when they were first made as graphic symbols.

The system needs to know at least three things for the nodal figure to be correctly inserted

1. The name of the nodal figure
2. The size it is to be given
3. The location of the nodal figure

There may be other things that the system may also have to know, depending on the drawing requirements, such as orientation and layer, which are included in the command if needed. A typical command for insertion of one of these parts looks like this:

```
#INS NFIG ET.S.RES.H SCL1: dig D
```

This command states that the nodal figure having the name ET.S.RES.H is to be inserted at a scale of 1:1, at a location that is digitized by the digitizing pen.

It would seem that, with each nodal figure having a different name, the designer or operator would have considerable difficulty using nodal figures to construct a schematic. The operator would have to know or look up the name and then laboriously type out the name on the keyboard. However, with the use of the menu, the insertion of a symbol into a schematic could be made very simple. Practically the whole command is programmed as a function key on the menu. All that the operator has to do is operate the digitizing on a function key that is marked with a notation that represents the symbol, and the command is given. All that remains for the operator to do is to digitize where the symbol is to go, using the digitizing pen. If the symbol is to be moved or changed in size, a command is available to do that easily. Again, those commands can also be programmed onto the menu. Frequently, an entire drawing can be made using only the digitizing pen without once using the keyboard. All that is required is a well-prepared menu.

Now nodal lines are drawn between the connect nodes on each symbol. The nodal lines are inserted onto the drawing by use of a command like

#INS NLIN LAY1: ent D dig DD

The designer or operator identifies the connect node by the first digitized entry and then routes the nodal line to its destination by additional digitizing entries. The final digitized location must be at a connect node, marking the other end of the electrical connection. The designer then repeats this operation for each electrical connection to be made on the schematic.

Nodal text is then inserted on the drawing at the text nodes that have been established for this purpose. A typical command for inserting the nodal text is as follows:

#INS NTXT $$R1$C1$C2$$ TNOD: ent DD

Two delimiters (the $$ entries) represent the beginning and ending of text that is being subdivided. In this case, R1 is inserted at the first digitized location, C1 is inserted at the second digitized location, and C2 is inserted at the third digitized location. After the second set of double delimiters ($$) TNOD is entered to indicate to the system that text is to be inserted at the digitized text nodes.

The text nodes and connect nodes are used on the drawing only during its construction. When the drawing is completed, the operator enters the commands:

#ECH TNOD OFF

and

#ECH CNOD OFF

and these two nodal entities are removed from the picture, although they remain in the database. The command:

#ECH SORG OFF

removes the subfigure origins off of the drawing.

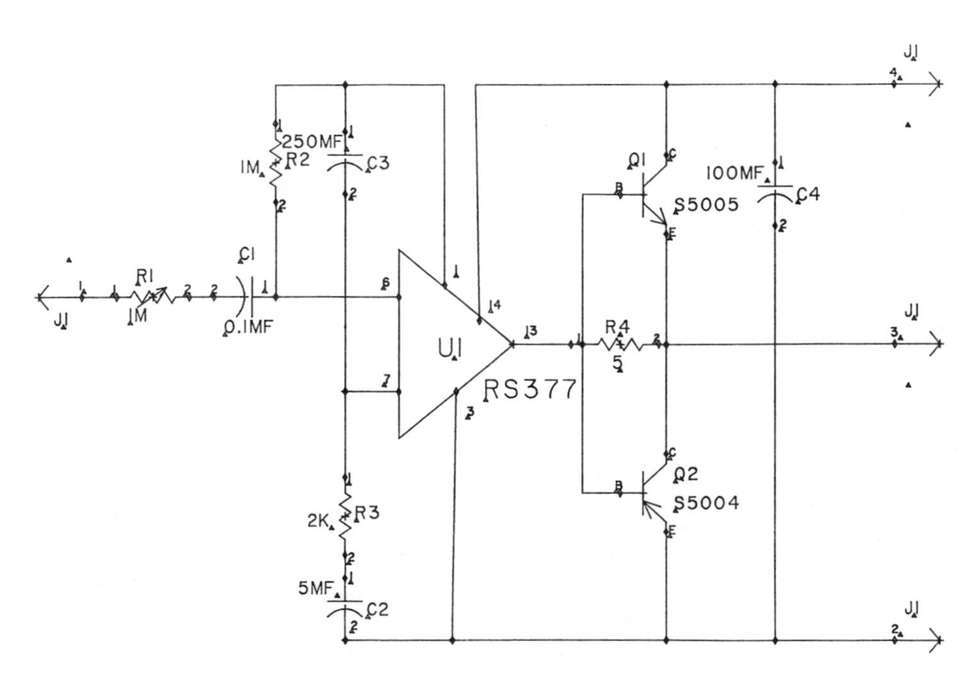

Figure 10.18 Schematic, as made by computer graphics system, with connect nodes, text nodes, and subfigure origins all echoed on.

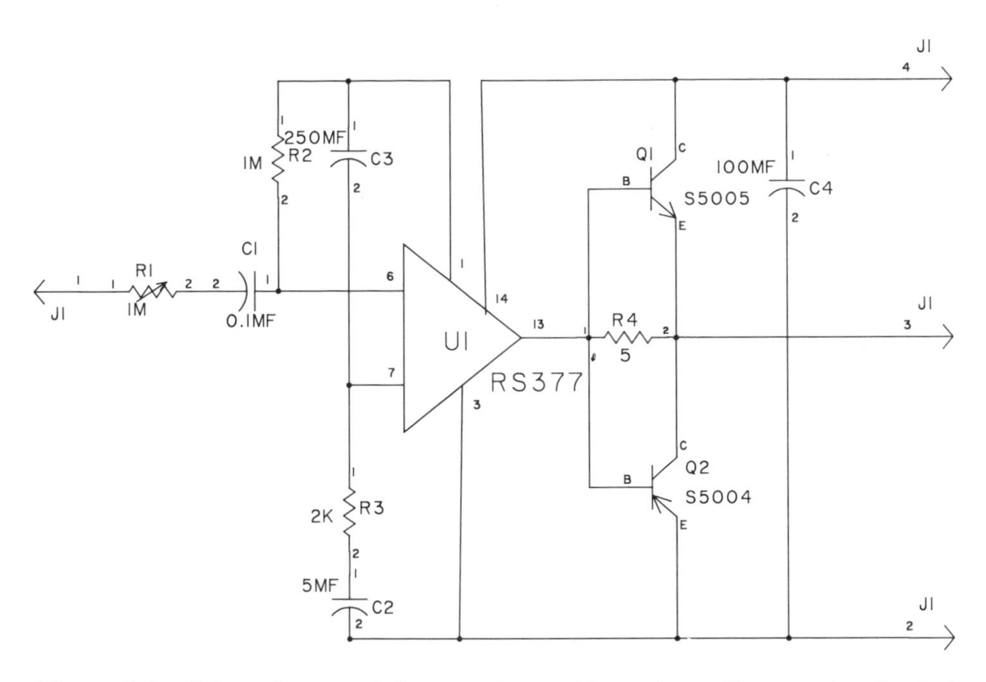

Figure 10.19 Schematic, as made by computer graphics system, with connect nodes, text nodes, and subfigure origins echoed off.

10.4.5 Checking

The system software provides the designer with the opportunity to have the drawings automatically checked. To do this, the operator may need to build and store various text files that instruct the system as to the specifications that the drawings must meet. The drawings must have been prepared by use of the standard layering format, correctly specified properties of entities and symbols, and correctly inserted connect nodes, text nodes, and nodal lines. With these preparations done, a schematic may be checked for

1. Correct labeling of components, terminals, and connecting lines
2. Parallel conducting paths
3. Connecting points to which connections have not been made
4. Connecting lines that do not terminate at an actual component
5. Correspondence to a circuit board layout or integrated-circuit layout which has been based upon the schematic

The first four items in the list are accomplished by means of a LIST NET command. This command causes a list to be printed out of the signals in a circuit, the reference designators of the components to which a given signal is connected, and the terminals to which the connections are made. The system identifies the number of unused connect nodes there are, thereby flagging down the number of connections that have not been made. The system identifies the number of floating nodal lines there are to determine connecting lines that do not terminate at an actual component. The system also, in the same printout, identifies the number of multiple paths that occur in a given signal, thereby determining the parallel conducting paths.

Correspondence of a schematic to a circuit board layout or integrated-circuit layout is checked by means of the COMPARE NET command. This command compares the specifications of an identified signal on a schematic with its specifications on the printed-circuit board or integrated-circuit layout. It is easy for the system to do this because the reference designators and terminal identifiers on the schematic must be the same as the reference designators and terminal identifiers that have been recorded on the physical layout of the printed-circuit board or integrated circuit. The connective relationships between the component symbols of the two drawings must also be the same for any given signal. Even though the graphics of the symbols and connecting lines may be different, the labeling is exactly the same.

For ladder diagrams, there are frequently a number of relays used in the circuit. These relays can best be shown on the diagram by separating their contacts and coils physically at a great distance from each other. They may even be on different drawings yet still be part of the same system of electric connections. The correct connections are assured by cross-referencing drawings and contact locations. The system aids in determining whether the correct connections have been made by checking to see that

1. The coils are labeled properly
2. The contacts are labeled properly
3. All coils have labels and that there are contacts associated with them
4. All contacts have labels and that there are coils associated with them

If the coils have not been labeled properly, the reason might be that they are not connected properly. If a coil or some contacts are missing or not labeled, a connection could be missing to them or they could be misconnected.

10.5 PRODUCTION OF A PRINTED-CIRCUIT BOARD DESIGN

10.5.1 Symbol Development

To make the greatest use of the computer graphics system for designing printed-circuit boards, there first must be

1. A library of standard component symbols
2. Text files for checking and autoplacement of components
3. Software available that can be used for fast and efficient component placement and connection layouts.

The component symbols used for printed-circuit boards are made in a similar manner as the schematic symbols. They contain

1. Graphics that show the shape and size of the component
2. Connect nodes for showing connections to the components
3. Text nodes for labeling the components

The component symbol graphics include a full-scale outline of the top view of the component as it appears on the board. The graphics are produced so that the lines and curves on the symbol have some specified thickness. With this feature, when the resulting symbol is plotted on a photoplotter, a line drawing appears clearly on the film. The graphics are put on layer 0.

Each printed-circuit symbol has one or more terminals that locate where connections are to be made. Since each symbol is the top view of a component, the terminals are arranged to be viewed from the top of the component. If the terminals are underneath the component they will appear on the symbol layout as if the symbol were transparent.

The graphical and nongraphical characteristics of the symbol terminals are composed of a number of entities that are inserted one on top of the other. Each terminal contains pads, solder masks, a connect node, and a drill symbol. The contents and description of each of these items is discussed in the following paragraphs.

CONNECT NODE

A connect node is placed at the center of each terminal. For one of the terminals, the connect node marks the subfigure origin of the symbol. For multiterminal components, the location of the connect node that marks the subfigure origin is located at some standard position on the symbol, such as at terminal 1. Various properties may be assigned to the connect node. These properties perform the function of identifying for the system certain characteristics of a connect node that allow for full use of the system capabilities in preparing complete specifications for a printed-circuit board, with little help from the designer. Such properties may perform functions like controlling areas to avoid while routing the circuit board or specifying drill sizes for holes that are to be drilled through the board at the terminal locations.

PADS

Each terminal contains figures that represent pads on the circuit board. These pads are built as separate library parts that are inserted onto a terminal whenever a symbol is constructed. They are inserted onto a terminal so that their subfigure origins are located at the same position as the connect nodes that have also been placed on the terminal. If the board is a multilayer type, there must be a pad inserted on every layer. For example, a printed-circuit board with copper on both sides will have a pad inserted on the component side as well as the connection side. A standard layer format is to put the component-side pad on layer 9 and the connection-side pad on layer 2.

SOLDER MASKS

If a printed-circuit is to be assembled using an automated soldering process, each component symbol must have solder masks placed on the terminal locations. To make the solder mask, a figure is inserted at the terminal location to mark the boundaries of the area that solder will be allowed to make contact with the pad. The solder mask is typically larger than the pad, and its subfigure origin is placed in the same location as that of the pad and connect node. If automated soldering is used for both sides of the board, a solder mask is placed on different layers, representing each side on which it is to be placed. For example, for a board with copper on both sides, a standard layering format uses layer 49 for the solder side and layer 42 for the component side.

DRILL SYMBOL

The drill symbol is a figure shaped like a cross that is used as the graphic representation of a hole to be drilled in the board. The subfigure origin of the drill symbol is the center of the cross, and when inserted on the terminal, it is placed on the same location as the subfigure origins of the other elements that make up the terminal. The size of the drill symbol is based on the diameter of the hole to be drilled. Layer 60 is used for insertion of the drill symbol. This layer is used to identify the drill symbol locations when the database

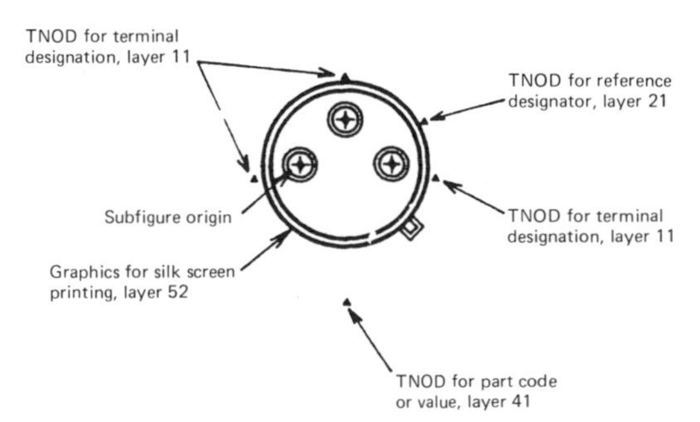

Figure 10.20 Printed-circuit symbol for a TO-5 transistor, as made by a computer graphics system, along with a description of its major parts.

is used in programming a numerically controlled drill press or for plotting a drill template to be used by the machinist who manually drills holes in the board.

10.5.2 Board Outline and Placement of Components

The designer uses the graphics system for printed-circuit design by first drawing the outline and shape of the board, inserting strings as graphic entities on the screen. An edge connector is then added for external connections to the board. The connector is defined by a figure that represents a standard connector configuration. This is inserted onto the board in the desired location. Again using the string as a graphic entity, the designer draws the boundaries of "keep-out" areas of the board. The keep-out areas define certain areas that are not to be used for component placement or for runs between components. Layer numbers or properties or both are used to identify the connector and keep-out areas to the system, allowing the automatic placement and automatic routing programs to put components and runs in preferred areas of the board.

The components are placed on the board layout individually by the system operator and moved around as desired to allow for the easiest layout pattern. The method of accomplishing this is much neater and faster than the designer can do on a traditional drafting board. The designer can be further assisted by the system if it is equipped with autoplacement software. However, the placement software must be backed up by a group of previously constructed text files. The autoplacement software accomplishes these functions:

1. Uses the schematic or other information to define the components to be placed into the circuit
2. Relates these components to those which are available in the component symbols library
3. Defines the orientation of the components with respect to their subfigure origins
4. Defines the criteria to follow for placing the components in the best position

If the plans of the designer are such that many similar components, circuits, and board layouts are to be used in design projects, the designer may find the automatic placement routine helpful in the design procedure. If the autoplacement routine is not used, there are other shortcuts that are available to the designer in placing components. If there are repetitive component insertions to be made, text files can be constructed that can be called on to have the system put a group of standard components on the board in

Figure 10.21 Board outline and shape, with edge connectors, as plotted by Interact IV plotter.

preselected locations. Even if components are placed individually by the designer, the routine is considerably simplified and speeded up over traditional methods using a drafting board. The entire drawing, including board outline definition, component placement, and routing, is performed by use of a grid system similar to that used when making a schematic. In addition, automatic checking routines are available to the designer, whether or not the board is designed with autoplacement and autorouting.

10.5.3 Routing the Board

The designer has the option of routing the board by placing individual runs or by allowing the system to route the board automatically. The system can route the board automatically if autoroute software is available and if the designer has properly placed and annotated the components on the board configuration in the database. If autoroute or autoplacement software is not available, the circuit-board designer still has powerful assistance in preparing the design.

First of all, the designer can, after insertion of component symbols, individually insert nodal lines to make connections to the components. Nodal lines represent runs on the board. The nodal lines are modified to have width, justification, endpoint extension, and other specifications as desired by the operator. They are inserted individually onto the board layout using a layer number that represents the side of the board on which they are to be placed. For example, layer 22 is used for runs placed on the component side, and layer 39 is used for runs placed on the connection side.

The designer can have all the connections temporarily identified for any signal. The system has knowledge of the schematic that the circuit-board design is based on and uses that knowledge to highlight the signals that the designer wishes to place on the board. The designer saves time by not having to refer to the schematic and there is less chance of overlooking a connection. Nodal lines are then inserted individually or collectively as desired, depending on designer software available.

The designer can insert all the nodal lines with one command for a particular signal by using the INSERT NET command. The system uses air-line routes that can be modified afterward by the designer. By having all the signal paths made and shown on the screen, the designer saves time and there is less chance of overlooking a connection.

If autorouting software is available, the designer can issue the ROUT BRD command, and the entire board will be routed automatically. The system will determine the path the nodal lines take and the locations of vias or feed-throughs, and it will draw nodal lines between all previously assigned connect nodes on symbol terminals. Prior to issuing the command, the designer must have taken the following steps:

1. Insert and annotate all component symbols.
2. Have a board outline drawn, with keep-out areas designated.
3. Have the system merge schematic information (stored in text files) with information that has been inserted into the circuit board drawing. (This is also required for utilizing signal highlighting and bulk nodal line insertion.)
4. Use any special modifiers with the command that will allow the board to be automatically routed in such a way that the designer's wishes are met.

After the board is routed, whether automatically or by individual nodal line insertion, the board must be edited. Editing may be required if

1. Insufficient clearance between entities is found
2. A more pleasing appearance is required
3. Undetected errors have to be corrected
4. Routes must be simplified for greater reliability and ease of manufacture
5. Engineering changes are made

Editing is accomplished by rerouting nodal lines, moving the ends of nodal lines, or moving vias or component symbols.

The board design is then checked for errors between the schematic and the board layout. It is also checked for insufficient clearances between entities. The system aids the designer in making these checks. Since the database contains both a schematic and a printed-circuit board layout that describes the same basic electric circuit, the system can compare the two data groups and highlight and print out errors that exist between them, using the COMPARE NET command. By the use of previously constructed text files, the system searches for insufficient gaps between runs, between runs and pads, pads and vias, or vias and runs. The system checks for overlaps between runs and pads or vias. The system also checks to see that the width of the runs are as specified.

10.5.4 Producing a Database for Use in Manufacturing Facilities

An unusual feature of printed-circuit board drawings is that many of them are actually used in the manufacturing process, not as reference guides, but as actual templates or tools. The drawing for a specific manufacturing process can be obtained by echoing on only those layers that are used by that process before the drawing is made. Thus, a master layout drawing can be produced by only echoing on layers 2, 20, and 22. These will show the pads, vias, and runs for one side of the board. The photoplotter will then produce a photographic film that is used to photoetch the board. A silk screen drawing can be made by only using layer 52 in the plotting process. The plotter will make a film that is used to mark the board, using a silk screen printing process. A drilling drawing is made by only plotting layer 60. This layer produces a drawing of the diameter and location of the holes to be drilled in the board. A solder-mask drawing is made by only plotting layer 49. This photoplotted film can be used to mark areas on the board that are to be soldered in an automated soldering process.

In addition to the drawings that can be produced, magnetic tapes can be made of the printed-circuit board database. These are fed to numerically controlled equipment through a postprocessor device. For example, the drawings can be made in such a way that the tapes of them can be supplied to a numerically controlled component inserter. The component inserter will recognize the location and identity of a component that is to be automatically inserted in a board. The component inserter is then used to reduce labor and increase speed in the assembly of components to the board.

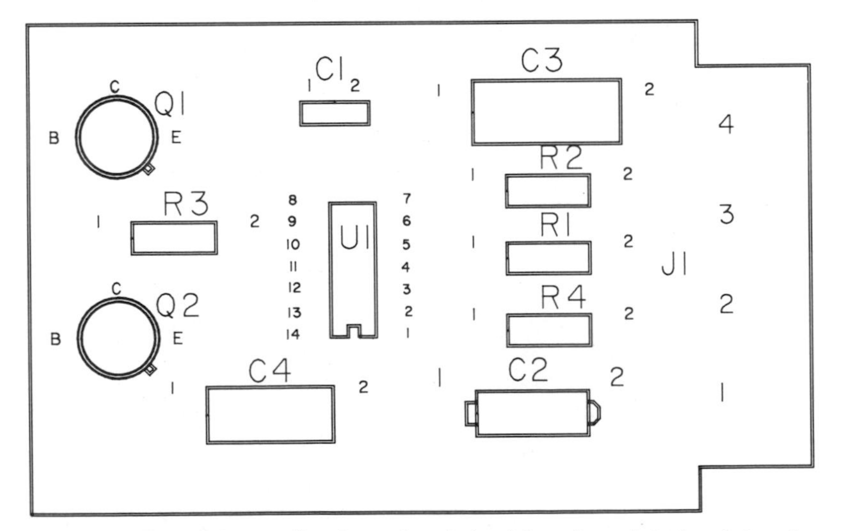

Figure 10.22 Silk screen drawing, printed-circuit board, as plotted on Interact IV plotter.

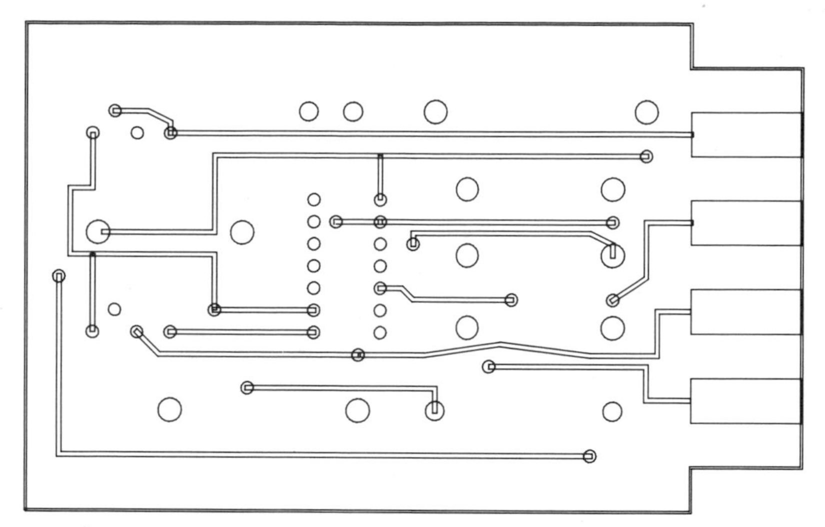

Figure 10.23 Board layout pattern, connection side, as plotted on Interact IV plotter (layer 22 echoed).

Holes can be drilled in the board by a numerically controlled drill press, based on tapes supplied from the system. A command can be issued during the board design process that will specify the size of holes to be drilled in the board, their location, and the path that the drill takes in going from one hole to another. The holes are located by having a "drill" property assigned to connect nodes that mark places where a hole is to be drilled. Another property specifies the size of the hole to be drilled.

10.6 DESIGNING INTEGRATED CIRCUITS

For integrated-circuit design, the operator uses a library of previously constructed parts called *cells*. The cells represent masking patterns for each elementary circuit to be made in the process of constructing the semiconductor circuit on the chip.

The cells are then inserted onto a larger drawing to make a layout representing a mask that is used in the fabrication process. The mask layout is based on a "floor plan" that represents the architecture of the integrated circuit. A predetermined grid is used during

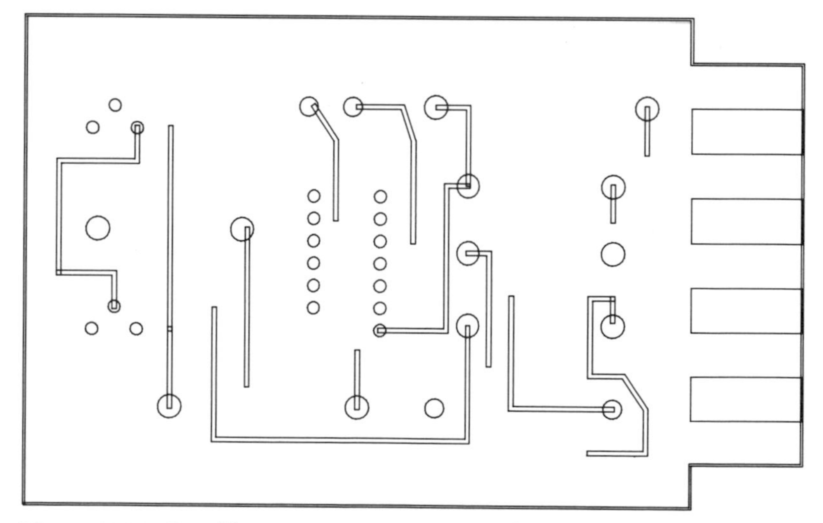

Figure 10.24 Board layout pattern, component side, plotted on Interact IV (layer 39 echoed).

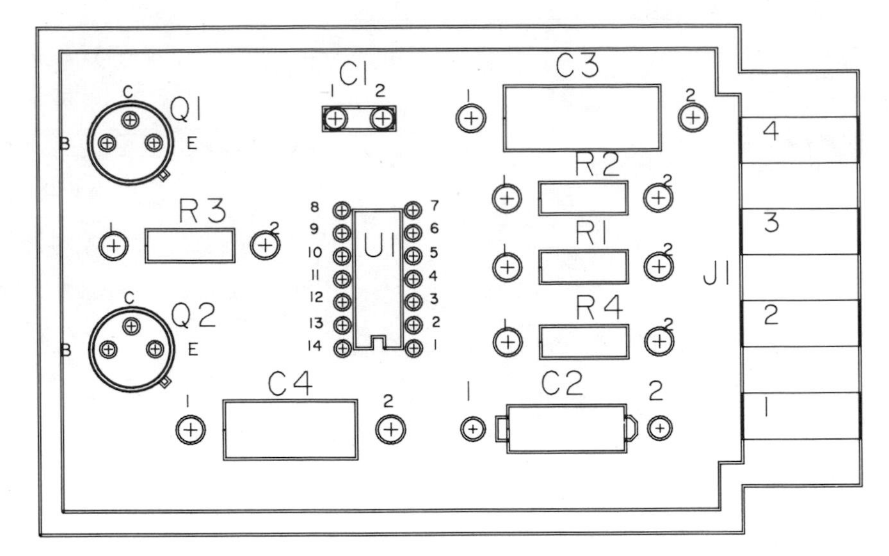

Figure 10.25 Silk screen drawing, printed-circuit board, layer 52 plotted on Interact IV.

insertion of cells to guide the pattern design. Each cell is given identification text similar to that used for the schematic symbols. Connections are then routed between the cells, using nodal lines having width. This is done for each mask that is prepared for the chip. This is also done to construct a pattern of commonly used cells. This group of cells and associated connections is called a *macrocell*. Both cells and macrocells are stored into the system memory as library parts that are inserted as one entity for construction of the circuit on a single chip.

10.6.1 Cell Development

To construct a basic cell, a different layer is chosen for each mask pattern required for the circuit layout. For example, layer 21 may be used as the mask for a diffusion process. Then layer 24 may be used for the mask that prepares an area to which a metal contact is to be made. Then layer 25 is chosen for the layer that determines the pattern that the metal

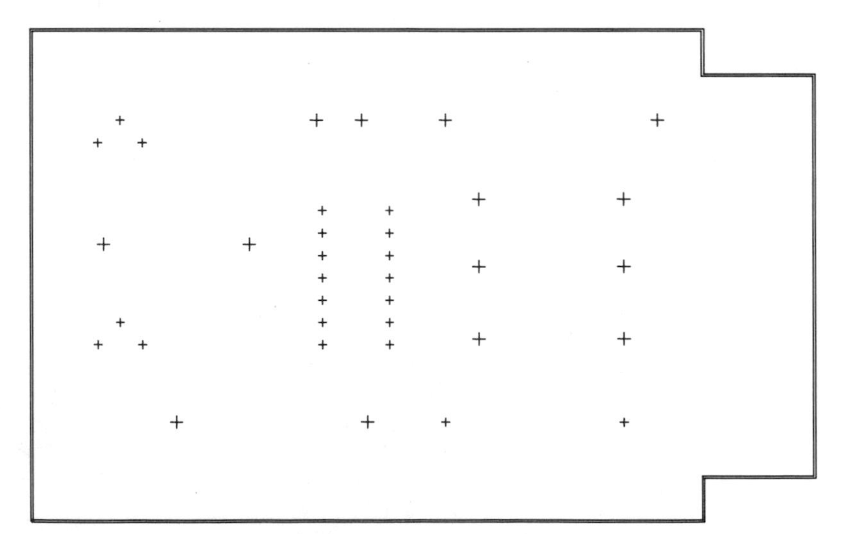

Figure 10.26 Drilling drawings, printed-circuit board, layer 60 plotted on Interact IV.

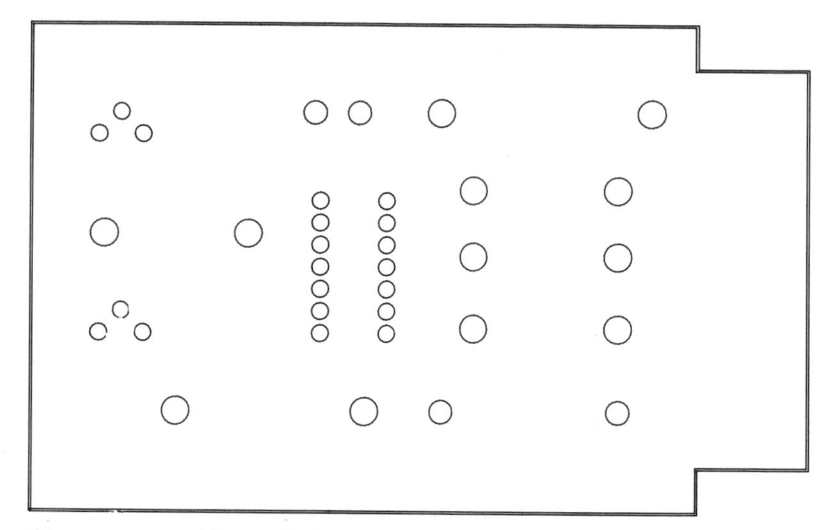

Figure 10.27 Solder-mask drawing, printed-circuit board, layer 49 plotted on Interact IV.

contact is to have on the chip. The entities used for the cell graphics are inserted as lines or strings, and the part is filed. Then a nodal figure, containing connect nodes and text nodes, is built. The connect nodes are put on layer 1 and are placed wherever a connection is to be made within the cell or to neighboring cells. When inserting connect nodes, a distinction is made between connect nodes that make connections within a cell and connect nodes that are used to make connections to neighboring cells. Text nodes are put on the cell layout to mark the seat of text for identifying connecting points and the name of the cell. The cell name is placed on layer 21 and the text identifying cell connecting points is placed on layer 11. The nodal figure, thus constructed, is then filed under a separate part name. It is then inserted onto the part that represents the cell graphics.

Now there exists a graphical representation of a cell, along with a nodal figure containing a group of text nodes and connect nodes inserted onto it. The connect nodes within the cell are then joined by nodal lines inserted on layer 1. This combination of

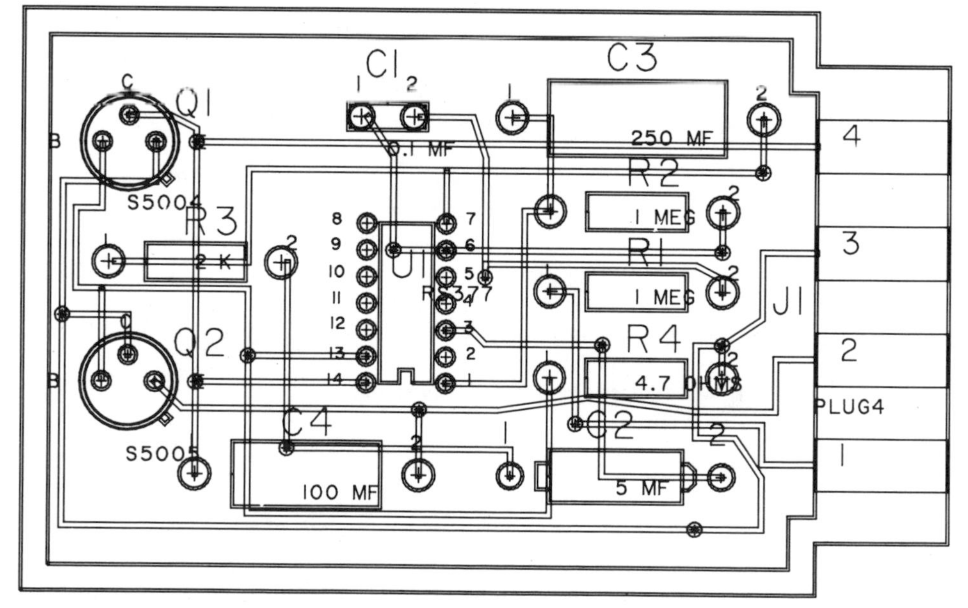

Figure 10.28 Printed-circuit board, all layers echoed, plotted on Interact IV.

graphics, connect nodes, text nodes, and nodal lines is needed for the command that automatically interconnects this cell with neighboring cells (the JOIN PANEL command). The JOIN PANEL command permits two or more cells (panels) to be merged into a larger part whereby the nodal lines from the different cells which meet along common borders will be joined together to make a macrocell.

10.6.2 Building the Chip

To build the chip, first a logic diagram or schematic drawing must be created. The schematic is then checked and edited so that nodal information on the schematic will match nodal information that is used on the chip layout. A list of signals is then created that serves as a net list to which a corresponding net list for the chip can be prepared. The net list is prepared using the LIST NET command available in the system repertoire.

The chip is then built in the following steps, using the graphics system.

1. A basic floor plan is prepared, based on the logic diagram or schematic diagram.
2. Nodal entities are inserted into the basic cell pattern and appropriate interconnections made to construct the standard cells or macrocells needed. The cells that are chosen must have connect nodes in the correct location and contain associated text nodes that are in correspondence with that of the schematic for which a layout must be created.
3. The mask layout is prepared by placing the cells and macrocells on the chip according to the floor plan. Channels are provided for interconnections.
4. The connect nodes of adjoining cells are connected together by using nodal lines. If autorouting software is available, it may be utilized at this stage.
5. A list is obtained of the signals (a net list using the LIST NET command).

10.6.3 Checking the Design

The design is checked by comparing the net list for the schematic with the net list for the chip layout. This is used to check for errors in the layout. The system can be used to aid this operation; however, the technique is different from that used for printed-circuit boards. There are structural and semantic differences between the two net lists, requiring that the format of one or the other be changed before the system can assist in making the comparison. This is done by applying the data-extract features of the system. To apply data extract, a group of text files is made available that will reformat the net list information after it is obtained from the diagram. The reformatting is accomplished in two major steps.

1. The basic interconnection data are obtained from the diagram, using the EXTRACT DATA command.
2. The data are reformatted, with the help of previously prepared text files, using repeated application of a MERGE FILE command.

The result is a net list that is provided in the same format as a net list produced during the chip layout procedure. The two net lists can then be compared for errors, using the COMPARE NET command. If any errors are found, either the circuit diagram or chip layout is edited, and the net lists are again constructed, reformatted, and compared for any additional errors.

10.7 SUMMARY

The building of electrical diagrams and the designing of printed-circuit boards and integrated circuits using traditional drafting methods or using a computer graphics system have been discussed. Only a survey of the main computer graphic techniques has been given because of the lack of space and because the techniques differ, depending upon the actual system used.

Limitations of traditional drafting techniques and advantages of computer graphics systems for electrical design and drafting were covered. The speed, precision, and efficiency of computer graphics systems far exceed conventional manual drafting and design methods. The need for an adequate parts library, text files, and system management has been mentioned.

The importance of nongraphical features of the system database has been emphasized, and the need for adequate training of new operators is made evident.

Specific techniques were covered using the Computervision system CADDS 3 electrical design software. To prepare the reader for the discussion, basic operating facilities and techniques were summarized. A brief discussion was included on the preparation of symbols for various electrical drawings and the use of them in preparing the diagrams and circuit layouts. Nodal entities were listed and defined as important parts of the database. Some salient features of autoplacement and autorouting software were explained.

There is a sizable amount of information needed for a complete explanation of the use of a computer graphics system in performing electrical design and drafting work. This discussion only provides a superficial coverage of the subject, but we hope it has stimulated the reader to seek further information on this important application of computer technology.

BIBLIOGRAPHY

CADDS3 Graphics Operator, Revision 11, Computervision Corporation, 1980, Bedford, Mass.

Evans, Charles H.: *Electronic Amplifiers*, Litton Educational Publishing, New York, 1979.

Horgan, James D.: "Network Comparison of a Mask Layout and a Logic Diagram," *Proceedings of the Fourth Annual International Computervision Users Conference*, 1982, Computervision Corp., Bedford, Mass.

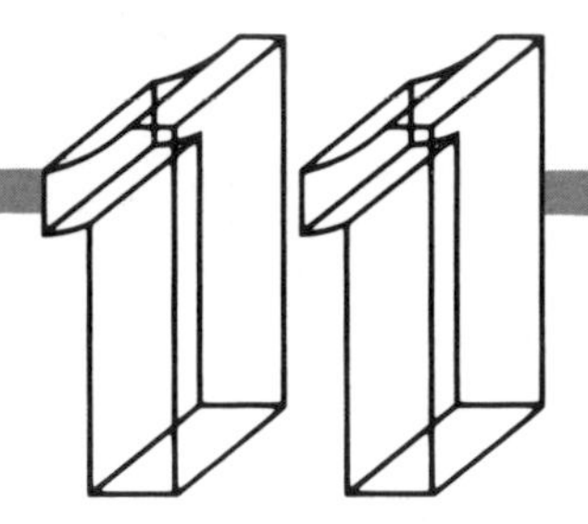

Architecture, Engineering, and Construction

by
William J. Mitchell

11.1 CAD'S ROLE IN THE BUILDING DESIGN AND CONSTRUCTION PROCESS

11.1.1 Overview of the Process

The building design and construction process normally involves investigation and documentation of the requirements for a proposed facility, generation and consideration of ranges of schematic design alternatives, selection, then detailed development, of one alternative, production of extensive documentation (working drawings, specifications, shop drawings, etc.) describing the developed design, negotiation of construction contracts based upon this documentation, construction management, planning and coordination of the move-in, and ongoing facility management. (See Refs. 1 and 2 for further details.) From an information processing point of view, this involves accessing catalog databases of various kinds (catalogs of construction components and materials, building codes, master specifications, standard details, etc.) to extract required information, developing a description of the proposed building (by making design decisions and recording them in drawings, written specifications, etc.), analyzing design concepts to determine their adequacy, producing and disseminating construction documents of a variety of different types (drawings, tabular reports, specification text, etc.), and managing the ongoing process (sequencing tasks, allocating resources, monitoring progress, maintaining data security and integrity, and so on). The project databases developed at the design phase may later be employed in construction management and ongoing facility management. Figure 11.1 provides an overview of this entire process.

The process has both a vertical structure of phases succeeding each other over time and a horizontal structure of parallel activities at any particular phase. This is illustrated in Fig. 11.2. Different kinds of organizations that play a role in design and construction are characterized by different degrees of horizontal and vertical integration.

A traditional architectural firm, for example, vertically integrates design tasks—from investigation of requirements (programming) to final documentation—then (to a carefully limited extent) supervises the work of the construction contractor. Some architectural firms (usually smaller ones) are more specialized, focusing primarily upon the programming phase, the schematic design phase, or the documentation phase. Drafting services (either manual or computer-based) are concerned solely with document production. Some larger architectural firms are attempting greater vertical integration—backward, by becoming involved in long-term facility planning, and forward, by offering construction management and ongoing facility management services. There are also an increasing number of specialized firms which deal with the vertical sequence of facility planning, programming, space planning, interior design, and facility management. Structural, mechanical, and other engineering consulting firms are usually integrated vertically over the design phases, in parallel with architectural firms. There is an increasing tendency for large organizations (universities, hospitals, major corporations, etc.) to do their own facility management and then to begin integrating backward to design tasks.

Some specialized firms integrate horizontally to provide comprehensive services at one phase of the process. Often this is tied to specialization in a building type. For

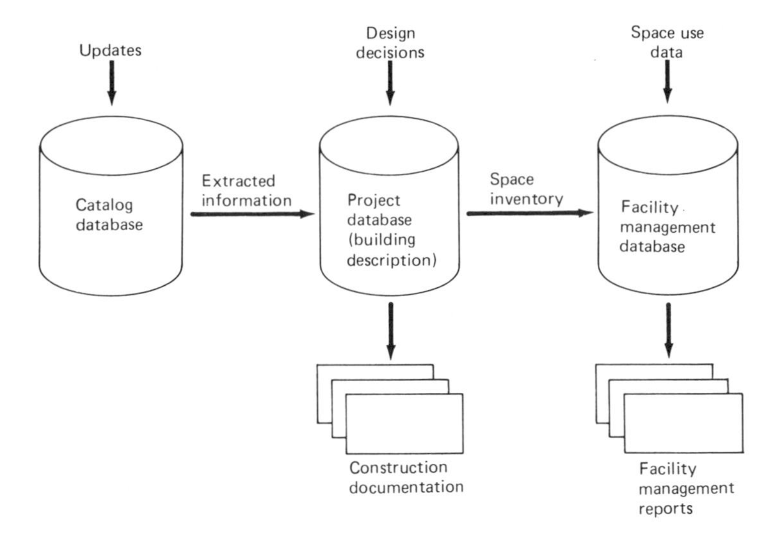

Figure 11.1 Basic flow of data in the building design and facility management process.

example, there are horizontally integrated firms that specialize in the planning, programming, and schematic design of medical facilities.

The latest available reliable data show that the numbers and sizes of architectural firms in the United States are distributed as follows:[3]

No. of employees	% of firms	% of total fee receipts
50+	3.3	26.9
20–49	11.4	23.4
8–19	34.1	29.5
4–7	51.2	20.2
	100.0	100.0

The approximately 150 large (50 or more employees) firms do a very large part of the total business, including almost all the very large and technically complex projects. These are the firms most able to make major investments in computer-aid design (CAD) technology. At the other end of the spectrum, over 2000 very small (seven or fewer employees) firms do only about 20 percent of the total business, and most of this is in domestic-scale, technically simple projects. These firms are most likely to make use of low-cost microcomputer hardware, off-the-shelf software, and service bureaus.

Construction firms are distributed in a very similar pattern. Numerous small firms undertake small-scale projects, while a relatively small number of large firms dominate the field and carry out the large and complex projects. The giants of the building design and construction field are the large architectural and engineering (AE) and architectural, engineering, and construction (AEC) firms. These are characterized by broad horizontal integration across the design disciplines. Some focus upon the design phase, some upon construction contracting, and some provide vertically integrated turnkey design and construction services.

Another important set of actors in the design and construction process are the suppliers of building materials, prefabricated construction components, furniture, and equipment. These are primarily concerned with the design of items for relatively extended production runs and factory production rather than the design of one-off objects for on-site construction. An issue of emerging importance, then, is how to achieve appropriate integration between industrial computer-aided design and computer-aided manufac-

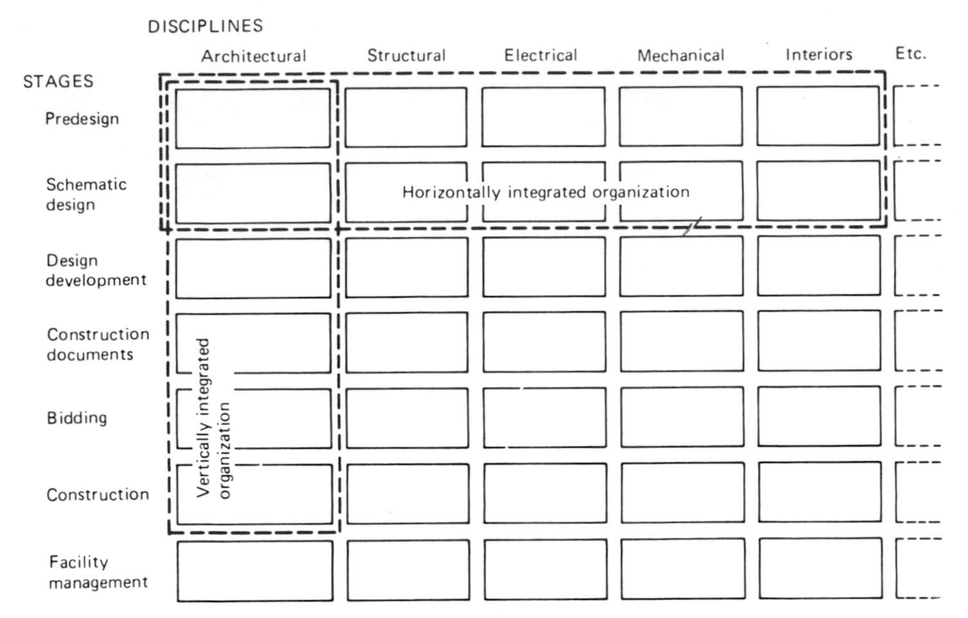

Figure 11.2 Horizontal and vertical structures of the building design, construction, and management process.

turing (CAD/CAM) systems employed by suppliers and the drafting and CAD systems employed by architects, engineers, and interior designers.

In summary, the AEC field in the United States is fragmented and balkanized in its structure (see Ref. 4 for further details). Furthermore, it is risky, and firms in it are subject to sudden and unexpected fluctuations in work load and cash flow. These factors have significantly slowed the penetration of CAD/CAM technology into the field. In some other parts of the world the pattern has been different. In Britain and many other parts of western Europe, for example, a very significant proportion of design and construction work is carried out by large government agencies which, in many cases, have been able to implement CAD on a broad scale (see Ref. 5 for further information on these efforts). (In the United States the role of public agencies in design and construction is much more limited, but some agencies, notably the Army Corps of Engineers and the Veterans Administration, have developed significant CAD capabilities.) In Japan there are a number of very large, well-established corporations which integrate AEC activities, and many of these have made major investments in development of proprietary CAD software for in-house use.

Except in the case where a large AEC firm or government agency provides a complete turnkey service, design and construction processes are characterized by the participation of numerous independent firms linked by contractual relationships. These contractual relationships establish the kind of information that flows back and forth between firms and the financial frameworks within which various kinds of firms work, and so have important implications for the design, marketing, and use of CAD systems within the construction industry. For example, there are well-established conventions governing the percentage of the construction cost (under various different circumstances) which goes to the architect's fee and governing the information which should be shown on working drawings (which play a role as construction contract documents). These kinds of conventions can be challenged, and new kinds of contracts, financial relationships, and patterns of information flow can be developed. Indeed, the potential of CAD often motivates reconsideration. However it is important to recognize that such conventions are always an important factor in the construction industry and that making changes in order to take full advantage of CAD is not often quick or easy.

Finally, it is worth noting that the construction industry deals with an enormous diversity of scales, methods of construction, and facility types. This means that effective CAD systems for use within the construction industry must be appropriately specialized to their contexts of application. For example, systems for the design of single-family tract houses, for space planning and facility management in large corporations, for hospital design and documentation, and for the design of large-scale pipework systems, all have very different performance requirements. This is obviously so on the plane of high-level application software modules and symbol and component menus. More subtly (and disturbingly, for vendors who would like to employ a standard CAD system infrastructure), the differences in context of application can have quite profound implications for the organization of databases, the semantics of graphic editing commands, display and plotting capabilities, and protocols for graphic interaction.

Against the background that has now been sketched, the following subsections will examine catalog, project, and facility management databases; the analysis requirements in building design, construction, and management processes; the role of CAD systems in design synthesis processes; the requirements for document production; and project management and accounting implications. This will provide a foundation for analysis of the potential benefits of CAD in architecture and construction, technical issues that arise in the application of CAD technology to this field, and current and future patterns of practical application.

11.1.2 Catalog Data

The process of designing a building (or other physical system) may be regarded (for our immediate purposes) as one of selecting standard items from various catalogs, adapting those items, where necessary, to the requirements of a particular context, and combining them with other items to describe a design proposal. In manual design, the catalogs are often implicit, as when an architect works with a stylistically characteristic vocabulary of room shapes and construction devices. Certain kinds of catalogs have traditionally been made explicit on paper: component catalogs for industrialized building systems, furniture and equipment catalogs, tables of steel sections, libraries of standard details, master specifications, and so on. For their effectiveness, CAD systems normally rely heavily upon the availability of extensive catalogs in machine-readable form, together with associated software to support indexing and efficient retrieval and menu selection operations. Thus a useful distinction can be drawn between two kinds of design activities: the investment of effort in developing and maintaining catalogs and the application of available catalogs in particular design projects. Since catalogs are often expensive to develop and maintain, a division of labor frequently evolves; a central organization develops and maintains catalogs, recovers costs by charging users, and spreads cost recovery over a relatively large number of users.

Catalog databases commonly employed in architectural and construction CAD applications may conveniently be grouped under the headings of tabular data, text data, graphic data, and physical component data.

TABULAR DATA

A good example of a tabular database in this context is one containing standard area and equipment requirements for the many types of rooms in a large hospital. Such a database requires constant updating in response to changes in patterns of patient care and can only be maintained effectively by a knowledgeable research group. It can be used to put together quickly a program of specific space and equipment requirements for a particular hospital project. Space inventories and furniture inventories employed in facility management systems also commonly take tabular form. Some analysis programs also rely on the availability of tabular data; cost analysis programs require current cost data, for example, and thermal analysis programs require weather data for particular locations.

TEXT DATA

The most familiar kind of catalog database in text format is a master specification. From this, blocks of text may be selected to generate the construction specification for a particular project.

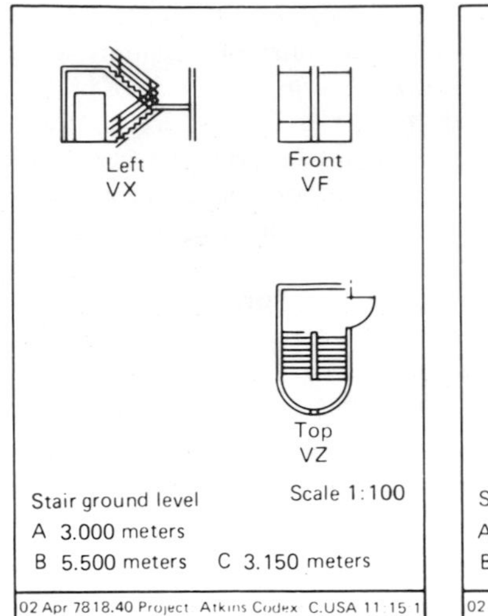

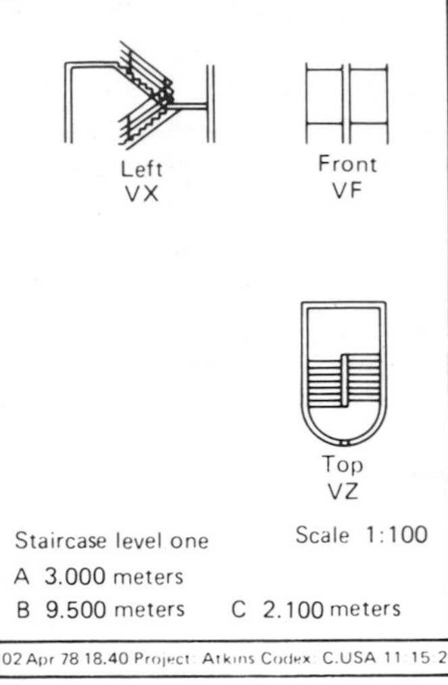

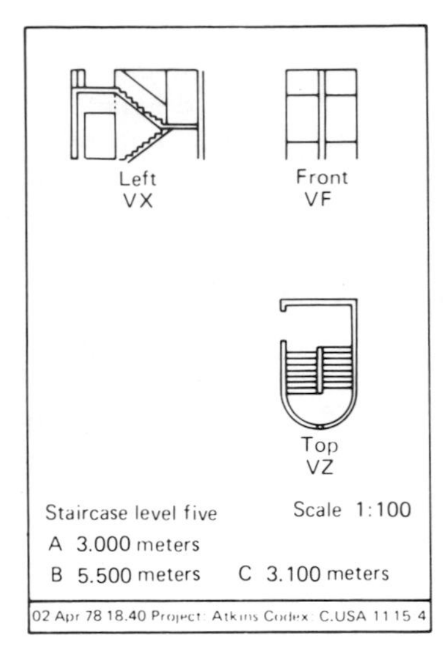

Figure 11.3 Part of a typical physical component database.

GRAPHIC DATA

Graphic databases are usually associated with drafting systems. Typically they are organized in several levels. At the lowest level is a menu of elementary geometric figures—arcs, rectangles, and the like—which may be instantiated by the system. These are employed to build an appropriate library of architectural symbols—door swings, windows, columns, standard furniture items, and so on. Groups of these elements may be associated into standard rooms, furniture groupings, etc. Finally, a system that has been in use for some time usually accumulates an extensive archive of completed drawings, which may be recalled and edited to adapt them quickly for use in new contexts. Generally, the level of productivity achievable by a drafting system in architectural applications is extremely sensitive to the relevance and extent of the associated graphic database.

PHYSICAL COMPONENT DATA

Physical component databases are usually associated with the more ambitious kinds of integrated CAD systems. Entries are physical elements, such as construction components, items of furniture or equipment, or standard room types (Fig. 11.3). Each is described geometrically at some appropriate level of completeness, ranging from a few key measures to a complete solid model, depending upon the objective and sophistication of the system. Nongeometric data, such as material properties, cost, supplier, and specification text, are also associated with each entry. This kind of catalog supports a design process of assembling instances of components to develop a full physical description of a proposed building.

11.1.3 Project Data

In a traditional manual design process, project data describing a design proposal (or alternative proposals) accumulate on paper as the process progresses. Drawings are produced, revised, and developed to higher levels of detail. In parallel, other information is recorded in the form of written notes; door, window, finish, and equipment schedules; and specifications. Eventually, a definitive and (one hopes) consistent description of the design is expressed in the final documentation.

The most elementary and obvious way to introduce computer aids into the design process is to parallel this organization of information development and recording so that a drafting system can be employed to produce and store drawings, a word processing system to produce and store specifications, and a database management system to produce and store tabular data. Furthermore, mathematical models of proposals may also exist in the form of input files for engineering analysis programs. This approach has evolved in many firms.

It is obvious, however, that this approach can generate some severe problems. It is likely to yield project descriptions which are both redundant and incomplete. Consistency of data held in different places is difficult to maintain as design changes are made. The economies that potentially follow from reuse of data in a variety of different applications are difficult to achieve.

An alternative is to organize a CAD system around a single, central, nonredundant database, maintaining a sufficiently complete description of the building to support a full range of alternative analysis, design synthesis, and document production applications. This organization is illustrated in Fig. 11.4. In practice, complete integration of project databases is difficult to achieve, and most CAD systems in practical use in the construction industry lie at some intermediate point between the poles of making no attempt at integration and of attempting full-scale integration.

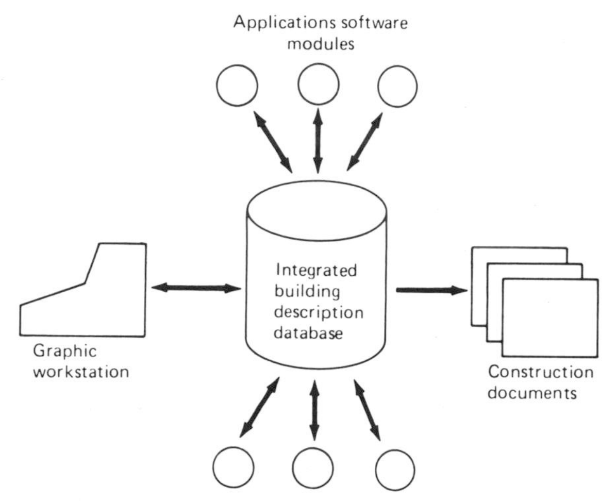

Figure 11.4 Integration of an architectural CAD system around a building description database.

Since there is a good deal of repetition of standard elements in most building designs, it is common to relate catalog and project databases as illustrated in Fig. 11.5. Each entry in the catalog fully describes a standard element type, while each entry in the project database records a type identifier, location, and other parameters which determine the instance. Thus the catalog and project databases jointly provide a concise but complete description of a building. However, this approach can cause problems if it is too rigidly implemented; sometimes it is convenient for a user to have the freedom to locate an element in a design without treating it as an instance of a cataloged type.

Vertical integration of project databases is also an important issue. It is highly desirable in an architectural CAD system to provide the capability to carry a project description all the way through the phases of architectural programming, schematic design, design development and documentation, and facility management. This is not straightforward, since both the contents and structures of project descriptions must change from phase to phase. Capabilities must be provided for transforming from one level of description to the next.

11.1.4 Facility Management Data

CAD systems used in facility management are usually organized around a space inventory and a furniture inventory database. These inventories may be tabular, with each entry recording characteristics of a space or furniture item. In this case, a database management

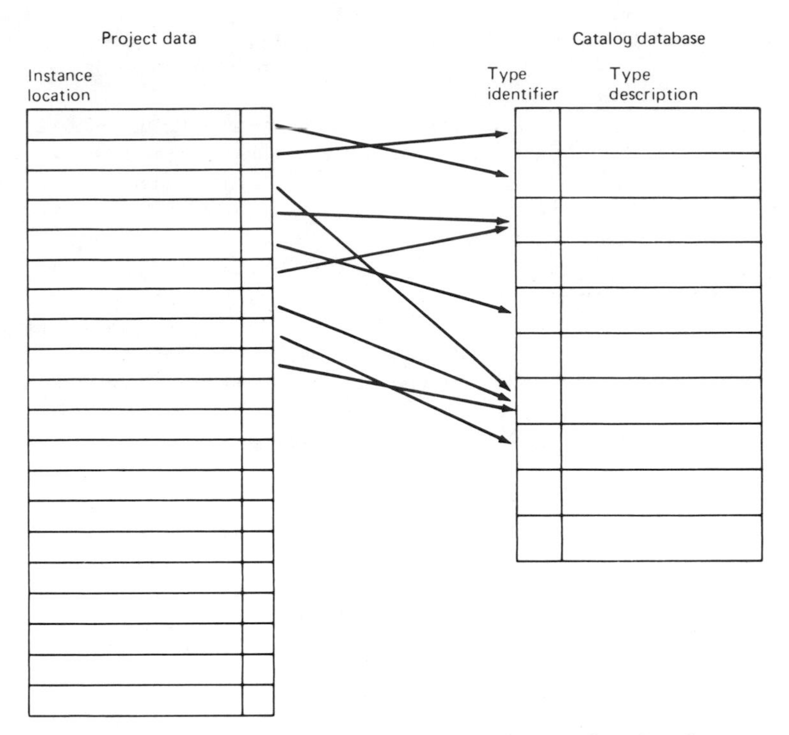

Figure 11.5 A building described as a set of instances of cataloged types.

system may be employed to maintain and report from the inventories. Alternatively, a drafting system may be employed to maintain the data graphically, in the form of plans. Usually, in this case, the drafting system is extended with at least some elementary database management capabilities, so that counts and tabulations of items may be generated.

The important link between CAD (as it has usually been understood) and facility management follows from the fact that the project database developed using a CAD system in the design of a new facility may potentially be taken over as the database of a management system for that facility. Obvious efficiencies and economies follow if this can be achieved. Furthermore, if the facility is later altered or extended, the architect can immediately gain access to an accurate current description of layout and space use; it is not necessary to conduct a survey of the facility or to rely upon out-of-date as-built drawings.

11.1.5 Analysis

A wide variety of performance and cost analyses must be carried out at each phase of the architectural design process to assure that the completed building is likely to meet specified performance and cost targets. Simple analyses are carried out by architects and more sophisticated analyses are performed as required by technical specialists such as structural engineers, mechanical engineers, electrical engineers, and cost consultants. At the early stages, when a design is defined only at a low level of resolution and detail, methods that require few data and quickly produce approximate results are employed. At later stages, when the design is more fully developed, more accurate, computationally expensive, and data-demanding methods are employed.

Numerous discrete programs for performing various kinds of analyses are in common use in architecture and construction. There are also comprehensive software libraries for particular technical disciplines. But the central technical issue, from a CAD viewpoint, is how broadly and effectively a CAD system can horizontally integrate by providing input data for analysis programs from the project database. This depends, of course, upon the nature of the project database. Two-dimensional drafting systems are incapable of achieving much integration of engineering analysis, for example, because they cannot supply the three-dimensional geometric and physical data required for structural analysis, energy analysis, etc. Systems which can maintain wire-frame three-dimensional geometric descriptions, or surface descriptions, can do considerably better. But only solid modeling systems, which maintain complete and unambiguous physical descriptions, are capable of integrating the full range of analysis applications. (See Section 11.3.4 for a discussion of wire-frame, surface, and solid modeling techniques.)

11.1.6 Synthesis

Any kind of CAD system provides the user with a repertoire of low-level design operations, such as instantiation of primitives; transformations; and perhaps sweep, extrusion, spatial set, and other operations for constructing solids. These constitute a set of basic tools with which, in conjunction with a catalog of standard elements, a design can be developed and manipulated.

More sophisticated systems also provide a variety of high-level design operations, which incorporate a certain amount of "architectural intelligence." Typically they are implemented as procedures which accept parameters describing a context and then attempt to instantiate a standard element of some kind. Typical examples are operations to lay out stairs between specified points in section, to lay out parking bays between points in a plan, and to route a duct through a ceiling from one specified point to another.

Where an instance must satisfy complex constraints (and where it may not be obvious that they are satisfiable), or where an optimal instance (such as a minimum beam section or an optimally efficient floor plan layout) is sought, software may be provided in a CAD system to perform the nontrivial problem-solving task that is involved in generating an appropriate instance. We usually think of this as automated design software.

A hierarchy is involved here. High-level design operations are built from sequences of lower-level design operations. The higher the level of a design synthesis procedure, in general, the more complex its control logic becomes, and the more difficult it is to anticipate the results that the procedure will produce in a particular context. Most current, practical architectural CAD systems are rich in low-level operations and very limited in their high-level "automated" design capabilities. However, the challenge is to discover how to build as much architectural intelligence into operations as possible so that designers using the systems can make their decisions at higher levels and eliminate as much routine work as possible.

In general, it is useful to think of an architectural CAD system as a machine which applies design operators (both low-level and high-level) in some domain of designs which is based upon a specified architectural vocabulary—just as a calculator is a machine which applies arithmetic operators in a domain of numbers. The available set of design operators will always, in practice, be limited. Furthermore, since complete generality is both inefficient and unnecessary in any specific context, there will be restrictions on the vocabulary of architectural elements and upon the ways in which elements may be combined. For example, a system might require all elements to be plane-faced polyhedra, or (more restrictedly) convex plane-faced polyhedra, or (more restrictedly still) rectangular boxes set out on a square grid. That is, an architectural CAD system has an associated language of architectural form and operators for exploring the possibilities within that language. Clearly it is of critical importance that this language should be technically and aesthetically appropriate to the context in which it is to be applied, and that it should be convenient and natural for the architect to manipulate using the available operators.

Some of the pioneering architectural CAD systems in Europe dealt with this issue by assuming a specific, well-defined industrialized component building system. In many other CAD systems, by contrast, the language is implicitly established by various implementation decisions, with the result that its characteristics and limits remain ill defined, and its appropriateness is difficult to evaluate. A sounder approach is to specify formally the architectural language that a system is to process by means of a shape grammar[6,7] or similar formalism, just as a computer language to be processed by a compiler might be formally specified in Backus-Naur Form (BNF).*

As yet, very few architects have much practical experience with the direct use of CAD systems in design synthesis. (Analysis and document production applications of computer technology have been much more common.) Hence, although one may speculate, there is very little evidence about the kinds of architectural languages, design operators, and user interfaces that might most effectively support architectural design synthesis. Nor is it at all clear how architectural design processes should be structured and managed to take maximum advantage of the potentials of CAD; architects are only just beginning to learn to think in terms of powerful CAD constructs such as parametric variation of shape, association of architectural elements and subsystems in instantiation hierarchies, and iterative or recursive procedural generation of regular geometric objects and arrangements.

11.1.7 Expert Advice

The design synthesis process can also be aided by providing expert advice to the designer at appropriate moments. In a conventional manual process, an architect gets advice by questioning consultants or by looking up references in printed texts. In the context of CAD systems, the interrogation of online databases is now beginning to play an important role. Such databases may be in-house or they may be made available by a database service. Reference 8 lists available online databases of interest in architecture and construction. For example, online building products databases are now available in the United States, France, and Sweden. In the United States, the *Avery Index to Architectural Periodicals* is now available online, and there are also available a number of construction cost and construction equipment databases.

As in many other professional and scientific fields, the recent rapid development of the technology of expert systems holds considerable potential for architecture. Landsdown has written a useful brief introduction to expert systems that discusses their potential roles in architecture and the construction industry.[9] An expert system in some specific field consists of software encoding facts and inference procedures, which together may be regarded as "a model of the expertise of the best practitioners in the field."[10] An expert system may be interrogated in a very flexible way and generally plays a role very much like that of a specialized technical consultant. Some prototype expert systems have been developed to provide advice on such topics as housing layout, diagnosis of timber defects, diagnosis of air conditioning problems, and architectural project administration, and it seems likely that expert systems will soon begin to play a serious practical role in architectural CAD.

11.1.8 Document Production and Dissemination

The traditional forms of design documentation in the architectural field are working drawings, shop drawings for certain elements, specifications, and tables and schedules of various kinds. In addition, there may be various sorts of nontechnical presentation documentation—perspective renderings, models, and so on. Production of working drawings and specifications by traditional hand methods is a slow and labor-intensive process, so it has seemed attractive to introduce drafting systems and word processors in order to enhance productivity at this phase.

However, it is not always possible, in practice, to achieve sufficient productivity benefits in this way to justify investment in computer technology. First of all, data preparation and input costs for the automated production of architectural drawings tend to be higher than in many other fields of drafting system application. Second, since the

* See Ref. 6 for an introduction to shape grammars. Reference 7 gives an example of shape grammar specification of a nontrivial language of architectural form.

architectural field is so fragmented, many firms do not have sufficient work flow to justify a major investment in drafting system technology. Third, an architectural firm usually has a job-shop mode of operation, with considerable and often unexpected fluctuations in work load, and this often makes it difficult to achieve adequate utilization factors on expensive equipment. For these reasons, successful architectural applications of drafting systems have been possible, so far, only under particularly favorable conditions—usually in large firms with a relatively steady flow of fairly repetitive work. Even here, very careful organization and management are required to assure success.

Of course, as drafting system costs continue to drop, the potential for cost-effective application in drawing production will expand to encompass a wider range of firms. But the development of libraries of standard symbols and details needed to make a drafting system productive in practice will still remain an expensive matter. It seems likely, then, that smaller firms will tend to make use of standard libraries provided by system vendors or by third-party sources. This parallels an established pattern with specifications; smaller firms frequently make use of standard master specifications provided by outside sources.

If automated document production systems are not operated in isolation but are employed instead as sophisticated "report generators" from the databases of integrated CAD systems which support the entire design process, then data preparation and input costs are spread over a wide range of applications, and automated production can become much more cost-effective. However, the achievement of such integration requires not only more sophisticated CAD systems but also, frequently, substantial restructuring of architectural offices. Many firms are divided internally into design and production departments—frequently with production much larger than design, and generating the majority of the firm's income. This separation makes very little sense, though, when an integrated system is employed, and much of the traditional role of the production department disappears.

Construction differs significantly from many other areas of CAD/CAM application in that large numbers of text and graphic documents must not only be efficiently produced but also rapidly disseminated to remote and scattered sites. It is not at all unusual, for example, for a construction site to be located in one country, the architectural firm based in another, and the construction contractor headquartered in a third. Furthermore, design amendments must often be made and documented as construction proceeds. In many cases, too, construction of one phase of a project is commenced before later phases are fully designed and documented. Thus speedy and reliable communication of drawings and text to and from remote locations is particularly important, and the digital transmission of data can produce substantial benefits. Architectural documentation will, increasingly, be transmitted electronically between CAD workstations rather than by physical transportation of paper, and online graphic teleconferencing will play an increasingly important role.

Another significant difference between construction and other CAD/CAM application areas is that realistic perspective rendering of designs is a more centrally important function. Architects are vitally concerned with the visual qualities of the buildings they design and with communicating these qualities to their clients. It is rarely worthwhile to input a detailed geometric description of a building *solely* for the purpose of generating a perspective rendering, but if the required geometric information can be extracted from the database of an integrated system, then computer production of renderings or animations becomes very attractive. Increasingly, architects will want access to sophisticated three-dimensional visual simulation software of the kind now in widespread use in the film industry for this purpose (see Ref. 11 for a survey of visual simulation techniques used in the film industry). They will also want high-quality color display devices—particularly as the costs of these continue to drop.

11.1.9 Project Management and Accounting

The management of an architectural project usually requires development of schedule, labor, and budget estimates for the project; negotiation of contract and fees based upon these estimates; ongoing monitoring of progress and expenditure of resources and production of reports on this for the project manager; and execution of payroll and billing functions. These are functions common to many organizations, and a great deal of software is available to support them. However, such software is most effective in practice when it is carefully tailored to reflect the categories of work and expenses that are commonly recognized in architectural practice, and to produce reports that are designed for effective use in architectural project management. Standard accounting and management methods developed by the American Institute of Architects provide some useful guidance here.[12]

Many architectural offices employ computer-based project management and accounting systems. Usually these are stand-alone systems, completely separate from any CAD systems. As a greater proportion of the work in an office shifts to CAD systems, however, it is increasingly advantageous to capture management data automatically as a by-product of workstation operation. For example, client billing information may be generated from records of workstation hours spent on projects, and percentage completion information may be generated from project databases.

11.1.10 Summary of CAD's Potential Roles

In summary, then, a wide variety of analysis, design synthesis, expert advising, document production and dissemination, and project management and accounting functions in building design and construction may be performed by computer systems. Most of these functions can be (and often have been) supported by stand-alone pieces of computer software. But a CAD system provides the potential to integrate a relatively wide range of functions through use of centralized catalog and project databases, digital transfer of data, and standard workstations and user interaction protocols. The broader the range of functions that can be integrated in this way, the more practically successful an architectural CAD system is likely to be.

11.2 MOTIVATIONS FOR COMPUTER APPLICATION

11.2.1 Technical Feasibility and Cost Effectiveness

The technical feasibility of automating an architectural function does not, in itself, justify an investment in computer technology for that purpose. The rational basis for introduction of a computer system is the expectation that certain benefits will result, that the benefits will outweigh the costs, and the benefit/cost ratio will lead to an acceptable return on the investment that is made. The major kinds of benefits typically sought from the introduction of architectural CAD systems may be classified broadly as enhanced productivity and reduced response time on projects, error reduction, and enhanced design quality. These will be considered, in turn, in the following subsections.

11.2.2 Productivity and Response Time Benefits

The total time and effort spent on a typical building design project is distributed very unevenly across the stages of the design process, as illustrated in Fig. 11.6. Most effort is spent at the design development and production documents stages, where a great deal of detailed decision making and documentation is required.

A typical architect's fee breakdown for a project (reflecting this pattern) is as follows: (see also Fig. 11.6):

	% of fee
Schematic design phase	15
Design development phase	20
Construction documents phase	40
Bidding or negotiating phase	5
Construction phase	20
	100

(Engineering consultants' fees at each stage are included in these figures.) This implies that productivity benefits of computer applications will mostly show up at the design development and construction documents phases, where even a small percentage reduction in expenditure of resources to complete the project is important.

Enhancing productivity may not only reduce costs but also the response time on projects. This can enable a firm to accept tightly-scheduled projects that otherwise could not be taken on. Furthermore, it provides the capability to make very rapid emergency revisions to designs where required, for example, by unexpected conditions encountered during construction, and thus to minimize losses resulting from construction delays. Under certain economic conditions, too, rapid response becomes a particularly crucial issue. In the context of a highly inflationary economy, for example, rapid design can lead to substantial reduction in eventual construction cost. And, in a context of fluctuating relative costs of construction methods (e.g., steel vs. poured-in-place concrete), ability to redesign at short notice can allow advantage to be taken of the fluctuations.

Productivity can also be particularly important in developing countries, where there is often ambitious construction activity but a severe shortage of technically skilled and experienced architects and engineers. In this context, enhanced productivity achieved through CAD can enable optimal use of scarce labor resources.

Typically, productivity benefits have been sought principally through automation of routine engineering calculations and data processing and word processing tasks, and through use of drafting systems for production of working drawings. As computer costs continue to drop and as architectural CAD systems become more broadly integrated, it becomes increasingly attractive to replace labor by capital in this way, and we can expect to see architectural firms generally become much more capital-intensive operations.

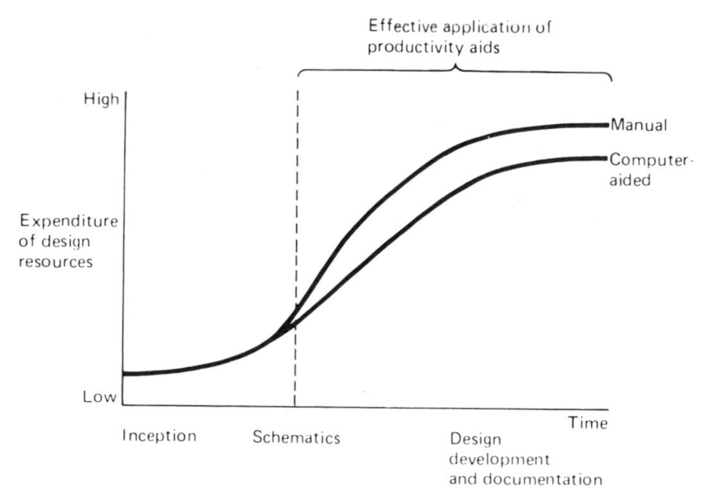

Figure 11.6 Distribution of design effort across a project.

11.2.3 Error Reduction

Design and documentation of a building involves making and recording a large number of individual decisions, coordinating the work of many different people, and producing a great deal of highly detailed information. Even in the best-run architectural firm, then, errors will occur with statistical regularity and can result in client dissatisfaction, redoing work, lawsuits, and high errors and omissions insurance rates. So reduction in errors is a very important potential benefit of computer application.

Specifically, architectural CAD systems obviously have the potential to reduce errors by automation of text and graphic data handling (thus reducing clerical and copy errors), and by automation of a considerable amount of routine decision making (through use of high-level design operations). Less obviously, automated production of counts of items, of measurement of areas, and of the performance of routine calculations, leads to reduction of errors in cost estimation and in ordering of items.

Perhaps the most important way in which architectural CAD systems can reduce errors, though, is by supporting maintenance of logical consistency of data in project descriptions—particularly as parts of a design are modified, propagating chains of logical consequence to other parts. Spatial clashes between physical elements (e.g., beams and ducts) are a common type of inconsistency in sets of drawings, for instance. A two-dimensional drafting system may be employed to help identify these by producing overlaid color-coded drawings of different building subsystems. A three-dimensional system allows the application of automated spatial-clash checking procedures.

More generally, it may be observed that a project description maintained by an architectural CAD system is a model of a proposed physical system, and, if this model is to be maximally useful, certain logical relations in the data should be automatically maintained as the model is manipulated. These relations may be defined formally by means of integrity constraints which establish the modeling semantics.[13] For example, the modeling semantics of a sophisticated architectural CAD system might establish that moving a wall results in appropriate movement of windows and doors in the wall, and automatic adjustment of all connected walls.[14] Generally, designers of practical architectural CAD systems have been content to treat modeling semantics in informal, ad hoc fashion, and to provide only rudimentary automated consistency-maintenance facilities—that is, to leave most of the responsibility for consistency maintenance to the user. But formalization of modeling semantics for architectural systems is an active research topic,[15,16,17] and it seems likely that future architectural systems will incorporate much more complete and rigorously defined modeling semantics. This should both make systems easier to use (by freeing the user from responsibility for low-level adjustments of a design to maintain consistency) and produce a significant reduction in design errors and inconsistencies.

11.2.4 Design Quality Benefits

The most major architectural design decisions, those with the largest impact on building cost (construction and life cycle) and performance, are usually made early in the design process. As the process continues, it increasingly becomes one of detailed refinement of a basically "frozen" concept, with decreasing impact on building cost and performance. This trend is sketched in Fig. 11.7. This implies that most of the design quality benefits of computer use will follow from software that applies at early stages in the design process, by contrast with productivity benefits, which mostly relate to later stages.

The basic way in which CAD can produce objective design quality benefits is by facilitating the rapid generation and analysis of relevant design alternatives—thus increasing confidence that possibilities have been thoroughly explored and that well-informed design decisions have been made. For example, an architect might employ a CAD system to model the essential geometry and other features of a high-rise office building, rapidly generate a wide range of parametric variations on the model, produce perspective drawings to illustrate the visual effects of variation, and produce preliminary engineering

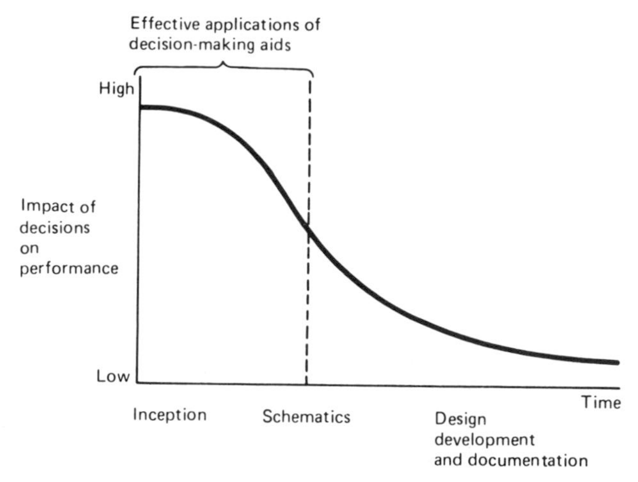

Figure 11.7 Impact of decisions on design cost and quality.

and cost analyses of each variant. This is likely to produce a technically better result than a manual process which must be restricted to consideration of a narrower range of alternatives, less extensive analysis, and less complete exploration of trade-offs.

It should be noted that achievement of design quality benefits requires rather different kinds of hardware and software than achievement of productivity benefits. Many productivity tools, such as large turnkey drafting systems, are expensive pieces of equipment which must be heavily and continuously utilized in order to achieve an adequate return on investment, and which are operated by trained technical specialists. Design aids, however, must be readily accessible to designers at the drawing board, easy to use by nonspecialists, and relatively cheap (so that continuous utilization is not necessary). This suggests that design aids are best developed in the context of low-cost, user-friendly personal computer technology.

11.3 CLASSES OF SYSTEMS

11.3.1 A Taxonomy of Systems

Architectural CAD systems designed to achieve these various kinds of benefits may conveniently be grouped under the following headings: two-dimensional drafting systems, drafting systems augmented with database management capabilities, and three-dimensional modeling systems. We shall consider these in turn.

11.3.2 Two-Dimensional Drafting Systems

Almost any reasonably capable two-dimensional drafting system may be employed for production of building plans, elevations, sections, and details (Fig. 11.8), and most major drafting system vendors have at least a few installations devoted to architectural drafting applications—mostly in the larger architectural and AE firms. However, as was noted earlier, the cost-effectiveness of a general two-dimensional drafting system in an architectural or AE office is by no means assured, and the record of such systems in practice has so far been very mixed.

One way to make drafting systems more cost-effective is to reduce the cost. This is particularly important in architecture, where many firms are small and where high and steady levels of work flow comparable to those in other fields usually cannot be assumed. Thus the emerging generation of very low-cost graphics systems based upon powerful

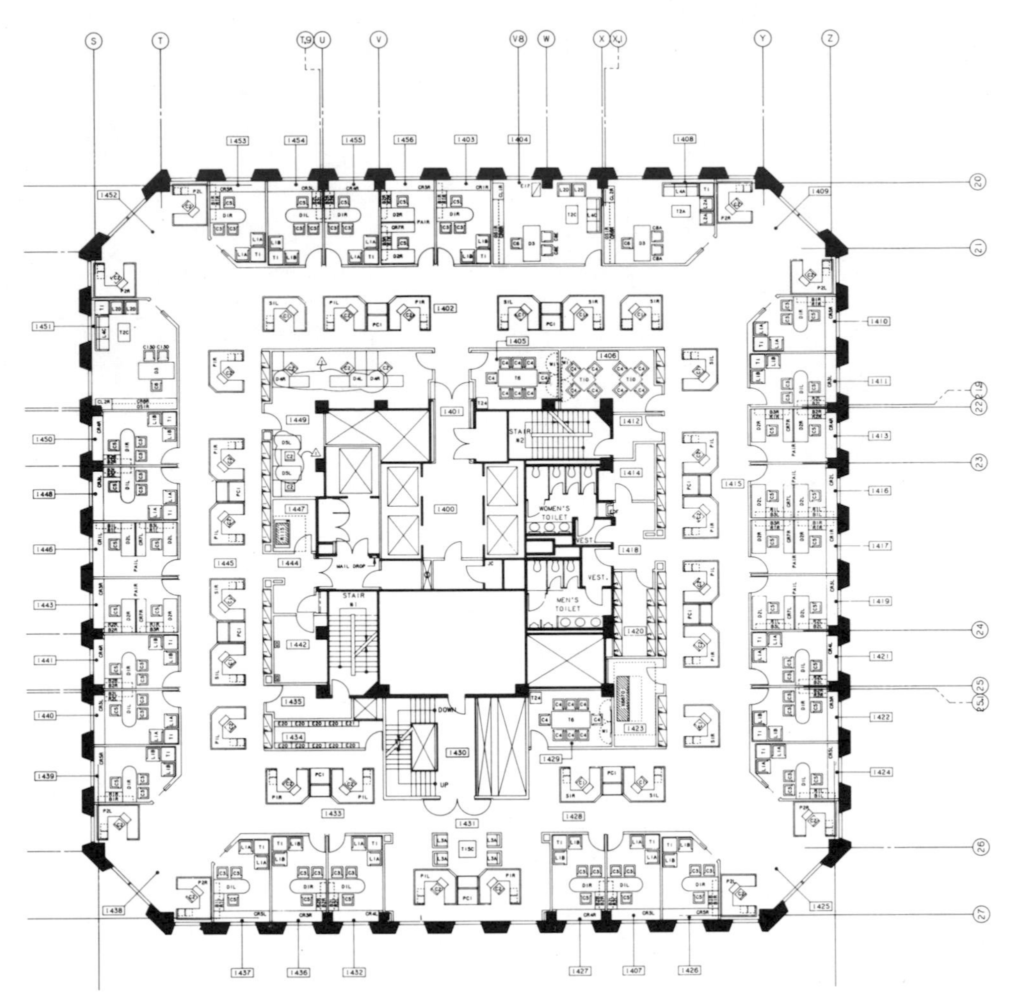

Figure 11.8 Building plan produced by McDonnell Douglas Corp.'s (McAuto's) GDS two-dimensional drafting system.

microprocessors, such as the Motorola 68000, and raster graphics seems likely to have a major impact in the architecture and construction field.

Another obvious way to enhance cost-effectiveness is to tailor general drafting systems to architectural applications by developing architectural symbol menus and by providing specialized operators for use in manipulating architectural drawings—for example, operators to insert doors and windows into walls in a plan. Drafting system vendors are finding that they need to provide such tailoring of their systems if they are to compete in the architectural market.

11.3.3 Drafting Systems with Database Management

A third way to enhance cost-effectiveness is to integrate a broader range of functions within the scope of the system. Recently, many drafting systems have been augmented with database management system capabilities in an effort to accomplish this. Typically, software is provided to automatically take off counts and measurements from drawings—numbers of instances of items of furniture and equipment, lengths of partitioning and ductwork, floor areas enclosed within rooms, and so on. In this way, files of numerical data describing a building can be constructed and later processed and reported from in various ways. Furthermore, additional nongraphic data (such as cost information, physical properties, and specification clauses) may be associated with graphic entities. Thus drafting systems can reasonably satisfactorily be extended to integrate a variety of quantity takeoff and costing, specification, schedule and inventory production, and facility management functions.

However, this technique suffers from a number of fundamental deficiencies and so is best regarded as a transitional technology. First, it results in a redundant description of a building (with the same information represented on drawings and, in a different form, in the nongraphic database), with resulting problems of efficiency and consistency maintenance. Second, it is backward. In principle it is better to treat two-dimensional drawings as reports from an integrated project database rather than to treat such drawings as the primary description of a design.

11.3.4 Three-Dimensional Modeling Systems

A system that maintains a complete and unambiguous three-dimensional building description, rather than a collection of two-dimensional drawings, provides the necessary foundation for integration of a full range of architectural analysis and design functions in a CAD system. However, it is essential, in consideration of this issue, to draw careful distinctions between wire-frame, surface, and solid three-dimensional models of building forms. (See Ref. 18 for a more detailed technical discussion of this point.) Figure 11.9 graphically depicts the differences.

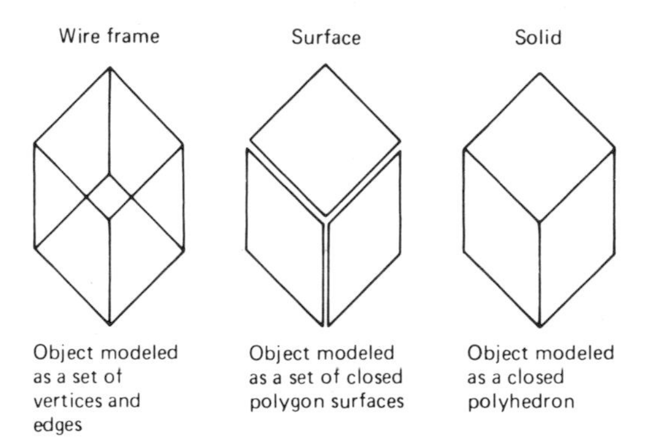

Figure 11.9 Wire-frame, surface, and solid models of polyhedral objects.

A wire-frame model represents a three-dimensional object as a set of vertices connected by edges. Such models are straightforward to implement, and many two-dimensional drafting systems have been augmented with wire-frame three-dimensional modeling capabilities. But wire-frame models provide no way to represent surface and volumetric properties and are often spatially ambiguous, so they are not particularly useful in this context. At best they can support generation of rudimentary perspective views (without removal of hidden edge lines) and a limited range of structural analysis applications (where edges model structural members).

A surface model recognizes not only vertices and edges but also closed polygonal faces of three-dimensional objects and allows properties of such faces to be specified. Such models are more complex to implement but can support the production of very realistic perspective renderings, with hidden surface removal, surface color and texture, shading, and cast shadows.

The most complete kind of three-dimensional model is a solid model, which recognizes vertices, edges, closed polygonal faces, and closed polyhedral solids, and allows properties to be specified for all these kinds of geometric entities. In a solid modeling system, a building is represented as an assemblage of polyhedra—both solid construction elements such as columns and beams, and bounded voids such as rooms. Such a complete physical description can be used to support a wide range of high-level design operations, engineering and cost analyses of designs, automated consistency maintenance as designs are modified, and production of documentation by reporting from the project database.

Many CAD/CAM systems intended for use in manufacturing industry now provide solid modeling capabilities. But these are not, in general, suitable for architectural applications. Whereas a solid model of, say, a mechanical part involves relatively few and relatively complex polyhedra, a solid model of a building typically involves thousands of relatively simple polyhedra (often just boxes, prisms, and cylinders). In this respect, building modeling systems have much in common with pipework design systems and systems used in the shipbuilding industry.

The implementation of an efficient, general solid modeling system that is capable of maintaining and manipulating a detailed description of a large and complex building is a formidable undertaking. It has been the subject of considerable research, and some prototype systems have been developed.[19,20,21] However, no such system is currently commercially available in a form suitable for production use. The closest approximation is the Building Design System (BDS), a large-scale CAD system developed in the United Kingdom by Applied Research of Cambridge, and marketed in the United States by McDonnell Douglas Corp. (McAuto). BDS can handle large and complex buildings with remarkable efficiency and integrates a wide range of design, analysis, and documentation functions. However, it does all this at the expense of imposing some quite severe (though intelligently chosen) limitations upon the building and component geometries that can be handled. Figure 11.10 illustrates some views of buildings designed, analyzed, and documented using BDS.

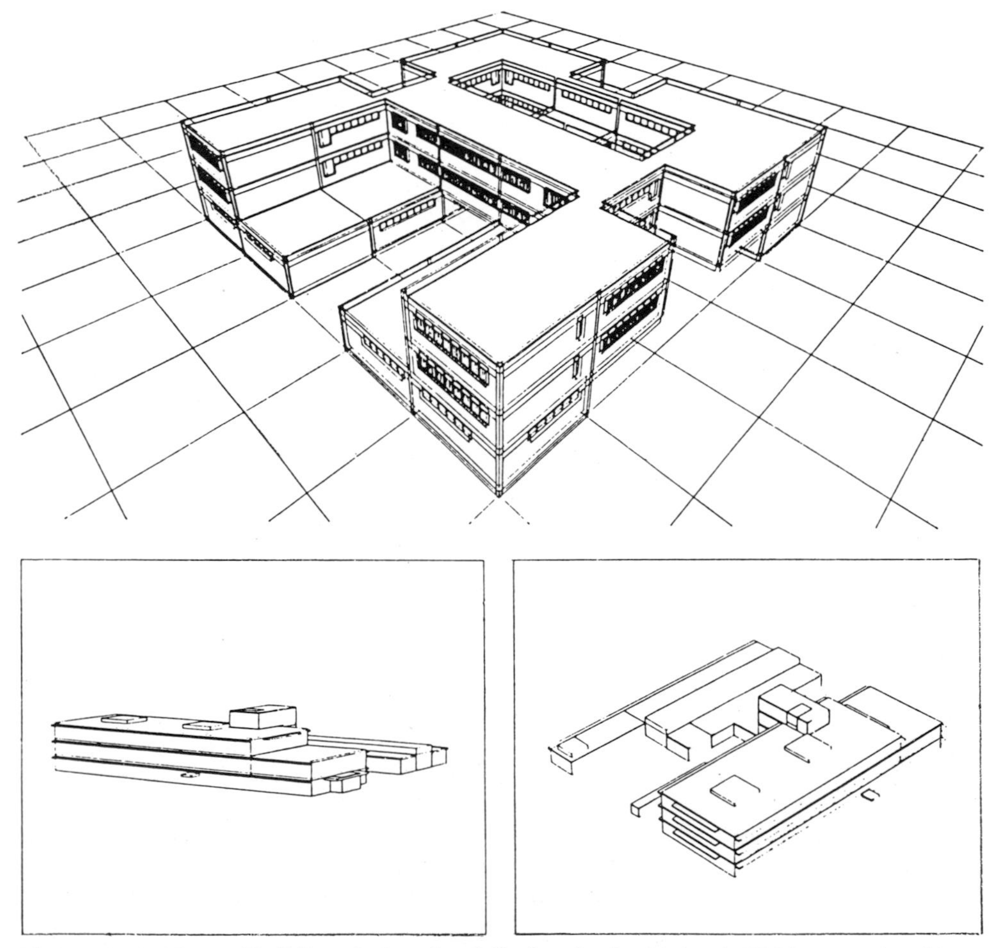

Figure 11.10 Views of buildings designed and displayed using McAuto's BDS integrated architectural CAD system.

11.4 CONCLUSIONS

The application of CAD technology in the AEC field is still immature, though now developing rapidly. The most important factors driving further development are likely to be continued cost reductions, broader integration of functions made possible through use of more sophisticated building modeling techniques, incorporation of more specifically architectural knowledge in software, more sensitive attention to issues of appropriateness of architectural language and design operators, and more careful formalization of modeling semantics resulting in more effective consistency maintenance.

At present, practical application of CAD technology is mostly confined to the largest architectural and AE firms and architectural drafting service bureaus. But, as increasingly effective systems become available, while costs reduce, much broader penetration of the field can be expected to evolve. Over the next decade, there will be a strong tendency for traditionally labor-intensive architectural and AE firms to become much more capital-intensive through investment in CAD technology.

REFERENCES

1. American Institute of Architects: *The Architect's Handbook of Professional Practice*, American Institute of Architects, Washington, D.C., 1973.
2. Royal Institute of British Architects: *Handbook of Architectural Practice and Management*, Royal Institute of British Architects, London, 1973.
3. Gutman, R., B. Westergaard, and D. Hicks: "The Structure of Design Firms in the Construction Industry," *Environment and Planning B*, vol. 4, 1977.
4. Midwest Research Institute: "The Building Industry: Concepts of Change (1920–2000)," in G. M. McCue et al., *Creating the Human Environment*, University of Illinois Press, Urbana, Ill. 1970.
5. Mitchell, W. J.: *Computer Aided Architectural Design*, Van Nostrand Reinhold, New York, 1977.
6. Stiny, G.: "Introduction to Shape and Shape Grammars," *Environment and Planning B*, vol. 7, 1980.
7. Stiny, G., and W. J. Mitchell, "The Palladian Grammar," *Environment and Planning B*, vol. 5, 1978.
8. Cuadra, R. N., D. M. Abels, and J. Wanger: *Directory of Online Databases*, Cuadra Associates, Inc., Santa Monica, Cal., 1983.
9. Landsdown, J.: *Expert Systems: Their Impact on the Construction Industry*, Royal Institute of British Architects, London, 1982.
10. Feigenbaum, E. A.: "Expert Systems in the 1980's," in A. Bond (ed.), *Machine Intelligence*, Pergamon-Infotec, 1981.
11. Greenberg, D.: "An Overview of Computer Graphics," in D. Greenberg et al. (eds.), *The Computer Image: Applications of Computer Graphics*, Addison-Wesley, Reading, Mass., 1982.
12. American Institute of Architects: *Financial Management for Architectural Firms*, American Institute of Architects, Washington, D.C., 1970.
13. Hammer, M., and D. McLeod: "Semantic Integrity in a Relational Database System," in *Proceedings of the International Conference on Very Large Databases*, Association for Computing Machinery, New York, 1975.
14. Yasky, Y.: "Transforming a Set of Building Drawings into a Consistent Database," *CAD80 Proceedings*, IPC Science and Technology Press, Guildford, Surrey, England, 1980.
15. Eastman, C.: "The Representation of Design Problems and Maintenance of Their Structure," in J. C. Latombe (ed.), *Artificial Intelligence and Pattern Recognition in Computer Aided Design*, North-Holland, Amsterdam, 1978.
16. Eastman, C.: "Systems Facilities for CAD Databases," *Proceedings of the 17th ACM Design Automation Conference*, Association for Computing Machinery, New York, 1980.
17. Eastman, C.: "Database Facilities for Engineering Design," *Proceedings of the IEEE*, vol. 69, October 1981.
18. Requicha, A. A. G.: "Representations for Rigid Solids: Theory, Methods and Systems," *Computing Surveys*, vol. 12, December 1980.

19. Eastman, C.: "General Purpose Building Description Systems," *Computer Aided Design*, vol. 8, January 1976.

20. Eastman, C., and M. Henrion: "GLIDE: A Language for Design Information Systems," *Computer Graphics*, vol. 11, Summer 1977.

21. Borkin, H. J., J. F. McIntosh, P. G. McIntosh, and J. A. Turner: "Arch: Model, Geometric Relational Database System," Technical Report, Architectural Research Laboratory, College of Architecture and Urban Planning, University of Michigan, June 1982.

Piping and Instrumentation Diagrams

by
Tom Bakey

12.1 INTRODUCTION

Piping and instrumentation diagrams (P & IDs) are schematic drawings designed to represent the flow and control of processes within a plant. They contain information on the various types of pipes, valves, and controls along with their connections to major vessels and containers within the process plant. P & IDs are considered the core schematics used in the design, development, and final construction process. Initial flow diagrams used to identify various processes, plot plans used as geographic reference drawings, and the many dimensioned physical orthographic drawings are referenced to the P & IDs. P & IDs have been called by many the *master schematics*, since they impact all major disciplines and are used in every facet of the design and construction process.

12.2 SETTING UP THE SYSTEM

Prior to the use of the CAD system to produce any P & ID drawing or sets of drawings, the CAD system must be programmed to address the particular needs of the user. Symbol libraries representative of the specific disciplines in use must be created and stored in the system. Specific commands such as ARC, SPLINE, and LINE BETWEEN POINTS must also be contained in the system. Menus with command and symbol listings must be available for optimum use.

P & ID application programs with names such as AUTOSET (enabling automatic setting of lines near an object) and FORWARD ANNOTATION (placing text automatically on drawings other than the one being created) must be implemented and placed in the system. Various drawing borders from A to E size should be available for use by the user. A general-purpose report generator should be incorporated to generate various types of listings and reports.

Once all of these capabilities are resident in the CAD system, then and only then is the user ready to operate the system. In any P & ID application, whether it is manual or CAD-system-assisted, several basic steps must be followed. The drawing must first be created. During this process, it usually requires several revisions. Once the graphics are developed, the drawing must be annotated and, quite probably, many revisions are added.

The drawing border must be formatted and the final drawing produced. In many instances either during or after the drawing is completed, a material takeoff is desired producing a bill of material (BOM). All these procedures can be executed by a CAD system when properly utilized and can be explained by applying the system to a typical situation.

12.3 APPLYING THE SYSTEM TO P & IDs

To demonstrate how the CAD system operates and creates P & IDs and reports under operator control, this section will describe the steps followed in creating a particular P & ID.

A P & ID (Fig. 12.1) is a schematic representation of pipe runs and instrumentation controls in a process plant. It is one of the major drawings used in plant design and development, originating in the mechanical discipline but used as a reference document in many others.

12.4 CREATING THE DRAWING

At the initiation of the drawing, the user starts with jottings, rough sketches, marked-up prints from previous projects, etc. Any one of these, or any combination is the initial information for the preliminary draft of the P & ID. These data are entered and digitally stored in the computer database, where they can be revised at the discretion of the user and reproduced as many times as necessary and from which reports, listings, and schedules can be obtained.

The primary building block of a P & ID is the equipment or device symbol. The CAD system offers a library of such symbols, conformant to American National Standards Institute (ANSI), ISA, and other recognized standards. These symbols can be changed easily should the user's company have different standards. Figure 12.2 shows a possible initial placement of symbols when starting a P & ID in the vicinity of a heat exchanger.

Symbols selected are for:

- Ball valves
- Heat exchanger
- Diaphragm valves
- Reducers
- Hose connections

Further attributes, such as ANSI or ISA codes, are optional.

The CAD system also provides the capability to magnify or reduce the size of the symbol. Figure 12.3 indicates several of the endless size possibilities and their relative appearance, in this case using the heat exchanger symbol. This rather simple feature already underscores the flexibility of the CAD system as opposed to the constraints of templates used in manual designing and drafting.

When symbols have been created and stored in the database, a copy can be recalled for placement in a drawing either by typing its designation or by touching (via the electronic pen) a predetermined square on a menu sheet. Menus, offered as part of the CAD system, contain a library of standard drawing elements (i.e., predetermined, often-used symbol structures), which are shown on the graphics screen and activated via the electronic pen (a sample menu is given in Fig. 12.4).

These menus also contain "touch squares" for specific commands, i.e., to rotate, copy, mirror, orient, etc., the placed symbols. Generic symbols for placement purposes are another part of the menus provided with the CAD sytem.

Figure 12.5 shows instrumentation balloons conformant to ISA standards. Symbolized instrumentation lines, conformant to ISA standards, are also offered (see Fig. 12.6).

For quick, correct connections of lines and symbols, the CAD system has an application program called AUTOSET. This means each symbol has established connection points, or nodes, which can be viewable on the screen around a symbol for the correct placement of a line identification or annotation. These nodes remain after a connection has been made, thereby making revisions or further connections (such as annotation) a simple process. Figure 12.7 illustrates the beginning stage of a drawing, using some of the symbols from Fig. 12.2 with connecting lines and AUTOSET nodes.

AUTOSET nodes greatly facilitate joining of lines, symbols, and text because the user does not need to indicate the exact point on the digitizer tablet or graphics screen in order to make the proper connection. The sensitive "homing" area around the AUTOSET node is between 2 and 7 millimeters (0.1 to 0.25 inch) in radius. By merely indicating the general area of connection, the connection is accurately and automatically made with much time and effort saved, resulting in more accurate drawings and higher productivity.

To begin a true P & ID, the symbols shown in Fig. 12.4 are connected with lines of type 01 and type 02, producing lines 1.0 and 0.7 millimeter wide and adding arrowheads for the direction of flow (see Fig. 12.8).

The drawing can then be expanded by adding instrumentation symbols (see Fig. 12.9). Note that in this view all AUTOSET nodes have been suppressed from presentation.

In most drawings there is much redundancy, namely the repetition of basic constructions. The very tedious manual work is alleviated by the CAD system's DUPLICATION command. The time and effort saved by this command is easily recognized when, for example, the top half of an E-size drawing must be copied onto the bottom half. In such a case, the CAD system could effect the copy within seconds. Also, this copying, or duplication, can be performed as many times as necessary without restriction. Taking the example in Fig. 12.9, duplicating part of the heat exchanger subassembly, placing it in parallel, and adding connecting lines and other associated symbols would result in the drawing shown in Fig. 12.10.

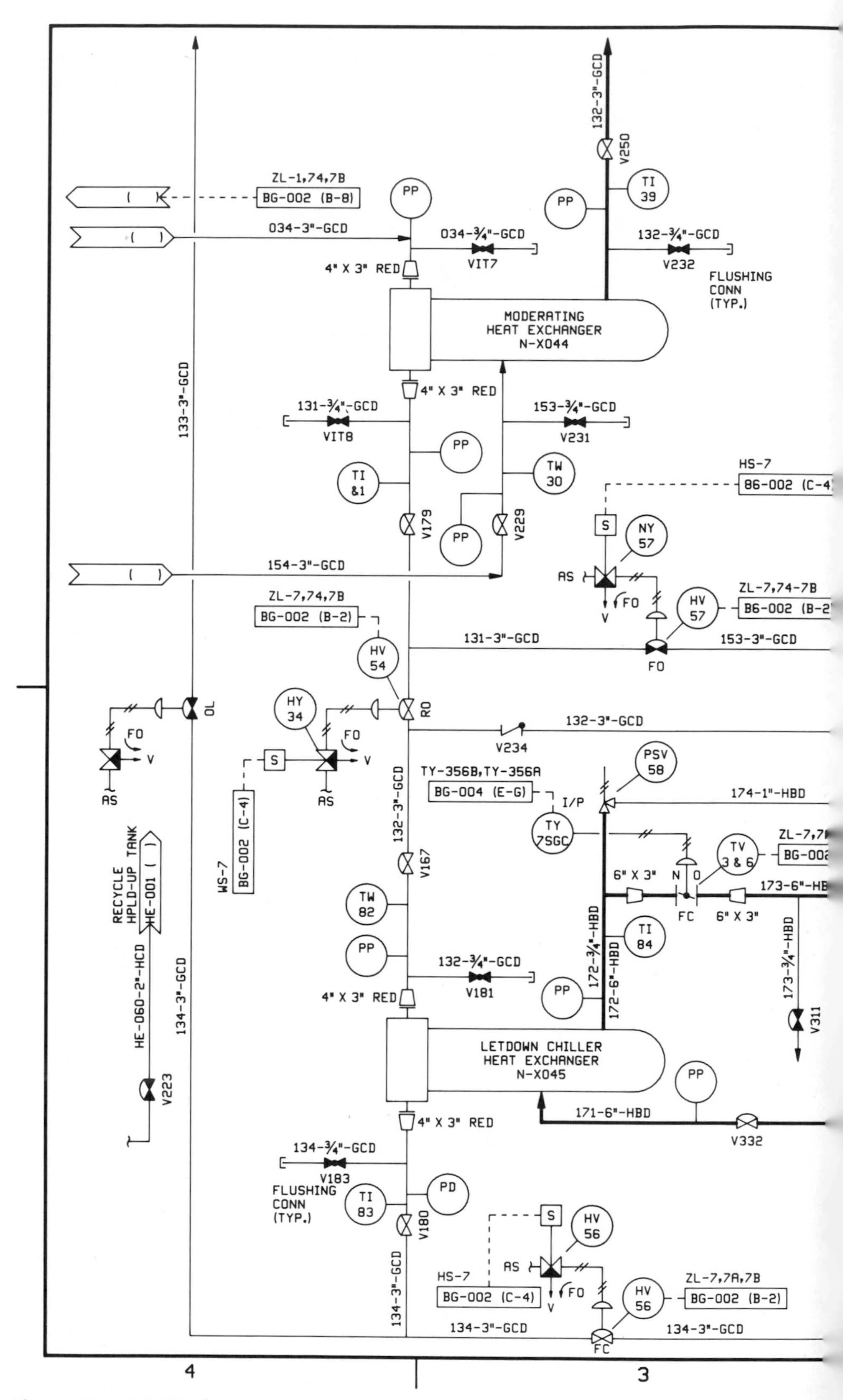

Figure 12.1 P & ID schematic.

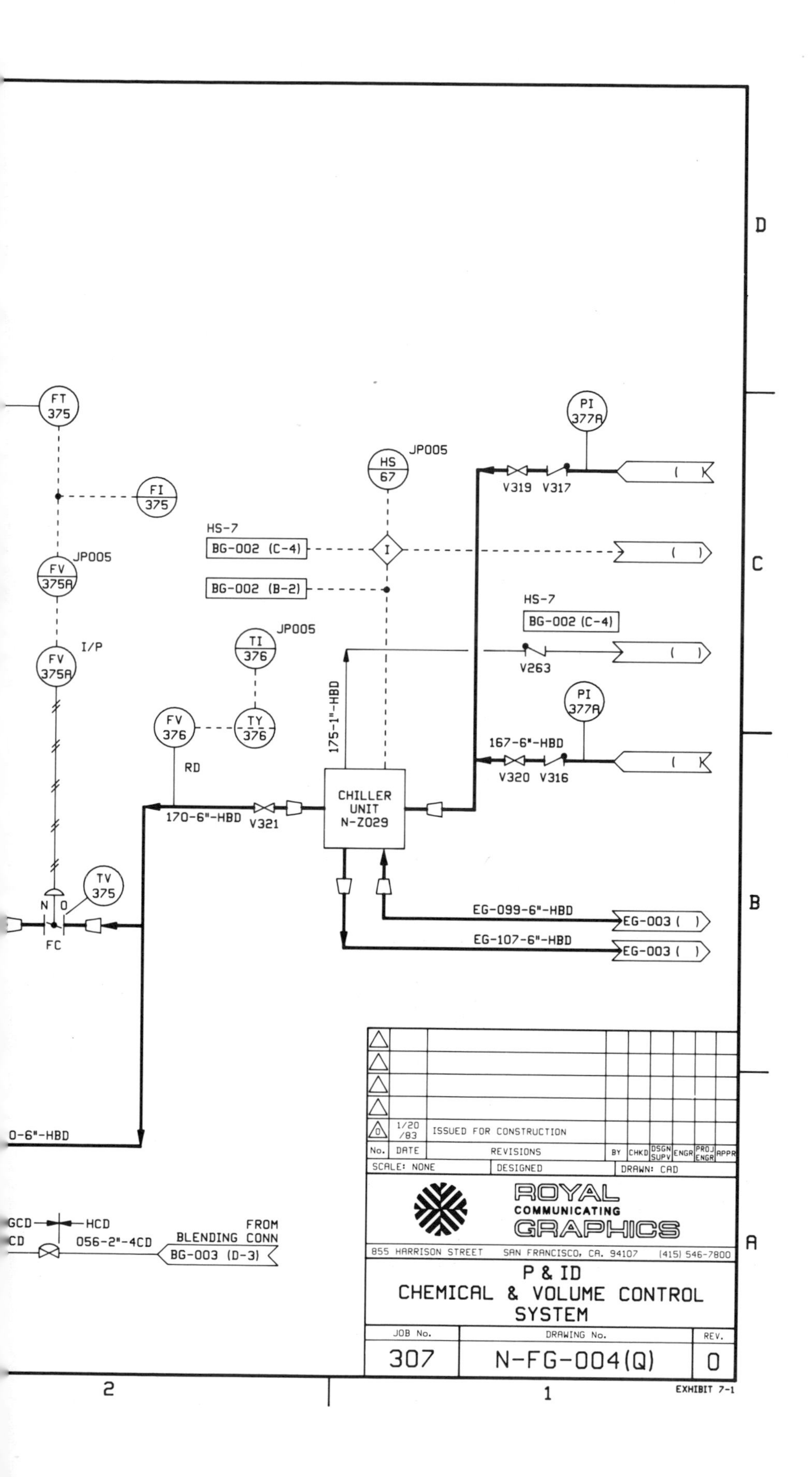
D
C
B
A
FT 375
FI 375
JP005
FV 375A
I/P
FV 375A
TV 375
N O
FC
HS 67
HS-7
BG-002 (C-4)
BG-002 (B-2)
I
TI 376
TY 376
FV 376
RD
175-1"-HBD
CHILLER UNIT N-Z029
170-6"-HBD
V321
PI 377A
V319 V317
V263
167-6"-HBD
V320 V316
EG-099-6"-HBD
EG-003 ( )
EG-107-6"-HBD
0-6"-HBD
GCD
HCD
CD
056-2"-4CD
FROM BLENDING CONN
BG-003 (D-3)
1/20 /83
ISSUED FOR CONSTRUCTION
No. DATE REVISIONS BY CHKD DSGN SUPV ENGR PROJ ENGR APPR
SCALE: NONE
DESIGNED
DRAWN: CAD
ROYAL COMMUNICATING GRAPHICS
855 HARRISON STREET SAN FRANCISCO, CA. 94107 (415) 546-7800
P & ID
CHEMICAL & VOLUME CONTROL SYSTEM
JOB No.
307
DRAWING No.
N-FG-004(Q)
REV.
0
2
1
EXHIBIT 7-1

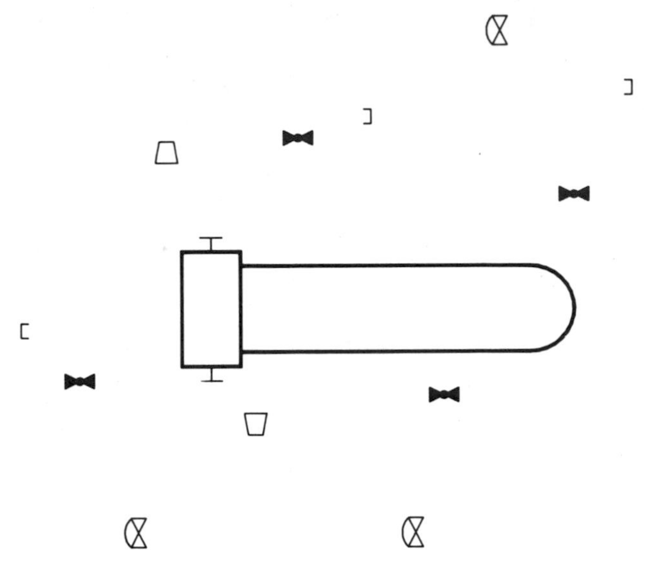

Figure 12.2 P & ID symbols.

Basic constructions can be used as many times as necessary, since they are stored in the database and can be recalled at any time. These patterns can also be scaled and changed. Only several minutes at the CAD workstation are necessary to further expand this area of the drawing, as shown in Fig. 12.11.

12.5 DRAWING REVISIONS

Revisions of line work and symbols are easily and quickly effected by the CAD system. This is of great importance, since changes, additions, deletions, and refinements are so commonplace in diagram production. The user points to a section of the drawing, gives the command to magnify or reduce it for better viewability, then enters the command for computer-aided deletion or addition of the desired lines or symbols. This capability also encompasses the deletion of entire sections of drawings by noting the boundary of the area via electronic pen and entering the DELETE command. Then, replacing lines and

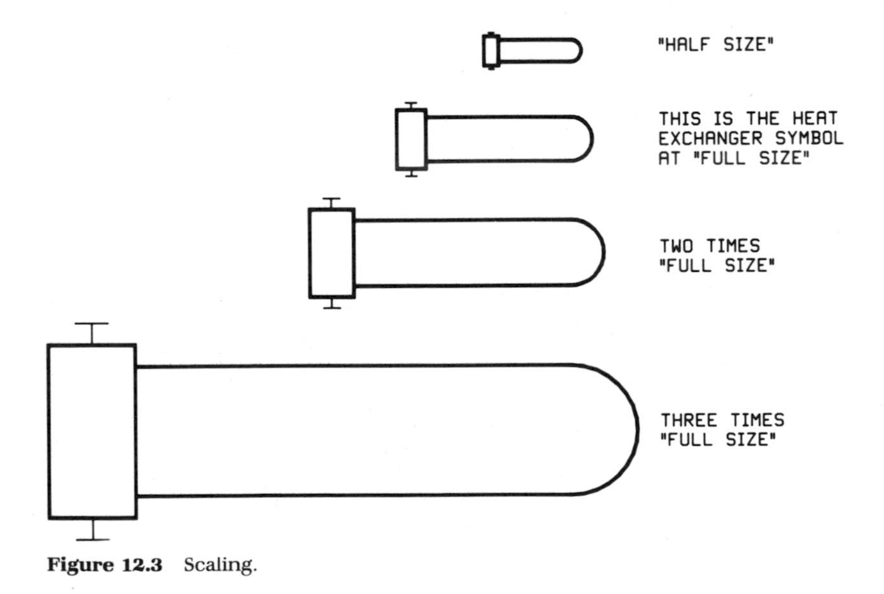

Figure 12.3 Scaling.

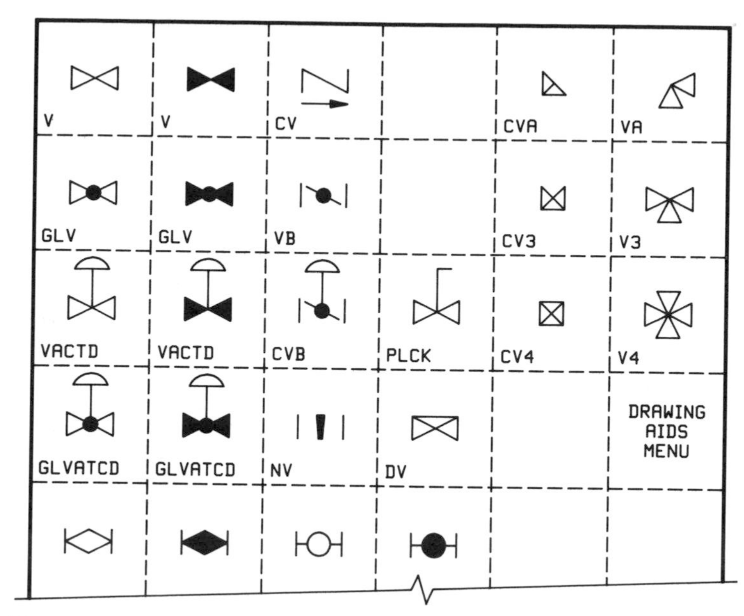

Figure 12.4 P & ID menu.

symbols is exactly like creating them in the first place. Deleting, however, not only "erases" the lines and symbols from the drawing but also erases any connected annotation, because of the AUTOSET node associativity feature described previously. Revision of line types, for instance, would be reflected by new line weights on the drawing when plotted. This revision process is no different from any other method.

Should the user's symbol standards be different from those offered in the symbol library, the CAD system permits making changes quickly and easily. To the database, a symbol is merely a small drawing. Therefore, revision of a symbol is the same as that of a drawing. Symbols already placed on a drawing may be revised singly, collectively by

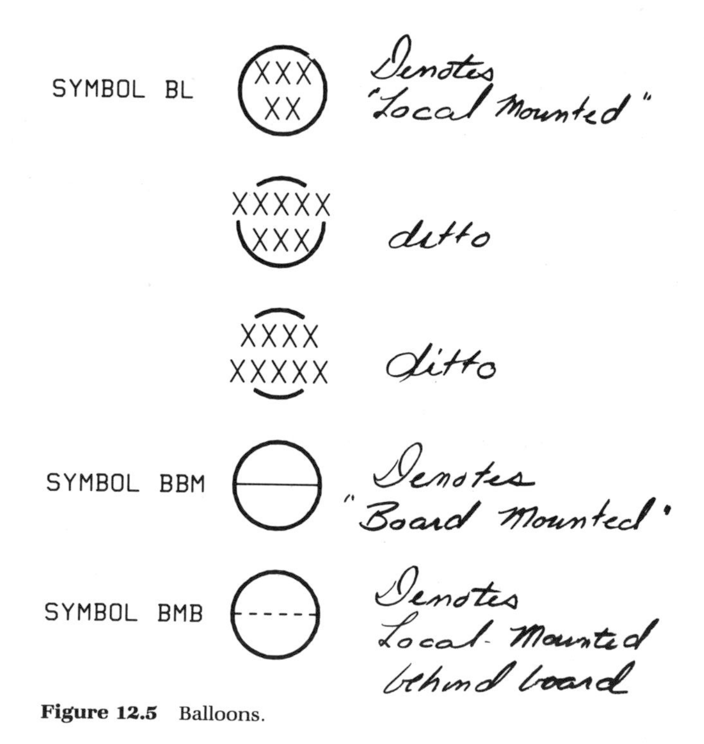

Figure 12.5 Balloons.

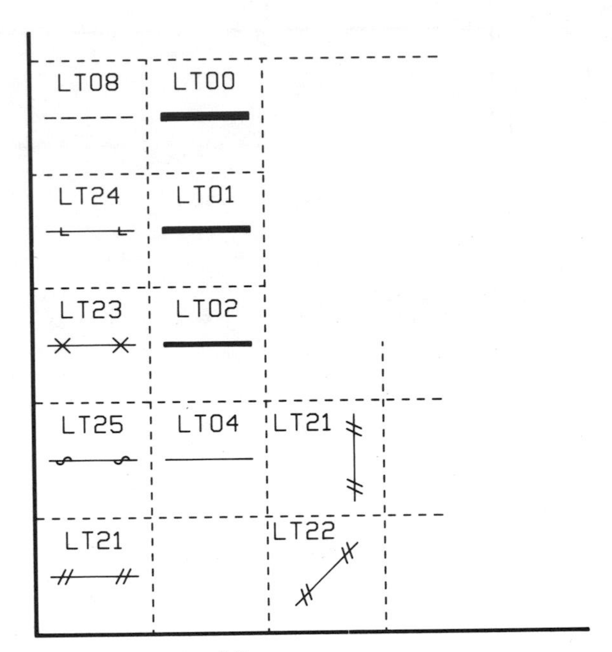

Figure 12.6 Signal lines.

drawings, or throughout a set of drawings. An example of how timesaving this feature can be is illustrated in Fig. 12.12.

Given this part of a drawing for a safety injection system, let us assume numerous omissions and misrepresentations of original nodes have been flagged in a review cycle. Manual drafting techniques would require changes affecting not only this part of the drawing but also references of the changed or new lines and symbols on other drawings.

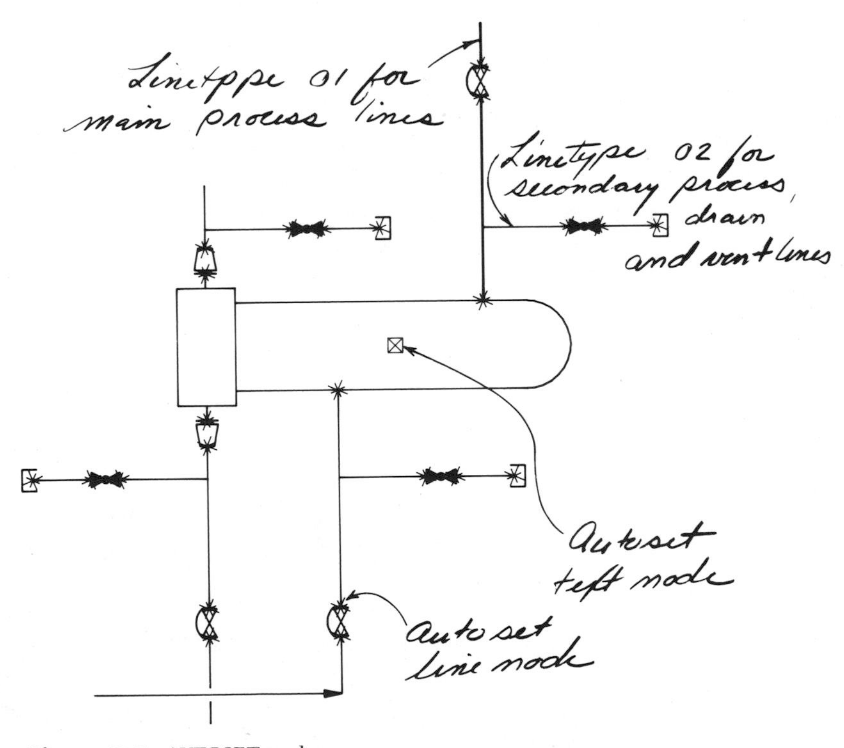

Figure 12.7 AUTOSET nodes.

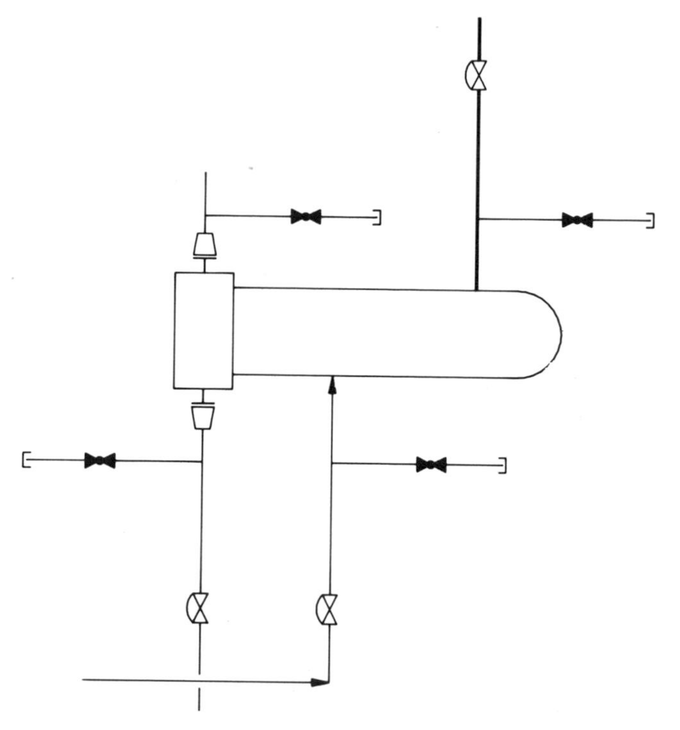

Figure 12.8 Instrumentation symbols added.

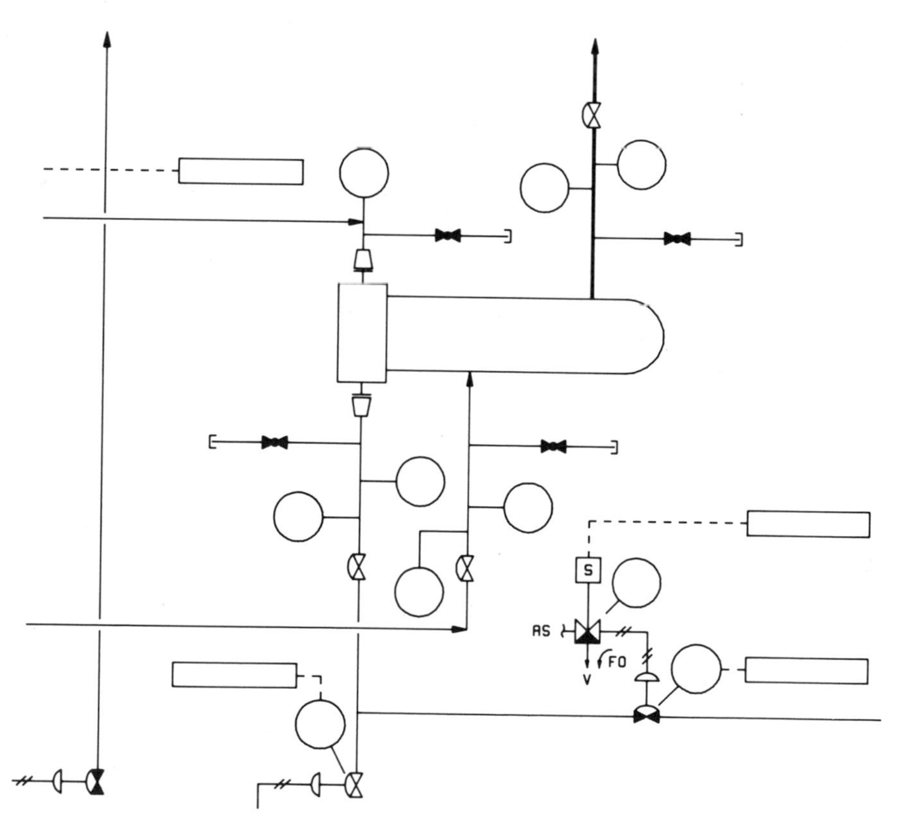

Figure 12.9 Expanding the P & ID.

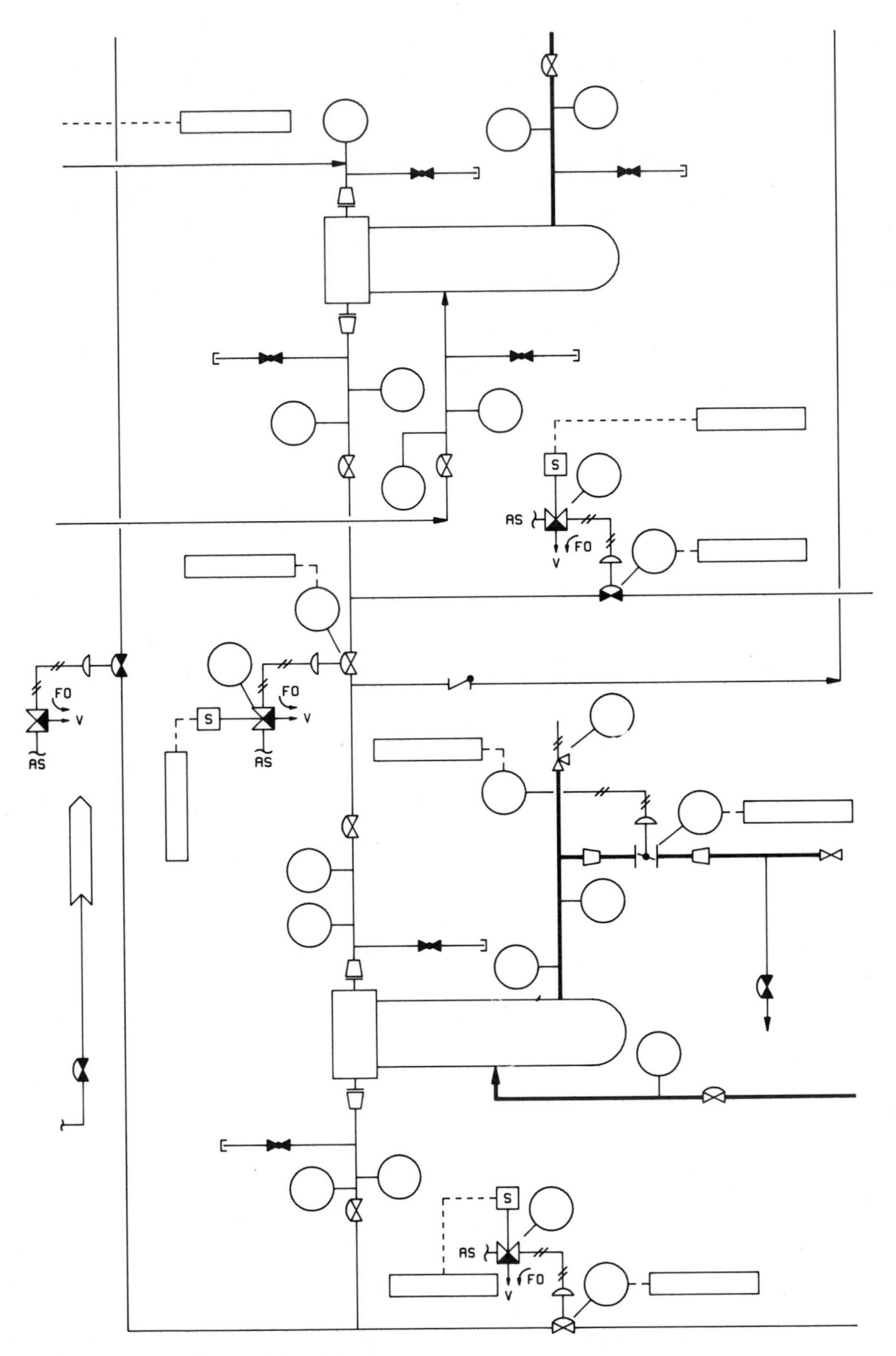

Figure 12.10 Duplicating information.

The CAD system allows the user to make the necessary changes once and have all references to these changes selected automatically. This not only saves much productive time but also ensures absolute consistency. Figure 12.12 indicates the changes to be made. Figure 12.13 shows the changes.

Another example of a timesaving feature is illustrated with a part of a drawing for a chiller surge tank (Fig. 12.14). Let us assume that all balloons (circular instrument symbols) must be represented elliptically. P & IDs for a nuclear power plant could contain as many as 10,000 instrument symbols, which would mean a very lengthy and costly revision. The CAD system user merely changes the designation of the symbol to be placed from balloon to ellipse, and all reference instances on the revised drawing can automatically reflect the change (see Fig. 12.15).

12.6 TEXT DRAWING ANNOTATION

Adding text or numbers to individual symbols or designator coding to process lines on a drawing produced with a CAD system is quickly and easily done. Alphanumeric designations can either be typed, or, if already stored, be automatically placed onto the drawing by using the menu control. For typing in the annotation, the CAD workstation keyboard may be used. The system Text Editor is a versatile and powerful word processor as well.

Shown are examples of alphanumeric notations flush left, flush right, and centered.

Text flush LEFT	A-P026 BORON INJECTION RECIRCULATION PUMP
Text flush RIGHT	A-P026 BORON INJECTION RECIRCULATION PUMP
Text CENTERED	A-P026 BORON INJECTION RECIRCULATION PUMP

These variations are quickly achieved by use of the electronic pen and on-screen menu. The menu contains alphabetic and numeric characters, which can be implemented by using the electronic pen. This obviates manual typing at the workstation keyboard. The user also has the choice of entering some annotations via keyboard, others by the on-screen menu.

AUTOSET is also used to aid in the placement of alphanumeric notations onto the drawing. Like device and equipment symbols and lines, text also has nodes for easy and accurate placement. Figure 12.16 contrasts the accuracy and the resultant orderliness (bottom) when using AUTOSET with instrumentation symbols and their code markings with a misaligned "manual" version (top).

The time and judgment involved in manual text placement are greatly reduced, and, therefore, many errors are automatically eliminated. Another feature of the AUTOSET program is that the text, when placed, need not be displayed. It may be suppressed or shown by a single command. The important factor is its proper connection with symbols and lines in the database. The user can, therefore, have uncluttered graphics on the screen when creating complex or dense drawings yet also obtain complete documentation for FROM-TO tracking, bills of material, etc.

Figure 12.17 shows the AUTOSET nodes for placement of annotation to a control valve

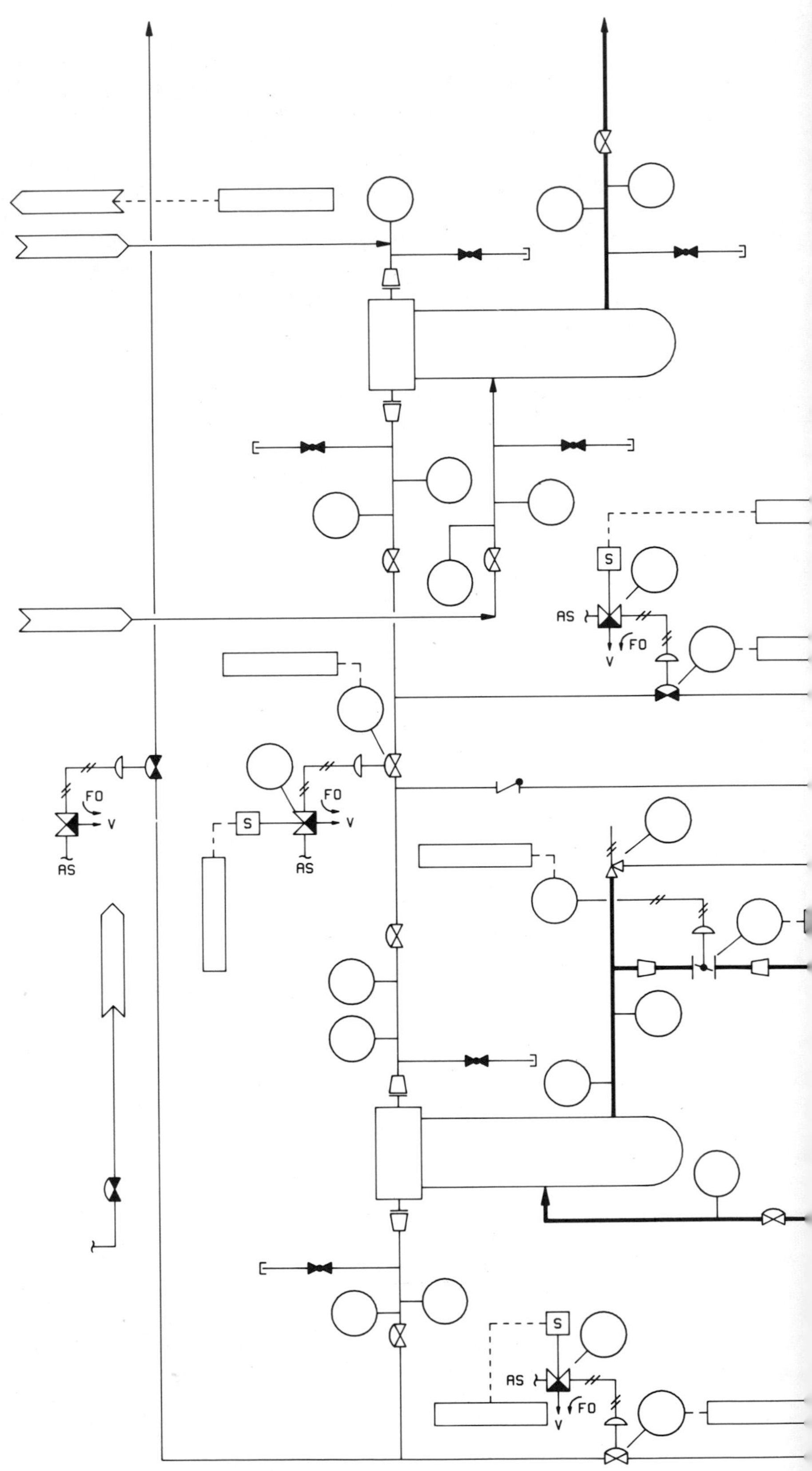

Figure 12.11 Further expansion of the P & ID.

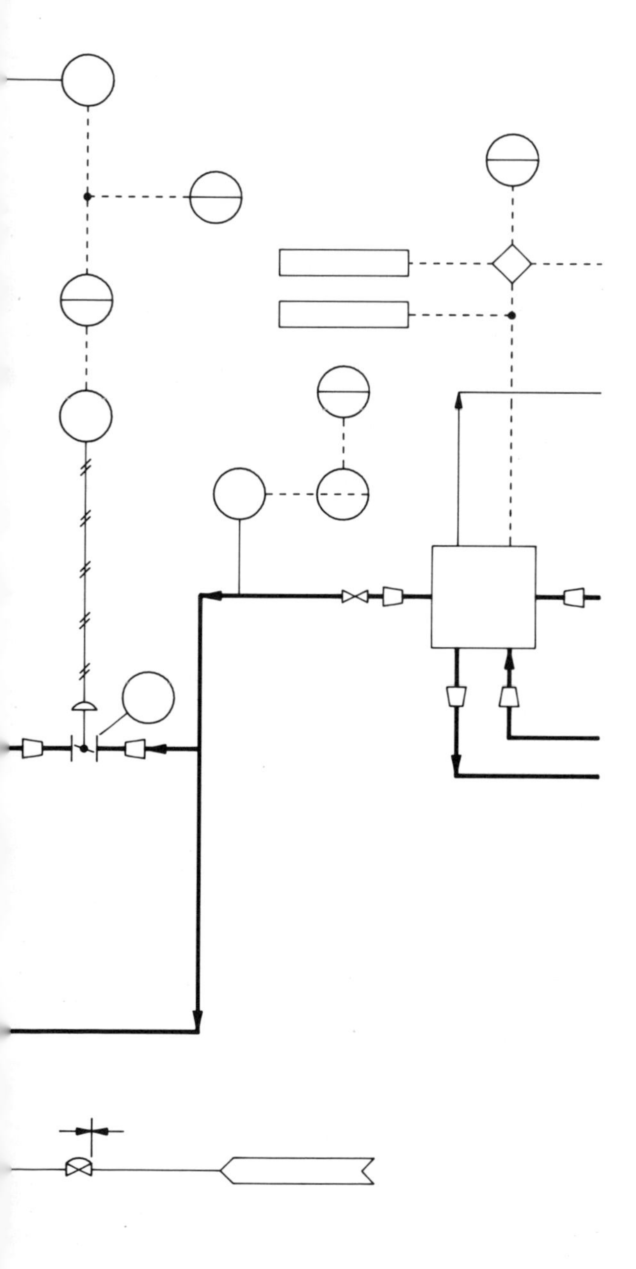

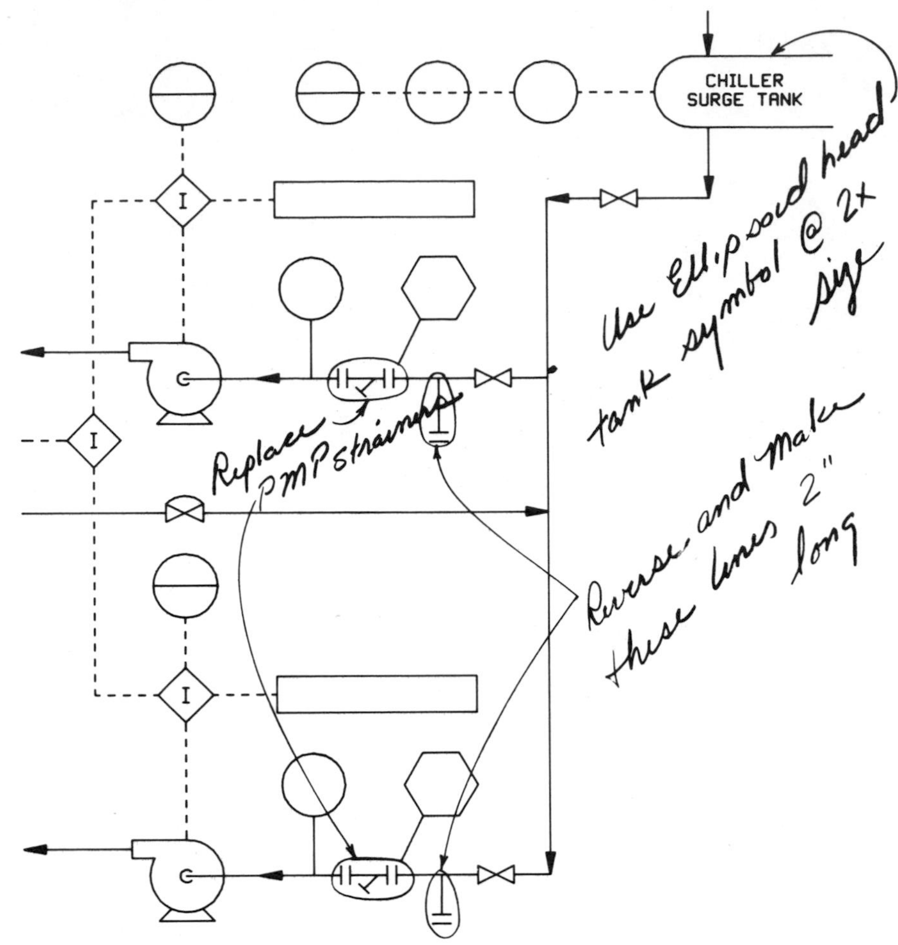

Figure 12.12 Symbol revisions.

and instrument symbol. To identify the symbols, the user types (or touches a menu square) the following characters at the workstation keyboard:

V-137, N.O., TV, 386, W, JP005

When the user enters a carriage return, the graphics screen will then automatically show these entries in their correct places (see Fig. 12.18). Note that the characters have been centered automatically, as per user request.

AUTOSET nodes determine the horizontal and vertical spacing of the annotation. This also means that text may be placed at any angle. Figure 12.19 shows the annotation placed on the line drawing from Fig. 12.11. As can be seen on this drawing, line-work annotation is no different from that for an equipment or device symbol.

AUTOSET nodes serve not only to generate drawings and place annotations quickly and accurately, they also have an important role as associators. That is, they identify which devices, symbols, and lines are connected, as well as noting their individual functions, sizes, specifications, and numbers. This associativity enables the user to generate complete BOMs, schedules, lists, and sorts by area, size, etc. When a device or equipment symbol, a line, or even an entire construction is duplicated, AUTOSET nodes ensure that any associated alphanumerics are also copied. The result is not only a uniformity in appearance but also a consistency in notation.

It is obvious that the greater the volume of data that must be managed, the greater the value of these features. However, smaller projects with less experienced designers and drafters can also benefit from the inherent consistency of a CAD system.

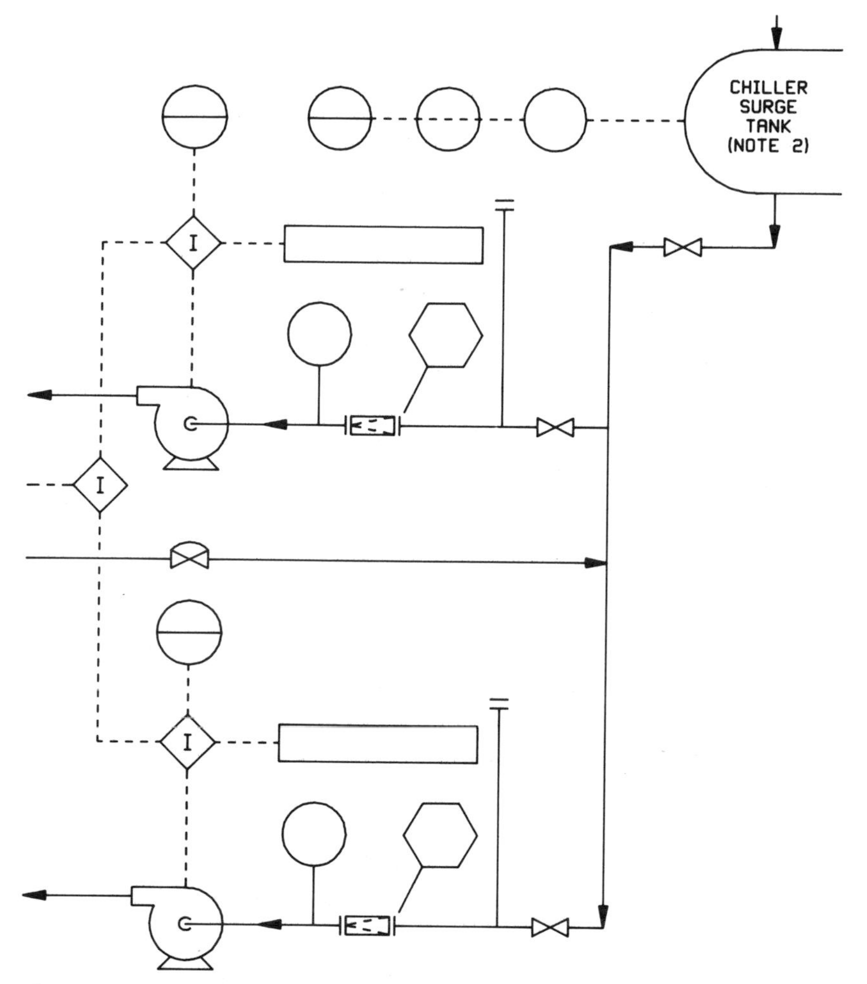

Figure 12.13 Revised P & ID section.

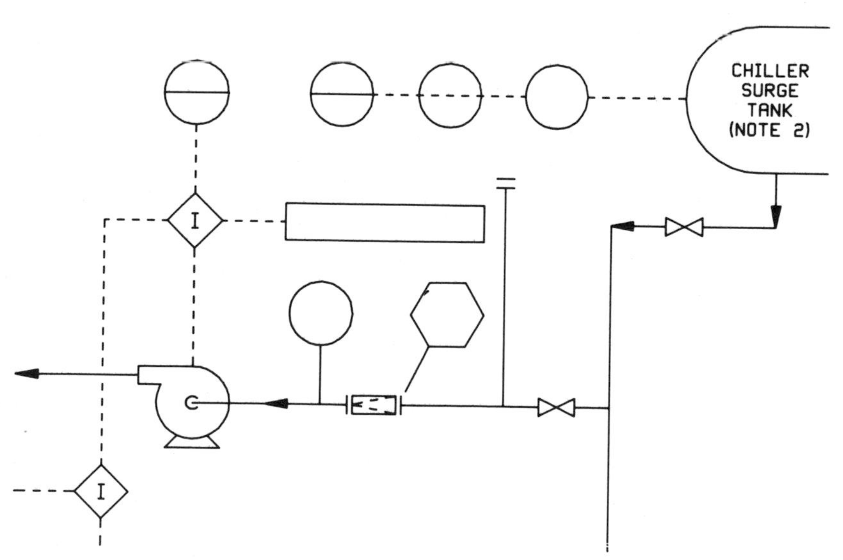

Figure 12.14 Conventional circles to be replaced.

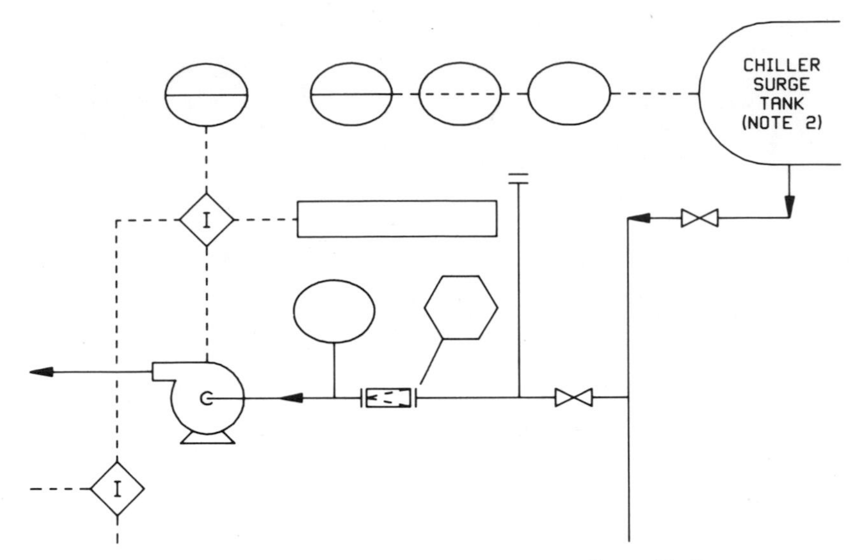

Figure 12.15 Revised drawing with circles replaced by elliptical balloons.

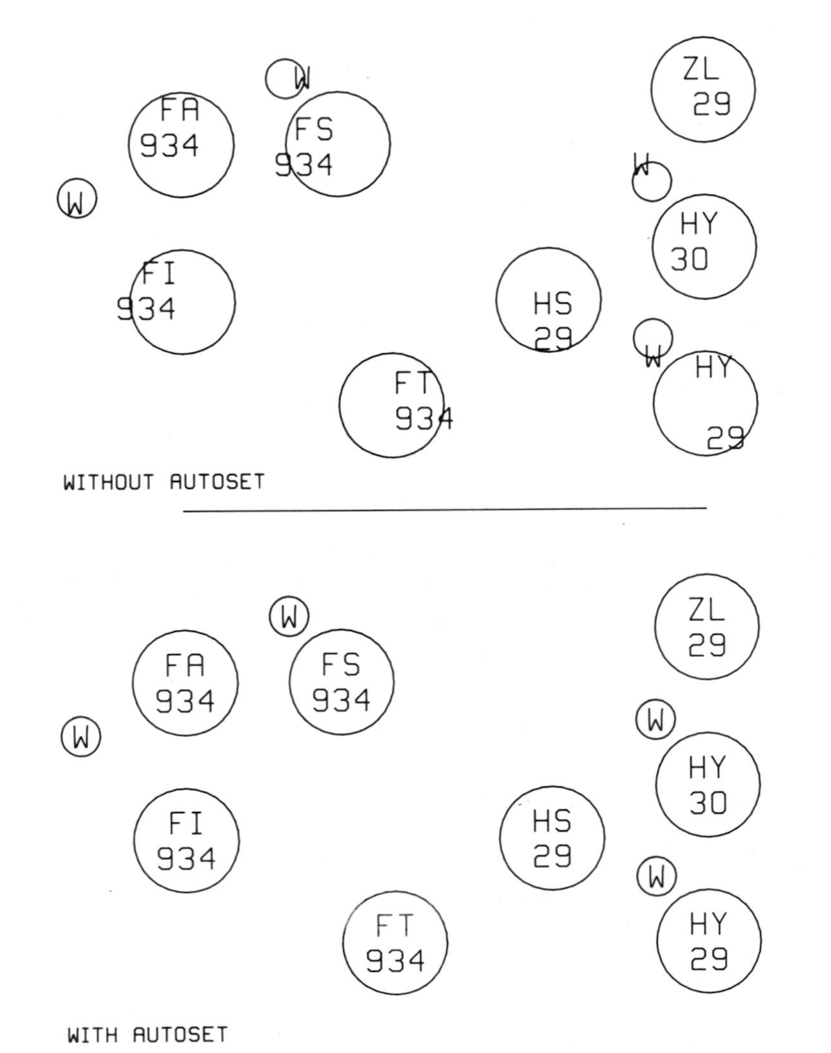

Figure 12.16 AUTOSET text placement.

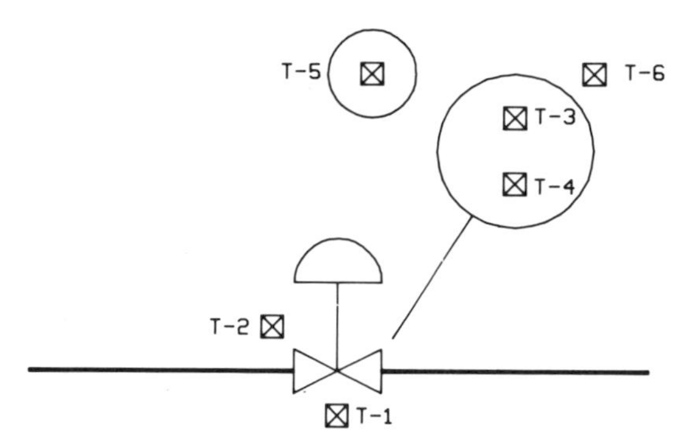

Figure 12.17 Automatic text placement.

The user can also construct original charts, schedules, or flowsheet tabulations using AUTOSET nodes. Figure 12.20 shows a part of a single-page, small-plant process flowsheet. The user merely joins the desired alphanumerics to the node for automatic placement. This can be accomplished easily by a typist, freeing the CAD user for more creative and demanding work. This placement capability is also used when annotating the title block of a drawing. Refer to Fig. 12.21.

12.7 TEXT REVISIONS

The CAD system allows the user to renumber, rename, or revise general notes to any drawing stored in the database. This feature permits text changes ranging from adding, deleting, or revising a single character in a word to complete reorganization of general notes for different or greater emphasis. Common revisions, such as correcting code numbers, adding alphanumeric text, or renaming equipment or device symbols are easily and quickly accomplished. To effect a revision of text at a symbol, for example, the user merely identifies the character or word to be changed, and then types in the desired change. The few seconds it takes a CAD operator to do this is significantly less than the time required for the manual method. Beyond that, this change is automatically reflected on all other drawings containing this symbol and its text. This associativity is very valuable for changing entire class designations. To do this, the user merely changes the class code; the system automatically updates all occurrences of that class in the database to the new designation.

If, for example, on a system all 2-inch lines of carbon steel were to be changed to stainless steel, the user would change the designation in the specification list from AB (carbon steel) to ST (stainless steel). The system ensures that all notations for 2-inch lines

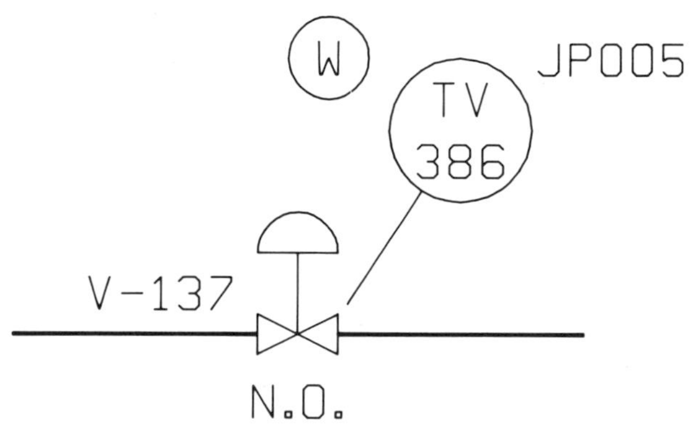

Figure 12.18 Automatic text occurrence.

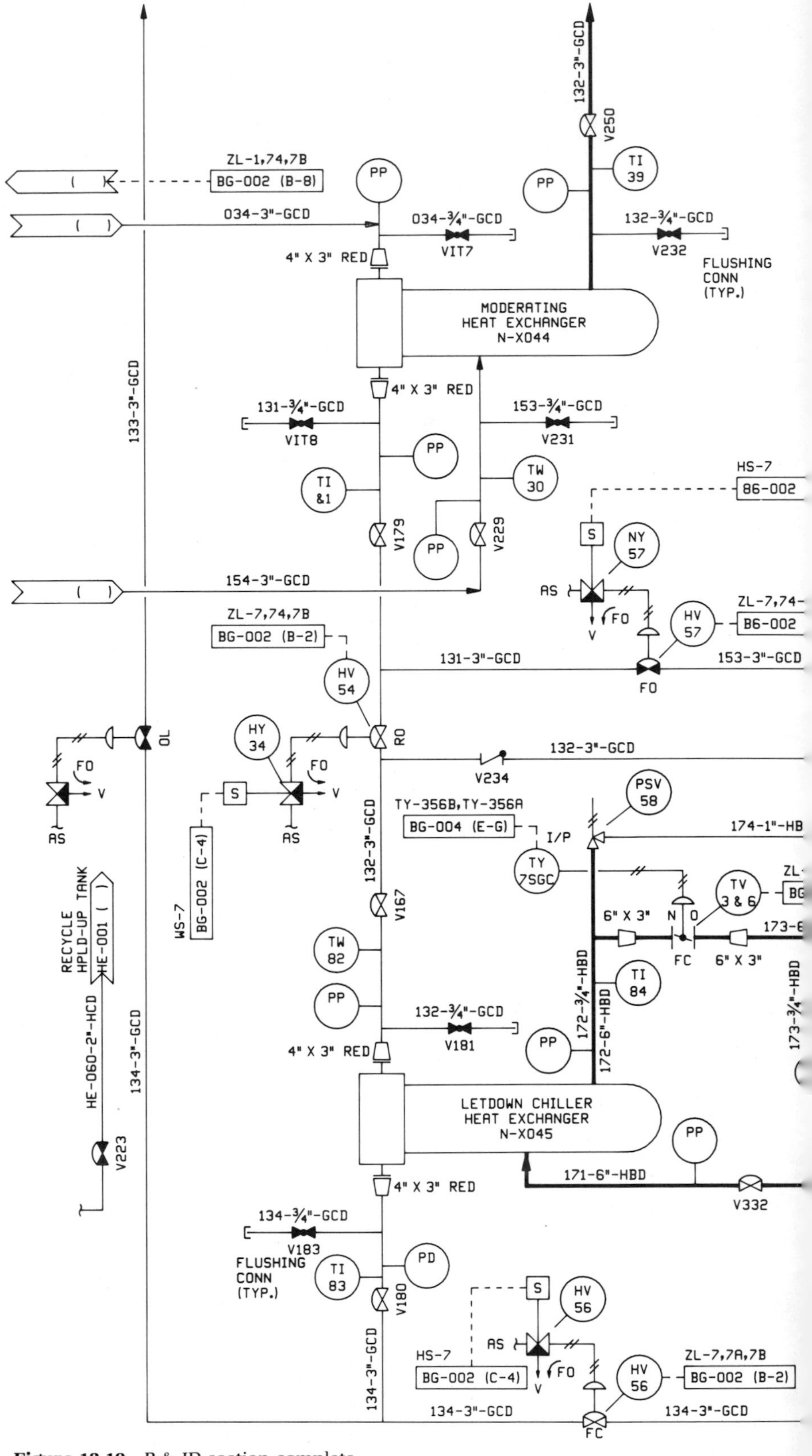

Figure 12.19 P & ID section complete.

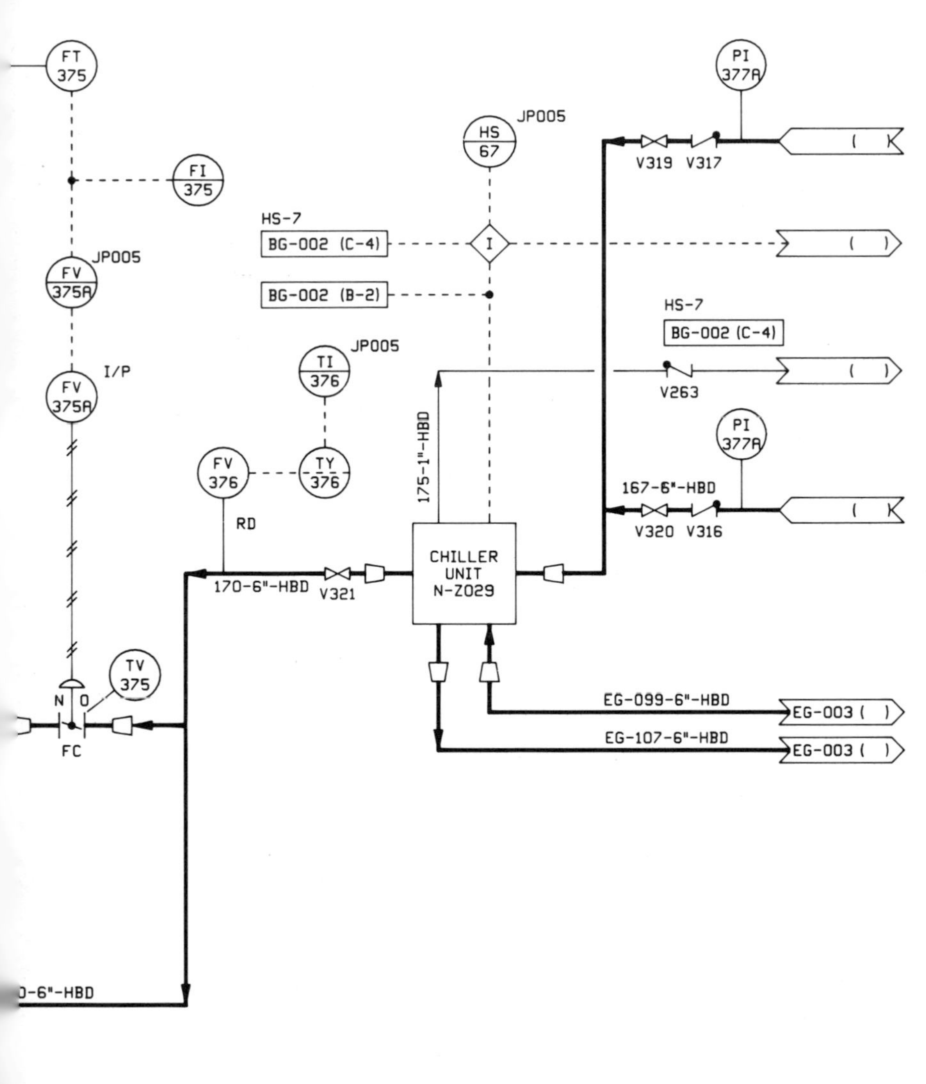

FT
375
FI
375
FV
375A
JP005
FV
375A
I/P
HS
67
JP005
HS-7
BG-002 (C-4)
I
BG-002 (B-2)
TI
376
JP005
FV
376
TY
376
RD
PI
377A
V319 V317
HS-7
BG-002 (C-4)
V263
175-1"-HBD
PI
377A
167-6"-HBD
V320 V316
CHILLER
UNIT
N-Z029
170-6"-HBD
V321
TV
375
N O
FC
EG-099-6"-HBD
EG-003 ( )
EG-107-6"-HBD
EG-003 ( )
0-6"-HBD
GCD
HCD
CD
056-2"-4CD
FROM
BLENDING CONN
BG-003 (D-3)

EQUIPMENT NUMBER	C201	X202	H203	C204	
NAME	QUENCH TOWER	FILTER	ABSORBER/ CONDENSER	KETONE ABSORBER	
SIZE or CAPACITY	4' - 6" DIA, 12" - 0" PKG	2,000 GPH	4,750 SQ FT	3' - 3" DIA, 19 PLATES	
MATERIAL HANDLED % Wt/Wt A	27	0	26	54	
C	34	53	35	4	
N	29	47	29	2	
GAS	(5+K5)	0	5 K5	37+K3	
WORKING PRESS PSIG	5	5	100 = TUBES 4 = SHELLS	3.5	
WORKING TEMP °C	700 = BASE	150	150→30 FLUID 23→35 WATER	25-35	
MATERIAL	ST STL 18/8/1/1	ST STL 18/8/1/1	ST STL 18/8/1/1	COPPER	
UTILITIES					
STEAM 150 LB	-	-	-	-	
STEAM 50 LB	-	-	-	-	
CITY WATER	-	-	67,500 GPH	-	
OTHER	-	-	-	-	
OTHER DATA	PACKED WITH 4" RASCH IG RINGS; LOWER 4 FT STACKED; REMAINDER RANDOM PCKD.	INSTALL FEED PUMP IF REQ'D TO REMOVE SOLIDS DOWN TO 100 MESH.	1,536 TUBES 1"OD X 12"-0" LONG; SIX PASSES ON WATER SIDE. 10 SHELL BAFFLES, 25% CUT ON 14" CTRS.	37 BUBBLE CAP PER PLATE; 3" DIA WITH 38 SLOTS, 1/8 WIDE X 1"HIGH CAPS ON 4 1/4 TRIANGULAR PITCH. PLATE SPACING AT 15	

Figure 12.20 Process flowsheet material.

and other documentation reflect this change. Revision of letters, numbers, words, sentences, or even their left-to-right justification is effected just as easily.

A CAD system should also allow revision symbols to be readily placed on drawings. Such symbols have AUTOSET nodes for the placement of revision identification numbers and can be positioned anywhere on the drawing.

12.8 DRAWING FORMATS

The ability to size drawings so they conform to standard American (A to E) or SI metric (A4 to A0) sizes is standard with most CAD systems. The user can change these measurements should the company format be different; this includes title-block sizing. Format measurements for borders and title blocks can be stored and recalled whenever needed, facilitating the judging of the percent reduction or magnification necessary.

To make a complete or partial drawing conform to a particular standard often requires that the drawing elements be reduced or magnified. The CAD system allows for variable reduction and magnification in the x and/or y direction independently.

The CAD system gives the user the capability to align orthogonally the major axes of drawings to borders either prestored in the database or preprinted on the final plot sheet. The user also has the option to assign a drawing origin (0, 0) to the lower left trim-line corner, ensuring correct drawing orientation and plotting within border lines.

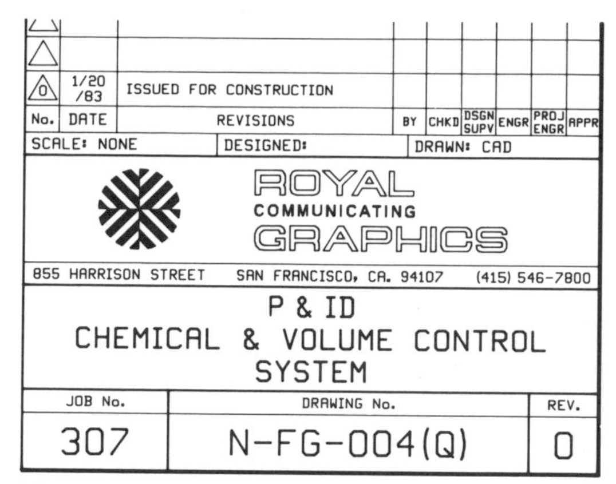

Figure 12.21 Drawing border.

12.9 REPORT GENERATION

12.9.1 Lists and Schedules

The CAD system allows the user to generate customized reports, which list specified data in user-selected format and organization. The following is a partial overview of the kinds of reports the user can generate with a typical P & ID program.

- Listings
- Schedule sheets—line, vessel and tank, equipment pump, motor or drive, FROM-TO
- P & ID tabulations—BOM
- Accounting—job, project
- Sorts, tallies, totals

All reports are in user-designated formats and are usually output on a line printer, including drawing-associated data and sorts by class, area, size, etc. These may be obtained at any time during the drafting and documentation process.

Listing may not necessarily reflect data associated with entire drawings; any part of a drawing can be "windowed," and a list for only that section generated. The user also has the capability to have lists "lettered" onto a preassigned portion of a drawing as well as "typed" on the line printer.

12.9.2 Revision

Should a drawing be changed, any lists associated with the changed items would automatically reflect this change. This automatic compilation feature of a CAD system also permits the user to cross-check between data on a flow diagram and P & IDs.

An example of an automatic schedule update is given using the thermal regeneration subsystem example in Fig. 12.22. The preliminary BOM for this subsystem is given in Fig. 12.23 (see pages 12.24 and 12.25). Once the original drawing (in this case Fig. 12.22) is changed, as illustrated in Fig. 12.24 (see pages 12.26 and 12.27), the attendant preliminary BOM is automatically updated to reflect these changes. In all cases the upgraded information is consistent between drawing and report; typographical or code errors are impossible since all data have been extracted from the same database.

The only data not updated automatically in this manner are information placed on a drawing and not associated with any device or equipment symbols, such as general notes.

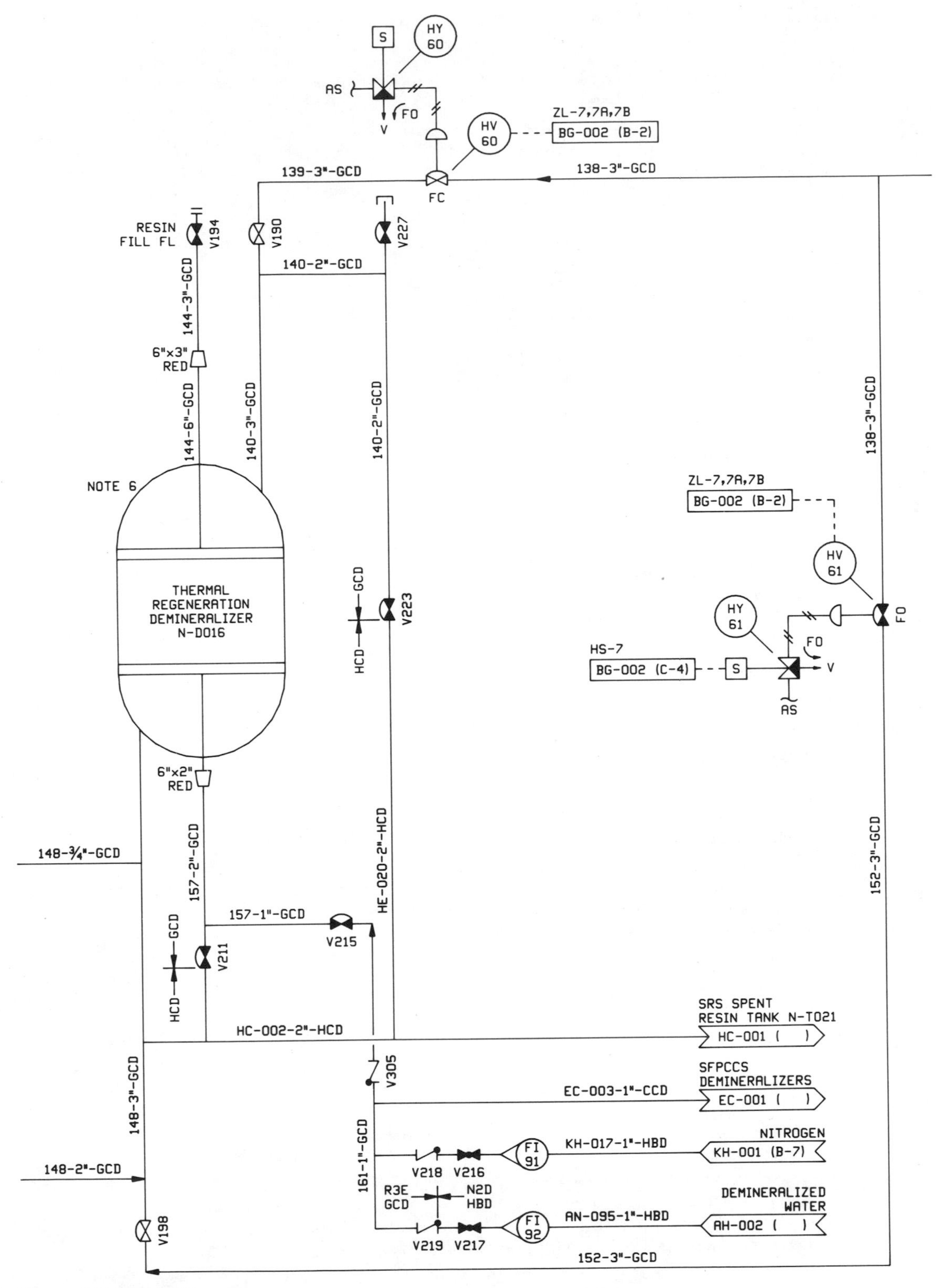

Figure 12.22 P & ID section.

12.10 DOCUMENTATION: PLOTTERS

The user has many options for obtaining hard copies of a partial or completed drawing. The CAD system interfaces to a variety of plotters. They can produce drawings in formats up to E size (A0 size). Hard-copy units are available for immediate A size (A4 size) facsimiles of data as shown on the graphics cathode-ray tube (CRT) screen.

Large plots of data selected by the user can be obtained from ball point or wet ink, drum, flatbed, belt-driven, matrix, or computer microfilm plotters. To start a plot, the data are first windowed on the graphics CRT. In this way the user can determine exactly what is to appear on the plot. For offline plotting, the data are then formatted for output to the plotter; then they are transmitted from the tape drive to the plotter in background mode so that the user can work on other designs while the plot is running.

12.11 SUMMARY

A CAD system can be one of the most effective and productive means for developing P & IDs. The particular P & ID application must be identified and studied, using the methodology outlined in this chapter. For optimum effectiveness, symbol libraries, pertinent command files, and application programs should all be established and resident in the system prior to use.

Operators must be trained and versed in P & ID drafting techniques. Once the system commands and functions have been mastered, the operator is in a position to perform useful work. With a properly programmed system operated by a trained user, the inherent drafting capabilities of the system will improve the quality of the work and increase overall productivity for P & ID applications.

CLIENT______________________ P&ID______________________ REV___ DATE__________

JOB NO.______ ______________________ TAPE NO.________

BOM LIST CURRENT ON __________ SYSTEM ______________________ Sh___of___

P&ID BILL OF MATERIAL LIST SUMMARY: See Sh____ of ____

SEQ. LINE NO.	LINE DESIGNATOR	NPD -in.-	LINE ORIGIN AND LINE TERMINATION	LINE VALVE			CONTROL VALVE			OTHER	INSTRUMENT		PR SEQ. NO.
				SIZE	TYPE	ID NO.	SIZE	TYPE	ID NO.		TAG	SP	
1	AN-095-1"-HBD	1.0	COME FR AN-002 V219	1.0	BV	217	-	-	-	FLOW IND	FI-92	-	1 2 3
2	EC-003-1"-GCD	1.0	161-1"-GCD GO TO EC-001	-	-	-	-	-	-	-	-	-	4 5 6
3	HC-002-2"-HCD	2.0	V211 V212 GO TO HC-001 SRS SPENT RESIN TANK N-T021	-	-	-	-	-	-	-	-	-	7 8 9 10 11 12
4	HE-020-2"-HCD	2.0	COME FR HC-001 SRS RESIN SLUICE PUMP N-POB V206	-	-	-	-	-	-	-	-	-	13 14 15 16 17 18
4A	KH-017-1"-HBD	1.0	COME FR KH-001 NITROGEN V218	1.0	BV	216	-	-	-	FLOW IND	FI-92	-	19 20 21 22
5	138-3"-GCD	3.0	xxxxxxxxx CV HV-60, HV-61	-	-	-	-	-	-	-	-	-	23 24 25 26
													27 28 29 30

Sh___of___

SEQ. LINE NO.	LINE DESIGNATOR	NPD -in.-	LINE ORIGIN AND LINE TERMINATION	LINE VALVE			CONTROL VALVE			OTHER	INSTRUMENT		PR SEQ. NO.
				SIZE	TYPE	ID NO.	SIZE	TYPE	ID NO.		TAG	SP	
6	139-3"-GCD	3.0	138-3"-GCD V190	-	-	-	3.0	dia	6.0	-	HV-60 HY-60	- -	1 2 3
7	140-#"GCD	3.0	139-3"-GCD N-D016	3.0	DV	V190	-	-	-	-	-	-	4 5 6
8	140-2"-GCD	2.0	140-3"-GCD V223	2.0 2.0	DV DV	V223 V227	-	-	-	HOSE CONN			7 8 9 10
													11 12 13
													14 15 16
11	144-6"-GCD		144-3"-GCD N-D016	-	-	-	-	-	-	6"x3" RED	-	-	17 18 19 20
12	144-3"-GCD		RESIN FILL FL 144-6"-GCD	3.0	DV	V194	-	-	-	-	-	-	21 22 23 24
													25 26 27
													28 29 30

Figure 12.23 Bill of material.

Sh____of____

SEQ. LINE NO.	LINE DESIGNATOR	NPD -in.-	LINE ORIGIN AND LINE TERMINATION	LINE VALVE SIZE	LINE VALVE TYPE	LINE VALVE ID NO.	CONTROL VALVE SIZE	CONTROL VALVE TYPE	CONTROL VALVE ID NO.	OTHER	INSTRUMENT TAG	INSTRUMENT SP	PR SEQ. NO.
15	148-3"-GCD	3.0	152-3"-GCD N-D016	3.0	DV	V198	-	-	-	-	-	-	1 2 3
16	148-2"-GCD	2.0	HC-020-2"-HCD 148-3"-GCD	2.0	DV	V206	-	-	-	-	-	-	4 5 6
17	148-3/4"-GCD	0.75	HOSE CONN 148-3"-GCD	0.75	DV	V201	-	-	-	-	-	-	7 8 9 10
													11 12 13
													14 15 16
													17 18 19 20
21	152-3"-GCD	3.0	138-3"-GCD 144-3"-GCD	-	-	-	3.0	dia	61	-	HV-61 HV-61	- -	21 22 23 24
													25 26 27
													28 29 30

Sh____of____

SEQ. LINE NO.	LINE DESIGNATOR	NPD -in.-	LINE ORIGIN AND LINE TERMINATION	LINE VALVE SIZE	LINE VALVE TYPE	LINE VALVE ID NO.	CONTROL VALVE SIZE	CONTROL VALVE TYPE	CONTROL VALVE ID NO.	OTHER	INSTRUMENT TAG	INSTRUMENT SP	PR SEQ. NO.
22	157-2"-GCD	2.0	N-D016 HC-002-2"-HCD	2.0	DV	V211	-	-	-	6"x2" RED	-	-	1 2 3
23	157-1"-GCD	1.0	161-1"-GCD 157-2"-GCD	1.0	DV	V215	-	-	-	-	-	-	4 5 6
													7 8 9 10
													11 12 13
26	161-1"-GCD	1.0	AN-095-1"-HBD 157-1"-GCD	1.0 1.0	CV CV	V219 V305	-	-	-	-	-	-	14 15 16
													17 18 19 20
													21 22 23 24
													25 26 27
													28 29 30

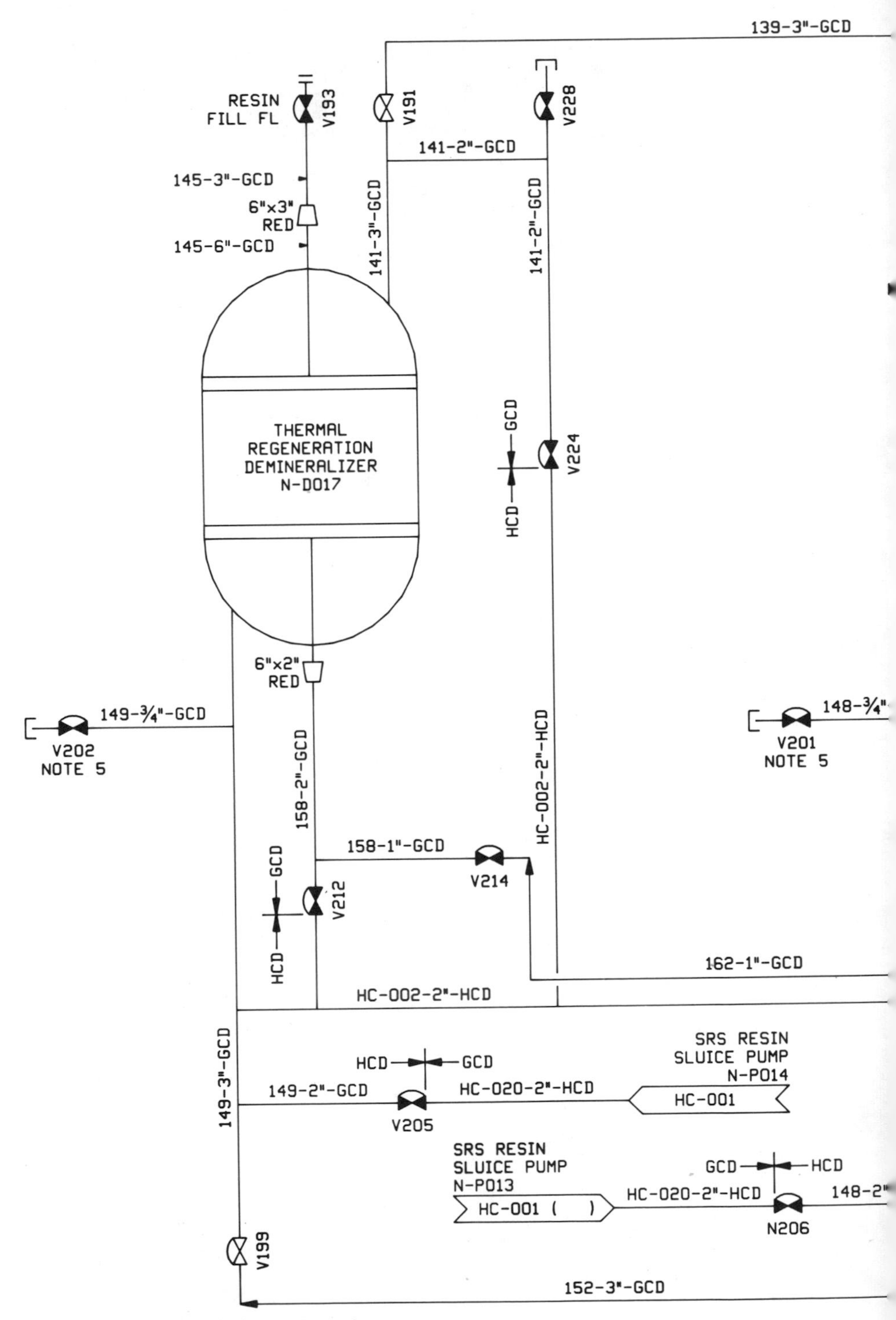

Figure 12.24 Extended P & ID section.

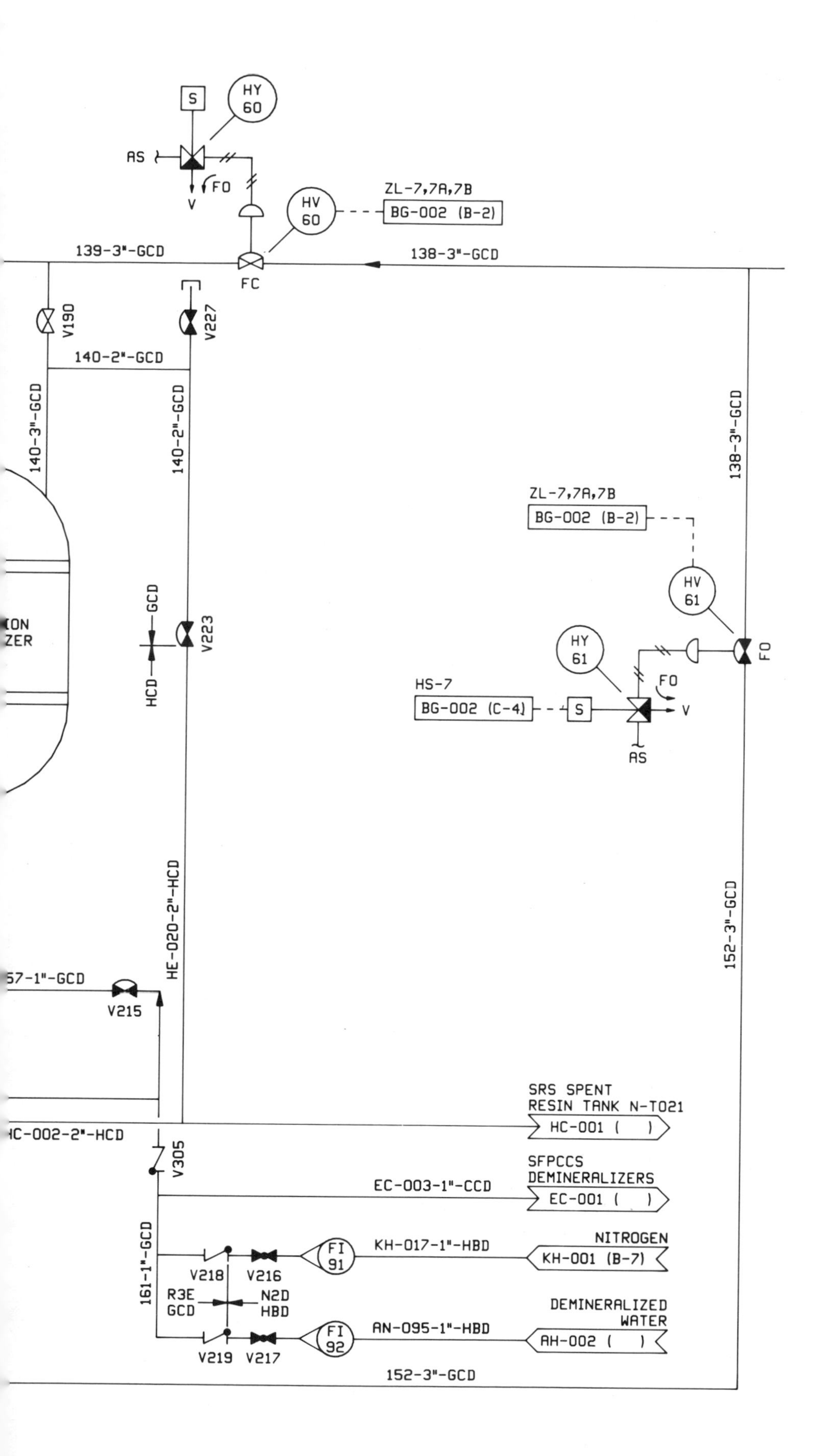

S
HY 60
AS
FO
V
ZL-7,7A,7B
BG-002 (B-2)
HV 60
139-3"-GCD
138-3"-GCD
FC
V190
V227
140-2"-GCD
140-3"-GCD
140-2"-GCD
138-3"-GCD
ZL-7,7A,7B
BG-002 (B-2)
HV 61
GCD
HCD
V223
HY 61
FO
HS-7
BG-002 (C-4)
S
V
AS
HE-020-2"-HCD
152-3"-GCD
57-1"-GCD
V215
SRS SPENT
RESIN TANK N-T021
HC-001 ( )
HC-002-2"-HCD
V305
SFPCCS
DEMINERALIZERS
EC-003-1"-CCD
EC-001 ( )
161-1"-GCD
FI 91
KH-017-1"-HBD
NITROGEN
KH-001 (B-7)
V218
V216
R3E GCD
N2D HBD
DEMINERALIZED
WATER
FI 92
AN-095-1"-HBD
AH-002 ( )
V219
V217
152-3"-GCD

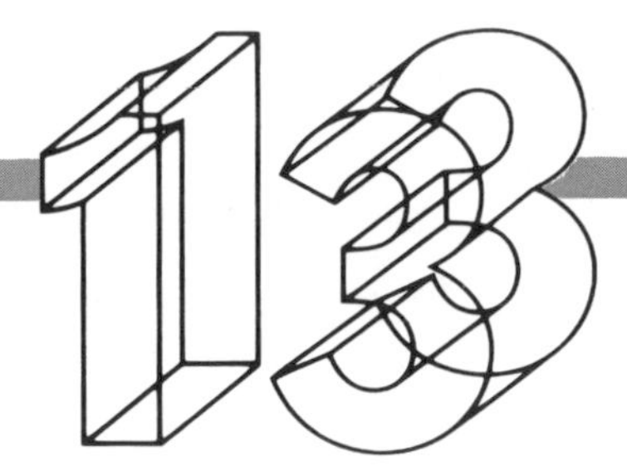

Solid Modeling

by
Jerry Borrell

13.1 INTRODUCTION

Solid or geometric modeling has become an indicator of two important considerations for computer-aided design (CAD) systems. First, solid modeling (SM) software represents the forefront of converging software developments in design, analysis, and engineering. Second, the possession of SM capability is considered an indicator of a vendor's awareness of the ensuing changes in CAD over the next decade and whether or not the manufacturer is attempting to keep abreast of software and hardware developments in order to remain competitive. Because of these two factors there remains a great deal of contention in the marketing of systems and in discussing them.

The basic definition of an SM system might be one that allows for the storage and manipulation of a geometrically accurate and unambiguous description of an object. To do so the system should be able to determine whether any point lies adjacent to, concurrent with, or inside a plane. Beyond these characteristics, systems may be able to determine moments of inertia, mass properties, or interface with other software packages in order to perform engineering analysis.

Terry Palmer of the CAD Centre in Cambridge has noted in several technical papers on the field of geometric modeling that the earliest attempts to design CAD systems provided for the storage of designs based upon their source as engineering drawings. The shortcoming of this approach is that the material being stored in memory is a description of a drawing and not a model of the design itself. One outcome of such a technique is the inability to display more than stored views of objects—the reason being that the two-dimensional descriptions are insufficient for three-dimensional picture processing of an existing object.

The solution developed over two decades ago is to describe objects in terms of three-dimensional points and lines—the wire-frame approach to CAD. From such a database of points, edges, and vertices, it is possible to produce displays of isometric, orthogonal, and other projections. However, several problems remained with this stage of development. For example, in order to provide unambiguous displays of complex wire-frame drawings, hidden-line algorithms had to be applied which could remove those lines that would not be seen by the viewer. However, if the system is capable of working only with dimensional wire frames, the viewer may still be unable to determine absolutely where a face or boundary actually lies.

The next step then was to implement limited surface information with the wire-frame model so that individual faces could be identified and displayed. The final development before today's work in surface-shaded SM packages, then, was to add not only surface information but to provide a means by which the database could be accessed by the computer to determine how the surfaces related to one another. This latter capability allows the system to make the crucial determination mentioned earlier of whether or not a point lies within, adjacent to, or outside a plane.

It remains unclear whether possession of SM capability is a fair indicator of a firm's viability in CAD. However, because SM software requires significant computational power and operates primarily on 32-bit computers, it has become one of the reasons for the shift of manufacturers to more powerful systems. This need, on the other hand, may act as a deterrent to SM implementation.

While another important trend in CAD is the effort to provide individual workstations for designers, many of the current generation of workstations are unsuitable for SM. It has also become popular to refer to graphic systems with color surface shading as solid modelers, an unfortunate practice at a time when potential users of computer-aided manufacturing (CAM) and computer-aided engineering (CAE) are attempting to evaluate uses of SM.

13.2 THE MARKETPLACE FOR SM: CONVERGING TECHNOLOGIES OF CAD, CAM, AND CAE

SM represents one of the areas in which the software of CAD, CAM, and CAE are converging. The uniting factor for these traditionally separate areas lies in the acquisition of the geometric database required to display the solid model. This database can provide the information required to display typical 2½- or three-dimensional engineering drawings, to drive numerically controlled devices such as milling machines, or to assist in the construction of models which can be subjected to analytic evaluation for the design process. Because these areas overlap and because of the current inability of most SM systems (hardware and software configurations) to be used in all of these applications, the present applicability of SM to all three is limited. Many industry observers feel that available SM systems provide the most benefit in applications to the communication of design concepts.

13.2.1 Barriers to the Growth of SM

Of all of the problems associated with the use and development of SM, the complexity of the software may be most problematic. Typically a package might contain thousands of lines of code. The result is the need for almost exclusive central processing unit (CPU) time if designs are to be displayed with anything approaching interactivity—even with 32-bit minicomputers this may not be practical. A related problem is the storage of both the code and the data associated with solid shapes.

In reality the nature of the data and CPU demands are dependent upon the user. And, as systems such as the Hewlett-Packard HP 9000 desktop become available, CPU time can be affordable for the individual designer. Despite changes in computer technology, SM packages have application in CAD primarily for design and drafting functions but remain impractical for new areas of CAD development such as technical illustration, architectural, and electrical-electronic applications. High cost, relatively slow designer interaction and lack of applications software tend to limit SM to areas within mechanical design. One exception is the application to animation such as that seen in the Disney film *Tron*. Even here the application remains relatively limited and of extremely high cost.

Within available interactive design and drafting software, SM does not compare well with two- or 2½-dimensional software. Construction of complex solid models not only requires a longer period than with ordinary two-dimensional methods (because of operator interaction, computation, and rendering), but there are many applications for which a solid would not be suitable.

There are even questions about whether SM drawings would be acceptable under existing technical and legal codes defined by administrative or professional groups—where an architectural plan for a building might be a typical illustration. In mechanical design applications, however, in which a drawing may only need to convey sufficient information to a design shop engineer, an SM may well be acceptable. There are questions even about the latter case, as most engineers would not be familiar with a design made with SM. Traditional methods of design are so well established that a great deal of information is conveyed by implication or convention rather than by explicit notation. The unmarked but unmistakable 90° angle is often cited as an example here.

Proponents of SM in CAD applications justifiably note that solids do, however, provide designers with a great deal more freedom once the initial model has been created. To support this, they point out the ability of many SM systems to generate rapidly sectional views of an object along any desired plane. While this is not a capability possible with two-dimensional drafting systems, the latter are proficient at producing different projections (isometric, orthogonal, etc.) of objects.

Many two- and three-dimensional systems today offer multiple window views of the object being designed. Those critical of solid modelers also note the inability of most of the systems to provide annotations vital in the design process such as dimensions, text, and notes.

The problem of hard-copy output is another barrier to the wide use of SM in CAD. Commercially available two- and three-dimensional CAD systems provide an interface to a drafting device such as a plotter. This ability to draw automatically on different media (paper, Mylar, film) or to transmit the output data to remote plotters provides one of the greatest advantages for CAD.

To date there are few suitable methods for producing hard copy with an SM CAD system—ink-jet and camera systems being the two most valuable—that are also acceptable in an engineering environment. Applicon initially provided a high-cost ink-jet plotter with its SM package and reintroduced a lower-cost device in 1983, but this remains a solution suited more for design communication and not engineering drawings. Other companies such as Printacolor, Diablo, and Sharp are making progress in offering lower-cost, high-resolution output on ink-jet plotters.

This insufficiency indicates yet another area where SM does not rival the available CAD systems, technical illustration. As computer technology has modified the printing process by introducing phototypesetting or laser typesetting, it has been possible to interface CAD systems with devices that allow illustrators to combine technical drawings and text for the printing process. IDI and XYVision are two of the most advanced systems.

SM is not yet suitable for this area because of the inability of the current-generation CAD systems used for the production of technical publications to support color output at acceptable costs. To be certain, manufacturers, such as Hell and Crossfield, provide such systems, but they are cost-effective only for full-page color workstations rather than the monochrome line art and text typical of technical publications such an manuals and handbooks. Another factor which will slow the application of SM in printing applications is the manner of storing data on objects, usually as descriptions based upon boundary files of points and lines in objects, or as volume models of objects (constructive solid geometry models) discussed in Sec. 13.3.

Few of the current manufacturers of full-color pagination systems have sufficient knowledge of CAD to develop applications packages for SM.

Users of existing CAD systems note that their systems offer designers and drafters a broad repertoire of software and hardware interaction. SM to date remains relatively limited in this way and based primarily upon keyboard interaction rather than the tablet or screen menus so effective in most design and drafting workstations. Lexidata has addressed this issue and now offers a three-dimensional joystick-controlled cursor for SM—however, the system awaits use with a major SM software package. This limitation of software interaction is based partially upon the complexity of the software itself and the computational time required to generate display.

Finally, because solid models with shaded surfaces have become the de facto standard, vendors must support not only extensive computer programs for modeling but also the algorithms needed to render color, light sources, and shading. Until recently this type of software was implemented primarily on minicomputers and superminicomputers (16- and 32-bit systems). During the past year the Romulus SM package has been implemented on the Terak and IBM PC microcomputers. An obvious disadvantage of using these relatively small systems is that their processors are not powerful enough to support as wide a range of software and interaction as larger computers.

Again, one of the limitations which prevents system integrators from combining modeling with analysis, such as finite-element software, is that both are intensely demanding of the CPU. Most analysis packages, for example, are run on superminicomputers or mainframe computers. The need to draw and render solid shaded surfaces is no less complex, as witnessed by the recent announcement of Floating Point Computers that its largest array processors will be used to support solid software packages. Thus while computers are becoming more powerful, the demands of both SM and analytic software for design require an extraordinary amount of CPU time.

13.2.2 CAM and Solid Models

The application of SM to the manufacturing process remains one of the most promising uses of SM. The data about a geometric figure required to display, render data surfaces, and perform analysis are ideally suited to provide output for numerically controlled machine tools. To date the programs devised in creating solid models for analysis, such as finite-element mesh generation and analysis, and those used in numeric control applications are separate, but most of the major CAD system manufacturers or software houses are attempting to integrate capability from each group into packages.

At present there can be said to be only a few actual solid modelers in active use for CAM. GM Solid, the SM package developed and implemented by General Motors, is one of the few that is part of a production research program. It should be noted that this is true of color-shaded systems; however, the boundary file representation systems of Medusa or Gino in the United Kingdom and Euclid in France have been used for CAM for several years.

13.2.3 CAE and SM

There are three primary areas of application for engineering analysis and SM with current CAD systems: the determination of mass properties, clearances (or interference), and mesh generation. The calculation of mass properties is the best understood and includes the analysis of volumes, weight, center of gravity, moments of inertia, volume, and surface area. For example, the design of a bottle is made easier if the relationship of the volume of the bottle vis-à-vis its shape can be precalculated. Center of gravity data can prove invaluable as input in the design process because they can allow engineers to consider factors such as the possible positions for machine parts in automatic inspection, or to test a machine part for torque and stress before the actual part is built.

The generation of the mesh may be made easier if a solid model is present because calculations to test stress or other aspects of a model can be related to the actual product, not to an idealized model. Some of the developers of SM systems maintain that the unique capability of SM systems to generate cross sections is also useful for engineering analysis.

While most CAD systems can generate different perspective views of a design, they do not contain as much information as a solid. But one may be able to create sectional views of the internal construction of a model, or to display selective parts of a design with a minimum of effort, particularly with the constructive solid geometry–based modelers.

An additional benefit of some SM systems is that the operator can calculate clearances of working parts in three dimensions to determine if the design is viable. Some system developers claim to be able to support such a "kinematic" capability, that is, the ability to perform motion analysis with their SM systems. At the very least one can expect to be able to move objects through a series of precalculated views to examine possible overlap, interference, or improper tolerance.

13.3 CURRENT TECHNOLOGY

The commercially available SM systems discussed in this section are primarily based upon two software approaches: constructive solid geometry (CSG), otherwise known as the geometric primitive approach; and a boundary file representation (B-rep) approach, the latter sometimes known as the wire-frame approach, in which files describe the edges of all surfaces of the objects being modeled.

The former type of system has, until very recently, been the predominant system in the United States, probably because of its ability to render models in color. The latter systems are based upon work done the late 1960s at the University of Cambridge and the CAD Centre, both located in Cambridge, England. Today almost all of the earlier-developed European SM systems are being interfaced with color-rendering capability. The development in American SM systems has, conversely, been to develop an interface with analysis and engineering software packages.

SM software developed in the United States has also had the distinction of being associated with specific vendor hardware systems, although this is changing. European software has stressed system independence—at the cost of developing surface display capabilities. One additional trend among American system providers, which borrows from both CSG and B-rep approaches, is shown by firms such as Intergraph, California Computer Corp. (CalComp), and Auto-trol—who take a traditional B-rep approach to CAD but who are developing additional capabilities of surface modeling and rendering. While not true SM systems by the definition given here, these software packages may represent a transitional step toward the development of such systems.

Exceptions to these types of broad generic modelers are those systems that maintain both boundary file and CSG representations. Included in this class are programs such as MAGI, PADL-1 and PADL-2, and the Geometric Modeling System. Although there exist other approaches to SM, few of these are commercially available.

There are many trade-offs with each type of system. One of the most obvious relates to the manner of operator interaction. While the CSG systems perform certain types of operations more quickly than B-rep systems because of their storage of information as a complete geometric volume, B-rep can perform other types of calculations more quickly because certain data about the object's edges, vertices, or faces are more easily calculated than having to deal with the enormous amount of information associated with a solid volume.

13.3.1 Constructive Solid Geometry Modeling Systems

Probably the most well known of the CSG systems is that of the Mathematical Applications Group, Inc. (MAGI) of New York. MAGI began to work with solid models as a result of its research into the penetration of armor by projectiles for the military.

This work not only led the firm into developing SM but also into methods for rendering output. MAGI's modeler, called Synthavision, has become the basis for several commercially available SM products including Control Data's ICEM Modeler and the initial SM package from Applicon—Solid Modeling. Synthavision gained public attention recently when it was used to create key animation sequences for the Disney film *Tron*.

Another system that has been the basis for several other packages is the PADL software developed at the University of Rochester, Production Automation Project. PADL (versions 1 and 2) were used in developing GM Solid (the proprietary package of General Motors) and McDonnell Douglas Corp.'s (McAuto's) UNISOLID. While PADL-1 is largely considered a teaching tool, PADL-2 is much used by manufacturers to demonstrate the principles of SM to its staff and has over 50 installations worldwide.

Another CSG modeler, developed at a university, is the TIPS system originated at the University of Hokkaido in Japan. TIPS is sold in the United States by CAM-I. While TIPS is also considered a teaching tool, it has strong interface functions to CAM applications such as finite-element modeling and numerical control output. A lesser known CSG modeler, the Interactive Computer Modeling Corporation's Geographic Modeling System, is said to incorporate both CSG and B-rep modeling.

One of the more comprehensive systems for both engineering analysis and modeling currently available is produced by a company called Prototype Development Association, and is reported to incorporate "Parametric" solids.

The last of the available CSG systems is sold by Compeda of Great Britain, recently acquired by Prime, and a company called CADTRAK. The package is called PDMS, Plant Display Management System, and was developed in cooperation with the CAD Centre. While PDMS is a very expensive package, it was developed with specific design applications in mind—the design of chemical plants. Thus the developers envision that while there are only 150 potential purchasers, the market is lucrative. The repertoire of solid shapes developed for this package includes objects ordinarily used in the construction of a major chemical facility: pipes, joints, and pressure vessels. PDMS is unique in that it was developed for only one application.

13.3.2 B-Rep Systems

One of the most confusing perceptions about SM systems is caused by the predominant use of color shading by the suppliers of CSG systems. The public has come to associate SM with color and has developed a certain prejudice for monochromatic boundary file–based systems that have developed from the wire-frame approach to CAD.

During the past year, however, most of the European-developed systems have been converted for use with shaded surfaces. The Romulus package, formerly sold by Shape Data Limited of Great Britain, is now sold by Evans and Sutherland (which purchased the firm). Romulus is being written for shaded surface display at the graphics laboratory of Purdue University.

Another firm, GRAFTEK, of Boulder, Colorado, has developed an SM package, based upon Romulus, with color-rendering capability for use on Gould Electronics' SEL superminicomputers. GRAFTEK has also been named as a software development organization for Hewlett-Packard (HP). The HP project will involve writing the package for use on the 9020 version of the newest HP minicomputer. The new package will operate under UNIX operating system and provide one of the only desktop configurations available that will support SM. Catronix of Atlanta, Georgia, has also been working with Romulus. This firm's product called CATSOFT has been written to operate on a 16-bit Terak microcomputer.

One of the more recent announcements related to SM software has been that of Cubicomp Corporation of Berkeley, California. Cubicomp is writing its own B-rep software to run on a single-board display processor that is used in conjunction with the IBM PC. Despite the obvious limitations of operating under UNIX on an 8088, 8/16-bit microprocessor, the package offers a surprisingly powerful entry-level system for SM.

The Euclid SM package, developed in France by Matra Datavision, is much like Romulus in that it is now being sold in the United States and in that there are ongoing efforts to obtain original equipment manufacturer (OEM) agreements with hardware manufacturers who would both sell the software with their systems and write device drivers allowing the wire-frame images to be rendered in color. To date the models have been displayed on Lexidata, Digital Equipment Corporation, and Raster Technologies systems. The package may require extensive revision, since it was developed for Tektronix systems and has features specific to those devices (such as a cross-hair cursor for interaction). Prime Computer supports a British-developed SM package called Medusa and has recently announced additional CAD/CAM packages for its line of minicomputers.

Among the B-rep systems, several model not by manipulating stored files of edge data but rather by storing the information about planar surfaces. Included are IBM's proprietary package GRN/GDP, Manufacturing and Consulting Services (MCS) ANVIL, and others. MCS is a California-based firm with a long history of developing software for different minicomputers and display devices. MCS also currently has a turnkey agreement with Genisco allowing it to sell its ANVIL series of systems.

General Electric now has two subsidiaries involved in SM: Structural Dynamics Research Corporation (SDRC) and Calma. SDRC software is similar to many of the British-developed packages in that it is device-independent but more advanced than most of the other packages available today in terms of its display capabilities and user interaction. The company also has a long-standing history of work in preprocessors and postprocessors for engineering work. GEOMOD, the software package offered by the company, has a wide repertoire of commands for manipulating models.

Calma has been offering a solid package called DDM for the last 3 years and offered major enhancements for the package in 1984. One of the major reemphases of the company in the near term is its focus on mechanical design.

13.3.3 Hardware Systems Developed for SM

Because the user demands of SM software are so great, several hardware manufacturers have developed systems that are particularly well suited for processing color-shaded surfaces associated with B-rep SM software. Lexidata's Solidview and Imageview are the first of such products. Raster Technologies has also announced a product for SM processing. These systems are said to provide special advantages to the implementer of SM software by providing high-level graphics processing commands as firmware, thus offering the designer more interaction with the SM system.

13.4 INTERACTING WITH SM SYSTEMS

Depending upon the point of view of the perceiver, SM packages are either tools with a potential for freeing a designer's creative abilities or systems that are unnecessarily restrictive. There is some truth in both perceptions. The ease with which complicated designs may be built depends largely upon the quality of the system's software. Some SM systems can genuinely improve design efficiency for accomplished operators.

One should be able to determine the relative facility of a specific package by several basic criteria. Can irregular surfaces (B-spline types) be modeled? How are shapes built? There are also questions relating to the structure of the software's interaction—that is, whether it is prompt-, menu-, or command-based.

13.4.1 Boolean Operations

The ability to create and manipulate shapes is made a great deal easier if the basic boolean operations of union, subtraction, and intersection are available. AND OR, and NOT commands provide operators with an effective means of manipulating shapes. Most commonly found on CSG systems, boolean operations are most efficient when used forming complex shapes with a library of geometric primitives. Those B-rep systems allowing for input with boolean operators include Build, Design, and Romulus.

System users should be aware, however, that different systems have different approaches to boolean operations, and some have rigid procedures for their use—requiring, for example, that the operator finish a design with a union action.

13.4.2 Surface Operations

A set of operator interactions more common to both CSG and B-rep systems may be referred to generically as surface operations. These include surfaces of revolution, sweeping, tweaking, deformations, and other types of similar functions that may be known in various systems as bending, blending, scaling, rotations, or reflections.

One of the most important of these is the sweeping function. Although this may have other descriptions, the process is based upon translating a two-dimensional figure across a space to create a three-dimensional figure. Translational sweeping most often refers to moving a planar surface to create box or cube figures, while rotational sweeping most often refers to revolving curves for up to 360° around a central axis.

13.4.3 Geometric Primitive Operations

All systems, whether CSG or B-rep, will have the ability to manipulate their models. One of the most efficient aspects of CSG modelers is that they provide the operator with a library of geometric primitives upon which boolean operations or surface operations may be performed.

While the number of primitives in a library varies from system to system, it is held by some that beyond a few crucial shapes there are only repetitive forms. The basic primitives might be planes, cones, cylinders, tori, and spheres. Systems such as MAGI offer as many as 17 different primitives, including one for irregular surfaces.

Most systems should allow the operator to create primitives of "convenience." For example, a mechanical modeler might want to develop primitives such as a filleted surface that one might expect to need with some regularity. Among the B-rep systems, similar libraries might be made up of lines, points, curves, or irregular curves.

13.5 DISPLAY REQUIREMENTS

There are two considerations of displays in SM, the manner of producing the display and the physical requirements of a display system. There are two basic techniques for rendering colored shaded surfaces; ray-cast methods (MAGI, PADL) and polygonal approaches (Lexidata, Raster). To date, the ray-casting technique is said to be superior to others in that the amount of computer memory required for storing and manipulating the solid is less.

The questions relating to the number of pixels displayed and the horizontal and vertical resolution required for high-quality displays vary with the perception of the viewer. At a recent trade show it became apparent that a 1280 × 1064 pixel resolution is the new de facto benchmark. There are, however, several systems that are able to produce displays of very high quality at 512 × 512 pixel resolution. The key factor in producing quality displays at the lower resolutions appears to be the amount of pixel memory available for each color. Sixteen-bit planes appear to be the minimum to create the impression of a smooth shaded surface (as demonstrated by Cubicomp). Raster Technologies uses up to 24-bit planes and has superb quality displays.

It has also been mentioned that most systems were developed in the United States for specific hardware, necessitating that the system supplier develop software devices (called *drivers*) for a variety of display devices with different resolutions in order to have wide application. Until such time as a "virtual device interface" is adopted as a technical standard, there is likely to be a great deal of difficulty in ensuring that software will be easily applied to specific display devices of different resolutions.

13.6 SUMMARY

In the final analysis, there are many types of systems that may qualify for the name solid modeler. However, the usefulness of the system is probably the most valuable indicator of the worth of any individual package. While one cannot expect a 16-bit microcomputer to support the rich interactive capabilities of systems provided on superminicomputers, the solution offered by implementing the modeler on a smaller system may be appropriate for the right application.

Further, solid modelers cannot expect to have the practically unqualified acceptance of today's best three-dimensional CAD systems until they are able to provide the user with techniques of interaction that have proved so useful in the former area. For example, a designer can legitimately expect to be able to drag, rotate, or translate a solid model of a mechanical part in order to view it from different perspectives. The demands made upon a display system required to perform such functions approach the computational capabilities ordinarily described as image processing.

The cost of processors, random-access memory, and logic required to perform such tasks is significantly more than most system users would be willing to pay, particularly given the lack of formal acceptance of solid modelers. Thus one might most profitably view today's efforts as transitional attempts to develop the software of SM that will eventually be implemented in hardware for fast application.

A problem that still needs to be solved is the inability to transfer data between the two types of modeling systems. The measure of a system's adaptability (mentioned earlier as definable through its ability to describe irregular surfaces) is a function of the presence of its type of algorithmic processing capability. This type of processing is CPU-intensive and not available with most of today's systems.

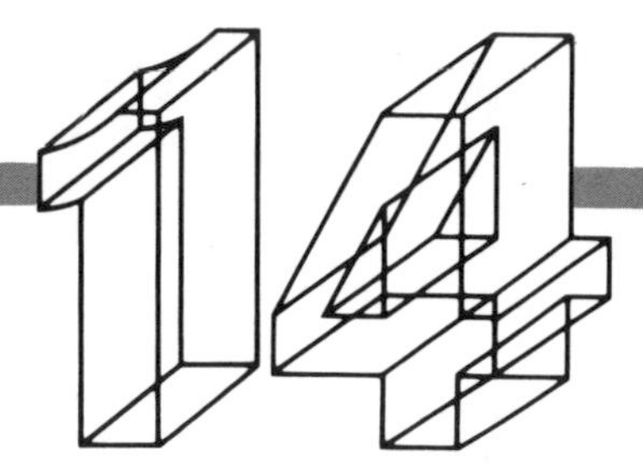

Cartography

by
Allan H. Schmidt

14.1 INTRODUCTION

The preparation and use of maps has a long and remarkable history. However, during the last 20 years computer technology has begun to introduce major changes not only into the preparation of maps but also their use.

Section 14.2 begins with a brief description of the various applications of maps in terms of their uses and users. Section 14.3 sketches the procedures and resources traditionally involved in preparing a map. Section 14.4 discusses automated cartography objectives, processes, and technological resources. Section 14.5 concludes with comments regarding trends in the supply of and demand for computer-generated maps in relation to data availability, new technologies, and future uses of maps.

14.2 MAPPING APPLICATIONS—USES AND USERS

Major categories of mapping applications include (1) geographic reference, (2) natural resource exploration and management, (3) land improvement, construction, and facilities management, and (4) analysis and display of economic and demographic data.

The use of maps as sources of information for geographic reference is their oldest and most fundamental use. Navigation maps are an example of geographic reference maps whether for use on land, on water, or in the air. Other examples include geodetic and topographic maps which are used to record locational information required in the preparation of special-purpose maps.

Natural resource exploration and management activities require the use of maps as an aid in locating, managing, and productively using natural resources for commercial as well as public purposes. Examples of such users include government agencies responsible for public land management and environmental protection programs as well as commercial firms involved in mineral or energy extraction and wood and paper production. Because of the small scale and high density of information, maps for these purposes are increasingly in the form of, or derived from, satellite imagery and aerial photographs. Climatological maps which contain data concerning air pressure, temperature, wind direction and velocity, precipitation, and cloud cover also can be considered natural resource maps.

Maps used for land development involving engineering, construction, and facilities maintenance are necessarily at a much larger scale (smaller geographic area) than those used for natural resource exploration and management. Land development maps frequently include elevation contours to allow for terrain analysis and estimates of land movement (cut and fill), as well as vegetation, geologic, and hydrologic data which would affect construction activities. Construction maps record the location and type of improvements built on or beneath the earth's surface. Land development activities within an urbanized area frequently involve preparation of engineering maps which include descriptions of public utility equipment such as telephone, electric, gas, and water lines. Such maps are essential not only for construction but also for subsequent maintenance of these facilities. A related map use is as part of public records for land ownership. Land ownership maps supplement legal written descriptions of land boundaries. These maps are provided by land surveyors and assist in the identification of land boundaries for the property owner, land developer, builder, and tax assessor.

The analysis and display of economic or demographic data is another category of map use. Such maps are referred to as *thematic maps* because they are used to represent the geographic distribution of one or a small number of specific topics or themes. Alternatively, a general reference map, such as would be found in a general-purpose atlas, usually contains numerous topics on the same map. Thematic maps are of growing interest for use in commercial market research as well as in government planning activities. They are used in a manner similar to that of military maps; that is, they allow for the identification of problems or opportunities of interest to commercial firms or a government agency and provide a valuable source of information for assessing the effectiveness of current allocations of resources and assisting in the determination of where resources should be allocated in the future.

14.3 MAP PRODUCTION

Preparation of a map involves the combination of several kinds of information. These include (1) locational data which provide a spatial reference frame and answer the question of "where," (2) geographic attribute data which describe various natural and cultural features or human activity patterns and answer the question "what," and (3) selection and placement of graphic symbols used to categorize and graphically portray geographic attribute data at their proper location on the map. When several different subjects are to be displayed on the same map, for example, political boundaries, natural features, and cultural features, a separate drawing may be prepared for each subject and the final map produced as a layered composite of several different images for the same geographic area. The final map is recorded as a graphic image on paper or film and saved for subsequent retrieval, modification, and printing.

14.3.1 Locational Data

GEODETIC CONTROL

Maps which accompany land records or are used in conjunction with land development activities must include reference to previously established ground control points. Such control points in the United States are determined by the National Geodetic Survey and exist as monument markers with known latitude, longitude, and elevation. A local surveyor may then establish the position of other locations by measuring distance and direction from these known control points.

BOUNDARIES

Political and administrative boundaries reflect regions of human activity and provide a geographic framework for partitioning a physical map, such as by nation or city. Federal, state, county, and local government boundaries are well defined and provide not only a location reference but also a regional definition for recording, analyzing, and reporting statistics regarding each region's economic and demographic characteristics (see Fig. 14.1).

PHOTOGRAMMETRY

Aerial photogrammetry provides a rapid and efficient means for acquiring graphic images of the earth's surface and is commonly used to produce maps. By use of multiple overlapping photographs and stereo triangulation devices, it is possible to establish

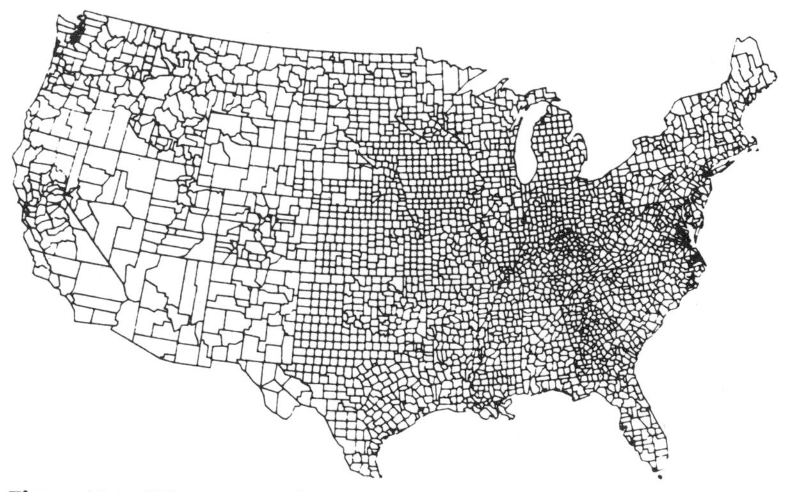

Figure 14.1 U.S. county outlines from a digital cartographic database.

precise *xy* coordinate locations on the ground as well as their vertical elevation. Procedures used include the ability to correct for errors within the photos due to tilt, skew, and rotation of an airplane during the photographic process.

MAP PROJECTION

Although locational data may be recorded with great precision, the fact remains that the surface of the earth is curved, whereas the surface on which a map is displayed is a flat piece of paper or film. The larger the geographic area, the greater the curvature and therefore the greater the potential map distortion. Maps of small areas are relatively unaffected by such distortion. However, to correct for this distortion on a small-scale (large-area) map, geodetic coordinates are converted to rectangular cartesian coordinates by use of one of many possible map projection algorithms. The resulting map will not preserve true direction, shape, and equal area, but depending upon the projection chosen, two of the three measurements may be preserved to varying degrees at specific locations on the map.

MAP SCALE

The scale of a map (the ratio of distance on the map to distance on the ground) is of critical importance in determining not only distortion introduced when projecting data describing a curved surface onto a flat surface but also the information content of the final map. When a larger geographic area is included on a map of fixed size, it obviously becomes necessary to combine and generalize features on the map and delete detail. The relative precision of locations shown on a map also is reduced at small scales. It is for this reason that maps which are to be used for establishing or finding precise locations, such as for engineering or construction purposes, are at quite large scales. Conversely, for maps which are intended for navigation over long distances, it is of greater importance to portray large areas on a relatively few map sheets and rely upon navigational markers to establish actual locations by visual or electronic means.

14.3.2 Geographic Attribute Data

Information which appears on a map typically is concerned with describing the earth's surface, physical features on or below the surface, or human activities which have occurred at various locations.

TOPOGRAPHY

The elevation or height of the earth's surface above sea level is typically shown on a map by use of contour lines, each of which describes a line of constant elevation. The distance and value between each line may be used to estimate degree and direction of slope. Orientation and value of the lines also indicate the location of critical surface features such as peaks, pits, passes, pales, course lines, and ridge lines. Topographic maps also may be prepared as oblique views of three-dimensional surfaces. (see Fig. 14.2).

NATURAL AND CULTURAL FEATURES

Specific naturally occurring features and physical features of human origin on or below the earth's surface may be included on a map to the extent that they serve a map's purpose or intended use. Natural features include not only topography, described above, but also rivers and streams, geologic and soil data, vegetation and wildlife, and other naturally occurring phenomena. Cultural features reflect the physical impact of human occupancy and include transport systems (roads, canals, railroads, airports, etc.), communication facilities, buildings, urbanized areas, and agricultural areas. The scale of a map will determine the detail possible and the intended use will influence the selection of features desirable for inclusion on a specific map.

Figure 14.2 U.S. topography using data from a digital terrain model.

ECONOMIC AND DEMOGRAPHIC DATA

Information concerning human activity patterns typically represents measurements related to economic and demographic conditions and their change over time. Because such data are a description, or a measure of change for a group of individuals, they frequently cannot be represented on a map in the same manner as a physical object on the earth's surface. Because of the volume of data involved and the scale of a map, it is usually necessary to aggregate the data to a region prior to their display. The most common examples of such data are those collected by the U.S. Bureau of the Census every 10 years concerning U.S. population and housing (see Fig. 14.3). Numerous other government agencies also record data regarding their activities as does every commercial firm, for example, concerning each customer, employee, and supplier. Since most such data include street address and postal delivery (zip) code, it is necessary to aggregate the data to an area such as a city block, neighborhood, town, county, sales area, state, or other region appropriate to the purpose for which the data are to be interpreted.

14.3.3 Graphic Symbols and Conventions

POSITION, DIRECTION, AND SCALE

Position on a map is indicated by use of lines or tick marks which define *xy* coordinates in terms of latitude and longitude and state plane coordinates, universal transverse Mercator grid, or an arbitrary grid imposed by the mapmaker. Orientation of a map has north at the top by convention plus an arrow or other symbol to point in the direction of true north. On maps intended for navigation, a second arrow will also be provided to indicate the direction of magnetic north, as would appear on a compass. The scale of a map may be given in one or more of three different ways. (1) A graphic measuring scale may be included with tick marks and numbers illustrating the ground distance represented by the distance

Figure 14.3 U.S. population density by county (1970).

between tick marks on the map. (2) Comparable information may be provided by a statement which equates 1 inch or centimeter on the map with the equivalent ground distance in miles or kilometers. (3) A numerical ratio or fraction may be given which equates a unit length on the map with its equivalent distance in the same units on the ground.

GEOGRAPHIC FEATURE SYMBOLS

The United States Geological Survey (USGS) is the primary government agency in the United States responsible for creating and distributing cartographic products. The symbols which appear on a USGS map are used consistently for all USGS maps to describe geodetic, topographic, political, natural, and cultural features. Their topographic map series covers most of the United States at a scale of 1:24,000 plus the remainder at 1:63,630 and is considered to be the standard reference map series from which commercial and other government organizations produce other maps, such as for a city or state, at the same or a smaller scale.

THEMATIC MAP SYMBOLS

In representing quantitative and qualitative information such as economic and demographic data on a thematic map, four basic types of symbols are used: dots of varying density, lines with various width and spacing, icons of various size and shape, and tones or color. The process of selecting symbols and assigning them to a set of quantitative data assumes that the data have been grouped into a number of classes or categories, each of which may then be represented by a specific graphic symbol. By limiting the number of different classes and therefore types of symbols, for example, to 5 to 10, the data as displayed on the map are able to show spatial patterns which may be inherent in the data (Figs. 14.4 and 14.5). Three-dimensional symbolism also may be used to illustrate differences in quantitative values and to eliminate the need for prior grouping of the data into a small number of classes (see Figs. 14.6 and 14.7). The resulting maps are usually more informative and have significant visual impact. However, it may be necessary to produce several such maps with views from different directions to examine the resulting data surface fully.

14.3.4 Graphic Media

For most applications, paper represents an economic and convenient medium for recording, storing, and transporting maps. However, paper maps are easily damaged and are unreliable if precise measurements are required because of paper's dimensional

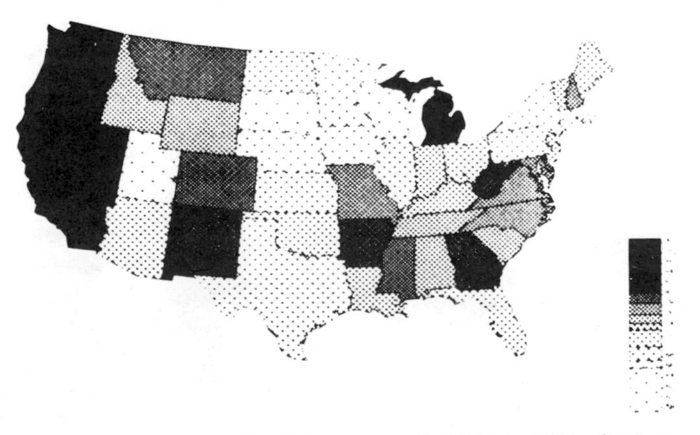

Figure 14.4 Projected grocery store productivity in 1977 using two-dimensional symbolism.

Figure 14.5 Montreal cancer rates in 1972 with two-dimensional symbolism.

instability as a result of age and humidity. For purposes of photographically reproducing a map, the dimensional stability and long life of Mylar and similar film materials make them superior to paper, although at a higher initial cost. Film also allows for the superimposition of several different separation sheets to produce composite maps which retain their registration with one another.

14.4 AUTOMATED CARTOGRAPHY

14.4.1 Objectives

The two major objectives of automated cartography are increased productivity and new utility. Increased productivity in the preparation of maps because of the use of automated cartography results in the reduction or total elimination of manual drafting operations and the substitution of electronic digitizing and computer-generated graphic displays. The precision of computer graphic drawings, automated error detection capabilities, and associated standardization of procedures and, therefore, map products all contribute to the potential for an improved cartographic process and product. The greatest savings, however, result from the elimination of the need to redraw an entire map in order to

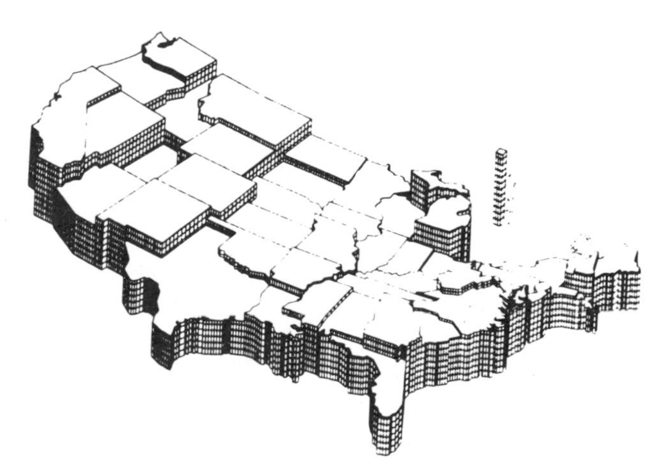

Figure 14.6 Projected grocery store productivity in 1977 using three-dimensional symbolism.

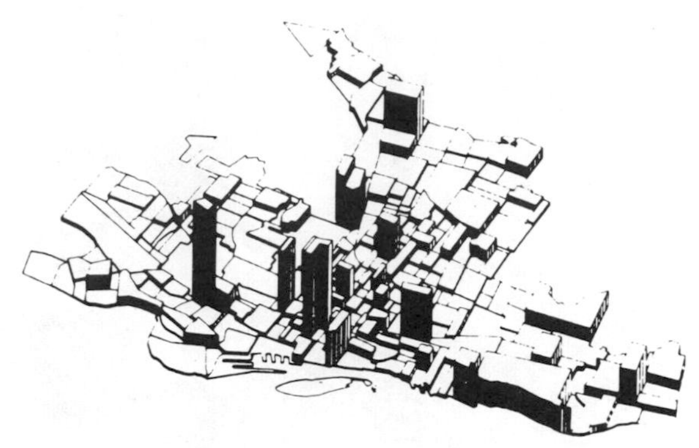

Figure 14.7 Montreal cancer rates in 1972 using three-dimensional symbolism.

incorporate revisions. The ability to maintain and continually reuse all or any part of a digital cartographic database when adding new information is a significant savings over the continual redrafting of maps by manual methods.

New uses for maps result from the ability to manipulate a digital cartographic database in a manner not possible with purely graphic map products. Applications involving land subdivision design, land suitability studies, geologic exploration, and commercial site location analyses involve the creation and interpretation of digital map products which go far beyond traditional capabilities and uses of manually prepared maps.

Automated cartography uses the capability of a computer to improve the productivity of cartographers responsible for the preparation of a broad range of map products such as those described in Sec. 14.2. In doing so, the traditional procedures and resources used in manual preparation of maps and described in Sec. 14.3 must be accommodated in a digital environment. The role of the cartographer as map designer becomes increasingly important in the process because although some traditional operations, such as redrafting of prior drawings, are susceptible to automation, the increased range and application for which maps economically can be prepared creates many new opportunities for the use of maps. It also provides new tools and potential technical skills for professional cartographers. Although the changing role of cartographers is not an initial intent of automated cartography, it is a realistic result of the introduction of computers into cartography as it is into many other professions.

14.4.2 Process

DATA SOURCE TYPES

The primary sources from which cartographic databases are prepared are imagery, prior maps, or field notes. Imagery may be in a digital format such as a computer-compatible tape obtained from remote sensing, as with a satellite, or a photographic image, as with an aerial photograph. Alternatively, prior maps may exist as traditional prints on paper or film or in a digital format as a cartographic database. Field notes include data obtained by a survey crew and could be used in either a digital or paper form depending upon the survey equipment used.

GRAPHIC ENCODING

Nondigital graphic data sources such as maps or photographs are converted to a machine-readable form by a digitizing process. Digitizing converts a graphic image into an equivalent numerical form which is recorded as a digital database. The resulting database may be organized either as a series of points and lines with *xy* coordinate values for each vertex or as a large matrix with a value for each grid cell. Point and line databases are referred to as *vector databases*. Matrix databases are known as *raster databases* to reflect the fact that they are usually processed sequentially by row, each row being contained in one raster of a cathode-ray tube display. Raster databases also may be used to produce vector databases by extracting the point and line information which is implicit in an image recorded as a matrix of values.

Vector databases are particularly well suited to applications where precise positional data are required, such as in land record or engineering maps. However, when small-scale geographic features are of primary concern, such as in natural resource exploration and land management, data are normally acquired in the form of an image stored in a raster database.

GRAPHIC DATA MANAGEMENT

Creation of a digital cartographic database implies use of the database for more than a single point in time with associated maintenance and revision of the data. The data management activities involved necessarily require that the data be in a form and of a quality which will minimize costs of data management as well as subsequent retrieval, analysis, and display. As a result, the data need to be structured in a manner which allows individual components of the map to be added, deleted, or changed. In a vector database, map components include point, line, and areal objects which have locational as well as categorical attributes. The ability and efficiency of data management becomes increasingly important as a cartographic database grows in size and complexity. Retrieval and update operations require an efficient database design which allows a database to be accessed with flexibility and efficiency. Flexibility includes the ability to construct, retrieve, and modify data for arbitrary geographic regions regardless of the map sheets which originally were used to define an arbitrary partitioning of geographic space. Efficiency requires that all such operations be possible quickly and with a minimum of computing resources and time.

DATA ANALYSIS

Automated cartography provides an ability to measure the current and potential future location and character of geographic features such as topography, natural resources, geology, land use, and socioeconomic characteristics. Data which are acquired for several time periods allow for time-series analysis to detect and forecast change over time.

Topographic analysis includes determination of slope, aspect, and orientation. Geologic, soil, hydrologic, and vegetation data are also frequently included in studies of suitability of land for future use. Natural resource exploration for minerals, energy sources, and water are other examples of applications which are heavily dependent upon the use of data derived from geographic data sources. Land management activities for natural resources in the public as well as the private sectors are using automated cartography to inventory, monitor, and develop timber, rangeland, recreation areas, and agricultural resources.

Land records and related map products are being automated in several cities in a manner which will allow for the development of multipurpose land data systems. Such systems have the potential for providing substantial economies in the preparation and use of map products by numerous government and private organizations. Traditional development and use of map products by local government organizations involve substantial duplication of effort and exhibit a serious lack of standardization.

Similar capabilities are being developed to support the creation of utility maps for one or more utility systems within a given metropolitan area. Such automated systems are capable of substantially improving the ability to create and maintain vital engineering drawings regarding the location and nature of a utility system's physical plant, both above and below ground. Given the description of a utility network, it also is possible to use that same database in the context of a mathematical model to determine existing capacities and simulate future loading, as well as to evaluate alternative modifications to the system in anticipation of changes in usage levels over time.

In the design of a new utility network, such as a cable television system, a schematic description of the network can be used to evaluate alternative routings and placement of specific components within the system to optimize and balance its performance. In this respect the use of network design tools appropriate for computer-aided design of electronic circuits have their counterpart in the design of larger circuits, be they for electric transmission, water systems, or highways.

DATA RETRIEVAL AND GRAPHIC DISPLAY

Computer graphic images are in themselves pictorial representations of numerical data. As a result, these data may be saved for subsequent use to produce additional computer graphic images either of the entire file or of specific geographic "windows." Examples of subsets include an extracted region with the exterior deleted or a region with a smaller interior region blanked out. A superset would result from the combining of two or more data sets, each obtained from a different map sheet but representing adjoining geographic regions.

In addition, a graphic database may be updated to incorporate new information. Computer graphics also may be used to compare an original image with later information in order to detect the location and extent of changes that have occurred over time.

Although symbols are used to represent information visually on a computer-generated map, the graphic symbols themselves need not be stored as part of a database but may be defined as symbol tables in the computer software. The database only would need to specify a location and its feature code. Text strings, such as place names, also may be displayed at specific sizes and with particular orientations which are determined at map display time rather than being prestored in the database. This is particularly important for a database used to produce maps at different scales or with different overlays of geographic features which may produce conflicts in symbol placement.

14.4.3 Hardware

INPUT DEVICES

Vector databases are typically created by use of electronic digitizing devices. A map sheet is placed on a digitizing table and an operator traces the location of each line, recording its *xy* location as individually selected points or as a stream of *xy* coordinates. In addition to recording the geometry of each line, the operator also may use a keypad to enter an identifying code for each line along with other information such as the topological identifiers for endpoints plus left and right coboundary identifiers. Data produced by a digitizing device are stored on tape or disk for subsequent editing and organization prior to being stored as a database.

Raster databases normally are created using scanning devices which detect by optical sensors the reflectance of each *xy* location on a map sheet as it passes through the scanning device. The resulting data are stored as a large matrix. However, for storage efficiency the matrix will normally be compacted by use of run-length encoding or other techniques to reduce its size prior to being saved for future use.

Note that the above description of input device hardware assumes an initial map sheet which only contains black-and-white point, line, and area graphics. In practice, maps are far more complex and include colors, special symbols, numbers, and text strings as well. Such maps normally are the result of offset printing of several separation sheets, one for each color. Prior to its use with colored ink in a composite printing process, each separation sheet physically exists as a black-and-white drawing. Special symbols, numbers, and text strings also may be treated as separate data layers.

CENTRAL PROCESSING UNIT AND STORAGE MEDIA

Computing devices used for automated cartography tend to be of the 16- or 32-bit word length size because of the precision required for storing *xy* coordinates plus the need to address large blocks of memory. Hard disks normally are used to store and provide immediate access to cartographic databases in active use. Magnetic tape serves as a backup or archival storage medium.

CATHODE-RAY TUBE (CRT) DISPLAY DEVICES

Display devices used with automated cartography range from high-resolution (4096 × 4096 addressable points) vector storage tubes to medium-resolution (512 × 512 pixels) raster refresh tubes. Applications requiring high-resolution real-time displays, such as for air traffic control, would use vector refresh displays.

Color CRTs are particularly useful when several different types of information are to be displayed on the same image, in effect a color composite comparable to what might be produced by color separation plates in printing. However, on a color CRT opportunity exists to experiment with the visual interpretation resulting from use of different colors for a given set of data.

PAPER OR FILM HARD COPY

The vast majority of automated cartography applications are intended to produce hard-copy documents for subsequent interpretation and general use. These documents frequently will be larger than the image shown on a CRT screen and capable of containing more information. They may be produced on paper or film by pen plotters, laser plotters, ink-jet plotters, electrostatic plotters, or any of a variety of other computer-driven drawing devices. In each case the resulting image may be in black or white or multicolored.

Photographic drawings also may be produced as black-and-white or color images drawn with light on a photosensitive emulsion, ranging from 35-millimeter transparency films to 24 × 36 inch or larger paper prints.

14.4.4 Software and Data

LANGUAGES AND PROGRAMS

The predominant language used for automated cartography is Fortran, although other languages such as PL-1, APL, Pascal, and C are also used. The reason for Fortran's popularity reflects its common use in the scientific community plus the availability of standards. Input and output routines frequently are written in assembly language for greater efficiency.

The majority of automated cartography systems are sold as hardware and software combined. However, in the area of thematic cartography a number of programs are available from organizations such as the Harvard Laboratory for Computer Graphics, Geographic Systems Inc. (GSI), Environmental Science Research Institute (ESRI), and others. Combined hardware and software system vendors include large companies such as IBM, Intergraph, Synercom, Computervision, and Scitex, as well as newer firms such as ESRI, GSI, Urban Systems Applications, Iconx, GeoBased Systems, Comarc Design Systems, and ERDAS.

DATABASES

Physical vs. Logical Map Databases

Visual images are physical pictures. A physical map database has a 1 : 1 correspondence to a physical picture except it is in digital form. Examples are (1) a bit map matrix used to produce a virtual display on a CRT or (2) a simple vector or matrix database resulting from the digitization of an image. In both cases, the physical database contains only the information required to produce a physical picture by the direct substitution of graphic symbols for their data values.

A logical map database has a different purpose, namely the logical and arithmetic manipulation of map information content such as the graphic objects and relations on the map. As a result, a logical database benefits from the inclusion of information regarding the locational and geographic attributes of named graphic objects within the image and their logical relationship to each other, such as their topology. Given that information, it becomes possible to perform logical as well as arithmetic operations upon the graphic objects contained within a map database. It is important to note, however, that the operations need not and should not be restricted to the pixel level. Far more valuable is the opportunity to include within the database geometric, topological, and geographic attributes for higher-order, named graphic objects such as lines and areas. These in turn may be aggregated to larger, complex objects which also would be described by their geometric, topological, and geographic attributes.

Coordinate Manipulation

Computer mapping involves three different coordinate transformations. Initial database creation by use of a digitizer results in a database expressed in terms of digitizer table cartesian *xy* coordinate space. Because the source map document will usually include known geodetic coordinate control points in latitude and longitude plus a specified map projection, it is possible subsequently to convert the digitized data into geodetic coordinates by use of an inverse map projection algorithm. This is necessary for merging data derived from two separate but adjoining map sheets in order to treat the final database as one continuous description of the earth's surface regardless of how many separate map sheets are used to create the total database. At the time of map display it is necessary once again to convert the coordinates, this time from geodetic to cartesian coordinates. This requires use of a map projection algorithm to produce coordinates which reflect the location of origin and min-max coordinates for the display device.

External Database Organization and Content

At time of vector database creation (digitizing), there are many possible record and file structures which may be used. The most common techniques involve the definition of coordinates for lines of varying length which describe continuous runs of *xy* coordinates. The length of these runs is usually determined by the endpoints of a given line. The endpoints may be at the terminus of a line or at its intersection with one or more other lines. Each line will have an identification number as well as a feature code to indicate the type of information it represents. Other attributes of that line may be included as part of the same record or contained in a separate record keyed to the line by its identification number.

Procedures originally developed by the U.S. Bureau of the Census and extended by others at the Harvard Laboratory for Computer Graphics and also at the USGS have introduced topological relations for lines as an explicit component of a cartographic database. This is in addition to the essential description of spatial geometry for the lines (their *xy* coordinates). Each record describes a line which is treated as though it were an arc within a graph. Endpoints of a line are defined by its terminus or the point at which it intersects two or more other lines. These endpoints are termed *nodes* to distinguish them from points at vertices intermediate to the endpoints.

The topology for each arc is described in terms of the connection its two endpoints have with other lines, plus reference to the two adjacent regions which lie on either side of the line. Connectedness is described by an arc's two endpoints (nodes) and their from-to relationship as determined by a clockwise cycling of the graph. Adjacency relations are based upon the identification codes for the regions to the left and right of an arc, relative to its from-to nodes.

One of the principal benefits which a topological data structure provides is the ability to detect automatically missing or extraneous nodes and lines resulting from the digitizing process. As a result, significant savings are possible in the cost of accurate database creation. An additional benefit of a topological database is its potential for geometric intersection and integration with other topological databases.

Algorithms

Because of the large size of most cartographic databases, it is desirable to use a "divide-and-conquer" approach when processing data. For example, it is often possible to segment the data by geographic regions as well as by geographic feature types. When a map can be decomposed and stored as a series of feature overlays, the amount of data which must be in active memory at any one time is reduced. It also is helpful to use local processing techniques which deal with the map in a stepwise fashion using a band-sweep approach. This allows for concurrent processing of input and output and efficient use of available memory. Such an approach requires that a file first be sorted on its x and y coordinates, but it eliminates the need for random-access files and allows the data to be processed in a sequential fashion.

Two operations used in the processing of cartographic data include line smoothing and line generalization. Line smoothing adds points to a line to achieve a smooth curvature. Line generalization selectively removes points from a line to reduce unnecessary detail in situations such as reduction of map scale or use of a display device with a resolution less than that of the graphic data.

Internal Data Structure

Cartographic data can be organized hierarchically with global descriptors for each file followed by header records for each arc with its summary statistics, extrema coordinates (xy min-max), and topological identifiers. Detail records which contain the bulk of xy point data may then be maintained separately in secondary storage. Geographic attributes for each arc also may be stored in this manner. Directories can be used to index the point and geographic attribute files to the header records. Similarly, graphic symbol files may be maintained separately for access at time of graphic output.

GEOGRAPHIC ATTRIBUTE DATA

Geographic attribute data sources reflect the nature of the application and the map scale. Large-scale maps of engineering projects, such as utility maps, acquire data attributes from the engineering drawings for a facility. Such maps necessarily are very precise in terms of location and feature attributes. However, the density of graphic information is relatively low.

Medium-scale thematic maps, such as for an urbanized area, acquire attribute data from commercial and government records keyed to location by a geo-reference code such as a street address. Locations are less precisely defined than for engineering maps but with numerous attributes for each geographic feature.

Small scale, large region maps such as for natural resource exploration make significant use of satellite imagery and aerial photographs to acquire multiple attribute information over large areas, with location being less precisely defined relative to large- or medium-scale maps. Imagery, whether from satellite or aerial photographs, is a rich source of information, especially concerning physical geographic attributes.

Economic and demographic data produced by commercial and government organizations are usually aggregated to predefined administrative regions. Unfortunately, the boundaries used are frequently unique to each organization, therefore making comparisons difficult. For example, postal zip code districts, which could be used to summarize and display customer data for a firm, have different boundaries from census tracts for which total population data are available.

The ability to combine information from two or more sources, be they imagery, traditional cartographic sources, or various economic or demographic databases, is frequently desirable for applications such as land suitability studies or regional planning. However, because of the differences in geographic recording units for each data source, integration of information from diverse sources requires that one of three approaches be used: (1) each source may be used to produce separate graphic products with unique boundaries and these are manually superimposed for visual comparison, (2) the cartographic and economic and demographic data available by administrative regions are assigned to imagery pixels, thereby using pixels as a common unit of geographic analysis, or (3) imagery data available by pixels are aggregated to extract graphic patterns. These data zones may then be geometrically overlayed with one or more topological cartographic databases and their attributes to produce a single composite database composed of least-common geographic units (see Fig. 14.8*a* to *f*).

The alternative chosen is dependent upon the objectives sought and the resources available. They are described above in order of increasing cost and capability for subsequent analysis. The advantages of topological files over pixel files result from the preservation of predefined spatial objects, their boundaries, and their spatial relation to each other plus the ability to perform logical and arithmetic operations upon the data.

14.5 TRENDS

14.5.1 Data Availability

The 1970s and 1980s have seen the beginning and rapid growth of digital cartographic data and related sources of geographic feature data. Current sources of such databases include the U.S. Bureau of the Census, with databases containing coordinate descriptions of major metropolitan areas by census tract and census block as well as U.S. state and county boundary and congressional district boundary files. Several files also are available which contain *xy* coordinate centroids for U.S. counties and places. All of the above files are distributed by the U.S. Bureau of the Census in Suitland, Maryland.

The USGS has for several years been developing and distributing digital databases which describe patterns of land use and land cover at a scale of 1:100,000 for various sections of the United States based upon aerial photographic interpretation. They are also in the process of developing digital line-graph databases at a scale of 1:200,000 with three separate sets of data: boundaries, transportation features, and hydrographic features. Elevation data in a matrix format are also available at a scale of 1:250,000. USGS databases are distributed by the National Cartographic Information Center in Reston, Virginia. USGS digital databases will be especially important because they will serve as national standard maps and provide the digital base maps onto which additional information will be added by others. Another federal agency, the U.S. Soil Service, is in the process of creating digital descriptions of soil patterns across the United States based upon their soil maps.

Each of these federal organizations has adopted a topological structure for their databases. The specific formats vary, but each contains the essential information necessary for performing topological error checking and, potentially, file integration.

NASA's Landsat satellite data collection system, now administered by the National Oceanographic and Atmospheric Administration, has its data products distributed by EROS Data Center in Sioux Falls, South Dakota. They have produced a continuous stream of multispectral scanner imagery, the latest of which, Landsat-D, is providing images with a pixel resolution of 90 feet on the ground. Use of Landsat imagery for natural resource exploration and management purposes continues to grow and includes applications such as mineral, fossil fuel, and water exploration.

Multipurpose land data systems have been initiated in several metropolitan areas including Milwaukee, Wisconsin, and Philadelphia, Pennsylvania. These systems have begun to demonstrate procedures and capabilities required for government computer mapping systems on a citywide basis. Special-purpose cartographic systems also have been developed in Nashville, Tennessee, and Houston, Texas, focusing upon multiuser public utility systems. Future developments of these and other municipal mapping systems will continue to grow as experience in their development and use accumulates and costs decline due to technological advances.

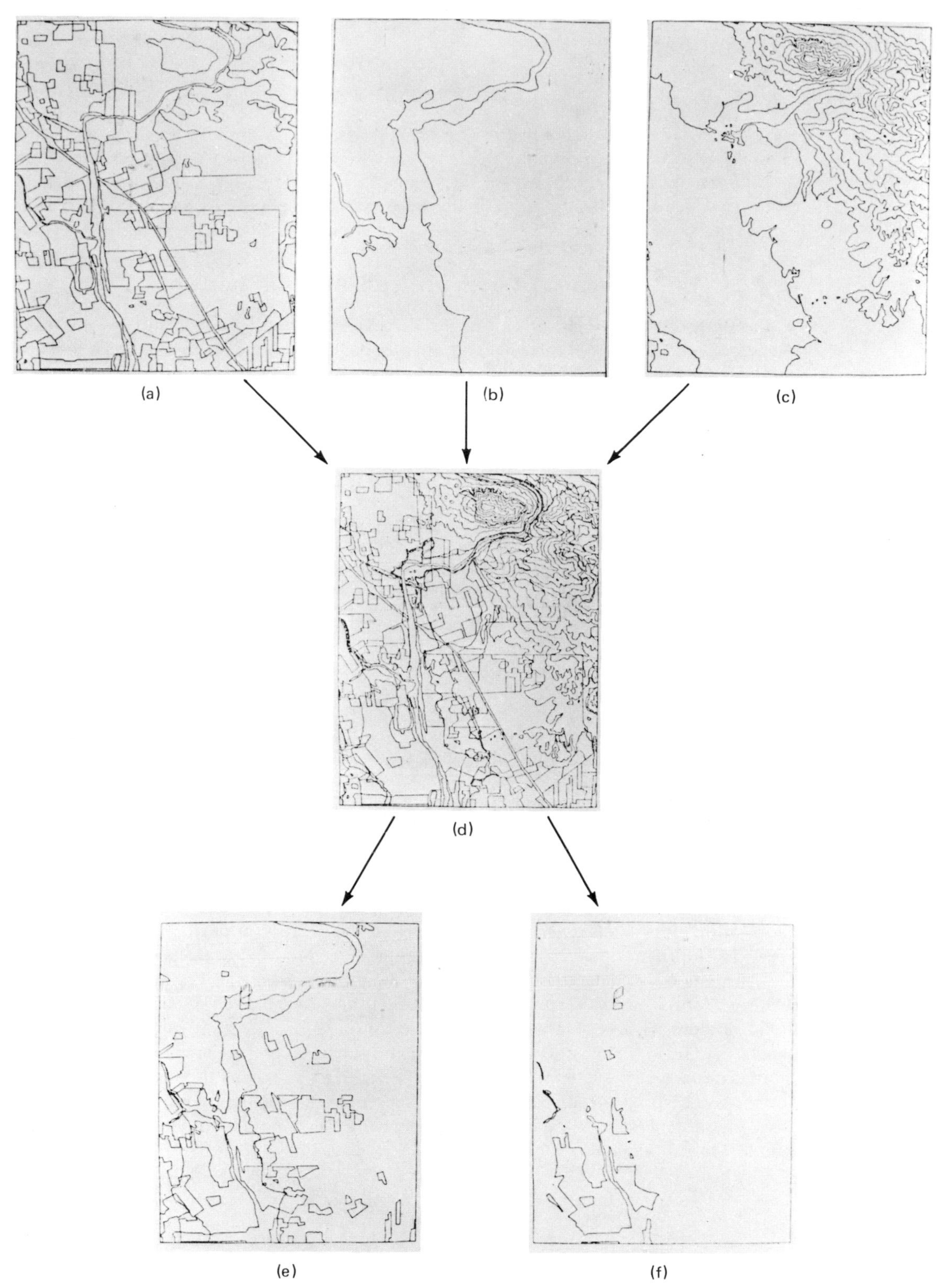

Figure 14.8 Examples of polygon overlay and analysis in the Russian River valley north of San Francisco. (*a*) Land use; (*b*) flood plain; (*c*) elevation; (*d*) combination of land use, flood plain, and elevation boundaries; (*e*) combination of vineyard land use and flood plain (logical OR); (*f*) combination of vineyard land use and flood plain (logical AND).

14.5.2 New Technologies

PARALLEL PROCESSING

The development of parallel processing capabilities with multiple processors will be of value for automated cartography applications where band-sweep operations can occur simultaneously at several locations over a map. Image databases as well as topological vector databases will benefit from increased processing speed and the ability to handle larger and more complex sets of data with greater efficiency.

HIGH-BULK DATA STORAGE REQUIREMENTS

As the bulk of imagery grows due to the expansion in both number and resolution of image collection systems, there will be increased difficulty in satisfying storage requirements and a corresponding need to be able to preserve essential information contained within such images. Topological databases created by automated extraction of graphic objects offer potential savings in storage as well as analytic interpretation.

VIDEO TECHNOLOGY

The continual development of video recording, storage, retrieval, and communications suggests that optical data management will become increasingly important for all areas of computer graphics. High-density optical recording with microprocessor-controlled image retrieval is likely to offer significant benefits, particularly given the availability of read-write video disks.

14.5.3 Future Uses for Maps

Technological capabilities in support of computer-aided natural resource exploration and management undoubtedly will continue to grow as will demand for its use, particularly by energy exploration and commercial forest companies as well as developing nations. Agricultural and commercial fishing activities also benefit from an opportunity to monitor the status of agricultural crops and changes in fishing resources.

Business uses of computer-generated maps have begun to offer new and valuable forms of information for market research purposes. The ability to display the location of current sales in relation to potential sales provides vivid and immediately useful information for evaluating effectiveness of current sales efforts, opportunities for additional sales, development of advertising strategies, and selection of sites for new stores.

Navigation maps have always been essential resources for travel by air, water, or land. However, future navigational systems are likely to use information obtained from navigational satellites. These data will be displayed on maps produced by digital cartographic databases. The availability of portable graphic display devices, satellite receivers, as well as cellular radio systems creates the capacity to produce truly dynamic mobile maps. These devices will display the current position of the receiver in relation to roads, landmarks, or other identifying features regardless of whether the receiving device is in a plane, boat, or auto or on an individual's wrist.

BIBLIOGRAPHY

Chasen, S. H., and D. W. Dow: *The Guide for the Evaluation and Implementation of CAD/CAM Systems,* CAD/CAM Decisions, Atlanta, Ga., 1979.

Davis, John C. and M. K. McCullagh (eds.): *Display and Analysis of Spatial Data,* Wiley-Interscience, New York, 1975.

Goldberg, Mark, A. H. Schmidt, and N. Chrisman: "Integration and Analysis of Multiple Geographic Data Bases: An Application of ODYSSEY," in *Harvard Library of Computer*

Graphics, vol. 2, pp. 81–97, Harvard Laboratory For Computer Graphics, Cambridge, Mass., 1979.

Monmonier, Mark S.: *Computer Assisted Cartography*, Prentice-Hall, Englewood Cliffs, N.J., 1982.

Moore, Patricia (ed.): *The Harvard Library of Computer Graphics*, 19 volumes, Harvard Laboratory For Computer Graphics, Cambridge, Mass., 1981.

Muehrcke, Phillip C.: *Map Use*, J. P. Publications, Madison, Wis., 1978.

Need for a Multipurpose Cadastre, National Academy Press, Washington, D.C., 1980.

Procedures and Standards for a Multipurpose Cadastre, National Academy Press, Washington, D.C., 1983.

Robinson, Arthur H., Randall D. Sale, and Joel Morrison: *Elements of Cartography*, John Wiley and Sons, New York, 1978.

Rosenfeld, Azriel: *Digital Picture Processing*, 2 volumes, Academic Press, New York, 1983.

Taylor, D. R. Fraser (ed.): *The Computer in Contemporary Cartography*, John Wiley and Sons, New York, 1980.

Robotics

by

Ronald C. Reeve, Jr.

15.1 THE INDUSTRIAL ROBOT DEFINED

The word "robot" has been used to describe a variety of mechanical devices, from simple axis manipulators to full human analogs. It carries the connotation of replacement of human function. The meaning of the term robot will continue to evolve, driven by its genetic heritage: technology.

According to the Japanese Industrial Robot Association (JIRA), the definition of industrial robots includes six categories:*

1. ***Manual Manipulator.*** A manipulator that is worked by an operator.
2. ***Fixed-Sequence Robot.*** A manipulator which repetitively performs successive steps of a given operation according to a predetermined sequence, condition, and position, and whose set information *cannot* be easily changed.
3. ***Variable-Sequence Robot.*** A manipulator which repetitively performs successive steps of a given operation according to a predetermined sequence, condition, and position, and whose set information *can* be easily changed.
4. ***Playback Robot.*** A manipulator which can produce, from memory, operations originally executed under human control. A human operator initially operates the robot in order to input instructions. All the information relevant to the operations (sequence, conditions, and positions) is put in memory. When needed, this information is recalled (or played back) and the operations are repetitively executed automatically from memory.
5. ***Numerical Control (NC) Robot.*** A manipulator that can perform a given task according to the sequence, conditions, and position, as commanded via numerical

* Japanese Industrial Robot Association, Tokyo, Japan.

Figure 15.1 Industrial robots are changing manufacturing methods around the world. This automotive spot-welding robot work cell produces 72 car bodies per hour with 14 robots working together. (*Cincinnati Milicron.*)

data. The software used for these robots includes punched tapes, cards, and digital switches. This robot has the same control mode as an NC machine.

6. ***Intelligent Robot.*** This robot with sensory perception (visual and/or tactile) can detect changes by itself in the work environment or work condition and by its own decision-making faculty, proceed with its operation accordingly.

The Robot Institute of America takes a narrower view and defines a robot as: "A reprogrammable, multifunctional manipulator designed to move materials, parts, tools or specialized devices, through variable programmed motions for the performance of a variety of tasks."*

It is anticipated that the definition of a robot will further change during the latter half of the decade to require that robots be readily reprogrammable. In fact, the future definition probably will narrow to include only those devices that are controlled by computers, thus excluding categories 1 and 2 of the Japanese definition.

15.1.1 Mechanical Manipulation

A robot has the ability to manipulate objects in the real world. This mechanism, connected to a computer, enables the computer to interact physically with the real world. Literally, robots are the arms of the computer.

Robots vary widely in their skills and capabilities. Some manufacturers produce general-purpose robots that are capable of a wide range of tasks. Others manufacture robots for specific applications. However, all robots have in common the ability to interact with the physical world.

15.1.2 Programmability

The concept of programmability is implicit in the definition of a robot. Nonprogrammable mechanisms, no matter how simple or complex, do not fit the true sense of the term "robot." Instead, they fall into the category of machines or mechanisms. Computer-

* Robot Institute of America, Dearborn, Michigan.

controlled industrial robots are usually programmed by (1) lead-through teaching, (2) walk-through teaching, or (3) offline programming.

1. Lead-through teaching requires the programmer to physically manipulate the robot mechanism, or a replica of the mechanism, through the desired motions. Lead-through programming is popular for spray-painting robots which require complex, dynamic changes in robot motion and velocity.
2. Walk-through teaching is commonly used to program the current generation of industrial robots. A handheld pendant is employed to send signals to move the robot via its own servo system. The operator directs the robot with the pendant to a series of points in space and instructs the robot control to record these locations. During the playback of these locations, the robot trajectory and velocity are determined by the control system.
3. Offline programming is a new technology for robots and will be required in the factory of the future. Offline programming provides the ability to create or modify a robot program without interrupting the robot's activities. But, more significantly, it provides a means to communicate abstractly with the robot.

15.1.3 Computer Control and Interfaces

Although the definition of industrial robot will constrict to include only computer-controlled devices, there will remain a wide range of control capabilities. Robot control, in its simplest form, can be a programmable-logic controller (PLC). The PLC establishes a sequence of events to be performed. These events may be measured by simple limit switch closures.

Advanced robot control will be a hierarchy of computers linked together. These hierarchical control networks will be used in artificial intelligence and adaptive-controlled robots. The National Bureau of Standards has published a scheme for a generalized hierarchical robot control system. This hierarchical network can expand as additional computing power is required.

The specific computer model or control architecture used by a manufacturer is not a critical factor, as long as the robot meets its performance specification. However, the interfaces between the robot control and the computer-integrated manufacturing (CIM) system are critical. At this writing, no interface standards have been adopted by the robot industry. The RS232C and the IEEE488 interface standards are supported by most robot manufacturers. But most proponents of offline programming for robots foresee the need to adopt a communication standard of greater capability to support the integration of robots into computer-integrated manufacturing. The Ethernet standard has the largest following at the present.

15.2 THE ROBOT'S ROLE IN COMPUTER-INTEGRATED MANUFACTURING (CIM)

Today we are seeing the beginnings of CIM. However, we have yet to transform these concepts into practiced engineering disciplines. The role of the robot in CIM is also new, and we are beginning to see robot manufacturers promote features and capabilities which will meet the challenges of CIM.

There are many prototypical installations where robots are performing CIM functions. Offline programming of robots via host computers is already a reality. But the technical and economic need has not yet been defined by the marketplace. Aggressive young U.S. robot companies are active in CIM technology, while the major robot manufacturers are more cautious in entering this market. The government has assumed a leadership role in the development of working demonstration CIM facilities via the Air Force I-CAM program and the National Bureau of Standards. The Japanese have already constructed commercial plants which demonstrate the economic viability of CIM.

The robot is a major ingredient of CIM technology. It appears to be the nucleus around which the technology is forming. As a commercial, low-cost, flexible manufacturing device, the robot can bring the beginnings of CIM to every production floor.

15.2.1 Overview of the Computer-Integrated Factory

The computer-integrated factory will be a coordinated grouping of machines and equipment which perform tasks together to create a product, all under the control of a hierarchical authority. Each machine will be linked by a communication port to an hierarchical network of computers responsible for production flow and scheduling. Each machine will receive instructions and information regarding its task and the sequence in which the tasks are to be performed. They will execute their tasks and report back their accomplishments, operating status, and state of being.

In the course of this century, machines have grown complex in function and capability. Witness the evolution of the simple lathe of the 1800s to the computer-controlled numerical turning machines on modern factory floors. We are, however, approaching practical limits in the complexity and functions that should be built into a single machine. Further increases in machine capabilities will require additional specialization. Specialization limits the total market potential for a specific machine design. Increased complexity adds to the design, manufacturing, and service costs. The limited market reduces product lot sizes, further increasing costs.

The tendency in CIM will be to integrate multiple machines, each with a range of capabilities, into flexible work cells with multiple function capability. The work cells will be programmed and scheduled to perform complex tasks as dictated by inventory and manufacturing requirements. With flexible work cells, the manufacturer will produce product in low unit quantities, on demand, reducing investment in inventories, work in process, and production facility floor space.

The industrial robot will perform three distinctly different roles in the computer-integrated factory. One role will be assisting other equipment, such as robot machine loading. A second role will be performing semiskilled tasks such as assembly. The third role will be controlling complex processes, such as arc welding, in a highly skilled manner.

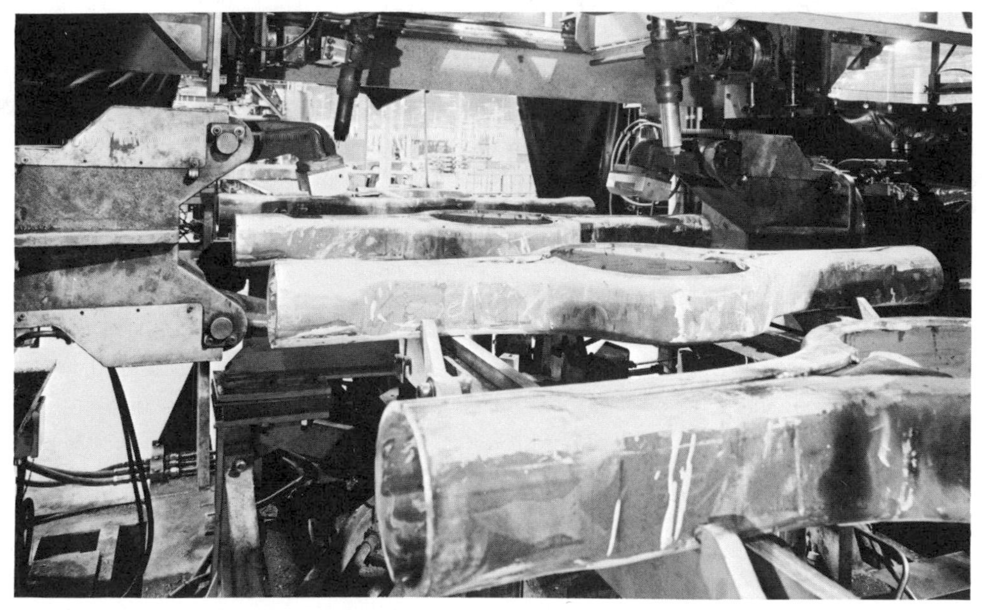

Figure 15.2 Two arc-welding robots stand poised while truck axles are automatically transferred into one work cell of a seven-work-cell computerized fabrication facility. (*Advanced Robotics Corporation.*)

15.2.2 Material Handling and Machine Loading

Material handling and machine loading will be important tasks for robots in the computer-integrated factory. A low-cost mass-produced industrial robot with multiple degrees of freedom and sufficient load capacity and reach can perform handling and loading tasks that would otherwise require specialized and costly custom engineering and manufacture. Specialized handling and loading systems will continue to be used to move high volumes of material or material over long distances. However, robots will be used to provide complex services such as part orientation, decision-based parts transfer, or unloading and loading functions.

Material-handling robots can perform routine complex tasks with the aid of special features and capabilities. For example, palletizing programs can be used to locate and stack objects with a mathematically defined accuracy. Object orientation is easily performed with the inherent dexterity of a five- or six-axis robot. Vision may be used to ensure proper object orientation. Vision may also be used to locate and recognize or inspect objects. These functions add value to the robot's activity.

Figure 15.3 A material-handling robot is an integral member of this automated machining work, servicing machine tools from conveyor lines. (*Prab Robots.*)

15.2.3 Semiskilled Tasks

Many other semiskilled tasks can be performed by robots. Spot welding has been the largest single application of robots in the United States during the past 10 years. Hazardous human working conditions and improved performance predictability have motivated investment in this robot application.

Many new applications are being developed, such as deburring, drilling, routing, machining, inspection and assembly. The integration of robots into semiskilled tasks will be led by the resourcefulness of application development in each specific technology. Robots will be employed to replace manual skills, thus improving production predictability, and will replace mechanized alternatives where economics can justify the investment in applications technology.

Figure 15.4 A machine-loading robot performs hazardous duty in the hot and humid die-casting environment. (*Unimation.*)

15.2.4 Skilled Tasks

Robots have been applied in many skilled task areas, most notably painting and arc welding. Other skilled tasks would include specialized assembly, glueing, or complex machining functions. In a skilled application, the robot typically has control over a process and performs a skilled motion and a coordination of actions.

The advantage of a skilled-task robot is improved predictability of the end result. Improved predictability will yield higher quality and reduced production costs. Robots applied to skilled tasks are generally continuous-path robots. They have more powerful control systems, provide more sophisticated servo control, and usually directly regulate the process being performed.

The boundary between skilled and nonskilled tasks is not yet clearly defined. The

Figure 15.5 Skilled arc welding is performed on these large machinery components by this specialized arc-welding robot. (*Advanced Robotics Corporation.*)

classifications exist to draw attention to the evolution of robot control, which is maturing to provide highly skilled capabilities. This maturation process is generally termed "the development of artificial intelligence and adaptive controls."

15.3 CAD/CAM INTERFACES FOR ROBOTS

15.3.1 Task Input

For maximum efficiency, a robot in a flexible manufacturing work cell should obtain its task program directly from a supervisory control via a hardware interface. This link enables rapid changeover of work-cell activities with minimum disruption of productive time.

A program download link requires protocol to assure that the robot is in a condition to receive the program and can do so without interfering with safety and operations in the work cell. This link must also verify that the data transmission has been received correctly. A means must also be provided to assure that the transmitted program is appropriate for the task to be performed in the work cell and contains the correct data for proper execution of that task.

In order to input a task to a robot, there must be a method to create that task for that specific robot as it relates to its work cell. Inaccuracies in the manufacture of the robot and defining the relationship of the robot within the work cell create programming errors. These must be accounted for via a robot signature and a work-cell signature to avoid costly down time for reprogramming. Additionally, calibration, component drift, or equipment repair may alter these signatures, requiring a means to verify and to update their accuracy.

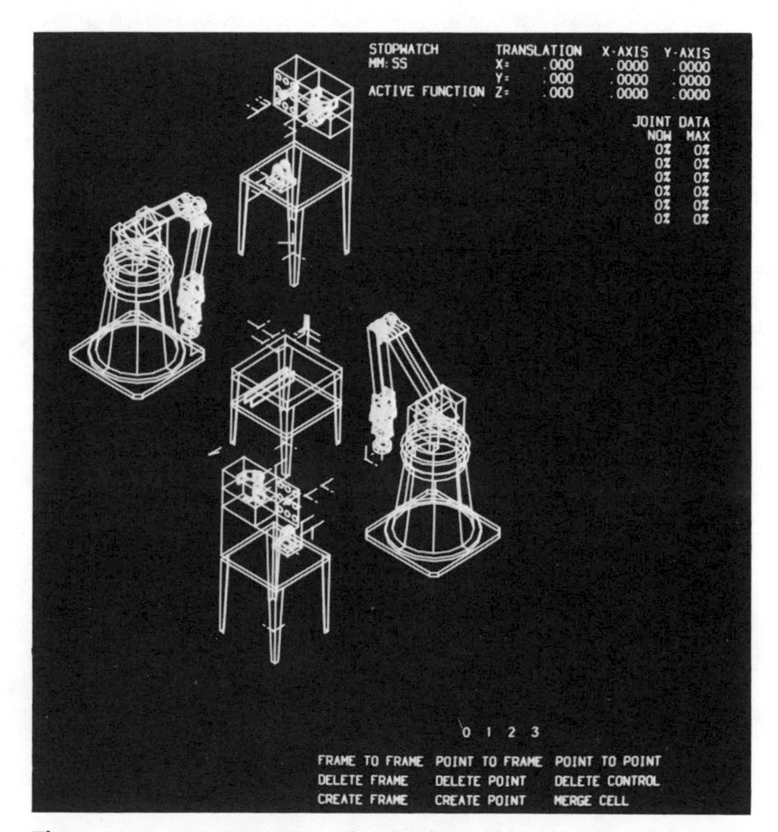

Figure 15.6 CAD system is used to develop and test a multiple-robot work cell. (*McDonnell Douglas Automation Company.*)

15.3.2 Task Definition

Some type of database is required to define a task for an offline robot. For example, a computer-aided design (CAD) database can provide information related to part geometry. A computer-aided manufacturing (CAM) database can provide machine and tool information. But in most cases, new or enhanced databases must be developed for offline programming of robots.

First, a database is required for robot simulation. Robot tasks can be designed with computer-aided simulation. Simulation allows the system programmer to test the procedure and concepts without tying up the work cell. Second, a database is required for clearance and interference checking. Robot paths can be checked and optimized with computer-aided programs to verify clearances and test the interaction of machines, tools, and workpieces in the cell. Third, a database for the specific robot process is required. In material handling, for example, this database may include weight, center of gravity, surface features, surface quality, and gripping or handling constraints.

Most CAD/CAM databases do not currently contain these types of data. It may be desirable to expand the CAD/CAM database to include robot, task, and work-cell variables which can be used to define the specific task for a robot and to define relative tasks among robot and machines which operate in the same work cell.

15.3.3 Control and Supervision

Efficiency in the CIM facility requires supervisory and control interfaces between robots and the factory. These interfaces will take a variety of forms and require different rates of data transmission. The interfaces must be robust, provide adequate handshaking and protocol, and have sufficient bandwidth to accommodate the required data transfer rate.

An example of high data transmission would be two continuous-path robots performing simultaneous tasks on the same moving part. At present, this type of relative motion control is typically done within a single robot control. However, it is anticipated that robots must communicate between controls to allow close dynamic coupling.

Large multiple robot installations are prevalent in the production of automobile bodies. As many as 26 robots operate in conjunction with transfer devices through standard input-output interfaces. Many of these systems use programmable controllers for overall sequence management. Some installations have host computers supervising the interaction. Supervision requires a lower data rate than control.

Figure 15.7 Twenty-six spot-welding robots perform their tasks in concert, efficiently supervised by a host controller. (*Unimation.*)

The role of supervisory systems will greatly increase as CAD/CAM is integrated with the factory floor. The tasks performed within the factory will be subdivided into individual tasks, each with its own level of control. Tasks will be linked together in a supervisory control loop to orchestrate the entire system performance.

15.3.4 Feedback and Feedforward

All control loops use some type of feedback or feedforward. In the computer-integrated factory, feedback and feedforward will perform the quality assurance task. For example, one stage in the manufacturing process may feed back information regarding part size to another work center. This information will contain data from which changes at earlier stages of manufacture may be made to produce the component more accurately.

This same type of logic is used in feedforward control. A work cell can feed information forward to work cells that will perform subsequent tasks. This information could contain data which would assist the subsequent work cell in performing its task.

The design and development of feedback and feedforward controls are critical to optimize productivity in the factory of the future. The goal of low inventory levels for the factory of the future will invalidate current statistical quality control technology.

15.4 BASIC ROBOT MECHANISMS AND GEOMETRIES

Robots have one or more axes of motion. These axes are typically rotary or linear. The number of axes and their relative orientations determine the degrees of freedom. The type of axis determines the working volume of the robot. In general, a robot uses three axes of motion to define points in space and three additional axes to approach that point in space from any angle. A robot with six degrees of freedom is considered a totally flexible manipulator.

The relative orientation of the motion axes is important in defining degrees of freedom. Axes of motion about the same centerline can be redundant and therefore not contribute to the degrees of freedom. Some mechanical linkages cause motion axes to become redundant under certain conditions. Such conditions are called *degeneracy.*

15.4.1 Cartesian Geometries

The primary axes of motion for a cartesian robot are linear. Typically they make three mutually orthogonal planes and resemble a cartesian coordinate system. Orthogonality, however, is not a necessary condition. A cartesian robot geometry usually has a rigid structural path that mechanically transfers loads to the robot base, providing stiffness and load-carrying capacity. The robot's working envelope is usually defined by its structure. As its motions are linear, they are usually of a lower velocity than rotary motions. The base axis of a cartesian system is often extended to enlarge the working volume or to move the robot from one position to another.

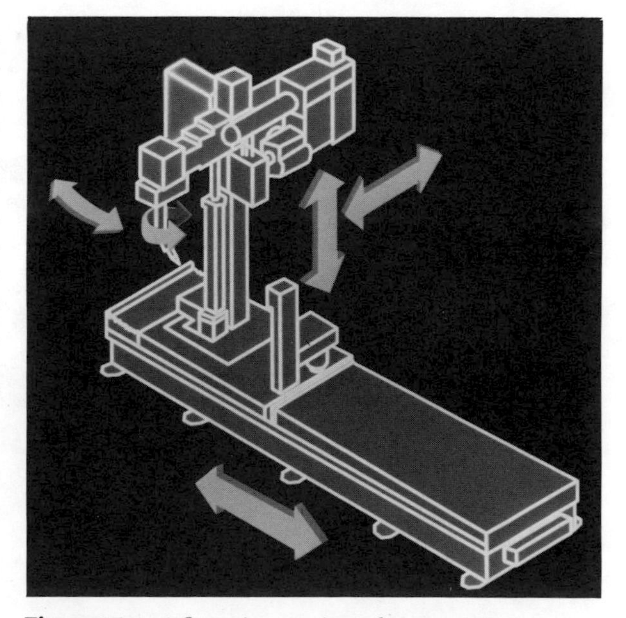

Figure 15.8 A five-axis cartesian robot geometry.

15.4.2 Cylindrical Geometries

Cylindrical geometries are similar to cartesian geometries except that the base axis is a rotary motion. The working envelope of the robot is a cylindrical section whose external diameter is the maximum reach of the horizontal axis and whose internal diameter is its minimum reach. Cylindrical systems offer similar structural stiffness and load-carrying capacities as cartesian systems. The rotary base axis can provide a rapid movement between locations. This geometry is commonly used in material-handling robots.

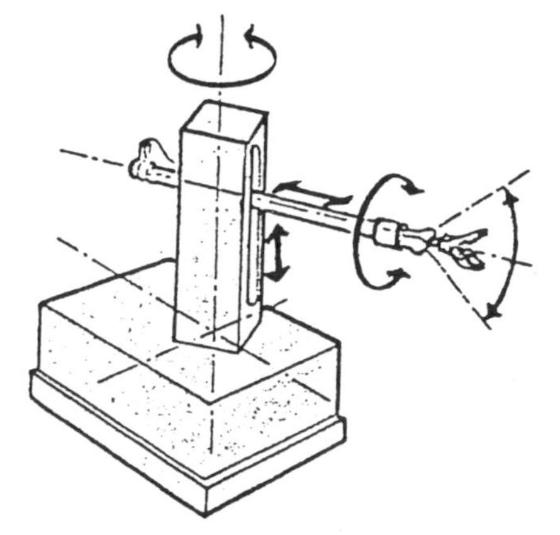

Figure 15.9 A five-axis cylindrical robot geometry.

15.4.3 Spherical Geometries

The spherical robot geometry has two rotary axes combined with a linear axis. The base axis is a rotary axis with a second rotary axis providing vertical motion. The linear axis makes the radius of the sphere. The working envelope of a spherical geometry is the area between a large sphere defined by the maximum extension of the linear axis and a small sphere defined by its minimum extension. These spheres are truncated by the mechanical travel limits of the rotary axes.

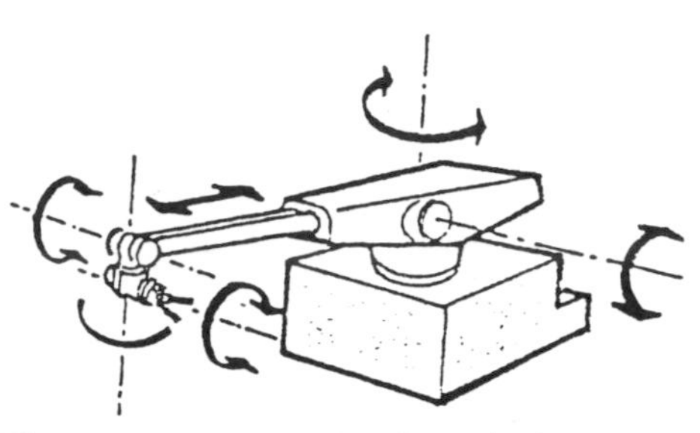

Figure 15.10 A six-axis spherical robot geometry.

15.4.4 Articulated, Revolute, and Anthropomorphic Geometries

Articulated, revolute, and anthropomorphic geometries are those which combine a series of linkages and motions. Typically, these robots use a series of nonparallel rotary motions. Their action often resembles that of human motion and some manufacturers refer to specific motions by the names of their human counterparts: waist, shoulder, and elbow.

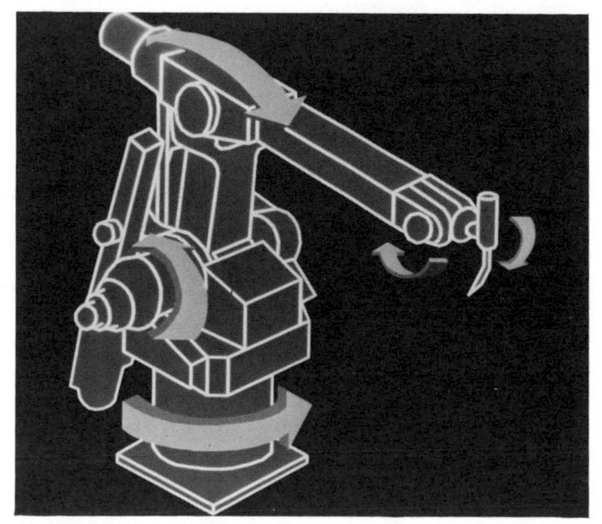

Figure 15.11 A five-axis articulated robot geometry.

15.4.5 Wrist Geometries

The wrist provides the robot with the ability to change orientation to a point in space. Wrist motions are angular, and at least three motions are required to uniquely define all orientations in space. Robot wrists can be designed with many different combinations and permutations of motion axes and their relative orientations. Wrist geometries can have unique advantages in specific circumstances.

Some process tools are circular or spherical at their working point. If the tool can be used omnidirectionally, it can provide an additional degree of freedom for the robot wrist. The coupling of the tool to the wrist, its effect on robot geometry, and the process constraints are important in robot applications.

15.4.6 Servo Control

Robots differ from other mechanical devices through their reprogrammability and manipulative capabilities. Feedback systems are required to achieve these functions. Various types of feedback are used in robots. The basic robot feedback is position. In simple robots, position feedback can be provided by mechanical stops that limit travel. These are inexpensive and repeatable but are difficult to reprogram. Position feedback in reprogrammable robots is commonly provided by encoders, resolvers, or potentiometers coupled with microprocessors, computers, or hard-wired electronics.

Resolvers and potentiometers are analog devices that transmit signals relative to the angular relationship of their components. They can provide absolute position information but may be subject to drift or calibration errors, depending upon implementation.

Incremental encoders transmit digital pulses relative to linear or rotational displacement and direction of travel. Incremental encoders require initialization and may be susceptible to electromagnetic interference. Servo-controlled robots require velocity and acceleration feedback. A tachometer is often used to generate this feedback. Some manufacturers are using microcomputers to differentiate position feedback to obtain velocity and acceleration feedback.

Air and hydraulics are used as motive power in industrial robots. Air is the least expensive to implement but is compressible and difficult to servo-control. Most air-powered robots are point-point robots with mechanical or electromechanical stops. Airmotor–driven, servo-controlled robots are under development, using pulsed air columns to regulate power to the air motor. Hydraulics has been broadly used as a power source for robots because of its power density. Hydraulic power is economic in all but high-precision servo control. Hydraulic-powered robots have dominated spot-welding, material-handling, and painting applications.

High-precision servo-controlled robots are usually powered by electric motors and drives which provide accuracy and smoothness for servo control. Mechanical transmissions, levers, or screws are used to increase torque at a sacrifice of speed.

15.5 PROCESS MANIPULATION AND CONTROL

A robot by itself has little utility. When interacting with other equipment or performing a skilled task, however, the robot greatly leverages its value. The amount of economic leverage it can provide is related to the robot's capability to interact with its surroundings. This is determined by the robot control.

15.5.1 Inputs and Outputs

Interfaces are used to link robots with their surroundings. One common interface is an analog or digital input or output.

Inputs provide signals to the robot from external sources. For example, when a part is delivered to a material-handling robot on a conveyor, a light-beam sensor could detect the presence of a part and send a signal to the robot that the part is present. This signal is used in the robot's program to initiate the robot action. Inputs are provided in digital or analog form for the convenience of the user. Digital inputs can be contact closures or voltages to provide binary information. Analog inputs transmit variable information to a robot. For example, a weighing system might provide a voltage to the robot relative to the weight of an object to be moved. Depending upon the object weight, the robot may select from alternative instructions in its program.

Outputs are signals sent from the robot to other devices. Outputs are often used to activate events in conjunction with the robot program. For example, the robot may signal a machine to clamp an object that the robot has just placed into a fixture. Outputs are usually available in the same forms as inputs. Digital outputs are typically contact closures or voltages. Contact closures are convenient for interfacing with binary logic systems such as programmable controllers. Signals of 115 volts are often used to directly energize relays, valves, or solenoids.

Some robots also provide analog outputs. Typically a 0- to 10-volt dc signal is provided to control an external device. For example, a robot can control the speed of a welding wire feeder by varying the value of an analog output. This output can be varied as a part of the robot's program, allowing the robot to control changes in the welding process.

15.5.2 Synchronous and Nonsynchronous

Robots interact either synchronously or nonsynchronously with other machines, devices, or robots. Nonsynchronous interaction is relatively simple to communicate. The interacting equipment sends an input signal to the robot advising the robot of its status. It continues its activity until an input command exists in its program. The equipment then halts until it receives an output signal from the robot. This is repeated as often as required to complete an interactive nonsynchronous task. Nonsynchronous interaction may require waiting time for the robot and/or the interacting equipment to establish proper relative conditions.

Synchronous interaction, on the other hand, requires a higher level of control between the robot and the interacting equipment. An example would be a robot tracking a conveyor line to place or remove an object from the moving conveyor. Synchronization can involve position, motion, or process control.

Synchronous control requires high-data-rate communication. Currently most synchronous control is performed within one control system. In the future, however, it is expected that high-level robots will have the capability of synchronous interaction with other robots and equipment.

15.5.3 Monitor and Status

As the industrial robot executes its task in the CIM facility, its performance and actions must be capable of being monitored. Monitoring is required to guarantee equipment and personnel safety and to assure that parallel events and activities occur efficiently. Monitoring may be performed actively or by exception. One form of monitoring is status reporting from the robot to a host system. Status reporting can include production data, errors, faults, sensor data, process variables, or other values. To date, no standard interfaces have been developed for status reporting.

15.5.4 Regulation

The robot control can be used to regulate processes, tools, and task-related systems. Regulation may be open- or closed-loop, depending upon requirements. Typically analog inputs and outputs are used for regulation. Some processes may have internal regulation loops where the robot control provides only a set point. This technique is common where the regulation loop is critical or peculiar to the process being controlled. It is possible, however, for the robot to provide closed-loop regulation for external processes. An analog input would be used to provide feedback to the robot. A control algorithm relating the feedback to the desired output must also be provided in the robot control.

15.5.5 Servo Control

The major task of a robot control is the servoing of robot motions. Servo control requires regulation of individual axis power to provide the desired robot trajectory and velocity. Manufacturers provide a wide range of robot servo systems depending on the application.

The range of loads and velocities imposed upon a robot presents a challenging servo-control problem. It is difficult to optimize a robot servo system based on current analog servo-control technology, since the robot must operate under a wide range of loads, arm extensions, and tip velocities. The development of computer servo controls is improving robot servo capabilities.

In addition to motion control, the robot control is often called upon to servo other mechanisms such as grippers, tools, sensors, or nonintegrated degrees of freedom. By providing servo control to such functions, the robot can closely synchronize external events. For example, an inspection robot might servo-control its inspection head to adjust magnification.

15.6 OFFLINE PROGRAMMING

Offline programming is necessary to the implementation of robots in CIM. A robot's productivity will be related to its ability to abstractly communicate with the CIM system. Computerized graphics, modeling, and simulation techniques will aid in the implementation of offline programming for industrial robots.

Offline programming is the abstract definition of tasks to be performed by a robot without involving the robot or the robot control system. Offline programming enhances robot productivity, as robot time is not lost to the programming activity. In addition,

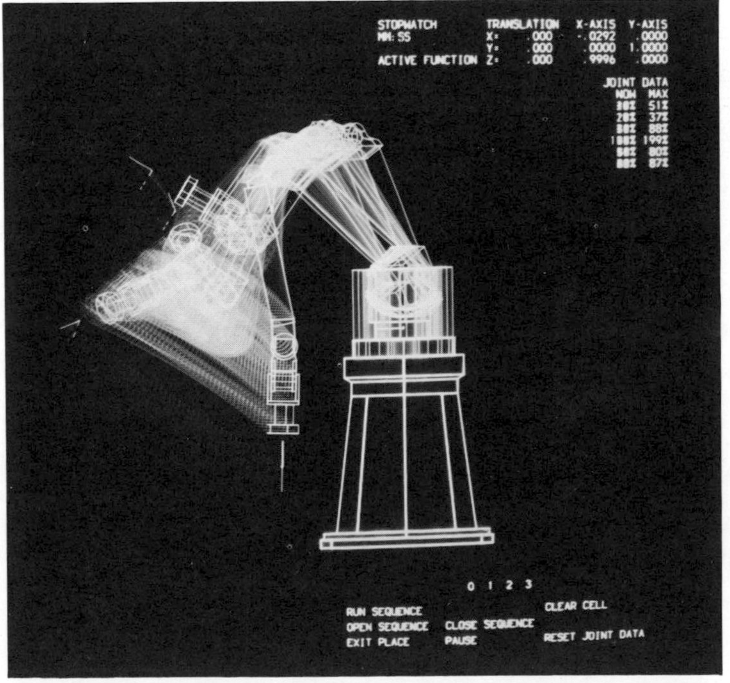

Figure 15.12 CAD system assists in developing programs for an industrial robot. (*McDonnell Douglas Automation Company.*)

complex tasks can be simulated, analyzed, and refined with computer aids for optimal robot performance.

In its simplest form, offline programming can be performed by programming an offline robot identical to an online robot. The coordinate reference frame of the offline robot is used to generate the program, which is played back in the coordinate reference frame of the online robot. Program transfer can be made via memory storage (tapes, disks, or bubble memories) or through a physical communication link. However, inaccuracies in the robot manufacture and calibration will cause position errors in such transported programs. These errors must be corrected by interrupting the offline robot for reprogramming or by mathematical alteration of the program based on premeasured values for each robot (robot signature).

Offline programming is best performed through transmission of abstract position data to the robot. The coordinate reference frame for these data are typically (1) joint coordinates (the coordinate system relative to the robot structure), (2) tool coordinates (the coordinate system relative to the tool (end effector) of the robot), (3) world coordinates (a coordinate system defined in real space), or (4) workpiece coordinates (a coordinate system relative to the workpiece). Position data in these abstract coordinate reference frames are usually generated with the aid of a computer. Software programs and graphic aids assist in writing sequences for specific robot models.

Robot accuracy is a key factor in offline programming. Accuracy is the measure of a robot's ability to position itself relative to an abstract reference frame. Robot accuracy is effected by design, encoding techniques, methods of manufacture, and calibration. No industry standards have been proposed to date and few robot manufacturers include accuracy in their product specification.

15.6.1 Robot Databases

A database with geometry and path information is required to define a robot's task abstractly. Many robot tasks can utilize a CAD database; others can utilize the CAM database; and in certain cases, the database can be mathematically derived. However, additional data or unique databases must be created in order to program most robot tasks offline.

A facilities database is required to define the relationship of the robot to the manufacturing environment. It must contain information on the exact physical location, orientation, and performance characteristics of the equipment and robots that must interact. These data must be accurate, transportable, and complete for each machine.

In addition, a workpiece database is required to define the parameters of the task to be performed. For example, a robot performing a drilling task requires a reference location on the component and the location and size of the holes to be drilled. CAD/CAM databases contain most of the required information for machine tool tasks. Additional data are required to define robot tasks that do not have a machine tool equivalent, such as material handling, welding, and painting.

15.6.2 Programming Languages

McDonnell Douglas Corporation, under the funding of the U.S. Air Force, has developed an extension of the APT language known as MCL for offline robot programming. Other offline programming languages for robots have been developed by robot manufacturers, but no industry standards have been established to date.

15.6.3 Coordinate Systems

Four basic coordinate systems are used to describe robot positions: (1) joint coordinates, (2) world coordinates, (3) tool coordinates, and (4) workpiece coordinates.

Joint coordinates describe points in space relative to the robot's mechanical joints.

Joint coordinates simplify robot servo control but are of little value for user programming and data storage or transfer. Joint coordinates are unique to a specific robot but programs may be transferrable among robots of the same manufacturing series.

World coordinates are the reference frame that describes robot position with respect to the earth. World coordinates are universal and can be transferred. They are a useful system for user programming and data storage but have deficiencies for certain robot applications. World coordinates are useful to abstractly program robot interactions with other machines, such as machine loading and material handling.

Tool coordinates are the reference frame defined with respect to the end effector or tool attached to the robot. This is a convenient frame of reference for use in programming tool-related robot functions. Applications, such as assembly, machining, and arc welding, are easier to program abstractly when tool coordinates are available for reference. However, these are rarely used as the primary programming coordinate system.

Workpiece coordinates are a reference frame relative to the object being worked. This coordinate system is the best for abstract programming of robot functions that are workpiece-related. Workpiece coordinates also are a compact and transferrable storage means for program data.

15.6.4 Multiple Robot Coordination

The offline programming system must be capable of dealing with interactive motion and multiple robot coordination. Many tasks cannot be performed without coordinated interactive motion, and, for efficiency, some tasks are enhanced by interactive motion.

Interactive motion can also be employed to optimize the position for performing tasks. Gravity often has an effect upon work and can be used to advantage. Interactive motion can also increase a robot's work envelope. Components too large to lie completely within the robot's work envelope can be robotically manipulated into the robot's envelope.

Figure 15.13 The coordinated motion between a part-handling robot and an arc-welding robot improves production efficiency. (*Advanced Robotics Corporation.*)

15.7 ARTIFICIAL INTELLIGENCE AND ADAPTIVE CONTROL

Adaptive control is the ability to modify a program in real time based upon sensory data. Robots can make use of abilities such as orienting parts based on features, following a changed path, or recognizing workpieces. Adaptive control requires sensory input and the ability to respond to that input.

Artificial intelligence is the level beyond adaptive control where learning occurs. Whereas adaptive control is a direct response to a stimulus, artificial intelligence anticipates changes based upon prior events or conditions. Both require sensory data, but artificial intelligence may use adaptive control to compensate for short-term aberrations while deducing trends.

15.7.1 Adaptive Robot Control

Adaptive controls will greatly enhance the industrial robot's role in the computer-integrated factory of the future. The robot endowed with the ability to adjust to its environment reduces the cost of workplace rationalization. Adaptive controls reduce the manufacturing costs of scrap and rework, and a robot equipped with adaptive controls can perform quality-control functions integral with its tasks.

Adaptive control sensors for robots are found in the same general categories as the human senses: touch, sound, vision, and process-related sensors (functionally similar to taste and smell). Sensor input can be used at different levels in the robot control hierarchy. Commonly, they are used for robot path or position alteration. Sensors may be used to adaptively control processes being performed by the robot. Sensor data may also be sent by the robot to other machines. The physical integration of sensors into the robot structure has been dictated by the specific task to be performed and the properties of the sensors. As sensor technology matures, standard robot configurations will emerge.

Figure 15.14 The welding arc is used to sense the weld joint location for adaptive weld path control. (*Advanced Robotics Corporation.*)

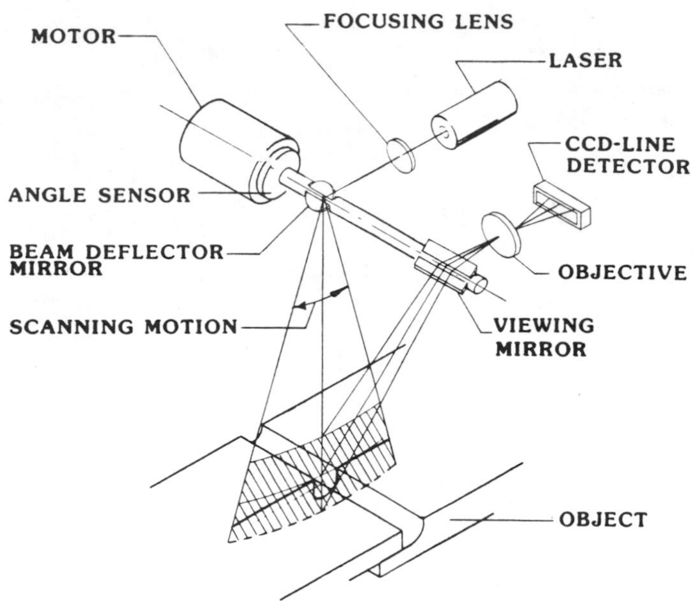

Figure 15.15 Robot vision system for arc-welding uses laser scanner. Diagram of the sensor camera. (*Advanced Robotics Corporation.*)

15.7.2 Tactile, Sound, and Other Sensors

Tactile and force sensors provide feedback for gripping and grasping. They are used to regulate forces or to locate objects and surfaces. Tactile and force sensors are important in assembly tasks where alignment, insertion, and fastening are required. Tactile sensing can be used to detect component presence and for surface mapping and adaptive position control. Tactile and force sensors are also important in material-handling and machine-loading applications. Certain process applications, such as deburring, rely heavily upon tactile sensors for adaptive feedback.

Sound can be used to detect the location size and shape of objects. Scanning techniques and sound sensor grids have been used to create topographical maps. Sound sensing is reasonably accurate and resolution can be increased by using frequencies in the ultrasonic region.

15.7.3 Vision

Industrial robot vision is generally classified in three distinct categories: laser gauging, structured light, or pattern recognition. Laser gauging is a mapping technique where a laser light source is reflected on a surface and a triangulation process establishes the dimensional relationships between the laser source, the reflected surface, and the light receiver. The mapping may be performed in two or three dimensions. A variety of laser beam projection scanning methods and sensing techniques exist which can generate a complete topographical map of objects and surfaces.

Structured light systems project beams of light of known geometric form. Object locations and shapes are determined through mathematical and logical analysis of the image. The size and shape of a simple object can be deduced from the bending of the structured light beam by the object surface. Locations are measurable by triangulation.

Pattern recognition vision systems extract features from thresholded reflected light images. Pattern recognition is usually sensitive to lighting intensity and illumination direction. Automatic thresholding techniques are used to account for these effects. Pattern recognition vision tends to be computation-intensive and requires significant data processing power. Array and pipeline processing are commonly used to achieve useful data output rates.

Template matching is a high-speed technique that also employs thresholding and feature extraction. It is commonly used in high-speed continuous production applications where ambient conditions can be controlled.

Gray-scale processing is a flexible pattern recognition technique. The image is processed over a wide range of gray-scale values to extract desired features. Gray-scale processing is fairly tolerant of changing illumination environments. Its wide dynamic range helps minimize feature definition requirements.

The solid-state miniaturized array camera is playing an important role in robotic vision systems. Cameras are being integrated into the robot's end effectors for close-proximity viewing. Cameras are being mounted over working-cell areas to provide inspection or provide data. Interpretation of visual images is a complex art, not yet reduced to science. Techniques have been developed to extract meaningful data from observed input. Each technique provides superior performance in certain applications.

15.7.4 Adaptive CIM

The production quality and productivity of the CIM facility will be directly related to its adaptive capabilities. During the manufacturing process, integral inspection systems and sensors will make quality and condition measurements. This information will be routed via communication networks to supervisory controls and to work cells where the information can be used to establish product quality.

The factory will be self-maintained to assure efficiency. Variations in materials, tool wear, and equipment performance will be dynamically sensed and compensated for. Random-error conditions will be detected and resolved with recovery programming techniques and artificial intelligence. Critical process variables will be sensed, corrected, or compensated for via adaptive controls.

15.7.5 Regulation and Feedback

Efficient CIM will be regulated through open and closed feedback loops. Feedback regulation requires a quality and quantity of data to stabilize the control loop. The type of inputs required will depend upon the manufacturing processes being performed. The feedback loop must have sufficient bandwidth and response to perform in real time. Production rates will dictate the data frequency, the complexity of tasks will dictate the bandwidth, and the quality of data will determine stability.

Figure 15.16 Autovision vision system (center) monitoring quality on automated inner tie-rod assembly line. (*Automatix Incorporated.*)

One type of system feedback will be the transfer of correction data to previous steps in the production system. Depending upon the character of this feedback and control employed, the system can develop overdamped, underdamped, or oscillatory states. Divergent oscillations are detrimental and must be totally eliminated. Underdamped or overdamped conditions are also not desirable. The optimum control loop is a critically damped network with a decay time of one component.

Feedforward control techniques can be utilized in the automated factory. For example, a noncritical component dimension that is incorrect may be compensated for by modifying the component that joins it in a subsequent assembly. Feedforward can reduce scrap and rework as well as improve overall product quality.

Figure 15.17 Improved product quality is achieved through continual program changes that optimize the robotic fabrication of truck axles. (*Advanced Robotics Corporation.*)

15.8 ROBOT APPLICATION

Although a robot is a general-purpose device, readily programmable and adaptable to many tasks, the technology of robotics is developing along specific areas of robot application. This specialization will continue until the technology of robot application is a more developed service and the robot tools and accessories required to perform tasks have been invented and standardized.

15.8.1 Spot Welding

The automotive companies worldwide have invested heavily in robots for spot welding. This application represents the largest installed base of robots. Spot welding is a point-to-point robot task. It can tolerate a modest degree of positioning inaccuracy. It has been favored by automotive manufacturers because of its ability to allow model mixing, model changeover, and tuning to meet changing manufacturing needs. Previously, automatic spot welding was performed with hard-tooled dedicated automation.

Reliability and serviceability are also key attributes for spot-welding robots. The robot may be removed from the production line for repairs that would normally shut down a hard-tooled spot-welding line. If a robot is removed from the line, it can be replaced with another robot, or another robot on the production line can be programmed to assume its duties.

Figure 15.18 Four spot-welding robots working together on an automated production line. (*Chrysler Corporation.*)

Spot-welding process control has been a major concern. The spot-welding process is sensitive to the mechanical condition of the welding electrodes and the quality of electrical contact made with the material. Resistance can steal energy that would normally be used in making the welding bond. Advances are being made in adaptive spot-welding controls for improved weld reliability.

The spot-welding robot market is maturing. The automotive and appliance manufacturers are aggressively automating high-volume spot-welding applications. The use of spot-welding robots in job shop applications has been slow because of lack of application expertise and overhead costs.

15.8.2 Painting and Finishing

Figure 15.19 Spray-painting robot finishes decorative shutters. (*De Villbiss.*)

Painting was an early and natural application for industrial robots because of the toxic fumes and hostile environment. Painting, however, is not a simple task. The condition of the material, the temperature, the humidity, the paint viscosity, and chemical properties all have an effect upon the quality of paint application. The human painter relies heavily upon visual feedback to obtain the desired gloss and coverage. Visual sensors for painting robots have not yet been commercially produced, so that for high-quality paint applications, stringent constituent and environmental controls are required.

For finishes where gloss and visual characteristics are not critical, the industrial robot is readily applied. Robots are used to apply primers, base coats, and rust inhibitors.

Control of robot velocity and trajectory are important in spray-painting applications. The robot must move smoothly, since its servo quality will be permanently recorded in the painted surface. In balance, however, accuracy requirements are modest.

The programming of painting robots can be difficult. Most painting robots use a leadthrough technique where an experienced painter guides the robot while painting a part. As backdriving a robot's servo motions can be cumbersome, some manufacturers have developed lightweight counterbalanced robot emulators for offline program development. Computer-aided offline programming can greatly facilitate the programming of robotic painting.

15.8.3 Material Handling

Material-handling applications will utilize large quantities of industrial robots. Although first employed to perform handling tasks under hostile conditions, robot use has expanded to include almost every imaginable material-handling task. Robots have the ability to work tirelessly around the clock at a predictable rate, performing repetitive tasks with movement dexterity. Their cost-benefit performance makes them an efficient automation device for most medium- to low-volume material-handling tasks.

Material-handling tasks include component transfer to and from conveyors and machines, palletizing, and the movement of components in a manufacturing process. Special algorithms have been developed to simplify material-handling programming, particularly for palletizing. Interfaces between material-handling robots and other devices are easy to establish to customize a robot installation. Standard grippers are being developed by third parties to enable cost-effective application of material-handling robots in most production environments.

Figure 15.20 Glass tubes are handled safely by an industrial robot. (*Unimation.*)

15.8.4 Machine Loading

Machine loading is a specialized form of material handling where a robot transports objects or tools to and from machines where operations are performed. The ability of the robot to interface and interact with machines is important for performance of this task. An early machine-loading application was the loading and unloading of die-casting presses. The die-casting environment is hot and dangerous, and the robot is ideally suited for this tedious multishift task. In addition to machine loading or unloading, the robot performs deflashing or part orientation functions.

Figure 15.21 Two multispindle machine tools are loaded and unloaded from feed conveyors by a robot. (*Prab Robots.*)

Machine-loading grippers are usually able to handle more than one part simultaneously. These grippers allow the robot to load and unload a part with a single major movement, reducing cycle time.

15.8.5 Arc Welding

The arc-welding environment is hot, smokey, and bright, not suited for humans without special protective clothing and equipment. But arc welding is a highly skilled task that has demanded the development of more sophisticated robots in order to be practical. Arc-

Figure 15.22 Intelligent arc-welding robot adaptively controls the weld process in a three-robot production cell. (*Advanced Robotics Corporation.*)

welding robot applications are now growing rapidly and have become a major application area for industrial robots.

Arc-welding robots require different capabilities and features than other applications. They must be continuous-path robots, with smooth servo-controlled motions and the ability to control the arc-welding process variables. The arc-welding task has little in common with spot welding. The arc-welding process is affected by gravity, speed, absolute position, and numerous component-related variables. It needs special robot skills and adaptive robot and process controls.

Arc-welding robots can use companion robots that position the workpiece to optimize the gravity effect on the molten welding puddle. If these companion robots can be coordinated with the welding robot, improved weld quality and production efficiency can be obtained. Additional productivity and quality are also provided by welding robots that have control over the welding process variables.

Adaptive controls provide the arc-welding robot with the ability to compensate for variation of a weld scan location, a common problem. Advanced adaptive controls enable the detection of variations in weld joint size and adjustment of weld process parameters to compensate for the amount of weld metal applied. The most sophisticated adaptive systems also recognize weld fit up and gap conditions and compensate by adjusting the process variables.

Productivity improvements in robotic arc welding extend beyond simple labor cost savings to a predictable quality product. Quality improvements decrease indirect costs and can provide large material cost reductions because of enhanced product performance predictability.

15.8.6 Assembly

Assembly will be the largest single application for industrial robots, but its requirements are diverse, complex, and technically challenging. At this writing robots have made only initial inroads into production assembly tasks. Demonstration systems have been made by a number of research centers, technology groups, and manufacturers. These have helped to expose the requirements of assembly and to classify the problems into manageable objectives.

Component weight and size are two major factors that divide assembly applications. Assembly tasks which involve components under 5 pounds and which are smaller than the human hand are receiving major attention. Automotive engine component insertion applications are also being addressed with significant resources. And the electronics industry is being addressed for printed-circuit board, keyboard, packaging, and memory device assembly tasks.

The difficulty of assembly lies with the number of possible error events that can occur. Point-to-point servoing, with repeatabilities of between 0.002 and 0.004 inch, is acceptable for most assembly operations. The capability to sense and deal with events such as missing components, out-of-tolerance components, calibration errors, drift, variable sequencing, and misalignment are the major obstacles.

Sensory systems for tactile, force, and vision feedback are important in assembly. These sensors help to address the error conditions that routinely occur. In addition, software routines will facilitate error recovery techniques and speed correction of the fault or provide alternative courses of action to maintain productivity under less than optimal conditions. Component feeders, grippers, material-handling robots, inspection robots, and other devices will be required by assembly robots to accomplish these tasks. Software flexibility, system design ingenuity, and equipment interfaces will be required in assembly robot work-cell design.

15.8.7 Machining

Robots are not destined to replace efficient machine tools. However, many machining tasks, such as deburring, drilling, tapping, and routing, can be performed effectively by robots. Often these can be integrated with other work-cell tasks to distribute the

Figure 15.23 Intelligent machining robot reads part identification, selects correct drill heads, and performs a complex drilling operation. (*Cincinnati Milicron.*)

production functions effectively and minimize material transfers and additional work-cell handling.

Most robots are not designed to handle the reactive forces present in heavy machining tasks; nor do robots typically provide the accuracies required. But the flexible industrial robot is well suited for tasks that do not require high accuracy or high-reactive-force capacity.

Numerical Control

by
Roger S. Pressman

During the past decade, a vision of computer-aided manufacturing (CAM) and the fully automated factory has presented engineers with unsurpassed challenges in system theory, has enticed managers with promises of precise control and better productivity, and has concerned social commentators with specters of human displacement. Numerical control (NC)—one of the oldest technologies associated with programmable automation—is the forerunner of modern CAM and an integral part of any vision of the fully automated factory.

16.1 INTRODUCTION

NC is a mature technology. Combining electronic hardware with increasingly sophisticated software (computer programs), NC systems are used in applications that span fabric cutting to laser welding, placement of integrated circuits to machining of metal parts, furniture making to inspection of mechanical and electronic components. The NC machine actually encompasses (1) a control system comprised of microprocessor-based hardware and software and (2) a servo system that includes transducers to measure speed, motion, and other data related to the machine's environment; actuation devices that accomplish accurate positioning and motion; and mechanical and electronic peripheral components that are required for specific applications.

In this section NC is introduced as an important component of factory automation. The important elements of an NC system are described, and a brief history of the technology is presented.

16.1.1 The Impact of Programmable Automation

The potential impact of computers on the manufacturing process has been called "a new industrial revolution" or the "factory of the future." Much of the technology required to achieve the computer-based factory already exists. Computer and communications capabilities have achieved considerable sophistication and continue to evolve rapidly. Manufacturing and assembly and fabrication equipment (e.g., NC machines and robots) are available at many levels of sophistication. The factory floor can be linked to engineering information by computer-aided design (CAD) and engineering (CAE) systems. Manufacturing control can be achieved with planning systems [e.g., manufacturing requirements planning (MRP)] that attempt to coordinate production flow under a set of complex constraints. Why, then, do we speak in the future tense? Why is the factory of the future not the factory of today?

The answers lie in the difficulty arising from integration—the requirement to connect CAM components to one another so that coordination, information transfer, and broad-based planning can occur. To accomplish integration, the architecture of manufacturing must be revised into a hierarchy that supports computer-based CAM components (including but not limited to NC).

NC systems are a relatively small but extremely important part of the "new" manufacturing architecture. The architecture is defined by a hierarchy, noted in Fig. 16.1, that encompasses the following levels:

- ***Process Equipment.*** Nonprogrammable machines such as conventional machine tools and, in some cases, high-speed transfer machines
- ***Workstations.*** Programmable equipment that includes NC machines, robots, and the computers
- ***Manufacturing Cell.*** A group of workstations combined with material-handling equipment that produces a subassembly or major component
- ***Manufacturing Center.*** A group of cells that are combined to produce a major subassembly

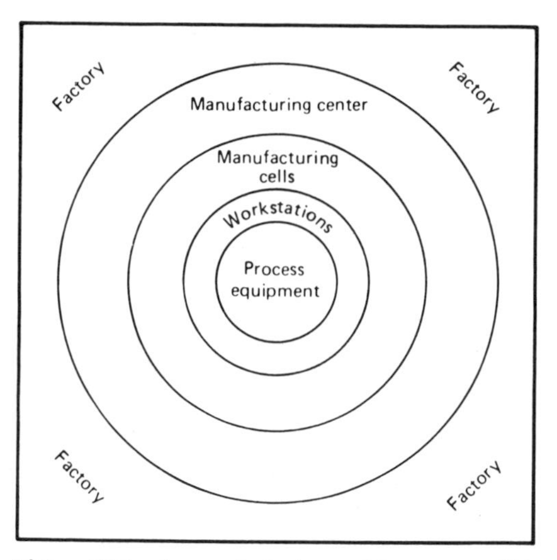

Figure 16.1 A manufacturing architecture and hierarchy.

- ***Factory.*** Integrates all of the above levels with centralized computer control for process and capacity planning; manufacturing, quality control, and tracking; and engineering data interface

It is clear from the manufacturing hierarchy that NC and CAM are not synonymous terms. It should be noted, however, that NC can receive and transmit information that is processed at the factory level and can have a significant impact on the overall activities associated with CAM.

16.1.2 NC Systems—An Overview

NC, a term coined in the late 1940s, refers to an electronic device that can be programmed to coordinate the operation of a machine. In the modern context, an NC is a microprocessor-based control system that accepts a set of program instructions, processes output control information to a machine (e.g., a lathe, a fabric cutter, a laser welder), accepts feedback information acquired from transducers placed on the machine, and based on both instructions and feedback, assures that proper motion, speed, and operation occur.

An NC system, regardless of its application, may be characterized in terms of three major elements: hardware, software, and information. NC hardware includes the microprocessors that effect control system functions and peripheral devices for data communication, machine interfacing, and machine status monitoring. In addition, certain elements of the machine can be considered part of the NC system (e.g., transducers and actuation devices). The NC hardware environment is illustrated schematically in Fig. 16.2.

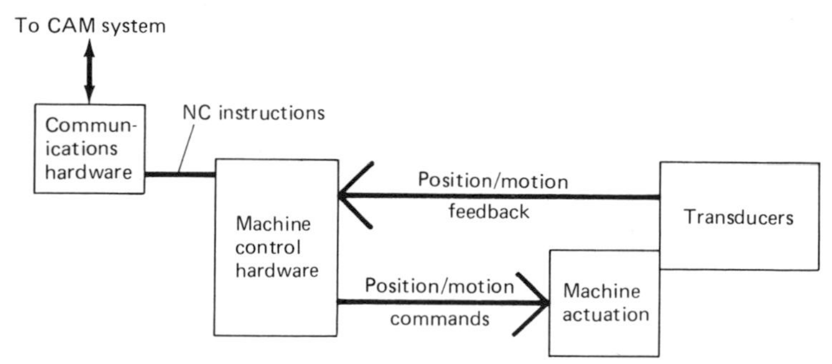

Figure 16.2 NC hardware environment.

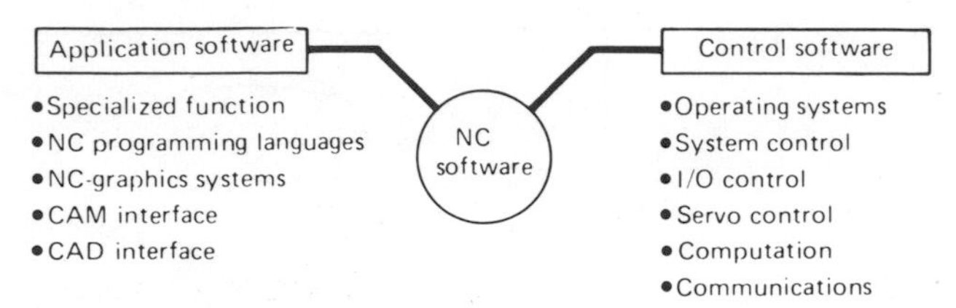

Figure 16.3 NC software domain.

NC software includes the programs that execute on the control system microprocessors. These programs process input and output instructions and control information, make all necessary computations for machine functions, coordinate the functions of the NC itself, and provide a mechanism for communication with other levels of the manufacturing architecture. NC software also encompasses computer programs that are external to the NC. The stream of instructions that drive an NC are frequently generated using special programming languages or interactive systems (see Sec. 16.4). NC instructions are often generated with the assistance of programs that execute on computers other than the microprocessor residing within the NC. Figure 16.3 depicts the primary domains associated with NC software.

Because NC is a computer-based system, the information that is processed becomes a system element. NC information includes (1) the program instructions that are input to the NC and are intended to control operation of the machine to which the NC is attached, (2) machine operator inputs, (3) control information passed to and received from the machine, and (4) CAM information that is passed to or from other levels of the manufacturing architecture.

An NC machine makes use of hardware, software, and information to accomplish some manufacturing function. Regardless of the application area, the process flow for NC can be represented as shown in Fig. 16.4. Referring to the figure, instructions are passed to the NC [sometimes called a machine control unit (MCU)]. The instructions may be contained on punched tape or magnetic media or may be transmitted from another computer in the CAM hierarchy. Software within the NC transforms the instruction stream into a set of positioning, motion, and function commands that are passed to actuation components attached to the machine (e.g., pulse commands passed to a stepping motor attached to a drive screw on a milling machine table). Transducers pass feedback information to the NC. Software processes the feedback to assure that proper machine operations have occurred and corrects the machine commands to compensate for error inferred from the feedback.

The NC process flow described in the preceding paragraph is a gross oversimplification of a very complex system. Even with microelectronic miniaturization, NC hardware must still be implemented on many densely packed printed-circuit boards. The software that drives control system functions can result in well over 50,000 lines of programming language source code! Further information concerning the NC process flow is presented in later sections of this chapter.

16.1.3 NC—A Brief History

An early ancestor of the NC machine was developed at the beginning of the nineteenth century by Joseph Jacquard. The textile industry was evolving rapidly and Jacquard saw

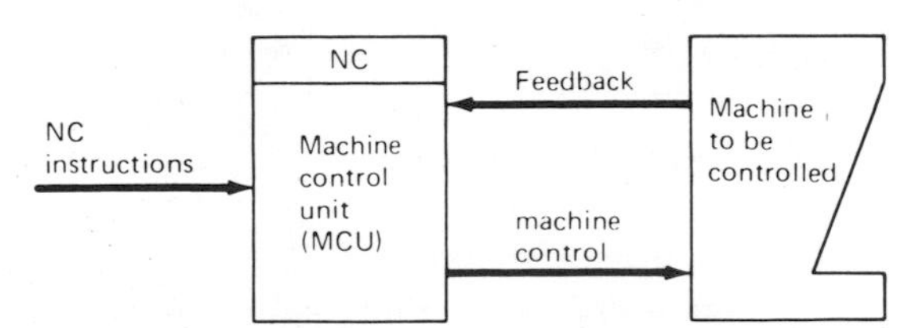

Figure 16.4 NC process flow.

an opportunity to develop a loom that could be "programmed" to produce the same pattern repeatedly. The new loom achieved consistency and quality that could not be attained with manual looms. The Jacquard loom was programmed with a wide paper tape into which punch holes were placed. The holes contained "instructions" that defined the weaving pattern.

NC as we know it today was proposed in the late 1940s. John T. Parsons recommended a method of automatic machine control that would guide a milling cutter for the generation of smooth profiles. In 1949, the U.S. Air Force commissioned the Massachusetts Institute of Technology (MIT) to develop a practical implementation of Parsons' concept. Scientists and engineers at MIT built a control system for a two-axis drill press that used perforated paper tape as the instruction medium. This first NC machine prototype was refined, and by 1957 NC machines were in use throughout the United States.

During the late 1950s and early 1960s, machine tool builders refined the NC concept. Programming languages, such as APT, were developed to assist the engineer in defining the proper instructions for an NC. As programming languages became popular, the term *part programmer* became widely used as a description of one who defines instructions for NC machines.

Through the 1960s, NC manufacturers made use of hard-wired logic to accomplish control functions with the MCU. Low-cost, high-speed computing capability was unavailable, so all functions within an NC were accomplished with relays and control circuits. In fact, it was not until the mid-1970s that computer-based NC became widely used, and many hard-wired NC machines are still in productive use today.

During the decade of the 1970s, NC matured as an automation technology and early attempts at integration with other CAM system elements began. CAD system vendors developed interactive methods for the generation of NC instructions. New concepts such as computer numerical control (CNC) and direct numerical control (DNC) focused on NC's role within the manufacturing hierarchy. Microprocessors made computer-based systems both inexpensive and extremely powerful. Retrofit of existing conventional machine tools became practical and the population of NC machines grew.

In the early years of the 1980s, NC systems are viewed as one element of the automated factory. Methods for integrating NC into computer networks are well underway. Manufacturing flexibility and product quality have become primary factors for industrial growth. The NC system, although an old-timer in the CAD/CAM arena, is an important contributor to factory automation.

16.2 THE NC SYSTEM

The purpose of NC is to control and monitor the operations of a machine. Therefore an NC system encompasses not only the computer-based MCU but also components of the machine that are being controlled. In this section, important components of the NC system are described.

16.2.1 Fundamental Aspects of Machine Control

The primary objective of NC is machine control. Although every NC application requires special control activities, all NC machines are programmed to accomplish three major objectives:

1. ***Positioning.*** The position of a tool (e.g., a metal-cutting bit, an inspection probe, or a welding rod) is controlled in two or three dimensions.
2. ***Motion.*** The direction and speed of a tool is controlled so that the motion of the tool is predictable.
3. ***Function.*** Other machine functions (e.g., controlling the flow of coolant for metal cutting or moderating the energy in a laser welder) are controlled so that the tool can better adapt to its environment.

The vast majority of all NC systems use a two- or three-dimensional cartesian coordinate system (x, y, [z]) to accomplish positioning. In addition, some NC machines have tools that can be rotated through one, two, or three axes of rotation. In some cases, the workpiece (the component that the machine is to produce), rather than the tool, is moved or rotated.

The machine workspace is the bounded plane or volume in which the tool and workpiece can be positioned and through which controlled motion can be invoked. When NC instructions are generated by a part programmer, the geometry of workpiece must be transformed into a coordinate system that is consistent with the workspace origin and coordinate reference frame. Figure 16.5 illustrates this concept for a two-dimensional milling application.

Tool motion within the workspace is accomplished under direct control of MCU. Depending on the sophistication of the NC system and the requirements of the application, motion may be point to point or continuous path. Referring to Fig. 16.6*a*, point-to-point motion guarantees that the tool will move from a start point (x, y) and arrive at the precise endpoint (x', y') coordinate. However, the tool path between the two points is not defined by the part programmer. Point-to-point motion is ideal for positioning systems such as integrated-circuit (IC) inserters for printed-circuit boards or hole-drilling machines. In both cases, the path between points where the tool must be used is unimportant and need not be precisely controlled.

The control problem for point-to-point systems is a relatively simple matter. Endpoint coordinates are loaded into control registers, and individual stepping motors (or other actuation mechanisms) for each axis are driven until each coordinate value is achieved.

Continuous-path control, illustrated in Fig. 16.6*b*, requires that the tool move along a precisely defined curve. All continuous-path systems implement linear interpolation; that is, the endpoints of a linear path are specified and the MCU controls the actuation system so that a line between endpoints is precisely followed. Other curves can also be approximated with linear interpolation. A series of nominal points is defined along the curve (Fig. 16.6*b*) and connected with a series of straight lines. Some continuous-path systems implement higher-order interpolation to produce smooth curves using very few nominal points.

Machine function is also controlled so that position and motion can be supplemented with other capabilities of the NC. For example, a metal-cutting machine requires cooling oil to reduce cutting-tool temperatures—NC instructions can be provided to control oil flow. An inspection machine may use three or four different measuring probes—NC instructions enable the machine to replace a probe at the appropriate time.

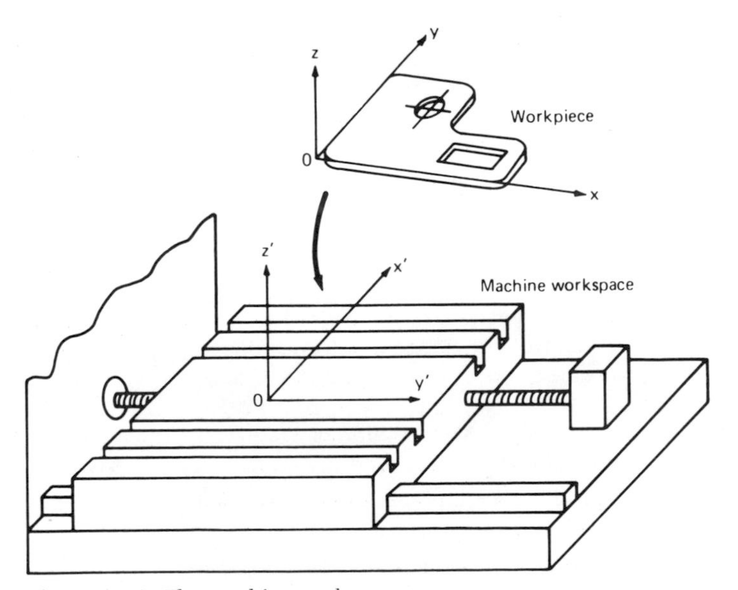

Figure 16.5 The machine workspace.

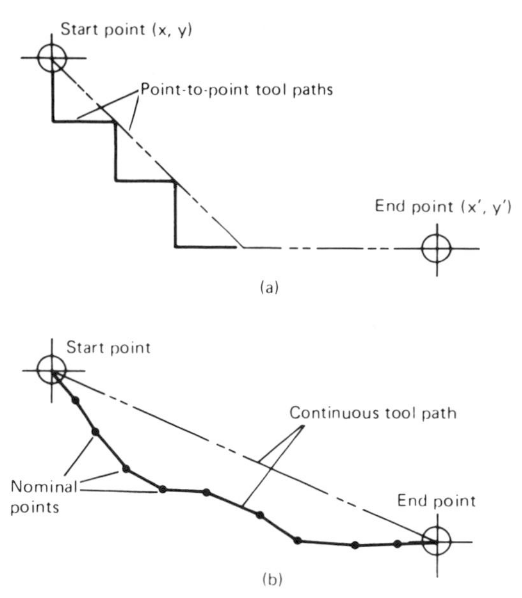

Figure 16.6 Tool motion. (*a*) Point-to-point motion; (*b*) continuous motion.

The control system functions described in this section rely on MCU hardware and software, machine feedback components, and the actuation elements that control the tool. In the next section, each of these system components is described.

16.2.2 NC System Components

In the early days of NC, all logic functions performed by the MCU were implemented with hard-wired circuits, relays, and other primitive (by today's standards) hardware. Modern NC makes use of microprocessors to control machine operations as well as perform internal coordination and monitoring. Hence, the modern MCU is a combination of hardware and software that effects all control system operations described in Sec. 16.2.1.

Prior to the early 1970s, all MCU functions—NC instruction format recognition, interpolation, axis control, function control, feedback reconciliation, and many more—were accomplished with analog and digital electronics that were designed explicitly for the NC and the machine it was to control. A modification of MCU function (or an optional feature) required that circuitry (usually a circuit board) would have to be replaced or added.

General-purpose microprocessors and associated software began to replace hard-wired controls and the CNC was introduced. With CNC, software took over many of the functions that were relegated to hardware in older NC systems. Options that were extremely costly in hard-wired systems were relatively easy to provide without additional cost in CNC systems. MCU hardware remains the same regardless of the machine that is being controlled. Modifications to MCU software (sometimes called the *executive program*) adapt the NC to different applications.

All NC systems delivered today are computer-based. In fact, the terms NC and CNC can be used synonymously. It should be noted, however, that the range of features can vary dramatically among the many MCUs on the market. Cost and performance are controlling parameters. The following features are available as part of many MCUs:

- ***Internal NC Program Storage.*** NC instructions are stored within the MCU and edited by the machine operator or via input provided by another computer.
- ***Improved Communications Capabilities.*** Computer-to-computer and network communications eliminate the need for punched or magnetic tape and provide control necessary for modern manufacturing architectures.

- ***Computational Capabilities.*** The MCU performs computations that the part programmer was required to perform on older systems, making part programs simpler to specify.
- ***Code and Units Flexibility.*** MCU software enables instructions to be provided in different formats (EIA and ASCII formats are common) and can convert between English and metric units.
- ***Adaptive Control Capability.*** The MCU can monitor conditions associated with the tool's environment and modify machine operations to optimize one or more preset production characteristics.
- ***Interpolation.*** Computer-based MCUs can apply software to accomplish linear, circular, parabolic, and/or cubic interpolation for continuous-path motion.
- ***Standard Operations.*** Computer-based MCUs perform all standard operations performed by hard-wired systems.

The MCU produces control information that is passed to the NC machine and receives feedback from the machine. All machines receive control information. However, some low-cost NC systems, called *open loop*, do not provide feedback.

Control information is received by actuation components that consist of three elements: the power amplifier, drive motor, and drive transmission devices. Input to actuation components is in the form of low-level signals that control power amplification equipment to produce sufficient energy conversion for drive components. NC systems use one or more of three basic actuation systems: electromechanical, hydraulic, and pneumatic.

Electromechanical actuation systems use electric motors to accomplish positioning and motion functions. Stepping motors—motors that convert a digital pulse (generated by the MCU) into a small-step rotation—are frequently used in applications where relatively low torque is required. Direct-current (dc) motors provide higher-torque output and are also common in electromechanical actuation systems. The electric motor drives a leadscrew, rack-and-pinion mechanism or gearing to accomplish motion transmission. Typical configurations are shown in Fig. 16.7.

Hydraulic and pneumatic actuation systems make use of a fluid (oil and air, respectively) as the power source. The hydraulic pump and the pneumatic compressor provide energy to valves that are controlled by MCU input. In most cases hydraulic or pneumatic cylinders are used to transmit the appropriate power to the machine.

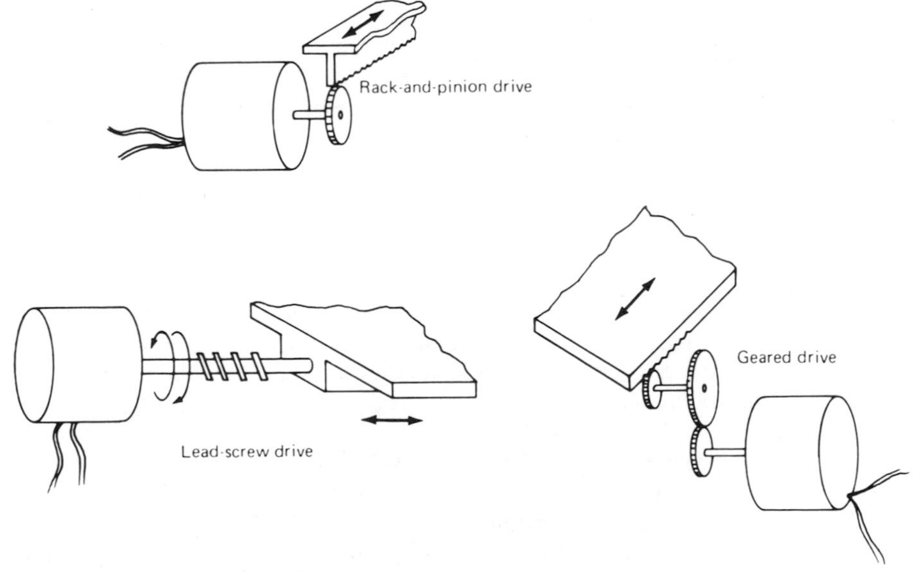

Figure 16.7 Motor drive configurations.

Hydraulic systems are used in applications where heavy loads and good response are required. Pneumatic systems require less maintenance than their hydraulic counterparts but offer poorer response and less power.

Feedback—position and motion information reported continuously to the MCU—is produced by transducers that monitor the machine. Three classes of transducers are used in NC systems: digital encoding devices, pulse summation devices, and analog devices.

Digital encoding devices (called *numerical encoders* or *pulse-generating encoders*) use a rotating disk or linear rule that is specially encoded to be read with photoelectric, magnetic, or electrical techniques. The encoded pattern provides position information that is transformed to feedback by the encoder. Pulse-summation devices count electric pulses generated by each angular or linear motion of the drive mechanism and transmit pulse count as feedback. Finally, analog devices, such as the linear voltage differential transducer (LVDT), translate linear displacement (or velocity/acceleration) into a voltage that must be converted to digital feedback for computer-based MCUs.

A schematic representation of NC system components is shown in Fig. 16.8. In the section that follows, the hardware and software elements of the MCU will be considered in greater detail.

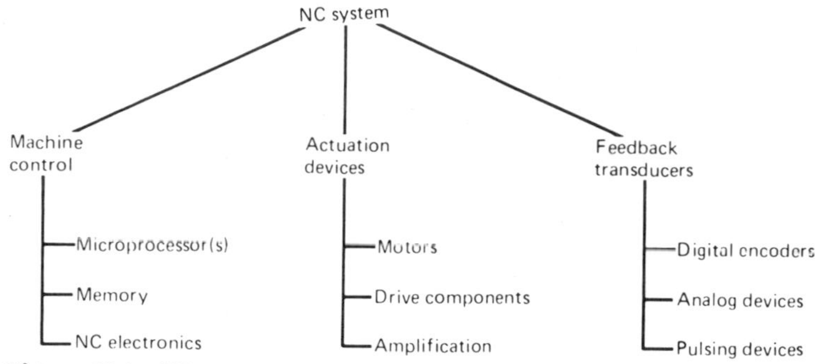

Figure 16.8 NC system components.

16.3 THE MCU

The MCU is the "brain" of an NC system. The functions that the MCU performs and its place within the NC system have already been discussed. In this section, the hardware and software subsystems that comprise the MCU are considered in more detail.

16.3.1 MCU Hardware

The term MCU can be interpreted broadly to encompass all electronics associated with the NC or, more narrowly, to encompass only those components that cause direct control of the machine servo system. We adopt the former interpretation because CNC systems (the most common NC sold today) perform a variety of functions including, but not limited to, control of the servo system.

There is no *typical* hardware architecture for CNC. Each NC manufacturer combines one or more microprocessors to accomplish the following functions:

- ***Overall System Control.*** Coordination of all data transmission and timing for other microprocessors within the system
- ***Input-Output Control.*** Processing of all input (NC instructions) and nonmachine control output such as cathode-ray tube (CRT) displays at the NC site and other operator interface data
- ***Servo Control.*** Processing of NC instructions that accomplish axis control and positioning
- ***Arithmetic Operations.*** Computation of all mathematical functions (e.g., interpolation and acceleration-deceleration calculations)

Each of the above functions may be accomplished with a separate microprocessor. In some cases, a single microprocessor accomplishes two or more of the functions. Figures 16.9 and 16.10 illustrate typical hardware configurations. Figure 16.9 illustrates a hardware hierarchy in which a main microprocessor controller coordinates other microprocessors in a treelike hierarchy. Note that four microprocessors are used to accomplish the functions noted in the list above. Figure 16.10 illustrates a hardware configuration that uses a number of communication pathways (called *buses*) to coordinate microprocessors. Again, multiple microprocessors accomplish functions such as axis control, input-output (I/O) processing, system control, and other functions.

As the CNC becomes more "intelligent," it can perform functions that were once performed away from the machine site on large mainframe computers. A few toggle switches and/or thumbwheels coupled with simple numerical readout were used for operator I/O on early NC units. Today, a front panel (Fig. 16.11) often couples a CRT with keyboard functions that enable comprehensive instruction editing and other sophisticated I/O. In the next section, the capabilities accomplished by NC software are discussed in detail.

16.3.2 MCU Software

If MCU microprocessor hardware is the brain of the NC, then MCU software is the "soul" of the system. Software must be developed to drive each microprocessor in the system and, in fact, actually performs the functions that are often attributed to the electronics. To illustrate the family of computer programs that can be used in modern CNC, we consider a description of software used to control the hardware architecture shown in Fig. 16.9.

Referring to Fig. 16.12, software (shown as labeled boxes) is partitioned among the four microprocessors according to the functional application of the microprocessor. Task-control software is driven by an external clock and monitors information from other microprocessor central processing units (CPUs). Task-control software reads machine status including servo-system feedback, data flow requirements, and task status (from other CPUs) and coordinates when other tasks begin execution, receive needed data, and communicate with one another.

Display processor software handles all I/O operations that occur via the CNC front panel. Program elements control CRT display, read keys as they are depressed, and invoke "macro operations" or "canned cycles" (e.g., a major function such as tracing a circular

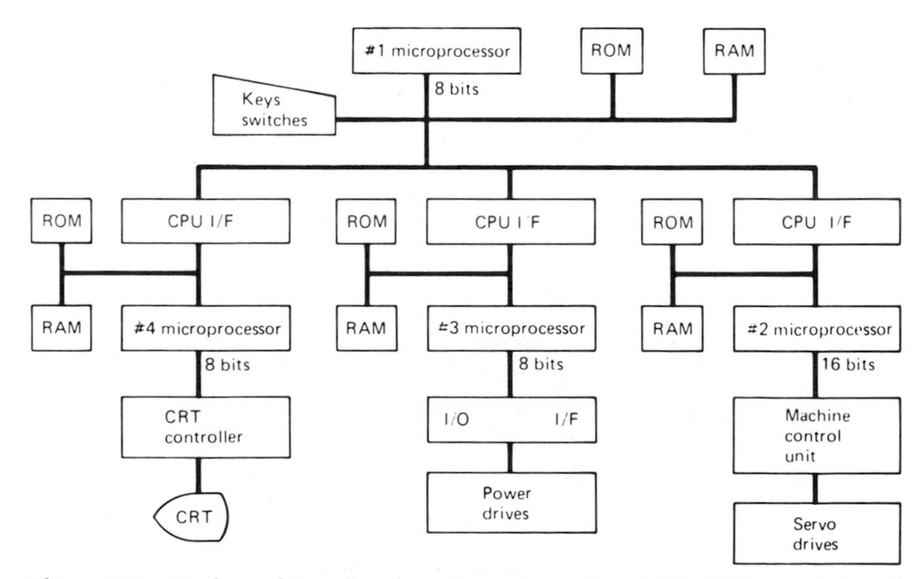

Figure 16.9 Hardware hierarchy of a microprocessor-based NC. (*With permission of Mitsubishi Electric Corp.*)

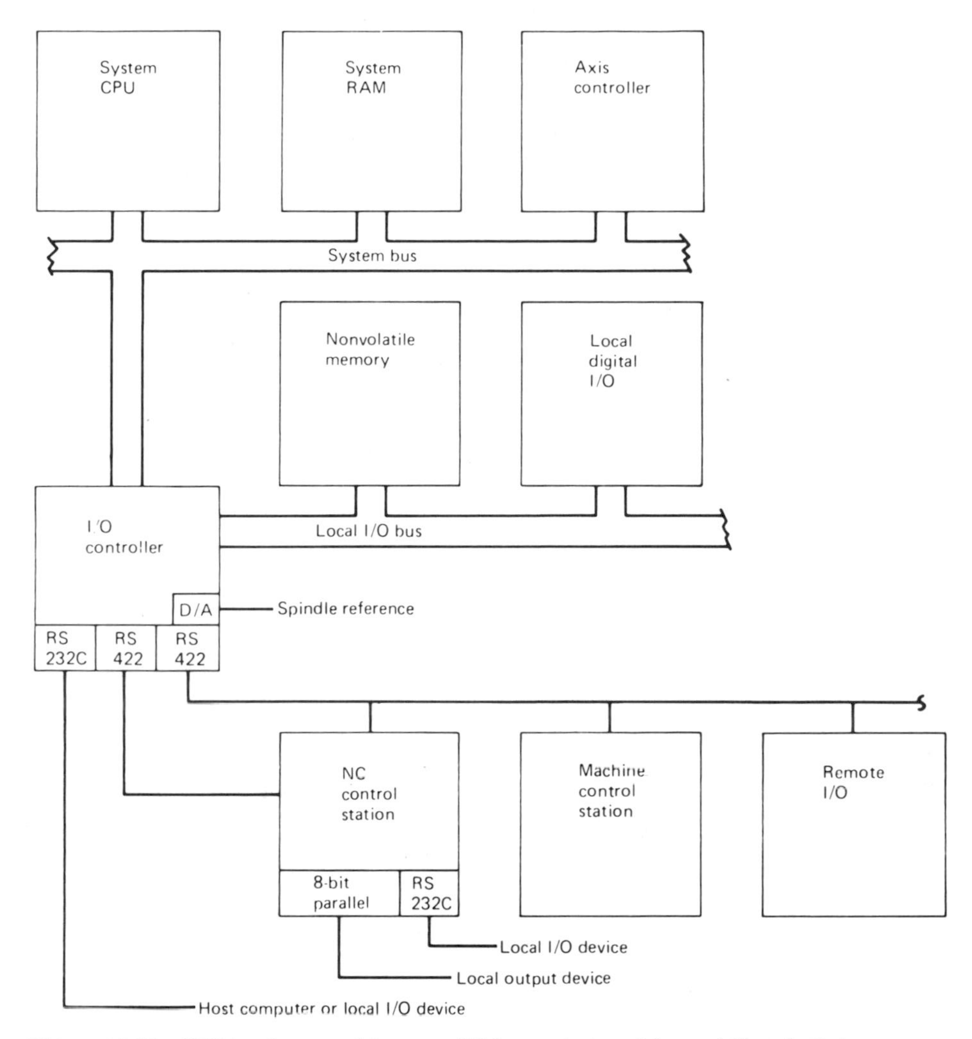

Figure 16.10 CNC hardware architecture. (*With permission of General Electric Co.*)

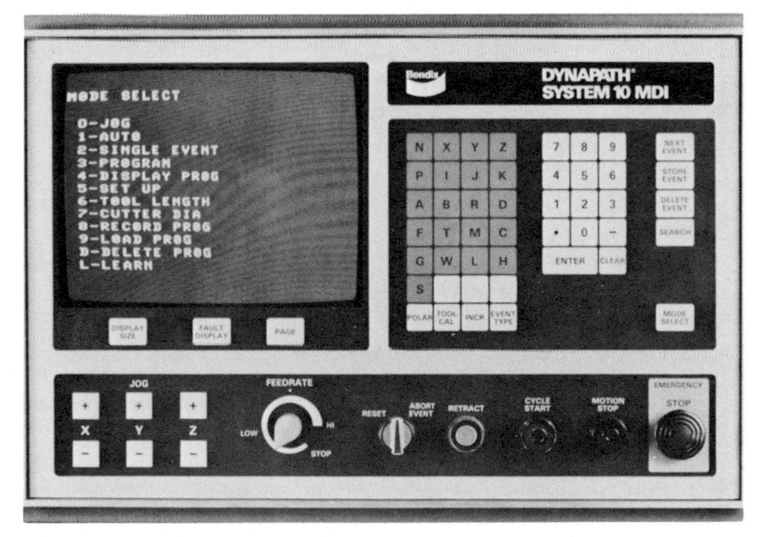

Figure 16.11 A CNC front panel. (*With permission of Bendix Industrial Controls Div.*)

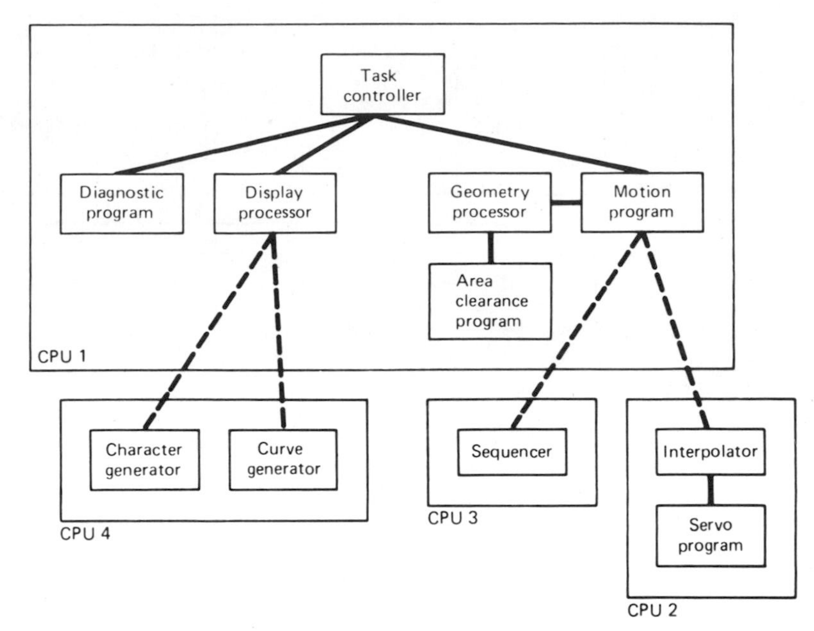

Figure 16.12 CNC software—a representative system. (*With permission of Mitsubishi Electric Corp.*)

path with a single instruction) that are implied by a key. In addition, display processor software enables the operator to edit NC instructions and (in sophisticated systems) create program files, machining data files for metal cutting, and tool files. The files comprise a database that is maintained within the CNC memory. Display processor software may also be coupled with general-purpose I/O software, enabling communication with other computers in the CAM architecture.

Display processor software invokes subprograms such as character generators and curve generators that create alphanumeric and machine-path representations on the CRT. For some advanced systems, CRT displays are generated in color.

The geometry processor performs all arithmetic and transformation tasks necessary to translate NC instructions into machine-level commands. Today, most CNCs receive an NC instruction file (see Sec. 16.4) from another computer or from punched tape. Because most geometric processing has already been done, the role of the geometric processor is confined to calculations that result from file editing or special operator requests. Current trends in CNC (see Sec. 16.5) may result in little more than the component design description being passed to the CNC. In such cases, most or all geometric computation will be performed locally by the geometric processor.

The geometry processor invokes area clearance and motion control subprograms that generate actual tool paths and servo-control motion, respectively. The use of area clearance and motion control is dependent on the level of processing required of the geometry processor.

The interpolator program performs linear (and, if required, higher-order) interpolation between supplied nominal points. Output from the interpolator is passed to a servo program that actually drives the actuators for the machine. A sequencer program is invoked to control communications with the servo system.

In addition to the major programs described above, many CNC systems incorporate applications software that provides canned cycle capability for specific NC applications. For example, a set of canned cycles for metal cutting may allow an NC operator to create an NC program via key strokes on the CNC front panel. Macros for machine motion, tooling, and many other machine functions can be accomplished with applications software.

The MCU incorporates sophisticated real-time capabilities that challenge even the most experienced software developers. For sophisticated CNC, MCU software can account for more than half of the development cost of a system and comprise 50,000 or more programming language source lines. Like other computer-based systems of the 1980s, the success of a CNC is based largely on the capabilities provided by the software that has been developed to control it.

16.4 NC PROGRAMMING

NC programming is a term that refers to methods for the generation of instructions that drive the NC. For two-dimensional components with little geometric complexity, NC instructions can be derived using little more than paper and pencil. However, as geometric complexity increases and three-dimensional NC becomes commonplace, more sophisticated techniques are required. In this section, the spectrum of methods for NC programming is examined.

16.4.1 The Changing Face of NC Programming

In the early days of NC, instructions that "programmed" the NC were generated manually. A part programmer would analyze a blueprint and translate physical coordinates, dimensions, and geometry into an appropriate tool path for the NC machine. As part geometries became more complex, manual methods were replaced by part programming languages—specialized computer languages that facilitated the description of a component geometry and assisted in the computation of tool path and position. Today, NC programming is coupled with CAD systems—enabling a predefined component already stored in the CAD database to be interactively translated into appropriate NC instructions.

There are four distinct techniques that are used to generate NC instructions:

1. Manual NC instruction definition
2. Computer-assisted NC part programming
3. Computer graphics–based systems tied to CAD
4. Solid modeling systems

Techniques 1 and 2, sometimes called *conventional* approaches to NC programming, continue to be the most widely used. However, computer graphics–based systems (technique 3) have gained widespread acceptance and will probably displace the conventional techniques by the early 1990s. Finally, solid modeling systems (technique 4) show enormous promise and have already been adopted for CAD/CAM applications in high-technology industries.

16.4.2 Conventional Approaches to NC Programming

In the early days of NC, the only method available for NC programming was the manual approach. Although it is still applied today, manual NC programming is reserved for relatively simple geometries and applications.

Manual part programming begins with careful study of the component design. The component geometry is discerned from design drawings, and after supplementary calculations are made, the NC tool path is described by offsetting the tool from the component. Each NC instruction is then defined using a code that takes the form

n g xyzab f s t m *eob*

where n = instruction sequence number
g = preparatory function
xyzab = coordinate and angular data
f = feed function

s = speed function
t = tool function
m = miscellaneous function
eob = end of block indicator

The code shown above, often called an *NC block*, is defined in a number of different formats and is then committed to punched tape using either EIA or ASCII codes (standard formats for NC instructions, see Bibliography). The g, f, s, t, and m codes refer to specific functions that control the operation of the NC machine or its environment.

Today, another form of "manual" programming is gaining acceptance. Using sophisticated CNC software, the NC operator can develop a set of NC instructions at the machine site. Basic tool motion commands are combined with canned cycles—predefined NC machine sequences such as drilling operations or pocket milling—and may be selected using the CNC front panel (Fig. 16.11). In some advanced CNC devices, the programmer can enter component geometry information via the front panel, examine the geometry on the front panel CRT, provide supplementary information about tool path, and cause the NC program to be generated automatically. There is no need for the programmer to generate NC blocks.

The second mode of conventional NC programming applies a specialized computer programming language. The language is coupled with software that enables complicated components to be accurately described for NC. In the section that follows, the computer-assisted part programming process is considered in detail.

16.4.3 NC Languages, Processors, and Postprocessors

Thousands of instructions (NC blocks) are often required to accomplish NC machining of complex, three-dimensional components. Without computer assistance in the generation of these NC instructions, it would be impractical, if not impossible, to produce many high-technology products. NC languages and the processors and postprocessors that translate languages into instructions were the first attempt at computer-aided NC part programming. Their use continues to be the most widely applied NC programming method.

For NC applications, a part programmer needs a language that allows:

- Geometry description based on the design drawing dimensions that describe a product
- Methods for the description of tool motion relative to the component geometry
- A means for the specification of machine-specific information (e.g., feeds and speeds for metal cutting)

In addition, an NC part programming language must have (1) the versatility to describe both simple two-dimensional components and sophisticated three-dimensional components, (2) built-in computational features that relieve the programmer from performing tedious and error-prone geometric calculations, (3) error-checking and diagnostic features that will uncover defects in the specification of part geometry and/or tool motion, (4) the ability to process NC programs for different NC controllers and machine tools, (5) output that can be represented in a verifiable form, and (6) accessibility via mainframe computers, minicomputers (and even personal computers), or timesharing networks. Each of these characteristics must be offered at a cost that can be justified by improved NC programming productivity.

Although many NC programming languages are used throughout the industry, two languages, APT and COMPACT II, are generally considered to be the most widely used. Both languages exhibit all of the features of NC programming languages described above. To illustrate the function and form of an NC programming language, we consider APT.

APT (automatically programmed tool) was developed in the late 1950s as a solution to the problems associated with manual NC programming. APT, like other part programming languages, has statements that support geometry description, tool motion, and other miscellaneous functions. APT statements are organized in the following manner:

major word/minor word(s), data, qualifiers, data

where major and minor words and qualifiers describe the statement type (geometry, motion, miscellaneous) and the operations to be performed.

The following excerpt from an APT program illustrates the general form of the language:

```
MACHIN/KTM01,1
FEDRAT/20.0
CUTTER/2
.
.
.
START = POINT/0,4,2
PT1 = POINT/0.25,1
PT2 = POINT/5.75,1
BASLIN = PT1,PT2
CIRC1 = CIRCLE/CENTER,(POINT/1.5,1.5),RADIUS,0.5
LIN1 = LINE/(POINT/1,1), LEFT,TANTO,CIRC1
.
.
.
PSIS/(PLANE/0,0,1,0),0.375
INDIRP/PT1
GO/PAST,BASLIN
TLRGT,GOLFT/BASLIN,PAST,LIN5
GOLFT/LIN5,ON,(LINE/5.5,0,5.5,9)
GOFWD/LIN4,TO,LIN3
.
.
.
STOP
```

The APT source code is divided into three segments separated by the vertical ellipses (. . .). The first set of APT statements describes the machine tool on which the NC program will operate and other characteristics about the machining operation. The second set of statements begins the description of the component geometry. In this case, the geometry is defined by a series of points, lines, and circles. Note that tangency (TANTO) and many other geometric relations can be specified among geometric elements. The third set of statements describes the tool motion relative to the geometric description. Hence,

GOLFT/LIN5,ON,(LINE/5.5,0,5.5,9)

defines motion moving left along line number 5 (defined as LIN5 in an APT statement not shown) and stopping ON (i.e., the center of the tool will stop on the line) the unnamed line defined within the GOLFT statement.

The APT language contains hundreds of major and minor words and requires formal training to be used properly. The language is described in American National Standards Institute (ANSI) standard number X3.37-1977, *APT Standard Programming Language*, and in manuals supplied by many computer and NC vendors.

Each statement in an APT program must be translated and analyzed by a special program called the *APT Processor*. The processor examines the syntax of each statement and then translates geometric and motion information into a generic NC tool path. That is, the processor produces tool-path information that is independent of a specific controller–machine tool combination.

The generic data (called the *CL data file*) is passed to a postprocessor that converts the generic information into specific NC blocks for a specified controller and machine tool. In general, one postprocessor exists for each NC or family of NCs. The overall flow of events and information associated with NC language processing is summarized in Fig. 16.13.

16.4.4 NC Instruction Generation via Interactive CAD/CAM

The technical characteristics of CAD systems (a topic treated extensively in other chapters of this handbook) provide for natural extensions for an interactive approach to NC part programming. All facets of a component design are created and stored as part of CAD system operation. Because the design exists in a database, it can be retrieved and processed for NC applications using additional software.

Two approaches for interactive NC programming are currently used. In the first approach, a turnkey CAD system is augmented with additional software. NC programming occurs directly at the CAD workstation. In the second approach, specialized NC workstations are used to retrieve design data from the CAD/CAM database. Regardless of the approach that is taken, the overall sequence of events for interactive NC programming follows the flow depicted in Fig. 16.14.

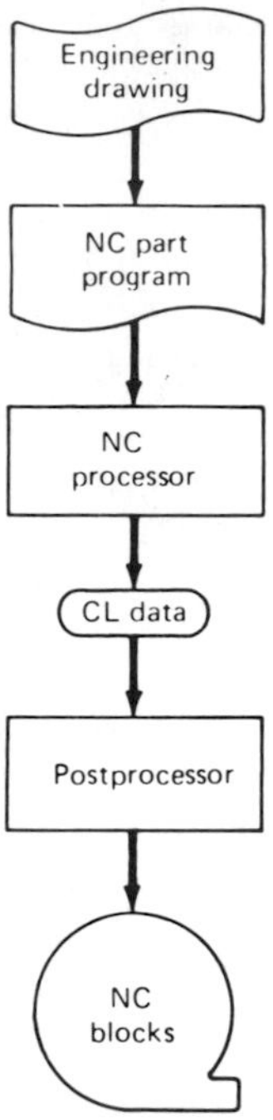

Referring to this figure, the CAD-NC workstation becomes the focal point for programming activities. From the workstation, a part programmer retrieves a component geometry from the CAD/CAM database and displays the geometry on a computer graphics display device. Using interaction devices (function keys, light pen, tablet, etc.), the

Figure 16.13 NC language processing—information flow.

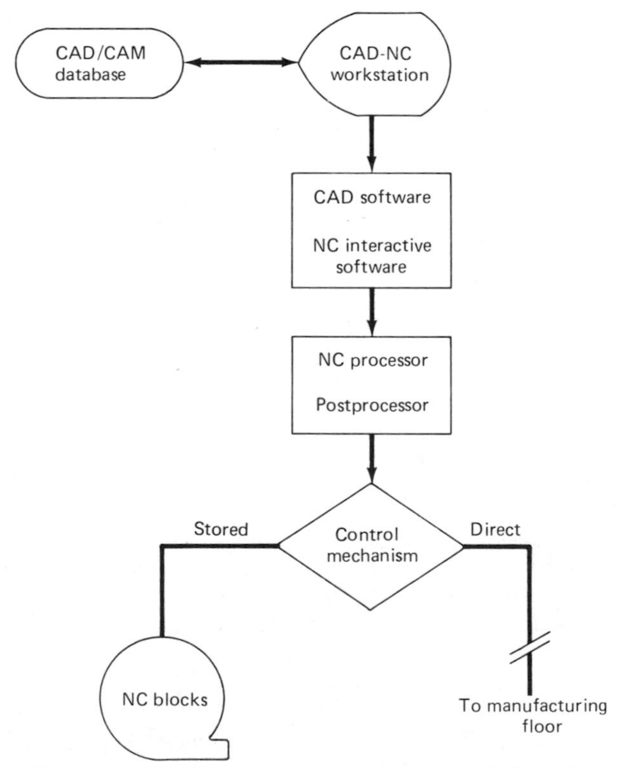

Figure 16.14 Interactive NC programming—information flow.

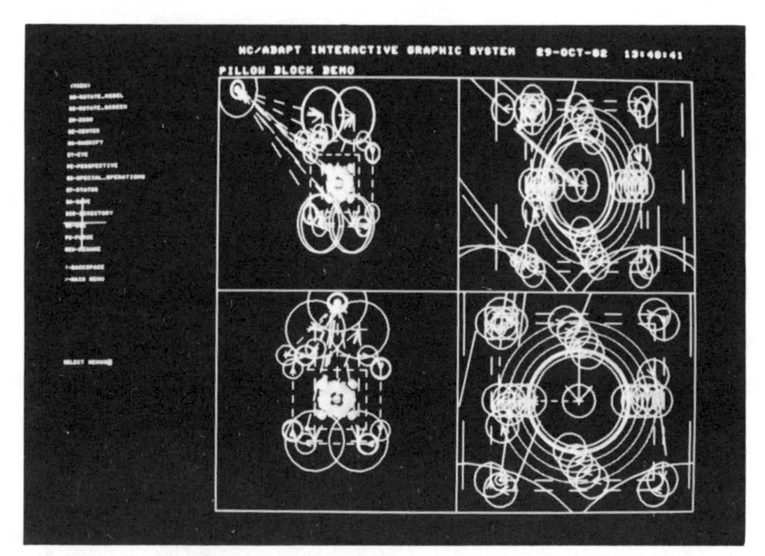

Figure 16.15 Interaction NC programming screen display. (*With permission of General Electric CAE International, Inc.*)

programmer describes geometry elements and the tool path pictorially on the screen (Fig. 16.15). NC software makes all calculations to define the tool path, and the path itself is displayed on the computer graphics screen. The programmer may view tool-path motion in different reference planes and replay the entire NC operation to determine correctness. No programming language statements are written by the programmer!

After the programmer validates tool motion and position by replaying the NC sequence, an NC program is generated (Fig. 16.16 illustrates a COMPACT II program generated automatically for the component shown). An NC processor and postprocessor are invoked to generate the actual instructions that drive the MCU. All NC information may be stored in the CAD/CAM database and associated with the design geometry and other component information.

Interactive NC programming using the approach described above can provide significant productivity improvement over language-oriented part programming. A productivity gain of 4:1 or better is not uncommon. In fact, an important part of CAD system justification may be reduced cost and improved turnaround associated with NC programming.

16.4.5 Geometric Modeling

Geometric modeling systems (described in Chap. 13) may someday replace conventional CAD as the method of choice for automatic NC programming. Modeling enables a designer to define a component using solid volumes rather than line drawings. Because manufacturing relies on the production and manipulation of solids, there is enormous potential for coupling NC and geometric modeling.

Currently, a number of commercially available geometric modeling systems can be interfaced with conventional CAD systems, thereby supporting both design and NC programming functions. A geometric model and the resultant design representation are shown in Fig. 16.17. The design representation can be processed as described in the preceding section. Ultimately, geometric modelers may produce NC programs directly from the solid model description of a component.

16.5 NC AND THE AUTOMATED FACTORY

In the preceding sections of this chapter, the nature of stand-alone NC systems has been described. As the factory of the future evolves, the expanding role of CAD/CAM will link NC with a wide variety of engineering and manufacturing information. Because CNC systems

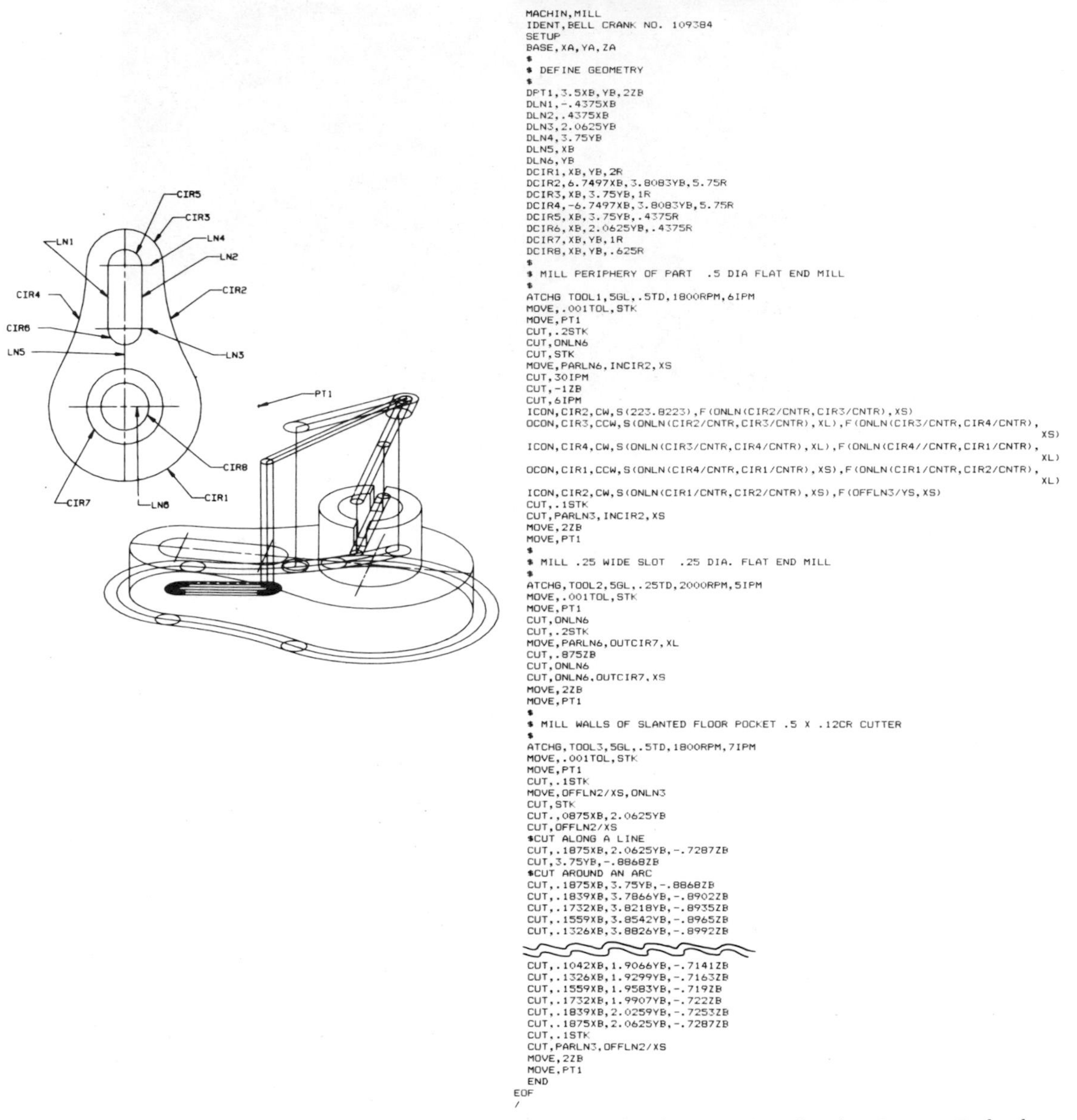

Figure 16.16 Automatic NC program generation. (*With permission of Gerber Systems Technology, Inc.*)

are computer-based, the MCU can become an intelligent node in a CAD/CAM network, accepting information from other nodes and producing information for transmission to other nodes.

16.5.1 Networks and DNC

A computer network is a set of computers and computer-based systems that are connected via communication links. For CAD/CAM, the network concept provides a means for interfacing many different devices and systems (each is called a *network node*) and for communicating the information produced by each node. Although many different

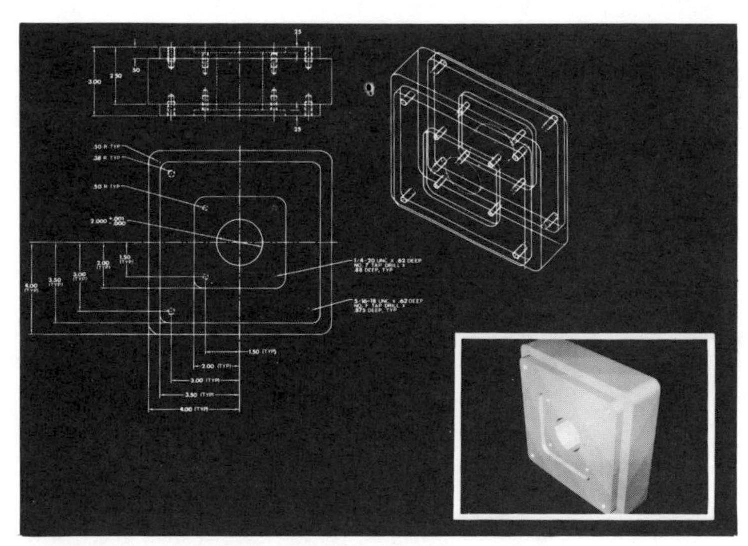

Figure 16.17 Geometric modeling and NC programming. (*With permission of General Electric CAE International, Inc.*)

network architectures exist, the four most common are illustrated in Fig. 16.18. Referring to Fig. 16.18, computer and computer-based devices (nodes) are represented by circles; communication lines among nodes are represented by lines. Each of the networks shown can be applied to CAD/CAM and may be used to implement factory automation.

The application of NC to computer networks was proposed in the mid-1970s and is called direct numerical control (DNC). In terms of today's technology, DNC implies that information (e.g., NC instructions) generated at one node of a network (usually a computer system) is passed via communication links to another node (usually a CNC system). In fact, the abbreviation DNC might be better defined as "distributed numerical control."

Referring to Fig. 16.18, DNC can be implemented using a star network in which all CNC systems are directly connected to a central host computer that maintains a database

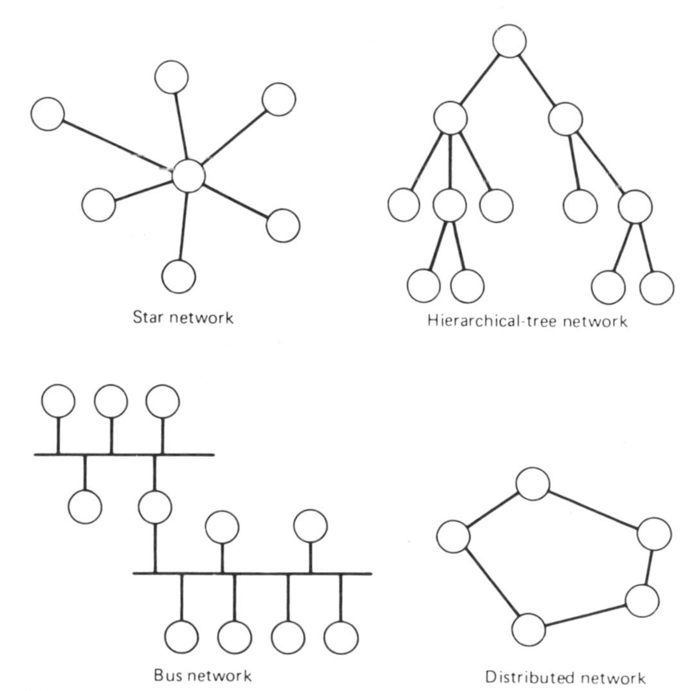

Figure 16.18 Computer networks used in CAD/CAM.

of NC instructions. DNC may also be implemented with a hierarchical-tree network in which satellite computers act as intermediaries between a central computer (the node at the top of the network) and CNC systems (the bottom nodes). Finally, CNC machines may be placed along bus networks and can, under certain circumstances, become a node on a distributed network.

In all applications of DNC, the network serves as a communication and control pathway. The factory production schedule is used to control the dissemination of NC instruction files to specific CNC machines (nodes). If the CNC is equipped with capabilities that enable it to transmit machine status back to control nodes, network communication can proceed in two directions.

Networks have far wider applications in CAD/CAM than NC alone. In the next section, the impact of networks on automated engineering and manufacturing (the automated factory) is examined.

16.5.2 Networks and CAD/CAM

In recent years, the local area network (LAN) has been proposed as a communication pathway that can connect disparate elements of the manufacturing architecture with information that is generated by CAD/CAM tools. The LAN is a bus network (Fig. 16.18) and is depicted in Fig. 16.19. Computers, CAD systems, and a variety of CAM systems (DNC, robots, assembly machines, etc,) may all be connected on the network.

The marriage of CAD and NC programming (described in Sec. 16.4) can be accomplished using the LAN. Advanced network-oriented workstations (Fig. 16.20) provide powerful local computing capability that can access design drawings and manufacturing and industrial engineering data, producing NC programs that can be transmitted through the LAN (Fig. 16.19) to the manufacturing floor. Workstations, such as the CADLINC system illustrated in Fig. 16.20, use advanced display and microprocessor technology to represent "pages" of information to the engineer or NC programmer. Each page contains different engineering information (e.g., a drawing, a bill of materials, or a process sheet) and all can be displayed simultaneously. Drawing upon this comprehensive information packet, the station operator can produce NC program files that feed DNC on the network.

The network arrangement depicted in Fig. 16.19 places NC on the same information

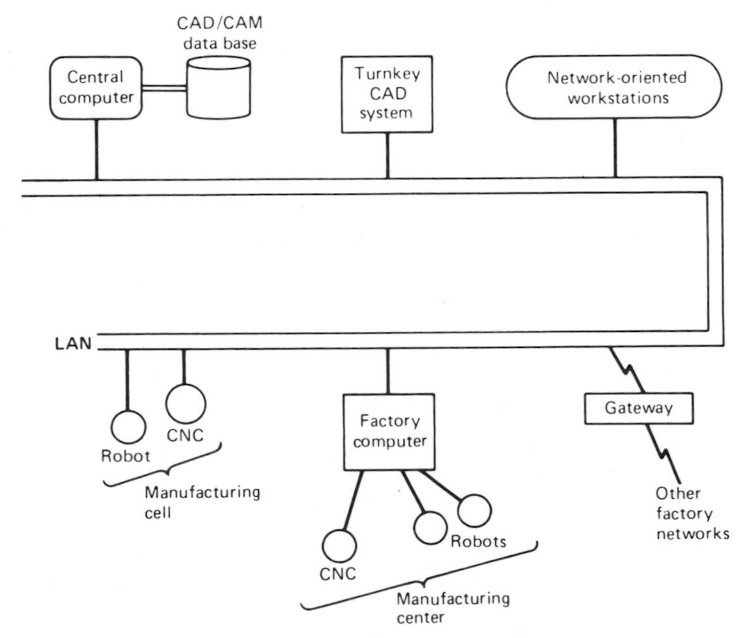

Figure 16.19 CAD/CAM—the local area network (LAN).

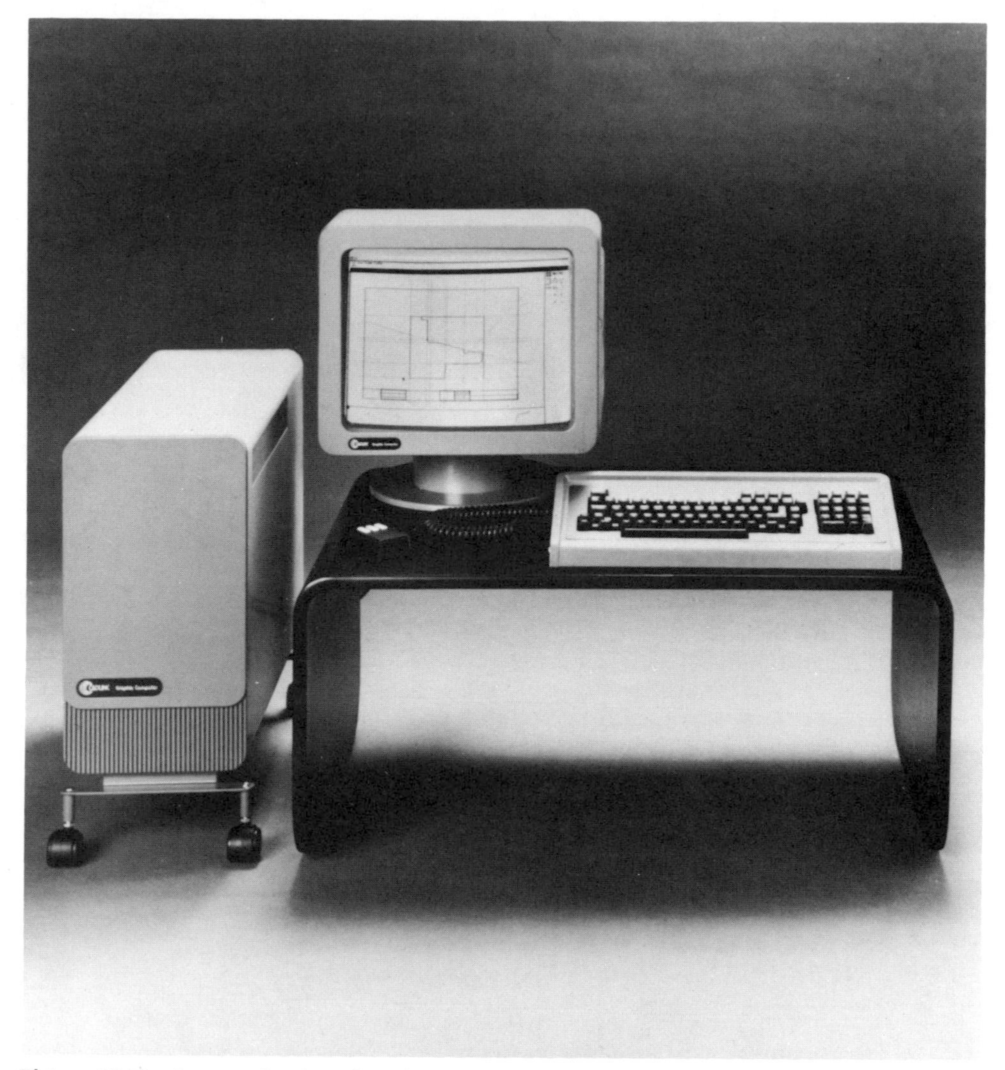

Figure 16.20 A network-oriented workstation. (*With permission of CADLINC, Inc.*)

bus (the LAN) as other components of CAD/CAM. Each of the levels of a manufacturing architecture (Sec. 16.1) can be accommodated on the network. Workstations and manufacturing cells can be coupled with a local computer to form a manufacturing center. Each manufacturing center is linked to the LAN, and in combination they form the automated factory.

16.5.3 Integration with Other CAD/CAM Elements

The CAD/CAM network described in the preceding section enables NC to be integrated with other physical levels of the manufacturing architecture. In addition, the network serves as a communication path so that other relevant manufacturing data can be used to plan and produce NC program files.

The concept of the manufacturing cell (introduced earlier in this chapter) combines NC machines with process equipment, robots, and other hardware. When a cell is used in stand-alone fashion, a local computer coordinates activities among cell components, but information to and from the cell does not move dynamically to other sources. When the cell becomes a node on a LAN, dynamic information transfer can be achieved and a higher level of automation results. In the future, it may be possible for computer-based elements of one manufacturing cell to produce information that is communicated to specific CNC machines in other cells. In this way, variations in manufacturing can be accommodated by information transfer along the CAD/CAM network and flexible manufacturing will become a reality.

The CAD/CAM network also provides the potential for associating manufacturing planning data and process data with NC. As an example, group technology (a method for parts classification using geometric and material properties) is considered. Parts classification information for a new component (derived from the CAD description) can be used to select existing NC program files (defined for similar components) from the CAD/CAM database. Using the NC workstation discussed in Sec. 16.5.2, the existing program could be modified for the specific attributes of the new component. Significant time savings can be achieved.

The network also connects NC, or an entire manufacturing cell, with the automated inspection facilities (and, possibly, NC inspection machines). Dimensional tolerances for each component are passed to the inspection facilities from the CAD/CAM database. If out-of-tolerance situations occur, the inspection facilities can communicate with NC machines, producing the part in question and automatic corrections can be implemented. This sophisticated feedback loop requires comprehensive software support and monitoring so that factory management can be appraised of changes to the manufacturing operation.

The network also enables NC machines to report status information back to a main computer. In the future, it may be possible to integrate these data with manufacturing requirements planning (MRP) systems and other process planning and control tools. In an ideal setting, the network, coupled with hardware and software tools, will provide a communication gateway that can (1) maximize both engineering and manufacturing output, (2) minimize actual manufacturing times, (3) improve the flexibility of the manufacturing process, and (4) maximize utilization of critical resources.

16.5.4 NC and CAM—Future Trends

The future of the automated factory and CAM is tied more closely to new methods for acquisition and use of manufacturing information than it is to specific hardware. However, NC will undoubtedly remain as a key element in the automated factory and will evolve from a stand-alone device to one component in an intelligent manufacturing cell.

Within the NC itself, system elements will evolve, but it is unlikely that revolutionary change will occur. The MCU will become increasingly dependent on the sophistication of software that accomplishes current and many new functions. In addition to basic machine control, the MCU may become an automatic NC programming device that maintains its own program libraries, communicates with other CAM system elements along a LAN, and coordinates other slave machines (e.g., robots) in a manufacturing cell. Finally, the MCU will take on additional diagnostic capabilities. That is, the NC will monitor itself and the machine, determining when maintenance is needed and reporting this information to other nodes of the CAD/CAM network.

The NC servo-system actuation and feedback elements will also evolve. Lower cost, smaller size, and increased energy efficiency are likely for all actuation components. High-resolution feedback systems will enable precision manufacturing at relatively low cost.

The CAD/CAM network (described in the preceding sections) provides a mechanism for accomplishing the kinds of information transfer that are necessary to achieve the automated factory. As powerful, low-cost computing expands the capabilities of CNC systems, NC machines will become more intelligent. In addition to servo-system control, CNC will provide record-keeping and reporting facilities, optimization analysis for manufacturing operations, coordination with robots and other manufacturing-cell elements, and general communication facilities for the CAD/CAM network. It should be noted, however, that the primary function of the NC system—programmable manufacturing through machine control—will remain unchanged.

CNC systems of the future will require less information from the part programmer. CNC software may ultimately encompass an expert system for the generation of NC program files. Such a system may operate in the following manner:

1. The CNC will be connected to a CAD/CAM network and will have access to design files created at CAD workstations; such design files will be passed directly to the CNC.
2. Special software that reflects the knowledge base of an NC programmer (an expert system) will analyze the design and other relevant manufacturing specifications and automatically create a production approach for the NC machine.
3. Other software will transform the production approach into a part program that will be translated directly into machine instructions by a processor that resides within the CNC; all calculations and processing are performed at the CNC site.
4. The program may be appended to the design file for repeated use.

Obviously, the scenario described above assumes advances in CAD design methods, online manufacturing data, and significant computer processing power within the CNC. Both hardware and, more important, software to achieve this superintelligent CNC will be available within the next decade.

As local computer power within the MCU makes additional computational and monitoring functions inexpensive, CNC systems may incorporate adaptive control (AC) features. AC—a concept introduced in the late 1960s but never widely adopted—incorporates feedback from the machine environment (e.g., the workpiece). AC uses this feedback along with conventional position and motion feedback to optimize the manufacturing operation. For example, a metal-cutting machine may sense tool temperature, vibration, and other environmental characteristics and automatically control feeds and speeds to minimize tool wear or maximize metal removal rate. AC has never been widely adopted because of high cost and insufficient optimization algorithms. Future CNC systems may make AC a low-cost option, enabling manufacturers to justify it for the first time.

Future CAM architectures will integrate NC data with other manufacturing information. The combination of NC data with group technology characteristics, process planning, manufacturing control systems (e.g., MRP), and the LAN will help to achieve the information technology that is essential for advanced factory automation.

16.6 SUMMARY

NC is the most mature element in the CAM architecture. NC has evolved from primitive hard-wired machine controllers to programmable microprocessor-based systems that perform machine control and many other functions. NC encompasses computer hardware, servo-system hardware, and a growing array of software that supports machine control and computation functions.

NC machines are driven by part programs that may be generated using programming languages of specialized options within CAD turnkey systems. The part programmer uses the language or a computer graphics terminal to describe the tool path that is translated into NC machine instructions. In addition, advanced NC programming workstations can access a wide array of design and manufacturing information.

NC is one element of CAD/CAM networks. The network is a communication pathway that couples engineering design data with manufacturing data and automated machines on the factory floor. The CAM architecture already incorporates NC as an element of the manufacturing cell and the manufacturing center, NC—the forerunner of a field we now call CAM—will remain a vital part of a technology that holds the best promise for improved industrial productivity.

BIBLIOGRAPHY

The following references provide the reader with further information on many NC-related topics. A comprehensive NC bibliography may be obtained from the *Numerical Control Society*, 520 Zenith Drive, Glenview, IL 60025, Industry standards on NC can be obtained from the *American National Standards Institute*, Inc., New York; the *National Standards Association*, Washington, D.C. and the *Electronic Industries Association*, Washington, D.C.

GENERAL REFERENCES

"The Automated Factory," special feature in *Mechanical Engineering*, February 1982, pp. 20–31.

CAD/CAM Alert, The Management Roundtable, Inc., Chestnut Hill, Mass., a newsletter published monthly.

CAD/CAM Digest, CAD/CAM Publications, Peterborough, England, published bimonthly.

Computer Aided Engineering—Systems and Software Annual, Penton/IPC, Inc., Cleveland, Ohio, published yearly.

Gunn, T. G.: *Computer Applications in Manufacturing*, Industrial Press, New York, 1981.

Kinnucan, P.: "Computer Aided Manufacturing Aims for Integration," *High Technology*, vol. 2, no. 3, 1982, pp. 49–56.

Lerner, E. J.: "Computer Aided Manufacturing," *Spectrum*, vol. 18, no. 11, 1981, pp. 34–39.

Lillehagen, F. M.: "CAD/CAM Workstations for Man-Model Communications," *Computer Graphics*, vol. 1, no. 3, 1981, pp. 17–28.

"Micros and Minis in CNC," *Machine Design*, vol. 54, no. 6, 1982, pp. 66–71.

Modern Machine Shop—NC/CAM Guidebook, Gardner Publications, Cincinnati, Ohio, published yearly.

Pressman, R. S., and J. E. Williams: *Numerical Control and Computer Aided Manufacturing*, John Wiley and Sons, Inc., New York, 1977.

TECHNICAL PAPERS AND ARTICLES

Bacheler, A. T.: "Using EIA Numerical Control Standards in Manufacturing Systems," *Proc. 25th IEEE Machine Tool Conf.*, October 1981, pp. 40–44.

Crossley, T. R., et al.: "Microprocessor-Based Direct Numerical Control Systems," *CIRP Annals*, vol. 28, no. 1, 1979, pp. 273–276.

Hammer, H.: "NC Programming Systems for Direct Machine Interconnection," *Engineer's Digest*, vol. 42, no. 2, 1981, pp. 17–20.

Levin, B. K., and V. A. Ratmirov: "The Principal Algorithms for NC Microprocessor Systems," *Machines & Tooling*, vol. 49, no. 9, 1978, pp. 6–8.

Li, D.: "A Microprocessor Based Numerical Control System," *Proc. IECI Annual Conf.*, 1981, pp. 154–158.

Okamoto, K., and M. Isomura: "Application of Microprogramming in Numerical Machine Controllers," *Euromicro Journal*, vol. 6, no. 5, 1980, pp. 288–295.

Oshima, Y.: "Recent Trends of Manufacturing Technology in Japan," *Automatica*, vol. 17, no. 3, 1981, pp. 421–440.

Rogers, D.: "Interactive Graphics and Numerical Control," *Computer Aided Design*, vol. 12, no. 5, 1980, pp. 253–261.

Teschler, L.: "Software vs. Hardware: Trade-offs for Machine Tool Electronics," *Machine Design*, vol. 52, no. 19, 1980, pp. 101–105.

Zwitter, T., and V. Hom: "Current Direction of Numerical Control," *Proc. 25th IEEE Machine Tool Conf.*, October 1981, pp. 2–6.

Process Planning and Group Technology

by
Alex Houtzeel

17.1 BACKGROUND

Beginning with the industrial revolution, a great deal of research and development has been devoted to the optimization of design and manufacturing in mass production. When production rates of hundreds of thousands or millions of units are involved, very small gains in efficiency can lead to significant production or cost savings. There have been many improvements in mass production technology over the years, and the twentieth century would have been a much different time without them.

Most manufacturing is not done with endless assembly lines or other mass technologies, however. Even in the United States, today approximately 75 percent of all manufacturing is carried out in smaller batches—in lots ranging in size from one or two to a few thousand. Until recently, very little has been done to improve batch manufacturing, despite its importance. The seemingly random nature of both design and manufacturing activities in the batch environment have made it difficult to even define approaches to their optimization. There were approaches to queuing and sequencing programs in batch manufacturing and to standardization of certain design and manufacturing activities, but these efforts have been somewhat limited and never had a great impact. A basic problem is that it is difficult to invest large sums for research and development into operations which may produce a few washers here, a few shafts there, a half-dozen gears, etc. It is one thing to shave a fraction of a penny from an item which is to be produced in the tens of millions; it is another to justify efforts to save pennies on the cost of producing an item made in a lot size of two or three.

The problem, of course, is that improvements made to batch manufacturing must be generic if they are to be cost-effective. They cannot focus on the production of specific products but rather must deal with principles which can be applied to all, or at least almost all, the items produced in a batch manufacturing environment. If the random nature of batch manufacturing is taken into account, one realizes that solving this problem has not been easy.

There have been scheduling programs, sequencing programs, and, more recently, material requirements planning systems which have been developed to help improve manufacturing productivity. All of these types of systems are ultimately geared to the production of parts to be finished at the right time for final assembly. While this is a worthwhile objective, it is often accomplished at the expense of other things.

Constantly meeting deadlines does not mean that assets such as people and machine tools are effectively utilized. In fact, such systems can increase production costs, because additional people and machines are required to fulfill their objectives. It is not difficult to do more with more, but it is not easy to do more with less, especially in batch manufacturing environments.

Since World War II, there has been an increased awareness of the problems of batch manufacturing. The general feeling, however, has been that more and more items would be made in mass production environments and that the importance of batch manufacturing would decrease. That has not been the case. We are now beginning to see that the trend is to smaller and smaller lot sizes, in mass production as well as in batch manufacturing. Government regulations, energy costs, the demand for more personalized products, marketing considerations, and other factors are resulting in smaller lot sizes, even of basically standard items. An automobile may be a mass-produced standard item, but when the purchaser specifies a certain type of stereo system, air conditioning, a special steering wheel, and other factory-installed options, the car is ultimately produced in a very small lot size. As specialized features become more integral to basic products, the trend will continue.

All of this could have a tremendous impact on future costs. An automobile manufacturer can produce a car at a cost of $2000 to $5000. The same car would cost a job shop $500,000 or $1,000,000 to manufacture. If more and more things move from mass production to small series production, the impact on the costs of consumer goods and inflation rates could be dramatic, not to speak of the need for more production personnel.

Skill levels are another factor. In mass production operations, the skill levels required for standardized jobs are relatively low. In batch manufacturing, however, much higher skills are required. With an increasing shortage of skilled machinists and others, this could be an important problem. Whatever the reasons, in recent years there has been a sharply increased recognition of the problems of batch manufacturing and an increase in efforts to help overcome them. Advances in computer technology have encouraged these efforts.

17.1.1 The Search for Similarities

It is apparent that when a company makes a particular series of a type of product, there are inevitably underlying similarities among at least some of the parts in production. For example, a company producing centrifugal pumps may manufacture many different types of such pumps. In doing so, however, it will make many similar impellers, housings, packings, etc. The same is true in the manufacture of airplanes, machine tools, and all other mechanical, electrical, or electronic products.

The fact that there are such similarities is obvious and has long been recognized. Until recently, however, it was difficult to take advantage of those similarities. A supervisor on the shop floor might organize the sequence of parts awaiting production on a given machine tool to help minimize the setup times required to produce those parts. There have been other types of informal attempts to organize parts by similarities. Very recently, flexible manufacturing systems have been developed based on part similarities. These systems tend to deal with larger lot sizes—less than mass production, but more than small batch quantities.

There have been other approaches to the utilization of underlying similarities in the batch manufacturing environment. In the manufacture of machine tools, for example, certain types of similarities are obvious. Lathes may be manufactured with different horsepower ratings, feeds and speeds, and sizes, but many spindles, gears, shafts, etc. are really very similar, even though the main frame may be different. These types of perceptions were the basis for work carried out in the forties and fifties. The basic principle was that if numerical values which reflected similarities could be assigned to parts, then it might be possible to take some advantage of these similarities. This was done through classification and coding systems, which were means to classify parts according to similarities, assigning code numbers which reflected those similarities. The code number could then be used as a tool to find classes of similar parts.

The initial applications for these concepts were in design retrieval. If a designer had a means of knowing whether or not the same or a similar part had been designed in the past, unnecessary designs and duplication could be avoided. In the fifties, a number of systems were developed to facilitate design retrieval. They became popular in Europe, especially in the United Kingdom, in the eastern bloc countries, and in the United States. Essentially, they were systems which permitted the designer to describe a part in numeric or alphanumeric values. When a new part entered into the design process, the designer could code it and, with the code designation, retrieve the same or similar drawings from a file cabinet (Fig. 17.1).

The early systems were manual. The designer had a handbook illustrating various design features and their associated code numbers. He or she would manually code the part using this code handbook as a reference. The drawings themselves were stored in manila envelopes or folders in file cabinets. While these systems were quite useful, they

Figure 17.1 Classification and coding and design retrieval.

had their limitations. For the most part, they were tied to the particular products of specific users. They were highly customized to meet individual needs.

A second problem was size. Retrieval with a code number is relatively easy when the filing cabinets contain a few thousand drawings. When the number of drawings gets into the hundreds of thousands, however, complications set in, both in the coding process and in the retrieval process.

Another significant problem grew out of the design application itself. Design features are not the only criteria for similarity. A group of parts may look somewhat the same (Fig. 17.2), but if part 2 is made of tungsten carbide, part 3 of stainless steel, and part 4 of cast iron or if lot sizes or other factors differ significantly, different manufacturing techniques will be required to produce each part. Therefore, although they may look the same, they are not the same from a manufacturing point of view.

At the same time, parts that look different may in fact be the same from a manufacturing point of view. Figure 17.3 illustrates a group of apparently dissimilar parts. However, all are castings and the only operation to be performed on each of them is a holing operation. From the manufacturing point of view, they are indeed similar.

17.1.2 Meeting Design and Manufacturing Needs

In the Federal Republic of Germany at the University of Aachen and elsewhere, the emphasis shifted from classification and coding for design retrieval purposes to the development of classification and coding systems which addressed similarities in manufacturing processes. This was a very important step, because it led to a realization that the grouping of manufacturing elements could lead to an inexpensive way of mass production, with groups of machine tools especially set up to manufacture families of similar parts. In other words, work cells of dedicated machine tools could be formed to produce families of parts with similar manufacturing requirements. This was the beginning of group technology for manufacturing (Fig. 17.4).

In addition to work in the Federal Republic of Germany, efforts were made in the United Kingdom, France, and the eastern European countries to optimize batch manufacturing using these group technology principles. The question was not only how to find parts with similar manufacturing requirements but also how to balance the manufacturing

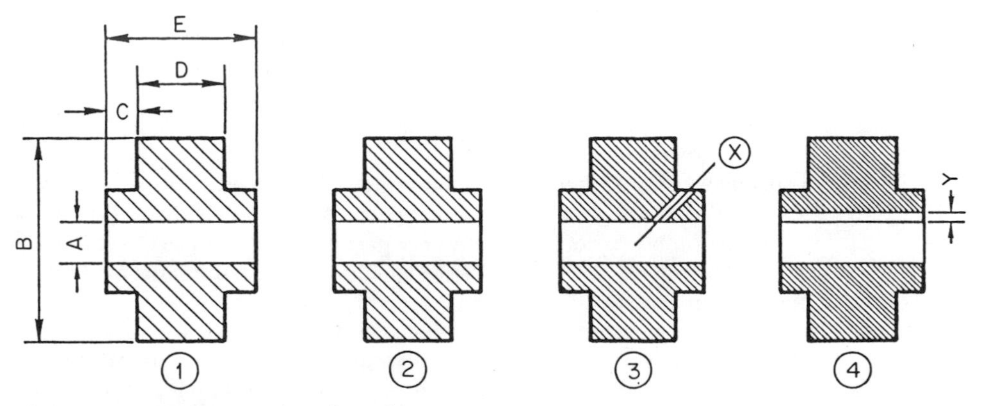

Figure 17.2 Similar parts based on shape.

Figure 17.3 Similar parts based on manufacturing process.

load requirements with available machine tools to make those parts. The work-cell concept could not be effective unless loads were balanced so that existing resources—both personnel and machine tools—were effectively utilized.

Experiments in work-cell implementation were successful primarily in small European companies, where load balancing and grouping could be done manually. In the United States, where batch manufacturing was often on a much larger scale, the approach was not very successful.

A major breakthrough occurred in the late 1960s in The Netherlands. The first classification and coding system which served both design and manufacturing needs was developed, and the system was implemented on a computer rather than operated manually. New computers which could interface with users interactively rather than working in batches helped to make this possible. It marked the beginning of the relationship of the computer to classification and coding and was a major step forward in the development and use of computer-aided manufacturing (CAM) software. This was also the first use of classification and coding as a tool to interface with a computer design and manufacturing information database (Fig. 17.5).

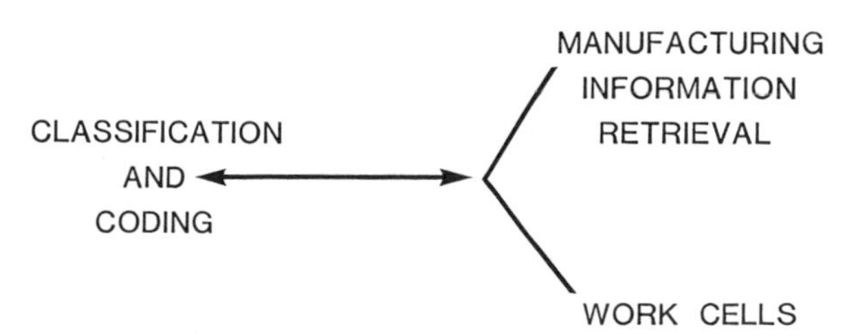

Figure 17.4 Classification and coding and manufacturing information retrieval and work cells.

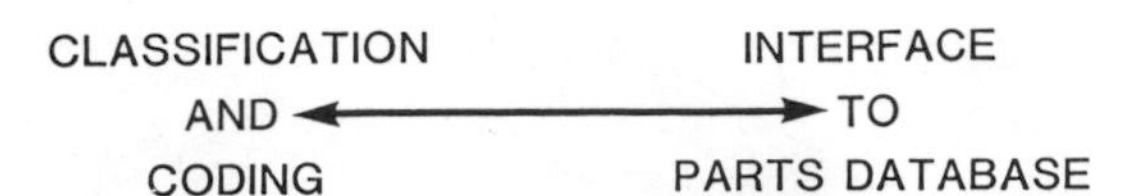

Figure 17.5 Classification and coding and interface to parts database.

17.2 CLASSIFICATION AND CODING

With its application to both design and manufacturing, classification and coding came of age. It had evolved from a means of manually indexing drawings for retrieval purposes to a compact vocabulary for the storage, recall, and use of large amounts of design and manufacturing information. With the developments in The Netherlands, classification and coding embraced designs, manufacturing information, cost data, and much more.

In classification and coding, code numbers are used to identify parts by specific characteristics. In doing so, they make it possible to classify parts—group them according to their characteristics. In a sense, this is a sifting of all of a company's products and detailed parts by similarities. It is a major step in the translation of the seemingly random nature of batch manufacturing operations into a rational order.

When handled manually, the length of a code number was significant. The longer the number, the more tedious the coding process and the larger the chance for error in the transference of a code number from one piece of paper to another. With the computerization of classification and coding, code length was no longer as critical. Thus the earliest truly comprehensive classification and coding system for design and manufacturing application was a matrix of 300 positions—a "sieve" with 300 holes (Fig. 17.6). Within this system, a code number could be as long as 30 digits, and each digit had a possible value ranging from 0 to 9. This meant that 30 different parameters could be coded, each with as many as 10 different attributes.

The growth in code length somewhat paralleled the evolution of computer technology. The computer not only was able to handle the lengthier codes with ease but also made it much easier to assign them to parts. In the interactive mode, the computer would ask a

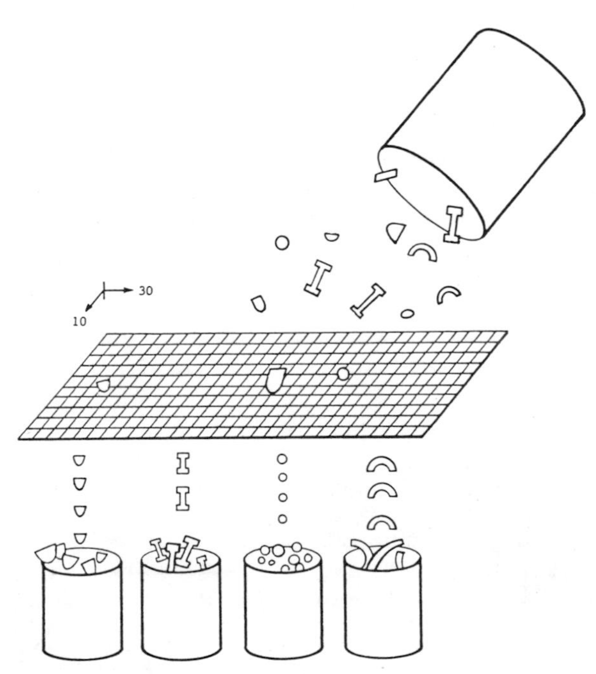

Figure 17.6 The "sieve." A classification and coding system can be compared to a sieve which sorts parts by specific attributes. The system works like a sieve with 300 holes.

series of questions requiring yes, no, or numerical answers and would then generate the code number. As the process became easier, different departments became interested in using classification and coding. What began with design and then spread to manufacturing now began to find applications in quality control, testing, purchasing, and other areas. The code length grew from the original 7 or 8 digits used for drawing retrieval in customized systems to more generalized codes of 18 to 25 or more digits.

17.2.1 What Do You Code?

In the development of a classification and coding system, the most basic question is "What should I code?". Different departments require different types of information (see Table 17.1). For example, the purchasing department is interested in information about the type of material, its rough shape, its dimensions, and, of course, the batch size. The design office, on the other hand, deals with such things as main shape, shape elements, and dimensions. Batch size is much less important. Process planners need still more information. It is very easy when developing a multiple-purpose system to attempt to capture so much information that the entire system becomes cumbersome and unworkable. The key is to be able to define the information that is really needed.

Table 17.1 Part Attribute Information Required by Various Departments in a Company

	Department			
Data	Purchasing department	Design office	Work preparation	Manufacturing planning and scheduling
Main shape	—	X	X	X
Shape elements	—	X	X	X
Type of material	X	X	X	X
Rough shape	X	—	X	X
Dimensions	X	X	X	X
Dimensional accuracy	—	—	X	X
Batch size	X	—	X	X
Production time	—	—	—	X
Processing sequence	—	—	X	X

An important issue in the development of this definition is the number of different shapes and manufacturing methods which the system will have to embrace. There are some basic principles involved, which most people have difficulty in accepting at first. The experience of a centrifugal pump manufacturer is illustrated in Figs. 17.7 and 17.8. The company had between 65,000 and 75,000 part numbers and produced parts in batches

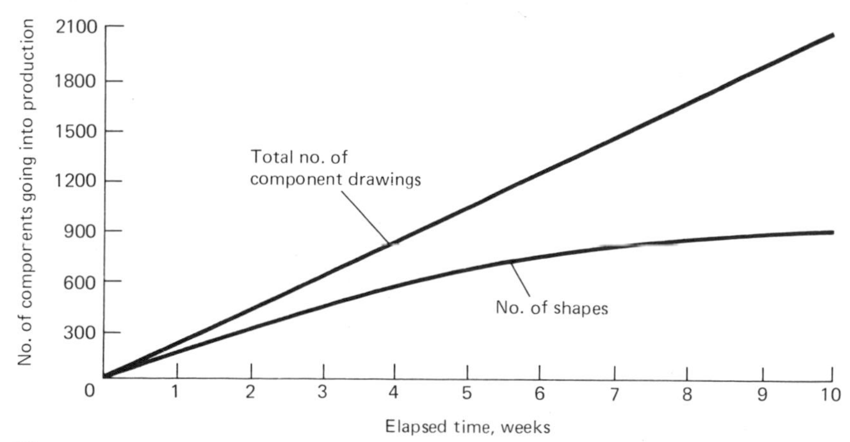

Figure 17.7 New component shapes for manufacture.

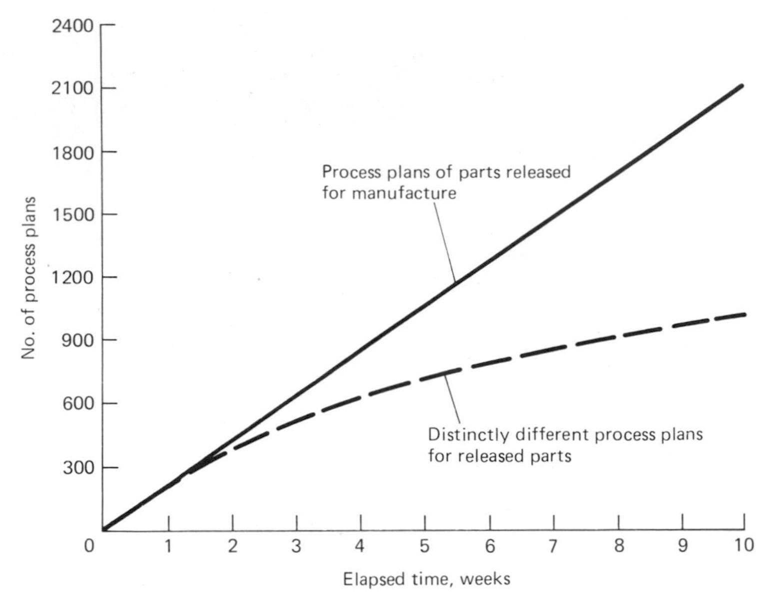

Figure 17.8 New process plans for manufacture.

ranging in size form 1 to 50. Management's assumption was that everything was different and that all parts would need to be included in the classification and coding database in order for the system to be truly effective. A random sample of parts going into production was coded—roughly 200 parts a week for a period of 10 weeks. At the end of the 10-week period, 2100 parts had been coded. As Fig. 17.7 indicates, the number of different shapes leveled off at 900. All others entering into production were essentially of the same shape. In other words, instead of 65,000 to 75,000 different shapes, the company actually had 900.

As illustrated in Fig. 17.8, the same type of phenomenon occurred with respect to new process plans. The number of distinctly different process plans leveled off at around 1200. All of the other process plans created by the company were essentially reinventions of the wheel.

One may argue that all centrifugal pumps are essentially the same and that the results cited above are not surprising. Since then, however, the author has observed the same type of experience at nearly 100 other installations. Within 10 to 20 weeks of the beginning of the coding of representative samples of parts going into production, the curves for both the number of distinctly different shapes and the number of distinctly different process plans will flatten out. Even in the very largest of organizations, the total number rarely, if ever, exceeds 4000 to 6000 different shapes or process plans. Thus, a company may have 500,000 part numbers or process plans but no more than approximately 6000 of them will be different. Invariably, company personnel will argue that these principles do not apply in their organization. An actual test, as indicated above, will always demonstrate otherwise.

There is still further argument, however. "What happens next year, when we change models?" Unless a company drastically changes its business, from machine tools to airplanes, for example, the mix of parts will stay about the same. Washers, gears, spindles, and other components that are basic to large classes of products do not change easily.

Thus the size of the classified universe for many companies can be defined by looking at all the produced parts over a period of about 10 to 20 weeks. In that time, it is possible to identify all of the design and manufacturing attributes of importance. This assumes, of course, that one has started with a coding system which is capable of capturing these different attributes. Assuming that this is the case and that roughly 10 to 20 weeks of production has been classified and coded, it is possible to analyze the coded data to begin the development of relevant design and manufacturing families of parts for standardization and retrieval purposes. The results can be impressive, even in the early stages of implementation.

17.2.2 System Criteria

A classification and coding system is a tool to capture relevant design, manufacturing, and other features of parts. It is also a tool to analyze and retrieve parts by design and manufacturing features, and it is a communication tool with an information database which can ultimately be used to link different computer-aided design and computer-aided manufacturing (CAD/CAM) systems.

A basic issue in the creation of a coding system is its form—should it be numeric, alphabetic, or alphanumeric? In the development of such things as postal zip codes, telephone numbers, and other coding systems, a great deal of research has been conducted into the effectiveness of various ways of creating a code number. It has been found, for example, that blocks of no more than four digits are most effective for lengthier codes. It has also been found that numeric rather than alphanumeric systems are least prone to errors. With each digit being decimal-based (10 possible values), the numbers are easy to understand and work with. There appears to be no doubt that the best type of code designator is a series of decimally based numeric values expressed in blocks of four digits.

What should one look for in a classification and coding system? What characteristics correlate with ultimate effectiveness? A very basic requirement is that the system be product-independent. If it is customized to specific products, it will not last. The day that a somewhat different product is developed, the system will fall apart if it is too product-dependent. A product-independent system will meet all needs for now *and* the future. It is also essential that the system be capable of classifying all parts. While its application may begin with machined parts or some other specific type of product (such as purchased parts or assemblies), it should ultimately be capable of handling assemblies and subassemblies, tools, purchased parts—any and all components which may at some time enter into the manufacturing stream.

Reliability is yet another essential component. There should be checks within the system to help assure accuracy and to minimize coding errors. One of the functions a classification and coding system serves is to capture experience so that it is not lost when personnel leave or retire. Reliability is essential to the retention of this experience.

The system should also be extendable. As indicated above, its first applications may only account for a small portion of its ultimate uses. It should be capable of ultimately capturing quality control information, for example, or testing data. In line with this, it should be conceived with the current and future needs of all departments in mind. In order for different departments of a company to get the information they require, the code should capture information about manufacturing operations as well as about shape and other part attributes.

Potential interfaces with other types of systems must also be considered. For example, when part families are established, it should be possible to create a master numerical control (NC) tape for a family. Such a tape would require only changes in dimensions when used to manufacture parts within the family and would consequently save considerable time in NC tape preparation costs. The capability of interfacing with computer graphics is another important feature. The system should allow graphic systems to access information about design, NC requirements, manufacturing requirements, etc.

In terms of these applications and others, the classification and coding system should not create a duplicate database. The classification and coding system should interface with existing parts information databases or provide the framework for a new comprehensive database if none exists.

17.2.3 Computerization

As indicated previously, classification and coding systems were initially manual. The design engineer compared the sketch of a new part to drawings of part features contained in a handbook, derived a code number, and then searched for a similar drawing in a file cabinet.

Although classification and coding were first linked to a computer in The Netherlands, with the advent of convenient interactive modes of computer accessibility, its real growth and the evolution of computerized classification and coding took place in the United States as the computer found its way into the manufacturing environment.

Manufacturing companies first began to use computers as accounting tools. In the early seventies, when interactive capabilities were still relatively primitive, design and manufacturing engineers had low priorities in the allocation of computer time. The introduction of the minicomputer was an important turning point. The minicomputer freed design and manufacturing engineers from the need to access corporate mainframe computers. Its evolution coincided with the development of increasingly sophisticated interactive capabilities.

The introduction of computer graphics systems in the seventies also helped to stimulate the use of computers in the design environment. By the end of the 1970s, minicomputers were no longer unusual in design or manufacturing offices. Computerization greatly enhanced the effectiveness and efficiency of classification and coding systems. It not only significantly reduced error rates, particularly when coding was done in different locations, but also greatly speeded the retrieval of design and manufacturing information.

A modern minicomputer takes the user through a decision-tree process, asking questions appropriate to the identification of relevant part features and manufacturing requirements. The computer can do this very well and then can integrate the results with applications such as computer graphics, NC tape generation, and computer-assisted process planning.

17.2.4 Code Structures

There are two basic types of code structures: hierarchical, or monocode, and attribute, or polycode. In a hierarchical code, each position relates to the previous position. Thus if the first digit defines a main shape, such as rotational, the second digit will define a feature related to a rotational part, and the next digit will define a feature related to the feature defined in the second digit. This is the basic philosophy of a hierarchical code such as the Dewey decimal system, which is used in libraries.

Figure 17.9 illustrates a typical hierarchical code structure. As the diagram illustrates,

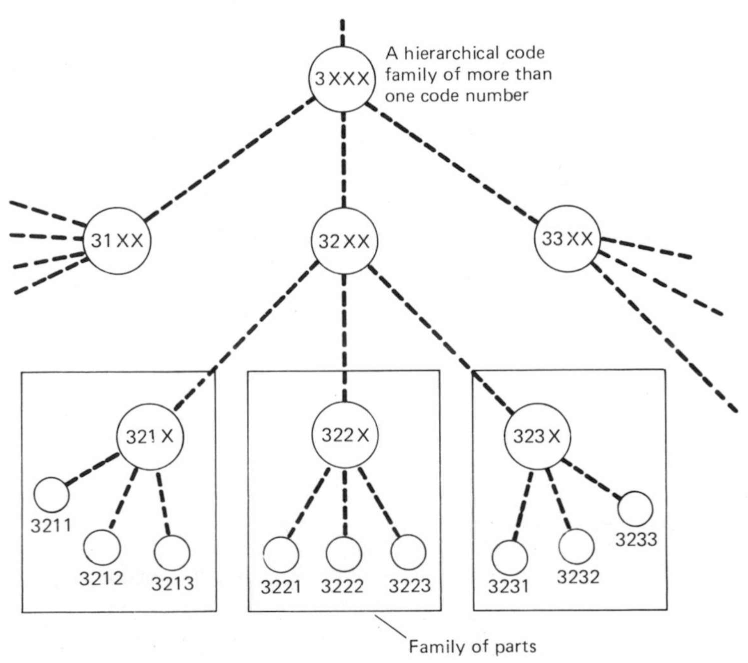

Figure 17.9 The structure of a classification and coding system based on hierarchical principles.

each digit is directly related to the previous digit. Thus the first digit, 3, may define a rotational part. The digit in the second position may then define the size of the outer diameter of that rotational part. Thus a 1 in the second position may refer to a size of ½ inch or less, a 2 may refer to a size of ½ to 1 inch, etc. In the third position, if a 1 is preceded by 2, then a 3 may define an inside diameter of a particular dimension; or if a 1 is preceded by 1, then a 3 might have a totally different meaning.

As the process continues, parts may be grouped into families with increasingly specific feature definitions. Each digit fine tunes the information contained in the previous digits. The meaning of any number in any position (a 2 in position 3, for example) will rarely, if ever, be the same.

Hierarchical codes are compact—it is possible to include a great deal of information in a few digits because each digit is an exponent of the preceding digit. The hierarchical approach is very useful in highly customized applications for retrieval only. It also works well in a manual system.

While a hierarchical code is good for design retrieval, it is not useful for much else. Because the same digit in the same position may have different meanings at different times depending on the preceding digit, hierarchical codes do not lend themselves to computerization or to easy analysis. Their usefulness is thus limited when analysis and comparisons of data are desired.

Attribute or polycodes are based on the total population of different attributes. A typical attribute code structure is illustrated in Fig. 17.10. As the figure illustrates, each digit and each position (value) of each digit has a specific meaning. Thus, for example, the first digit would always describe external shape, the second internal shape, the third the number of holes, the fourth the type of hole, etc. A complete code number would identify all of the part's major attributes. As a result, the meanings of digit values for any given part would be consistent in the system.

Digit	Class of feature	Possible values of digits							
		1	2	3	4	5	6	7	8
1	External shape	Shape$_1$	Shape$_2$	Shape$_3$	—	—	—	—	—
2	Internal shape	None	Shape$_1$	—	—	—	—	—	
3	# holes	0	1-2	3-5	5-8				
4	Type holes	Axial	Cross	Axial and cross					
5	Flats	None	Internal	External	Both				
6	Gear teeth	Spur	Helical	None					
7	Splines								

Figure 17.10 Attribute code structure.

This opens the door to detailed computer analysis and the definition of the specific operations required to make all the parts in a specific group. If, based on the Fig. 17.10, the user needs to know how many parts require cross holing, for example, all the computer needs to do is to check on the number of times the value 2 appears in the fourth position. The same is true of much more complex comparisons.

The problem, of course, is that there are a great many possible attributes in the total universe of parts, and so a purely attribute code number would have to be very long to accommodate all of the possibilities. The solution to this problem is a hybrid structure—a combination of a hierarchical code and an attribute code structure. The first digit in such a structure could refer to the main shape configuration (Fig. 17.11). An attribute matrix is then tied to each main shape. Since attributes are different for different types of parts (e.g., sheet metal or turned parts), computer analysis is still possible. The hybrid code offers the benefits of attribute coding but in a much more compact form. Most contemporary classification systems are based on the hybrid approach.

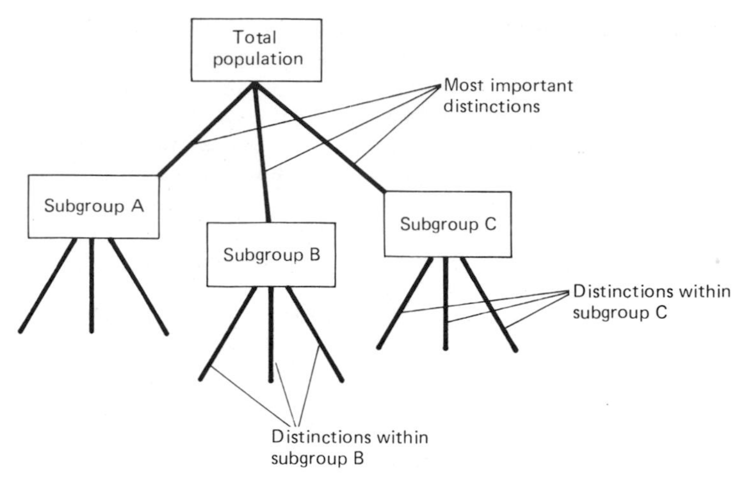

Figure 17.11 Hybrid code.

17.2.5 Attributes

Experience has demonstrated that there are certain attributes which need to be coded in order to accomplish the design and manufacturing objectives of a classification and coding system. Some of these are universal—they seem to apply to every company in every industry; others are more industry- or company-dependent. The universal elements include:

- ***Main Shape.*** Rotational, box form, sheet
- ***Shape Elements on the Main Shape.*** Cones, holes, slots
- ***Element Position.*** Where are these shape elements?
- ***Dimensions.*** A main dimension, an auxiliary dimension, and the ratio of dimensions
- ***Accuracy.*** How critical are the tolerances?
- ***Material***

Beyond that, there are a number of pieces of information which are more industry-, factory-, or operation-dependent. These include such things as lot size, piece time, setup time, the relationship between necessary operations, and other specific factory information (relating to such things as testing, assembly, and quality control).

17.2.6 Developing Your Own System

In the preceding paragraphs, we have discussed the types of attributes to be captured in a classification and coding system. Many companies have chosen to develop their own classification and coding system rather than purchase one from a vendor of such systems. The results have ranged from moderate success to absolute disaster. It is a process which can be described in relatively simple terms but which is much more complex in actual operation. To begin, one must consider that there are parts which are designed and manufactured in-house, others which are designed in-house and manufactured elsewhere, and still others which are purchased. Ultimately, the system should accommodate all of these parts.

The first step in the development of the classification and coding system in-house is to sample the existing parts database. The size of the sample will vary with the size of the total base, of course. It may be 20 to 25 percent of a small database of perhaps 2000 active parts and considerably less for much larger active part files. Generally speaking, the sample might range from 1000 to 6000 parts.

The next step is to assemble the sample drawings into families. This, to say the least, is not easy. It requires a good-size room, tables on which to stack drawings, sharp eyes, and a great deal of design and manufacturing experience.

Basically, one should look for classification "buckets" defined by different features. Industry standards may be a useful guide for the definition of these features. The characteristics which are cited in industry standards or specifications are worth considering. One must identify the frequency of occurrence of the chosen features in the drawings contained in the selected sample, work out a rational hierarchy of these features based on the sample, link them to the machine tool capabilities of the company in question, evaluate the results, and then continue.

It is a continuing process of examination, analysis, review, adjustment, reassembly, and reanalysis. It is a very elaborate activity which requires many labor-years of hard effort. In some companies, the work started with perfectly cylindrical parts and initial results came quickly. Unfortunately, as these companies discovered, perfectly cylindrical parts do not reflect the complexity of the total task. Thus, projects which started off with high optimism ended in disappointment.

It is possible to develop successful classification and coding systems in-house, and it has been done. For most companies, however, it is not really cost-effective, and the usefulness of such systems has been limited.

17.3 MANUFACTURING APPLICATIONS

Up to now, we have looked at the need to find similarities and how to classify them, and at the nature of code designations. We have also briefly mentioned design retrieval as the basic application of coding and classification systems. There are other, more important applications of classification and coding and group technology which emerged in the seventies and are now the focus of these technologies. The use of classification and coding in group technology applications in manufacturing was the biggest step forward in the evolution of classification and coding systems.

It was one thing to discover ways of codifying similarities in part features and using those features for design retrieval. As pointed out earlier, this type of approach had limitations, particularly with respect to computerization. With the introduction of the attribute type of structure, it became possible to begin to look at the total design and manufacturing picture in different ways.

Group technology is a means of increasing productivity in design and manufacturing by taking advantage of underlying part similarities. Obviously, classification and coding could relate synergistically to it. Classification and coding, as part of a group technology system, could ultimately impact the total design and manufacturing process in a number of significant ways. It could greatly improve batch manufacturing efficiencies and lower batch manufacturing costs by standardizing design and manufacturing processes and by defining the most practical cost-effective methods of producing each and every part.

Standardization refers not only to the elimination of unnecessary duplication but also to the selection of the "best" way of doing things. The best way involves the optimal utilization of personnel, time, materials, and equipment. This in turn requires a thorough understanding of the flow of parts through the manufacturing facility, the load on each of the machine tools within that facility, and the relative costs and cost trade-offs of production on those machines.

The development of highly efficient and relatively inexpensive computers and of sophisticated software programs helped to make these objectives attainable. At the same time, however, the "ultimate" ingredient remained the knowledge of experienced design and manufacturing personnel.

17.3.1 Analysis for Standardization

Perhaps the most important use of modern classification and coding systems is in the analysis of data based on similarities of parts, and the use of that information for design and manufacturing standardization. This process can be illustrated with an example.

The management of a large machine tool company felt that the introduction of classification and coding would provide a good vehicle for the retrieval of existing designs and process plans. Their parts were coded, but it soon became apparent that there were significant duplication problems. For example, it was found that there were 521 gears with the same or similar code number; the differences among them were minimal. If a design engineer were to use the classification and coding system for retrieval, he or she would have found 521 gears. Instead of checking each one of the gears, it would have been easier to design gear 522. In fact, this is what happened.

It was also found that the 521 gears had 477 different manufacturing process plans associated with them. If each process plan were four to five pages long, a process planner using the system for retrieval would have to deal with 2000 pages of manufacturing information. Again, obviously, it would be easier to develop a new process plan. When these and other problems became known to top management, a vigorous standardization program was undertaken, both for design and manufacturing. After a good deal of work, the 521 gears were reduced to 30 standard gears, with 71 manufacturing process plans (taking into account different manufacturing methods for different lot sizes). All of the other designs and process plans were eliminated.

17.3.2 The Standardization Process

Design and manufacturing standardization requires a considerable amount of effort. The first problem is how to deal with a database of 50,000 or 100,000 parts or more. It is virtually impossible to look at all the designs and all the manufacturing process plans. It is here that the principle of similarity of designs and manufacturing methods becomes valuable.

As pointed out earlier, the number of truly different part manufacturing process plans in any manufacturing environment is limited. All of a company's distinctively different part attributes will be captured by coding only a few thousand parts, usually somewhere between 2000 and 7000, depending on the company and its products (Fig. 17.12). Once the curve of different shapes and manufacturing process plans (Figs. 17.7 and 17.8) flattens out, there is no need to code any more for analysis purposes.

The next step is to analyze the code numbers to define families of parts. These families may be design- or manufacturing-oriented. By looking at individual part attributes and the frequency with which they occur, it is possible to begin to determine the major families. For example, families may be defined by certain rotational parts within certain diameter ranges and within certain tolerance ranges.

The product mix analysis is a major tool in the differentiation of parts and their division into families. Once the major families are defined, the process continues with the breaking down of those families into smaller and smaller families—each with code numbers describing more detailed aspects of each part and its attributes. For example, from a manufacturing point of view there might be a major separation in rotational parts and nonrotational parts. The rotational parts may be then divided into those which are

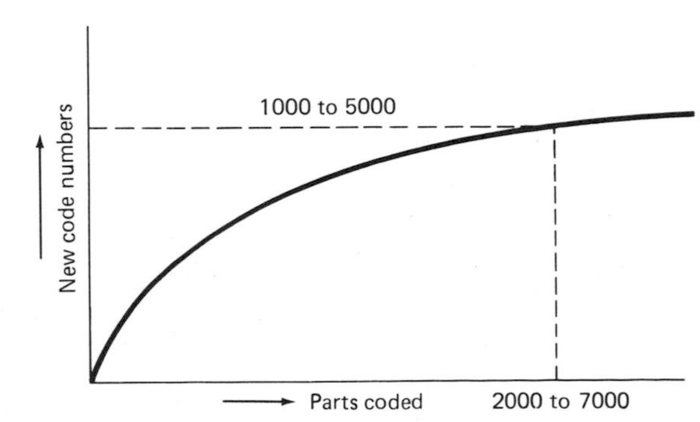

Figure 17.12 Coding of parts to capture distinctly different attributes.

turned only and those which are turned and milled. Further separations may depend on such things as grinding features and special features like hardening, surface hardening, and surface treatment. Thus by separating a representative sample of the parts in production, manufacturing families of parts can be established.

After the establishment of families, experienced engineers and designers are then required to consider each particular family and to decide on the standards required for optimal design and optimal manufacturing of that family. Following the optimization by family, the impact of standardization from a manufacturing point of view must be considered, particularly with respect to the availability of machine tools. The optimum manufacturing methods may not be appropriate to the available machine tool capacities. It is obviously essential that loads be balanced so that capital equipment—machine tools—are effectively utilized.

17.3.3 Load Balancing

For proper load balancing, the code numbers should include such factors as lot size and number of releases per year. With the inclusion of such information, it is possible to relate each family and each part within each family to load demand over a period of time. One must next look at the individual machine tools available for the production of families of parts. Information about the parts and information about the machine tools available to manufacture them can be combined in matrices.

The principle of a code number matrix is that as one can identify the features of a part by code number, one can also use the same code number to identify the attributes which can be manufactured on a particular machine tool. For example, two different parts are identified in Fig. 17.13. One is a shaft type, with a collet on it, and the other is a shorter flange type. The first part has a code number of 1220 3251 1141; the second is 1210 3911 1132. Could both these parts be manufactured on a specific lathe?

The part attributes which can be manufactured on that lathe are expressed in the code number matrix. A part with a code value of 1 in the first position could be, because in the matrix there is a meeting at that position. However, a part with the code value of 2 or 4 in the first position could not be manufactured on that lathe. Figure 17.13 thus is a "nameplate of capabilities" of the lathe, expressed in the matrix.

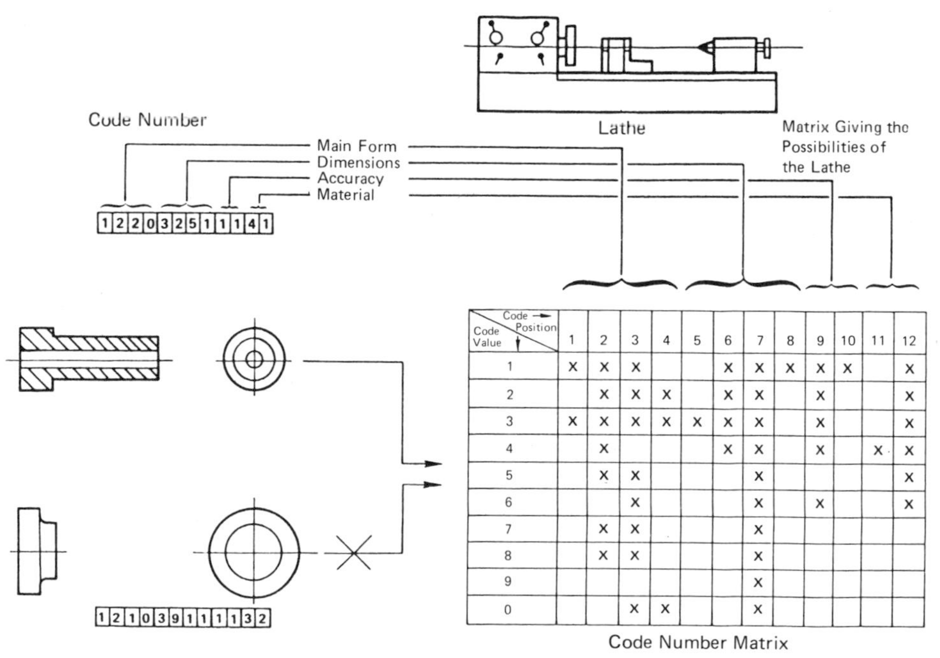

Code Value ↓ / Code Position →	1	2	3	4	5	6	7	8	9	10	11	12
1	X	X	X			X	X	X	X	X		X
2		X	X	X		X	X		X			X
3	X	X	X	X	X	X	X		X			X
4		X				X	X		X		X	X
5		X	X				X					X
6			X				X		X			X
7		X	X				X					
8		X	X				X					
9							X					
0			X	X			X					

Figure 17.13 Matrix of capability for one machine tool expressed in code numbers.

Looking at the first part, one can see that the code number matches the machine tool matrix, and the part could thus be manufactured on that lathe. Looking at the second part, one can see that the sixth position, with a value of 9, does not match with the machine tool matrix. Since this particular position defines dimensions, it is apparent that the part in question is too large to be manufactured on the particular lathe. This process opens the road to matching families of parts with code numbers to dedicated machine tools or groups of machine tools, as illustrated in Figs. 17.14 and 17.15.

17.3.4 Practical Application

In day-to-day operations, this is how the results of the standardization process are applied (Figs. 17.14 and 17.15). The design engineer, working with a sketch of a flange, codes it interactively and is given the number 1772 3231 3144. Going into the parts database, the engineer finds an existing design, part number 2576707. This is the design-retrieval process of the fifties and sixties.

The second step is the most important one. The computer system automatically checks the code number to determine if it fits into a matrix represented by the capabilities of machine tools as identified in Fig. 17.15. In this particular case, the code number fits the matrix, as identified in the same figure, and the designer is given a set of preferred standards for the part which appear on the screen (Fig. 17.14) in order to fit on the machine tools as identified in Fig. 17.15.

If the design engineer accepts the material, tolerance, surface finish, and other standards, then the code number will lead him or her through the same matrix to a set of machine tools which has been specifically set up to make that part. In other words, the design and manufacturing standards are coupled together so that the classification and coding system is used as the key to the implementation of optimal designs and manufacturing methods.

Once this is done, it is possible to go further and link the manufacturing process plan with automated time standards, cost calculator modules, and shop floor control programs. Even in its earliest stages, standardization can lead to significant results.

17.3.5 An Example

The way this works can be illustrated with the following example. In a manufacturing facility, 150 very similar parts were routed over 51 tools. The parts were so similar that differences were hard to find. There were 87 different process plans for these very similar parts, however (Fig. 17.16).

There were so many different process plans because planners have a tendency to route parts over machines with which they are most familiar. It is not at all uncommon, of course, for two machines or even more to be capable of performing the same operation on the same part. Through group technology analysis and standardization, it was possible to look at all of these parts and the manufacturing requirements for each, including such factors as releases per year and lot size. The total load requirement was determined and analyzed.

Simulation and analysis programs were used to create a group technology work center which could produce the parts in question. It was found that the 150 parts could be manufactured on only 8 tools, using 31 standard routings. (See Fig. 17.17 and Table 17.2.)

This type of analysis and cell formation was made possible by the work carried out in the 1970s. With new computers and new group technology software, it is possible to do what had been impossible before.

17.3.6 Computer-Integrated Manufacturing

CAD/CAM became a fashionable term in the 1970s. The introduction of minicomputers with their superior interactive capability and ease of use made it possible to dedicate computers to new specific tasks. At the same time, it marked the beginning of the physical

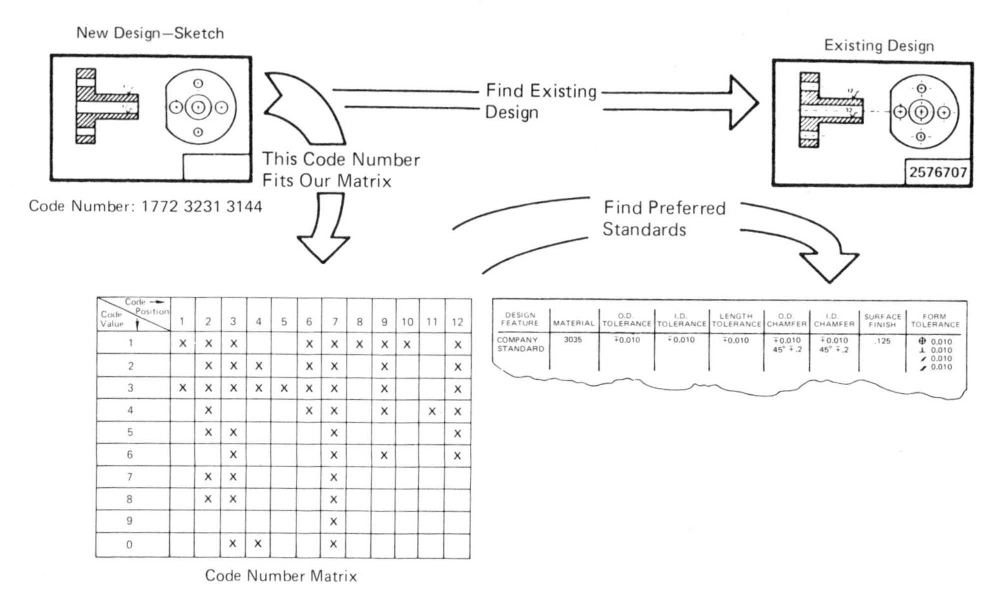

Code Value \ Code Position	1	2	3	4	5	6	7	8	9	10	11	12
1	X	X	X			X	X	X	X	X		X
2		X	X	X		X	X		X			X
3	X	X	X	X	X	X	X		X			X
4		X				X	X		X		X	X
5		X	X				X					X
6			X				X		X			X
7		X	X				X					
8		X	X				X					
9							X					
0			X	X			X					

DESIGN FEATURE	MATERIAL	O.D. TOLERANCE	I.D. TOLERANCE	LENGTH TOLERANCE	O.D. CHAMFER	I.D. CHAMFER	SURFACE FINISH	FORM TOLERANCE
COMPANY STANDARD	3035	±0.010	±0.010	±0.010	±0.010 45° ±.2	±0.010 45° ±.2	.125	⊕ 0.010 ⊥ 0.010 ↗ 0.010 ↗ 0.010

Figure 17.14 Design standardization and retrieval.

spread of computers from the central data processing department to various operations scattered throughout a company.

Recognizing the problems of batch manufacturing inefficiencies, manufacturing management looked to these new computers and the software systems which accompanied them as the potential solutions to their problems. In fact, specific problems were

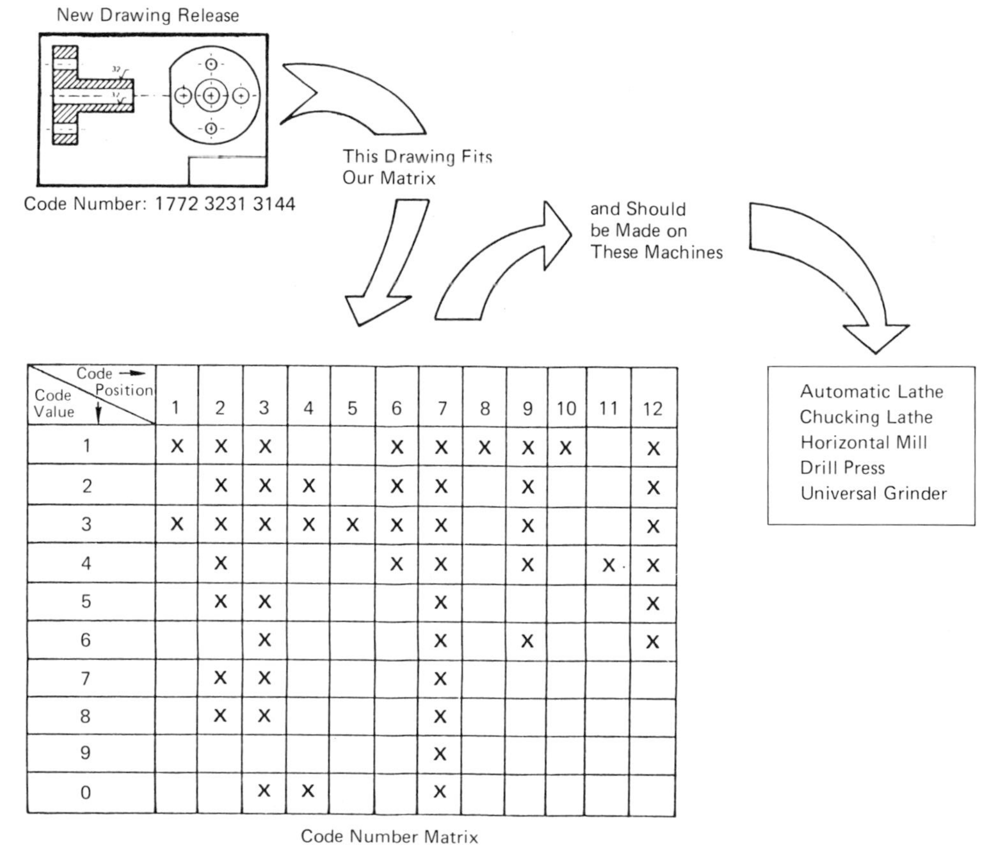

Code Value \ Code Position	1	2	3	4	5	6	7	8	9	10	11	12
1	X	X	X			X	X	X	X	X		X
2		X	X	X		X	X		X			X
3	X	X	X	X	X	X	X		X			X
4		X				X	X		X		X	X
5		X	X				X					X
6			X				X		X			X
7		X	X				X					
8		X	X				X					
9							X					
0			X	X			X					

Figure 17.15 Manufacturing process planning.

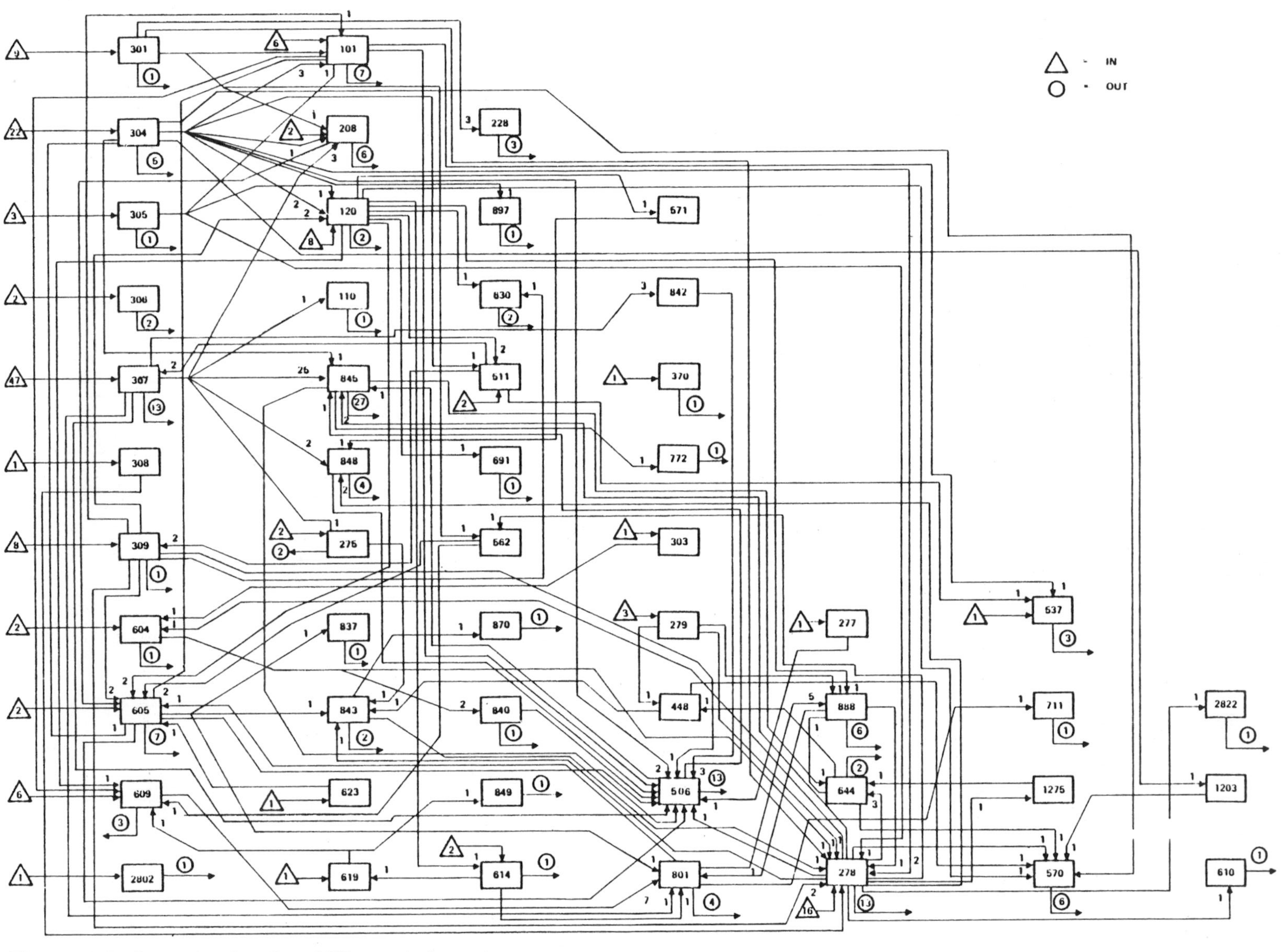

Figure 17.16 Conventional routing of 150 very similar parts.

Table 17.2 An Example of Current and Standardized Methods of Load Balancing

	Current method	Standardized method
Machines	51	8
Flows	87	31
Parts	150	150

solved, but over all manufacturing efficiencies did not increase very appreciably. Throughput time did not diminish significantly.

The phenomenon was somewhat analogous to expanding the diameter of a pipe in a few places (Fig. 17.18). The creation of 4-inch-diameter sections in a pipeline of 2 inches does not increase overall flow efficiencies. To the contrary, it only creates more turbulence, particularly at those points where the pipeline returns to its normal diameter. In other words, if you want to increase the flow, you have to expand the diameter of the entire pipe. In terms of CAD/CAM, this means that various computerized modules must be connected. As long as they operate in isolation, they will not increase total efficiency very much.

Computer-integrated manufacturing is the term used to describe the interrelationship of all of a company's computerized design and manufacturing activities. Group technology is the "glue" which can bring about the integration of CAD/CAM into computer-integrated manufacturing (Fig. 17.19) because it provides a common vocabulary for users, and because it is the vehicle for the creation of a database which includes design and manufacturing attributes, processes, and machine tool capabilities. Perhaps even most important, a group technology–based classification and coding system also provides the means for extracting data in usable formats for a variety of different users.

17.3.7 Decision-Tree-Handling Systems

Until recently, group technology–based classification and coding systems were geared to detailed parts, particularly mechanical parts. When one considers a user-oriented interface to a computerized database of information, it becomes clear that the system

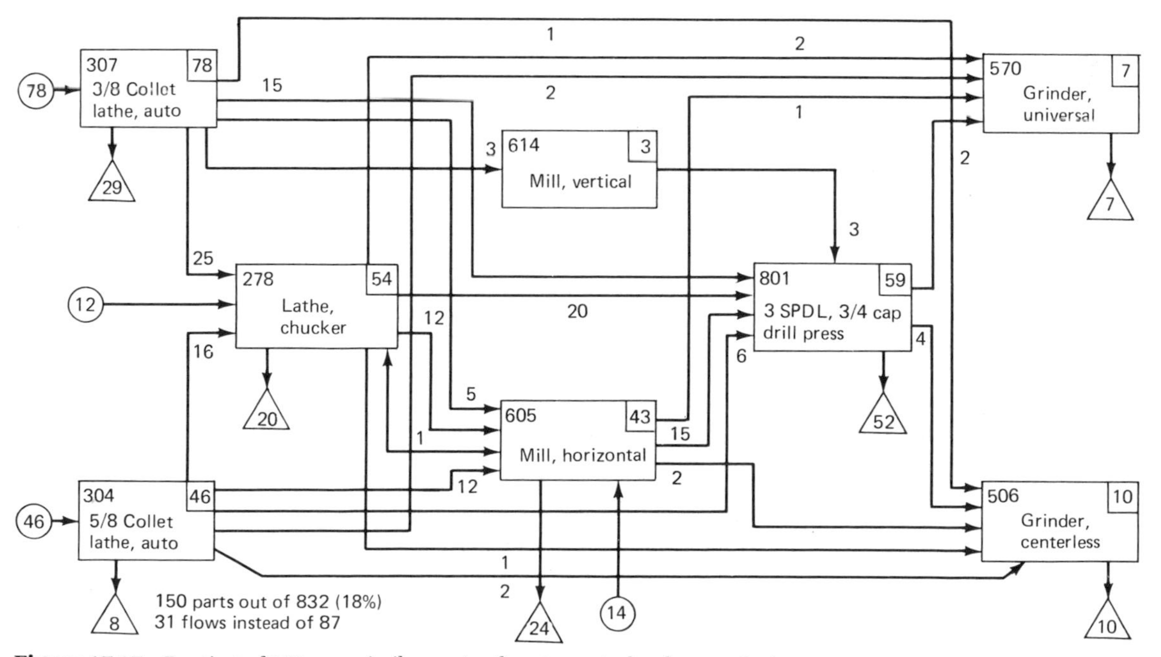

Figure 17.17 Routing of 150 very similar parts after group technology analysis.

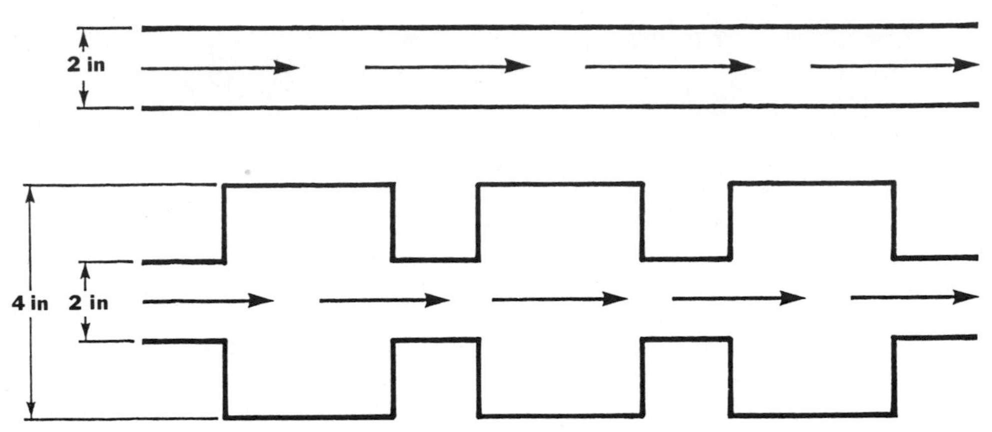

Figure 17.18 Independent computer modules do not necessarily improve productivity.

should include other elements, such as electronics, assemblies, subassemblies, and purchased parts.

Older computerized coding systems were "hard-coded." Such systems were relatively inflexible and could not be extended to encompass different components without major software changes. This led to a new approach: the design of entirely new decision-tree-handling systems which could handle different coding structures, depending on user needs.

Ultimately, a coding system is an interactive means of leading the user through a decision tree to arrive at a string of digits which can be used to retrieve information and for other purposes. With a generalized decision-tree-handling system, it is possible to use one basic structure and software system instead of a number of hard-coded systems with their usual software problems. This type of approach also gives the user the opportunity to short-circuit decision trees after major standardization has been accomplished. Figure 17.20 illustrates a decision-tree-handling system with multiple applications.

Such systems take full advantage of state-of-the-art computer hardware and software technology and also recognize the different needs of different elements of any manufacturing company. The hardware makes it possible to work interactively, easily, and quickly, and the software makes it possible to create coherent, usable code numbers and classifications regardless of the specific attributes under consideration. In looking at a piece of equipment, a manufacturing engineer may be interested in the surface hardness of the main shaft, bearing tolerances, etc. The design engineer may be more concerned with horsepower, rpm's, mounting devices, etc. The purchasing agent may look at horsepower and shaft diameter. These new systems meet all of these needs in a single decision-tree structure. They can also be tailored to meet increasingly specific needs, to the point of providing the retrieval vehicles for generative process planning.

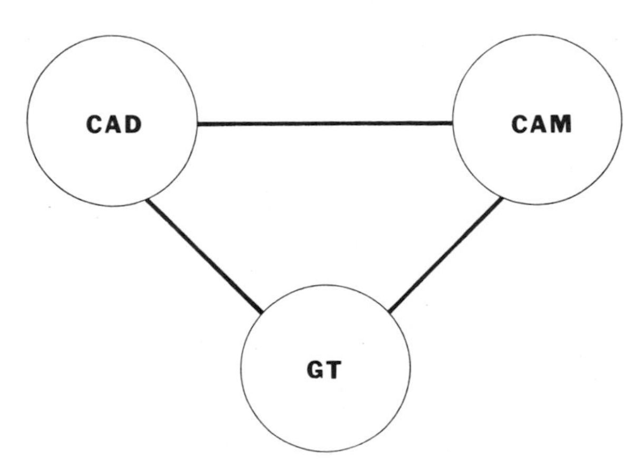

Figure 17.19 Group technology links CAD and CAM.

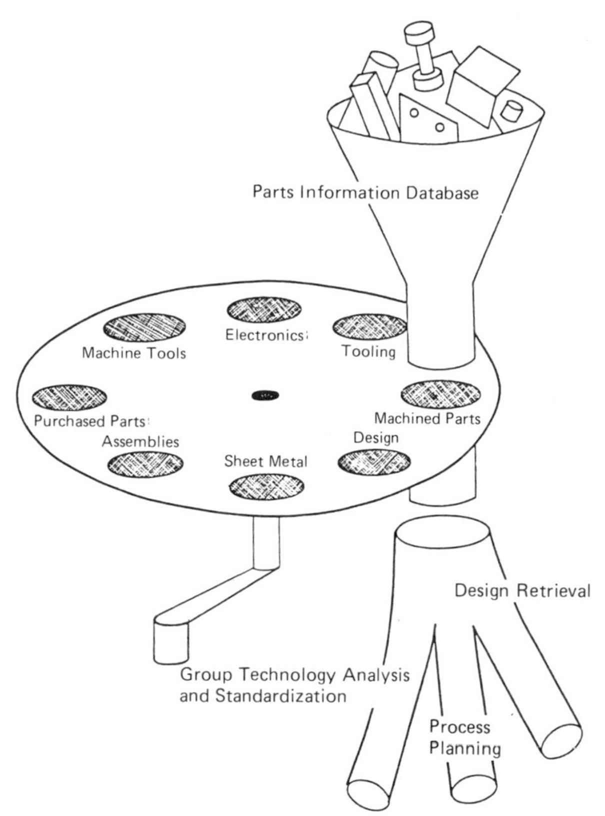

Figure 17.20 Multiple classification and coding system and applications.

17.4 APPLICATIONS OF GROUP TECHNOLOGY

17.4.1 Design Retrieval

It costs between $2000 and $12,000 in manufacturing preparation for a typical part—costs for tool design, jigs and fixtures, process planning, NC tape preparation, and other elements of the preproduction process. Important savings can thus be derived by avoiding the unnecessary design of new parts. A "new" part is often created when the designer varies a tolerance or creates some other design variance which is not absolutely necessary. Or, if the designer does not know that exactly the same part was previously designed, an unnecessary new part may be created.

Design retrieval and the standardization of the designs are very important applications of group technology and classification and coding. Even in a batch production facility, the time spent on such standardization and classification and coding can easily be amortized within a 1- to 2-year period.

Within the design activity itself, 2 to 15 percent of design costs can be saved with an effective design retrieval system. The real payoff, however, as the above demonstrates, is in the manufacturing area. It is therefore important that design and manufacturing understand each other's needs. The system must be implemented in the design area, where the savings are less significant, in order to effect savings in manufacturing.

In CAD applications, an effective design retrieval system can be even more useful. Because designing a new part on a computer graphics terminal is relatively easy, there is less motivation to spend time attempting to retrieve and review existing designs. Unnecessary part design can therefore proliferate rapidly.

Group technology classification and coding and design retrieval have been linked to CAD systems as well as being applied to conventional design operations. The use of these technologies with computer graphics will grow and dramatically increase the usefulness of computer graphics systems.

17.4.2 Process Planning

Manufacturing costs are not only determined by the design of a part. The process planner plays a major role in the cost of production. It is the process planner who determines the tools and manufacturing methods. A 2-inch shaft can be made on a small lathe or on a five-axis milling machine—the choice is the planner's. The manufacturing cost varies greatly. Manufacturing costs for the same part can vary by factors of 2 to 5.

There is a shortage of experienced process planners which is likely to become more severe in the coming years. As planners retire, their experience could be lost, unless it is captured in some way. The importance of the process planning function, the growing shortage of process planners, and the need to retain the experience of retiring process planners are all arguments for computer-assisted process planning.

Computer-assisted process planning systems are becoming increasingly common in the manufacturing industry. With a proper system, payback is almost immediate. Even in its simplest form—as an "electronic pencil," or word processor—such a system can increase process planning efficiencies by 20 to 30 percent. This results from the elimination of the manual labor associated with writing or typing process plans.

A computer-assisted process planning system should be much more than a word processor, however. With a group technology–based system utilizing classification and coding, code numbers can be used for retrieval of existing and "preferred" manufacturing information. The storage, retrieval, and editing of process plans from a computer-assisted process planning database greatly increase process planning efficiencies. Going an important step forward, however, it is also possible to standardize process plans and to develop preferred routings for part families. The retrieval is done by code number or code number matrix, as explained previously. This preferred routing is in fact the optimal routing for the part, based on the experience of process planners and the tools available to do the job.

Cost information can be included in a computer-assisted process planning system. Cost calculation modules help the process planner and others to realize the cost implications of a decision and also make it possible to predict costs. This can be done most effectively when an automated time standards (ATS) system is linked to the process planning system. Companies using such systems have reported that it is possible to predict the manufacturing cost of a finished part within 5 to 10 percent, based on a code number. In other words, code numbers can be used for cost estimating.

A group technology–based computer-assisted process planning system linked with ATS and material requirements planning (MRP) can be very effective in improving shop floor productivity.

17.4.3 Pictorial Process Planning

While a process plan can be a very simple document, it is often lengthy, with many steps and many details accompanying each step. Interpreting lengthy instructions is not always easy, especially in this age of visual communications. People are reading less and looking at pictures more. It is now possible to link computer-assisted process planning and computer graphics to create pictorial process plans which contain not only verbal instruction but illustrations as well.

The text of the process plan itself is developed on an alphanumeric or graphics terminal. It is then formatted on the graphics terminal. For example, all text may be on the left side or right side, and the graphic information, such as setup, machining details, jigs, and fixtures, is created on the remaining part of the graphics screen. (See Fig. 17.21.) Furthermore, the tool path can be visualized to prove out the operation before going to the shop floor.

The finished process plan, with verbal and visual instructions, is then sent to the shop floor for machine operator use. As common databases are used for both graphics and process planning, the use of this type of approach will undoubtedly increase.

PART NO:190105 PART NAME: FRONT PLATE FORMAT: NC9

PLNG REV: 1 DWG REV: A PLANNER: ADAMS

CODE # 8798-3711-1189-3433-1400-0000-0000-00

0040	5002 MACHINE PER TAPE #1
	SET UP IN FIXTURE #1
	WITH STD ANGLE PLATE
	#A123 PER SKETCH
	ROUGH & FINISH FACE
	- HOLD .25+-.02 DIM.
	USE 4" DIA FACE MILL
	C-DRILL (3) HOLES
	DRILL (1) HOLE 3/8 DIA.
	DRILL (2) TOOLING HOLES
	5/16 DIA.
	DRILL (2) TOOLING HOLES
	.365/.370 DIA
	AND REAM TO .376/.370 DIA
	SET UP = 2.50
	PIECE TIME=.350

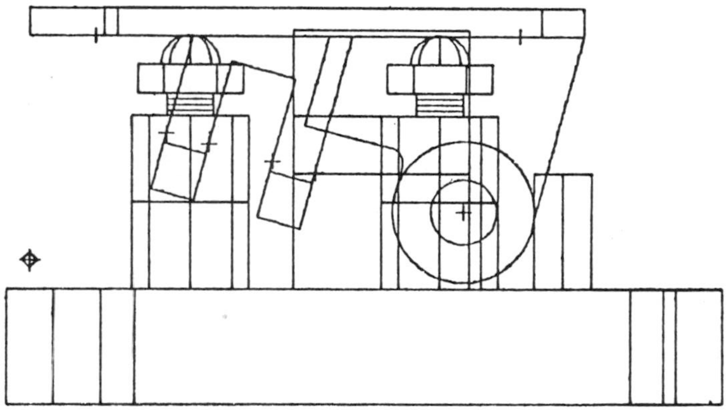

Figure 17.21 Pictorial process planning.

17.4.4 Generative Process Planning

There are two types of computer-assisted process planning. In a variant system, a process plan is retrieved by part number, code number, or some other key. If the retrieved plan is for exactly the same part entering into production, it can be used without change. If the part is in any way different, the retrieved plan can be varied to meet its specific requirements. In a generative system, the part under consideration is described to the computer, and the computer immediately produces the plan to manufacture the part exactly based on manufacturing logic available.

In the variant mode, standard or prepared process plans are stored for future use (Fig. 17.22). In a generative mode, manufacturing logic is stored to create process plans on "the fly." In general, all systems used today are variant. Although the terms are often used loosely, there are very few, if any, real generative process planning systems yet. Work is being carried out on the development of such systems, however.

One approach to generative process planning is artificial intelligence. Using artificial intelligence, the computer would look at those attributes of the part in question and using decision rules programmed into it, would decide exactly how to manufacture the part. Artificial intelligence is a very desirable means of generating a process plan, but current technology falls far short of its realization because there are very few established and accepted manufacturing rules.

Another more practical approach is through the use of multiple classification and coding systems and group technology. This approach begins with the development of a manufacturing database which can be accessed by part number, nomenclature, or code number. Using group technology, optimized processes can be developed for each part attribute and part family. Design and manufacturing considerations can be optimized to the point where all factors are considered so that the plan provides the best design and manufacturing technology for the specific facility in which the part is to be produced.

Using a multiple classification and coding system, these optimized process plans can be fine-tuned to a high degree. Matrices, such as those discussed earlier, can be developed for both parts and the tools available to manufacture them. Tight parameters must be devised for the specific facility to meet exacting needs. In other words, going from variant process planning to design and manufacturing optimization using classification and coding and group technology, one arrives gradually at a manufacturing rationale (logic) for individual part families. These rationales are specifically geared to an individual production facility.

The system can be continually refined to the point where it would be possible to ask the computer to generate a plan for such things as a gear or a shaft. The system would ask

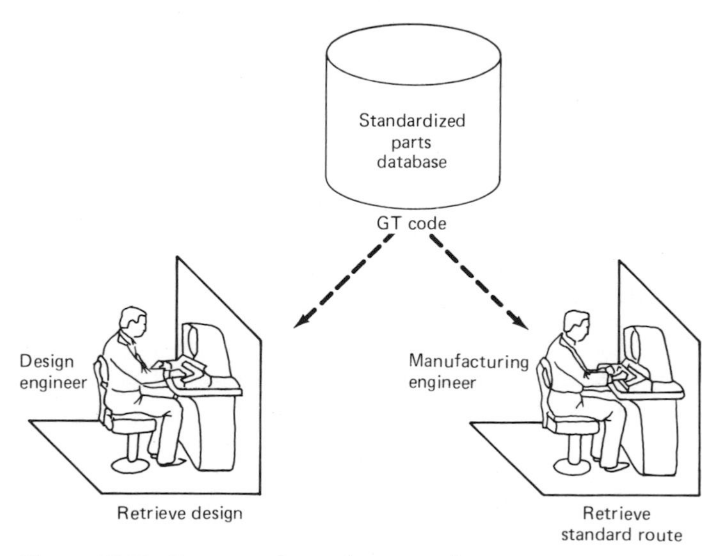

Figure 17.22 Storage and use of process plans.

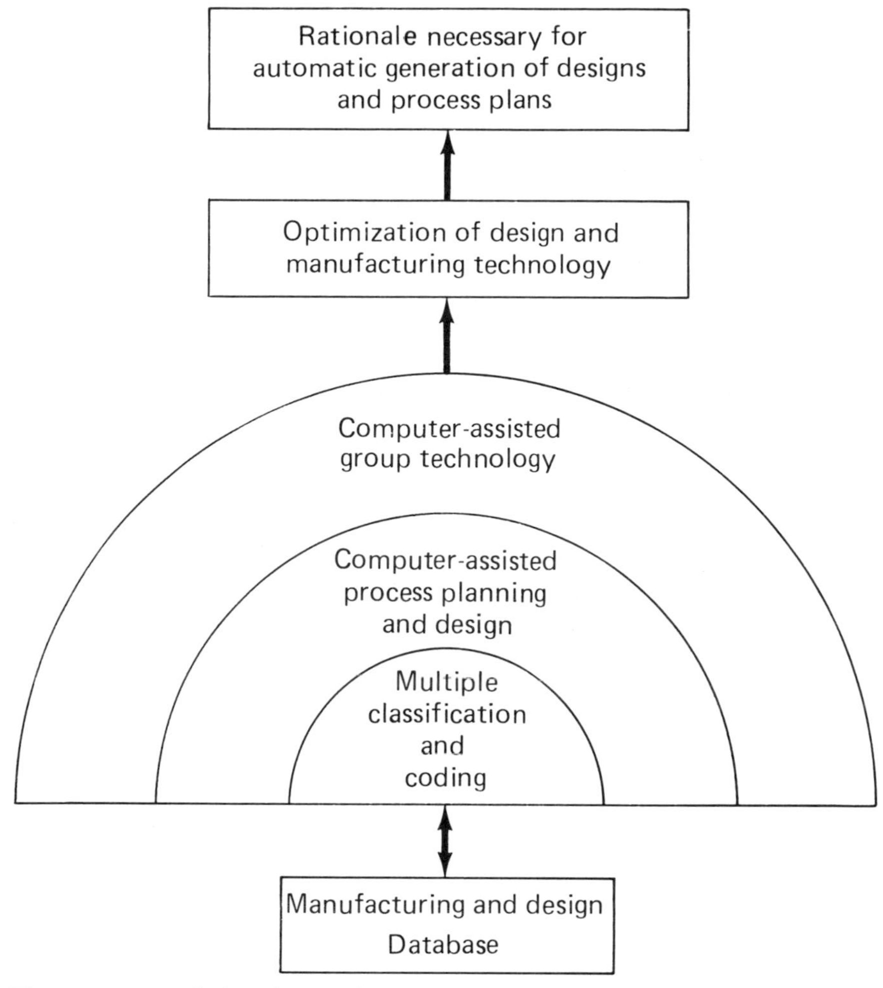

Figure 17.23 Evolution of generative process planning.

the user several questions to further define the part, then search through its matrices and generate a process plan which would describe the optimal method to manufacture it. The group technology multiple classification and coding approach to generative process planning is possible with today's technology and will lead to the rationale to generate process plans (and designs) automatically. (See Fig. 17.23.)

17.4.5 Numerical Control

Group technology can be used to cut significantly costs and time in the preparation of NC tapes. The principle is simple. In a properly implemented system, the code number matrix for each family of parts contains all pertinent design and manufacturing information. Each member of a family falls into a particular design envelope. Standardized NC programs (tapes) can be developed to produce parts within the family. These macro tapes require only the addition of small amounts of specific information (shaft diameter, for example) to be put to use.

This application of group technology broadens the potential uses of NC equipment. Lot sizes of 15 to 20 are necessary to amortize the cost of preparing an NC tape in the conventional way. Using prepared macro tapes, however, the preparation costs can be amortized with 1 or 2 parts. In other words, parts which would otherwise be made manually can now be made on NC tools.

17.4.6 Manufacturing Requirements Planning

The purpose of an MRP system is to have the right part in the right place at the right time. Parts are scheduled through the manufacturing process, either on an order-launching basis or scheduled through all operations. This can be an elaborate system, involving the scheduling of all manufacturing operations of all parts. Consequently, proper process plans are required—plans which will assure that parts are manufactured on schedule. In order to meet delivery schedules, MRP schedules which parts should be manufactured, on what machine tools, and in what sequence. The problem is that the batch manufacturing environment is nonstandard with many different production methods for the same part.

In conventional operations, the supervisor picks similar parts from a queue to reduce setup times. In an MRP system, however, parts are scheduled in terms of delivery and the supervisor does not have that option. Since the supervisor has no choice, he or she cannot optimize setup times. As a result, setup times increase and the time available for metal removal per machine tool decreases. There is thus a loss in production capacity and a decrease in asset utilization.

There is ample evidence that group technology and MRP can be implemented together and complement each other's success rate. Through group technology analyses, a part family can be defined and optimal routings developed. The group technology system tells the planner what parts to send out on what machines. The key is that families of parts are routed consistently to dedicated groups of machine tools. The MRP system recognizes this group of machine tools as one machining center (a black box) where parts enter one side of the center and leave in finished form at the other side. The flow of materials inside the center is scheduled by group technology considerations. MRP is only related to the schedule of material and parts to and from the center. Some companies call these centers GT1, GT2, etc.

It is essential to implement group technology first. With group technology analysis, it is possible to deal with issues such as optimized family production, production flow analysis, and load balance by families. Parts can then be produced in families for maximum efficiencies, without interfering with MRP operations in any way. This has been done in several companies, with high rates of success.

17.4.7 Machine Tool Selection and Shop Layout

Since the code number reflects a preferred design or process plan, frequencies of occurrence of code numbers in certain time periods can be related to manufacturing requirements, and thus to the machines needed to manufacture the parts over the course of time. In other words, it is possible to predict with a high degree of accuracy exactly how many hours of time will be required from each machine based on the occurrence of code numbers.

Since group technology analysis can also be used as a simulation tool, it is also possible to examine variables in future manufacturing operations and look at future machine tool use with those variables. In short, it is possible to predict machine tool use, and thereby make purchasing decisions, based on current manufacturing patterns or on expectations of future changes.

With group technology it is also possible to form work cells, of course. With the definition of work cells and production flow analyses, it is possible to determine specifications for an entire manufacturing facility and to lay out the facility based on these specifications. This has been done with great success, improving asset utilization dramatically and decreasing the investment budget for new machine tools.

The same principles can be applied to the purchase of robots. Robots as such are not tools, but they are material handlers. Based on production flow analyses and the positioning and production expectations of work cells, it is possible to determine where and how robots can best be used.

What has become an increasingly attractive method of selecting machine tools and for layout of machine shops is also very applicable to the selection of flexible manufacturing systems (FMS). The manufacturing database has all the information available to retrieve those parts (by code number) to be run on an FMS. It can thus be utilized to lay out the specifications of an FMS to be used (or not to be used) most precisely.

17.5 THE FUTURE

There is no doubt that computers will be increasingly important in manufacturing in the future. The parameters for future use of computers in manufacturing environments have been established by experience to date. Certain trends appear to be firmly established, and technology is evolving consistently with those trends. For example, computer-integrated manufacturing will require a single integrated database of design and manufacturing information. This database will not only contain conventional design and manufacturing data but also information on cost, testing, quality control, and other elements of the process from initial design through assembly, testing, and shipment. The key to retrieve all this information can be most effectively done by sophisticated multiple classification and coding structures, interfacing the user directly with relevant information for the computer database.

Concurrent with this, microcomputers will play an increasingly important role in batch manufacturing. Microcomputers on the shop floor and in the design and manufacturing engineering offices can handle local processing needs at the workstations, interfaced with larger computers which will be used to process and store data. Linked systems will accommodate both alphanumeric and graphics hardware and software.

A major breakthrough will be the implementation of solid modeling in computer graphics. Once a computer can actually recognize a part, not as a wire diagram but rather as a physical entity, it will be possible to generate code numbers automatically. These code numbers, invisible to the user, will become the means to tie all database elements together automatically. Interactive communication will become even more efficient.

With a group technology classification and coding system as the key, it will be possible to create designs automatically, link them to the process plans required for manufacturing, produce NC tapes as needed, program robots, and oversee all other aspects of the total integrated manufacturing process. When this is done—and it will not be done easily—the concept of the automated factory for batch manufacturing will be well on its way to realization. It should be realized that these features are not long-term expectations but rather realities to be expected within this decade.

Glossary of Computer Graphics Terms

by
Megatek Computer Graphics*

Absolute Vector A vector whose endpoints are defined in terms of units from the specified origin.

Additive Color The colors produced by adding varying intensity levels of the red, green, and blue color components.

Address Space *See* Device Space.

Addressability The range of addressable points or device coordinates.

Addressable Point Any position specifiable in device coordinates.

Aiming Symbol *See* Tracking Symbol.

Aliasing The visual effects that occur when the detail of an image exceeds the resolution of the device space, i.e., a stairstep line on a raster display.

Alphanumeric Display A CRT display used to display text strings.

Analog Color The assignment of black-and-white video signal levels to an RGB value. *See* Density Slicing.

Analog Vector Generator A device which takes endpoint coordinate data and converts it to deflection signals for the electron gun.

Annotation The presence of textual descriptions on a display.

Antialiasing A process which removes the effects of pixel addressing on a raster display, i.e., stairstep lines appear continuous.

Appearance A primitive attribute which specifies an intensity level on a calligraphic display or a color on a raster display.

Area Fill Processor *See* Fill.

Assembly Drawing A CAD/CAM display which represents a major subdivision of a final product.

*The Glossary of Computer Graphics Terms appearing on pages 18.1 through 18.11 is reprinted by permission of Megatek Corporation, San Diego, Calif., copyright 1981 by Megatek Corporation.

Associative Dimensioning The updating of the respective dimensions of CAD/CAM display groups as the dimensions of their display entities change.

Attribute Any characteristic of a display item (color, linestyle, character font, etc.) or segment (visibility, detectability, etc.)

Back Annotation The extracting of information from a completed printed-circuit board to create a CAD/CAM display.

Background Display List A display list the refresh of which is not time-critical. *See* Foreground Display List.

Baseline Fill The fill between a string of vectors and a vector specified as the baseline.

Beam Penetration CRT A CRT display which produces color by varying the electron-beam penetration of a multilayer phosphor display surface.

Bit Plane The hardware used as a storage medium for image bit maps.

Blackness A characteristic of color defining its percentage ranking on a scale from dark to light, specifying perceived brightness.

Blanked Region A bounded area in display space, inside which display elements are not visible.

Blanked Vector A vector having no intensity, which effectively changes the current position without creating a visible line segment.

Blinking The technique of alternately displaying and not displaying a display entity. A method of highlighting a display entity.

Bounding Box A rectangle whose dimensions are the same as the width and height of a symbol, and therefore can contain the entire symbol.

Boxing A visibility test incorporated in clipping which uses a bounding box to test the relationship of an entire symbol to the clipping boundaries.

Brush A marker generated by painting in computer animation.

Buffer A storage area which receives and subsequently releases transient data.

Button Device A button used as a graphic input device.

CAD Computer-aided design.

Calligraphic Display A display device which can present images composed of line segments.

Calligraphic Drawing A line drawing, as opposed to a raster scan. From the word calligraphy, the art of stroke drawing.

CAM Computer-aided manufacturing.

Cathode-Ray Tube An electron tube in which electron beams projected onto its display surface excite the phosphor coating, producing luminous spots.

Center of Projection The common point from which all projectors emanate in a perspective projection.

Character An instance of a numeral, letter, or other linguistic, mathematical, or logical symbol.

Character Font A primitive attribute of text strings defining the style of the character set.

Character Generator A hardware device which accesses character patterns in a ROM and generates them at user-specified display surface positions.

Character Plane A primitive attribute of text strings defining the plane in which characters are generated.

Character Size A primitive attribute of text strings defining the size of characters in terms of the bounding box.

Choice A graphic input device composed of a number of buttons from which a selection is made.

Clip Boundary A boundary in display space, beyond which any portion of a display element will not be visible.

Clipping The process of determining which portion or portions of a display element lie outside the specified clip boundary and making them invisible.

Coded Graphics The specification of a display as a set of display instructions.

Coherence A property used in raster scan which recognizes that adjacent pixels are likely to be similar in characteristics.

Color Look-Up Table A table designed to provide a range of colors by defining different mixtures of the color components. A component in indirect color specification schemes, where colors are specified in terms of elements in the table.

Color Map *See* Color Look-Up Table.

Color Space A conceptual geometric model used to describe the characteristics of color, i.e., hue, whiteness, blackness, RGB, hue, saturation, lightness.

COM Computer output microfilm.

COM Recorder A display device for placing displays on microfilm.

Comparator A device which compares the proximity of a cursor to the vector currently being drawn.

Component A CAD/CAM marker which has physical meaning, i.e., resistor, capacitor, switch.

Composite Color A color described in terms of its hue, whiteness, and blackness and encoded in a single video signal.

Composite Video A single video signal encoding RGB data. *See* NTSC Converter.

Computer Animation The use of computer graphics to generate motion pictures.

Computer-Independent Graphics A graphics package which can be used on more than one type of computer.

Construction Plane A plane in a CAD/CAM display used for the projection of digitized information.

Context Switching The controlling of the visibility of layers in a CAD/CAM display by shifting between groups that share common attributes.

Contrast The ratio of the highest available intensity level to the lowest.

Contrast Enhancement A linear expansion of the gray scale.

Contrast Stretching The use of density slicing to emphasize portions of a black-and-white display.

Control Dial A valuator device whose inputs are determined by an incremental scale the user assigns to its rotatable movements.

Coordinate The location of a point in terms of units from the specified origin.

Core System A proposed graphics standard developed by the ACM Special Interest Group on Graphics (SIGGRAPH).

Cross Hairs Two intersecting perpendicular lines incorporated in a cursor, with the intersect being used to indicate desired device coordinates.

Cross-Hatching The filling of an area of the display surface bounded by vectors with a pattern of crisscrossed line segments.

CRT Cathode-ray tube.

CRT Display A display device employing a cathode-ray tube.

Current Position The beam position on the display surface prior to invoking a display instruction.

Cursor A recognizable display entity that can be moved about the display surface by a graphic input device to return either device coordinates or a pick stack. *See* Puck.

Cut Plane A plane which intersects a three-dimensional object at a specified point, used to view a cross section at that location.

Data Tablet A flat-surfaced graphic input device used with a stylus for inking and cursor movement, or with a puck for digitizing.

Decluttering The selective erasure of display items when the display is too dense to easily discern details.

Delta Gun *See* Triad.

Density Slicing The assigning of RGB values to black-and-white video signal levels.

Depth Queuing A technique used to suggest depth in a three-dimensional display item by varying intensity levels in relation to distance from the view point.

Detectability A dynamic segment attribute which determines if display items can be identified by a pick device.

Device Coordinate System A coordinate system which represents the internal digital limits of the display device. Typically uses integers with finite limits along each axis recognized by the display device.

Device Driver A device-dependent software which generates display instructions from the invocations of a graphics package.

Device-Independent Graphics A graphics package which can be used on more than one type of display device.

Device Space The area defined by the device coodinate system.

Digital Vector Generator A device used with raster displays to interpolate the straightest possible pixel string between specified endpoints.

Digitizer A data tablet that generates coordinate data from visual data through the use of a puck or stylus. A large data tablet.

Dimensioning The measuring of distances on a CAD/CAM display.

Directed Beam The technique used in calligraphic displays to produce vectors by having the electron beam stroke them in a selected order.

Direct-View Storage Tube A type of CRT whose display is maintained by a continuous flood of electrons.

Disable A display command which prevents further inputs from a graphic input device.

Display A collection of display items presented on the display surface.

Display Background The static backdrop against which displays are presented.

Display Command A processor-generated instruction to the display device.

Display Console A configuration containing a

display device and any associated graphic input devices.

Display Cycle *See* Refresh Cycle.

Display Device An output device used to display computer-generated graphical data.

Display Element *See* Output Primitive.

Display Entity A logical grouping of output primitives which forms a recognizable unit on the display surface.

Display File *See* Display List.

Display Foreground That portion of the display which has display items accessible while in interactive mode.

Display Group An assemblage of display entities controlled as a unit.

Display Image The portion of an image visible on the display surface at any one time.

Display Instruction The coded information passed to the graphics processor specifying the display items to be drawn on the display surface.

Display Item A display element, display entity, or display group.

Display List A collection of display instructions assembled to create a display.

Display Segment *See* Segment.

Display Space The portion of the image space which is viewable on the display surface.

Display Surface That part of the display device which actually displays graphical data, e.g., a CRT, the plotting surface of a plotter, or the film in a COM recorder.

Dithering The increasing of the variations of color or intensity on raster displays by trading picture resolution for patterns of pixel arrays.

Dot Matrix A pattern of dots taken from a two-dimensional array.

Dot Matrix Plotter *See* Raster Plotter.

Double Buffering A technique used to speed data access by alternatively addressing two buffers; while one buffer is passing data, the other can receive data to be transmitted in the next access.

Dragging The interactive mode technique of moving a display item by translating it along a path determined by a graphic input device.

Draw The generation of a vector by creating a line segment from the current position to a specified endpoint, which becomes the new current position.

DRC Design rules checking.

Drum Plotter A plotter whose display surface is a rotatable drum and whose plotting head can only move parallel to the drum's axis of rotation, with movement at angles to that axis provided by the drum's rotation.

DVST Direct-view storage tube.

Dynamic Range The ratio of the minimum to the maximum brightness of an input image.

Dynamic Segment Attribute The attributes of a segment which can be changed after its creation: visibility, highlighting, image transformation, and detectability.

Echo The mode of a graphic input device which provides visual feedback to the operator, e.g., a cursor, text strings, etc.

Electron Gun The part of a CRT which focuses and emits the electron beam.

Electrostatic Plotter A raster plotter which produces display images on paper sensitized to electrostatic charges.

Element *See* Display Element.

Elementary Diagram A CAD/CAM ES display containing components, logic elements, wire nets, annotation, etc.

Enable To cause a graphic input device to be in the mode which marks it as ready to produce input.

Endpoint Either of the points that mark the ends of a line segment.

Endpoint Matching The accuracy of the vector generator in drawing two or more vectors emanating from the same point.

ES Electrical schematic.

Event An operator action which prompts an event device to produce an input.

Event Device A graphic input device which notifies a user task of an event by placing an event report in the event queue.

Event Queue A list of event reports, generated in the order of their occurrence.

Event Report The status of an event device when an event occurred.

Exploring Spot The point of focus of the electron beam of an image digitizer on the input image.

FEM Finite-element model.

Fill To fill an area of the display surface bounded by vectors, e.g., with a solid color or a pattern of line segments.

Finite Element Model A mathematical model of a continuous object which divides the object into an array of discrete elements for the purpose of simulated structural analysis.

Fixing The positioning of a display item at a set location after dragging.

Flatbed Plotter A plotter with a flat display surface fully accessible by the plotting head.

Flicker A noticeable flashing of the display during each refresh, caused when the refresh interval exceeds the phosphor persistence.

Flying Spot *See* Exploring Spot.

Flying Spot Scanner A device for scanning a picture to record it as a pixel array.

Foreground Display List A display list whose refresh is time-critical. May be refreshed several times for each refresh of a background display list.

Frame One refresh of a raster display image.

Frame Buffer *See* Image Bit Map.

Frame Update Rate The time required to rewrite an entire frame buffer.

Function Button *See* Function Switch.

Function Key A key on a function pad which causes execution of special program functions defined by the user.

Function Pad A graphic input device with user-programmable function keys.

Function Switch A button on a button device which can operate in either momentary or latchable mode, and whose value may be retained.

Fusion Point The point at which the refresh rate reaches a frequency that makes a display appear steady, as opposed to flicker.

Graphic Input Any inputs entered by a user through a graphic input device while in interactive mode.

Graphic Input Device The hardware which allows the user to enter data, or pick a detectable display item.

Graphic Primitive *See* Output Primitive.

Graphics The visual presentation of data as a series of output primitives.

Graphics Package A series of software routines which provide the user access to the graphics hardware for the purpose of generating a display.

Graphics Processor A controller which accesses the display list, interprets the display instructions, and passes coordinates to the vector generator.

Gray Scale An ordered description of the tonal levels of an input image.

Grid The uniformly spaced points in two or three dimensions within which an object may be defined.

Halftone Images A display of three-dimensional objects using shaded surfaces.

Hard Copy A copy of a display on a permanent medium, e.g., paper or microfilm.

Hatching The filling of an area of the display surface bounded by vectors with a pattern of parallel line segments.

Hidden Lines The line segments which should not be visible to a viewer of a three-dimensional display item because they are "behind" other parts of the same or other display items.

Hidden Objects The objects in a three-dimensional display which should not be visible to a viewer because they are obscured by other objects.

Hidden Surfaces The surfaces of a three-dimensional display item which should not be visible to a viewer because they are obscured by other surfaces of the same or other display items.

Highlight To force a display item to stand out by blinking or varying its intensity.

Hit Detection The returning of a pick stack when a valid pick is made by a graphic input device.

Hither Plane The front clipping plane used in z clipping to define a finite view volume.

Homogeneous Coordinates The coordinates used in matrix transformations to convert objects described in n-space to a representation described in $n + 1$ space, i.e., x, y, z become wx, wy wz, w, where w is a homogeneous scale factor.

Horizontal Retrace The turning off and repositioning of the electron beam down and to the left during raster scan in order to begin the sweep of the next scan line.

Hue A characteristic of color which allows it to be named, i.e., red, yellow, green, blue, and which is often defined by an angle representing its graduation.

Image A view of an object.

Image Bit Map A digital representation of a display image as a pattern of bits, where each bit maps to one or more pixels. Multiple-bit maps may be used in color graphics to assign values to each pixel, which are used as indices into the color look-up table, if one exists.

Image Data Data composed of an array of points, each with a specified color or intensity level. *See* Pixel.

Image Digitizer A video camera tube incorporating an electron beam to scan an input image, sense the light emitted, and produce video signals.

Image Enhancement A technique which displays user-selected portions of an input image in great detail.

Image Graphics The creation of an image from data stored in pixel form.

Image Plane The plane containing an input image.

Image Processing The inputting of image data to a computer and processing it for output to a display device.

Image Space The view plane defined in world coordinates.

Image Transformations The applying of a transformation function to an image after projection to the display space.

Imaging *See* Image Processing.

Inline CRT A color CRT display whose electron guns are in an inline configuration and whose phosphors and shadow mask are arranged accordingly.

Inbetweening The generating of the movements of a figure between two specified extremes in computer animation.

Incremental Plotter A plotter which produces a display in discrete steps defined by the limited movements of the plotting head.

Incremental Vector A vector defined by a relative component and an absolute component.

Inking The technique of using a graphic input device to sketch freehand with a stylus.

Ink-Jet Plotter A plotter which uses electrostatic technology to first atomize a liquid ink and then control the number of droplets that are deposited on the plotting medium.

Input Image A picture to be digitized.

Instancing The repetitious use of a marker or subroutine on a display.

Intensity *See* Blackness.

Intensity Level One of a discrete set of brightness levels attainable with a CRT.

Interactive Graphics A method which allows users to dynamically modify displays through the use of graphic input devices.

Interactive Mode A setting which permits a display console to be used for interactive graphics.

Interconnection A line segment used in CAD/CAM displays to connect display entities having logical, electrical, or mechanical functions.

Interlace A raster scan technique which alternately refreshes the even and odd scan lines with each pass.

Joystick A graphic input device which employs a moveable lever to control the position of a cursor, for returning locator or pick information.

Kernel A subset of routines from a graphics package which permits construction of elementary displays.

Key A button on a keyboard device which transmits a single character or control information to the user program.

Keyboard Device A graphic input device which allows the user to enter characters or other key-driven values.

Key-Frame Animation The animation of figures by defining successive frames containing slightly changing fundamental movements.

Laser Plotter A plotter which produces display images on photographic film, in raster or vector formats, using a laser.

Latchable Mode A mode setting for function switches which allows a switch to toggle between two states when depressed by a user.

Layer The logical subdivisions of the data contained in a two-dimensional CAD/CAM display, such that the subdivisions may be viewed individually or overlaid and viewed in groups.

Layout A completed CAD/CAM display drawn to scale.

Light Button A detectable display item which functions as a button device.

Light Pen A graphic input device which generates a hit detection when a pick is made while pointed at a detectable display item.

Lightness *See* Blackness.

Line Follower A graphic input device which detects and traces lines in vector format. Branching and bridging decisions are handled either by sophisticated software or through operator intervention.

Line Segment A portion of a line bounded by two endpoints.

Line Style A primitive attribute of lines which defines whether they are to be solid or dashed, and a possible dash pattern.

Line Type *See* Line Style.

Line Width A primitive attribute which defines the thickness of a line segment.

LIS Large interactive surface.

Locate To provide coordinate information with a locator device.

Locator Device A graphic input device, such as a joystick or data tablet, which uses a cursor to provide coordinate information.

Logic Element A CAD/CAM marker which has logical meaning, i.e., gate, flip-flop.

Mapping Function A method of transforming an image definition expressed in one coordinate system to another.

Marker A user-defined symbol which can be invoked repeatedly on the display surface.

Memory Management A scheme used to allocate and deallocate memory to the segments composing a display list.

Menu A list of program execution options appearing on the display surface which prompts the user to choose one or more through the use of a graphic input device.

Metafile A device-independent file for storing a display and transporting it from one system to another.

Mirroring The creation of a mirror image of a display item.

Model The definition of an object in world coordinates.

Modeling System A system which allows models to be defined and transformed using world coordinates.

Modeling Transformation *See* World Coordinate Transformation.

Model Space The world coordinate system in use by a particular model.

Momentary A mode setting for function switches which places a switch in an active state only while it is pressed by the user.

Mouse A hand-held device used with a data tablet that positions a cursor on the display surface by the movement of two wheels against the tablet's surface. The wheels are perpendicular to one another, with one for the x coordinate and one for the y coordinate.

Move To change the current position without producing an output primitive.

Name To associate a label with a display group to allow it to be identified and addressed.

NDC Normalized device coordinates.

Net A logical linking of pins in a CAD/CAM display using interconnections.

New Frame Action A refresh of the display surface which produces an updated display.

Node The intersection of two or more interconnections.

Noninterlace A raster scan technique which refreshes every scan line with each pass.

Nonretained Segment The segment which is open when all retained segments are closed.

Normalized Device Coordinate Space The addressable area defined in terms of normalized device coordinates.

Normalized Device Coordinates The device-independent coordinates in the range of 0 to 1 which are mapped to the device space.

NTSC Converter A converter used to encode video signals into National Television Standard Committee composite video. Normally RGB signals are converted to a single-color video signal.

Object A display item created with output primitives described in world coordinates.

Operator The user of a display console in interactive mode.

Optical Scanner *See* Image Digitizer.

Ordered Dither The setting of the intensity level or color for each pixel according to its relation to a set of threshold values applied to the pixel array.

Origin The point in a coordinate system whose components are all zero.

Orthographic Projection A parallel projection whose direction is determined by a vector perpendicular to the view plane.

Output Primitive A basic graphical entity, i.e., a point, line segment, character, marker, or text string. A basic component of a display entity.

Overlay A pattern used as the display background.

P & ID Piping and instrumentation diagram.

Painting A technique similar to inking, but used only on raster displays where line width and color may vary.

Pan To translate horizontally.

Parallax The apparent displacement of a display item from where the viewer perceives it and where a light pen is pointing.

Parallel Projection A projection in which the projectors are all parallel to a specified vector.

Passive Graphics A method allowing no operator dynamic interaction with a display.

Passive Mode A setting which specifies a display console as usable for passive graphics.

Pattern Fill Repetitively using a user-defined pixel array to perform fill.

Pel Picture element. *See* Pixel.

Perspective Projection A projection in which the projectors all originate at a specified center of projection.

Phosphor One of a number of chemical compounds used to coat the display surface of a CRT and which glow when excited by an electron beam.

Phosphor Persistence A measure of the time it takes for a phosphor's brightness to drop to one-tenth of its initial value. The tendency of a phosphor to continue to emit light when no longer excited by an electron beam.

Pick An event triggered by a pick device which generates an event report containing the pick identifier of the detected display item and the name of the segment containing it.

Pick Device An event device, such as a light pen or a locator device with a comparator, which causes picks when pointed at detectable display items.

Pick Identifier A name associated with a detectable display item.

Pick Label *See* Pick Identifier.

Pick Stack The information returned by a pick device in an event report, including the segment name, pick identifier, and the display item coordinates.

Picture Structure The way in which a display is subdivided into segments and subroutines for use in interactive mode.

Pin The connection points on logic elements and components in CAD/CAM displays.

Pixel The discrete display element of a raster display, represented as a single point with a specified color or intensity level.

Pixel Array *See* Raster.

Pixel Replication The repetition of each pixel in a display when an operator zooms in.

Plasma Panel A type of display device whose display surface consists of a matrix of gas filled cells which can be turned on and off individually, and which remain on until turned off.

Plotter A computer-controlled device which produces a hard copy of a display.

Point A line segment of zero length.

Polygon Fill The fill performed on any defined polygon.

Posting Setting the visibility segment attribute on.

Primitive *See* Output Primitive.

Primitive Attribute A characteristic of an output primitive, i.e., character size, line style, blink rate.

Projector A line passing through an object to intersect with the view plane in a projection.

Prompt Any action of the display console which indicates an operator reaction is needed, normally in the form of a message or menu on the display surface.

Properties *See* Primitive Attribute.

Pseudo Color The color assigned to noncolor data, i.e., using color for different stress values in a FEM.

Puck A hand-held device with a transparent portion containing cross hairs that is used for inputting coordinate data from a data tablet through the use of programmable buttons. *See* Cursor.

Raster A rectangular matrix of pixels.

Raster Count The number of scan lines in a raster display.

Raster Display A CRT display whose display surface is covered by a raster and which generates displays using raster scan techniques.

Raster Plotter A plotter which produces displays in dot matrix form.

Raster Scan The generation of a display on a raster display by having the electron beam follow a set pattern through the scan lines, applying varying color or intensities to each individual pixel.

Raster Unit The physical distance between the midpoints of two adjacent pixels.

Read To query a graphic input device and await operator action.

Refresh The process of repeatedly drawing a display on the display surface of a refresh tube.

Refresh Cycle One refresh of the display surface.

Refresh Display A display device employing a refresh tube which permits dynamics due to high refresh rate.

Refresh Rate The time needed for one refresh of the display surface.

Refresh Tube A CRT which must be refreshed in order to maintain a display.

Relative Vector A vector whose endpoints are specified in reference to the current position.

Repaint To refresh a display surface with an updated display.

Repeatability The accuracy of an analog vector generator in minimizing the deviation from precise overlap when redrawing vectors.

Reproducing Spot The point of contact of the electron beam of a raster display with the display surface.

Resolution The precision of a CRT, measured as the number of line pairs distinguishable across the display surface.

Retained Segment A user-named and user-defined segment whose segment attributes may be modified at any time.

Reverse Video The specifying of a color by reversing the value of an existing color to yield its complement.

RGB Color A color described in terms of its red, green, and blue intensity levels.

Right Complement *See* Reverse Video.

Roam To translate a window about the view plane.

Rotate To transform a display or display item by revolving it around a specific axis.

Routing The positioning of interconnections in a CAD/CAM display.

Rubber-Band Line A line segment that extends from a specified fixed point to a cursor and moves along with the cursor.

Rubberstamping The invoking of a brush.

Run Length Encoding A scan conversion technique used to compress scan line information by storing counts of the number of identical consecutive pixels and their respective colors or intensities across each line.

Sample To query a graphic input device to determine its current state.

Sampled Device A graphic input device which a user task may sample.

Saturation *See* Whiteness.

Scale (1) To transform the size or shape of a display or display item by modifying the coordinate dimensions. (2) The ratio of the actual dimensions of a model to the true dimensions of the subject represented.

Scan Conversion The process of converting a display to an image bit map.

Scan Line A horizontal line of pixels on a raster display that is swept by the electron beam during refresh.

Scanning Pattern The path followed by an exploring spot.

Scanning Spot *See* Exploring Spot.

Scissoring *See* Clipping.

Screen Coordinate System *See* Device Coordinate System.

Scrolling The translating of text strings or graphics vertically.

Segment A named portion of the display list that defines a display item.

Segment Attribute A characteristic of a segment, i.e., detectability, visibility.

Selective Erase The ability to delete portions of a display without affecting the remainder.

Shading (1) An image processing technique which indicates light sources in a three-dimensional image. (2) The changes in sensitivity of the video camera tube of an image digitizer.

Shadow Mask A metal plate positioned behind the display surface of a color raster display and pierced with small holes, such that when the triad is focused on a hole, the electrons from each gun only strike their respective phosphors.

Shielding The defining of an opaque viewport or window in which to display a menu, a title, or a message to the operator.

Signal *See* Net.

Signal Highlighting The distinguishing of the pins in a net.

Soft Copy A copy of a display in video form, as on videotape.

Spot Size The smallest area on the display surface of a CRT which can be excited by an electron beam, determining the line width on calligraphic displays.

Static Segment Attribute The segment attribute which specifies what transformation functions are available for the segment.

Stipple Pattern The pattern fill chosen in dithering.

Storage Tube A CRT which maintains a display on the display surface without refresh.

Stroke Writing *See* Calligraphic Drawing.

Stylus A device analogous to a pencil which is used in conjunction with a data tablet to input coordinate information.

Subfigure *See* Marker.

Subroutine A named display item description contained in the display list, used to create multiple views of the item without repeating the display instructions.

Subtractive Color The color produced by filtering out the red, green, or blue color components of another color.

Surface of Revolution The surface which results from tracing the path of a curve as it is rotated about an axis.

Surface Patch A piecewise component of the surface of a three-dimensional object.

Sweep Plane The plane defined by the end-points of a line segment and the view point.

Tablet *See* Data Tablet.

Text String A collection of characters.

Thematic Mapping The use of maps as a display background over which to display geographically oriented information.

Thumbwheel A graphic input device consisting of a rotatable dial which controls the movement of a line across the display surface, horizontally or vertically. They are normally found in pairs, one horizontal and one vertical, and are used to input coordinate data.

Touch-Sensitive Display A display device whose display surface can register physical contact.

Track Ball A graphic input device which employs a mounted rotatable ball to control the position of a cursor, used for producing coordinate data.

Tracking The following of the movements of a pick device on the display surface.

Tracking Symbol A cursor on the display surface which indicates where a pick device is pointing.

Transformation Function A function which modifies a display by introducing rotation, scaling or translation.

Transformation Matrix The matrix defining the multiplications to be performed on existing vectors to produce the desired transformation function.

Translate To transform a display item on the display surface by repositioning it to another coordinate location.

Triad Three electron guns grouped in a triangle for use with a shadow mask, with each gun responsible for either the red, green, or blue color component.

True Scale The introduction of more detail to a display when an operator zooms in.

Tumbling The viewing of a three-dimensional object by continually changing its axis of rotation.

Unposting The setting of the visibility segment attribute to off.

Valuator Device A graphic input device, such as a control dial, that inputs scalar values within a user-defined range.

Vector A directed line segment.

Vertical Retrace The turning off and repositioning of the electron beam to the upper left corner of the display surface after the last scan line has been drawn during raster scan.

Video Signal An electric voltage representing image data in terms of its brightness.

Viewing Direction The inclination of a window with respect to the axes of a world coordinate system as defined in the viewing operation.

Viewing Operation The process of defining and using a mapping from world coordinates to NDC or device coordinates.

Viewing Transformation The conversion of an object definition to NDC using the viewing operation.

Viewing Vector A vector emanating from the view point and passing perpendicular through the view plane to define the viewing direction.

View Plane The projection plane used in three-dimensional viewing operations.

View Plane Distance The distance from the view plane to the view reference point.

View Plane Normal A vector specified relative to the view reference point, to which the view plane is perpendicular.

View Point The originating point of a field of view.

Viewport A specified rectangle on the view surface within which a window's contents are displayed.

View Reference Point A coordinate point near the object being viewed, normally the origin.

View Site A coordinate point on the object being viewed which intersects with the viewing vector.

View Surface A two-dimensional display surface mapped to normalized device coordinate space.

View Up Vector A vector specified in world coordinates and relative to the view reference point, which if projected onto the view surface would be upright. Used to define a window's rotation.

View Volume The portion of the world coordinate system to be projected onto the view plane, whose boundaries are defined through window clipping and z clipping.

Virtual Coordinate System The result of mapping a portion of the world coordinate system to the finite limits of the device space.

Visibility A dynamic segment attribute which defines if a segment is currently visible on the display surface.

Voice Input Device A graphic input device which accepts and interprets vocal data.

White Graphics The overlaying of image data with vector data.

Whiteness A characteristic of color defining its percentage difference from a gray of the same blackness.

Window The specified area on the view plane containing the projections to be displayed.

Window Clipping The bounding of a view volume in the x and y directions by passing projectors through the corners of the window to define its sides.

Wire Frame An image of a three-dimensional object displayed as a series of line segments outlining its surface, including hidden lines.

Wire Net A subset of net which shows those interconnections having common characteristics.

Wiring Elementary *See* Elementary Diagram.

Workstation *See* Display Console.

World Coordinate System The device-independent coordinate system used to define objects meant for display.

World Coordinate Transformation A transformation which transforms the world coordinate system of a model to the default world coordinate system of a graphics package which is in effect immediately prior to a viewing operation.

Wraparound The positioning of a display item such that it overlaps the border of the device space, resulting in it being displayed on the opposite side of the display surface.

Write Protect A feature which prevents the updating of a bit plane.

Yon Plane The back clipping plane used in z clipping to define a finite view volume.

z Clipping The bounding of a view volume in the z direction by defining a hither plane and a yon plane parallel to the view plane.

Zoom To scale a display or display item so it appears to either approach or recede from the viewer.

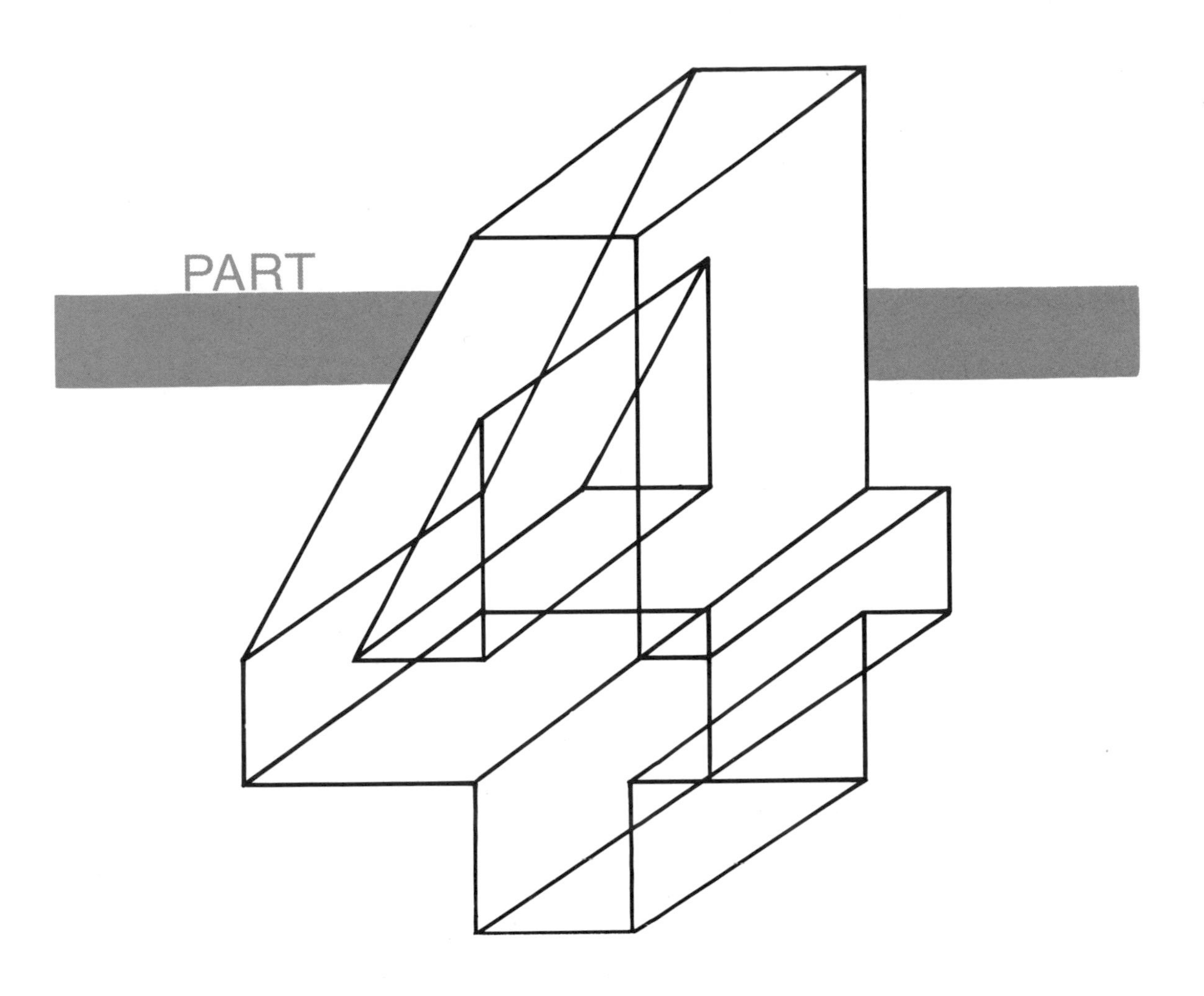

PART 4

APPENDIXES

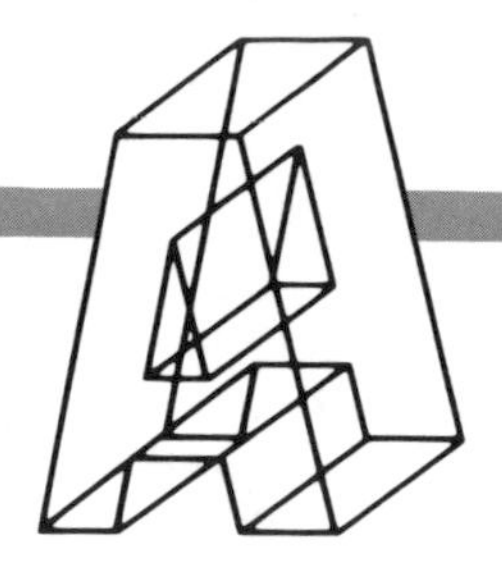

Microcomputer Systems

by
Eric Teicholz

A.1 INTRODUCTION

The use of microprocessors as the basis for stand-alone computer-aided design (CAD) systems is a relatively recent phenomenon. Until 6 or 7 years ago microprocessors mostly had 8-bit word architectures that were both too slow and had too little addressable primary memory to serve all but the most limited of drafting and engineering applications. With the general availability of 16-bit word and, still more recently, 32-bit word architectures and the use of intelligent input and output peripherals, the true stand-alone microcomputer turnkey CAD system represents an ever-increasing alternative to general-purpose minicomputer and mainframe CAD systems.

There are currently over 100 vendors offering low-cost CAD systems (with entry prices starting under $100,000) for the mechanical drafting, general electronics, printed- and integrated-circuit (PC/IC), architectural, engineering, metalworking, and mapping markets. Most low-cost vendor offerings are built around microprocessors, but some represent entry-level minicomputer systems. As a rule, users of low-cost systems tend to be relatively unsophisticated technically and prefer to deal with a single vendor for hardware, software, and support rather than procure systems piecemeal.

Current users of microcomputer CAD systems generally consist of either small design and drafting firms or drafting departments within large companies. Vendors have so far concentrated on the mechanical drafting and electronics markets, which tend both to be somewhat focused and often to not require the full software capabilities of general-purpose minicomputer and mainframe computer-aided design and computer-aided manufacturing (CAD/CAM) systems.

The potential market for low-cost microcomputer systems is extremely large and is currently only minimally using CAD technology. Some industry experts are predicting a growth rate of over 70 percent for such systems—over twice that of minicomputer and mainframe CAD/CAM systems. It is estimated that there are over 60,000 firms in the United States selling in excess of $3 million per year that comprise the potential microcomputer-based CAD marketplace.

A.2 BACKGROUND

This section covers advantages of microprocessor CAD systems, types of vendors currently selling software and turnkey microcomputer-based systems, types of applications currently served by vendors, and industry trends.

A.2.1 Definition, Types of Systems and Vendors

Microprocessor CAD systems and complete stand-alone turnkey systems are currently selling in the $20,000 to $100,000 range. In the higher price range, systems compete against several entry-level minicomputer systems such as Intergraph Corp., Calma, Gerber, California Computer Products (CalComp), Auto-trol, Technology Inc., Applicon, and Computervision Corp. Typical microprocessor systems include the following components:

- Either 16-bit word [such as Digital Equipment Corp.'s (DEC) LSI 11/23] or 32-bit word chips (such as the M-68000)
- Medium-resolution (500 × 500 pixels) graphic display for the edit workstation
- Ten to fifty megabytes of secondary storage (either floppy or Winchester hard disk)
- Alpha keyboard
- Menu tablet
- Plotter
- Digitizer
- Drafting software

- Training
- Installation
- Hardware and software maintenance for the warranty period

There are three broad cost ranges for microprocessor CAD systems:

1. Very low-cost systems (Cascade Graphics Development, T&W Systems, Inc. Summit CAD Corp.) often based on personal computers, that perform training, education, or limited two-dimensional drafting functions
2. Medium-range systems costing from $40,000 to $75,000 [Interactive Computer Systems, Inc. (ICS), Formtek, BruningCAD, SKOK Systems, Inc., Racal-Redac], based on 16-bit (and increasingly 32-bit) processors, performing mostly two-dimensional drafting and some applications software functions
3. High-end systems, costing over $75,000 (Sigma Design Inc, Aydin Controls, and Tricad), using 32-bit word single or multiprocessors and performing two- and three-dimensional design, drafting, and general-purpose applications.

Table 3.1 in Chap. 3, Sec. 3.5 compares vendors on the basis of the size of the word used by the processor. Vendors of microcomputer CAD systems come from a variety of backgrounds. Surprisingly, only about half the vendors are start-up companies. Vendor classifications consist of the following:

- ***New Companies.*** Most start-up companies (Avera Corp., Mentor Graphics Corp., VIA Systems, Telesis Corp.) have been founded by previous employees of existing minicomputer CAD companies. These start-ups try to fill a market niche not met by the parent company.
- ***Software Houses.*** Many software companies (ICS, EGS, Holguin Associates, Grafcon) have developed general-purpose applications software which they subsequently integrate and sell as part of a turnkey CAD system. If the company is large enough, it will buy hardware from an established manufacturer on an original equipment manufacturers (OEM) basis, perhaps develop proprietary hardware, and market and service the entire system.
- ***Engineering Supply Companies.*** Several engineering supply companies [e.g., BruningCAD, Keuffel & Esser Co. (K & E)] seeking new high-growth markets have turned to microcomputer CAD systems.
- ***Computer Peripheral Equipment Vendors.*** Several companies [e.g., Bausch & Lomb, Summagraphics Corp., Data Technology Inc. (DataTech)] that produce computer input and output (I/O) equipment, such as plotters, displays, and digitizers, are now supporting integrated turnkey systems for design and drafting applications.

A.2.2 Advantages and Limitations of Microcomputers

Chapter 1 lists a number of advantages of CAD/CAM over using manual methods for design and drafting, There are, additionally, several other reasons for selecting microprocessor systems rather than traditional larger mini and mainframe systems. Lower graphic workstation costs are the most obvious reason. Others include:

- ***Ease of Use.*** Larger mini and mainframe systems often require a 6- to 9-month learning period before an operator is functioning at the projected efficiency rate over manual methods. Microcomputer-based CAD systems, which are often more specialized in nature, normally require a third to a half of this time.
- ***Application Features.*** Several microcomputer systems dedicated to particular applications (mostly in electronics) are quite powerful and are less expensive to

operate on the smaller systems. Some microcomputer-based vendors who are marketing PC/IC board software, for example, have capabilities that include routing, design rule checking, and net list generation.

- ***Specialization.*** Many firms have specialized design or drafting needs (e.g., school or hospital design, some mechanical part design) that justify the lack of generalization offered by most microcomputer CAD systems.
- ***Decentralization.*** Many large firms, often already using large CAD/CAM systems, have remote offices that can effectively make use of microcomputer-based systems. Many of these systems currently can be networked either to other small systems (usually of the same make) or to a remote host computer in order to either access a centralized drawing database or use an application package that exists on the host machine.
- ***Education.*** Although some firms can initially afford only low-cost microcomputer systems, these systems can serve the function of providing a bridge (intermediate step) to procuring larger CAD/CAM systems purchased at a later date. Using a microcomputer system can educate a firm in basic CAD techniques such as drawing overlays; menuing; and computer drawing creation, editing, and output—plus provide insights into the management and organizational implications of using CAD. If a microcomputer system is used in this way, particular attention should be paid to telecommunications and networking capabilities so that the small system will not be "dead-ended" in terms of growth or future integration with other CAD/CAM systems.
- ***Database Compatibility with Large CAD/CAM Systems.*** Several low-cost system vendors (e.g., Cascade, VIA, Avera) offer functional and database compatibility with larger minicomputer systems. The microprocessor CAD system can therefore serve as an inexpensive data entry and edit station for the larger system or be used for system training without utilizing expensive workstations or degrading the larger system's performance.

Microprocessor CAD systems are not currently equal to larger systems in all aspects except cost. In general, microprocessors do not currently have the same computation speed or the same addressable memory space as larger systems. Computationally demanding applications, such as solids modeling and large drawing file handling, cannot be effectively handled with microprocessors. Additional limitations include the following:

- ***Two-Dimensional Databases.*** Most personal computer microcomputer CAD systems incorporate two-dimensional data representation. The mid- and high-range systems will often use either 32-bit chips or multiprocessors to permit true three-dimensional data geometry.
- ***Limited Applications Software.*** In general, low end microcomputer CAD systems are specialized in nature. Because of hardware limitations and the relative newness of the industry, there is nowhere near the breadth of software that is offered by traditional minicomputer vendors (see App. B).
- ***Support of I/O Equipment.*** Microcomputer CAD systems do not yet offer support for the large variety of digitizers, plotters, and displays currently supported by the minicomputer and mainframe vendors.
- ***Limited Workstation Support.*** Minicomputer CAD systems generally support at least four workstations simultaneously. Microcomputer systems will usually support only one workstation per processor. Most vendors will, however, offer local networking of processors. This networking, plus graphic database standards such as Initial Graphic Exchange Specifications (IGES) (see next section), will help alleviate the current limited upward migration path of microcomputer CAD systems.

A.2.3 Trends

It is always difficult to predict future developments in industries that are evolving as rapidly as the microprocessor and the CAD/CAM industries. One can, however, expand on developments already occurring in these industries to ascertain near-range (perhaps 3 years) implications. Some of the current developments that will have strong impacts within this time frame include the following:

- ***More Mobile Upward Migration Paths.*** As microcomputers become faster and incorporate 32- and 64-bit word architectures, systems will develop virtual memories and be much more extensible in terms of hardware and software growth than is currently the case.
- ***Emergence of Database Standards.*** A major factor impeding CAD/CAM use is the lack of database standards. Not having cross-system standards for data formats means that systems are incompatible with one another. One such neutral format for exchanging data between noncompatible CAD/CAM systems is the IGES developed by the American National Standards Institute (ANSI). Over 40 vendors have stated their intention to develop IGES translators as of January 1984. Only a few microprocessor CAD vendors currently support IGES.
- ***Development of Stand-Alone Workstations from Display Processors.*** With the increased use of microprocessors for graphic functions normally performed by a host minicomputer or mainframe computer, it is just a matter of time before vendors of display processors offer general drafting capabilities. Lexidata Corporation's SOLIDESIGN firmware (using M-68000 processors) already generates shaded, hidden-surface solid models using simple polygon data as input from a host computer.
- ***Emergence of Very Low-Cost Workstations.*** Personal computers, such as the IBM PC, DEC's Professional, and Apple computers, will have functional compatibility with larger CAD/CAM systems and increasingly be used for both training and "front-end" drafting applications.
- ***More Competition.*** If the low-cost CAD marketplace approaches anything like $0.5 billion projected for 1986, current microcomputer CAD vendors can expect significant competition from existing minicomputer CAD systems, from large companies such as IBM not currently having low-cost CAD products, from start-ups employing experienced CAD/CAM personnel (such as Avera and VIA Systems), and from reprographics and engineering supply companies with established distribution channels (such as K & E).
- ***New and Improved Software.*** As the microcomputer market matures, better software for existing and emerging applications will appear—both from independent software houses and from system vendors.
- ***Application Integration.*** As microcomputers proliferate, scientific applications will increasingly be merged with business programs. Using common command languages, networking, and database standards, vendors will offer integrated software packages encompassing CAD, business graphics, word processing, project management and control, and other generic applications.

A.3 USER CASE STUDIES: LOW-COST SYSTEMS

Most turnkey microprocessor CAD systems have been designed by vendors to fill a particular application need. Applications have been designed either for small companies (from 20 to 75 employees) where it would be difficult to justify the entry prices of mini and mainframe systems or for narrowly defined application tasks that do not require the general-purpose capabilities of larger systems. In general, microprocessor development is just reaching the point where general-purpose integrated systems are being developed that can operate on very large databases. Small system applications that have been targeted to date include the following:

- Mechanical drafting
- Architecture, engineering, and construction

- Electronics [including IC and very large-scale integration (VLSI) design and PC boards]
- Mapping

Other case studies of small firms are included in Chap. 2.

A.3.1 Mechanical Drafting

Most of the current vendors, except perhaps for those marketing electronic systems, offer a general-purpose drafting capability. Most microprocessor CAD systems support two-dimensional geometry (Vector Automation, Inc., BruningCAD, Holguin Associates, ICS) although some support three-dimensional data representation (Vector Automation, Inc., Tricad).

Basic to any CAD system is mechanical drafting software—consisting of capabilities for graphical data input, editing, manipulation, and analysis. Input relates to the types of building blocks or primitives accessible to the user by a particular package (e.g., points, lines, arcs, circles, splines, curves, surfaces). Manipulation relates to graphic transformation capabilities of a system, such as the ability to move, mirror, stretch, merge, scale, delete, and perform group operations on a drawing. Typical analytic capabilities of a drafting package include point, angle, centroid, perimeter, area, volume, and moment calculations.

One east coast equipment manufacturer interviewed for this case study analysis is using Bausch & Lomb's (B & L) PRODUCER CAD system (Fig. A.1) for general drafting related to ferrous and nonferrous industrial furnaces. The system is used by three CAD drafters, each of whom works 5 hours a day, to create a 15-hour workday for the computer. Each shift works on its own project rather than picking up where the previous shift left off. When not working on the system, the operator's time is devoted to planning and creating a relevant symbol library for furnace equipment.

B & L's PRODUCER system sold in 1983 for $58,000 and consisted of a DEC LSI 11/23 16-bit word central processing unit (CPU), dual-density floppy disks (a 5- to 10-megabyte Winchester hard disk is optional), a digitizer, plotter, and a Tektronix 4010 cathode-ray tube (CRT) (subsequently upgraded to a color refresh CRT) edit workstation with a tablet menu (see Fig. A.2). For service reasons, system sales or rentals were restricted to sites within 1 1/2-hour driving distance from sales offices.

The chief operator of the furnace equipment manufacturer maintains that "the PRODUCER system is most helpful in making electrical wiring diagrams. We can already

Figure A.1 The PRODUCER electronic drafting system by Bausch & Lomb. (*Courtesy of Bausch & Lomb.*)

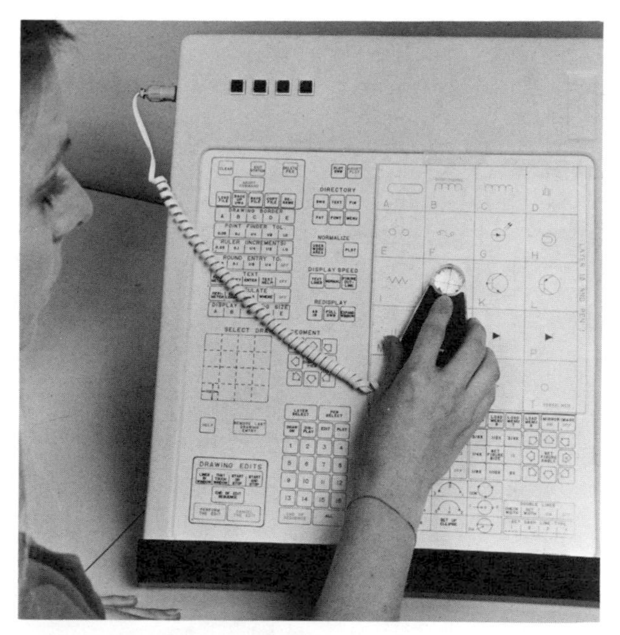

Figure A.2 The PRODUCERS's menu tablet. (*Courtesy of Bausch & Lomb.*)

produce these twice as fast as we did manually. It produces picture-perfect drawings with great accuracy." Drafting applications work best when there is repetition—either in terms of features within a drawing or for modifying previously stored drawings. The firm maintains that, so far, complex (one-of-a-kind) drawings are best accomplished manually rather than on the CADD system. Finally, the firm maintains that the system "would not replace any of the people we have, but we are expecting not to have to hire as many people as we have in the past."

A.3.2 Architecture, Engineering, and Construction

Crosier, Kilgour and Partners, Ltd., an engineering and architectural firm, has five offices in western Canada. The Calgary office consists of 14 people (mostly structural engineers) using an Omnitech Graphic Systems, Inc. ERGOS 240 CADD system (Fig. A.3). The $87,000 to $150,000 system (in 1983) uses a CA 240 16-bit word minicomputer processor, a

Figure A.3 The architectural CAD system based on the Hewlett-Packard 9836C Computer. (*Courtesy of SKOK Systems.*)

Summagraphics' digitizer, a vendor-manufactured CRT (as part of the dual-screen edit workstation), and either a Hewlett-Packard (HP), CalComp, Zeta, or Versatec plotter. Applications software from Omnitech includes automatic bill-of-material extraction, finite-element modeling (FEM) for mechanical parts and buildings, drawing management, central database or distributed network support, and chart booking (record keeping of a project over time).

At Crosier Kilgour, the system is primarily used for structural, architectural, precast concrete, and steel drafting and detailing. Production drawings constitute 50 percent of the CADD system use, and steel and precast detailing another 50 percent. Five operators work on three systems, each operator working 4 days on, 3 days off—which gives approximately 200 hours per week from the three systems.

Rick Scheidt, a partner at the Calgary office, reports that the system is best-suited for repetitive drawing.

> Revisions can be reflected in new, original drawings, eliminating the need for low-quality sepias. Corporate details—client logos, for example—can be put into memory and reprinted on a drawing. The system greatly impoves accuracy and quality; lettering and numbering appear uniform, rather than being subject to different drafters' styles. The system can draw at any scale, and dimension using either Metric or English standards. Complex and non-repetitive items are more efficient and cost-effective done manually. The only liability I'd associate with the system is that we need to maintain a constant flow of work to justify the cost of the machine.

A.3.3 Electronics

Major vendors of IC and VSLI circuit systems include Avera, Mentor Graphics, VIA, Valid Logic Systems, Inc., and ICS. Printed-circuit board (PCB) vendors include Design Aids, Inc., Racal-Redac, Summit Cad, Telesis, and Gerber Scientific Instrument.

The Nelson Electric Marine Division of General Signal uses an ICS CADD 2000 series system for electrical switchboard design for ships and submarines for the U.S. Navy. The ICS system has software to support electrical ladder diagrams, schematics, and control circuit analysis. ICS systems sell from $50,000 to $93,000 and are based on DEC LSI microprocessors, Altec, CalComp, or Summagraphics digitizers, a Tektronix 4014 CRT edit workstation, and CalComp, HP, Glaser, or Tektronix plotters.

According to Larry Bowles, computer graphics operator, "the overwhelming advantage of the system is having a parts library. With this, anything on a drawing that is going to be repeated on future drawings can be called up from memory, edited if necessary, and inserted." Bowles reports that their library of assembly parts has reduced their drafting time in design layout by 35 to 40 percent. He maintains that complex drawings can undergo substantial revisions in quality control with minimal effort. As for limitations, "the speed of drawing displays, edits, and load times is significantly slower than with larger systems. However, the slow speed, which is common to all small systems, is a small price to pay for a system that has so many benefits associated with it."

Triad Engineering Corporation is a PC design service bureau. They own four Gerber Scientific Instrument (GSI) minicomputer CAD systems. GSI applications software includes tape plot generation, drill tape output for NC drills, a database language package, component insertion, and design rules checking software. GSI's basic drafting package has the ability to generate parts lists; solder masks; and silk screen, pad, and art masters for PCBs. GSI's PC 800 series CADD systems cost from $35,000 to $45,000 (exclusive of plotter or digitizer) and are based on an HP 2109EK processor.

Triad staff uses the GSI systems for PCB digitizing and design and operates in three shifts, each shift picking up on projects started by the preceding shift, so as to provide a continual digitizing effort. PCB design is a labor-intensive task which lends itself especially well to volume production, automatic testing, and automatic assembly. The payback on CADD in PCB design is almost immediate. It can increase speed, accuracy, and productivity in virtually every phase of design—from conception to delivery of the product to the customer.

Frank Haigh, sales manager at Triad, states that the low-cost GSI system can automatically interconnect points and provide design checks (e.g., check clearances between two conductors and report if there is a violation of design standards). Haigh believes that the system's forte is in assisting in the actual design of digital circuits.

> The system can display both sides of the PCB at the same time, to enable the designer to view the interconnections from side to side. It can automatically repeat similar patterns; make corrections; move components, or whole areas of the circuit on the screen; display grids; assign different colors to the different layers to make them more discernible; and display all the connections, as they are indicated on the schematic, to enable the designer to determine if and how they should be rearranged. Not only does the system generate film masters, but the same data base can produce the associated documentation (drill drawings, drill tapes, assembly drawings, etc.) with absolute accuracy.

A.3.4 Mapping

Major low-cost mapping vendors include Earth Resources Design Analysis Systems (ERDAS), HASP, Inc., DataTech, and GeoBased Systems. The James W. Sewall Company is a consulting firm of some 100 civil engineers and foresters. Their GeoBased Systems low-cost STRINGS (storage and retrieval of informative graphics) CADD system (Fig. A.4) consists of a PDP 11/23 16-bit word microprocessor CPU, a Talos digitizer, Houston Instrument and Soltec plotters, an AED 512 color CRT, and three digitizing stations—one interfaced to a Kern PG2 stereoplotter. GeoBased Systems CADD systems in 1983 cost from $25,000 (for a digitizing station) to $180,000. Applications software includes parcel mapping and timber information management systems.

One of the primary applications of STRINGS at Sewall is for forestry. Using the stereoplotter, a base map showing planimetric detail is compiled; forest data delineated from aerial photos (e.g., types of tree stands) is then superimposed on the base map. Attributes of stands such as the value of the stand reflected in the cords of wood it contains, the stand number and type, zoning, and soil and slope data are likewise encoded. The CADD system can then analyze and draw a map showing any combination of file attributes requested.

Earl Raymond, Director of Field Surveys and Photogrammetry, and Ted Tryon, Director of Forestry at Sewall, maintain that "what we're doing on the system would have been prohibitive or impossible by hand; for instance, we have not been able to afford to do color maps since the mid '50's. The system's ability to replace reams of tabular data with a color map to display the same information graphically is invaluable, as is its ability to reduce, enlarge, and change data."

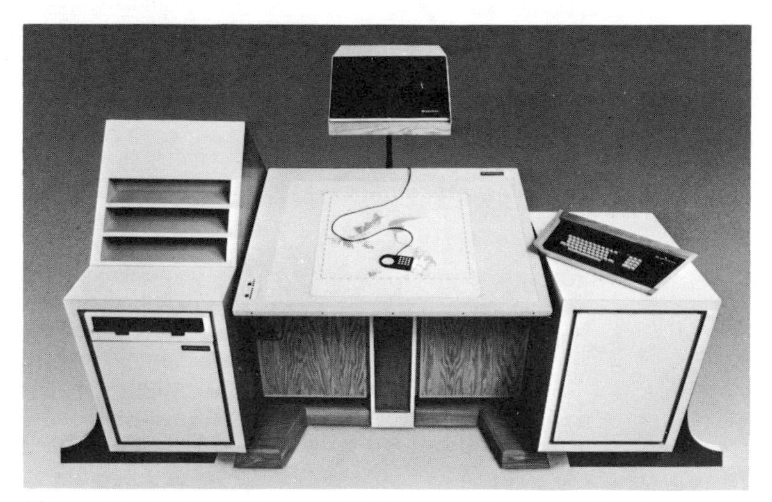

Figure A.4 GeoBased System's CADD system. (*Courtesy of GeoBased Systems.*)

VENDORS

Applicon, Inc.
32 Second Ave.
Burlington, MA 01803
(617)272-7070

Auto-trol Technology
12500 N. Washington St.
P.O. Box 33815
Denver, CO 80233
(303)452-4919

Avera Corporation
200 Technology Circle
Scotts Valley, CA 95066
(408)438-1401

Aydin controls
401 Commerce Dr.
Fort Washington, PA 19034
(215)643-0600

Bausch & Lomb
1212 E. Anderson Lane
Austin, TX 78752
(512)835-0900

BruningCAD
6111 E. Skelly Dr.
Tulsa, OK 74135
(918)663-5291

Cadlinc, Inc.
700 Nicholas Blvd.
Elk Grove Village, IL 60007
(312)228-7300

California Computer Products, Inc. (CalComp)
2411 W. LaPalma Ave.
Anaheim, CA 92801
(714)821-2011

Cascade Graphics Development
1000 S. Grand Ave.
Santa Ana, CA 92705
(714)558-3316

Comarc Systems
150 Executive Park Blvd.
San Francisco, CA 94134
(415)467-1300

Computervision Corp. (CV)
201 Burlington Rd.
Bedford, MA 01730
(617)275-1800

Control Data Corporation
Computer Systems Marketing
HQW 09G
P.O. Box O
Minneapolis, MN 55440
(612)853-8100

Data Technology, Inc. (DataTech)
4 Gill St.
Woburn, MA 01801
(617)935-8820

Design Aids, Inc.
27822 El Lazo Blvd.
Laguna Niguel, CA 92677
(714)831-5611

Engineering Systems Consultants, Inc.
1801 Staring Lane
Suite 103
P.O. Box 80318
Baton Rouge, LA 70808
(504)769-2226

Earth Resources Data Analysis Systems (ERDAS)
430 Tenth St., Suite N206
Atlanta, GA 30318
(404)872-7327

Formative Technologies, Inc. (FORMTEK)
5001 Baum Blvd.
Pittsburgh, Pa 15213
(412)682-8000

GE Calma
5155 Old Ironsides Dr.
Santa Clara, CA 95050
(408)245-7522

GeoBased Systems
725 W. Morgan St.
Raleigh, NC 27603
(919)834-9313

Gerber Scientific Instrument (GSI)
83 Gerber Road West
South Windsor, CT 06074
(203)644-1551

Gerber Systems Technology, Inc.
40 E. Gerber Rd.
South Windsor, CT 06074
(203)644-2581

Grafcon
5510 South Memorial
P.O Box 54909
Tulsa, OK 74145
(918)663-5291

Gravitronics Systems Engineering
3014 Shattuck Ave.
Berkeley, CA 94705
(415)644-2230

HASP, Inc.
1411 W. Eisenhower Blvd.
Loveland, CO 80537
(303)669-6900

Holguin Associates
5822 Cromo Dr.
P.O. Box 12990
El Paso, TX 79912
(915)581-1171

Interactive Computer Systems, Inc. (ICS)
13541 Tiger Bend Rd.
Baton Rouge, LA 70816
(504)292-7570

Intergraph Corp.
One Madison Industrial Park
Huntsville, AL 35807
(205)772-2000

Keuffel & Esser Co. (K & E)
20 Whippany Rd.
Morristown, NJ 07960
(201)285-5160

McDonnell Douglas Automation Co. (McAuto)
325 McDonnell Blvd.
P.O. Box 516
St. Louis, MO 63166
(314)232-8021

Manufacturing Consulting Services
17942 Cowan Ave.
Irvine, CA 92714
(714)540-3921

Mentor Graphics Corporation
10200 SW Nimbus Av. G7
Portland, OR 97223
(503)620-9817

Omnitech Graphic systems, Inc.
City Centre Building
880 Wellington St.
7th Floor
Ottawa, Ontario
Canada K 1R 6K7
(613)232-1747

Prime Computer Inc.
1 Speen St.
Framingham, MA 01701
(617)872-4770

Racal-Redac
One Redac Way
Littleton, MA 01460
(617)486-9231

Sigma Design Inc.
7306 S. Alton Way
Englewood, CO 80112
(303)773-0666

SKOK Systems, Inc.
222 Third St.
Cambridge, MA 02142
(617)868-6003

Summagraphics Corp.
35 Brentwood Ave.
P.O. Box 781
Fairfield, Ct 06430
(203)384-1344

Summit CAD Corporation
5222 FM 1960 West 102
Houston, TX 77069
(713)440-1468

Tektronix, Inc.
P.O. Box 500
Beaverton, OR 97077
(503)682-3411

Telesis Corporation
21 Alpha Rd.
Chelmsford, MA 01824
(617)256-2300

Tricad
1655 McCarthy Blvd.
Militas, CA 95035
(408)942-8800

T&W Systems, Inc.
7372 Prince Dr., No. 106
Huntington Beach, CA 92647
(714)847-9960

Valid Logic Systems, Inc.
650 North Mary Ave.
Sunnyvale, CA 94086
(408)773-1300

Vector Automation, Inc.
Village of Cross Keys
Baltimore, MD 21210
(301)433-4202

VIA Systems
76 Treble Cove Road
N. Billerica, MA 01862
(617)667-8574

BIBLIOGRAPHY

NEWSLETTERS

A-E-C Automation Newsletter, 7209 Wisteria Way, Carlsbad, CA 92008, (714)438-1595, monthly, $96/year.

The Anderson Report, 4505 E. Industrial, No. 2J, Simi Valley, CA 93063, (805)581-1184, monthly, $125/year.

CAD/CAM Alert, The Management Roundtable, Inc., 824 Boylston Street, Chestnut Hill, MA 02167, (617)232-8080, monthly, $167/year.

ECAN: Engineering Computer Applications Newsletter, 5 Denver Tech Center, P.O. Box 3109, Englewood, CO 80155, (303)771-5307, monthly, $60/year.

The S. Klein Newsletter on Computer Graphics, P.O. Box 89, Sudbury, MA 01776, (617)443-4671, biweekly, $145/year.

BOOKS

Allan, John: *A Survey of Computer-Aided Design and Computer-Aided Manufacturing*, Productivity International Inc., P.O. Box 8100, 5622 Dyer Street, Suite 225, Dallas TX 75205, (214)739-3056, 1980.

Chasen, S. H., and J. W. Dow: *The Guide for the Evaluation and Implementation of CAD/CAM Systems*, CAD/CAM Decisions, Box 76042, Atlanta, GA 30328, (404)255-5271, 1979.

Drawneck, B. A., J. R. Gurd, and B. S. Walker: *Interactive Computer Graphics*, Crane, Russak and Co, Inc., 3 E. 44th Street, New York, NY 10017, (212)867-1490, 1976.

Foley, James, and Andries Van Dam: *Fundamentals of Interactive Computer Graphics*, Addison-Wesley Publishing Co., Inc., Jacob Way, Reading, MA 01867, (617)944-3700, 1980.

Hulbert, L. E.: *Interactive Computer Graphics in Engineering*, American Society of Mechanical Engineers, 345 E. 47th Street, New York, NY 10017, (212)644-7713, 1977.

Stasiowski, Frank A.: *How to Select Data Processing Systems*, Annual Report, 56 Van Brunt Ave., Dedham, MA 02026, (617)326-4103,

Summer, Claire, and Walter Levy: *The Affordable Computer: The Microprocessor for Business and Industry*, The American Management Association, AMACON Division, 135 W. 50th Street, New York, NY 10020, (212)586-8100.

Taraman, Khalil: *CAD/CAM: Meeting Today's Productivity Challenge*, Society of Manufacturing Engineers, One SME Drive, P.O. Box 930, Dearborn, MI 48128, 1980.

DIRECTORIES

Computer Graphics Industry Service: The Low Cost CAD/CAM Systems Market, International Data Corporation, Pacific Technology Center, 1448 15th Street, Suite 101, Santa Monica, CA 90404, May 1982. Market study of low-cost system vendors.

Construction Computer Applications Directory, Construction Industry Press, 1105-F Spring Street, Silver Spring, MD 20910, (301)589-4884, $95(includes 2 updates). Contains over 1000 software program descriptions from over 150 vendors.

DATAPRO, Datapro Research Corp., 1805 Underwood Boulevard, Delran, NJ 08075, (800)257-9406 or in N.J. (609)764-0100. Reports on hardware, software, and buyers' guides.

Design Compudata, Graphic Systems, Inc. (publisher), 180 Franklin St., Cambridge, MA 02139, (617)492-1148. Annual, $95 + $3 postage. Lists over 400 software packages.

Low Cost CAD Systems, Leading Edge Publishing Inc., P.O. Box 8100, 5622 Dyer Street, Dallas, TX 75205, (214)739-0340, November 1981. Lists vendors, tabular comparisons, and management considerations for low-cost vendors.

NTIS: A Directory of Computer Software and Related Technical Reports, Walter Finch, Software Product Manager, Office of Data Base Services, NTIS, 5285 Port Royal Road, Springfield, VA 22161, (703)487-4807. Report PB 80-110232, $40. Listing, including abstracts and prices, for 450 computer programs.

The S. Klein Directory of Computer Graphics Suppliers: Hardware, Software, Systems and Services, Stanley Klein (publisher), P.O. Box 89, Sudbury, MA 01776, (617)443-4671. Annual, $47, 128 pages. Lists vendors, services, systems, and software including business graphics and image processing.

Turnkey CAD/CAM Computer Graphics: A Survey and Buyers' Guide, Charles M. Foundyller, Daratech Assoc., P.O. Box 410, Cambridge, MA 02238, (617)354-2339, 1980 with updates, 3 volumes. Volume 1 has background data on CAD/CAM components, volume 2 has data on how to compare vendors and volume 3 is a directory of vendors.

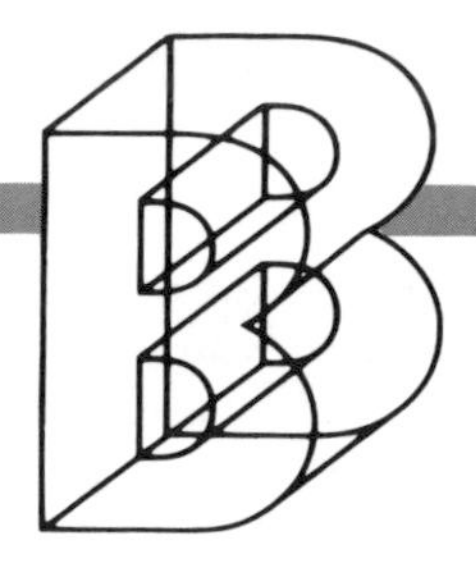

Minicomputer Systems

by
Joel Orr

B.1 WHAT THIS CHAPTER COVERS

In recent years, computer-aided design and drafting (CADD) systems have been constructed around computers of various sizes. The size categories of the computers have given rise to distinctions among the CADD systems based on them. Let us examine these categories and their members.

Mainframe-based, or large, CADD systems were the earliest size category to appear. In the late 1960s, the General Motors Design Augmented by Computer (DAC) program was developed, in conjuncton with International Business Machines (IBM). It ran on large IBM machines, with the 2250 vector refresh graphics display and light pen serving as the major components of the interactive workstation.

Minicomputer-based systems first came out around 1970. These are also called medium-size systems. Taking advantage of the then new Tektronix direct-view storage tube (DVST), two spinoffs of Massachusetts Institute of Technology (MIT) began marketing simple drafting systems that contained minicomputers; Applicon used the Digital Equipment Corp. (DEC) PDP-11, while Computervision selected the Data General NOVA for its computational "engine."

Microcomputer-based, or very small, CADD systems made their debut in 1977, in the form of the Bendix microNOVA version of its pioneering System 100. This size system is now becoming much more popular as microcomputers increase in power.

This chapter deals with CADD systems of the second category—medium-size systems. We look at system and vendor comparison issues.

B.2 SYSTEM ISSUES

Examining and comparing medium-size CADD systems is a major undertaking. The following are some points of comparison.

- ***Type of Computer.*** One of the principal distinguishing characteristics of the various systems on the market is the type of computer they use. Low-cost systems, use either a minicomputer or a microcomputer. The main difference between these two types is that a microcomputer has its central computational function embodied in a single chip, or integrated circuit. Minicomputers contain a computing facility made up of a number of integrated circuits.

  Minicomputers are usually larger—both in terms of physical size and of the number of tasks they can handle concurrently—than microcomputers. The dividing line between the types is not always sharp and clear.

  Another way computers differ is in the number of bits per word. A *bit*, or binary digit, is the smallest unit of digital information; a *word* is the basic number of bits a given computer handles at one time. Most minicomputers have 16-bit words; microcomputers have 8-, 16-, or 32-bit words. While word length is not an absolute indication of computer power, if all other factors are equal, a 16-bit-word computer is more powerful than an 8-bit-word computer.

  Beware of applying this generalization too broadly; well-written software on an 8-bit-word microcomputer can outperform poorly written software on a larger machine. You are seeking *function*, not raw computing power.

  If the system vendor does not provide its own maintenance, the type of computer will have some bearing on the maintainability of the system by other parties.

- ***Two and Three Dimensions.*** Engineering drawings are always two-dimensional; they are made on flat, two-dimensional pieces of paper, and so cannot be otherwise. Some CADD systems, however, can store three-dimensional images by retaining x, y, and z coordinates for each point. This representation of the object of interest is more faithful to reality than the two-dimensional one; clearly, we live in a three-dimensional world. The principal practical benefit of the three-dimensional representation is that views—drawings of the object from a particular viewing angle—are easily created by the CADD system automatically from the image stored in its memory.

Figure B.1 A medium-size interactive CADD system. (*Courtesy of CalComp.*)

If a change is made to the three-dimensional model, any view of that model will reflect the change. This is, in general, highly desirable; errors are frequently introduced in projects when changes are made to some views but not to others.

In most instances, working in three dimensions is more productive than working in two dimensions because it is not necessary to draw the different views; these can be automatically created by the system. On the other hand, engineers, designers, and drafters are accustomed to working in two dimensions. Though many profess to conceive designs in three dimensions, the available drafting tools have constrained them to producing two-dimensional views. It may not be easy for them to learn an entirely new way to express their designs. Of course, some disciplines have no use for three dimensions, for instance, electrical schematic drafting and process and instrumentation drafting.

Most low-cost CADD systems are strictly two-dimensional; those that do permit three-dimensional drafting are not all easy to use. In sum, drawing in three dimensions offers great productivity gains to those who can take advantage of it. But where it is unnecessary, it may be a burden to the CADD system in terms of both cost and performance compromises.

- ***Drawing Commands.*** As an electronic drafting board the CADD system has much to offer. It takes the tedious aspects of drawing creation upon itself, leaving the user free to deal with the creative aspect. When using a CADD system, there is no need for the user to be concerned with the straightness of lines, the sharpness of a pencil point, or the precise position of a ruler or compass; the system sees to those things.

  Lettering-related issues are also simplified by the CADD system; all the user needs to do is to select the place, type, and justification of the lettering, then type in the text. The system sees to its accurate and clean creation and placement.

  Different engineering disciplines, however, necessitate different drawing aids. For instance, an architect wants the system to make it easy to create a column grid.

That user also wants to add thickness to lines to represent walls and to have the overlapping portions of such thicknesses disappear in the appropriate places. An electronic engineer is more concerned with symbol definition and placement, as well as with vertical and horizontal alignment of components in a schematic diagram. The mechanical engineer using a CADD system looks for a variety of dimensioning and tolerancing capabilities and perhaps the ability to change from English to metric measure and back again. Each engineering discipline imposes certain requirements on the drafting capabilities of the system. "The more, the better" does *not* apply in this case. The designer of integrated circuits has no use for a smooth spline, while it may be essential to the mapper. Determine your needs and select a system accordingly.

- ***Simultaneous Plotting.*** In manual drawing creation, the drawing is directly produced in its hard-copy form; in CADD, this is not the case. The drawing is first produced in digital form and edited in the computer memory. Only then does the user select the form in which the hard copy is to appear. Of course, it is just this segmentation of the process that gives CADD its power; an endless variety of drawings, at different scales and with different components, can be produced from a single digital drawing.

    In many small CADD systems, the computer is capable of handling only one task at a time. This means that, if the system is being used for designing, no plotting can take place; similarly, no designing can be performed while the plotter is in use. This can seriously limit the overall productivity of the system—particularly if it is to be used for designing on a full-time basis. Here are some remedies for this situation:

    - Have a clerk run plots after normal working hours.
    - Acquire one system strictly for plotting that can serve several design systems.
    - Consider only systems that permit simultaneous plotting and design.

- ***Data Storage and Backup.*** Since CADD systems put drawings and designs into electronic form, it is clear that normal drawing storage techniques cannot be used. Most small CADD systems store drawings on flexible diskettes, with online storage on nonremovable Winchester disks.

    Typically, the Winchester disk holds between 5 and 600 million characters (bytes) of data; while this factor varies from system to system, this represents between 50 and 6000 drawings, at 100,000 characters per drawing. (Since different internal representations are used by all the system vendors, the same drawing might occupy three times the amount of space on one system that it does on another. Furthermore, some systems have fixed drawing file sizes so that a drawing takes up the same amount of room no matter how sparse it is.)

    In planning your CADD operation, an important factor to determine is the number of drawings to which you need immediate and concurrent access; this could include symbol tables and subdrawings. In systems that have Winchester disks, some procedural provision must be made for periodically copying the contents of the disk onto some removable medium, such as diskette or magnetic tape. Good computer operating practice dictates that this type of copy be made periodically—once a day or once a week, depending on the volume of new data added daily to the system. This copying, or backup, protects you in the event of a system failure; the hours of work invested in creating the data will not be lost if the drawings can be retrieved from the removable medium.

    Another less-than-obvious consideration has to do with naming conventions. If the system restricts the names you may give to drawings to a small number of letters and numbers, you might find it difficult to keep track of a large number of drawings.

- ***Color.*** Once considered an interesting but useless frill, color has been found to be a real help in CADD displays. The more complex the drawing, the greater the advantage of being able to display it in a number of different colors, so that its component parts can be distinguished from each other. This is particularly true in applications such as integrated-circuit or printed-circuit-board design, where the drawing elements are all similar in shape and, hence, difficult to tell apart.

Unhappily, the price of color is still high compared to the price of a system with a monochromatic display. Color may add as much as $20,000 to the system cost. Color hard-copy output is available with almost any pen plotter; pens of different colors are used to produce colored lines. Ink-jet plotters are dropping in cost and will soon be competitive in price and resolution with pen plotters.

- ***Interface to Other Systems.*** In many cases, it is desirable to interface the small CADD system to other computing systems. For instance, if there is already a bill-of-materials application program in operation on another computer, it might be possible to tie the CADD system to it, so that information regarding materials might be extracted as drawings are created.

  Another example: If you have two or more CADD systems, you may want to transfer data between them over telephone lines rather than by trading diskettes. Not all systems have this capability. Others are able to communicate only with systems of the same brand. Still others are electronically capable of such communications but have no software for that purpose.

- ***Expansion.*** If you are expecting your organization to grow, you must consider what will become of the CADD system you now acquire. Will it be able to grow in a manner that accommodates your growth? Or will you be able to tie together other systems of the same type to make expansion possible? While these questions may appear to be premature, bear in mind that you may create a large database of drawings and designs which will not be translatable into the format of any other system! Thus, today's choice of CADD system may severely limit future system growth.

- ***Running Other Software.*** You may be interested in using the computer of the CADD system to perform other functions within your office—perhaps word processing, financial analysis, or payroll processing. While some of the systems have the features that allow such use—a widely used operating system, such as CP/M, for instance—many do not. Systems that do not permit the running of other programs usually cannot be modified to do so later.

- ***Display Resolution.*** The "niceness" of the picture on the system display is determined primarily by the display resolution—the number of individually addressable points on the screen. The more there are, the smoother and less jagged the image. When resolution is low, the image appears to have "staircases" along all its diagonal lines. It is very important to remember, however, that the jaggedness of the image on the display is not a function of the stored image but only of the display. Consider the following analogy: Projecting a 35-millimeter slide onto a picket fence yields an image with gaps in it, but the image on the slide remains whole. Zooming in and out with the system will demonstrate that the staircases remain the same size, while the image gets larger and smaller.

  Plots produced from the system database will *not* exhibit the jaggedness of the display; their resolution will be limited by that of the plotting device. In general, resolution costs money, i.e., the greater the resolution, the more expensive the display. You should determine if you really need high resolution or if you can make do with less as part of your system selection criteria.

- ***Ease of Learning.*** Some systems are extremely tutorial in nature. They instruct the user precisely what to do at every step. Other systems require the user to learn a set of commands in order to operate the system. Those that are very helpful are sometimes *too* helpful for the experienced user. The helpful menus and prompting messages seem to get in the way after the user is familiar with them.

  Systems that are to be placed in a "casual use" environment in which several people will use them from time to time should be easy to use. Otherwise, the casual user may feel frustrated by being forced to learn a set of commands each time.

- ***Ease of Use.*** Contrasted with ease of learning, ease of use is an indication of how proficient a user can become through frequent use of a system. The easy-to-use system may *not* be easy to learn, and vice versa. Both features are important and should be separately specified.

Figure B.2 An interactive CADD system workstation. (*Courtesy of CalComp.*)

- ***Reliability and Service.*** As your CADD system gains in importance in your organization, you will become more and more reliant upon it. If it malfunctions, the effect on your business could be very negative. You will surely want, therefore, to acquire a reliable system; one that does not break down frequently. Unfortunately, none of the systems come with little signs telling how often they break down. This information can be obtained only by research among current owners of the system type. Ask people who own one—but do it in such a way that the owners recognize you as someone to help not as someone who has come to critically analyze their selection. That way, you will obtain useful information.

  Entropy is at work in the universe—the tendency of all systems to go from order to disorder. It is thus in the nature of things that even the most reliable of systems will, on occasion, cease to function. That is why you need good service. Find out from each candidate vendor what their service arrangements are; then, go back to the friendly users you have contacted and check on the vendor's *performance*. Reliability and service should be high on your list of important features.

- ***Application Programs.*** In some disciplines, there is special software available for performing certain tasks. For example, one CADD vendor offers a program for design of sprinkler systems, while another has a time analysis program for integrated-circuit design. The application software can turn out to be more valuable to you than the basic CADD system; it should therefore be considered carefully in the selection process.

- ***Cost Issues.*** The costs you must consider include the cost of the system itself; costs of any optional devices or software you may acquire; the cost of service; the cost of materials, such as diskettes, plotter paper, and plotter pens or toner; the cost of training, if any; the costs of site preparation; and the cost of financing.

- ***Timing.*** The ability of a vendor to deliver the promised system varies with market conditions. When the vendor is experiencing good times, you may have to wait as long as 6 months for the delivery of a CADD system; at other times, the delivery may be almost immediate. Furthermore, system delivery may be adjusted if your purchase is contingent upon receiving the system by a particular date. All vendors, even the largest ones, have some flexibility along this line. However, if you are preparing an installation location, be sure that the completion of the preparations coincides with the delivery of the system; otherwise, you may have labored for naught.

Another time period to be aware of is the learning curve—the time it takes the system user to become proficient in system operations. Your productivity projections should take this time period into account. Since it varies from system to system, you will have to rely upon user accounts to estimate its length.

B.3 VENDOR ISSUES

Acquiring a CADD system is not a simple commercial transaction; it is the beginning of a relationship between the vendor and the purchaser. It behooves the purchaser to examine the character of the vendor thoroughly *before* agreeing to such an arrangement. Here are some points on which to evaluate both the vendor and the likelihood of the relationship having a positive and lasting existence.

- ***Stability.*** Is the vendor going to be there next month? Next year? If you expect your system to be fully useful for 3 to 5 years, take the time to determine the likelihood of the vendor's continued existence. Use Dun and Bradstreet ratings, annual reports, the vendor's business plan (if the company has one!), and any other indicator you can obtain.
- ***Integrity.*** What is so rare a commodity as old-fashioned business integrity? Consistency, honesty, fairness, faithfulness—these are traits no longer held in high regard. They are also not easily discerned; time and experience are needed. Although integrity is hard to discern and hard to define, it *is* worth looking for. A good many system deficiencies can be overlooked if the vendor is faithful in its business dealings.
- ***Training.*** A common misconception is that the vendor supplies all the necessary training. The truth is that vendors *do* supply all the training necessary to operate the CADD system; that training, however, is only part of the story.

  In order for an operator to be fully trained to perform in your work environment, system training must be integrated with work skills. Procedures and standards must be developed for the new mode of operation so that your work can be produced to the standards you expect.

  The vendor's portion of the training typically constitutes 5 to 10 percent of the overall training ultimately required. This is not due to the vendor holding back; it is simply a requirement that the user develop the full scope of training. If the training is to take place at the vendor's facility, there may be travel and living expenses involved for your operators. On small systems, however, training is usually at the customer's site.
- ***Strategy.*** Before entering into a long-term relationship with anyone, it is essential to know what their long-range plans are. You must choose a vendor whose goals coincide with yours to some degree. A vendor that sees its future in robots and robot programming systems while it is still engaged in selling CADD systems to architects is not going to be of much use to the architects for long.
- ***User Group.*** A very important aspect of your relationship with your vendor is the user group. This is an organization consisting of users of the vendor's equipment. They meet to share information about using the system and to join forces in obtaining software improvements from the vendor.

  The user group is also an important forum for exchanging information on operating techniques; in some cases, user-written software is also exchanged. A good (meaning active and user-run) user group can be very helpful, especially to the beginning CADD user.
- ***Application Knowledge.*** Applying CADD technology to your area of interest is not always simple. Having a vendor that is knowledgeable in the application of your interest can greatly facilitate implementation.

B.4 CADDBUCKS

This section contains a description of a fictitious CADD vendor and its products and is a composite of the leading firms in the field and their products.

CADDBUCKS, our nonexistent CADD vendor, was founded in 1970 by several aerospace engineers and MIT and IBM graduates. The firm's first product, the CADDastrophe, used a DEC PDP-11/20 minicomputer, a Tektronix 611 storage tube, and an SAC Graf-pen for input. The simple two-dimensional drafting system could draw anything, as long as it consisted of lines, points, and circular arcs, and the system offered "one style fits all" text.

CADDastrophe was promoted as "a revolution for the engineering designer"; the founders of CADDBUCKS started catching up on their late mortgage payments by 1971.

SYSTEM DETAILS: CADDASTROPHE

Computer. The founders picked the DEC computer line for two reasons: price and brand recognition. Even in 1970, DEC had become known as *the* supplier of small computers. The gravity of this decision can better be grasped when one realizes that it required CADDBUCKS to write their own operating system for the computer, as DEC did not offer an interactive one at the time.

Software. The application software was written in Fortran II and assembler language. User programming? At your own risk. File structures were very simple, for maximum speed; graphics and text were stored together. Security? None.

Workstation. The workstation consisted of an alphanumeric display and the Tektronix graphics tube, sitting alongside a large, "home-grown," gantry-style digitizer board. The operator of this advanced system had to stand up to reach many of the digitizer functions; sales personnel were quick to point out this feature, which increased circulation and prevented cramps.

Plotter. Output was directed to a large Calcomp flatbed plotter, which required its own room and operator. Then, as now, the plotter was the most popular stop on the CADD system tour.

MARKET

Early efforts on CADDBUCKS' part were directed to selling the systems wherever it could. The first purchasers were electronics and mechanical device manufacturers; CADDBUCKS thus developed expertise in these application areas, to the exclusion of others, such as architecture and mapping.

CADDBUCKS TODAY

Since 1970, CADDBUCKS has grown at an average annual rate of 40 percent. The firm experienced a serious management crisis when annual sales were $20 million, resulting in the departure of three of the founders—the president and two vice presidents. The board of directors hired a professional manager from a Fortune 300 company, who quickly brought the "bottom line" in line and took the company public in 1979.

Once considerd a "glamor" stock, CADDBUCKS is looked upon with some caution by Wall Street analysts, who now show a preference for vendors whose systems are based on stand-alone workstations.

SYSTEM DETAILS: RECENT PRODUCTS

Computers. CADDBUCKS stuck with DEC and after some early traumatic conversions to DEC operating systems, today supports the 32-bit VAX line. PDP-11's are still supported but no longer sold by the company. While the enclosure is constructed almost entirely by CADDBUCKS, who also buys memory from other sources and builds their own disk controllers, the computer and operating system are "vanilla" DEC VAX. CADDBUCKS justifiably claims that any software that can run on a VAX will run on its version.

The company produced a relatively low-cost system for a time, based on the PDP-11. It soon realized, however, that the economics of the CADD market are such that it could not make a profit on small systems and dropped them. Customers, however, continued to clamor for lower-cost workstations. This has led CADDBUCKS to add intelligence to its fairly expensive ($65,000) workstations, so that they can be sold in $125,000 stand-alone packages—with the promise of expandability in evidence.

Software. Today's CADDBUCKS software is almost entirely written in highly transportable Fortran 77. It has an extensive and powerful user programming language and an interface to a real DBMS provided by another company.

A large part of CADDBUCKS' initial lack of software was remedied by early customers. Many of these developed their own codes, which were bought by CADDBUCKS and enhanced for sale to subsequent customers.

While in the past software was only sold "bundled" with the CADDBUCKS system, today the company has unbundled its codes. You can buy a computer from DEC and run CADDBUCKS programs on it. This has also led to a more realistic allocation of costs on the part of the vendor. Previously, software appeared to be given away while hardware components were heavily marked up. This led to disgruntlement among users, who learned they could buy the hardware for less elsewhere—except the CADD vendor would not support their system if they did. Today's approach reflects the perception that the vendor's "value added" lies primarily in the area of software.

Workstations. The primary CADDBUCKS workstation of today has a 1000 × 1280, 60-hertz, noninterlaced, color raster refresh display. The display is fast enough to allow image dynamics, but the display controller does not quite. Interaction is permitted with multiple nonoverlapping views by means of a digitizing tablet cursor that is looking more and more like a "mouse" with each new release.

The top-of-the-line workstation is almost a complete system in itself. It contains multiple microprocessors and performs most graphical manipulations without communicating with the main system computer. This has become a requirement for CADD systems, as most users are sensitive to the need for quick response time, which is only possible by giving each user his or her own computer.

CADDBUCKS now offers other workstations—some with text only and others with medium-resolution graphics—to meet the broad range of demands it is encountering.

Plotters. A wide range of output devices is now available to the CADDBUCKS user. These include pen plotters (Calcomp, Zeta, HI, HP), electrostatic plotters (Versatec, Benson, Calcomp), and "quick-copy" color ink-jet and thermal devices (Tektronix and Gulton). Furthermore, plots can be "queued" to any device—that is, placed in line for later plotting.

Raster output units, such as electrostatic plotters, are provided with data by a special piece of hardware called a *rasterizer*. The task of converting the vector-format CADD file into raster format is highly computer-consuming; this device relieves the processor of that burden.

Communications. CADDBUCKS systems can now talk among themselves as well as to other computers. Rather than design its own networking software, the company relies upon DECnet and has implemented the full range of DECnet products in complete integration with the CADD system.

MARKETS

Competition in the markets CADDBUCKS used to dominate has heated up; it lost market share in IC design to start-ups whose system technology leapfrogged that of the venerable

CADDBUCKS system. Joint ventures and company acquisitions are planned to overcome these shortcomings.

Some of CADDBUCKS' markets have integrated themselves into units for example, the CIM (computer-integrated manufacturing) area. Although two-dimensional drafting and NC (numerical control) were previously viewed as separate markets, CIM now demands workstations, computers, networks, and software at a rate that is attracting many industrial giants, such as GE and Westinghouse.

LONG-TERM STRATEGY

Today CADDBUCKS is a major provider of automation products and services. Training and maintenance, once afterthoughts, are now important revenue producers for the company—and are conducted accordingly. Upward compatibility with future products is no longer a question. Although smaller, newer companies may be more "state of the art" and have better price-to-performance ratios, CADDBUCKS guarantees performance and expandability.

B.5 SUMMARY

Medium-size systems are the most common form of CADD systems in use today. Their characteristics are complex and must be understood in terms of the prospective user's needs. When selecting a system, emphasis should be placed on functions dictated by application rather than on raw speed or responsiveness. It is also important to carefully examine the system vendor.

Large Systems

by
William L. Howard

Barth's Distinction:

There are two types of people: those who divide people into two types, and those who don't.

The purpose of this chapter is to divide computer graphic geometry systems into types to make it easier for you to wander through the maze of myriad competing systems and more quickly understand what you are seeing.

C.1 DEFINITION

The authors of these appendixes have had sufficient conversation to mutually agree that there is not a sharp dividing line between micro and mini and mini and large systems. Where we overlap, you, the reader, will have the benefit of two opinions. To keep the chore to a manageable size, systems are divided by size, cost, and processor definitions.

All devices which have direct, online, real-time, etc. access to common system and application software, but particularly to a common set of user-defined geometry, are to be considered part of a single system. A large geometry system must have the capability to support multiple graphics terminals. In the usual case the effective lower limit is four, but there are two-terminal configurations available that do not significantly differ from their larger brethren.

Online storage in a large system is on a hard disk and is measured in megabytes. A typical lower limit is 65 megabytes. If the primary storage medium is a floppy disk, it is not a large system. Very few large systems are useful for long with less than hundreds of megabytes.

Large systems will support multiple functions. Geometry construction, analysis, storage and retrieval, and a variety of hard-copy outputs can all occur simultaneously and under the direction and control of the users at the display units.

The advent of small systems within the last 2 years has made price a significant differential. Mini systems, today, carry list prices of $150,000 and below. Large systems with four or more terminals, fully configured, generally cost $350,000 and up. There is no theoretical upper limit. A fully configured system includes terminals, processors, storage, hard-copy outputs, and software.

There is no adequate definition of processors that can differentiate between large and mini systems. However, most graphics vendors are either promising or offering machines with 32-bit words because they are faster, more effective machines.

C.2 GENERAL COMMENTS

The widely assumed differences between mainframe-based systems and minicomputer-based systems are far more apparent than real. There are dedicated systems of each type wherein the entire system went from packing crates to production use in less than 72 hours, with weeks of subsequent operation virtually unattended except for data backup. There are differences: Mainframes typically provide more flexibility, can be shared, and are more easily upgraded; minicomputers have lower entry cost and, when dedicated, require less attention. One of the most significant differences is that the quality and professionalism of large computer vendors has been superior to that of the mini system vendors. As the small companies have grown large or have been acquired by large companies that, too, has changed and is not nearly the problem that it was as late as 1982.

The lowest entry cost for a full-function system is to attach terminals to a paid-for mainframe. The lowest-cost system for more than a half-dozen or so terminals is mainframe-based. There is no rule for what is least expensive in the middle range. In any case, cost should be a tertiary consideration behind capability and vendor support.

There are some clear advantages to mainframe-based systems. The vendors are larger companies who can generally provide better support at more locations. Mainframes tend to have more sophisticated system software, which eases accounting, security, communications, and database management problems. More terminals per processor means that more terminals have direct access to the same database. Better communications means that terminals can be further from the mainframe. Perhaps the biggest drawback inherent in using a large computer to drive a graphics system is the high probability that the processor will be shared with other applications that tend to degrade graphics performance.

In comparing one system to another, the differences in productive use will be quite small. Virtually any system on the market can provide large productivity gains. It matters more how the system is implemented and managed than which system is used. There are, however, two fundamental philosophical classes which make systems different from each other. Not necessarily better or worse, but different.

The first philosophical class is in the user interface. There are three types, menu-driven, command-driven, and function key-driven. Unigraphics (McDonnell Douglas Automation Company) is the purest form of the first, Computervision Corporation of the second, and Gerber Systems Technology, Inc., of the third. How this affects the system in productive use will be discussed within the individual descriptions.

The second philosophical class is defined by who developed the system. Virtually all of the application code and all of the menus in CADD were written by people who are experienced aircraft designers and have been taught a minimum of Fortran. Computervision, among others, has depended upon the Boston-area computer science geniuses. This, too, affects the systems, as is described below.

As a final general comment, every large computer system, including graphics, has had to undergo a major rewrite to permit further progress. Incompatability with new hardware or new operating systems, system architecture limitations, and conversion from two to three dimensions are examples of blocks that can be removed only with a major rewrite. During the rewrite few enhancements are made to the system. The ideal time to acquire a system is long enough after the rewrite that the bugs have been worked out but not so long that another major retrenchment is due.

C.3 VECTOR REFRESH TERMINAL SYSTEMS

C.3.1 CADAM*

CADAM is the Lockheed-developed system now being marketed by CADAM, Inc; IBM; and VG Systems. It shares with the other systems in this category the advantage of enormous hardware flexibility. IBM; Adage, Inc.; VG Systems CGX; and Spectragraphics Corp. each sell compatible terminals. Any IBM-compatible mainframe, storage, and communication devices will work. Color raster is available from each of the vendors.

CADAM is one of the oldest systems in the market but has had major system rewrite over the last 3 years. Its development has been firmly controlled by design and manufacturing engineers within Lockheed. As a result, CADAM provides an outstanding compromise between menu- and function key–driven use. The combination of this excellent user interface and the speed provided by the refresh terminals makes CADAM the most productive drafting system available. The breadth of application is limited. CADAM is an enhanced two-dimensional system. It is far from the best design tool. But if your application involves a large amount of drawing, CADAM has proved to be the best there is.

C.3.2 CADD

CADD was developed as an effective design tool within McDonnell Aircraft Company by 1971. It was, and it remains, the very best three-dimensional wire-frame and surface geometry system in the world. CADD is not an efficient drafting tool, but it does in three

* CADAM is a registered trademark of CADAM, Inc.

dimensions what most other system developers are just beginning to comprehend. Along with outstanding direct user development, McDonnell Douglas has shown a genius for providing elegant solutions to the wrong problems. They developed a sophisticated minicomputer-based distributed software system just as low-cost mainframes were being announced. The other problem is that CADD is not marketed. McDonnell Aircraft (McAir) paid for the development, while McDonnell Douglas Automation (McAuto) receives the benefits of any profit. There is a disincentive for McAir to support external customers.

C.3.3 CATIA*

CATIA was developed within Daussault (Avions Marcel Dassault-Breguet Aviation) as a design adjunct to their use of CADAM. It is being marketed by IBM as the three-dimensional complementary to CADAM. CATIA has a very effective wire-frame, surface, and an attractive solids package. The capability to generate a numerical control (NC) program for compound area milling based on a solid model is particularly effective. However, CATIA, though primarily menu-driven, is very cumbersome to use. Even with extensive training and experience it is unlikely that a user could be so proficient at CATIA manipulation that he or she could give a dazzling demonstration with a complicated design.

C.4 CURRENT AD2000-BASED SYSTEMS

C.4.1 Autol-trol Technology Corporation

Auto-trol enjoyed success early in the marketplace with a system tailored to the energy-related companies. They profitably acquired a large market share but had serious problems when they tried to expand into the broader, more competitive manufacturing industry market. Their current prime offering is the first successful product based on conversion of AD2000. It is an effective system with relatively broad application but little product differentiation in the software system. Improvement continues, but there are still some problems left from the AD2000 base. The design of the workstation is the best in the industry. Ergonomics has been applied.

C.4.2 Control Data Corporation (CDC)

The current system is the product of a very long, painful implementation of AD2000 by both CDC and their first customers, but it now appears to work effectively. Other than current CDC computer users, the only particular advantage that CDC offers is the ability to enter graphics easily through time-sharing on the CDC network.

C.4.3 Graphics Technology Corporation (Graphtek)†

This is one of the new companies, a spinoff in the sense that experienced people left their parent company to develop a new system. All reports are very positive about the system. Choosing Graphtek is primarily a judgment that a small, new company will go farther and faster than their larger, older, more bureaucratic competitors.

* CATIA is a registered trademark of Daussault Systems.
† Graphtek is a registered trademark of Graphics Technology Corporation.

C.4.4 Manufacturing and Consulting Services, Inc. (MCS)

The chief executive of MCS is Pat Hanratty. Most of the systems on the market were at one time based on Hanratty software. Only those in this section retain much, if any. The history of MCS is that the software is brilliant in concept, poor in execution. Witness the travails of Tektronix, Auto-trol, and CDC in bringing a production tool to the market. ANVIL is the first production tool from MCS. The software is about as portable as it is possible for a large system to be. If you need a software base upon which to develop your own system or to place on one of the less popular computers, MCS is a good place to look.

C.5 OTHER SYSTEMS

C.5.1 Applicon

Applicon has long been the favorite system of the academicians, researchers, and more arcane applications. It is a very effective system with a significant market share. Applicon is a command-driven system with the heavily advertised feature of symbol recognition for command execution. A user can instruct the system to recognize any cursor movement pattern as a command. That has never worked as well nor been the advantage that Applicon thinks. Applicon was the first to make effective use of color and includes a broad spectrum of special applications such as FEM and printed-circuit board design. Applicon includes a solids capability as good as any on the market.

Applicon is owned by Schlumberger, who clearly intends to remain among the industry leaders through acquisition and integration. NC programming is provided through University Computing software. Engineering analysis capability is provided through software from Structural Dynamics Research Corp. (SDRC). Since that arrangement was completed, General Electric purchased a 48 percent share of SDRC and announced a joint agreement that puts SDRC and Calma together. Schlumberger has also purchased Benson, the plotter vendor. All of this gives Applicon significant breadth and the backing of a very strong company.

C.5.2 McDonnell Douglas Automation–Unigraphics*

As CADD is not being marketed, many of its best features are being implemented in Unigraphics. McAuto is the only minicomputer-based system vendor who genuinely understands three-dimensional CAD and how to most effectively use it. Unigraphics was an acquisition by McDonnell Douglas. The strength of the original company (United Computing) was in NC programming. The strength of Unigraphics is still NC. It is a totally menu-driven system. That makes it very easy to learn, but weaker in experienced user proficiency. This is not the most powerful drafting system. Implementation of more CADD features will improve it as a design tool but may weaken its drafting effectiveness even more. McAuto, very intelligently, does not know yet what to do with solids, although a capability is offered. A robotics programming module is available.

C.5.3 GE Calma Company

Calma has suffered over the last several years with having a good system and a poor sales force. Its acquisition by General Electric (GE) may have some impact on that. It has already impacted the breadth of system capability with the addition of engineering analysis

* Unigraphics is a registered trademark of McDonnell Douglas Automation Company.

software from SDRC. Calma has long had an effective printed-circuit board capability. Someday GE is expected to offer the further benefit of direct interface to its MIMS manufacturing information system software and to its machine controls and robots. Calma has signed an agreement with IBM that is expected to result in an IBM-hosted version.

C.5.4 Computervision Corporation

Computervision (CV) had the largest market share until 1983, when only IBM sold more. This success was accomplished with a marginally competitive system, less-than-excellent product support, and a superb sales force. Computervision offers the broadest range of capabilities of any system on the market; it does more things than any other single system. All modules are command driven; thus, this is one of the most difficult systems to learn and to use.

For the last several years CV has built its own hardware. This has led, twice, to placing the installed base in the position of either continuing to use an obsolete system or replacing hardware in order to use the latest software. Recently announced third-party processors may solve that problem.

C.5.5 Intergraph Corporation

Intergraph has employed a flexible command structure coupled to clever hardware use to capture a large market share in architecture and engineering, cartography, and energy industries. They do not understand the manufacturing industry and have not done well there. They are, however, the fastest growing vendor.

The Intergraph system does not retrieve an entire geometry model from disk storage to core memory. It only brings into core those geometric entities which are affected by the immediate command. These unique disk-resident data permit very efficient use of very small processors without getting into large-model problems. Intergraph is also adding an array processor to their system to speed complex data manipulation.

The hardware efficiency and command structure flexibility might be reason enough to buy from Intergraph, if you decided that you need to tailor your own system.

C.5.6 Gerber Systems Technology, Inc.

Gerber is the most function key–driven system on the market. As such, it is probably the easiest to learn to use. However, it shares with Unigraphics a constraint on how fast the user can drive the system. Partly because of this and partly because circumstance caught them in the rewrite cycle just when the market boomed, they have not been particularly popular in the last 2 years.

C.5.7 Synercom Technology, Inc.

Synercom has concentrated in the architecture and engineering and energy company markets and offers one of the best systems for those specialties. Included are unusual capabilities such as one for the design of transmission towers. Synercom is lightly regarded and has had little impact in the manufacturing industry. They are strong in AEC and cartography.

C.6 CONCLUSION

It should be obvious, but I feel compelled to issue the standard disclaimer that the above remarks are entirely personal opinion based not on extensive research but upon close observation and involvement with computer graphics over many years. My comments are not more detailed because the facts on these companies change within 6 months.

> There aren't enough tubes in this world.
>
> *James Daues, 1971*

VENDORS

Adage, Inc.
1 Fortune Drive
Billerica, MA 01821
(617)667-7070

Applicon, Inc.
32 Second Avenue
Burlington, MA 01803
(617)272-7070

Auto-trol Technology Corporation
12500 N. Washington Street
Denver, CO 80233
(303)452–4919

CADAM, Inc.
1935 N. Buena Vista
Burbank, CA 91504
(213)841–9470

CGX Corporation
42 Nagog Park
Alton, MA 01720

Computervision Corporation
201 Burlington Road
Bedford, MA 01730
(617)275-1800

Control Data Corp.
Manufacturing Industry Marketing
P.O. Box 0
Minneapolis, MN 55440
(612)853-8100

GE Calma Company
5155 Old Ironsides Drive
Santa Clara, CA 95050
(408)727-0121

Gerber Systems Technology, Inc.
40 Gerber Road East
South Windsor, CT 06074
(203)644-2581

Graphics Technology Corp
1777 Conestoga Street
Boulder, CO 80301
(303)449-1138

IBM Corporation
1133 Westchester Avenue
White Plains, NY 10604
(914)696-1960

Intergraph Corporation
One Madison Industrial Park
Huntsville, AL 35807
(205)772-3411

Manufacturing and Consulting Services, Inc.
2960 South Daimler Avenue
Santa Ana, CA 92705
(714)540-3921

McDonnell Douglas Automation Co.
P.O. Box 516
St. Louis, MO 63166
(314)233-2299

Spectragraphics Corporation
3333 Camino Del Rio South
San Diego, CA 92108
(714)584-1822

Synercom Technology, Inc.
500 Corporate Drive
Sugar Land, TX 77478
(713)491-5000

VG Systems, Inc.
21300 Oxnard Street
Woodland Hills, CA 91367
(213)346-3410

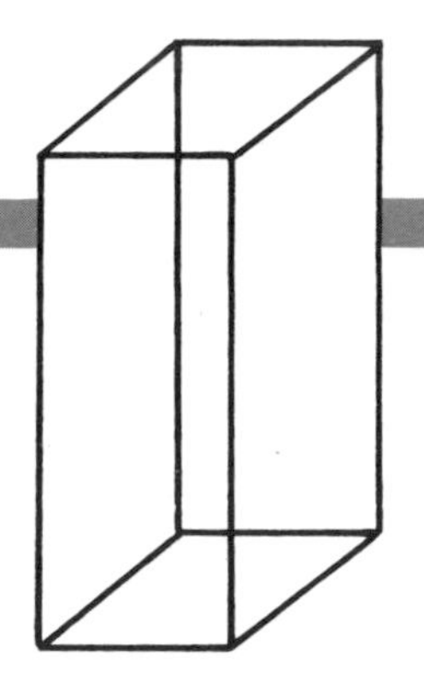

Index